Mirrors in the Cliffs

EDITED BY JIM PERRIN

Mirrors in the Cliffs

with cartoons by Sheridan Anderson

DIADEM BOOKS LTD LONDON

First published in 1983 by
Diadem Books Limited, London

All trade enquiries to:
Cordee, 3a De Montfort Street, Leicester (UK, Europe and Commonwealth)
Royal Robbins Inc., P.O. Box 4536, Modesto, California 95352 (US)

Mirrors in the cliffs
   1. Mountaineering — Correspondence, reminiscences, etc.
   I. Perrin, Jim
   796.5'22 GV199.82

ISBN 0-906371-95-3

Printed in Great Britain by
St. Edmunds Press, Bury St. Edmunds, Suffolk

ACKNOWLEDGEMENTS My thanks are due to all the authors for permission to use their articles. In addition I would like to thank the following publishers, agents, executors, next-of-kin, etc., who have given permission to quote where they hold copyright or where authors were unavailable or deceased: Geoffrey Bles and Co; Mrs J. Carleton, Faber and Faber, Frederick Grubb and the Carcenet Press; Constable and Co.; Mrs P. Davis; Rev. S. Z. Edwards; Eyre and Spottiswoode; The Countess of Essex; Glasgow University Press; Victor Gollancz and Nyphenburger Verlagshandlung; Mrs A. Haston; David Hyam Associates; Eva Altmeier-Karl and Limpert Verlag; The Mountaineers Books; Mrs J. MacIntyre; Thomas Nelson; Reynard House; The Estate of Lord Schuster; Nick Shipton; Sierra Club Books and Granada Publishing; Mrs Smith; Mrs W. Unsoeld.
   I am also indebted to the editors and publishers of various journals and magazines for their support and assistance: *Alpin* (*Alpinismus*); *The Alpine Journal; The American Alpine Journal; Ascent* (Sierra Club Books); *The Canadian Alpine Journal; Climber and Rambler; Climbing; Climbers' Club Journal; The Edinburgh University Mountaineering Club Journal; The Fell and Rock Journal; High* (*Crags*); *La Montagne; Leeds University Mountaineering Club Journal; Mountain; Mountain Gazette; Wild.*
   For translation services I would like to thank Tim Carruthers, Ian Dickson, Tony Pearson and Jane Taylor.
   For advice and sundry assistance I have to thank Geoff Birtles, Robin Campbell, Moira Irvine, Martin Lutterjohann, Michael Kennedy, Tony Shaw, Dick Swindon and Doris Venning.
   And for photographs: the credited photographers; the Editors of *High* and *Mountain* for permission to cull material from their files; George Greenfield and Trish Plumb; Pat Hughes; Mr and Mrs Tasker.
   To Sheridan Anderson for another collection of his cartoons and to Royal Robbins for his Foreword.

Contents

FOREWORD *Royal Robbins*   *page* 13
INTRODUCTION   17
COAST TO COAST ON THE GRANITE SLASHER
  Greg Child   19
END OF A CLIMB *John Menlove Edwards*   28

Part 1: Roots

ON THE PROFUNDITY TRAIL *Doug Scott*   41
NIGHTSHIFT IN ZERO *Dougal Haston*   51
THE LAST STEP *Rick Ridgeway*   54
SPEEDING DOWN SOUTH *Jim Bridwell*   60
NO BIG CIGAR *Geoff Birtles*   66
THE INSCRUTABLE BREGAGLIA EAST *Robin Campbell*   71
WITH GOD ON OUR SIDE *Terry King*   75
OUT OF THE MIDDAY SUN *Ed Drummond*   82
SNAKES AND LADDERS *Robin Smith*   85
THE ROPE *Sir Douglas Busk*   89
WITH TWO MEN ON THE MATTERHORN *Yvette Vaucher*   91
BERNAT'S HORSE *Harold Drasdo*   95
CENGALO, CENGALO *Emil Zopfi*   101
THE ONLY BLASPHEMY *John Long*   107
ON TREE CLIMBING *H. E. L. Porter*   110
TRAPDOOR FANDANGO *Ron Fawcett*   115
MOMENTUM ON MAKALU *John Roskelley*   117
THE SHROUD SOLO *Ivan Ghirardini*   121
ABOVE AND BEYOND *Reinhold Messner*   126
FORTUNATUS *Dorothy Pilley*   133
ALL THAT GLORY *Georges Bettembourg*   135
GLASGOW *John MacKenzie*   136
PASS THE MIRROR *Arlene Blum*   139
BALL'S PYRAMID *Keith Bell*   141
WELSH INTERLUDE *Nea Morin*   145

MOSES *Fred Beckey* 148
BELTANE FIRE *Geoff Milburn* 152
STATES OF THE ART *Max Jones* 155
SOLO ON CLOGGY *Wilfrid Noyce* 159
THREE BEGINNINGS *Jeff Schwenn, Gwen Moffat and Dennis Gray* 161

Part 2: New Found Lands

KAMET SEEN AND CONQUERED *Raymond Greene* 169
DAY OF THE FOX *Chris Baxter* 171
BOTTERILL'S SLAB *Fred Botterill* 175
ROBBINS — ON THE PLANK *Pat Ament* 178
ASGARD OUTING *Paul Nunn* 181
HETCH HETCHY: FIRST IMPRESSIONS *Galen Rowell* 185
AFRICAN ESCAPADE *Eric Shipton* 190
POTATO MEDALLIST *Colin Kirkus* 197
PATAGONIAN VIRGIN *Chris Bonington* 200
JACK OF DIAMONDS *Royal Robbins* 204
WINTERING OUT *Alan Rouse* 209
THE MASK OF DEATH *Pierre Mazeaud* 213
GENTLEMEN'S RELISH *H. W. Tilman* 217
CONSOLATION FOR A TRAGEDY? *Dave Roberts* 221
DANGEROUS DANCING *Alex MacIntyre* 226
TAXATION NO TYRANNY *Jim Perrin* 229
HENNA HORROR *Mick Fowler* 234
BOREDOM AND THE BIG NUMBERS *Reinhard Karl* 238
IMAGINED HEIGHTS *Hudson Stuck* 247

Part 3: The Moral? It's the Travelling

ONCE IN A WHILE *G. F. Dutton* 251
UNINVITED GUESTS *H. W. Tilman* 257
HITLER AND LENI *Anderl Heckmair* 259
AN EXCURSION IN SCOTLAND *Royal Robbins* 265
THE MOUNTAIN TOURISTS *Sir Leslie Stephen* 271
NOTES FROM A FUND-RAISING BROCHURE *Anon.* 273
ALASKA: JOURNEY BY LAND *Galen Rowell* 274
TRAVELS WITH A DONKEY *Pete Livesey* 281

THE SOLOIST'S DIARY *Jeff Long* 288
CONFUSIONS OF AN ODIUM MEETER *Robin Smith* 306
RAWALPINDI TO RAWTENSTALL *Don Whillans* 308
CROOKED ROAD TO THE FAR NORTH
  Lito Tejada-Flores 319
YOUR LOVELY HILLS ARE VERY DANGEROUS
  Kevin Fitzgerald 326
HIMALAYAN HOPEFULS *Greg Child* 331
BUT I NEVER RETURNED . . . (A THIRTIES IDYLL)
  Raymond Greene 338

Part 4: Cast List

CLIMBERS *James Morris* 347
LETTERS FROM HERBERT *Don Lauria* 348
LOCK UP YOUR DAUGHTERS *Laura and Guy Waterman* 351
THREE OBITUARIES:
  GLACIER PILOT *Jim Sharp* 353
  I'M ALIVE — HOW CAN HE BE DEAD?
    Dietrich Hasse 356
  WHO WAS OSCAR ECKENSTEIN? *David Dean* 361
TWO EIGER FAILURES:
  A SHORT WALK WITH WHILLANS *Tom Patey* 371
  UNDER STARTER'S ORDERS *John Barry* 381
THE EYEGLASS *Tom Longstaff* 385
LE GRAND MELCHIOR *Ronald Clark* 385
ARNOLD KÜPFER *Claude Benson* 400
TENZING NORGAY *Michael Tobias* 401
SAHIBS AND SHERPAS *Mike Thompson* 405
ALPINE FLEAS *T. G. Bonney* 417
THE LLANBERIS MOVEMENT *John Cleare and
  Robin Collomb* 418
REFLECTIONS OF A BROKEN-DOWN CLIMBER
  Warren Harding 421
BRICK-EDGE CRUISER *Alex MacIntyre* 429
TRUE-BORN ENGLISHMEN *Claud Schuster* 430
PRATT *Pat Ament* 435
A SUPERIORITY COMPLEX *E. L. Strutt* 437
ROSS TALKS . . . *Paul Ross* 440

NEW BREED *Kim Carrigan* 453
A WORD FOR WHYMPER: A REPLY TO SIR ARNOLD
 LUNN *T. S. Blakeney and D. F. O. Dangar* 456
WHYMPER AGAIN *Sir Arnold Lunn* 478

Part 5: Contingencies, Catastrophes, Death

A CREVASSE ON THE ECRINS
 Geoffrey Winthrop Young 487
"SIR, I REFUTE IT THUS." *Sir Douglas Busk* 490
ON THE EDGE *Sue Geller* 491
OTHON BRON *Janet Adam Smith* 495
THE BEGINNING OF A NEW LIFE *Fredi Rölli* 496
THE DEATH OF GARY ULLIN *Robert W. Craig* 503
A FEW MOMENTS *Merv English* 515
NANDA DEVI UNSOELD *Willi Unsoeld* 518
EARTHQUAKE *H. Adams Carter* 521
A MOUNTAIN VISION *Frank Smythe* 522
SALT-WATER CURE *Pat Littlejohn* 524
FIVE INTO EIGHT WON'T GO *Georges Bettembourg* 528
SHUFFLING OFF THIS MORTAL COIL
 Geoffrey Winthrop Young 529
PRISONER OF WAR *W. H. Murray* 530
THE PITY OF WAR *Lionel Terray* 536
WAR IRONIES *Armand Charlet* 539
A BREACH OF FAITH *Rob Taylor* 540
HENRY BARBER REPLIES *Henry Barber* 550
THE END OF A CHAPTER *Sir Arnold Lunn* 554
THE GREEN LAKE *Michael Roberts* 558

Part 6: Controversies, Tactics, Histories, Distractions

THE AESTHETICS OF RISK *Mike Thompson* 561
THE FINAL GAME *Glenn Randall* 574
BOULDERING AS ART *John Gill* 580
LOVE IN THE MOUNTAINS *Karl Lukan* 584
THE BLUE CRAMPON BRIGADE *Anne Sauvy-Wilkinson* 593
NO WONDER MALLORY DIDN'T MAKE IT *Robert Reid* 603

LARGE OR SMALL? *Eric Shipton* 617
T. GRAHAM BROWN AND THE BRENVA FACE
  Lord Tangley 621
BACKDOOR DIPLOMACY *Eric Shipton* 628
TWO EVEREST REVIEWS *H. W. Tilman and*
  Robin Campbell 630
HANGING AROUND *Dave Roberts* 636
A CLANDESTINE PLEA *Rick Sylvester* 645
THE CLIMBER AS VISIONARY *Doug Robinson* 648
THE POETRY AND HUMOUR OF MOUNTAINEERING
  Michael Roberts 656
SCAFELL PIKE *Norman Nicholson* 669
POSTSCRIPT *Claud Schuster* 670

NOTES ABOUT THE ARTICLES 680
SUBJECT INDEX 686
INDEX OF AUTHORS 688

Photographs in the Text

Frontispiece: Bouldering buskers, Yosemite. *Photo: Reinhard Karl*

between pages 128 and 129

1. Ice climbing techniques in use on the chalk cliffs at Dover: Phil Thornill and Chris Watts on the first ascent of Great White Fright. *Photo: Mick Fowler*
2. Andy Meyers leads The Thing, Bowles Rocks, Sussex. *Photo: Dave Jones*
3. Andy Barker leads Miller's Tale, Water cum Jolly, Derbyshire. *Photo: Steve Wright*
4. Jerry Moffat on Sole Fusion, Joshua Tree, California. *Photo: Chris Gore*
5. Chris Gore and Skip Guerin tackling the overhang on Equinox, Eldorado Springs Canyon, Colorado. *Photo: Gore collection*
6. Combined tactics in use on a sandstone climb in Czechoslovakia. *Photo: Karel Vlcek*
7. Tomas Cada leading Paprika, Teplice Rocks, Czechoslovakia. *Photo: Karel Vlcek*
8. Ron Fawcett and Pete Livesey in action on Craig y Forwyn, North Wales. *Photo: Geoff Birtles*
9. Gorge du Verdon, France. *Photo: David Belden*

between pages 256 and 257

10. Tobin Sorenson on the Kor Traverse, Eiger North Face. *Photo: Alex MacIntyre*
11. A fatal accident
12. Phil Burke solos Mongoose, Tremadog, North Wales. *Photo: John Stevenson*
13. Kalanka and Changabang, Garhwal, India. *Photo: Joe Tasker*
14. Latok 1 and the Choktoi Glacier, Karakoram. *Photo: Dave Potts*
15. On the North Face of Kanchenjunga. *Photo: Doug Scott*
16. The Titan, Fisher Towers, Utah. *Photo: Craig Martinson*

between pages 416 and 417

17. The North-East Ridge of Everest. *Photo:Chris Bonington*
18. An ice cave on the Lho La, Everest. *Photo:J. Altadill*
19. 20. 21. On the West Ridge of Everest. *Photos:Stane Belak*
22. 23. 24. 25. On the West Face of Makalu. *Photos:Alex MacIntyre*
26. Reinhold Messner on the summit of Nanga Parbat
27. Camp on the Diamir Face, Nanga Parbat
28. Reinhold Messner approaches the summit of Everest. *Photos:Messner collection*
29. K2 from the east. *Photo:Iwa to Yuki*
30. House's Chimney on K2's Abruzzi Ridge. *Photo:Joe Tasker*

between pages 544 and 545

31. Garbage being collected from below Half Dome's North-West Face. *Photo:Ron Partridge*
32. Gustaf Diessl and Leni Riefenstahl in the pre-war film The White Hell of Piz Palu.
33. The Swiss location for the 1982 film Five Days in Summer. *Photo:Courtesy of The Ladd Company*
34. The stars of Five Days in Summer. *Photo:Courtesy of The Ladd Company*
35. Naomi Uemura receives the International Award for Valour in Sport. *Photo:Julie Tullis*
36. Climbers as bodybuilders. *Photomontage:Courtesy of High*

portraits of some of the contributors

37. Greg Child
38. Reinhold Messner
39. Don Whillans and Chris Bonington
40. Galen Rowell
41. Anne Sauvy-Wilkinson
42. Pierre Mazeaud
43. Max Jones and Mark Hudon
44. H. W. Tilman
45. Rick Sylvester
46. D. F. O. Dangar and T. S. Blakeney
47. Alex MacIntyre
48. Jim Bridwell
49. Anderl Heckmair
50. Mick Fowler
51. Ivan Ghirardini
52. Claud Schuster
53. Willi and Nanda Devi Unsoeld
54. Kim Carrigan
55. Doug Scott
56. Kevin Fitzgerald
57. G. F. Dutton
58. Michael Roberts, Janet Adam Smith and Othon Bron
59. Dave Roberts

Photos: Doug Scott, Dave Roberts, Claude Taccoux, Ken Wilson, W. G. Lee, Julie Tullis, H. Munroe Thorington, Jozef Nyka, Joe Tasker, Phill Thomas, Geoff Birtles, John Krakauer, and the archives of High and Mountain.

Cartoons in the Text

Jailbreak	*page* 2
"Phil could be a great climber . . ."	38
Midi Tobacco and Pervatin	40
"Wow, the Salathé Wall!"	43
"The next pitch varies in difficulty . . ."	83
Best Wishes and Good Climbing. Your Friend — Mac	132
The Mirror	140
Cobwebbed Climbers	154
Baby with Toy Mountain	166
Nest on Ledge	168
"Don't laugh, it only encourages him"	207
Von Mabel's Suitcase	250
Golf on the Cliffs	344
Prusik to Putt	346
Working out Aggression	352
Golden Oldies — Tenzing and Hillary	403
A large percentage of people met on climbs are quite normal	421
Harding with a bottle of 'Red Mountain'	427
"Watch out for the ants . . ."	486
"Beautiful dynamic belay . . ."	494
Abseil around tree	560
Tying a novice to the rope (*Fell and Rock Journal*)	592
"Guess what we girls did today?"	602
Abominable Snowman with Oxygen	616
Von Mabel's Lecture	641
Skeletal Snapshot	679

Foreword

ROYAL ROBBINS

There is a natural affinity between mountaineering and literature. How else to account for the vast outflow of words on the subject of climbing mountains? In the first place, climbers tend to be readers, and many cut their idealistic teeth on books about climbing. I certainly did. To me the romantic (and it is that – not over-romantic, as many nowadays, following fashion, would claim) picture of mountaineering drawn by James Ramsey Ullman in his book *High Conquest* was intensely attractive because it contrasted so vividly with the sordid business of growing up in Los Angeles.

As climbers are readers, so too they tend to be writers; they value the power of the written word. The body of climbing literature is amazing in its disproportion to the number of participants. There are, for example, many more skiers than climbers, yet the literature of ski-ing is paltry compared to that of climbing. Then there is the question of quality. On the whole, this has been impressively high – enough to vie with those other two literary outdoor pursuits, exploration and war.

Climbing, more than most sports, comes alive in the pages of literature. In it, man can experience exploration and battle, but on a sporting basis. Messner, for example, in his solo ascent of Nanga Parbat: his description of the outer limits of solo mountaineering is engrossing in its cool, objective view from the top. It is a game which he plays very well. Ivan Ghirardini plays it less well, and his anguished description of getting in over his head in the French Alps is one of the better things in the book. He suffered, but he learnt something along the way; the valuable lesson of humility.

Humility – a whole essay could be written on the relationship between pride, humility, and mountain climbing. Pride is the first of the seven deadly sins. C. S. Lewis calls it "the great sin". The nature of climbing – which tends to put a man on top of a small point high above the Earth's surface – a place which he has reached through efforts by definition *extra*ordinary, and a place from which he literally looks down on the rest of the world – tends to develop in the climbers a growth, perhaps even a malignant growth, of pride.

The mountains, then, are a battleground between a man's weakness and his strength, between his pride and his humbleness. The best mountain writing will often mix these four elements. A perfect example is John Long's *The Only Blasphemy*, a short narrative which is the most vivid writing about pure rock-climbing I have ever read, a minor masterpiece about a hair's-breadth escape from death through which the protagonist learns a lesson in humility. Afterwards, Long is content to pick flowers and relish the skyscape. Not such an unusual occurrence! You will find it hinted at in other articles here; as when Yvette Vaucher says, near the top of the Matterhorn, "All I want to do now is to get back to the real world, to become a wife again, Michel's wife . . ." Or again, Pierre Mazeaud, after a desperately close shave on the Civetta: "We are a club with three members who now want only to walk with wife and child, to pick flowers." What climber has not made a variation of the promise: "Please God, let me out of this one and I won't tempt fate again"? He means he won't let *pride* lead him into tempting fate again.

There have been many anthologies of mountaineering literature, but this is probably the richest collection of writings about the mountains and mountaineering ever assembled. A strong statement, and all the more remarkable since this book follows hard on the heels of its predecessor, *The Games Climbers Play*. I say remarkable because *Games*, of course, had first pick of the litter. *Games* was a good book, but this in some ways is better. Its level of excellence is more consistent. *Games* was a bit like the Cascades, its pieces of writing tending to stand alone and separate like volcanic peaks in that range. The Cascades have their connecting foothills, but what one tends to notice is the apartness of the peaks. *Mirrors in the Cliffs* is a more organic collection. It is more like the Sierra Nevada – a range with peaks as high as the Cascades, but which stand together as one unit, connected by the granite bedrock underlying the entire massif, which in its turn holds high even the slighter peaks of the range.

Saying how the metaphor of the granite bedrock holds in relation to this anthology is difficult. I know it does, because that is what makes this collection so special. This is definitely not just another collection of mountain writing. It is inspired. Even though the articles came from all over the place, and are often quite dissimilar, they have a unity which sets this collection apart from any other.

Perhaps it is a certain unity of perspective on the mountain experience, whether it be female, male, virtuoso, modest climber, Italian, English, American, women's liberationist, women's traditionalist, rock-climber, mountaineer, philosopher, joker, polemicist or poet. Whatever it is, Jim Perrin has captured it in this collection; he is a very shrewd judge of climbing literature, who has brought out here the underlying kinship of climbers everywhere.

As diverse as climbers or climbing or these articles are, there is a central thread of high-mindedness, a searching for the same heights, literal or metaphorical, which inspired me when I first opened the pages of *High Conquest*. Climbing is a noble sport after all, even in the articles reveling human pettiness – the controversies over Whymper's character, or over the early ascents of Mont Blanc's Brenva Face, for example. Yet even in these articles the battles are over whether people are measuring up to the highest standards; there is an implicit acceptance within them.

Yes, this anthology derives its strength from Perrin's synthesizing vision, from his ability to see in each piece that granite bedrock of love for men and mountains, love for the struggle upwards, love for the effort to defeat our weakness, love for the perfecting of spirit which lies at the root of man's desire for the mountain peak. In the final article in the book Claud Schuster – one of many neglected or underrated authors whom Perrin recalls to our attenion laments of time – "wasted through sloth, or failing courage, or lack of imagination." He follows with "where you seized on life with both hands, whether you succeeded or failed, there you triumphed." This sums up the essential climbing ethos; we could not be left with a message more instructive, hopeful or wise.

The title of the book comes from *End of a Climb*, a fantasy by John Menlove Edwards which is one of the book's two lead essays. It is apt, for these stories hold the mirror up to nature, as the cliffs do a mirror to ourselves, enabling us to see inside, giving us the potentiality of a clearer view through into our true spirit.

Introduction

Inescapably, the anthologist makes a naked confession of taste, and is privileged to do so. The sort of writing which I like is different, in the main, to that of *The Games Climbers Play*. Writers whose work was not included in that book – Rowell or Tilman, for example – I would have refused to go to press without. Such a remark is not coat-trailing. Rather it points up the richness of the available material. That a sport's literature can sustain two large anthologies within five years is a sign of health.

One of the main purposes of any anthology is that its parts should reflect upon each other to produce a satisfying pattern and whole. It is not simply a random collection, but a statement of belief on the part of its compiler and a commentary on aspects of the sport. The two pieces which lead off the selection are a firm indication of what is to come. Greg Child's Yosemite saga, *Coast to Coast on the Granite Slasher,* is a considerable piece of work from this young Australian. Clear narrative direction controls its impressionistic grasp of detail and sure sense of human perspective. It sits well alongside J. M. Edwards' *End of a Climb,* where the implied question in the title is answered in a manner subtle, comprehensive, and profound.

Choice can be either the airing of prejudice or the striving after objectivity. There is not much in this book about large expeditions, but there is a good deal about adventures which, whilst apparently on a smaller scale, are far larger in terms of personal achievement. To my mind, it is the individual, and not the impersonal and over-organised which possesses the appeal, the risk, and human flavour of climbing. On the side of objectivity, I have tried to present as many as possible of climbing's multiple aspects. Distinctions blur at the edges; some of these pieces flow over into travel-writing or anthropology. In some areas the problem was one of a dearth of good material – why has so little of real quality been written about rock-climbing, for example? Is it a sphere where matter has finally triumphed over mind? I cannot think so when one of the best stories in this book, *The Only Blasphemy*, is a pure rock-climbing experience.

No matter and never mind—there's more than enough left from past, present, and peripheries to entertain, stimulate, and delight.

Dolwyddelan, 1983   JIM PERRIN

17

Coast to Coast on
the Granite Slasher

GREG CHILD

Never trust the written word. At best it's a second rate account of
reality. How can you duplicate the enormity of the moment? How
can you truthfully record the feelings or events when the intricacies
of each second of thought would fry the circuits of a computer?
And how can you honestly describe the moments that throw you to
your knees in humble awe in the face of the event? No – it's like
rendering colour memories into muddy monochrome negatives. It's
vernacular butchery. It's slashing at reality.

Like sub-titled movies something vital is lost in the translation.
This missing link between the actual abstract thought and the
recorded outcome has led me to believe that the finest moments,
thoughts and images fail in print or never even make it. How could
they?

Talking to a friend once I launched into an animated rave about
a previous personal experience, faltered on my inadequate words,
shrugged and concluded. "Well, you really had to be there." What
truth! So obvious yet so profound. It is in involvement, and not
through any armchair account, analogy or metaphor that meaning
to this pile of words, and justification for man's insatiable appetite
for escapism will be found. No one can find it for you. You will not
read it here. All you will find here is another razor murder.

A surfer planing down a wave or a biker leaning into a fast
corner isn't thinking of board dimensions or mechanics. They're in
there for the ride. Our intellect has given us technology, which has
given us a specific variety of devices suited to escapism, which in
turn stimulate our emotions. A full circle where man has used his
intellect to stimulate that intellect. Technology is the conveyance to
put one in these distant situations. On arrival the metaphysical
becomes as apparent as the physical, and ideas, feelings,
surroundings and events merge into a total experience that leaves
one slashing for words.

The notion of mountains or big walls as a medium for enlightenment is nothing new. Climbing literature is full of it; it's all the

rage. These high places are magnets to the escapist, allowing one to wrest one's mind from the humdrum of standard reality and focus on things otherwise inaccessible. Realities nonetheless, but so separate from the norm as to be unique to the human experience.

Strangely juxtaposed in an ex-wilderness setting is a monolith that epitomises the big wall image, indeed gave birth to the term. Vast sweeps of scalpel-sliced granite, huge bays and inlets formed of glinting sheets of surreal patterns and tones, dwarfing tall pines in size and age. Standing at the head of Yosemite Valley, humans at this point in time call it El Capitan.

Gazing from the meadows, I felt like a pinpoint against it; it seemed so huge, so unattainable. Yet in the spring of 1977 I found myself manteling over the grey headwall of Mescalito, a line near the fabled Dawn Wall. As I waited for my partner, Eric, to jumar up and join me I noticed how my metabolism was still vibrant with the energy that had accompanied us for six days. A surging and anticipatory energy that we felt could have kept us going for another week. As dusk filled the high country we found a clearing amid twisted hemlocks and slabs, and dropped into a deep sleep. By morning that energy was gone. Waking slowly, stretching stiff limbs and swollen fingers, stained black with oxides from the ever-clutched 'biners, I realised that the energy was controlled by the subconscious. Now, on top, our minds told our bodies that the journey was over so the flow of vital chemicals had diminished. Above all, our minds were exhausted, taxed by the continual concentration on each placement.

We jettisoned the haul-bag laden with iron down the steep east face. With a hammock clipped to the top as a parachute it sailed to earth like a returned space probe, landing with a distant thud on the talus below.

Descending to the fleshpots of the valley, hearing the bustle of civilisation it seemed that the energised clarity our minds had known was being smothered by our re-entry. That night, with heads full of wine that energy was briefly refound. We talked to all who came to sleep, then talked for hours to each other. Yet on the wall we hardly spoke. It just didn't seem the place for small talk. Suddenly the origin of that sureness and clarity became apparent. Up there, isolated from society and its trappings, our minds had no use for the babble and clutter, the ever-racing mental chatter that usually fills it. Our 'internal dialogue' had switched off, letting us focus on the task at hand, revealing a crystalline confidence and oneness with the rock that heightened each day. The night slurred on and we spoke of the afternoon breezes that lifted our ropes in aerial dance and of the kamikaze swallows that strafed us from sight unseen and made us cringe as from the buzz of falling rock, such was their sound.

It wasn't long before the post-wall high left and the horizontal world of Yosemite became old. In the central section of the east face where a vast black diorite intrusion has mapped a likeness of the North American continent, is a sea of calms and swells along the West Coast. By midsummer I was part of a team of four sailing across what was then the epitome of the epitome; the Pacific Ocean Wall.

Our number bolstered our confidence against the aura of the route. The night before we embarked, Darryl, our mad-dog Canadian, downed a fifth of vodka and demolished a building with a broomstick in a bicycle joust. Eric, Kim and I agreed that the pact was sealed with madness.

For a week our team and life-support units tapped slowly upwards. We were modern Michelangelos working gently and carefully, each placement a crucial work of art, copper and chromolly on granite. The wall swept drastically away beneath us. While jumaring a slowly spinning thread of nylon, 50ft. out from the rock, I felt so frail and dependent on technology, helpless without it yet at the same time suspicious of its hold over us. Perhaps there is a harmony, a delicate interplay between man, technology and the environment, but as I hung there with the valley revolving sickeningly around me, a healthy distrust of my immediate dependancy rocketed me to the belay.

The last hours were chaos. Kim screaming at a crack, Eric singing reggae tunes while beneath them Darryl and I beat hammers to a neolithic chant, water gone, sun baking our brains. Then suddenly it was all over. The top again. As we commended the bags to the deep it all seemed so ephemeral, like a dream, or an opiate euphoria. That timeless, fleeting state of mind only found on the vertical.

The summer baked on. From my patch in the meadows I felt as one of many drawn to the walls above. I wondered what it was like when those first adventurous climbers lay here and stared at the then virgin walls until the gaze fell on the obvious striking line that slices through the centre of El Cap. Perfectly hewn cracks and corners, as if the rock had been designed to climb. I wondered then if in 1958 when the Nose route was climbed if the team ever imagined the changes that El Cap would witness – the lacework of routes weaving about it, a pin in every crack, and the changes to the Valley itself; from the valley that John Muir wrote of to the wilderness Disneyland of today. Throwing my mind further back I wondered what the Indians, who must have revered the monolith as something sacred, would think of all this. The roads and cars that sped between myself and El Cap, the phony shops like the Pohono Indian Gallery where knobby-kneed tourists in garish check shorts can buy vinyl table mats with the laughing face of Geronimo beaming forth (before he was shot in the back), and where the nearby Indian village is a caucasian version of the past. Whatever happened to them anyway? Then I remembered that this very meadow had once been forest, cleared by settlers in the 1800s. For a while I felt somehow guilty and implicated in this web.

So I escaped to the anonymity of the Nose with a tall glib Englishman named Tom and a young local, Charlie. By climbing in the early fall we avoided the hordes that usually swarm up the route though we had to contend with the usual dry heat. The Imperial Japanese Climbing Army had just retreated from El Cap Tower, booted honourable haulbag off, Banzai! Too hot for numerous sons of Nippon.

Three days later, bivying on Camp Six with tongues like dry leather I would give the larger Tom the larger half of an orange and for this gift of moisture he would pledge eternal gratitude. Camp Six is an exfoliated flake with a wide crack behind it full of a mixture of tins, empty water jugs, gear and shit. With a skyhook we fish out a few relics. Jamming up long hand-cracks we pass mutilated iron and nuts. Man's presence is scattered everywhere.

Another half-day and we stand atop the shimmering bulwark, weak and parched. The view of the sparkling Merced meandering below tantalised our thirst as we hiked down.

"Christ youth, I'd give anything for a swig o' water," rasped Tom as we passed by a boulder at the edge of the Tangerine Trip.

"The hand is quicker than the eye," I retorted, plucking, from behind a boulder, a gallon jug that I'd stashed from Mescalito three months before.

"That's twice I owe you, youth," replied an astounded Pom. The green water was guzzled down in seconds.

Two years passed before I returned, during which time I spent a season pottering around the base of FitzRoy in Patagonia, a place that eats men forever. All that time I dreamt of the friendly walls of El Cap, so gentle against the icy, windswept towers of the Torre Valley.

Jetting out of the poverty of South America I headed straight for Yosemite, and a northern spring. When the spring deluge ceased I joined up with a fellow wanderer and doctor of rockaneering, Matt Taylor, on the soaring Magic Mushroom route. A nail-up in the classic sense that penetrates the Shield headwall via continuous groove systems.

The route was a celebration of spring. Green shoots sprouted from cracks while hummingbirds hovered by our bags, searching for flowers. In the morning sun, chunks of ice fell in clusters about us, blown in swaying flocks from the rim.

On the third afternoon I came across a moist crack with an angle peg jutting from it. Raising my hammer to reseat it I heard the croak of a frog. Pulling the loose pin out with my fingers, I found a tiny grey frog inhabiting the fold of steel. Apologising for the intrusion I put him aside, slammed the pin and was on my way. What a strange symbiosis. The small creature utilising the piece of iron placed by man as a shelter against the harsh winter. Silent, unquestioning desperation. A fragile, vertical oasis held together by the interaction of water, soil and tiny organisms. A delicate balance where too much or too little of one factor can mean the end.

The oasis and I, a clumsy oaf laden with 40lb of jangling junk, bungling into it, severing roots and disturbing the life cycles of creatures I couldn't even see. Reaching the belay I wondered if our physical trespass had an intellectual justification. It seems that wherever man goes he does nothing beneficial for the environment. Even amid 3,000ft. of stone he commits crimes against nature. The sunset glows pink with smog, the river below parallels a stream of tar. And inevitably as man spreads the wilderness shrinks before him.

"What right do we have to be here, Matt?" I asked as he joined me. His quizzical silence was my answer.

A couple of days later the frog had its revenge. Two pitches from the top, on a slightly expanding flake, my mind wandered and I popped a couple of placements and crashed feet first into a flake. Numb at first I finished the pitch, but soon sharp rhythmic pain tore at my ankle which had swollen to the size of a balloon. Matt took the helm for the last few hours as I tried to jumar and clean one-legged, the slightest twitch agonising. Of course we feared the worst and diagnosed it as broken, or rebroken since it was the ankle that surgery had bolted back together after a power dive years before. The final 30ft. roof was merciless, dangling and grinding my teeth for ages only to turn the lip and find Matt belayed a mere 15ft. from the top. The rope had just ended. He led off and hauled me up to the top. Release from the vertical was like a shot of morphine.

Next day, closer observation showed it to be a sprain. A gnarled stick of hemlock in hand, I began the four-mile hop, crawl and slide down slabs and tearing mazanita to the rappels and valley floor. The friendly gold stone had showed its mean side. The loose flakes, caved-in skulls and helicopter extravaganzas had only been stories until then. Human error is a reckless luxury in an environment where trespassers are merely tolerated.

By the fall I was locked into the trap that Yosemite can be, lazing by the river, gazing at El Cap's profile. Hanging around the social hub of the valley, the parking lot, I felt claustrophobia building in me. Too long penned between the walls. Just as I felt the roots of stagnation anchoring me to the kerb, a hyperkinetic hotshot from the Bay Area named Zacher talked me into a free repeat of the West Face of El Cap. He talked so fast I had no chance to refuse.

That's the parking lot though, a market place for partners, gear and simple amusements. People you hardly know will ask you to launch off on all manner of routes. All manner of people too. Sometimes the walls echo to the screaming matches of teams in the throes of divorce. Small issues take on strange dimensions on walls.

Sleeping at the base gave us a dawn start and a burst of energy that launched us up pitch after pitch. We took nothing but the clothes on our backs, a nut/friend rack, some water and Dextrose for energy. The rock was a similar texture to Middle Cathedral Rock, richly brown, about 80° steep, with fine incut holds linking hand- and finger-cracks. It's hard to recollect the climbing, it happened so fast. But even more than before I felt my subconscious guiding me. Almost as if I wasn't thinking, my body would perform. It knew exactly where to go.

By noon the pines looked like pencils and by dusk we scuttled over the final slabs. Once a Grade 6 nail-up, now an all-free marathon. Refinement of attitudes and techniques had led to the ultimate expression of the form.

Weary after the solid 2,000ft. push, we watched the sun sink into a red earth. Too late to make the rappel descent and too cold for a bagless bivy, we hiked the eight miles down the Falls Trail, staggering in at midnight to Camp Four. Rummaging in the steel locker for a blanket I heard a snotty grunt from the tree in front of me. Looking up I saw a bear silhouetted in moonlight, staring face to face, a whole three feet away. Behind him was his mother, looking very protective and much bigger. Rational panic prevailed – I grabbed a blanket and slammed the lid just as he made a move for a food box. Foiled, he snorted and continued up the tree to harass a screeching gang of racoons, no doubt thinking me a strange and scruffy animal as I curled up on a bed of pine needles.

There is always a feeling after a wall that it never really happened. It felt inconceivable then to wake up in the same old trap a day after starting a route I'd gone up on specifically to escape that very trap. Though a sudden rush of excitement, it was nothing like the satisfaction of a full-on Grade 6. Masochistic as it may sound there is a subtle beauty in the anxious rope-clutching and waiting at belay to the tune of distant tapping, the gadgetry, logistics and sweating. The tense concentration of climbing an expanding flake, placement by slow placement, your spine tingling with nervous care as the piece you're on shifts as you place the one above it. Then the relief when it holds. Even the feeling of self-destruction at the end of the route is an integral part of the experience. And the music of steel against steel, clashing and ringing, releasing the pent-up steam of living in the real world. Perhaps this brinksmanship, this contrast of calm and savagery satisfies our dual egos of aesthete and barbarian, our yin and yang.

A short time later, with a wall-climber by the name of Tim

Washik, I made a long, strange journey into the Atlantic side of the North America Wall, on to the steep and jagged face called the Iron Hawk. Deriving its name from a huge diorite fresco, the likeness of a surreal bird of prey, we found the hawk everywhere. Circling on silent thermals peregrine falcons watched our every move.

We started from El Cap tree, an 82ft. pine that sprouts 300ft. up the wall. Nailing a 40ft. ceiling level with the tree-top, exposure was total as we swung about in slings, looking at piles of bleached pigeon bones on the ledge below, the morsels of the hawk.

Features invisible from the ground revealed themselves to us as flake led to flake. A rope length of traversing on tipped-in blades led to a pair of curving arches. Delicate hooking then led out on to the blank face midway on the journey, which showed us subtle features and led us to strange stacks of steel in the arches above. Never had we driven so hard on our pins, so steep and insecure was the feeling. Everything jutted out at crazy angles.

On the fifth afternoon we were engulfed in a swirling mass of cloud. That night it rained, a flash flood on the vertical desert. In hammocks under an overhanging arch, we stayed fairly dry. Interludes in the morning cloud showed the team who's been paralleling us on Mescalito, bivvied in a water streak, soaked and severely miserable, climbing to a ledge 200ft. above them. We stayed put and watched the eerie mist-enshrouded castles and gothic towers of the Cathedral Spires.

During the afternoon the temperature dropped and we donned every stitch of clothing. From beneath us we heard music wafting in the breeze. Someone had mounted car speakers toward us and was blaring the Hendrix version of All Along the Watchtower. The words rang up at us on a gust . . . "There must be some kinda way outta here . . ."

As the sun set a front moved in at high speed, interrupting our dinner with a wind that filled our hammock-flies like parachutes and lifted us perpendicular to the wall. Before we could batten down the hatches we were being lifted and slammed into the wall mercilessly. This lasted all night. Our flies tore and rain gushed in. The only respite from the beating was to sit upright and pull the flies tightly around us. No one slept that night on El Cap and above the roaring gale came the staccato chatter of Tim's teeth. Neither asleep nor awake, but more tranced, my mind glowed orange within while outside my skin shrivelled white after thirty-six hours enhammocked in a gale.

By morning we were saturated despite layers of Goretex and technology. As the sunset had heralded the wind, the sunrise saw it leave. Numb to the bone we tried to make the most of the dim sunshine. Tim was still shivering. Our ropes, uncoiled by the wind, looked in bad shape and pins that we'd been anchored to hung loosely out of the crack. Even our gorp had turned to porridge. We tipped the vile slop out and scree-scrappers later enquired if it was our puke spread over the talus.

But we were in one piece after a helpless ordeal at the hands of the Iron Hawk. This I felt proved my theory that all bad scenes are transient – it's only a matter of time before the bad part ends.

We decided to climb out to dry ourselves and escape. Since Tim was wetter he led off on a hard double pendulum and stunt pitch to a corner. By dusk we were back in our damp bags, snowflakes pattering on our tattered rainflies.

The eighth day dawned clear and warm. As I swung over to a hand-crack a helicopter hovered by us. We waved it on; no rescues yet thanks. Another swing and we were on a small but flat ledge. The first thing we'd stood on for a week, we were determined to sleep on it no matter how small it was. Tim removed his damp socks and produced two wrinkled lumps of flesh he called his feet. He plucked a dead toenail from the sock and sat staring at it, mumbling something about frost-bite.

"It was a cruel storm," I consoled. Coyotes howled at a moonless sky and rockfall thundered down Sentinel Gully, dislodged by the first snow of the season.

The last day was warm. Free moves on diorite led to the summit roofs. Tim traversed under them, tensioned right to a fixed pin, clipped it and came hurtling back at me, the pin hanging uselessly from his aider. A cursory exchange and an hour later we arrived at the total calm of the summit. Half Dome and the high country were crowned in snow. Suddenly the place was alive with people, friends with food for the starvelings. We told them we were OK – six days' food stretches to ten easily. They poked our ribs and added that 140lb drops to 120 just as easily.

Ordeal by piton over, we reached the valley floor to find Tim's van had been robbed. Perhaps our luck was better on the wall after all and our ways parted after this strange encounter of ten days.

My last hours in the Valley saw another storm move in. I wondered what the place would look like next time I saw it. The Park Service has great plans here. Phase cars out of the valley, construct a huge car park at the west end. A grapple for franchise and exploitation; remodelling, greed, tourism, telephotos and tinsel pollute the valley floor. Yosemite is slowly going under. There's even a disease that's killing the trees by the dozen. I almost wonder if the Park Service hasn't conspired with the bugs for this chance to break out the buzz-saw. They call it developing the natural resources for the people. Some would give it another name. The great days of the valley floor were over when the first white man moved in.

But the walls are a refuge that the masses can't invade so easily. A few bolts and pins here and there, a fallen flake every few years, some dabs of chalk through the summer but essentially they remain unaffected by human erosion, while man just comes and goes.

If only he knew how the walls laugh at his smallness.

from ROCK 3 *1980*

End of a Climb

JOHN MENLOVE EDWARDS

It was an easy route, but I made a mess of it. My friend had to rub my middle for me, and that more than once all over, before I could get up the bad pitch. Even so I trembled violently all the way up.

Courage comes and goes so stupidly. I have never been able to discover the way of it myself, nor whether it was a good or a bad thing. Some people seem to get firmly into the habit of it and then it seems usually a bad thing. Perhaps it is that bravery is an accident, something to be explained away, or deprecated, or at the very least something to be kept very secretly to oneself, to use for one's own personal admiration. One can use it too instead of wisdom and so on in one's decisions, and it can then make life much easier, both to live and to take a pride in. As for the question of how to get this courage, I am myself convinced that here again it must almost always be accidentally come by: either it is put upon one because the world has left one too empty here and too full there, or else one catches it as one might a cold, from some odd circumstance, a friend rubbing one's middle for instance, in just the correct manner.

Anyhow, be the reason what it may, we did get up the climb, standard probably easy V.Diff., and at the top I was so exhausted with the conflicting emotions of fear and pride that, instead of thanking my friend for his kindly ministrations, I lay down full length in the heather and fell straight away into a deep sleep. The chief reward of virtue had come to me: but unfortunately my happiness was not complete, for out of the depths of an otherwise princely portion of unconsciousness there came to me a dream, a long and difficult dream.

Perhaps it was due to the inner conflict of feeling I had been through, or perhaps it was that while laying my upper half carefully on the heather I had left the lower half to fend for itself on the rocks: one way or the other I dreamt that I was in two parts, and that each was frankly annoyed with the other. For some time indeed they glared at each other without a word spoken. Then the legs could hold back no further. "Look here," they said, "we've been doing this all up the climb: it's about time we had it all out." And to my alarm and disgust they began to pull yard after yard of the most unpleasant-looking material from their insides. It was plain enough that the wretched halves were simply doing this to annoy each other. The atmosphere of hate was in it, and they were showing how rotten the inside of a person can be when brought unexpectedly outside. I could do nothing to prevent it, and the cliff was rapidly getting into very nasty condition. They went on shouting and cursing and throwing out half-digested material on either side until the climbs were no longer worth doing: excellent routes covered with this, as I say, half-digested stuff that one usually prefers to stow away and take for granted.

In sheer disgust at the sight they made I took to flight, and floated off into the fastnesses of the Alps. But alas, speed as I might, they were there before me standing there still, for I might as well be honest, strewing their guts all over the mountains. I rushed rapidly on through the air towards the Himalayas. I never got there. Whether it was my hurry, or perhaps that the lower part of my bed was not only hard but a little slippery, I suddenly felt myself drop. Down I fell into the sea, then a sick, heavy tremor crept along the marrow of my bones and I sank slowly through the dull water. What sea it was I do not know, but it was quite warm and may well have been the Persian Gulf. It must have been deep, too, for I seemed to sink for a long time before subsiding on the bottom. That may have been deceptive though, for I certainly remember that even the last few feet took ages to go by. I hated it, and as I sank, I cried out my fears. "It is no earthly use trying to get to the Himalayas," I cried. "What shall I do now?" Then with a sudden dead calm I stopped breathing.

You may think that was a highly satisfactory ending for a man's more fine desires, but it was never to be consummated, for, soon after I had stopped breathing, I was surprised to find that by far the greater part of me was still perfectly well alive. Either it did not require air at all, or it could get it from some internal source. The apparent necessity of logic was being dispensed with, and as I realised this I began to rouse myself from the mud of the sea-floor in which I was being already systematically fossilised. I struggled hard, but the words were still floating about above me and it required a terrible effort to grasp them. "Er – er – oxygen's a farce," and as I gasped it out I rose at once to the surface of the water. "I need air?" I went on, "but dash it all I'm full of sorts of air, and anyhow you know nothing about it." Apparently, for without the slightest sign of breathing or anything that might support its further existence, my love detached itself and sailed strongly down the wind to the cliff where it had started, flicked off the mess and began climbing again without a qualm.

I was pleased at this, and not hesitating to put my mind at rest I seized the chance as it came and rose half a mile into the full heat of the sun. There, from that elevated and pleasant position, I was able to survey the operations below me at a proper distance and with a proper detachment.

It seems wrong to pass straight from dream to reality, yet, as this is what actually happened, I do not wish to falsify the truth in any way and will stick to the facts. I fancy I slept on undisturbed until I finally awoke. Awoke, but it was with a not very definite awakening. I became conscious of a calmness in the air, then of faint sounds of the hillside. One might wake up a little more.

It was indeed a warm day and a good spot. The cliff was below us and its height carried us up above the rest of the steep valley side in a little castle of rock. On this was our patch of heather, dry and thick. The other side of the valley stood over against us in a ridge, hard and dark, for beyond and behind it the sun was declining into the faint mists of a still further horizon, somewhere over the flatlands beyond our range. Its rays lit the hillside round us, and down the pass we could see their straight lines slant across with the light in their arms. There was no need to move. The comfortable heather pressed into my back, filling out its angles of restlessness.

The sunset, the grinding of atom against its neighbour atom, force against its neighbour force. Fortuitous, perhaps, but moulded now into this by its necessities and a long chain of use. Moulded now into a colour of paradise, then driven away again along illimitable change. And a little figure looks up out of his own preoccupation and catches perhaps something of the size. He, too, is nature. He knows the change, the decay and long births, the mills grinding, and he, too, standing aside at the end of his climb can see, spread in his eyes, a terror and a glory within him. That his poor feelings are nature, but are no aim for nature. They are incidents, instruments, to be excited in him and caught up in him, dazzled and torn by him and used as goads upon him fully while there is any power left in them and until they are quite done. Use, and not satisfaction with nature, except that we can imagine ourselves dead a little.

Yet my mind would not gather together its profundities in that pause at the end of our climb. There was some tune that turned round and round in front of me, and my mind refused to recognise the silly jazz and put a stop to it. Poor, sleepy mind. The energy in us has always been like that. It kicked on and on inside of us until it was tired, and then only it let us stand aside. For once it gave leisure to look around us at the end of the climb in suitable perspective, but – the mind, too, had finished its climb, and was gone to sleep. When we have truly come to a pause, and this is often a pity.

My mind was in fact vaguely on the subject of climbing. Fancy lying about on the heather like this, after a single short climb halfway up the pass. This was not what they used to do in the old days. The heights for them; and some good solid foot-slogging, to work the city life out of stale muscles. We have it in the matter of standard though, and quality of what we do; and presumably they will get better still later on. The next generation would be quite exciting in the Helyg log, if we could see it now. Think of the efficiency required.

> . . . From this ledge a small sod is detached (6″ × 4″) and placed on the extreme edge at a point marked by a little scratched arrow. Stand on this and slide over the overhang. 110ft. below there is a small ledge and here, with careful attention to balance, the climber will come to rest. The sod will fit the ledge exactly and is necessary for friction. Those not familiar with the technique may find it wise to fasten the turf to the feet with a loop of rope. Now the route becomes more obvious. A layback leads slightly left for 180ft. to a small nail stance. . . .

And:

> . . . Found some new scramble on Clogwyn du'r Arddu. The rock is seldom even perpendicular for any distance and is literally covered with small holds. Yet novices may like it.

Then a note by that ambitious young party of rock-gymnasts.

> Repeated Outward Bound Route. Three falls, only two fatal.
> A B C, X Y Z, F W B, OK.
> (Signed)
> (Signed) Ferdinand Bounce.
> RIP

Yes, but perhaps, one never knows. For oneself it is nice to be a bit old-fashioned. There were those awkward moments one had on Charity. Besides that dry efficiency above one's own level is more depressing to the marrow than the bottom of the sea in the Persian Gulf. Baron Munchausen (*sic*) is more to taste. He would have been a hot lad on the rocks, and he would have told them all about it afterwards.

> Then, judge of my surprise, there I was hanging stuck by my coat collar in a position whence there was no possible means of escape. Neither above me nor below was there anything to which I could hold, and for a moment I was at some loss as to the proper course to pursue. My mind has become accustomed, however, to work at an unusual speed under the stimulus of instant danger, and after casting about a little I hit upon a plan. I rubbed the nail of my forefinger against the rock and pared it carefully down to a fine point. This I

was then just able to insert into a small hole high above my head and, thereupon, rotating about this as an axis, I brought my feet close to the summit, and with a last supreme effort leapt up feet first to safety.

That is better, one can afford to laugh at that.

We certainly do crave to excel, however little we may be prepared to give to the more difficult question of putting that into practice. But why should we always think like that about standards? Alternatively thinking that the standard of climbing has risen so rapidly that it must necessarily go on rising fast, and then that the standard is already so dangerously near the limit that for sane men it can go no further. And if one turns up the tablecloth and looks beneath, behold, both these ideas rest on the delightful notion that we ourselves are such extremely fine climbers and so immeasurably better than those others. No wonder we keep such ideas going. It satisfies our craving for height and with a minimum of effort, so long as we keep our eyes shut. The standard progresses towards the infinite of what is ideally possible to our physique, and we add a little or a lot or nothing to the advance, but concentrating on personal achievement, we credit ourselves with the excellence of the whole attained. A path is being steadily lengthened, but it is something definite in the way of success that we wish to add to ourselves when we climb, and we do it by walking along the path and stamping it in when we get as near as we reasonably can to the end of it, then we credit ourselves with the whole gain. The path has undoubtedly lengthened, but as for whether we, the particular people, are better than those before, it should be judged on quality, intensity or something, rather than on the precise position and amount of the stamping. In any case in climbing the aim and direction must be a thing to consider, and in climbing there is the complication that the aim is, we hope, not climbing.

I remember once, years ago, in Skye, I was talking, happy and excited:

Sir, I said to the weather-beaten old man with his iron grey hair. Sir, we have discovered a New Route. It lies up the Northern Buttress of Sgurr-a-Gumain and starting at a point 12ft. to the left of a little dagger crack it goes up, though both steeply and awkwardly, to a point on the summit ridge just halfway between two very obvious stones. A large one on the right shaped just like a baby, and a small one on the left shaped like nothing on earth. We climbed, sir, in rubbers, but it seemed to each one of us to be very, very severe.

He sipped slowly at his whisky, and the thin runnels of heat swelled out among the vessels of his throat:

Young man, he said, in the winter of '83 I remember cutting my way up that very buttress in ice and snow. We experienced considerable difficulty in the ascent and there have been one or two points about it graved on my memory ever since. I can see it now. A yard or two to the right of where we started I stood and put a match to my old pipe in the shelter of a small, dark crack formed like a dagger. It was growing dark when we came out on to the ridge, but looking around me I could discern dimly through the driving snow a large stone, and it looked ugly like a babe new-born. We turned away to the left and as I strode forward my foot caught, I fell full length, and my old briar lay on the ground, smashed to atoms. It was a small stone, young man, and it looked like nothing on earth.

Yes, but perhaps I have stressed it all the wrong way. It seemed to make it nicer for ourselves. We allowed that some of them might perhaps by some accident have been in some way as good as ourselves, but we did it by way of a joke, and then only as if some of those elders must have been quite incomprehensible supermen.

What twistings we make in our minds: and on these rocks, too; pulling them and pushing them as if we wanted to make some difference to them, as if it had results beyond those of our own manifest contortions. It is just as well we pull and push all the rest of the circumstances in our lives; as if it were they that had to be re-arranged and not ourselves. Yet circumstances would hardly make so bold as to laugh at us, nor would the cliffs, for we are giving ourselves good exercise and giving them little trouble. We are avoiding unpleasantnesses such as getting stiff and dying, and since it is all very real to us there is no harm surely in allowing ourselves the conceit that it is equally real to the rest of the universe. Imagination makes our game of life seem so much more noble and we so important, and that in turn helps us to help ourselves to more of this living. If we had to wait on reality to show us our importance we would never get any thrill at all. Besides we will drop each conceit when it has served its turn. When it no longer directly deceives us enough to help we will keep it near for a time for the odour of its sanctity, and when that is forgotten—well, it was never more than a figment of the brain, so it should go easily.

We draw ourselves out and educate, and climbing has come to be part of our education. We naturally make a mess of the things we educate ourselves on, and that thing is naturally the world. It is not easy for a limited number of people to make a mess of things so comparatively large as cliffs and hills, for instance, but we do our best, and the mountains are likely sooner or later to be placed on the altar of man's education. Meanwhile we had better cling tight to the old that we love, the grandeur, the isolation, the things untouched as yet by this man, aesthete at one end and vulgarian at the other, a species to which we are unpleasantly accustomed. These things, things from outside, help us to keep our little spark glowing. A spark of readiness for something further and different; for one must keep clear of the crowd even to be in touch with it. That little spark will indeed move heaven and earth before it is done, all to keep itself as clear away as possible. To consider it, it is just this struggle for individuality that is the greatest necessity of the greatest affection, as well as perhaps its only prize. It is the necessity of all mountains, whether of the earth or of the mind, if they are to remain mountains. And education? Education in its turn will not worry its head much in practice about the high places of our feelings. The two certainly work to the same end, but they are only powerful while they oppose each other, each wanting the full mastery over us. To be alike and then to be different, and dreams must always be at war with reality. For the time being the mountains are still the mountains, and we can keep our heads well away on their slopes. We will each make a little image from what we like to see of ourselves in the mirror of the hills. One will laugh at the image, so one-sided. One will make it into a grey God and will then fall down and worship himself. Another will set it up for the great spirit of Man, and will lay down to his own image.

The eyes could close themselves that night and miss nothing, for there was a mood of waiting in the air; the evening was waiting: the heather still moulded round me, and there was a diffused glow over the whole surface of the sky. The sun's rays fell higher up the hillside now: like narrow arms carrying the weight of the evening warmth across the valley. Above them the air was deep with colours. There were many blues and there was silver down towards the sea. There was gold on the slope above us, and the hillside opposite was sheeted in fold upon fold of the emperor's purple.

We were small to that. So many generations has man been lifting the stones, little stones, big stones, to clear a small pasture: stones of all sizes, lifting, carrying them, pushing them out of the way. Those men who years ago worked and made their walls, and fought and cursed each other down the secrecy of the pass. Then strolled out into the evening and the door banged to behind them for a minute.

Dreams of a little people. I remember a boy we saw climbing two or three times, on the Idwal Slabs. He would stand and gaze at the foot of the rocks, scanning them to right and left for some path in their expanse that the foot of man had not yet utilised. Then he went to the foot of the Ordinary Route. As he ascended, however, it was clear enough that he was no ordinary climber, for every now and then he stood, and looked around him with that air of expectancy that is the true explorer's heritage. We realised that at any moment, maybe without the least warning, he might break out on to fresh ground. Rather to our surprise he did actually continue up the Ordinary Route. Perhaps there was something in store for us now, for there he was, gazing with a wide purview above, below and to either side. The preliminaries were over. Clearly he knew these cliffs well, but was now eager above all things for fresh endeavour, new pasture. Sure enough he made no pause for rest, but turned round and with every appearance of one whose mind is set to conquer or to die, he made his way laboriously down the Ordinary Route. We laughed at him at the time and called him the Idwal Slab. He looked queer, too, and just fitted a rhyme we had then in our heads.

What a wonderful thing your face is
That its nose can begin without basis.

Yet he was an excellent youth, and we would have been dull indeed not to admire something at least in that devilish abandon with which our slot-machine culminated time and again in that grand finale of liquorice all-sorts. Indeed we had gone through just the same antics ourselves, only a few yards higher up. We both found mirrors in the cliffs like that. Perhaps it is really just that look of his that is the true explorer's heritage: the man lifting stones, little stones and rather larger stones, clearing a small space round him for pasture and dreaming that they are all very big.

We got up and shook ourselves, for the warmth had left our rock now, and the thin arms of the sun were rising steadily as their burden grew lighter. The colours, however, went still deeper, and then, as if the liquid of the sky became oversaturated with its intensity, it suddenly seemed to sigh and as it did so, it shed a slight greyish precipitate, that gathered and clung nervously together in a thin strip down the centre of the blue. As it formed, the earth seemed to come out a little and its detail began to rise coldly up the sides of the hill. The arms of the sun, as if driven into quick motion, lifted their beams clear of the earth, and the particles of their warmth, despairing, concentrated their last effort in a soft rose light along the western aspect of the strip of cloud. Down on the rocks a squat yew tree, clinging to the face, shivered and drew itself up. The shadows came together and lay cramped stiffly over it.

We turned our backs finally to the hills and began to chatter: setting about to make our minds easy. But behind us, fighting their slow wars, the forces of nature also shifted steadily on.

from THE CLIMBERS' CLUB JOURNAL *1937*

"Phil could be a great climber, but he lacks the
necessary self-discipline."

PART 1

Roots

The first section of the book is devoted to a series of accounts of individual climbs. The explicit emphasis is not on character or motivation, unexplored terrain or humorous situations — but more directly on the central experience of the sport, in all its variety.

Variety is perhaps the keynote here, for though all these accounts dwell on the detail of particular climbs, they do so in widely differing ways. There are sharp contrasts to be drawn. Dorothy Pilley's description of a Welsh climb in *Fortunatus* is light-hearted comedy shot through with an awareness of human foibles, whereas Max Jones brings the intense technical awareness of the modern athlete to bear on his American rock-experiences.

The style and seriousness of the situations differ too. Geoff Birtles' little domestic comedy *No Big Cigar* stands next to Jim Bridwell's taking monster falls in his stride during his momentous piece of super-alpinism on Cerro Torre. Yet the types of experience of which both write have a characteristic flavour, a validity, a body of adherents, within the wide-ranging territories of the sport which contains them. The title of the section is *Roots*, but see from the central preoccupations what flowers grow.

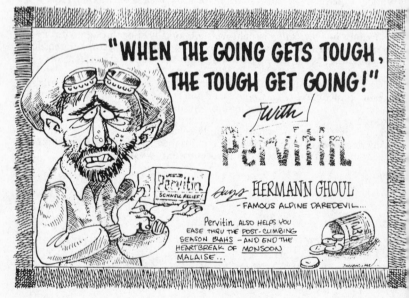

On the Profundity Trail

DOUG SCOTT

Most of the acid heads, wrapped up in old blankets, were lying huddled in a heap around a burnt-out fire. A few more were reflecting by the Merced, smoking weed as the mist rose out of the river into the cold morning air.

Peter Habeler arrived, threading his way down the camp road between the jutting caravans and cars of the tourists who were now swelling the camp to capacity.

Peter was also on his first visit to Yosemite, and it was a fortuitous set of circumstances that brought us together. We had both served a rather hectic apprenticeship in the Valley. Peter had got involved, briefly, with Yvon Chouinard, while I had tried to follow Royal Robbins with limited success. On the lower crags, we had both led free climbs comparable in difficulty with the hard pitches of Salathé; and we had made competent ascents of the Leaning Tower, which involved 900ft. of pegging. In theory we could manage Salathé, providing we kept our heads at altitude.

"Come Doug, it is time to go," hissed Peter, trying not to wake the tourists or our climbing friends still asleep in their tents between the caravans and trees. It wasn't the first time he was to ask me to hurry!

I scrambled round, bundling gear into my day sack (I should have packed it the night before), and we left this corner of Camp 7, heading towards El Capitan, for we were going on the profundity trail via Salathé Wall. Not for us popping a pill or drinking spiked apple cider to get eight hours of unimagined sensory splendour, but a hard, upward, four or five day slog.

We had none of the usual doubts that assail the mind when one is approaching a big climb. It wasn't that we had acclimatised ourselves to them — it was simply that we had committed ourselves the day before by putting our 100lb haul sack some 300ft. up the wall. This is one of the customs the Valley climbers have developed to cut back the odds to more manageable proportions; we were glad to adopt it.

No photograph I have seen really shows the characteristics of the solid, squat bulk of rock that is El Cap. It is monolithic from a distance, but on closer inspection the surface rock is far from uniform. On the contrary, it is highly featured: the granite has been sculptured into elegant buttresses and deep bays, which merge into the spreading slabs and walls that drop down to the forested screes and glacial drift below. When the light shines obliquely, casting shadows across the face, a closer scrutiny reveals long, vertical cracks, precariously perched flakes and splinters of rock, jutting overhangs, and wide expanses of unbroken rock rippled by glacier ice.

Our route included many of these features. It was not at first direct, but it was obviously a natural line and gave a variety of climbing at a continuously high standard. We reached our 'third man', as we called the haul sack, and took out another little helper in the shape of a topo map of the route. This ensures that climbers don't get lost and are not troubled by the unknown, for every pitch is graded and every feature marked, as is each pendule and abseil, and the number of pegs needed. But to us, as we looked up from the third pitch, the topo was not at all encouraging; it showed only too clearly that we had thirty-four pitches to go and that reaching the top was a very remote possibility. To overcome these problems we broke them down into four daily objectives, which loomed so large in our minds that they became like summits in themselves. For the first day we aimed to make Heart Ledge, and forgot about everything beyond.

The first day's work was not the best exercise in European collaboration. We were both humiliated into using sky hooks whilst leading the two 5.9 slab pitches. Neither of us had the slightest idea how the pioneers had stayed in place to put in the bolts which we so thankfully grabbed. Peter made up for this by leading the huge shield of rock known as the 'Half Dollar' in fine style. He couldn't pull the haul sack up and I cursed him as I climbed the narrow chimney pushing the sack in front of me. This procedure was repeated on another 5.9 jam crack above. Peter was in a rage at the restriction the sack was imposing on our progress. We hadn't hauled anything like that weight before and had not yet come to terms with it.

I slung the sack over my shoulder and walked along Mammoth

Terrace to the abseil bushes, looking for all the world like a drunken sailor. We both descended to Heart Ledge and our first bivouac site. It should have been a happy occasion, but I could only think bad thoughts about my partner, while he, no doubt, was wondering what he was doing up there with me! It was like this: he wouldn't stop moaning – about the haul sack, about my hitting the pegs too hard, and then about my moving too slowly up the free climbing. All of which was true enough. But I couldn't help laughing – he was such a smart little bugger, always plastering his blond hair down with the palms of his hands. Unknown to him, however, he was rubbing aluminium dye all over his face. In the end, he looked as though he'd spent the day down a coal mine. Then he was very fastidious. He would take boiled eggs out of a plastic container and slices of bread and butter from his snap tin. And *then* I found he had put salt into the four gallons of water to stop us getting cramp. I nearly threw a fit at home when they put fluoride into the local reservoir and now we had to quench our thirst with salt water!

No, we were not very happy – and if he'd been anyone other than a bloody Kraut, I'd have gone down. And if I had been anyone else but a patronising Englishman I'm sure he would have gone down too. Nothing was said, mind, but that was half the trouble; we couldn't communicate emotionally.

The only generous and charitable thoughts that came to mind were for the first ascensionists – Tom Frost, Chuck Pratt and Royal Robbins. They first climbed up to Lung Ledge, just above Heart Ledge, and then descended, leaving ropes fixed. Returning a few days later, they removed their 'life-line' and went for the top, over 2,000ft. higher, taking six days to negotiate the unknown and uncharted rock. It was a fantastic achievement, as we slowly realised over the next few days; it was also a considerable breakthrough in big wall climbing, paving the way for single-push first ascents.

Next morning, Peter was up and about bright and early. I cursed him (under my breath) for breaking into my fantasy world.

"To rest is not to conquer," I mumbled, sarcastically, and had some cheese and water before leading off from the ledge. I took ages on the first few feet, until Peter used some basic psychology to get me moving by offering to do it himself! That was all I needed to reach a pendule and a surprise bolt at the end of it.

"Get a shot with my cameras," I shouted to Peter.

"Doug, we have not the time," he replied, quite truthfully.

"Get those bloody cameras working," I yelled, and, as an afterthought: "to rest is not to rust."

Well, that did at least clear the air, and we carried on in better style and better humour.

Actually, I think the reason for the improvement was that we now felt more or less committed to the climb. Up to Heart Ledge we had not had that feeling, but now, nagging doubts about continuing were removed. There was only one way out – up and over the top.

We were both putting pegs in and ripping them out with an increased economy of effort. After Hollow Flakes the climb steepened, and sack-hauling was less of a drag. Wide jam cracks and sinuous aid cracks followed one another. In between the stances were remarkably spacious. Peter led the Ear, a flared horror chimney which opens out at the bottom to disgorge the failure into space. Peter was no failure and his wiry figure went up and into it with ease, just as the sun left the face. Although it was early April and the sun had not been anything like as hot as it can be in July and August, being in the shade was as good as a cold drink.

There followed a 150ft. pitch which was A1 and 5.9, and I led it in half-an-hour – the only good thing I'd done all day. This burst of energy was prompted by the long shadows and the thought of not reaching El Cap Spire (our next 'summit') before dark. Peter led the chimney behind the Spire in the dark, with the pegs jangling and the bongs booming behind the big black tower. An hour later I joined him, climbing up behind the sac and taking the few pegs out by the light of glowing granite chips that momentarily flared into life under my badly-aimed hammer.

The bivouac on the flat-topped 'Spire' was magnificent. It had been eroded into minor undulations and we each found a hollow in which to sleep. But first we ate and drank in true communion, chatting about the route and our reactions to it – quite a change from the previous bivouac. Before, my irrational fears of the route had caused me to build up a shell of self-pity and, as a sort of defence mechanism, to castigate my companion. That also was irrational, for he was a first-class climber and companion. A wave of contentment swept through my tired mind as I lay flat out, looking up at the clouds scudding across the night sky, and felt the blood oozing around my worn-out fingers.

That day we had climbed ten pitches of hard jamming and long, tedious pegging. Every peg had to be placed, and the sack hauled; then the second, using Jumars, prussiked up behind, removing all the pegs and slings and racking them ready for the next pitch. Wear and tear on the hands could not be avoided, but we both climbed as carefully as time would allow, so as not to cut the flesh. A sharp burr of chrome moly could easily open the finger-end, making climbing an agony. As it was, granite crystal in the cracks chafed the backs of our hands badly. But it was de-pegging that caused the most damage, because we soon found that it was quicker to take the pegs out under tension. That is, whenever it was convenient, the prusik rope was left attached to the peg which was being extracted. On overhanging walls and diagonal traverses, the sudden release of tension as the peg came out made for some exhilarating swings, but we had to look sharp so as not to catch our knuckles as we went.

Next morning we stepped across from the Spire, pegged up the wall above, and continued to peg for most of the day, from dawn to dusk. Despite the intense concentration I gave each pitch, whilst placing pegs or removing them, I can barely remember features and details. Yet I do recall seemingly trivial thoughts and actions that occupied my mind and time at the belays. On Broad Ledge, a frog leapt on to the scene. My surprise changed to wonder as I contemplated that little frog and its place on the vast monolith of El Cap. How many more were there, I wondered. Perhaps enough to fill a ten-foot-square box. Then he hopped away into the rock, so perfectly camouflaged that I couldn't spot him again. I felt really good up there because of that frog; he seemed to show that we were all in it together – not just the El Cap scene, but the whole business of being alive.

I looked around with a new intensity and watched a drop of water trickle down the dusty granite, a clear crystal that flashed a brilliant light and was gone, to be burnt up by the sun that had momentarily given it life. I traced its wet patch upwards to a crevice and considered its route down through the rock from the melting snow hundreds of feet above. I felt completely relaxed, and my mind ranged over the problems that had been troubling me and saw them with a new clarity. I had found in Eric Shipton's book *Upon that Mountain* a very inspiring way of looking at mountaineering. One phrase stood out: he wrote that it was not the approach that mattered, but the climber's attitude of mind whilst actually climbing. And indeed it no longer seemed important that anything should come from this climb other than the sheer pleasure and satisfaction of having done it. I had been plagued with doubts about my approach to big wall climbing because I felt that I was doing it partly for the wrong reasons, such as making money and achieving fame whilst lecturing and writing about it afterwards. Well, they no longer had any bearing on the matter. It was not that I felt humbled by the vast sweep of rock, but that I had got so much out of the route already. I was thinking and feeling and experiencing all the elements of joy and peace to such a degree that tears welled up into my eyes.

"Doug! Let go the sack," yelled Peter. "I am ready for hauling." Tears of joy were soon replaced by tears of sweat as I hammered up another 100ft. taking out Peter's pegs. In fact, they didn't need much hammering, as they were mostly tied off, with only the tips biting into the rock. One pitch I do remember. Dirty and awkward, it was marked A3. It was also wet and deceptively 150ft. long. After using a variety of smaller blades and angles in awkward, blind cracks, I found a two to four inch fissure which went out under a block for 15ft. and then up another 25ft. to a ledge. It was here that I learnt to stack three angles across each other and put my full weight on them. We seemed to be short on bongs and I had to hand-jam the overhanging crack for 15ft. before I could use regular angles. I arrived on the stance soaked from the dripping lichen of the lower part and stripped off to dry my clothes in the sun, now hanging low above the Leaning Tower.

Peter came up fast after another pendule – this time from under the jutting block – forced on him after he had taken out the last peg under tension. We moved together on the next pitch and then, after some navigational problems, Peter led round some black flakes after a downward tension traverse and climbed up to our third bivouac, 'Sous le Toit Ledge'. Sack-hauling here was made awkward because of jutting flakes, and the sack had to be pushed from behind. I arrived at the bivouac ledge tired after these exertions and was a bit disappointed to find that we could not lie out flat. I had become soft after the other two bivouacs where ten men could have found space to stretch out.

Peter fixed the ropes up another hundred feet, to just short of the 20ft. overhang which undercut the leaning headwall above. When he came back down we made a sort of hammock from the sack-hauling rope and settled down for the night. Half-on and half-off the ledge, we watched the tourists going home, streaming down the valley back to civilisation. Really, they had hardly left it, for they had brought a cocoon of possessions with them, some in caravans so big that Bertram Mills Circus would have been proud to have owned them.

I told Peter how a group next to my tent arrived one evening: from the back of a bus-cum-caravan, a woman spread out a stair carpet and then shook out a large mat beyond. Having set up a table and chairs, she and the family then prepared the evening meal. During the whole of the first evening she had never set foot on the valley floor. Next morning, with her husband, she set off for the supermarket on a motorbike unhitched from the foot of the caravan. There were rumours that some families even brought maids with them — black blouses, white lace aprons and all!

Peter led up next morning towards the belay below the roof. Although it was our fourth day, I regretted that the end was in sight. It was, after all, as the result of a good deal of hard work that we were up there enjoying the climb. I reached Peter's stance and looked with some misgiving at the belay pegs poking out of shallow pockets. I was glad to leave him to put more pegs between us. The roof reared out in three steps and, though the pegging was reasonable, it was difficult to rationalise the situation; I was glad to pass over the roof to the headwall, for I found the sheer drop of 2,500ft. to the trees below quite harrowing. It was certainly more exposed than any other roof I had climbed, including the direct on the Cima Ovest. We were both surprised to find the headwall overhanging for some 200ft. above, and now when the topo indicated slings for stances it meant just that. Some of the nailing was quite thin on the headwall, but with a light haul sack we could move together, and soon Peter was traversing right to the first ledge in four pitches. Those hanging belays were very exhilarating, in retrospect. Quite a wind buffeted the face, throwing us from side to side. Clouds gathered at both ends of the valley, and wisps blew off, diffusing the sun's rays which slanted down and across the quartzy granite, giving a sheen of rippled light.

Although the climbing was getting easier and was no longer actually overhanging, the threatening weather reminded us of our vulnerable position and made us hurry. Earlier in the month we had seen snow storms and six inches of snow. The clouds disintegrated towards evening as Peter led the last pitch, a 5.9 chimney. We scrambled up the last few feet of easy slabs and the climb was over – but not the whole experience, for our body chemistry kept on reacting hours after we had stopped climbing.

As the light faded, we went our separate ways on to the dome of El Cap. My walk slowed to a half pace as I stepped out, feeling my boots sink into the soft, friable earth that had only recently emerged from the melting snows. Heaps of pine cones crackled and crunched loudly in the still evening air as I walked over them. Stopping, I smelt the pine trees with an intensity I had never before experienced. I lifted my head to take in this sensation, like an animal sniffing out its quarry. I saw for the first time the full range of subtle, mellow colours in that evening light. The wind-scalloped surface of lingering snow patches twinkled like jewels in the fading light and all to the east the peaks of the High Sierra were pink above a purple haze of forested valleys. The brown of the soils, and the green of the forest ahead, exhibited innumerable facets. There were browns that were darker and browns that were lighter, and greens that stood out against other greens. Something enabled me to discern colours where before I had only seen one. I stood guzzling in these new sensations like a greedy child, hoping this beautiful experience would never end.

Our paths came together and we walked silently along a vague track, finally getting lost in the snow. As we settled down for the night in a forest clearing, I nibbled with relish at my shrunken salami. I can still recall the succulence of each mouthful. Next morning we made our way down towards the Lost Arrow and by a zig-zag path to the camp.

Like the man who has come down and out of his LSD trip I found the experience at first to be beyond words, but like him I have searched hard to express what I felt – naively perhaps. As with him, a glimpse of my experience is recreated vividly months afterwards, sparked off by a cloud pattern, an expanse of blue sky, a smell of lichen – and any other such catalyst. The day trippers, in their eight-hour ecstasy, lose all sense of time, and this happened on Salathé Wall, especially after the first bivouac. Hours would go by in a rhythm of effort that at times seemed eternal. We had little regard for the past or the future, and thought only of the patch of rock a few feet ahead whilst climbing, or about things quite un-related to our present position whilst sitting on the belays. We felt that, given enough food and water, we could have gone on for a long time to come, for stopping the routine to which our bodies and minds had become accustomed was just as difficult as starting it in the first place. Why didn't we go down and back up the Nose or another El Cap special? I suppose because the spell was broken when we reached camp and anyway Peter had to go back to Austria. Probably there was no reason to go again, at least not until this trip had been digested and lived with. Not even North America Wall, with the promise of newspaper articles and lecture fees, could tempt me to go again!

On any multi-day, big wall route, the climber will discipline his body and its appetites, in the manner of the ascetics. Like them, he will probably experience hardship through extremes of heat and cold, lie uncomfortable and sleepless on a hard bed, go without washing, remain immobile in certain bodily positions for long periods, wear 'chains or other painful bonds', and go in for a certain amount of self-mutilation. Most ascetics, of course, also go in for chastity, a reduction in their food and water intake, extended periods of solitude, abstinence from alcohol, and, in some cases, breath control.

Any climber will be aware of this list of sufferings and will be able to cite instances in which he was afflicted by some or all of them whilst climbing. Indeed, I have not said much that any climber home from a weekend's cragging doesn't know about. He returns relaxed after escaping the anxieties and pressures of city life. What I am trying to say, however, is that with longer and more demanding climbs there are added ingredients of both suffering and reward.

Some of the young hippies in Yosemite are so profoundly affected by the pills and potions that they take that they tend to opt out of ordinary living, or at least claim to do so. This seemed to me to be not only futile, but hypocritical, because for their worldly needs they are so obviously and willingly dependent on the society they say they are rejecting. I am not suggesting that 'the doors of perception' were opened in the same way, or as wide, for me as for the acid heads, but after the trip I did seem to know positively where to go next – and that was back into society, relaxed, but with a new zest and enthusiasm, and without any worries about 'the current undesirable side effects' on mind or body.

If big-wall climbing is pursued in a more hostile environment and for longer periods, or if the big-wall climber climbs alone, as Bonatti did on the Dru, then the doors of perception will be opened wide. The climbers involved may experience a more lasting state of heightened awareness, and may even reach a truly visionary, if not mystical state of being which transcends normal human comprehension. Most of us will never make such climbs, but that is not to say that less demanding climbs could not have a similar effect. The climber who is willing to extend himself to the limit of his technical skill and endurance on any long climb is *en route* up the profundity trail.

from MOUNTAIN 15 *1971*

Nightshift in Zero

DOUGAL HASTON

I was sleeping off a scoop in the Clubrooms when Wightman came rolling in and said he wanted to go to Nevis so we spent the next night in the CIC Hut. The morning was clear and Zero Gully needed a second ascent but our rope had been forgotten in the rush from the foulness of the city.

A solution was on hand, however: the Hut was full of steadfast English muttering earnestly, up Three down Four, up Two down Five, and other Nevis gully permutations, so we waited until they had departed and went on a scavenge for rope. Sure enough there was a nice shiny one hanging on a hook so we swallowed a foul breakfast, grabbed it and staggered up the hill feeling like junkies on a cure.

There was enough blue ice gleaming in the Gully to satisfy the aesthetic eye, but discouraging to arms whose only exercise for a month had been a table to mouth motion of little use in the cutting of steps. Andy got stuck in a corner moaning the blues while I pecked miserably at the first pitch and had done ten feet in half an hour when he told me to get a grip and move and I threatened to drop on him and put 24 holes in his head which shut him up and the slanging warmed me up so I charged up 70ft. within the hour. Arm exhaustion then recalled my month in the city so I decided to go down and have a rest and a sleep and come back on the morrow. I moved down into Andy's corner and Andy thawed himself out with a try and, on failure, the unravelling of the rope and then we slunk off back to the Hut.

The evening was full of hateful mutterings about black rope-stealing and bed-thieving Scots and the Hut is fully booked. Bed had just been achieved when a grubby Smith arrived. He made a brew and we talked of scoops, birds, parties, punch-ups, draught E, draught C, honks, ulcers and all the happenings of city week before Wheech admitted that he too had no rope so we slept on it and waited to see what the afternoon would bring. To be with it in the Scottish winter you don't start to think about climbing till noon so when we woke the nail-booted early risers of the long axe had left, leaving, as all good university clubs do, a selection of ropes for use in emergency. 'Emergency' was, after deliberation, equated to 'Scotsman without rope', so a nice red and white one disappeared into our rucksack. About 1 p.m. a big effort was made and we shambled up past English parties returning from a good day's climbing, to the foot of Zero.

Fit from a holiday with Old James, Smith thought he should lead the first pitch, so we quibbled, tossed up and he won, so Andy belayed and I stomped around to keep warm as Wheech's middle name is not Speed. Two hours of Zero Gully on our heads later he was 30ft. higher than the end of my steps of yesterday when a manky belay was announced and as we didn't want to leave him there I followed in a blue reverse and was so shattered and icicle-like that I left him to lead the next pitch.

This was an evil winking little bulge which turned out to be a pseudo and even Wheech using my axe because it was better than his managed to outwit it in less than half an hour. In fact he got so chuffed that he battered my axe into the ice with so much enthusiasm that the pick came flying past me and just missed the coat of ice which was Wightman who was frozen and in a great huff 'cause he had thought we were fast.

I shouted on him to come up and he shouted on me to come down and said he was going to untie but then his hands were so cold that he couldn't get the knot out and I pulled in the rope so fast that he had to run up the pitch which wasn't bad for a wee boy on his second winter climb. Now Andy should be called Willie the Weeper for all the moaning he does and sure enough the manky belay set him off and I left him mumbling and grumbling to himself while I went up the bulge to curse at Wheech for breaking my axe.

We had a ten-minute session and then I got the urge to lead and started up the next pitch. This got me gripped and eventually I stopped under an ice-bulge leaving a line of buckets to salute the evening sun which was charging down with so much haste that it forgot to tell the moon to come up so that it was getting dark rather quickly. Andy was brought up to Wheech and Wheech was brought up to me and proceeded on to the bulge. This was mountaineering at its wonderful best; the still lonely silence of glorious nature in all its twilit splendour was broken only by the sweet schoolboyish voice of Wightman uttering foul vicious oaths and tirades against the certainty of the origins of his partners on the rope.

Wheech was up above carving great steps round the bulge and rejoicing in the safety of my traditional ice-axe belay, which kept popping in and out of its widening hole in the powder snow as if looking for the other half of its mutilated head somewhere down in the depths. Darkness fell completely just as he reached the top of the bulge, and Andy and I quickly followed up the line of pot-holes which would have done credit to any Manual on Snow, The Climbing Of.

On the first ascent the party had only taken an hour to climb from here to the top as all the difficult pitches are in the first 400ft. We now reckoned on half an hour as the first party were old men.

We sat eating Mars Bars and being all friendly again until only one torch was found in the rucksack, so we relapsed into the usual mutterings and proceeded upwards through a waterlogged snow bulge which made us all wet and more bad-tempered. For the next few hours we meandered around in the dark and kept seeing great winking bulges and black evil rocks which made us traverse back and forward with no appreciable gain in height.

We then decided to go rightwards and try and find Observatory Ridge. While scrambling around on a crummy snow arête with belays at a premium we suddenly caught in the torch beam a line of steps about 60ft. vertically downwards and rightwards. This set the party chortling again to the tune of great spark-producing leaps on the end of a pendulary rappel, which eventually landed us one by one in large English smelling steps. The rest of the way was a wee doddle and we stomped up quite fast to the windswept plateau.

It was all hell let loose up there so we quickly beetled off down Number Four Gully in the dim light of approaching dawn to face court martial for rope-thieving by the English dayshift.

from THE EDINBURGH UNIVERSITY MOUNTAINEERING
CLUB JOURNAL *1962*

The Last Step

RICK RIDGEWAY

Straight above them loomed the enormous ice cliffs of the summit pyramid. To overcome the obstacle they would be forced to traverse left over rock covered with loose snow and some ice. It looked spooky. Above the narrow catwalk was vertical ice; below, a 10,000ft. drop down the south face to Base Camp.

"You should probably use your oxygen," Wick [Jim Wickwire] said.

"O.K."

Lou [Reichardt] removed his pack to screw on the regulator, then fitted the mask. Shouldering the pack, he slowly led across the traverse. He gingerly made each crampon-step, trying to keep the metal points off the rock where they would more easily pop off. Wick belayed the rope around his ice axe, but they both knew the anchor might not hold a fall.

Making the moves across the traverse was hard enough, but it was even more difficult because Lou was having trouble with his oxygen apparatus. It didn't seem to be delivering any gas; his bladder was limp and only partially inflated. Balancing with one hand on his axe and his feet carefully placed on the ice-covered rock, he removed the mask with the other hand, took several breaths of ambient air, replaced the mask, and made several more steps, only to be forced to do the same thing. He fiddled with the flow rate, opening it to a maximum eight litres a minute. Even then the bladder remained deflated. Something wasn't working; it had been easier climbing without the mask.

He finished his pitch and belayed the rope as Wick crossed. He enviously noted Wick's bladder puffed like a tight balloon, and knew without doubt he either had an obstruction or a leak. Wick climbed past and Lou followed, continuing to fiddle with the apparatus. He mentally rummaged through his pack for something to jury-rig a leak.

Adhesive tape, he thought, but I don't have any.

Then he realised it was hopeless. He looked up and saw a rock above, the next 'goal', and knew he couldn't possibly reach that, much less the summit, carrying a 17lb security blanket that wasn't even working. He stopped, removed the mask, and examined the rubber tube leading to the bladder. There were several holes, possibly caused by a crampon puncture while being transported in the pack lower on the mountain. He removed his pack and set everything – mask, cylinder, even the pack – in the snow and continued to catch up with Wick.

Wick had been slowly punching steps up a long snow slope beyond the end of the ice cliff, realising the most technically difficult sections were now behind him. From there it would be a long, slow trudge to the top. It was already past noon and they had some 1,200 vertical feet to go. Much time had been lost while Lou worked with his faulty regulator. It would be all-important to keep a steady pace, and there would be no time for rests.

The snow had once again softened in bright noon sun, and Wick struggled to maintain his pace. He looked behind to check on Lou and was amazed to see him take off his oxygen mask, set his pack in the snow, unrope, and continue, leaving everything behind. Without the weight of his pack, Lou was much faster, and Wick waited for him to catch up.

Wick thought, is Lou going back down? What's up?

Before Lou arrived, Wick made up his mind to continue, even if Lou was planning to descend, alone to the summit.

"What are you doing?" Wick asked when Lou arrived.

"I'm going without oxygen. My oxygen set wouldn't work. There was a leak or something. It's a gamble, but there's no choice."

Lou was concerned; he didn't know what his body's reaction would be at 28,000ft. without oxygen, and he feared it might dangerously impair his judgment. Recalling stories of previous climbs to the earth's highest summits where climbers had got in to trouble when their oxygen ran out, Lou's subconscious notified him it was time to be careful and not to expect his judgment to be sound.

"Watch me, and tell me if I exhibit any bizarre behaviour," he said to Wick.

"O.K. I'll talk to you every so often, and that way tell if you start to act weird," Wick said, then added, "You realise, though, I'm going to the top regardless?"

"Yes," Lou replied.

Wick continued slowly. His hopes for better snow conditions dissolved as his feet, calves, and then thighs disappeared in the mushy snow. Another hour passed. He traded leads with Lou, then switched back. One foot, then another, then breathe several times. Wick looked behind to see that Lou had started an angled traverse towards the ridge to their left, and Wick realised he was searching for better snow. Both men forged separate paths for another hour until finally Lou reached the ridge and appeared to have better footing. Wick began to traverse to merge with Lou's tracks. By the time he was in them, Lou was some distance above.

Wick tried to catch up, but it was all he could do to match Lou's pace.

Maybe something's wrong with my oxygen, he thought. He checked the flow rate, looked at the bladder. It was puffed full, still pressurised, still delivering gas. But he couldn't understand why Lou was maintaining distance. Wasn't he, the one with oxygen, supposed to be faster than Lou – the one without?

As they climbed to even more extreme altitudes, Wick slowly closed the distance, then passed Lou. It was like a crossing of the performance curves, if you could have graphed the trade-off of going with or without oxygen. Lower on the slope, Lou had been able to maintain his lead on Wick who, while breathing oxygen, was nevertheless handicapped by the 17lb bottle and other equipment in his pack. As they approached 28,000ft. though, the benefit of the oxygen exceeded the difficulty of the added weight, and Wick slowly worked ahead.

Other than a few sips from Lou's bottle, they had climbed all day without water. The small matter of the water bottle lost from Wick's parka was having its effect. Lou, in leaving his pack behind, had also left his parka, and he was starting to shiver in the increasing cold. The sun dropped behind the summit ridge, and the cold intensified. It was 4.30 p.m. Above, they could see the silhouetted, nearly horizontal ridge. Would the summit be there, or some distance beyond? They would make it, there was no going back, but it would be late.

It seemed deceptively close, yet it receded with each footstep. Wick continued in the slow, steady pace. Neither of them had rested for more than a minute or two since Lou had set down his pack. With each step Wick thought of his family, his wife, his children, his mother and father – all who had given such support to his quest for this summit. He thought of several of the earlier climbers who, except for the vagaries of bad weather and bad luck, might have been the first Americans to walk those last steps. He thought of Dusan and Al and Leif.

There were only a few more steps to the ridge crest. Excited, Wick picked up his pace and made the final moves up the steepening snow face. Suddenly he stepped onto the ridge crest tinted gold in late afternoon alpenglow. He was gasping for air; he thought he had somehow pinched off the supply of oxygen, then realised it was because he had made several rapid steps. He fell on one knee, exhausted.

His head down, he slowly looked to his right, hoping he would see the summit only a few feet away. Instead, the ridge continued level, then seemed to drop away into China. He could see the burnt Sinkiang hills before the setting sun. He looked the other direction. To his surprise, Lou was only inches away, making the final steps up the ridge crest. For Lou, increasingly cold without parka, the psychological warmth of the direct sun rays — then so low on the horizon – seemed to raise the temperature 30 degrees.

Wick looked past Lou, and now the ridge gently arched up, wider than he expected. The snow was gold. About 75ft. away he could see the ridge round off, then descend towards the west. It was a little larger than he expected, but still no bigger than a large dining table. He was in no way disappointed. He stood up and said to Lou: "We've come this far. Let's make the last step together."

Arm in arm, they walked to the summit of K2.

The second highest point on the surface of the planet. The summit of his dreams. Wick stared across the mountains stretching endlessly below him, summit after summit painted gold. They were all below him. The world curved away, in all directions, falling away, below his feet.

For Lou it was an even more remarkable victory. He was the first man to climb K2 without oxygen. The magnitude of his feat was measured in his blue lips, in the ice frozen thick in his beard. Although the moment seemed dreamlike, he was still thinking coherently, and unlike Wick, one thought predominated: Get Down. It was 5.15 p.m. Ninety minutes until total darkness. There would be no moon. Lou had no parka. He was fiercely cold. He knew he could not survive a bivouac.

When the pair had crested the summit ridge a few minutes before, Lou had said, "I'm going to walk to the top, then turn around and come right down."

"You've got to at least stay there long enough for me to take a picture of you," Wick had replied.

There was a tacit agreement that Wick intended to stay longer and Lou would descend. But first there were several things to do, and Lou waited impatiently while Wick rummaged in his pack for the American and Pakistani flags, for an eagle feather we had promised the United Tribes of All Indians Foundation, who had helped the expedition raise funds, we would carry to the summit. There was also the microfilmed list of all who had contributed $20 or more. Wick handed Lou the flags and the feather and took several photos. Wick then handed Lou his camera, since Lou had forgotten his own when he abandoned his pack, and Lou took a duty shot of Wick.

"Let's go."

"I want to get a panorama first," Wick said. "But I've got to change film. Go ahead. I'll be along in a minute.

Lou was cold. It was nearly 5.30, and the sun was dropping below the horizon. The first stars emerged in the blackening sky. Without hesitation, he turned and began to descend rapidly. Wick fumbled to change film. He had to remove his mittens, then work quickly to open the camera and thread the film. It was too cold to work for more than a few seconds before replacing his mittens. He waited for his fingers to warm. The wind was blowing harder, and he had to be careful not to let spindrift in the camera. He concentrated on the task; he hadn't been using oxygen since reaching the summit, and everything seemed so weird, so hard to do. He took his hands from the mittens, worked, put them back in. Finally the camera was loaded, but then he noticed the lens had iced, and he gave up.

He studied the terrain around him. He could see down the west side, to where he had tried to climb in 1975. He noted the Savoia peaks to the west. All the peaks of the Karakoram and especially the Baltoro dotted the horizon. He followed the horizon 360°, trying to identify each peak. He was impressed by the brownness of China. All the peaks basked in gold light; the sky was nearly cloudless. Finally he thought to look at his watch. It was 6.10. He had stayed too long; he had to move fast. Shouldering his pack he descended the summit ridge, then glanced down the route. A thousand feet below he could see Lou nearing his pack. It was then Wick first knew he could not make it down; he knew he would have to bivouac, alone, without sleeping bag, without tent, just below the summit. The wind began to pick up, and already it was fiercely cold.

from THE LAST STEP *1980*

Speeding Down South

JIM BRIDWELL

Patagonia is a land where good weather is as precious and rare as water in the Sahara. With rapid weather changes and not infrequent twenty- and thirty-day storms generating winds well over 100 mph, the line between a climber's boldness and a climber's stupidity is razor-thin. In Patagonia, perhaps there is no distinction, and I questioned from the beginning whether we weren't playing a form of Russian Roulette with four chambers loaded. But I had become obsessed with climbing the beautiful rock tower called the Cerro Torre and was prepared to climb it at almost any cost. That's a dangerous frame of mind if it gets out of control, but while I was frustrated, I was also determined.

My frustration was rooted in the fact that after a year of organisation, preparation, money-making, equipment-designing, sacrifice, travelling and team-selection for this very climb, I had arrived in Patagonia only to have my two partners decide they had more important business elsewhere. They abandoned me to my own devices. Perhaps it was my resolve to do the climb, perhaps it was the climb itself, perhaps it was my stubborn personality, perhaps there was another reason; but after travelling all the way from California to Patagonia and seeing the problem in person, so to speak, my two mates decided the weather was better somewhere else. Who knows where the roots of determination are buried? All I know is that I was alone in Patagonia and I wasn't leaving until I got a crack at the Cerro Torre.

I was by myself now, sitting in the FitzRoy Park surrounded by some of the most scenic mountains on earth, watching my thoughts and contemplating a solo attempt on the tower. Then I remembered the young American climber I had met the day before. Steve Brewer had hitchhiked into the park looking for an expedition to join. I went to him with the proposal of joining my expedition as the other half of a two-man alpine-style attempt on the South-East Ridge of the Cerro Torre, one of the world's wildest mountains. Before thinking it over, he agreed and I was given a second chance.

At 3.30 a.m. we climbed simultaneously and quickly through the pre-dawn darkness up the lower ice pitches, Steve in the lead. A strong ice climber, Brewer moved methodically upward, placing a token ice screw every 150ft. in order to give me practice removing them. Their security was purely psychological, but I appreciated the illusion and the rest they gave me while removing them.

Our hope was to reach the lower col by dawn; Cesare Maestri, who has had some experience with the Torre, once wrote, "Hope is a vain word in the mountains." Previous expeditions had placed their advanced snow caves on this col and from there seized the upper ridge. Our strategy was different. We carried the minimum amount of clothing: jackets, pants, sleeping bags; food: oatmeal, sugar, soup; equipment: twenty-five pitons and nuts, twenty-five karabiners, six ice screws, small bolt kit and two 9mm ropes and, of course, courage in our rucksacks. I had spent three years planning this climb; studying photographs and magazine articles and talking with other climbers, designing clothing, doing extensive preparatory climbing and thinking. Nevertheless, I like to think that if you're not scared, you're not having fun; and, if that's true, the Cerro Torre is worth a couple of years at Disneyland. Treading close to the edge elevates the fear factor, but it also focuses the mind and, on one level, reduces the possibility of the dreaded slip of attention.

We were vain enough to reach the col a half hour after the sun bathed it in golden light. It was 5.30 a.m. when I took over the lead on the rock and headed up the first pitch, an overhanging chimney. At the end of the pitch, I tied off the rope so Steve could jumar, and I hand-hauled my pack. The pitches sped by in the blue. Some were pure rock, some mixed rock and ice, and some had sections of aid. One nasty 5.10 ice-lined crack carved its impression into my memory. I drove my ice hammer into its icy depths for a couple of moves until there was no longer anything solid within hammer reach. I was forced against my peace of mind to use off-width technique on the quicksilver surface of the interior walls. Going for something that difficult with no protection is called a calculated risk. When I finally reached safety an eternity later at a loose chockstone, my arms were cramping and I was tired. "What had everyone else done here?" I asked myself. The mystery vanished when I checked the photo we brought along and discovered we were off-route. There was easy nailing to the right.

In time, the climbing and hauling took its toll on my arms, and I was forced to rest. We stopped under a small overhang at the base of a flaring chimney. Above, huge chunks of ice clung precariously to the smooth, steep walls. Our tranquillity and rest were cut short by the resonant roar of ice rushing toward us. Steve and I smeared ourselves against the wall and moulded our bodies to the underside of the overhang. The sky splintered around us with crashing ice. When it had passed, the silence was disturbed only by the pounding of my palpitating heart. Ice crystals floated through the brilliant blue sky like tiny winged diamonds, all the richness and wealth we needed at that moment. I rocketed up the chimney as soon as the fall ceased with all the speed and skill at my command. Hungry, threatening white fangs of ice hung above. There was no telling when that might go. I reached a safe ledge.

I had but a few moments to enjoy safety and contemplate fear. As soon as Steve arrived, I tiptoed across awful ice slabs on the precarious balance of the bolts left by those who came previously. Steve joined me and we immediately began clipping up a long, diagonal bolt ladder toward the ice towers of the Cerro Torre. It was evening now, and bolts or not, I realised that we were higher on the Cerro Torre than anyone else had ever been in a single day. I knew that what Steve and I had just done was but a premonition of how fast and well the younger climbers will do the difficult technical routes in the future. We had probably climbed the fastest and farthest ever accomplished on any mountain of that 'technical' standard.

Everything was going according to my plan. Our hopes had been met. Let us rephrase the great Maestri's words, "Irrational hope is a vain word in the mountains." I thought we would reach the bivouac in the ice towers by dark. Steve graciously and skilfully took over the lead finishing the bolt ladder. He gave me, as he always did, a much needed rest just when I needed it. I led another short line of bolts by-passing Dickinson's A1 fragile flake. Steve did another, and then he rapelled back down after fixing a rope.

We had climbed 3,500ft. up the Cerro Torre that day. We were exhausted; we were also exhilarated. But we had to spend another hour and a half chopping a bivouac ledge out of the solid ice. We finished that around 11.30 p.m. and began cooking dinner. We used headlamps; eerie orbs flashed through the unreal sky illuminating an icy architecture of surreal but very real surroundings.

Meanwhile, far below, Giuliano Giongo, leader of the Italian Torre Egger expedition, had his own surreal but real experience. He crawled out of his tent at Base Camp to see a star sitting on the face of the Cerro Torre. He thought his eyes were playing tricks on him. Incredulous, he suddenly realised the star was our headlamp far higher on the mountain than he believed possible. Giuliano called his mates out of their tents to view the rare spectacle.

I periodically awoke to check the weather. The wind had changed and blew from the west with hints of storm. The inevitable in Patagonia. To be caught in a storm on this mountain would be an ugly situation. No fixed rope. Food for one more bivouac. No bivy sacks. Only two ropes with us. We had a careful decision to make.

Dawn arrived with puffy harbingers of an approaching tempest. How much time did we have? We circumvented the problem by ignoring it. Casting our fates to the Patagonian wind, we started climbing in a race with the famous predatory weather. Steve cramponed up the ice ridge past abandoned relics of former struggles. Coiled ropes, racks of hardware and karabiners hung from the wall, evidence of rapid departures. The early-morning ice was solid and we moved swiftly. Confidently, Steve led pitch after pitch, threading his way on the ice between blank pillars of rock.

The high point of the 1971 British expedition was fixed 40ft. short of a small bolt ladder up a short overhang. At this point the strain of the climb began to show. I dropped my north wall hammer and Steve dropped one of his etriers. He substituted a couple of runners tied together. From the top of this pitch another bolt ladder led up the edge of a huge overhanging tower. I took the lead and had to chop away six to twelve inches of ice to uncover each bolt. Steve dodged the ice I was knocking down on him. One more pitch and the final headwall loomed above us, beckoning.

The weather was rapidly deteriorating. Wispy clouds circled the summit, vapoury, icy cobwebs moving in many directions at the same time. We clipped up the bolt ladder in unison to speed progress. No doubt most of the headwall could have been aided without the bolts, but it didn't matter since pitons would have been fixed instead.

Menacing clouds swirled everywhere as I climbed past Maestri's compressor, which he had used to bolt his way up. I marvelled at it here near the top of this magnificent spire, and I thought that getting that hunk of machinery up here was a feat comparable to Hannibal's crossing the Alps.

Looking up, I saw seven broken bolts leading up and slightly right, but 80ft. of blank granite stretched between the last bolt and the summit snow. My God, I thought, Maestri must have nailed 80ft. of ice tenuously bound to smooth rock. It was a bad joke and inconsistent with the magazine articles. I took out the small bolt kit and went to work placing aluminium dowels, knifeblades and copperheads. I thought I was climbing very slowly. Steve boosted my morale by telling me I was moving fast and to go for it. Finally, I could almost touch the ice. One last copperhead and I was able to chop a groove in an ice-filled crack and place a friend. It held and I started free-climbing, traversing left with my feet on steep friction and the pick of my hammer in the ice above. I pulled myself onto the summit snowfield. Balancing on one foot and then the other, I carefully donned my crampons and finished the lead. The summit would be an easy walk, and I wondered why Maestri and his friend hadn't gone to the top.

Steve came up leaving all the pitons in place, and without stopping he climbed past me to the summit. Together on the top of the ice mushroom we shook hands and embraced. We took a few photos and got the hell out of there. The wind blew about 60 mph on the summit, but 100ft. down it wasn't so bad. We wasted little time descending and we quickly reached the top of the ice towers. At that point, the rappel route had to deviate from the overhanging climbing route. It was necessary to rappel straight over the face of those ice-encrusted pillars with the giant fragile icicle swords hanging on God knows what. Fortunately, we reached the bivouac site without mishap and took the evening meal of oatmeal and hot chocolate. Storm dragons darted across the maroon and slate-coloured sky. The wind is the stalker on the Cerro Tore, and the climber is a very tiny prey. We were trapped for the night 3,500ft. above the glacier.

The diffused light of morning confirmed my worst fears. Snow covered everything. The ropes were stiff as steel cables, and we hung up the first two rappels. I jumared up to free the ropes,

acutely aware in the claustrophobic emptiness of the sound of jet
engines mixed with the roar of avalanches. The day seemed surreal
and weirdly familiar, like some deadly dream of *déja vu*
experienced in another life. We finally reached the bolt ladder
traverse and commenced the slow and methodical task of clipping
back down each bolt, reversing the process of only two days before,
though it seemed a lifetime before. I would move 50ft. and then
bring down Steve, decreasing the immobile period so neither of us
would grow too cold.

And then I clipped into a bolt with a small sling attached to my
swami belt. I yelled through the swirling clouds that I was off
belay. Suddenly the panic light in my head flashed red. The sling
had ripped apart, but I didn't know it yet. I accelerated earthward
at an alarming speed. Terminal velocity, no pun intended. "That is
it," I thought, "the last act." Just like Toni Egger, my mind
shifted into hyper-gear and became subtly disconnected, assuming
the viewpoint of spectator. My thoughts were as clear and distinct
as a computer read-out. What had happened? What was going to
happen? Would I live to see my unborn child? Where is the end of
the rope? Would I go all the way to the ground? I could hear myself
screaming. "Shut up," I told myself. "Screaming doesn't do any
good."

Wham! The end of the rope! God, it stretched forever before
there was a wrenching jolt and I shot upward like a
yo-yo on a string. After I finally stopped, it took a few seconds to
collect my wits which were scattered all over the place. A certain
amount of pain speeded reaction time, and I quickly yelled up,
"I'm OK. Just slipped a bit."

Now that I was responsible for myself again, I had to climb up to
get my weight off the rope so Steve could move. I stood on tiny, icy
holds and held on while Steve clipped down and fetched my aid
slings. It took forever. I had fallen about 40 metres, broken some
ribs, chipped an elbow, badly bruised a hip and rearranged my
mind. No serious damage. Just a great deal of discomfort. Pain is
the main thing I remember about the rest of the descent. There were
endless rappels, but they passed without incident.

The weather treated us kindly and cleared as we reached the
glacier. I stumbled into the Italian glacier camp ahead of Steve. I
was warmly received with the congratulations of Italian

exuberance. They were astonished with the speed of our ascent. "*Muy rápido. Muy rápido*," they exclaimed over and over, speaking Spanish for our benefit. I told them we moved so fast because we were so scared, and I was only half-joking. We were pleased with ourselves, and it was wonderful to hear the praise. It was even more wonderful to be able to hear their praise. Our Italian friends made us soup and tea with rum to revive our weary bodies.

Afterwards, I lay on the edge of sleep digesting the meal and the experience of a lifetime, and secure within the satisfying knowledge that we had both met the challenge and gotten back to safety, I stepped out of consciousness.

from THE AMERICAN ALPINE JOURNAL *1980*

No Big Cigar

GEOFF BIRTLES

My fetish about Castellan on Matlock's High Tor, dates back to the early sixties when Barry Webb made the first ascent and I had my first glimpse of it. Maybe I was overawed that the ascent made a newspaper's front cover.

High Tor hardly has an abundance of natural lines. Castellan takes the only natural weakness through the biggest overhang on the Tor and was probably the last natural line to fall, although a peg route at that time.

The overhang is a formidable prospect, dwelling in its own shadow. White limestone folds round into a matted crumbling black cleft resembling the female groin. The fetish unfolds.

I even like the 60ft. of climbing up to the balcony cave that forms the overhang. Here there is a grand terrace that sweetens my comfort, where it pleases me to loaf a while and smoke a little before the battle.

Over the winter of 1975/76, there was a great shift of attention by new-route diggers into the rich pickings of the previously aid-dominated steep limestone valleys of the southern Peak District.

This process of rejuvenation grew to an almost ridiculous level as routes started going free even on weekdays. Tom Proctor and I had been fortunate enough to grab two of the big aid routes, Behemoth and Mortlock's Arête, early in this scramble. Both ascents pre-empted attempts by Pete Livesey and Ron Fawcett. In the case of Behemoth we made an 8.30 a.m. start and only had time to place the first runner before our Yorkshire rivals appeared. They hung about in a predatory manner and forced us into a shivery seven-hour ordeal to gain our prize.

Only a few weeks later the comedy became a farce on Mortlock's on Chee Tor on a Tuesday afternoon. Again we had the rope on the rock when, minutes later, Livesey arrived accompanied by John Sheard, Pete Gomersall and Jill Lawrence. Pete has a great weakness for the ridiculous and laughed at the irony of his second-near miss; Jill, on the other hand, was none too pleased and seethed with exasperation, cursing Pete, us, the world, anybody . . . This time they followed up with an immediate second ascent, hungrier than ever now should we fail.

They stayed in Derbyshire while we went back to work. Fawcett repeated Behemoth, eliminating our one point of aid, and Livesey snatched Bastille on High Tor. There remained a silent, unspoken but obvious focus on Castellan. Easter came, however, and we all went to Cornwall for our holidays – all except John Allen and Steve Bancroft.

It took Steve two days to lead the big overhang pitch of Castellan free. Allen did not bother to follow that pitch. They then abseiled down to the stance which Bancroft had reached, and Allen led the final pitch – so completing a fine performance of "while the cat's away".

I was impressed, and pulsating green with envy. Of all the big routes, I most fancied Castellan. We had now missed out on three big routes – London Wall, Bastille and Castellan – all because of dithering. Getting Tom on to biggies sometimes is like dragging a dead horse to water. He gets worried because he knows I am going to make him lead.

Well, that summer young Ron Fawcett frequented the Peak District and went through the card – like he does. Inevitably we ended up together on Castellan one fine Saturday morning. Ron tried the roof and managed to place two wedge-nuts in an upside-

down crack. These were backed up by a quarter-inch thread and a
peg with a cracked eye (funny farm protection).

He was climbing down for a rest when a hold broke and he shot
past the ledge and into space. The nuts held!

I went up for a look, although when Fawcett fails there isn't
usually much chance of making any improvement. And I didn't.

His next attempt took him into a position of leaning backwards
across the roof with an upside-down finger jam. Then he jumped
backwards across the roof and grabbed a pocket above the lip. I
could go into superlatives at this stage, but I was once warned
"Beware the adjective" — and without them I couldn't begin to
describe my feelings. It looked impressive.

Ron hung there from the lip, trying to pull over without success.
Then he put his foot above his hands and jammed it across the
groove, hanging gibbon-style for a while. "I'm having a rest," he
said.

He jumped off and lowered down for a real rest. Then he
climbed back up and went through all the flying routine again — but
again, no joy. So we went home.

It was during *Doctor Who* that we talked of the morrow, without
much enthusiasm for anywhere. It only took a "Shall we . . .?"
and a flick of the head, and he said: "Oh aye!" And so we went
back.

Sunday morning, we detoured through Stoney cafe for breakfast. Outside, John Woodhouse sat in his car, looking decidedly
lurky. When we pulled out to set off for Matlock, a little blue Mini
estate slipped out behind us.

We went through the whole sketch of overtaking and undertaking everything in sight, but still our man on assignment was
right there. He was going to earn his four-quid-a-photo today; as
we got into Matlock I swung left at the island, then left again back
towards Chesterfield, and lost him. It was total waste of time,
because when we got back to the main road he was waiting for us.

I put my foot down before he could slip into the traffic, and
zapped round a bend and up somebody's drive. That did work, and
we lost him for real this time.

It was a nice day again on the crag, and this time Ron jumped the
roof, pulled round with relative ease and progressed up the crack
above to the stance quite quickly.

Seconding was another matter. The natural drag of the rope for the leader was not unfriendly, and John Allen assured me that Steve Bancroft did not find it too hostile either – the point being that if your body swings wildly out after your hands, you stand a good chance of dragging yourself off. When you are seconding, the rope just loops out into a spacious void and offers the greatest incentive to pull on a runner, which I did. It was, after all, a difficult position in which to retrieve runners.

Excuses like these become natural after years of climbing – it's what the instruction books call experience.

Once I had hold of the pocket at the lip, I pulled up and found that I could put my foot in the pocket and wedge my shoulder in the groove, and so rest with one foot hanging in space and both hands off the rock.

It was a nice position to be in, perched in space. I looked down between my legs. Some other climbers stood craning their necks in amazement. I knew they were amazed, because I felt amazing at that point.

Then I looked up, at the straightforward HVS crack I would climb to join Ron. A little face peered over the top of the crag to my left. It was John Woodhouse. "Say cheese, sweetie."

That crack would be no problem under normal circumstances, but feeling roofed-out I grovelled up the ever-widening crack – grazing skin as the jams slipped – and felt grateful for a little pull at the end to complete the hard-traverse to the stance. I missed Tom at this point; he gives me big pulls.

The situation at the stance is a real eyrie, perched on the edge of a giant detached flake with the ropes floating in the breeze. Ron didn't ask how I had found the pitch, but I was sure he wanted to know. "No big cigar!" I told him.

In retrospect, I feel I could have led the next pitch – but I would have needed an hour to rest, and Fawcett is an impatient beggar to climb with. So I let him lead it. I do things like that. It turned out to be a nice pitch: one desperate move early on, laybacking on a twisted two-finger jam in a shallow flared crack; then it was better finger-jams and a reach over a jutting bulge to reach good but stretchy holds, easing gradually to finish on the summit meadow.

During the following week I received a photo of Ron on the roof from you-know-who. The attached letter informed me that this was a scoop and required an £18 fee for reproduction*. What I haven't told you is that on the Saturday, when John Woodhouse soloed up to the cave, I thought: "Old John's pushing it a bit." And he was — we had to rescue him later on. So if we charge him £20 for rescue — then dash it all, I'm a generous man, let's call it even.

from CRAGS 16 *1979*

*Birtles was editor of *Crags* at the time.

The Inscrutable Bregaglia East

ROBIN CAMPBELL

After three days chewing our knees in a minibus, Peter and I were anxious to be off. So while the others stuffed their faces in Chur we stuffed our sacks, stripping the roof-rack in the main street and exposing our crummy equipment to the supercilious stares of Swissers-by. Below the Albigna Barrage in the late evening we hopped down, straightened up, huffed and groaned sweatily up to the Hut. The guardian was civil, considering the hour: he fed us with beer and showed us to a tolerable room. He was a very tall man, his head cocked like a heron's from dodging the hut lintels. His cold eye fell on our English guidebook. He riffled:

"Dieses Buch ist schitt. Pfochenschitt," he explained. We should climb the North-West Ridge of the Punta da l'Albigna, it seemed, an easy training climb. Our book said Grade 5, but, as he said . . .

He was as good as his few bad words: the Punta was a nice easy day. In the evening we fell foul of his powerful wife for not ordering dinner in the morning. She banished us to the Winterraum and then accused me of stealing someone's sandals. Wrongfully. The Hut thronged with ugly German policemen who had taken turns through the afternoon to stand naked in the trough and soap themselves furiously. Eventually we found our adviser sloshing dishes in the kitchen. We brandished our guidebook.

"Cima Zocca? Ist gut? Schnee O.K.? Absteig Nordwand?"

"Ja. Ja," he grunted. But this was all we got.

The way up was straightforward, if laborious. We got there about one o'clock and tested the North Face with some boulders. Big scabs of snow sloughed ominously away, disclosing hard grey ice. We consulted our book. "Except in good snow conditions, the best descent on the Albigna side is the North-West Ridge." Ho hum. Down we went, slithering over loose slates. The Ridge worsened into the afternoon, with the slates getting looser and each descent couloir showing the same fierce grey ice. Benightment loomed. But we abseiled instead; 1,000ft., two pegs and about £1 of tape onto the glacier. Eventually we staggered into the Hut, late

71

for our ordered dinner. She mastered her fury, manfully, and shooed us to a corner along with some other unspeakables, Fred Mantz and George Chisholm from Edinburgh, who had brought their own food for her to cook. The idea. While we minched we grabbed a German guidebook and thumbed to the Zocca North-West Ridge. Gefahrlichen, schlechten fels it said, and well it might. We stared accusingly at Heron Head, busy with his pots and pans. Next day she insisted we go down.

"Many, many people come," she said. We went.

The next idea was to traverse the Disgrazia by the Corda Molla, a classic ridge. Our book was fulsome — "the finest mixed climb of its standard in the area." It also said something about getting from Maloja to the Bivacco Taveggia (a box at 9,500ft.) in a day, but we saw right through that one. We tried to buy some food in Maloja (a sort of alpine Aviemore), but all we got was chocolate and giggled at by a crocodile of pretty schoolgirls on their way to church. Then there was a whole long day plodding through the alpine flowers to the Passo di Muretto (a sort of alpine Lairig Ghru) then back through the flowers in reverse to Chiareggio. Finally, we dragged up to the Porro Hut with the Disgrazia sulking in the clouds behind.

Neither of us knew a word of Italian, but we'd both been to the better sort of school:

"Mangare. Dormire," we intoned, gesturing at a frightened girl. She fled, understandably. Then we found a man from Milan who spoke French and soon we were sitting down to an enormous meal. Afterwards:

"Il faut parler avec le guide. Venez."

We trooped out of the Hut and stumbled over a rival establishment. A bronzed gorilla opened the door and waved us all in. His wife, who would have done all right on the beach at Cannes, sat in a corner, knitting and drying mushrooms. She raised her golden head and smote us with a smile.

"Scozzese? Loro sono molto avari!" She chuckled throatily and returned to her chores. Embarrassed, we bought postcards. Cheap ones. The man from Milan chipped in.

"Tous les lombardiens sont avares, aussi. C'est la faute de capitalisme." The gorilla put us all to shame by producing a bottle of grappa and waving away our disgusting money. We spoke to the man from Milan in French, he spoke to the gorilla in Italian and soon we had the Corda Molla all ravelled up. We would go tomorrow to the Bivacco Oggioni, then the day after up the ridge to the summit (where there was a nuovo bivacco, molto bellino) and down the Preda Rosso glacier to the Rifugio Ponti. The ghiaccio, apparently, was not brutto; the tempo was, but this would pass. We talked on while the grappa lasted, agreeing that capitalism was bad, that Italy was beautiful and that national stereotypes were always false. We also put the gorilla straight about Raeburn and Ling's 'Spigolo Inglese' on the Disgrazia's North Face. Then we all shuffled back to sleep in beds with sheets in the Porro and dream about being on the beach at Cannes with the gorilla's wife, once she got her mushrooms all dried out of the way.

Next day the Disgrazia still sulked. We ploughed up the Ventina and over the Canalone della Vergine glaciers to reach the Bivacco Oggioni without incident. This turned out to be comfortable, if cramped. It sits on a ledge looking across the Disgrazia glacier to the North Face. In the evening the tempo turned buono, as promised, and we rubbernecked at the Spigolo Inglese and at the Corda Molla snaking up to an improbable ice ridge and the gleaming summit.

During the night it froze and so we made good morning progress up the steep snow to the start of the rocks. These were comforting rough red gneiss and we dawdled along the ridge in the sun, exclaiming about the route like juveniles. The ice ridge put a stop to all that: it was steep and steepened as we rose and as it steepened the névé changed to disobliging blue ice, finally to that hard grey stuff we met on the Zocca. Definitely brutto. On the last run-out Peter was in front and terribly slow and I railed and cursed at him from my exposed perch, eyeing the evidence of stonefall embedded all around. But then he reached the rocks and stood for a pointedly silent hour while I clawed sloth-slowly up the summit ice-grooves. Then there it was, the nuovo bivacco all bright and shiny. We clattered in to find a half-empty bottle of wine, two glasses and miscellaneous victuals – the remains of the Opening Ceremony.

"C'est la faute de capitalisme," we said, drawing up our chairs.

Later, we wobbled past the enormous summit crucifix and down the easy ridge to the Sella di Pioda and the Preda Rosso glacier. A long blistering descent got us to the Ponto at about 5 p.m. It was closed. We tried the cellar. Open, but a cold miserable place, foodless.

"At least, it's better than nothing," Peter said, reasonably. By way of an answer a noise came from the foundations, like some ancient beast stirring and rattling its grizzled claws. Five minutes later, it came again. "The pipes?" we wondered. Or the reason for the Hut's desertion . . . Wordlessly, we hunched in our sacks and headed for the valley, not looking back. Low in the valley and lower in spirits we found, unbelievably, the Albergo Scotti just as the evening thunderstorms broke. We rushed in to bewilder the albergatrice with our Latin. "Tedesci?" she asked. But we got it sorted out eventually.

In the morning we came down to Cataeggio in the Val Masino. After a big lunch we sat eating ice-cream in the main street cafe. We planned to go to the Allievi Hut, climb on the Zocca again, then go over the frontier ridge back to Maloja. Peter made enquiries:

"E aperto, Capanno Allievi?" We were learning fast. The cafe rustled with debate.

"Dovete Parlare con Pietro Bardini, a San Martino." They wrote it down. At San Martino, Peter turned to the first person in the street after leaving the bus. An old man.

"Cerciamo Pietro Bardini," he said, stabbing his chest with a rusty fore-finger. Perhaps they had telephoned. The Allievi was open. So up we went, a long enervating 5,000ft. of effort. Well up we passed a crucifix. For the Memory of Aldo Paravicini, it said, a Brave Mountaineer. Caduto, of course. On the way through Il Pianone, a box canyon containing amongst other oddities a herd of horses, we could see the guardian watching us from the Hut balcony on the canyon lip. We were his only guests. He invited us into his living room and we responded by ordering steaks and much wine. All went well until about nine o'clock when two English we pretended not to know burst in, boots and all, and asked him to cook tinned hamburgers. We were all bundled out into the cold hut after that. Discouraged, we asked him what to climb. Something not too hard.

"Via Paravicini," he said, indicating a menacing pillar overhanging the Hut. "Quintogrado," aping our Latin.

"Molto pitones?"

"Libero, libero," this was a disparaging wave of the hand.

We were late getting away – a bad mistake. Aldo Paravicini was a Brave One all right. We laboured up long unprotected pitches. Then came a 150ft. groove with pegs every three feet. Libero, libero, I muttered and swung up on tatty slings. With our meagre equipment, I couldn't get more than halfway, so we had a fearsome belay in slings. Then my hands started opening or closing involuntarily with cramp, I can't remember which, and I had to take a long terrifying rest. The afternoon wore on. Clouds gathered. We came out of the groove on to easy ground below the summit just as the storm broke. Nothing for it but down through the thunderbolts. We had several appalling abseils: on the second last one I hadn't thrown the ropes down properly and abseiled below the point where one had snagged. Peter clicked his tongue and sorted it all out while I cursed and panicked. On the last one the lightning struck the rocks a foot from the ropes. A shambles.

Then we were down at the Hut. We went on about his libero, libero, waving our guidebook at him. He held it at arm's length and leafed through it fastidiously.

"Ah!" he said. "Questo libro e crappa. Bladdicrappa." He beamed.

Next day, we fled to Maloja, and home.

from THE SCOTTISH MOUNTAINEERING CLUB
JOURNAL 1974

With God on our Side

TERRY KING

I was hanging around Fort William one warm, wet winter, occasionally enjoying the hospitable attention of the non-racialist sector of the community and quite often avoiding the hospitalising attention of their less tolerant other three-quarters, when I received a message from Nevisport to ring Mr Paul Sidoli in Manchester, and reverse the charges.

There was no further information, no indication who he was or what he wanted, just telephone at six o'clock. My imagination went to work on what it might be about. Rejecting the more obvious possibilities, such as winning £50,000 on the pools, I was left with the inevitable conclusion that some big film producer had decided to make me a star. Sidoli, an Italian name, so it was probably a Spaghetti Western. My stomach tightened as I dialled for the big break and asked if Mr Sidoli was available. "Oh 'ello," said a bright, cheery man with a tinge of Liverpool in his accent. "Is that Terry King?" he said, pronouncing the G in King. "Do you want to go climbing tomorrow?" So that was it. Never mind fame and fortune, but how's about another day off work?

Somewhat deflated but not totally disappointed by the prospect of a few days on the hill, I asked him what particular routes he was interested in.

"Orion Face Direct," he said.

"Oh, great. What have you done on ice before?"

"Nothing."

"Mmm, well, that's pretty ambitious, how long are you coming up for?" I asked.

"A day."

"What, from Manchester?"

"Yes. I'm driving up tonight; I want to do it tomorrow and then I'll drive back through the night again because I have to be at work on Wednesday morning."

"Jesus Christ," I said, "you must be bent, mate. Why can't you get two days off, what do you do for a living?"

"Well," he said, "I'm a Catholic priest actually."

I was, I admit, a little surprised, and in my confusion I stumbled out directions on how to get to my place without more ado. If climbing was his way of getting nearer to God, then doing the Orion Direct as your first ice route could turn into a fairly intimate little affair.

He reckoned to arrive about two o'clock in the morning and get a few hours' sleep before we started out. After a few words about the weather – which was surprisingly good, though I wondered if he could have a word with head office about the freezing level – we hung up.

I was living in a caravan about a mile outside Spean Bridge, in a desolate field which I shared with a bunch of sheep who enjoyed butting the thin walls in the dead of night and scaring me to death. When the rent was due the farmer, my landlord, would let some cattle into the field, usually about an hour before dawn, and these creatures would amuse themselves by using the caravan as a scratching block. I would wake up to the wild rhythm of hairy brown hides pulsating at every corner. The next scene was always the same, and this day was no exception.

"Geeet ooot, oh yi baastards. Yeeaaah." Then the sound of stampeding hooves preceded a rap on the door which opened to reveal a ruddy, whisky-beaten face with pale blue eyes and a thin-lipped smile. "Did the beasties wake you up? Och, I'm sorry. Mind you, while I'm here, do you have this week's rent?" Paul had not arrived during the night as expected, so I stumped back into my sleeping bag, but about 8 a.m. a car pulled up outside.

The stopping of the engine was followed by the sound of vomiting. From the comfort of my pit I shouted him to come on in, which was greeted by another bout of retching, and finally Paul Sidoli stepped inside.

"Ee, I've been 'onking all the way 'ere."

He was a shortish bloke with benevolent brown eyes behind thick-rimmed specs, and slightly balding.

"Sorry I'm late, but I had to stop for a bit. I think it's just travel sickness."

"It's OK," I said, sitting up. "Look, make yourself a brew; do you want to have a bit of a kip?"

"Well, I wouldn't mind, but would it make us too late? Mind you, I've got two days now."

On the strength of this we decided to do a shorter route, Observatory Buttress, and leave the Orion Face until tomorrow. Paul went to bed looking distinctly ill, and fell asleep within minutes. So did I, but unlike me he was up at 10 a.m. making bacon butties, a well-known cure for queasy stomachs, and raring to go.

I was a little worried that his vocation might cause him to object to breaking down the forestry gate. Fortunately this was not necessary, as it was open, and although I did point out that we were trespassing, I don't think he heard. Mind you, he was outside the car, bent over a ditch, regurgitating his breakfast at the time.

For once in my life, I anticipated beating someone up the track to the CIC Hut – taking idle rests, hands in pockets, while this poor debilitated wretch struggled up behind. But this was pure fantasy:

using the "straight-line Charlie" technique, he pounded through the bogs leaving me, as usual, trailing in despair.

From the hut onwards – by which time I was convinced that his miraculous progress was divinely assisted and I couldn't possibly hope to compete – the gap between us opened beyond the limits of shouting. Having driven all night defying a virulent stomach bug, he had to sit down in the snow and wait for me, well slept and supposedly healthy, to catch up and tell him where to go next – which is a problem for anyone who walks fast but has to rely on me for directions.

The first pitch was fairly straightforward – not too steep but very pleasant work, balancing up delicately on front points. Being the proud owner of two Terrordactyls helped a little, too. I belayed in a tiny ice niche and prepared to see what Paul was going to make of it. His sickness had almost cleared up. An occasional racking cough was all that remained, though haggis and chips in Fort William would soon reverse that trend. In fact, it's money back guaranteed to reverse any normal digestive trend.

He set about the pitch with great determination, creating each placement by a series of almighty blows, then heaving up with furrowed brow and resolute jaw to make the next one in the same way. But there was something very different about his technique: he was holding his axe not by the handle, but by the head, and using it like a giant dagger, stabbing furiously at the ice and only achieving moderate security. He employed the same system with his hammer. Now, I had heard that some kind of dagger was used to climb ice in the old days, when moderate security was the name of the game and Scotsmen ruled the winter scene. Mind you, daggers are an essential part of Scotsmen ruling anything, but as I was a new boy to the entire business, I was loath to criticise. It did seem to me, however, that he was maintaining contact only at the expense of huge amounts of energy and perhaps even a little help from Him above. So when he joined me at the stance, I decided to pass on some of the rudimentary knowledge which I had learned from an unusually forthcoming native.

The next pitch began with a little bulge and proceeded up a bubbly icefall which became very brittle near the top. This horrible splintering stuff demoted me instantly from my temporary status as teacher back to one of the lads again, feeling hopelessly frightened and hideously committed – and Paul and I became mates. As he started up the first bulge, whoops of delight echoed around the Ben. He came steaming up the pitch beaming at me, over the top of the steep section.

"Ee, it's much easier like this, isn't it?" he said, dangling effortlessly from his wrist loops – and then, with a sudden quizzical look: "What are Terrordactyls like?" He was obviously a quick learner. We were in a sort of snowy bowl which Paul led up, and all that remained was a short, not-too-hard pitch to the plateau. Well pleased with our day out, we plodded back to the car and straight down for a few pints.

"What about tomorrow then?" I ventured.

"Well, I'm still willing to have a go, what about you?"

I must admit that climbing with a priest gave me an unusual feeling of security. Not so much that nothing would happen, as that if it did, at least I would be entering the Pearly Gates in good company. With this in mind I took the plunge, and early next morning we stood below the Orion Face. It looked fairly impressive. In fact, it looked frighteningly impossible.

"Gr, I dunno if I fancy this," said Paul.

"Oh well, never mind," I said, very relieved. "I understand just how you feel. Listen, there's Bob Run round the corner and that's a jolly good route as well."

"Mind you," he continued, "we could always do the Orion Ordinary."

"Mmm yes, we could, although Bob Run's really interesting, you know."

But his mind was made up and nothing would deter him. At the top of the first pitch, which presented no great problem, we paused to chew some Orkney fudge and make quite certain that no opportunity for an early retreat had been left unconsidered. I tried to smoke a cigarette wearing damp soppy Dachsteins, and to discover where the next pitch went.

To my untrained eye, it looked very intimidating. All I could see was a kind of Strone Ulladale of the ice-climbing world leering above us – and in any case hadn't yet learnt to make Terrordactyls go round corners, it began to look as if I was supposed to take it direct.

In the absence of any of the favourite get-out clauses such as

warm weather, wet weather, wild weather or almost any kind of
weather (which are normally so readily available on the Ben), I set
out to try. It was certainly one of the most frightening climbing
experiences I have ever had.

Not that I climbed it, of course, absolutely no chance. Just
setting off and thinking that I was going to climb it was enough to
nearly drown me in adrenalin. Fortunately a kind of off-balance,
icy chimney ushered me away my self-imposed super-direttissima
and bore me safely to the left over some very wet ice, though still
good quality stuff.

At one point, about halfway up, I stopped using the Terrors, as
there were plenty of good holds sculptured by tricklets of water. A
thread behind an ice pillar provided a welcome runner, before some
steepish little walls led on to a small stance and a genuine, ring-a-
ding-ding, in-situ rock peg belay.

Paul came racing up to join me in an impressive series of
dynamic bounds, arriving with a dauntless but breathless smile,
saying: "Really great that, really great." He was right, too, the
climbing was absolutely superb – but when another no-nonsense,
in-to-the-hilt peg appeared at the end of the next pitch, making two
in a row on ground that I had always understood to be lethal, I
began to suspect that some spiritual assistance was being exercised.

In fact, they turned out to be relics from an epic retreat made
only a few days before, after an accident higher up. But you know
what they say about working in mysterious ways.

There was now only about 30ft. separating us from the Basin.
However, the ice had withered to nothing but a veneer of frosty
glass standing several inches proud of the rock. Blunted Terrors
bounced against impenetrable granite; leaden-footed crampon-
kicking made hollow echoes through the ice, while tinkling fragments rattled down the gap below it. It was very scaring, too.

We ploughed up the basin, and planted one Deadman below the
Epsilon Chimney. About 20ft. up it, yet another stance and peg
belay were provided. The comparative safety of the whole operation really surprised me, as I had been brainwashed into believing
that all Scottish winter climbing was suicidally dangerous. Of
course, with the advantage of hindsight and greater experience, I
now realise that only most of it is.

The Chimney itself is probably the best pitch I have ever done in

Scotland. Not desperately hard, though not devoid of technical interest either, it is a steep flow of ice, with a few little bulges, contained by grey flanking walls. The situation is immaculate and the ice was perfect: crisp, white snow-ice providing idiot-proof placements, with a feeling of security normally associated with five-foot seracs on Les Bossons Glacier, and all just a few miles down the road from Glencoe.

We emerged on to a small snowfield and one more pitch landed us on the North-East Ridge, with only the Mantrap barring our exit. This famous Nevis feature was intimidating me far more than its diminutive size justified. Although it is only seven or eight feet high and appears to be avoidable on either side, the whole aura of its reputation had impressed me sufficiently for me to wonder whether descending the Ridge would not be a preferable proposition.

Such is the power of Scottish mythology, and of years of mindlessly agreeing with almost anything that Glaswegians tell you, that a small rock step of crampon-scarred granite can wipe out 30 years of progress and make you feel marooned, high on the mountain, with this monolithic obstacle towering above.

But 30 years raced by and there, in front of my very eyes, was modern technology at work: a hard steel peg sticking out of a crack about three feet up. Paul belayed to it, I stood on it, and a sharp icy groove was all that remained before we were moving together up to the observatory, the emergency shelter, the trig point or wherever else people eat their sandwiches.

Paul was yodelling away to the tune of "And Did Those Feet in Ancient Times?"; I was trying to convince my heaving lungs and leaden legs that absolutely nobody suffered from altitude sickness at 4,000ft.

We trudged down the Carn Dearg Arête and on to the snow-slope. Below the abseil posts, our adventures were all over bar the bumslide and the bogtrot. I decided to see how well a Terrordactyl performed as an ice-axe brake. I discovered, as I slid to a natural halt at the bottom of the slope, that if it ever happened for real, the only thing that was going to break was my neck.

from CRAGS 6 *1977*

Out of the Midday Sun

ED DRUMMOND

"The brimming self confidence shown in your letters and elsewhere borders on audacity, and engenders in me irritation. . ." Robbins' words were a warning which nagged me as we slunk through the last of the scrub's defences to face the object of our desire in the broken dark.

The aspect shut us up for a while, sorting gear while obedient eyes crawled 1,800ft. up to the Lost Arrow Spire, its tip thrust from the great limb of the Lost Arrow Chimney into the upper air.

The affair had been carried off in one long day on the first free ascent by Chuck Pratt in 1966, but we were to spend a night out with her, my first, not having the push and acquired subtlety of the valley man, which opens the secrets of the least willing.

The first long drain-pipe crack, at about Very Severe, flattered our virility; obviously a snare; the lift of a casual eyebrow. Illusions of attainment at ease were abandoned to extreme climbing in the hammering sun up a shallow crack system on poor pinch grips, and made me long for the cool falls of great shadow above our heads where the chimneys began to close. The third pitch took us over a large 'gritstone' over-hang to the 'Horseman's Ledge', before the 'Safety Valve', a squeeze chimney which once it allowed admission would not admit of return. It had taken us some four hours to reach this point, a bad beginning and omen for the harder pitches above where my inefficient hauling and pedagogical belaying were to lose us hours. It was the most strenuous pitch that I had ever done to a technique born of panic, I am not a strong swimmer. Schneider, the young American with whom I had teamed up for the climb, led through on what looked an innocuous pitch. All that was innocuous was my sense of scale after the confines of the intestinal hole.

A frog leaping downhill with easy indifference to the world of exposure lapping below us. Tiny, mocking my gigantic effort in the skin-tearing jam-crack where for the first time I seriously doubted my ability to free-climb the whole route; if it got any harder. . .

"The Guidebook says this next pitch varies in difficulty
depending upon the season!"

Below, on a lower pitch, I had stopped my hammer from driving a peg into a tiny frog, occupying the gloom of a convenient crack. The strangeness of the climb, myself a stranger here with a stranger, made me respect a life that in its insecurity of lodgement seemed my own.

Schneider seemed inspired by the difficulties of the crack that I had led, in spite of his prusik up it, to lead through on a 15ft. wide chimney, and in the cold twilight find only the second adequate ledge of our 14-hour day. Seconding revived me to lead through and, after a rapid pendulum to bivouac as high as possible; I was relieved at a long easy-angled chimney stuck with overhanging chockstones.

The chimney gathers the winds to it at night and without a half-sack my duvet was insufficient to bring sleep for long. Long absurd sounds of empty cans clattering down the day below amused us before sleep came.

The next day was only four pitches in length to the groin of the Lost Arrow Spire with the trunk of the chimney, where we were to meet Josephine my wife, with friends who were to leave prusik lines from here, the Notch, as is usual to avoid the final artificial wall. These pitches took me all day to lead.

The third was very hard. Too hard to me at the time, but I had to do it or be faced with a next day of rappels, and days of shame. On the first fifteen feet of the pitch I had used some aid; tired, cold and scared. Halfway up the pitch I was aware of a further 70ft. of air up which, against my gravity and fear, I had to move. Up the lips of this repudiating gargoyle I had to squeeze myself with cross pressure between knees and heels, and with downward-pointing palms. My puffed and bloody knees, ripe from the night, softly exploded in crimson berries on my dirty trouserless legs. If you are thrown overboard with your wrists and ankles tied, still you will try to swim. I went inside the blackness of the mouth and waited. Nothing would happen; I had to make it so. I risked the flare again with 50 clear feet of air below; a nasty house to fall off. Back I go; look around. At the top of the chimney a nest of stones. I caved up the back and succeeded in threading these together. Less worried now I descended and climbed up the spouting flare from the out-side, protected from above. A dead mouse unwrapped itself in my slings as I climbed, lifted by the able wind that held my hair on end as well. No matter, not even that spectre mirrored me; I was succeeding. A few feet higher I had to remove my chest harness, and re-tie at my waist, as the chimney was too narrow to permit me, corset and all.

That day and that climb ended one pitch above, the alley of my inexperience ringing with my shouting American friend, shouting at my slowness, teaching me. But the prusik lines promised an end, and for a while I forgot myself, and just screamed back, as virtuous as a god.

from THE ALPINE JOURNAL *1969*

Snakes and Ladders

ROBIN SMITH

Here is a note in English on the first Scottish ascent of the least vertical wall in all the Alps.

We went for a week or two among the greater mountains, the first, of course, the Matterhorn, a noble pile, so a day or two later we came to the Dolomites.

We hairpinned up to Lavaredo, 3 in 1 and 2 by 2, S. and R. for the wheel and meals and Haston and me for the Cima West. The cold at dawn would have blackened the toes of a brass monkey. So around 10, Haston and me, we ambled round to under the North Wall (having made a cunning plan with S. and R.) with 300ft. of rope, doubled, 1 sack, 1 camera, 2 hammers, 6 slings, 8 etriers, 40 karabiners, and (cunningly) 300ft. of line to save us taking bivvy gear.

Cassin climbed it years ago, two men and three days and just a few pitons, 800ft. up the far right edge, then 500ft. of hairy traverse, above the biggest overhang you ever saw, in to the middle of the wall, then, 1,000ft. up a couloir and over the top in a thundering storm, babbling. But nowadays they go for Direttissimas, straight up the biggest overhangs with a great beating of pegs and drums. A first ascent can last for years, with time off for rest cures, with an average of more than a piton a yard, and just a few expansion bolts where the rock won't take pitons, and just a

few free-climbing moves rudely disrupting the rhythm of swinging
free. The powers of the pioneers to pitoneer and persevere are far
beyond the grasp of Stone-age Britons, but all the pitons are left in
place so that later ascents are comparatively easy. In 1959, inevitably, they finished a direct start to the Via Cassin; and here is how
we cunningly climbed it.

We tied on to the double rope, and divided the gear, and one
man took the sack, with the line and the camera, and the other took
the krabs and stepped up off the path. For 20ft. you climb the rock,
because it's only vertical.

The wall has the look of an elephant's hide, flat and smooth
from a distance, but riddled all over with pocks and warts, piton-
cracks, sharp little finger holds, crumbling jugs, loose flakes,
shallow grooves, sharp little roofs, and ledges to stand on once in a
blue moon.

The route is a wandering line of pitons, 400ft. hither and thither
up a shallow, gently overhanging bay, to under the monstrous arch
of a roof jutting out about 80ft., and then 200ft. along a magnificent zig-zag piton crack, twisting up and out and leftwards all at
once, and round the lip of the roof, and then by another 400ft. of
gently overhanging wall easing off to the plumb vertical just as it
joins the Via Cassin at the end of the hairy traverse under the
couloir.

But we had had but a nibbling foretaste of unelementary piton-
eering. So up we bumbled, up two down one, clawing krabs and
thrashing air, hurling holds at audiences, otherwise avoiding the
rock like a hot tin roof, but nonetheless trapping fingers, baring
knuckles, dripping gore on krabs and ropes and beating knees to
black and blue balloons. To play it cool, you harmonise your
ropes. "Tight on white, and slack a bit of red." Only ours were
both a dirty white, synchronically turning speckled red, obtusely
clipped at acutest angles, writhing into tumorous kinks, and
hideously twisted like a pair of loving snakes, with the man who
was climbing too throttled to speak and the man at the reins too
sleepy to listen and the two of us linked by nothing but hate and
discord. One man would follow the pitons till he ran out of rope or
krabs or couldn't drag the rope any further, then he would sit and
swing in his ladders while the other man followed, collecting all the
krabs, and clambered over the first man and up the next pitch.

Easy; but night fell at the end of four pitches, which is to say, right away out on the lip of the monster roof.

This was not cunning, but we had a cunning move in hand, and scanned the gloomy screes below and bawled to left and right. But no S. and R., so we passed a worried hour spinning our webs for the night. Haston was laughing, he was at a belay, a rugosity for his seat and one foothold. He faced out, lopsidedly crucified across a ring of pitons, head jammed under a bit of roof, and held in at the belly by criss-cross bits of hoary abandoned rope. I was 20ft. down and right, hanging free from a holdless scoop, but with pitons all around. So facing in, I wove a net of krabs and ladders and bits of sling, slung around me under my armpits, under my seat and under my knees, with toes against the rock an inch above the biggest bit of roof, seated, as it were, on a bottomless closet, and feeling that way too.

I had the sack, so while Haston yelled the odds I took out the line and unravelled it 300ft. down into the night. This was the first, but we feared it was the last of the steps of our cunning plan. But then the plaintive voice of S. rose from the screes. We answered warmly. They had driven down to town to buy us fruit and goodies and bread and jam and butter and chocolate full of brandy, and cooked a thermos of coffee and a dixie of stew and potatoes, and wrapped them in duvets and sleeping-bags with knife and fork and spoon, and tied them all into a great rucksack. But then, it seemed, they had taken the sack to the wrong mountain; and only by chance had S. happened to hear us. So S. went off to fetch the sack and R. By now it was so dark that I couldn't see more than a blur of Haston, but we both untied from the double rope, and undoubled it, with some confusion, into a single length of 300ft. Then Haston tied onto one end, and I tied the other end to the top end of the dangling line and carried on lowering so that the bottom end of the line would reach all the 500ft. to the screes. But meanwhile, hanging loops of rope had embrangled themselves around the dangling line, and as I lowered the rope the line came back up in a loop-the-loop, and I found myself lowering it all over again. A fankle ensued. So I went to work like a fizzling computer, speaking coaxing words to all the little knots, with Haston somewhere up above turning cold and repetitive. Meanwhile S., with the sack and R., had been back for quite some time; we could see them waving torches at the bottom. In two hours all but the kernels of fankle were solved, so I lowered as much as I could, and sure enough they caught it in the beam of a torch, snaking down to the screes 100ft. out from the base of the wall. They fixed the sack to the end, and I rigged up a pulley of krabs, and then they beetled off back to camp and I pulled up the sack.

From where he was, Haston was useless, he just froze and swore and moaned, while the rope came up in tiny jerks and down in the depths the invisible sack was monstrously spinning and leaping through the night.

The pulley was all wrong, and once in a while there were bits of fankle to get past the krabs, and the more I pulled in the worse the fankles grew, till even my arms were all seized up in knots, and not until the first faint glimmer of dawn did the sack swirl into sight. I gaffed it to a piton and slumped in my slings, but then I was roused by Haston's groans, so I put on a duvet and sleeping-bag, and gobbled coffee and handfuls of goodies and stew, and Haston pulled up his share, with goodies and stew unhappily all mixed up, and then we slept.

Well into the morning S. and R. returned, so loth as sloths we unbedded ourselves and packed the rucksack, keeping duvets and goodies. Then I lowered it, that was easy, but the ropes were so fankled it stuck half-way, so I had to pull it up (pull it up) and start all over again. Next time it stuck about 60ft. from the screes, but I wasn't going to pull it up, so Haston untied from his end of the rope, which gave me another 20ft., and I added a chain of tatty slings, and S. stood tip-toe on a rock and got hold of the sack and took it off, and the ropes sprung back so high in the air that I hardly needed to pull them up at all. Then I took our cunning line and hurled it back to the screes, and Haston recovered an end of rope and we tried to redouble it for climbing, but the strain had left it twisted and kinked in psychopathic convulsions, and not for a dismal number of hours did we start to climb.

The climbing was just the bleeding same, with nothing but the beginnings of cunning to balance the loss of blood and vigour. We reached the hairy traverse of the Via Cassin just in time for an hour of beating sun-set, and here was the very first ledge of the climb with plenty of room for two. So we settled for a reasonably typical hunched-up twitching, chittering, wriggling, burbling, hellishly freezing bivouac. Then half an hour of tepid sun-rise hustled us onwards. The Direttissima really finishes up a lot more pitons just left of the Via Cassin couloir. But it looked daft and we were sickened, so stuffing our ladders away, we finished up the crumbling, tumbling couloir. At noon we came out in the frizzling sun and hobbled down the other side all sweat and blood and stiff and sore, with fists rolled up like hedge-hogs, and they never opened till S. and R. had fed us full of food and wine and wheeled us home to the land of rolling Munros.

from THE EDINBURGH UNIVERSITY MOUNTAINEERING CLUB JOURNAL *1960*

The Rope

SIR DOUGLAS BUSK

Our night in the lonely cabin was disturbed only by the inroads of a porcupine, at which five of the party's six boots had to be hurled with heartfelt imprecations before it would cease its noisy mastication of a succulent board by the door. At 7.30 a.m. we were off on our superb climb.

Long's Peak is a granite monster over 14,000ft. high with a pleasing diversity of routes, none of them entirely easy. The famous East (or strictly speaking north-east) Face is a magnificently steep wall, rising it may be 2,000ft. in one splendid leap from screes to summit. About a third of the way up, a level ledge, known as Broadway, runs across the face and divides the climb into two sections. It is usual, and more elegant, to reach Broadway by Alexander's Chimney, which was explored by my Einsteinian Princeton professor, who was the first to climb the face, but early in the year this is iced from top to bottom and we were compelled to take to the steep snow couloir to the left of it, known as Mills Glacier. This leads easily and conveniently to the beginning of Broadway. The ledge is a curiously regular fault some six feet wide and is easy enough except where an occasional rib protrudes and thrusts the climber out over empty space. Half an hour along it we struck straight up the face.

At this point my emotions began to be subjected to a serious strain. The reader will have gathered that I am an exceedingly cautious mountaineer and will not be surprised to hear that I now suggested with some emphasis that we should put on the rope I had been patiently carrying in my sack. The rocks hereabouts are shockingly steep and I was appalled by the temerity of my two companions in climbing unsafeguarded. They were well ahead of me, and after a heated exchange of shouts suggested that I had better bring the rope up to them if I felt so strongly about it. I did so with resignation, only to find that by then one of them had wandered still farther up. The other pointed out maliciously that I had already climbed the most difficult pitch unroped, so it was not worth roping now. Having delivered himself of this crushing statement, he too departed upwards. I must admit that the climbing was not severe, probably not even difficult, and it was certainly within my powers or I should not be alive today, but it is not pleasant to climb for hours unroped over places where a fall could not fail to be fatal and I think that my indignation can be pardoned.

I soon exhausted my stock of profanity and in self-defence was compelled to see the funny side. Here was I, the most timorous of mortals, shinning for dear life up a preposterous precipice in vain pursuit of two swift-footed maniacs who from time to time enquired after my well-being in solicitous accents. As so often before and since, humour saved the situation and we finished the climb in an amiable wrangle – but still unroped.

I had my first revenge on the summit, when I took unkind care to emphasise that local publications assigned to the face a standard of difficulty equal to that of the Grand Dru. Long's Peak is a magnificent climb, but there can be no question of this. The rock is solid and there are no route-finding or ice difficulties. We ran no outrageous risks in climbing it unroped, but better mountaineers might hesitate before thus tackling the Dru. This was the burden of my song on the sun-warmed summit rocks, until my laughing companions bade me desist, lest the fair name of their beloved peak be smirched.

For the descent we chose the North Face, which sinks in chancy slabs, at first at no great angle, to a final cliff. There was some snow and much *verglas*, so the descent demanded the utmost caution, since a slip would have been difficult if not impossible to arrest. One can wander more or less where one will on the upper part of this face, and it was by sheer chance that I found myself on the better line at a point where the slabs steepened for the final downrush to the screes. The others were away to my right and between us the rock was smooth and holdless. My second revenge for the scurvy treatment they had meted out to me came when a plaintive suggestion floated across the slabs that the rope might be put on. With difficulty I resisted the temptation to return all their specious arguments, but the ground was in fact too dangerous for such badinage, so I slung over a knotted end. With some labour and research I could devise an unconvincing belay, and after a nasty descent on their own line, the other traversed warily across to mine, and, at last decently united, we finished the climb together.

from THE DELECTABLE MOUNTAINS *1946*

With Two Men on the Matterhorn

YVETTE VAUCHER

It is now two years since I fell under the spell of that sombre face. In its shadow I became Michel's wife; our marriage was blessed by the priest of the tiny chapel at Schwarzsee, 6,000ft. up in the mountains. That was shortly after my battle with the North Face of the Eiger, when a savage drop in temperature had shattered all hope of success. From Schwarzsee I gazed at the towering North Face of the Matterhorn, and was spellbound. Yet my thoughts were little more than an exciting game, a futuristic dream.

Zermatt was in a festive mood when Michel and I returned on July 10, 1965. Feverish preparations were being made to celebrate the centenary of the first ascent of the Matterhorn. Television and press representatives were among the many people there. Above them all stood the beautiful mountain, so long the object of my affections. Yet I was unhappy. Michel had a television contract to climb the North Face with some Swiss guides. And as for me? Was I expected just to stand and watch? I was furious with everyone who expected me to do that, even with Michel. And I was miserable

After all, had I not taken Michel as my sole partner 'from this time forth, for evermore'? And now was I to be a mere spectator?

The next day we took the telepherique up to Schwarzsee, where the path to the Hörnli hut starts. As the little chapel came into view, I turned to Michel:

"Do you remember, two years ago. . .?" Yes of course he remembered. Why shouldn't he? But he also knew what I meant to say: "Take me on the route with you!"

"You know that's impossible. The television. . ."

I knew alright. I just refused to believe it.

We reached the hut, the starting place for most of the routes on the Matterhorn. The activity in the hut had little to do with climbing. It was a hive of industry, with every available space taken up by the Eurovision men and their equipment. We met a few friends there, among them Toni Hiebeler, who asked me if I was going on the North Face. I had to tell him "No." Othmar Krönig from Zermatt was there, and he too was employed by Eurovision, although his job was just to ferry loads on the Hörnli Ridge. Michel reckoned that the television people would have too many things on their minds to bother checking the team which would actually climb the route, and he had a word with Othmar. Did he fancy doing the North Face with us? With us?

Othmar had his doubts. He wasn't really fit, and anyway he'd promised to carry for the television. But climbers are, after all, only human and once the idea is there. . . The hut custodian stepped in for Othmar. I saw myself already on the route. Spurred on by happiness and my own good fortune I raced down to Schwarzsee, drove to Zermatt to pick up my gear, and was back at the hut by evening. Meanwhile, Michel, Hilti von Almen and Michel Darbellay had been to the base of the wall to check out the conditions and the entry pitches. Things didn't look too good, they said. I had other worries, too. Daisy Voog of Eigerwand fame, was in the area, and the North Face of the Matterhorn was on her list as well. On the Eiger she had been faster than me, and this time I wanted to redress the balance. . .

Evening came and the weather looked good, everything looked good, my thoughts were racing, already high up on the route.

On July 13 we are up at 2 a.m., still drunk with sleep, moving like automatons. Breakfast at that hour is singularly unappetising — a quick bite, a drop of coffee. In the pale light of the hut kitchen we say our goodbyes; hands are shaken, kind words spoken. Then out into the night. I see stars in a cloudless sky and, far above, a dark, barely discernible mass. Our mountains.

To the right, where the vast shape is darkest, I can just make out the North Face. It is not fear which I experience in moments like this, but the excitement of anticipation. We do not talk much. Only our footsteps and breathing break the silence. The route to the base of the wall is not easy. We follow the steps cut by our friends the previous day. An hour later we find ourselves at the foot of the North Face. Like Michel and Othmar, I am silent. We each tie on. The pegs and the rest of the ice gear is divided between us. We are as one, a team, each dependent on the others.

Our ropework is odd: Michel is the middle man, but climbs first, with one rope to me and one to Othmar. After 100ft. or so he cuts a stance, hammers a peg in and brings us up together, belaying us both at the same time is hard work and rather dangerous, but he has found a safe stance. The first icefield is 1,200ft. long, at an angle of about 55 degrees, but a covering of hard snow allows rapid progress. Dawn comes, and the shadows of the night creep down the valley towards Zermatt, where the last of the revellers are making their way to bed. I don't envy them. I am happy, because I am on the Matterhorn North Face with Michel and a good friend.

The final 150ft. of the icefield are dangerous, a sheet of ice which shines like crystal. Every couple of feet Michel has to cut a step in the ice, which is exhausting work. Othmar and I have things easier. Then the hateful traverse leading to the diagonal couloir. We study every move Michel makes, not daring to speak, watching him anxiously. He dare not fall here. I think to myself, the belay pegs do not look good at all. But Michel will not fall, I keep repeating, over and over. . . In fact he deals with this horrific section with supreme confidence. I reach the end of the awful traverse panting furiously. I see Michel, feel his strength and his skill, catch his kindly eye, and we embrace. Without him, this wall would be too cold and hostile for me; now everything is wild and beautiful, exciting, wonderful.

Noon, and after all our exertions, we deserve a rest. But we cannot; we have not anticipated bivouacking on the face, and have brought neither the gear nor the extra food necessary. So on it has to be: The diagonal couloir proves hard. Under normal summer conditions, this is the crux of the route; a blanket of snow on the rock makes it hard, man's work. But that is the way I wanted it. After four hours the monster is below us.

"Michel, we have to move right!" shouts Othmar, but Michel disagrees. He has no route description with him, and has not really studied the face, but his obstinate streak tells him that the route lies straight ahead, so that is the way he goes. What Michel does, we must do. Time is now pressing. We are slowed down by soft snow. Another steep section; this time I tell Michel that he should traverse to the left. He does not listen to me either, and continues straight up as if he knew the route by heart.

The route now becomes an endless plod: snow-covered rock, ice, snow and more ice. Enthusiasm gives way to exhaustion, and to worry about not reaching the top today. Doubts set in. Evening comes. Suddenly I see above us one more steep section and above that the sky, no longer blue, but overcast. Michel struggles doggedly with the last 50ft.; disappointment – there's more snow above: I am shattered, I've had enough of this wall now, enough of the danger, the sheer hard work, the height and the perpetual drop yawning below us. All I want to do now is to get back to the real world, to become a wife again; Michel's wife. Up here that world is far away, so far away that it may just as well not exist. All that we have is a biting wind whipping the snow into a frenzy, the cold, ice, rock and the fading light. I have two fine people with me, which is a lot in this world. Without thinking I climb up to Michel, he puts an arm around me and says nothing. Bivouac? No. We climb on. That must be the last rope length up there. Soon we are beneath it. It is dark, but there is no stopping Michel. He is not moving as quickly or as precisely as this morning, but he keeps on climbing. Another hour, but the top is nowhere to be seen, just the ice and rock in front of him. Michel ties the rope off to a peg and comes back down to the tiny ledge where somehow the three of us must bivouac.

We hammer a few pegs in, and sit down on the sloping shelf. I can no longer see the drop below but know that we are nearly up. There is a small bivi bag in my sack and Michel has a two-man bag with him. He tries to drag it out of his sack.

"Shit!" A brief hideous rustle and the bag is gone. We are all dejected. I have spent many nights in the mountains, but this is the longest. Our food supply is modest. A piece of chocolate, a sip of tea. In spite of the cold I feel Michel's comforting warmth. I think and wait and think, hour after hour. At last, the sky grows paler.

Michel mutters a few insignificant words and sets off, soon vanishing into thick cloud. The rope comes tight, the signal that we are to follow. He's at the top! Soon we join him; first Othmar, then me. We put our arms around each other. I cannot speak. Soon I can control myself no longer. I cry. Like a happy little girl with the riches of the world laid at her feet. I cry and I am happy, so happy. I did not know that life could be so beautiful.

from ALPINISMUS *1965*

Bernat's Horse

HAROLD DRASDO

Montserrat! The serrated mountain, rises from the plains 40 miles north-west of Barcelona. It is less than 5,000ft. high and three or four miles long. The rock is a very firm conglomerate. Seen from the south the mountain is a maze of pinnacles, many of them some hundreds of feet in height; to the north it presents sheer walls of up to 1,500ft, almost without weaknesses. All this rock rises from a shrub-forest, everywhere as dense as a privet hedge. The mountain is famous for its monastery, fitted impressively into a cirque of pinnacles. The monks are nothing if not enterprising. They have provided excellent restaurants, cafeterias, food shops, wine shops, bookshops, gift shops, hairdressers' salons and toilets. The monastery has published a handsome rock-climbers' guide book. Vending machines dispense cooled beer and chocolate at all hours of day and night.

We arrived in the early afternoon. In the huge tourist car park an attendant stopped us. On our first visit his predecessor had been helpful.

"Could we camp somewhere near here?" we had said.

"There is a free camp site, courtesy of the monastery," he said.

"We have come to climb," we said.

"The climbing is superb, enquire at the monastery," he said.

This time it was late in the year and the attendant barred the way.

"The camp site is closed for the winter," he said.

We pointed to a small tent, just visible through the trees.

"The camp site is closed for the winter," he said.

This exchange repeated itself interminably until an emergency called him aside and we were able to continue to the camp. It was indeed closed and the gate locked but two climbers had persuaded the administration to grant them access. It was a special privilege, not to be extended to anyone else, because they were there only to climb the mountain, they explained.

"So are we," we said, pitching our tent.

Of these two climbers, one was a Swede, working in Czechoslovakia. The other was a Spaniard, working in Switzerland. They conversed in German. The Spaniard recognised me immediately but did not say so because we had met on our earlier visit when Jean Nicol caught him transferring armloads of food, climbing gear and motor oil from our tents to his own. I recognised the Spaniard immediately but did not say so because it seemed useful to win friends. Retribution still lay some months into the future when Dave Nicol was to find himself a day and a half above the Spaniard on the Nose of El Cap. "Pedro," the men in front would shout as they drank their Coca-Colas. And the Ave Marias drifted up as the Coke cans tinkled down. Pedro finally roped off.

At night the place changes character. The day trippers disappear and the illuminations and the moonlight emphasise the huge clean facades of the buildings. Beautiful to wander around the deserted plazas, arcades and flights of stairs at those hours. The monks are nowhere to be seen. Sometimes we wondered what they did with themselves. But often we would hear heavy rock music pounding out from tiny lighted windows five or six floors up, and, on two occasions at least, girls screaming. However, as if to remind the visitor of their essentially solemn purposes the monks bang gongs from time to time and they keep this up for most of the night backed up at intervals by regular strokes and chimes from an assortment of powerful clocks and bells.

A memorable incident occurred in the camp that night. The site, perched on terraces above a precipitous slope, looks straight across at the buildings, a quarter of a mile away. Looking at the view from the pitch-dark camp site, the note of a trumpet right at my side suddenly shattered the silence. My first sensation was of devastating shock. Then I discerned the Swede, sitting in a camp chair on the terrace. My next reaction was a rush of anxiety as the full cool message poured across towards the monastery. Surely the authorities wouldn't stand for this maniacal attack on their privacy. They'd be up within minutes to turn us all off; then, bewilderment. From the monastery itself, a cool clear voice came back. It was the most impeccably timed, most perfect echo I have ever heard. The squares remained empty and it began to appear that there was to be no immediate hostile response. I relaxed into listening to this extraordinary duet. With impressive certainty and authority the Swede played a long and plaintive number and to each phrase, after a dignified pause, the melancholy answer responded, filling the cirque. It seemed to me the most beautiful melody I had ever heard and one that would haunt me for the rest of my life. But with the first notes of the next piece it slid off my memory for ever.

The guide-book to Montserrat is written in Catalan. This is good because Catalan appears to be a sort of Latin attempt at pidgin English, or, perhaps the climber's Esperanto. I quote the description of the first climb I did, on my previous visit, L'Esquelet by the Xemeneia Torras-Nubiola:

> *Ruta (Route) actualment utilitzada (actually utilised) com a via Normal (as the ordinary route). Aquesta Xemeneia que solca totalment el monolit (this chimney which completely splits the monolith) es una tipica escalada de tecnica de "ramonage" o xemeneia (is a typical chimneying-up a chimney type of chimney-climb!).*

Now try a bit yourself.

> *Molt convenient per a l'escalador montserrati per a completar la seva formacio de roquista. Escalada catalogada en 4.ᵗ. Al final (sortida) pas de 4.ᵗsup. Escalada molt segura. Una mica atletica. I hora. Descens en rappel per darrera (via Normal).*

Not knowing a word of the language I may have got bits of it wrong but the rock fitted my reading.

I had been thinking about the Cavall Bernat, Montserrat's most famous pinnacle, climbed as long ago as 1935. Constant attempts had preceded this victory. Temptatives constants havien precedit aquesta conquesta (I think!). The successful party consisted of Costa, Boix and Balaguer and an iron plaque placed at the start of the climb twenty-five years later remembers them. Compared with English climbing of the period it seemed a notable achievement and one cannot help wondering why we have heard so little of the Montserrati climbers. But, of course, only a year later the Civil War began and for three years Barcelona became the focus of one side's hopes. Until General Yagüe marched in on 26 January, 1939. Costa, Boix and Balaguer, where are you now? Then World War II confined the Barcelona climbers to their own mountain. But perhaps they wanted nothing else? They kept on doing what they'd already learned to do, but harder and longer. Their rock gives very few crack lines and its horizontally-bedded pebble surface can only be used up to steep slab angle. So one by one the great pinnacles and walls were bolted. The bolt was an ordinary Barcelona coach-bolt, sawn-off; the hanger was simply a length of very strong wire, twisted into a loop. On these precarious ladders the Montserrati climbers pushed bravely upwards. And by the end of the fifties they had forced El Paret de L'Aeri, the Wall of the Téléférique. "It's as impressive as Half Dome," Dave Nicol had exclaimed.

Maureen and I walked up to the Cavall Bernat in an hour. It was a warm, sunny afternoon. We scrambled up the easy pitch onto the shoulder and arranged the ropes. The big pitch starts with a 30ft. traverse graded at 5 sup. It went easily to an ancient peg in a pocket. Then a couple of very thin moves on pebbles, the wall just easing from vertical. Someone had pecked tiny scars on the surface of the key pebble. There was no way to step across on it and I persuaded myself to do so and moved into the scoop at the foot of the big chimney-groove. It was more difficult to stand there than I'd guessed and a few awkward moments passed before I was able to fix protection. Then, slowly up the groove assisted by a dozen pegs, bolts and rotting wedges already in place. At 100ft. something novel and disconcerting occurred. To this point, although we couldn't see each other we were in perfect contact. Then, in the upper bulges, I shouted down. A long wailing echo from the Paret dels Diables, straight opposite, drowned my words.

I tried shouting one word at a time. No way. I tried clipping the syllables. No way. Each one extended into an idiotic howl, ringing like a bell. I continued up the corner hearing at one point the sound of a hammer, no echo, close by. Stretching the 150ft. ropes I reached the small ledge. Two ancient bolts and a peg. I tied on, feeling committed and a bit worried. How would Maureen cope with the traverse? I had protected it with one rope but there'd be enough stretch to let her into space. I remembered that she had never prusiked.

I took in, holding the ropes very tight, and inch by inch she came up. Curiously, a mist had veiled the sun and a cool little breeze began to blow and rapidly grew stronger. At last she came into sight. She looked anxious. "Don't worry," I said, "at least we've got company for the descent." I heard a hammer. I said, "Pedro must be on the Via Puigmal, the big route on the back." She said, "Pegging, no, no, it's that sodding monk!" She hung back on a sling and pointed. On the very edge of the mind-blowing wall of the Paret dels Diables a hooded figure was crouched. The mist swirled around him. He was squaring off blocks for a shrine or meditation cell on the brink of as fearsome a precipice as I have ever seen!

Maureen joined me and we pulled ourselves together. I arranged myself hastily for the top pitch which consisted of a short wall, easing into a slab, easing into the perfectly rounded dome of the summit. The first steep bit was easy but I came to a halt in the middle of the slab. Reasonable holds but not one of them incut: no protection, great exposure, and suddenly the wind was blowing in powerful cold gusts. Wasn't it oddly dull, too? No, it wasn't dull, it was getting dark, and just this frustrating barrier before easy ground and the summit. There was a little flake and I tapped a tiny peg in. I tested it. It moved. I tapped it again. The crack widened. I adjusted a sling to suspend my foot upon a small pebble and as the wind abated a moment I made three swift moves up to easy ground, and scrambled up in a final scariscurry. I was half-turned round, shouting to Maureen to cast off quickly, when I became aware somehow of a terrifying figure close behind me. I gasped aloud as the corner of my eye picked up this silver apparition. Relax, I told myself, it is the Madonna again. I had never expected to meet her on this off-beat perch. I tied the ropes around her waist while she gazed serenely into the deepening gloom. Maureen came up swiftly.

First British, we said, congratulating ourselves on getting up. It may have been a poor thing but it was our own. What about getting down? I remembered that Maureen had never abseiled. We forced ourselves to rest for three or four precious minutes.

It was the perfect teaching set-up for a first abseil: a pitch that graded evenly from horizontal to vertical; a figure-eight descender; myself holding the safety rope; the Madonna holding the abseil rope; the imminence of darkness. I outlined the idea and Maureen went smoothly down, no problem. I followed, retrieved the peg, dropped the hammer which stopped providentially on the edge of the stance, retrieved the hammer, retrieved the abseil rope. Now for the big one. It seemed to take ages to set it up, but at last she set off, straight for the shoulder. I composed myself with difficulty until indistinct shouts signalled that she might be down. I had arranged to protect my own descent, having 600ft. of rope with us and not liking the corroded bolts. I also wanted a peg I had left in the groove. I set off for it but in a moment of carelessness I lost my purchase against the slanting groove and floated out across the wall. I had to forget it. I dropped onto the shoulder. The Cavall leaned over us like the prow of a gigantic liner in obscurity, mist swirled around her. To my delight and pride the ropes came cleanly down. Then down the easy shoulder and in five minutes we were on the ground and stuffing the ropes, which became suddenly and inextricably tangled, into the sacks. A wild exultation was starting to well up in us. But we hadn't quite finished yet.

Deep inside the monastery buildings there is an extraordinary cafeteria. It is the only place open after six and then from eight until nine only. Each evening, from the interstices of the monastery, a strange assortment of night people emerges to assemble there. The counters are laden with delicacies and offer every sort of drink. It presented itself to our thoughts now as the essential conclusion to this expedition.

We had no watch and no torch. Our senses led us along the ridge and into the narrow corridor through the forest. Eventually the faint whitish stones of the path disappeared and we had to admit that we had lost the line, probably 500ft. higher. The concrete pilgrims' stairway to S. Jeromi could be only a few hundred feet down through the thicket. Our impulses were to crash on down and our bodies agreed. But experience recalled the sheer smooth walls terracing the forest at random. We went wearily back up and staggered around, casting about for the path. Eventually we found it and felt our way from branch to branch, the trees so dense now that we were unable to fall out of the tunnel. A half-hour in this lovely enchanted wood and we stepped abruptly onto the concrete trackway. Then down and down, counting the features we recognised until a pale glow slowly transformed into the effulgence the illuminations cast onto the rocks overhanging the monastery. On and on until the lights and buildings came into view and our way was clearly lit. In five minutes we would be down. A bell crashed out.

The cafeteria opens at eight and closes at nine. We froze and counted. One, two, three, four, five, six, seven, eight. An agonising pause. The silence lengthened and became rich and profound. We stared at each other weakly and broke into hysterical laughter. Then, in a collapsed and aching walk, we stumbled down for beer and Cinzano, a little food maybe, and a brief but full taste of that rich contentment, ecstasy even, that visits us so infrequently, consequent sometimes on such a day as this.

from THE FELL AND ROCK CLIMBING CLUB JOURNAL *1974*

Cengalo, Cengalo

EMIL ZOPFI

When you say Cengalo, I think of scaly plates of rock which burst through the ice like reptiles' backs and hide their tiny saurian heads in the white cornices like timid animals. And of the lofty ridge cutting a slice of blue sky like a keen blade.

Cengalo, Cengalo. . .

Cengalo sounds strange, sinister – Why. . .? Like the monotonous scrapings, perhaps, that fill black summer nights when the farmers down there in their rude log cabins sharpen their scythes. . . like that perhaps? Yes, just like that.

Actually, we wanted to do the North Face of the Dru. We wanted to get it over with quickly before the days got shorter. And then

Hori still had this course to do in September, this computer programming course, or whatever the hell it was. The new red climbing sack stood, packed and ready, out in the hall on the new carpet, on the quiet monotone green, on the artificial meadow with its synthetic curls. And the new wallpaper, damn it, was torn because I couldn't find the rubber end for the ice hammer, I was in too much of a hurry. Then the phone rang:

"There's a storm in the west. . . it's just awful."

"But I've already arranged my holidays for tomorrow. . . and the session, what about the session with the television crew."

"The others want to go down to the Bregaglia."

"The Bregaglia?"

"Cengalo."

"Cengalo, Cengalo. . . hang on a minute."

"Pick you up at one tomorrow."

"That pillar we saw after the Badile. . .?"

There are four of us. And our guide had ordained one pair of crampons and one axe per party. Which meant that Dieter and I, armed with our axes, toiled upwards cutting steps in the gleaming black, gritty ice, thrashed upwards so to speak, cursing and wobbling and poking around in the dismal damp light of the headtorches; while the other two, Hori and the Guide, strolled past us with their hands in their pockets. . . crunch, crunch, crunch. . . crampons like sharks' teeth, snap, snap, snap. . . someone else pops up below us, someone with a fearful rusty-red snout; one of the opposition, and with him, Anja.

"You all right?"

"For Anja we'd cut steps all the way up the Badile Couloir and down the Gemelli Couloir if need be."

Suddenly, we are overcome by sickness; yes, that dreadful sickness Kluckeritis, named after its first victim the guide Christian Klucker, who hacked his way up all the ice gulleys around here. God knows why. Kluckeritis overcomes us and. . . hack, hack, hack. . . Anja trots past, lightfooted as a deer, with Rednose. . . crunch, crunch, crunch. . . But wait, there's a light up there in the darkness, on the slabs below the cornices . . . people, people up there? The others see nothing, plod onwards. There it is again, hanging clear and quiet on the cold, dead ruins; not a gleam, not a

warm glow, no . . . just a pale, deathly pale light. How did the
story go again? A light on the mountain, a light on the cliff, alpine
lights . . . midsummer lights, midsummer nights . . . God knows,
that was a long time ago. The souls of the dead, perhaps, the souls
of the dead, restless, haunting the mountain? But the light there is a
quiet light, alone and far off . . . The cockerel, yes, the bitter,
forgotten king of the Alps, the old cockerel; it is his betrayed soul
sweeping lightly over the mountain and whinning like the wind . . .
cengalo, cengalo. . .

After the bergschrund we climb a series of loose, dusty gullies,
down which the rocks hum like swarms of buzzing, angry insects.
At last, at last, we reach the ridge, the dragon's back, which
disappears into the milky light of the morning far above. Our
breathing comes in gasps; damn, these sacks are heavy. The Guide
presses on.

"Come on, get a move on! We've no time to lose."

. . . But what does time mean, when over there the sunlight is
falling on the summit slabs of the Badile, in a flash, as if thrown
there, then it trickles slowly down, reforms as fine threads in the
cracks, cobweb-like, then falls in a silent cascade over the rock
steps to bounce glistening on the scales and drip down walls and
roofs until finally, finally it trickles into the cracked maze of the
Bondasca glacier. What does time mean . . . perhaps you still
know?

"How many years is it again?"

Hori chews on a tough bit of ham.

"Hang on. . ."

"It's '73 now, huh. . .?"

"And four, no five years ago I got married, or. . ."

"Of course, that was before the South Africa trip."

"Two years after I got my degree."

"'63, it was thawing outside I think.

"Then it must have been '62. . ."

"'62, you're right."

"Eleven years ago. . ."

Anja smiles. Redsnout gets out cheese sandwiches and a huge
water bottle, while the Guide and Dieter are searching in the grassy
grooves for holds, jugs, peg cracks, rocky protuberances and
whatever else they need to make upward progress. We gaze across

at the smooth sweep of the Badile and can hardly believe that it is eleven years since we climbed on it, in bad weather and after a bivouac at the foot of the wall.

"Hey. . ."

". . . hang about, the karabiner's jammed. . ."

"It only seems like it was yesterday."

"Damn. . ."

. . . The old, almost forgotten memories hang like milky clouds in our minds, and suddenly everything is there before us again, tangible and real. We feel first of all how the ice-cold, damp rock grows beneath our fingers, dusty and glistening, see how in the twilight it grows into a vast black wall, the excitement as morning overtakes us.

Seven parties below us on the glacier, closing in on us like glow-worms in the night, scarlet patches of cloud shoot over the summit ridge . . . bad weather, turn back. Turn back, to face a cold bivouac—this single, solitary dawn, was this what we had dreamed of for so many years?

No! and the wall slides past beneath our fingers like a silent, grey movie. Is this climbing? No, it is gliding, hardly touching the rock we glide upwards and into the milky, collness. After hours, the shaft of light breaks on the summit ridge, and we look down over the slabs, and there, far below, the others are walking away from the foot of the wall; tiny figures, like tired ants. Defeated. The guide was with them then. Was that yesterday? Is it today? Eleven years ago? And tomorrow; what about tomorrow?

As a fearful storm broke, we had left the summit. Rain and hail swept down over the slabs tearing off anything that was not rock, poured in a white waterfall into the void below the buttresses, and were whipped by the storm into a foaming cloud of spray.

What was the storm to us?

We came down.

The Guide is in a hurry.

"Come on, come on. . ."

He is an architect and his clients are waiting; time is money, money, money. Redsnout is on our heels. He climbs well, but his voice is dreadful, a real throat disease.

"How old are you then, Anja?"

"Twenty-seven."

"And him with the red nose, that idiot, what's up with him?"

"That is my husband."

. . . Cengalo, Cengalo. . . A strange and sinister word. We once wanted to go south, to pack up and take a road, anywhere—where the sea boiled below white cliffs; where the girls were dark-skinned and spoke in softly lilting voices, like Anja. Do you still remember? Cengalo sounds distant, sad, forgotten. . .

On the warm slabs of the huge summit ridge it was like climbing a majestic staircase. Higher and higher, towards the glistening shafts of sunlight. Above, on the horizon, the others were hanging like flies, silhouetted against the blue of the sky, crawling like insects with fragile, thin limbs, their backs shimmering as if they had wings. Two or three times the Guide hammered a peg in. . . . Cengalo, Cengalo, that is music. The farmers undressing on summer nights, when even in the early morning a hazy heat hangs over the fields. And the dark-skinned girls lie awake in their chambers. . .

Slowly our feet begin to burn on the tiny footholds, and our fingers are already ripped to shreds.

"Do you still remember. . .?"

The wall over there once gave us strength, it was both objective and aspiration; it was the epitome of our youth, and we believed, believed . . . and then we forgot. Fever had overcome us and no power on earth could have held us back, then. Two days later, as we walked through Bondascal we stopped again and again to look back, until the wall disappeared between the trees into the hazy midday shadows and all that remained was the pillar, flashing into the dark like an incredible burnished flame. . . We wanted to return, but who thought it would be eleven years?

"And now. . ."

"Hey, Anja and Redsnout have got a child, do you hear, a baby. He's called Anton."

Strange . . . something — God knows what — is missing today. We find the climbing easy, like a well-oiled machine or a programme repeated a thousand times. But the fever which once took our breath away is gone. The fears are no longer with us, the fears we had that night on the wall when the stones were crashing and flying about over in the Badile couloir. . .

"Hey, Hori, have we changed since then. . .?"

He shrugs his shoulders. Tomorrow it's through the glass door and up the stairs to the sixth floor again. It is like a film, but without the cold, hard holds which grow under our hands out of the night. A film which once in a while breaks, but without the summit ridge where we sit and look down at them as they crawl, ant-like, away.

After a final steep section, Dieter and the Guide are sitting on the boulders and have already coiled their ropes. The scaly plates of rock have become easy-angled and the summit cornice is only a stone's throw away at the top of a short boulder slope.

"Whoever wants to can go to the top. We're going down."

The Guide is in a hurry.

"Come on, before it gets misty. The hut's still a long way down and we want to be in the valley by tomorrow morning."

"Aren't we going to wait for Anja?"

The others shake their heads. When we are already quite a long way down the gully, she appears at the top of the last steep bit. We wave.

To sit on the warm granite boulders between the last pine trees. To sit and watch the slabs of rock grow black in the evening light; how the cornices, the reptilian heads cowering beneath them, fade into the night, and that light sweeping slowly, slowly over the walls, the slabs, the gullies. . . The cockerel, the lonely restless spirit of the mountain, swirling over the ridges and finding no peace. . . To sit and feel her warm body close to mine and run my fingers through her long black hair. . .

"Anja. . ."

"Ja?"

"Close your eyes, then whisper two words:

"Cengalo, Cengalo."

from ALPINISMUS *1975*

The Only Blasphemy

JOHN LONG

At speeds beyond 80 mph, the cops jail you. I cruise at a prudent 79. Tobin [Sorenson] drove 100 – did so till his Datsun blew. It came as no surprise when he perished attempting to solo the North Face of Mt. Alberta. Tobin never drew the line. His rapacious motivation and a boundless fear threshold enamoured him of soloing.

I charge towards Joshua Tree National Monument, where two weeks prior, another pal had tweeked while soloing. After his fall, I inspected the base of the route, wincing at the grisly blood stains, the grated flesh and tufts of matted hair: soloing is unforgiving. Yet I mull these calamities like a salty dog, considering them avoidable. Soloing is OK I think; you just have to be realistic, not some knave abetted by peer pressure or ego. At 85, Joshua Tree comes quickly, but the stark night drags.

The morning sun peers over the flat horizon, gilding the countless rocks that bespeckle the desert carpet. The biggest stones are little more than 150ft. high. I hook up with John Bachar, probably the world's premier free-climber. John lives at that climbing area featuring the most sun. He has been at Joshua for two months and his soloing feats astonish everyone. It is winter, when school checks my climbing to weekends, so my motivation is fabulous, but my fitness only so-so. Bachar suggests a Half Dome day which translates as: Half Dome is 2,000ft. high, or about twenty pitches. Hence, we must climb twenty pitches to get our Half Dome day. In a wink, Bachar is shod and cinching his waist sling from which his chalk bag hangs. "Ready?" Only now do I realise he intends to climb all 2,000ft. solo. To save face, I agree, thinking: Well, if he suggests something too asinine, I'll just draw the line.

We embark on familiar ground, twisting feet and jamming hands into vertical cracks; smearing the toes of our skin tight boots onto tenuous bumps; pulling over roofs on bulbous holds; palming off rough rock and marvelling at it all. We're soloing: no rope. A little voice sometimes asks how good a quarter-inch, pliable hold can be.

If you're tight, you set an aquiline hand or pointed toe on that quarter-incher and push or pull perfunctorily.

After three hours, we've disposed with a dozen pitches, feel invincible. We up the ante to 5.10. We slow considerably, but by 2.30, we've climbed twenty pitches. As a finale, Bachar suggests soloing a 5.11, which is a pretty grim prospect for anyone, period. 5.11 is about my wintertime limit . . . when I'm fresh and sharp. But now I am thrashed and stolid from the past 2,000ft., having cruised the last four or five pitches on rhythm and momentum. Regardless, we trot over to Intersection Rock, the 'hang' for local climbers; also, the local for Bachar's final solo.

He wastes no time and scores of milling climbers freeze like salt statues when he begins. He moves with dauntless precision, plugging his fingertips into shallow pockets in the 105° wall. I scrutinise his moves, taking mental notes on the sequence. He pauses at 50ft. level, directly beneath the crux bulge. Splaying out his left foot onto a slanting rugosity, he pinches a minute wafer and pulls through to a gigantic bucket hold. He walks over the last 100ft. which is only dead vertical.

By virtue of boots, chalk bag, location, and reputation, the crowd, with its heartless avarice, has already committed me. All eyes pan to me, as if to say: Well?! He did make it look trivial, I think, stepping up for a crack.

I draw several audible breaths, as if to convince myself if nobody else. A body length of easy moves, then those incipient pockets which I finger adroitly before yarding with maximum might. 50ft. passes quickly, unconsciously. Then, as I splay my left foot out onto that slanting rugosity, the chilling realisation comes that, in my haste, I have bungled the sequence, that my hands are too low on that puny wafer which I'm now pinching with waning power, my foot vibrating, and I'm desperate, wondering if and when my body will seize and plummet before those heartless salt statues, cutting the air like a swift. A montage of abysmal images flood my brain.

I glance beneath my legs and my gut churns at the thought of a hideous free fall onto the gilded boulders. That 'little' voice is bellowing: "Do something! Pronto!" My breathing is frenzied while my arms, trashed from the previous 2,000ft., feel like titanium beef steaks. Pinching that little wafer, I suck my feet up so as to extend my arm and jam my hand in the bottoming crack above: the crack is too shallow, will accept only a third of my hand. I'm stuck, terrified, and my whole existence is focused down to a pinpoint which sears my everything like the torrid amber dot from a magnifying glass. Shamefully I understand the only blasphemy: to wilfully jeopardise my own existence, which I've done, and this sickens me. I know that wasted seconds could . . . then a flash, the world stops, or is it preservation instincts booting my brain into hyper gear? In the time it takes a hummingbird to wave its wings – once – I've realised my implacable desire to live, not die!; but my regrets cannot alter my situation: arms shot, legs wobbling, head ablaze. My fear has devoured itself, leaving me hollow and mortified. To concede, to quit would be easy. Another little voice calmly intones: "At least die trying. . ." I agree and again punch my tremulous hand into the bottoming crack. If only I can execute this one crux move, I'll get an incut jug-hold, can rest on it before the final section. I'm afraid to eyeball my crimped hand, jokingly jammed in the shallow crack. It *must* hold my 190lb, on an overhanging wall, and this seems ludicrous, impossible.

My body has jittered in this spot for a millennium, but that hummingbird has moved but one centimetre. My jammed hand says "NO WAY!," but that other little voice adds "might as well try it." I pull up slowly – my left foot is still pasted to that sloping edge – and that big bucket hold is right there . . . I almost have it, I do!", and simultaneously my right hand rips from the crack and my left foot flies off that rugosity; all my weight hangs from an enfeebled left arm. Adrenalin rockets me atop that Thank God hold when I press my chest to the wall, get that 190lb over my feet and start quaking like no metaphor can depict.

That hummingbird is halfway to Rio before I consider pushing on. I would rather extract my wisdom teeth with vice grips. Dancing black orbs dot my vision when I finally claw over the summit. "Looked a little shaky," Bachar croons, flashing that candid, disarming snicker.

That night, I drove into town and got a bottle, and Sunday, while Bachar went for an El Capitan day (3,000ft.), I listlessly wandered through dark desert corridors, scouting for turtles, making garlands from wild flowers, relishing the skyscape, doing all those things a person does on borrowed time.

from MOUNTAIN 83 *1982*

On Tree Climbing

H. E. L. PORTER

Not long ago I had a nightmare, and I remember being irritated, as it approached its climax, by the refrain, "Why do climbers not climb trees?" Having failed to solve the riddle (if it was one), I was on the point of giving it up, when there sprang from my brain in full panoply the god Syllogismus himself, who, touching the ears of his votary, gave voice to this effect:

Trees are responsible for rainfall.
Rainfall is responsible for the levelling of mountains.
Trees are responsible for the levelling of mountains.

"Dim realisation of this truth," he continued, "has led to the boycotting of trees by climbers. As a protest against the unceasing steamrolling of their playground the mountains, they refuse to deal with the agency which works the steamroller."

I awoke after that somewhat comforted: the comfort was needed, for in the previous course of the dream I had been watching the face of the earth rolling itself out like a melting jelly, till it became as level and green and pocketless as a French billiard-table: the cloth, however, had not been brushed, and grit was visible everywhere in the shape of trees. I have mentioned my dream, because this article was written in revenge.

Tree-climbing, to judge by the silent contempt with which it has hitherto been treated, must be, so to speak, the Cinderella among the sister-branches of the sport, and no fairy prince has yet appeared to do her justice – not unnaturally, for climbers, unlike fishers, eschew fairytales. However, fairy princes can be dispensed with in these days of slums and sordid realism; we can revel in tree-dirt unashamed and play with Cinderella among the ashes. Rocks, snow and ice, sea-cliff, quarry and roof, have all found champions to sing their praises exhaustively in the word-tournaments of climbing journals: it is time the tree found a champion too. The true knight prefers his lady to be getting on in life, and if age be a

110

recommendation, tree-climbing is far more venerable than its more popular rivals; consider only prehistoric age merging into Darwinian man, to whom this was the only sport; wherein if an ape excelled, he became the king-ape or hero-ape: and perhaps King Pentheus in the glen of Cithaeron and King Charles in the royal oak were only displaying an atavistic tendency to imitate their ancestors and prove their fitness for kingship by proficiency in the one-time sport of kings: such methods of kingcraft being hopelessly out of date, both of them in accordance with the laws of survival came to a speedy and untimely end.

Such reflections will not serve as an apologia for modern tree-climbers, but plenty of other defences are available. Most of us feel it a more or less pleasant duty to find some substitute for mountain exercise in our everyday life. To be satisfactory, the substitute must provide open air, occasion to stretch every muscle, and, if possible, pleasant surroundings. It is hard to fulfil all three conditions together. Nothing but a very stern sense of duty or a double portion of youthful enthusiasm can reconcile one to a regular course of dumb-bells or Muller exercises, which fulfil my second condition best. Quarries fulfil my first, but they are generally uninteresting, often unsound, and not seldom unclimbable. 'Artificial rocks' (e.g. houses) are almost repulsive: who can get pleasure out of monotonously rectangular perpendicularity?

There remain for the town-dweller only two alternatives:

1. Natural excrescences such as Mr Laycock has recently classified and described for one district. These are admirable as a rule, but they are few and far between, and require time and trouble to get at: moreover, you climb too often before a crowded house of urchins, with the uneasy feeling that they may kill themselves in misguided attempts at imitation.

2. Trees: trees can be found everywhere at any time: they are of all sizes, sorts and shapes, so that you never exhaust the supply. You can get more exercise on one tree than in two quarries in half the time. You can get as dirty as you like, if you enjoy the process of getting clean again. You can learn the neglected art of quick and fearless descent, since you cannot evade the consequences of a rash ascent by the familiar method of walking down on the right or left. You can increase your value as a scout in war-time; it is a revelation how much the view expands in level country as you mount higher. If your tastes are scientific, you can study tree-botany between the pitches: personally, I received my first lesson in the mysteries of 'bracts' and 'stipules' from a diminutive sister with all an elder brother's condescension, while our legs dangled fearfully over what seemed to us then almost interstellar space – a sheer drop of 20ft. Finally, on a sunny day, you can revel in sylvan delights and rural peace among the 'green-robed senators of mighty woods'.

Aesthetic charm, however, is not very much to the fore in the sport: a tree-climb is in no sense comparable to the movements of a symphony blending into a harmonious whole; though it has its own accompaniment in the humbler music of bird and squirrel and the rustle of summer breezes. Still less can it lay claim to sensational interest: here are no hairbreadth escapes, melodramatic adventures or icy grapplings with death, no first-ascents or other exploits to be puffed in 'Ercles vein'. The charm when analysed resolves itself into very commonplace elements. I find it partly in the satisfaction of the 'Excelsior' instinct: it is, of course, a drawback that in tree-climbing this satisfaction can never be complete, for you never get to the top; nothing but a medieval angel dancing on a pin-point, or an enterprising microbe, could stand on a normal tree-top; the mere man, ensconced on the highest trustworthy bough, must comfort himself, as he gazes regretfully upwards, with the poor consolation that all true ideals are unattainable, and that he is in the mean between the celestial and terrestrial. But the real pleasure lies simply in physical exertion skilfully applied: the problems presented are sufficiently varied to require considerable skill, if they are to be overcome smoothly, gracefully and without visible effort. You can tell the novice here as easily as on rocks; he betrays himself by jerkings of legs, convulsive armpulls, pulmonary agitations, desperate ejaculations and amazing caution in descent. If he is teachable, he will soon pick up some points of climbing form: elementary principles of rope-management, too, can be demonstrated to him practically. In fact, the tree cannot be despised as a training ground for recruit-drill.

Which of the thousand and one species of tree is best for the purpose can be left for individual taste to decide. I prefer a full-grown oak, gnarled and weatherbeaten. Frontal attack by the trunk is not always successful, but you can generally turn the enemy's flank by executing a hand or stomach-traverse up a convenient bough; the ramifications up above are as interesting to the explorer as an ancient house to the child, with its obscure recesses and floors of different levels. Pines are the dirtiest of trees, and the preliminary swarm up to the first bough is apt to be undignified and exhausting; nor are there any compensating merits that I know of. Limes in their flowering season reward the nostrils of the persevering who conquer the girth of the bole. N.B. This is often done with a ladder.) Elms are attractive, but very treacherous; both elms and beeches have a habit of forking low down, which produces a species of chimney, differing from a rock-chimney in having only two walls instead of three. The absence of the third is serious, and the difficulty is increased by the extreme narrowness of the fork at the bottom and the gradual divergence of the two sides higher up. Backing up under these circumstances is peculiarly trying: you cannot ease your strained muscles by a change of position, and if you do get exhausted, your plight is perilous: both of the trunks are probably too stout for a firm clasp, and by hypothesis there are no branches within reach, or you would not be in the chimney: if you decide on retreat, your tired muscles may collapse; in that case you may fall out, or you may jam in the fork and remain suspended: the probability is that you will do one or the other. This kind of ascent, therefore, is only to be embarked on with circumspection.

Why should I speak of cedar and alder, hawthorn and willow, apple and pear, and whatever else of tree may grow? In the words of the immortal Greek play, why indeed? But the monkey-puzzler let no one think to mount with impunity, unless he be armed with triple brass and an enthusiasm which no pain can dim.

Tree-traversing is another dangerous game. I imagine the emotions of the man who walks across space on the unsteadfast footing of a branch must resemble those of the unfortunate victims of the buccaneers who are forced to walk the plank. Still, it is undeniably fascinating: The reaction and glow of success as you pass over the abyss and regain safety tingles like electric. I have sometimes tried to find a girdle traverse in woods of small extent on the Downs, but have not yet succeeded in making the buckles of the girdle meet; human beings have a constitutional aversion to launching themselves apewise through space, and without that manoeuvre the thing seems impossible.

I know a school with large and beautiful grounds, in which many noble trees flourish. Among them is an oak, which school tradition asserts to be mentioned in Domesday; there are other oaks of great antiquity and growth, also an abundance of stately limes and elms. Some years ago, till the practice fell under the displeasure of authority, the elder boys used each to be the proprietor of some special tree, a right which he bought from the previous occupant: the tree was his castle, and woe to the offender who trespassed thereupon. The oaks were the most coveted and fetched the highest prices. Ingenious steps were hewn, when necessary, to make direct ascent possible, yet not too easy. Up above a comfortable sanctum was constructed, with a substratum of sturdy boughs and a surface of cushions, in which an idle half-holiday could be dreamed away. Thus 'bosomed high in tufted trees', all but invisible from below, and secure from interruption, they were insulated from the current of school routine: This happy result they achieved by tree-climbing: we do the same on a larger scale when we rest on a ledge on Lliwedd or bask in the purity of an Alpine peak.

I would end on this solemn note, but for misgivings that my labour has brought forth at best a 'ridiculous mouse', although of a mountain-parent. Let me then confess that I have little expectation of making converts; admit the truth of a saying I learnt at school, "Non omnes arbusta juvant": and, in conclusion, plead guilty to the charge of having found a 'tongue in trees' instead of a 'sermon in stones'.

from THE CLIMBERS' CLUB JOURNAL *1915*

Trapdoor Fandango

RON FAWCETT

As I climbed further afield I soloed bigger, better things, often because the people I was climbing with have had enough after two or three routes and I class a good day out as one when I feel totally wasted at the end. It was a day like that when I soloed November and Shadow on Clogwyn du'r Arddu. We had done Great Wall, Silhouette and Medi and Chris [Gibb] wanted a doss in the sun so he wandered off round the lake. As I hadn't done either Vember or November I plodded up Drainpipe Crack onto the big ledge where the routes divide. Tom Jones had just strolled up November so I went for that.

I really surprised myself by not blowing my cool; every move seemed well within my mental capabilities and luckily there seemed to be a good jam or fingerlock after every hard move. I find it very reassuring once I can cram my meaty digits in some crack or other.

The worst fear I had was wondering if there was going to be a hard move high up which might require the use of a doubtful hold. When one is using a shaky fingerhold with a runner by your waist it is no sweat but when you are looking at a 200ft. ground-fall it is totally gripping. I find the worst situation to be in is one where you have to totally commit yourself on a series of moves that you couldn't reverse, doing a move that you couldn't get reverse and being faced with a similar move above; man, that is when soloing gets really scary. Luckily November was nowhere near like that. It was just very satisfying – a real buzz-route.

On another occasion I happened to be at Gogarth on my own, a stupid situation to start with, so I wandered along the sea level traverse wondering if I dare solo Big Groove. I had only done the route once before, about six years earlier, and I remembered finding it desperate even using the top peg for aid.

At the ledge below the crux pitch I recalled the last time I was there with a friend who tragically lost his life whilst climbing alone at Gordale Scar when a thin prusik sling failed. Other people were on the route so I couldn't sit around pondering all day. The first wall went with no bother but the little traverse right seemed really slippery. I don't like trusting my feet when soloing but there was no other way but to teeter across to the good crack. Up this, no sweat, then at the top I was in a quandary; which way now? The crack continued up to the right but would I be able to get back left onto the stance. The thin little corner above was where I had my past grip so I knew that it did 'go' in that direction. I teetered up into the corner; the rock seemed so smooth and I was really sweating – would my feet stick? I committed myself to the move and went for it . . . Right foot in the groove, left foot out on nothing. I was sure there must be a good crack in the back because there was no peg in now, but no way. I could hardly get my finger nails in never mind a digit. I kept trying to bridge up, gain a little ground, but my foot was slipping or so I had convinced myself. Luckily my left hand groped out onto the rib in the usual piano player's panic and, manna from heaven, a super little fingerhold appeared; a quick pull and I was on the ledge wondering if the Acapulco high divers could stand a dive from here.

The last pitch went easily but my legs ached with the bridging. When doing such a route in 'normal' style one has a rest on the belays but when soloing 'on sight' it's just go for it; to linger on hard ground I find gripping. The mind starts playing games, telling you that hold is loose or the EB is going to roll off that tiny edge, but that is all part of the game – to have one's neck in the noose and manage to pull it out at the last moment. But will the trapdoor ever open below my feet, I often wonder.

from THE CLIMBERS' CLUB JOURNAL *1978*

Momentum on Makalu

JOHN ROSKELLEY

The cold could have shattered glass two mornings later as Chris [Kopczynski] and I crawled out of our down bags at 7 a.m. An hour up the ropes and my feet were gone, the pain having given way to a pleasant numbness. Perched on a butt-sized ledge, I removed my boots and began to thaw my feet helped by Chris's warm belly. Soon we were at the end of our lines on a stance too crowded for two. Several aid pins enabled me to surmount a rounded flake and gain a 70° gully. A French cable ladder, frayed and broken in sections, stretched for 80ft. to a ledge system. I used the thing guiltily. The trip to the ledge was terrifying as several anchors popped and the ⅛-inch cable threatened to break.

Once Chris had arrived, I began a steeply ascending traverse, mantelling and chimneying through several solid, but blocky gullies. Chris cleaned the few pins and arrived as clouds began to filter in. I front-pointed up several feet of ice, then swung left into a vertical rock gully and corner system.

Another badly-damaged cable ladder hung from unseen points. Avoiding the ladder as much as possible, I used the good holds along the chimney's walls, occasionally stepping on a ladder rung to rest. On the top was a notch and the narrowest section of the West Ridge I'd seen. I climbed a flaring chimney, mantelled an ice-topped boulder and waded up the steep, short snowfield to the old French Camp 5, marked by a discoloured remnant of tent fabric.

The possibilities above were limited. To my left rose an awkward-looking off-width flake that the French had obviously climbed; to my right was a 95° blank wall, but hung with another 40ft., vile-looking, deteriorated cable ladder, partially separated, but begging to be used.

While I uncoiled our last 150ft. rope and Chris found a comfortable belay, my freezing sweat and the lateness of the day made me go for the cable ladder. I climbed down from the belay to a three-inch-wide ledge and traversed to the cable. My eyes were fixed on the break in the cable 20ft. above as I crept slowly toward it. By placing a single front-point on the broken ladder rungs, I was able to use my feet sparingly, depending almost totally on my shoulders and arms. My fingers started to freeze immediately from gripping the bare aluminium, but I finally passed the break in the cable and pushed hard for the lip of the wall. As I reached the end, I was pulled back by my haul line, which was jammed under a flake far below. I descended a few feet, shook the rope violently and it loosened.

My arms and shoulders were blown and I couldn't feel my hands when I surmounted the lip. Painfully, feeling came back, but I was still too exhausted to move for several minutes. I finished the strenuous pitch after jamming, front-pointing and stemming a wide groove for about 90ft. It didn't look far to Camp 4, but without rope we couldn't continue.

Over the radio the next morning, Kim [Momb] told us all that he had decided to descend to Base for good. His knee ligaments, continually stretched and torn from wearing converted ski boots, were too painful to continue carrying loads and descending. Jim [States], who was with Kim at Camp 2, also sounded depressed. It was time for the whole team to descend to Base to recuperate from the intense stress of the past several weeks. Moreover, the weather had deteriorated.

Within three days we were ready to go up for the last time. Chris and I, climbing quickly, reached Camp 2 on May 9 and Camp 3 the next day. We needed one more day to lead the final four severe pitches to Camp 4, at 25,000ft. Meanwhile, Jim, a day behind, climbed to Camp 3 to join us on the summit attempt.

The cramped two-man tent within the crevasse at Camp 3 became unbearable after a rest day. On May 14 all three of us willingly crawled out of the tent at 7 a.m. and slowly began jumaring the 1,300ft. of fixed line to Camp 4. Chris and I had already taken some camp gear to 4, but we still had 50lb. loads of food, kerosene, and personal gear.

By 1.30 p.m., I arrived at Camp 4 and picked a campsite for our tent. Hacking and shovelling, I finally had a perfect platform and pitched the tent before the others arrived. Cooking and rehydrating was a three-hour process made even more exasperating by a faulty stove pump.

In order to leave the tent by 2 a.m., at 11.30 p.m. we started to dress and cook. We climbed a steep snow gully in the moonless night more to gain altitude than follow a particular route. The pinpoints of light below helped me keep track of Jim and Chris as I left the centre avalanche slope for the windpack and rocks of a rib to our side. The rib ended abruptly on the West Ridge. Still in semi-darkness, we stopped for a rest and a candy bar where the west wall shot up sharply. The East Face of Everest, twelve miles to the west, suddenly flashed a brilliant sunrise orange. Encouraged by the perfect windless weather, we continued, climbing together despite the steep web of ice gullies criss-crossing the blocky granite.

The West Pillar butted into the South-East ridge at 27,000ft. It was noon and the days of effort, lack of oxygen and difficult, dangerous climbing called upon every ounce of will we could muster. Occasional deep snow had slowed us as we gained the ridge crest and followed it to an ominous rock buttress that barred further progress.

Chris took the lead as we all dropped off the South-East ridge to Makalu's east side. The lee slope had accumulated weeks of snow from wind and bad weather and in minutes it became obvious that our chances of success there were nil. With a disheartening yell, Chris told us what we already knew. The route was hopeless; we would have to return to the crest of the ridge.

The only solution was to climb the west wall of the buttress and regain the ridge crest above. Could all of us succeed? That answer was also painfully obvious. Although Jim's will to continue was there, his strength, which had been limited all morning, was not great enough. Regretfully, I ordered him to descend. Chris's strength was there, but he knew one climber could climb faster and have a better chance of getting down without a possibly fatal bivouac. In addition, he could assist Jim on the difficult descent.

Tears filled our eyes as I departed alone. For a few minutes, Jim and Chris watched my slow, steady progress, then turned and began their long, dangerous descent. Unroped, I gained the rock wall quickly and began clearing the icy holds of accumulated snow. A steeply ascending traverse of shoe-box width angled sharply toward the summit, but gained little on the rising ridge above. 100ft. up, I spotted a rappel sling from a past descent party to my right and near the ridge crest. Leaving the security of the ledge system, I mantelled and front-pointed my way toward the ridge with nothing sure for my heavily gloved hands. Soon, I was straddling the South-East ridge above the buttress.

Both sides dropped steeply away. I fought hip-deep, bottomless powder to gain inches at a great expense of effort. After 30ft., the ridge widened toward the west wall and the snow became hard and wind-packed, allowing me to gain ground much more quickly. The summit pyramid was now in full view a hundred yards off.

Keeping well to the west side because of immense east-facing cornices, I approached the final pyramid only to find deep, unconsolidated powder. By gaining a rock rib to my west, I was able to move easily to within 20ft. of the top. I quickly cramponed up the remaining distance on hard, summit ice.

Amidst rising clouds, but without wind, I crouched on the summit of Makalu. At my feet were the three great ridges rising from Tibet and Nepal. Three oxygen bottles, a bamboo wand and a package of rye crisp crackers were the only mementoes of man to crowd the summit.

I took pictures, then departed, collecting a large chunk of rock from the first outcrop as I descended. It was 3.45 p.m. Exhausted, I backed down the route for safety. At the top of the buttress, I knew I couldn't down-climb the west wall, so I pushed off into the cloudy east side, hoping I wouldn't kick off a large avalanche. Within a minute, I had shot through several rock bands and was at Chris's ploughed trough at his turn-around point.

Each ten to fifteen minutes, I would collapse intending to bivouac, but after a short, restless sleep, I would come to my senses and realise that if I bivouacked I would freeze to death in my sleep. A natural rock cave, 1,000ft. above Camp 4, was my lodestone and I decided that if I could reach that cave before dark, I might survive the night. As the sun disappeared behind dark clouds to the west, I arrived at the cave and immediately dropped asleep just for a few minutes. Out of my stupor, I heard Jim and Chris talking far below.

"Chris!" I yelled.

"John, is that you?" Chris replied.

Suddenly the tension and drama I was feeling evaporated. I thought, who does he think he is? A touch of humour had removed my building melodramatic stress.

The sun disappeared along with the voices far below. My sweat began to freeze and without the radiant heat of the sun, the air temperature dropped alarmingly. Again, I shuddered at the thought of falling asleep never to awaken. Down I stumbled until it was too dark to see and I had to put on my headlamp. Backing down carefully, I found the wind-blown, snow-covered tracks of that morning and followed those into the depths hoping to surface somewhere near Camp 4. I joined the fresh tracks of Jim and Chris as I entered a narrow section of the gully. Finally I rounded a boulder and collapsed into camp. It was 8.30 p.m.

We forced ourselves to leave Camp 4 at 4 p.m. the next afternoon in a violent storm because the stove had finally quit completely and we desperately needed fluids. We descended the route in three days, heavily laden with gear. Our only regret was that we were not able to remove the ropes on the descent.

Makalu had evaded American attempts for years and it was befitting that we had accomplished the task with a small team without artificial oxygen and without support members. No doubt it is the satisfying way to climb the Himalayan giants.

from THE AMERICAN ALPINE JOURNAL *1981*

The Shroud Solo

IVAN GHIRARDINI

The nurse's scissors disinterred me from my winding-sheet — my clothes, frozen stiff as a board on the outside and damp and clay-cold on my numbed body. It was with a feeling of faint surprise that I watched as my body emerged, emaciated, bruised by its days in the storm, without food or drink. My hands and feet were swollen and frost-bitten, purple and blue, and already on the toes were tell-tale black blotches.

I lay there with my eyes half-closed. Through the thick, stifling mists around me, I caught snatches of conversation: "Heart-beat's a bit irregular . . . Ah, that's better, body temperature's rising now . . . My God, his blood's so thick I can't even get a blood sample . . ." But I felt quite indifferent, unconcerned, unmoved.

Soon the drips were in place, the instruments set up. As I lay quiescent, in those warm, dry sheets, my shivers stilled; my knotted muscles relaxed; my very bones seemed to take up their normal stations. And yet I was unable to shake off a feeling of utter despair. Here I was, back in the world of men, surrounded by kindness, nursed devotedly, and yet I felt myself alone, most horribly alone.

Days passed. Lying on my hospital bed, I felt drained, finished, infinitely old despite my twenty-two years. I had had many visitors; plenty of people had been eager to see the young man who had dared, alone and in winter, to brave the Shroud on the North Face of the Grandes Jorasses. I had been deeply touched by the instinctive solidarity so many had shown. But had they understood? If so, how could they still speak of "exploit", of "uncommon physical resistance," of "courage," "will" and "daring"? None of these qualities were mine. No credit was due to me for having succeeded in my ascent, and it would have been vain of me to pretend otherwise. In going beyond my limits I had simply broken every law of nature, had put in danger not only my own life, but others. And yet one thing I could claim. There on the mountain I had lived for a few days the life of the visionary, the mystic, prey to a spiritual exaltation undreamt of before. Thus I had no regrets, no regrets even for the horrors of the descent. The intensity of the experience I had lived was above and beyond anything I had previously known.

At first sight there was nothing to orient me towards an Alpine and guiding career, indeed I had discovered the Alpine world only by accident through a book by Walter Bonatti. I had been fascinated by his account of his ascent of the Petit Dru. Fired by a spirit of emulation, I decided to become a guide, and to the distress of my parents, modest Italian immigrants, I gave up my studies. Alone and untutored, I acquired rock and ice-climbing techniques, learning painfully from my own mistakes. I improved rapidly — even perhaps too rapidly, becoming over-confident, cocksure. So perfectly at home did I feel at least on medium-standard rock that I undertook a series of long solo climbs for which in all probability I was not sufficiently competent.

My audacity paid off however, and I felt myself somehow protected. My greatest happiness lay always in my solitary bivouacs, on the summit of some great peak and after a difficult and successful climb. My finest memories are of days spent cowering on some great face in the teeth of the storm. It was then that I felt myself to be living in a sort of limbo which was no longer the world of the living but not yet the world of the dead. Many dismissed me as a tearaway, rash, sick or even deranged.

I find it difficult to isolate the factors which drove me to such feats, but one thing I feel is clear: my acts were only rarely willed by myself alone, only rarely freely undertaken. I felt myself something other, a plaything of impulses and inner compulsions which I did not control. I simply let myself be led, knowing that all was inevitable and that to oppose my will to this mysterious imperative would be an act not of self-assertion but of obstruction. Climbing solo taught me to control my thoughts, to discipline my fears, to debate with myself, in short was a process of self-education.

It was thus that I came to find my own mediocrity and that of the world around me intolerable. I recognised that I, like most of the other inhabitants of my planet, was degenerate. I was only twenty-one, yet I possessed not a single one of my own teeth, and was sick after virtually every meal. I realised that I was not a man in the full sense of the word, not worthy to be called 'man', and the realisation was so bitter that often I wept. We forget that we have the potential to be children of God, to be men in Christ's image. If I undertook the Shroud, it was precisely for that reason, to submit myself and my life to God's purpose. No longer could I tolerate my own mediocrity, no longer tolerate the unmistakable signs of my own degeneracy, physical and mental. And it was, of course, a wholly egotistic act. What I planned was entirely beyond my capability. I intended to follow the first third of the Desmaison Route on the Walker Spur, traverse out onto the Shroud above the gullies, and then climb direct to the summit over the wall where Serge Gousseault had met his death. I had determined to start my ascent on Sunday, February 23, come what may; I had an inner conviction that the weather would be good.

I had no down clothing and the rock was covered with verglas, and yet I felt no cold in my hands as I climbed the first 1,200ft. of the Direct Route. So heavy was my rucksack that I had to do each pitch twice; I had had to bring a large quantity of equipment to enable me to climb the overhanging walls which would confront me towards the summit of the route. At night, however, hanging from tape-slings on pegs (I had no ice-screws), I shivered, poorly protected by my little bivouac tent. Luckily, I had the comfort brought by hot drinks. . . The first four days were without incident; it would be pedantry to describe them. As I moved higher up the face, I lost all sense of time. In that utter solitude, I forgot exhaustion, thirst, hunger, cold. On the black ice of the Shroud, glassy, brittle, I was unaware of danger or difficulty. Without protection I would climb long pitches, balancing on my front points which bit only marginally into the ice. I would spend whole precious minutes, unknowing, studying air-bubbles trapped in the ice, or admiring the colours of a little patch of lichen on the rock. There were times when I forgot I had a summit to reach, and it was only when the vertiginous steepness of the face brought me to myself that I would shake off my inactivity and move on towards the summit.

On Wednesday, February 26, I bivouacked on the rock outcrop in the centre of the Shroud. As I was changing the gas cylinder on the stove, I dropped the valve screw. I had no option but to throw away my stove. Many other things too became useless: I threw away my spare gas cylinders, all the dried foods I had brought, my dried meat and ham which were now inedible. All that night, I broke off pieces of ice and sucked them to quench my thirst. My throat throbbed and burned, but I was not dismayed. I could so easily have retreated; some twenty abseils would have brought me safely to the foot of the face. But I was not master of my own fate; I had to go on. Reluctantly I left some climbing equipment, including my two 120ft. ropes, to lighten my load. I resolved to make for the Hirondelles Ridge. Every 30ft. I had to stop, exhausted, to control my breathing and ease the cramped muscles in my calves. Never had I suffered so. Any slightest mistake and I would have fallen to a certain death. Slowly, slowly, my fear grew, and as it grew, so did my exhaustion.

I was only 150ft. from the ridge when I heard a helicopter; it was the mountain rescue service. I drove a peg into the snow, belayed myself and raised my arms in a V-sign to signal my predicament; in the cabin I could see two men come to save me, and I wept. I stood there for several minutes, still as a statue, my arms raised, then extracted my peg and went on. The helicopter clattered away; I was convinced that they would come and collect me on the ridge. My momentary breakdown had given me a new surge of strength, and it was almost at a run that I finished that last pitch. The Shroud was conquered; I knew, however, that I was finished too, unless I was saved.

A freezing bivouac in a hollow in the rocks was followed by an unforgettable sunrise over the Valais. After five days in the sombre shadows of the North Face, I felt myself warmed and comforted, in spite of the biting wind, by the sun's welcome rays. I went on, despite my exhaustion, my deadly exhaustion. I had to throw away much of my equipment, items which had been with me since the beginning of my career as a solo climber and to which I was as attached as is the craftsman to his tools. There were moments when my eyes misted over, my legs tottered, and I had to stop and breathe deeply. All I had left were three biscuits and a few lumps of sugar, but I was not hungry. At about midday, I reached the point where the Tronchey and Hirondelles Ridges meet. There, in front of me, was the summit; I was almost there when the helicopter appeared again. As it circled round me, I made the standard distress signal. Then, inexplicably, I had the same reaction as on the previous day; I ran towards the summit. My would-be rescuers supposed I was quite well, and went away.

At the summit I collapsed on the snow, sobbing. It was no doubt a consequence of dehydration and of exhaustion. When finally I got to my feet, my head was spinning so that I nearly keeled over the cornice onto the North Face. I rested for a long time, then set off down to Courmayeur. At every step I sank into the snow up to my knees; after every ten steps I stopped, and sometimes crumpled to the ground. When I reached the Rocher du Reposoir, I came to a final halt; I was too low, but I could no longer summon up the strength to fight my way back up. That evening, a red helicopter came straight towards me from the Col des Grandes Jorasses. For the third time I made the distress signal, but although they passed directly over me, my rescuers failed to see me. On the horizon, to the west, a great wall of cloud was rising in the sky; the storm was coming.

I shall not attempt to describe the six days I spent up there at some 11,500ft., with no food or drink, buffeted by storm and avalanche; it would be impossible. I ought to have died, but thinking of my parents' grief, I fought for life. I prayed as I had never prayed before, but with this difference, that now I felt myself in direct contact with Him to whom my prayers were addressed.

On Monday, March 6 at about 11 a.m., the helicopter came. During that night I had been assured of its coming. With exemplary courage and skill, the pilot held his machine steady over me. At any moment, the cloud might sweep across between him and me. I watched as my rescuer came slowly down to me on a steel cable. He fastened me on in his place. I felt a jerk. I was saved from death. Never will I forget those seconds.

On the Shroud, I was using the mountains as a refuge from a life and a reality I was too weak and cowardly to face. Now that I have come back from death, I have embarked on a long and arduous process of regeneration which will require the dedication of my entire life, and a rigorous physical and mental self-discipline. Of what use are extreme faces? It is within that we find the most insurmountable barriers. We shall not find the seventh grade beyond the sixth, but in ourselves.

But enough of words.

from LA MONTAGNE *1976*

Above and Beyond

REINHOLD MESSNER

I am sipping my soup from a pan hardly bigger than a cup. My throat feels as rough and sore as if someone had gone into it with a rasp. It is an effort to force down a piece of corned beef out of the tin.

That's a mistake. I must vomit, out of the tiny tent into the snow. In so doing I spew up half the liquid which cost me so much effort in the course of the morning. And without enough liquid in the body (six litres a day, to be exact) I would be finished right away. My altimeter points to just over 19,700ft. I am on the West Face of Nanga Parbat in the Himalayas of Northern Pakistan.

I fetch in the socks and double boots which I had put outside the tent to dry in the sun. The fireball in the west dips amid a mass of clouds like atomic mushrooms, and sets.

It gets cold at once. As long as it was warm – even prickly hot in the sun – I melted snow in the bivvy tent. Before the meltwater can re-freeze in this sharp cold, I pour it carefully into a small pan and balance it over the gas flame. I must keep on drinking and replace the lost liquid so that my blood does not thicken. It's Monday, August 7, 1978 – the second day of my attempt to solo Nanga Parbat, 26,660ft.

This morning I stepped on to the 13,000ft. West Face, without a rope, without protection; crampons on my feet, an ice axe in my right hand and almost 40lb on my back.

In six hours I have gained more than 3,000ft. Hence I'm trembling with exhaustion; hence the cramp in my right forearm, which has been cutting steps continuously hacking out holes and pulling me over cravasse edges; hence the sickness. But I must go on drinking as darkness falls and the temperature drops to minus 15°C; I have to go on drinking and must not be sick again. Vomit once more, and I'll have to turn back if I wish to survive.

Solo. The only man before me to attempt an 8,000m. peak solo was Maurice Wilson. In 1934 he tried to climb Everest. Two years later his body was found at 21,000ft.

Solo the nearest people are now already 8,000ft. beneath me in the tiny Base Camp. Waiting there are Ursula Grether, a 27-year-old medical student, and Major Mohammed Tahir – 'Derry', my liaison officer.

Neither could help me in an accident. I have neither radio transmitter nor flares, nor any other emergency signal—there would be no point. The nearest place intermittently in touch with the outside world is Babusar, and is four days' walk away; they have a handcranked telephone which sometimes works.

To save weight, I have not even brought along a torch. The gas flame is my one source of light till I have drunk enough and prepare to sleep. And I sleep really well; at night nothing can happen to me. My mini-tent stands protected beneath an ice overhang and is tied to an ice screw. It ought even to resist being sucked away in the wake of any nearby avalanche. Ought to. . . .

From Europe I had only brought 45lb. Base Camp had been set up at about 13,000ft., at the end of the valley where the meadow stops and the scree starts.

Three weeks passed in reconnaissance. Day after day, if the weather was fine, I scanned the Diamir Face of Nanga Pargat to discover a route where I could climb as quickly and as steeply as possible without committing suicide. On July 30-31 I climbed the neighbouring Ganalo Peak, more than 19,500ft. high – my final training.

On August 2 I climbed from Base to the foot of the West Face. I bivouacked, but had to return next morning as the weather had turned foul. Not till August 6 could I try again. I left Base alone and without any mountaineering support. Absolutely solo.

On Tuesday, August 8 I wake up at 5 a.m. My altimeter shows 150ft. more than the previous evening. I haven't been lifted up in my sleep – air pressure has fallen. Not a good sign. I breakfast on tea and soup.

In the icy stillness of dawn there is suddenly a noise as if from some huge distant waterfall.

I tear open the iced-up tent entrance and poke my head out. Beneath me half the ice-face must have broken off. Everything seems on the move. On my left ice avalanches roar to the valley. Beneath me a wide avalanche sweeps like a tidal wave to the foot of the mountain. It consists of the ice which I climbed yesterday, and it pours over the bivouac spot that I left 24 hours ago. Spellbound, I watch the end which would have overtaken me had I started today.

No panic, though the blood is throbbing in my temples. I say to myself: there goes your descent route. You won't get down that now. You'll have to think of something else for the way home.

In the chill blue shadow of the face I fold up my tent and pack everything into my sack: two finger-thick foam mats, a down sleeping bag, cooking things, seven beercan-sized gas canisters. I have food for eight to ten days. Then the ice-screw, camera, rock peg of lightest titanium (which I don't use) lip salve against cracked lips, sun cream, two pairs of strong glacier glasses. This time I really must avoid being snow-blinded, as on Everest.

In addition: toilet paper. But I only use it once – in fact this morning, after the avalanche. Plasters, too, for minor injuries –

(Editor's note: It has since come to light that the cause of the avalanche was a local earthquake registering 5.5 on the Richter Scale.)

2 Andy Meyers makes the first lead of The Thing (6a) on Bowles Rocks in 1981,
climb regarded for years as one of the most difficult sandstone problems
of southern England. *Photo: Dave Jones*

3 (right) The limestone walls of the Derbyshire dales provide the ideal locations fo
the gymnastic rock-climbing of the eighties. Here Andy Barker makes the first ascer
of Miller's Tale (6b/c) on Rubicon Wall, Water cum Jolly. *Photo: Steve Wright*

1 (previous page) Phil Thornhill using ice-climbing techniques during the first
ascent of the Dover chalk climb Great White Fright (1983). *Photo: Mick Fowler*

4 (left) Jerry Moffat on Sole Fusion (5.12a), a typical modern problem at Joshua Tree, California, first climbed by John Bachar. *Photo: Chris Gore*

5 (above) The great overhang of Redgarden Wall, Eldorado Springs Canyon, Colorado – a magnet for climbers in recent years as its previously aided routes succumbed to free techniques. In this typical scene Chris Gore and Skip Geurin work out the problems of Equinox. *Photo: Gore collection*

6 7 The sandstone region of Czechoslovakia and East Germany has long been a centre for dynamic rock-climbing. Its isolation, in political terms, has ensured the development of a separate free-climbing tradition which is now recognised as one of the most rigorous in the world. Climbs of the highest standards have been made despite the lack of modern footgear and equipment.

Combined tactics, in use on Adrspach (left), are sometimes employed to overcome difficult sections.

Tomas Cada leading Paprika (above) a hard (7c) wall climb at Teplice Rocks. Note the 'specialised' footgear and rudimentary protection. *Photos: Karel Vlcek*

8 Ron Fawcett and Pete Livesey crossing Great Wall on Craig y Forwyn, North Wales. In the seventies these two climbers played a major role in the movement to eliminate aid from the main limestone cliffs.
Photo: Geoff Birtles

9 (overleaf) The Gorge du Verdon, France.
Photo: David Belden

with serious ones it would be all over anyway. Lastly 10 sleeping
and pain-killing tablets, but no stimulants at all.

I already know that I shall get into such difficult situations that
the temptation to take pills will be overwhelming. And if I take
them at this height I'm finished.

Perhaps I would have swallowed them today. I have the feeling
that no amount of movement will get me warm. The snow is
uneven, at times pure ice, at times crusty or powdery, and my feet
only feel secure when a firm base crunches under the crampons. In
the western sky are cirrus clouds, and on Nanga Parbat summit a
cloud is drooped in the colours of the rainbow. A cold wind blows
across my face. I fear it's going to snow.

At about 9.30 the sun hits me for the first time shining down
steeply from high up on the face. It turns warm, then hot. I feel the
rays as through a burning glass, even though the air remains cool. I
am now above 23,000ft. and reach gentler slopes surrounding the
trapezoidal summit block of rock, a summit block which rears up
in front of me, a whole separate peak by Alpine standards. This
mountain begins at a height about 8,000ft. above the highest peaks
in the Alps.

Gentler slopes – but as a result heavier, deeper snow where I sink
in up to my thighs. Foot after foot I struggle on. Five steps. Pause.
My breathing grates. Five steps. Pause. Pulse beats 130, 140.

In every cell of the body I now feel how alone I am. There's no
one to take over making the steps. No one with whom I can
exchange a few gasped curses and words of encouragement.

Finally I find a possible camp-site on the rocks of the summit
block. I am quite dehydrated, have no more strength, collapse in
the snow. I am not going to manage putting up the tent.

What on earth brought me to this misery? As if the ascent of
Mt. Everest without oxygen equipment, which Peter Habeler and I
had made only in May of this year, were not enough! But Pakistan
sent me permission for Nanga Parbat this same year, and after
staying only six weeks in Europe I was on my way again to the
Himalayas.

I have dreamt for ages of conquering an 8,000m. peak
alone – considered by mountaineers to be "even more impossible"
than the highest mountain on earth without breathing apparatus.
My physical condition was in favour of making the attempt im-

mediately, for after the many weeks on Everest my body was still acclimatised, and certainly more effective at altitude than it would be after a year's break.

Lying in the snow, I suck in the air and force it out in such a way that just before being exhaled it is briefly held again in the lungs. I must drink, melt more snow in the tent. With movements that seem very slow to me and must be even slower, I pitch my tent.

Beneath me is a sea of mist hiding all the valleys and mountains up to 21,000ft. But on the western horizon a reddish-yellow bank of haze promises good weather. While cooking and drinking, and now and then storing the air in my lungs, I gradually regain confidence. Another night without sleeping tablets. Tomorrow is the crucial day; I must get up in time.

I sleep badly and do not leave the tent until 7 a.m. The sky is overcast but I can see the summit. If there were firm snow or ice in between I would be up in two hours, three at the most. But here I am ploughing through bottomless snow, which is treacherous as quicksand.

At 10 a.m., after three gruelling hours, I realise that I'll never reach the summit like this. I know too that I won't get down again if I wear myself out any more. I must either turn back at once, or risk the last remaining chance: climb the steep rock barrier towering up on my left in a direct line to the summit. Rock-climbing has been my strength since childhood.

I climb carefully, but I give it everything, just as you must on a vertical Dolomite face. Dolomite faces, however, are unserious happy practice cliffs in comparison to this. Why I don't slip up here at 26,000ft., with my unwieldy double boots and my poor vision through the goggles, is something I don't know.

I balance along ledges the width of a hand, and struggle up a snowy groove. All my instincts are alert; inner reserves are touched on that I no longer thought existed.

I am there. It's 4 p.m., August 9. Standing on the summit plateau of Nanga Parbat, I see the *Silbersattel* where Willo Welzenbach and Willy Merkl were killed, and which Hermann Buhl crossed on the first ascent in 1953. On the right is the Rupal Valley, in between a vast precipice.

I, too, have stood here once before, eight years ago. My younger brother Günther was with me then and we embraced each other. It was our first 8,000m. peak. On the descent my brother was killed by an avalanche.

I now feel surprisingly calm, not excited as I did then. I fix my camera on to the head of the ice-axe, which is fitted with a screw so that it can be used as a tripod.

I photograph myself in such a way that the background cannot fail to be recognised. Then with my unused peg I fasten a metal container to the summit rock. In it is a parchment reproduction of the first page of the Gutenberg Bible: "In the beginning god created. . . ." It was given to me by a friend. I write the date and my name on the parchment and return it to the container.

I've often thought how it would be if I just remained sitting on an eight-thouander. Is it not a mountaineer's secret wish to stay up there? Not to return to the world which has only just been left behind with such an effort?

An hour later I descend, not down the rock barrier but round it – first along the South Ridge, then through the snow of the western slope. Descending the frosty quicksand is easier. Before dark I manage to reach the tent.

Next morning it's snowing, and thick mist. If I went on I would certainly lose my way like Franz Jäger and Andi Shlick, my two friends who disappeared when we descended Manaslu in a storm.

I wait. I have to ration fuel and food; the bad weather could last more than a week. I sit in the tent, dehydrated and very, very tired. Twice that day the full pan tips over. Part of my down sleeping bag is burned in the process. On the evening of August 10 the weather looks rotten. Three, four more days and I'll be too weak for the descent. I told Ursula Grether and Major Tahir: "If I am not back after 10 days you can strike Base Camp and report me missing to the authorities in Islamabad. Nothing can be done. A search would be pointless."

Three-thirty next morning. The weather seems to be improving. I feel giddy, but it doesn't stop me. At five I'm out of the tent, determined to risk everything. I abandon the tent, sleeping bag and various pieces of equipment: soups, stove, everything. I must try to reach Base Camp today, in one single mammoth stage. 10,000ft. of height loss in the steepest direct line. If I don't make it, I won't survive the ensuing night.

Traversing diagonally, I suddenly slip and can only stop myself through sheer speed of reaction. A sprained ankle or broken tibia would have meant the end. The shock forces me to concentrate all my efforts.

On the left of a vertical rock spur exposed to stonefall – the Mummery Spur – I descend 6,500ft. in one section, facing inwards on bare ice at 50°-60°. No other incidents, no avalanches. In the late afternoon, in the lower, more level reaches of the face, I leap over a dozen crevasses. I feel both half-dead and reborn.

At Base Camp they have seen me sometime ago. Ursula comes towards me across the vast scree slopes carrying my training shoes. We meet. I take off my clubfoot-boots and throw them away, don't want to see them again. With the keen insight of a medic she states that I look 'green'—like a mummy.

That's why there is not a photo of the return. Ursula thinks that a picture of me in this state would be 'in bad taste'.

from MOUNTAIN 65 *1979*

Fortunatus

DOROTHY PILLEY

Fortunatus was one morning at a loss for a party. We had watched him performing marvels on the crags and admired the dash which we ourselves did not possess. So when he asked us if we would care to come with him for an attempt on the Direct Route on Glyder Fach, we jumped at the suggestion. This climb has a distinct *cachet*. In the books it is classed as 'exceptionally severe'. It goes up the middle of the steepest crag in the Ogwen district. We had looked at it often from neighbouring climbs with longing eyes; so we were overjoyed and most grateful for the offer.

We set off gaily by the track that leads up to Llyn Bochlwyd. It was a fair summer morning and the pale grey crags of Glyder Fach were in their most inviting condition when we reached them. From their foot they tower up vertiginously into the sky and come much nearer than most cliffs to realising the non-climber's picture of the cragsman's 'dreadful trade'. Soon we were well on our way up them, Fortunatus clambering with all a monkey's agility from flange to flange of the massive grey shafts of which they are composed. We, 60ft. apart, followed either in more sedate or more laborious fashion. At intervals, ledges and niches occur, charming little halting-places, where two, or, at a crush, three can gather. Here Nature has provided a good supply of belays, strong pins of rock, very comforting to the party. The pitches between the ledges are solid and sheer. As you tiptoe up them you do really feel suspended over the valley with nothing but air below. 'Exposure', in other words, to use the climbing technicality, is continuous. When all is going well the experience is singularly exhilarating. As you look upwards from a ledge the soles of the leader's boots are what you chiefly see of him, and he is often stepping up on wrinkles no larger than the edge-nails of his boots.

We were rather more than halfway up and had taken the delicate little sideways movement known as the 'toe-and-finger traverse'. Above this the 'hand traverse' faced us. A crack slants diagonally up across a steep, smooth slab. It offers sloping and not very good hold to the hands, and the hold gets worse as it rises. The slab gives a little friction to the knees but not very much. Just below the leader's dangling feet in this passage the cliff drops to a small, turf-covered, but sloping, ledge. Thence it plunges down to the screes at the foot of the cliff. At the top of the 'hand traverse' the leader is about 18ft. above this ledge and so out of reach.

Our party had been repulsed by this traverse some days before and we were ready to take it with great respect. So I.A.R.* placed himself on the ledge with his heels dug in as deeply as the shallow, sloping turf would allow and Frazer and I held both his rope and our leader's from the best belays available some 25ft. over to the left. Fortunatus now threw himself on to the traverse. He arrived half-way quickly but stayed there rather a long time. His boots began to scrape about blindly. He exclaimed, "Find me a rugosity! Find me a rugosity!" with some insistence. Slowly he concertina'd out until he was dangling at full arm-stretch by his finger-tips. He made no attempt to return. Suddenly with a grating screech (I have never heard a sound quite like it before or since) his hands slipped off and he dropped clear through the air on to the ledge below, where I.A.R. pounced on him with a rugby collar. If they had rolled off they would have had a horrid sideways swing across the sheer face of the cliff and we could not have been certain that their ropes would have held them.

By this our ardour was a good deal damped. Not so with Fortunatus. Before we could discuss the matter he hopped up to the beginning of the crack and sprang at it like a cat again. This time his impetus carried him further—right to the upper end, in fact, and correspondingly further from us and higher up over I.A.R.'s head, who was clearly preparing himself for the worst. We were just hoping that he would win the good holds that lead up from the top of the crack when the same process began again. Knees and toes searched hopelessly over the smooth rock. Obviously his strength was going fast. Horrible moments, which seemed to pass very slowly. Little by little his arms stretched out, his fingers could not last much longer. We were ready, there was nothing further to be done except to stand taut and expectant. Again came the shrill, "Ar-r-r!" and, twisting in the air, down he bounced on to I.A.R.'s ledge. This time he landed squatting on its very verge and was in the

*I. A. Richards—later to achieve eminence as a literary critic.

act of diving off into the void, head-first, when he was clutched by the collar of his jacket and held for a second time. There he sat wringing his hands and ejaculating, "Curse me for a tailor! Curse me for a tailor!" again and again.

We should have laughed if the moment had not been still so full of suspense. For, entirely unshaken by these flights, he was all for reorganising the party for a fresh attempt. I was to work the belay while Frazer joined I.A.R. on the ledge. A long argument between him and Frazer followed. "We won't ask you to do anything, Frazer, that you don't want to, *but*, if you were to stand here underneath me you could take 40lb. off my weight or find me a rugosity for my feet, and then. . ." This was the moment when Frazer's adamantine streak came to our aid. With good sound sense he pointed out the weakness of the party's position if the ledge were still further crowded. Someone would be certain to be bowled off it. There was no hold there except a thin layer of soft grassy mud that was already much scored and cut up by our antics. The belay was too far to the side, whoever fell must swing through a whole quadrant of a circle. The probabilities were altogether too clear after these experiments. The vote went solidly three to one against a disappointed Fortunatus and we went off by an easier climb to the summit of the crags.

from CLIMBING DAYS *1935*

All That Glory

GEORGES BETTEMBOURG

In the sinister atmosphere of clouds and snow swirling about in the strong wind, for a few seconds, just a few, I caught a glimpse of the summital towers to our right, enlightened by the moon. Just as suddenly the view disappeared behind the clouds. Peter [Boardman] and I waited for the day to break, hoping for the weather to improve. We dug a little platform for our feet, anchored our axes, and started hitting our feet and hands to keep them alive.

"Peter, we can say we've climbed this mountain! We're so close to the summit. I feel I've already been on top and climbed it. . .''

". . . we're not yet on the summit!" Peter yelled into my face, cutting me short. Suddenly I realised that Peter and I were miles apart. His violent reaction stunned me. It shattered something inside me. Had I committed a crime by telling him my deeper feelings—that I felt we had already climbed the mountain? I had wanted to make him feel good by giving him a share in the effort produced to reach our high point. But he did not think I was talking to him. He must have thought I was talking to the people out there, the crowd for whom a summit is too often climbed. But I was no longer talking about the summit of Kangchenjunga, but my own summit. I had reached it and tried to tell him that. And now we were on a different wave-length, miles apart—a different species. I understood what Peter was concerned about—the glory—because I was concerned about it too. But he probably would have understood me if he had done what I had done on the mountain.

from THE WHITE DEATH *1982*

Glasgow

JOHN MACKENZIE

It is not commonly known that for a wet day or a spare evening in Glasgow there are alternatives to visiting the Whangie or staying at home. In fact there are no fewer than six separate areas within three miles of George Square where a climber may 'practice' his art. There are even a few places where, no matter how wet the day, he may climb without a drop reaching his head. Haston secured a permanent niche in climbing history for Edinburgh's Currie Walls by using the generous pages of the Tiso Eastern Outcrops Guide to show others the way; but the much greater scope of the Glasgow Walls remains unknown except to a few initiates.

The Currie Walls have an important advantage, in that the local law takes little notice, whereas in Glasgow sombre clothing and considerable guile are required to escape detection. Like the numerous small boys who peer over parapets with round eyes and open mouths, the police, if not so far professionally interested, are at least curious and a carefully-worded explanation usually gives sufficient satisfaction that we are not breaking the walls down, but are *bona fide* climbers who wish to be left alone; lunatics, perhaps, but essentially harmless.

For those who have never climbed a man-made wall before, the 'reason why' should not pose an insuperable problem. It is obvious that it is different — there's not much point in taking your ice-axe along, for example — and that exotic difficulties and objective dangers could be quoted *à la* Haston. But the real reason perhaps lies in the fact that most climbers, when sufficiently caged in, will somehow find a way of climbing out into the allegorical sunlight, constantly reaching for new nooks and crannies to climb, wriggle or squirm out of. More commonly, however, people say it strengthens the fingers.

There are traverses and straight-up routes and even diagonal routes leading nowhere in particular; they come in all shapes and sizes, from 60ft. high to 3,000ft. long! Sometimes a rope is needed but in others soloing is normal, often avoiding an embarrassing failure and that committed feeling when pirouetting gently on something over 130 routes of all grades, the grading being that of the southern British sandstone guides — grades 1-6, each subdivided into a, b, or c in increasing order of difficulty. The continental grades used by Haston in the Currie guide were found to be insufficiently accurate to capture all the obsessive technical nuances which these climbing grounds require.

The walls are a soft red sandstone, weathering into slightly sloping holds with good friction and occasionally into pockets. Jug handles are almost entirely unknown. Some fine cracks exist as well, especially in areas of prominent vertical jointing, as is found in corners.

Ground rules for first visitors are as follows: go dressed in old mouldies and retired PAs, take a rope and a couple of slings for the higher routes and stuff them in a bag, since house-breakers might mistake you for the Genuine Article, beating them to it.

The River Kelvin flows near all the climbing areas, the Kelvin Bridge being in a roughly central position about ten minutes' walk from the other walls. The bridge itself is one of the main straight-

up areas and is reached by descending the Gent's Lavatory steps at
the west end. If seen by the attendant hopping over the small locked
gate in descent, tell him what you are doing. Otherwise, being a
man of the world, he gets suspicious, particularly so if there are two
of you and he sees you changing your clothing beneath the bridge.
In such an occasion, he is liable to voice popular opinion, viz.,
    "Gerrabloodyellootatherryerrbleedenpoofs," etc.
This can be very embarrassing and is apt to bring a crowd quicker
than anything.

The main arches of the bridge were once the scene of a minor
epic, when an abortive attempt was made to cross them, using
slings for aid on the struts. Unfortunately the struts were 7ft. apart,
so that a cunning combination of lassoos and clamps had to be
used, assisted by 10ft. bamboo poles to reach and retrieve the
weighted lassoos, thus forming a series of endless loops, along
which slow progress could be made. A tremendous and horrifying
pendule started the process off, giving a satisfying sense of
commitment, there being only one way to go on, so to speak. Much
time was spent trying to lassoo struts whilst gyrating in the opposite
direction. The light began to fade after a miserable 70ft. or so,
lending seriousness to the operation. Eventually, total, sepulchral,
darkness fell when still 40ft. above the Stygian river. The trouble
was that, apart from the trifling inconvenience of sitting in etiers,
the abseil rope was still fully seven feet away, somewhere in the
darkness. This appalling situation was eventually resolved by
furious circling movements whilst lashing out wildly with the
bamboo pole. A further 1,000 calories or so resulted in a
satisfactory abseil position. All was prepared for a controlled
descent into the water. Regrettably the peaceful scene was then
disrupted by lamenting female voices from the far bank where a
good deal of confusion reigned as to what was going on! It was a
curious feeling, hanging there in mid-air like a trapped bomber
while torches stabbed at the surrounding bridgeworks, never quite
finding their target, and the slow descent continued.

There is one last area, somewhat exotic, which nevertheless
deserves a mention. This is St. Mungo's Cemetery—the famous
Necropolis—where climbs up to 50ft. may be had on a terrible
basalt called Teschenite. However, the objective dangers are so
high (rotten rock, poisoning and possible apparitions, spiritual and

temporal) that the risks are not worth it. Getting in after 'closing time' is the only solution and involves a difficult and very public climb over the railings.

These then are the climbing grounds of Glasgow so far discovered. No doubt others will be found — but the walls, particularly those of Finniston, will continue to provide the main challenge.

SMCJ Editor's Note: Since receiving this MS two important and unfortunate changes have occurred, which we feel should be mentioned. The Lavatory Attendant, by all accounts a pleasant man, was clubbed to death on New Year's Day and the Lavatory is now closed. Also Glasgow's last unconquered peak — The Tower of Babel — has been demolished.

from THE SCOTTISH MOUNTAINEERING CLUB
JOURNAL *1973*

Pass the Mirror

ARLENE BLUM

After the tent had been resurrected, we gathered in the kitchen, and Mingma shared his bottle of rum. Soon we were all laughing and joking. Vera [Komarkova] took out her mirror and studied her face intently. As usual it was covered with the thick pancake makeup she used as sunscreen.

"Let me look," I said, taking the mirror. I saw an unfamiliar, relatively slender sunburned face with prominent cheekbones. I wondered if John would recognise me when I got home.

"I don't want to see my new wrinkles," Vera W. said. But she couldn't resist the mirror for long. "Well, maybe I'll take just a peek." I handed her the mirror, and Vera looked at her face for the first time in several weeks.

"Oh," she complained, "I look so old."

"No, no, Vera. Your suntan is very becoming. You look beautiful." And she did indeed look classically lovely. In fact, the higher we climbed, the better we all looked — slim, tanned, and healthy. Many men, in contrast, take on a haggard look after a few weeks at high altitude.

But not all of us saw it that way. Annie made a face at herself in the mirror. "I look like a red-nosed booby," she laughed.

Margi took the mirror next and ruefully surveyed her short blond hair. "Blah! It looks like straw," she grimaced.

"It's great," Annie laughed. "You could be an English rock star."

"But I can't sing worth shit."

"Doesn't matter. Most of them can't either."

from ANNAPURNA: A WOMAN'S PLACE *1980*

Ball's Pyramid

KEITH BELL

A sense of isolation engulfed me as the boat disappeared behind the edge of the pinnacle. Memories flooded back as I gazed at the lonely sea. Three years before I had stood on the summit of Ball's Pyramid, one of a party of six who had pioneered a new route up the North Ridge. Now I had returned with Greg Mortimer to attempt the first skyline traverse of the Pyramid. We intended to climb the South Ridge to the summit, then descend the North Ridge. I had planned to do the traverse in 1972, but postponed the attempt due to an extraordinary amount of cyclonic activity.

Ball's Pyramid has unique approach problems. There are no bays, inlets or beaches to facilitate landings; bare rock rises sheer from the sea. The boat moors as close to the Pyramid as the swell will allow. It is up to the climbers to swim to the rock and climb to safety above the level of the swell. Previous expeditions had members put out of action before they landed. We landed twice – on the north end to cache supplies and on the south end to begin the climb. Fortunately, both landings were on the sheltered side of the Pyramid and the sea was like a millpool. The windward side was a different story, 15ft. waves smashing against the rocks.

By 1 p.m. on Monday, February 26, we had finished the preliminaries and begun the long climb up the South Ridge to the summit. Nightfall saw us safely positioned in an incut horizontal fault 1,000ft. above the ocean. The weather that day was fine and sunny with a strong north-easterly wind. Overnight it deteriorated and we awoke to find leaden skies. Towering above was one of the South Ridge's major features, Winklesteins Steeple. Alternating leads, we were soon moving into the slot between the twin towers of the Steeple. Some horizontal ridge climbing was encountered, during which we were subjected to unpleasant buffeting by the wind. The next major obstacle, the Pillar of Porteus, was followed by another *à cheval* ridge up to the final summit tower. Some hard and exposed climbing was covered as the Pyramid threw down its final challenge.

141

At 3.30 p.m., Tuesday, we were standing on the top of Australia's remotest summit, the greatest prize for an Australian climber; a ten-square-yard patch of real estate that barely a score of people had trodden. It felt good to be back. Little had changed in the intervening years. Lord Howe Island, now in view, straddled the horizon to the north, its two major peaks, Gower and Lidgeburgh, rising like beckoning sirens from the sea. We found the rum bottle left by the 1970 expedition, and added our jottings to the enclosed note, finishing with a confident, "and now attempting to descend the North Ridge." If we looked confident, we certainly didn't feel it.

Two airy rappels were made from the summit; I felt like a spider hanging from a fine thread 1,800ft. above the sea. Some roped scrambling followed to a series of terraces. On the end of these terraces and out on the East Face we found a comfortable cave, a fortunate discovery as it was 5 p.m. and the weather was threatening. For the first time since landing we were able to contact Lord Howe Island by radio, only to be told that a cyclone was moving south from the state of Queensland.

A comfortable night was spent, protected from the wind and rain by the large roof of the cave. The advance of the cyclone was heralded by low-lying mist and intermittent rain. The wind had ceased blowing in gusts and bore in at a constant velocity, fetching great waves before it. These waves smashed with frightening ferocity against the base of the rock. Our contact advised us to sit tight until the cyclone had passed, but our food and water were running low.

Two long rappels took us from the cave to the start of a traverse along the East Face. Four roped pitches along ledges poised above a 1,500ft. drop to the sea, led to the base of a crack system. It was raining heavily and the rock was running with sheets of water. I started leading up an incipient crack, bridging on minute slippery holds to a point where the crack opened up. I jammed my hand deeply into it, my first secure hold in 30ft. About 100ft. above Greg, I came to a good ledge and set up a belay. Greg joined me. Shaking with apprehension, I moved up the crack until it petered out into a bulge. This I pulled out over, teetering on small holds, the top barely feet away. My eyes wandered down 1,600ft. to the sea; fear welled up inside me. Suddenly I had it: reach for the loose flake and friction with my boots. The key was turned, the ridge reached and the traverse almost ours.

Dropping down and traversing under a huge gendarme, we then broke out onto a knife-edge ridge. It was an eerie sensation to sit astride the Pyramid with 1,500ft. voids on each side. Certainly it was no place to linger. A minute later we were off the ridge, preparing to rappel. As we swung down past all the familiar places, my mind moved back three years, reliving the moments I had shared with five others on the very same ground. The weather had been fairer then, warm and slightly overcast; perfect conditions for climbing. No cyclones, no wet clothes and shivering bodies; just the sensations of a pleasant, enjoyable climb.

Suddenly I was jolted back into reality as Greg landed on the ledge beside me. Now only 350ft. above the sea, we tried to retrieve the rope. We heaved and pulled to no avail; the rope was securely jammed. Greg jumared up, disappearing over the overhang 60ft. above me. Minutes later the rope moved, but his descent brought another problem. Under the overhang he touched some loose flakes, causing a barrage of rocks to come hurtling toward the ledge. I braced myself as they clattered around. A stab of pain shot through my leg as a rock the size of a man's fist crashed into my knee.

Two agonising rappels followed to reach the 1970 base camp ledge. It was a relief to get there, as my leg was collapsing under my applied weight. Up and 25ft. to the left was a small cave, our home for the next three days. We retrieved our ropes, climbed up to it, and collapsed, the rigours of the day having fatigued us both mentally and physically.

It was 5.30 p.m., Wednesday, February 28. Already a gloom had settled over the sea. 200ft. below us on the shoals at the northern end the sea was a turbulent, seething white mass. Waves were crashing in from all directions, sending froth and foam radiating out into a 500-yard circle. Right before our eyes, birds were plucked before the wind, their wings useless twisted appendages of their bodies. They were gathered up by the sea and drowned. Only the graceful gannets had the necessary strength to ride out the wind. The wafer shape of the Pyramid was dividing the wind into two streams. These collided violently at the north end with a resultant vortex 300ft. in width zooming up the face, its edge only yards from the mouth of the cave. We had a grandstand view of the awesome power of the cyclone. Never before had I seen such a release of natural energy.

Darkness came and clothed the drama in inky blackness. We prepared ourselves for the long ordeal of the night. Over saturated clothes and shivering bodies we placed our waterproof vests and pants, then slipped into large plastic bags that encased our bodies; scant protection against the rigours of the storm. Knowledge of the fact that our cached food and sleeping bags lay only 130ft. below did little to humour us. As the night progressed, the storm intensified. The mouth of the cave was the lip of a waterfall. On nearby Lord Howe Island roofs were torn off houses and palm trees flattened. Many people had their sleep disturbed by the violence of Cyclone Kirsty that night.

Dawn filtered through an oppressive mist and we again resumed our grandstand view of the fight below. We felt heartened by the weak light that now enveloped us. The night had passed slowly. It was the worst bivouac I had sat through, including those in the European Alps and on the highest peaks of Africa. It was Greg's third bivouac, all of which had been on the Pyramid. At least he had probably had his best and worst bivouac in one trip.

By 10.30 a.m. as the clouds scudded overhead, patches of blue began to appear. By 12.30 p.m. the sky was almost clear, though a trace of wind remained. Half an hour later, I was sitting sunning myself on the large ledge 20ft. below the cave. One could scarcely believe that there had been a cyclone. I was looking across brilliant blue water toward Lord Howe Island basking under a clear sky.

Late Friday morning an island fishing boat appeared, but it was too rough to attempt an evacuation. The afternoon was passed in dejected silence. Whereas before we had been fighting cold, the sun now bore into our cave, broiling us in a natural oven.

Mid-day Saturday another fishing boat came into sight. We had no choice this time; lack of food and water meant that we would have to attempt the swim. We packed our gear and ferried it down to the stowage ledge. Our confrontation with the surf at the lower level was frightening. Huge 15ft. waves, breaking 35 yards out from the rock. Getting our equipment off was out of the question; we would find difficulties enough without the added problem of valuable gear.

The boat anchored about 130 yards out. Greg and I stood on a platform with the surf boiling around our legs, waiting for a calm moment. When I dived at a wave's high point, the water level suddenly dropped, revealing a mosaic of rock and water. Miraculously I landed in water, surfacing only when I could hold my breath no longer. Continued diving to avoid crashing waves left me exhausted, but the thought of sharks spurred me on. At last the boat, only yards away! With my last ounce of energy I dragged myself to its side, where friendly hands hauled me to safety. Greg arrived and was lifted aboard in the same fashion. We both lay in the bottom of the boat like gasping fish, too exhausted to speak. The boat turned and headed for Lord Howe Island.

from SUMMIT *1974*

Welsh Interlude

NEA MORIN

So, from time to time, I could escape from the war to the hills, and early in the winter of 1943 there were a few glorious days spent at Ty Gwyn farm in the Nant Ffrancon Valley with Charles Marriott and other friends. This valley has the reputation of being the coldest in North Wales. As we sallied forth from the shelter of the farm house an icy blast, such as I have seldom encountered in the Alps, buffeted and tore at us. But it was fine, fine as I have rarely seen it in Wales. The hills looked treble their normal size with the detail of the lower slopes still indistinct in the early morning light, while the summits gleamed, snow-capped, far above. The sky was a uniform pale steely blue, the ground hard as iron, so that we walked dry-shod where normally one would sink into marsh.

Along the old road to Ogwen we passed many stone strongholds of the same grey as the mountain, but with oblong slits striking a sinister note and reminding us that this was wartime. We climbed the Sub Cneifion Rib, above Llyn Idwal, and decided it was too cold for pleasant rock climbing. So we made our way up the Nameless Cwm towards a likely-looking snow-gully. Mist came swirling down, unaccountably, from a clear sky, and whenever there was a break we looked quickly up, spotting and trying to memorise landmarks to guide us. The snow was ice-hard and gave out a peculiar hollow treacherous sound to the blows of the axe. We roped up. It was already late, for we had spent too long on the icy rocks of the Sub Cneifion Rib. By good luck we hit on the base of our gully, but decided to keep to a steep grassy rib bordering it on one side, thinking thus to gain height more rapidly. I was now to learn something quite new. We found ourselves on frozen turf at a steep angle on which the axe made not the slightest impression. Only an automatic drill might have been effective. We left that rib just as quickly as we knew how and dropped back into the gully with a sigh of relief. Progress here was slow for quite a lot of step-cutting was required, and when the slope curled up steeply into a small cornice I could almost imagine myself back in the Alps.

It was 4 p.m. when we scrambled out on to the summit plateau between Castell y Gwynt and Glyder Fawr to find a scene of unimaginable beauty before us. Castell y Gwynt, the Castle of the Winds, was transformed into a fairy fortress with the snow-plastered rocks glittering in the golden-red light of the setting sun, while the snow on the plateau was frozen into a brilliant sea of ripples shadowed now by the low sun and thrown into relief.

Back by the shores of Llyn Idwal we were under a clear evening sky, though mist still hung on the mountains. The wind had dropped and the stars appeared like so many pin-pricks into infinity. Ty Gwyn and its clump of pines made a dark blotch just visible from the road. We had been out for more than ten hours and the welcome of a blazing fire and a generous farmhouse meal heightened the feeling of escape from reality.

Another glorious and this time absolutely cloudless day, saw us clambering up the yellow bone-dry grass slopes of Mynydd Perfedd. Sheltered from the cutting wind, we were soon perspiring in shirt-sleeves; but for the frosty nip in the air it might have been a summer's day. From the summit plateau we looked up and across to Foel Goch and Y Garn and thought the gentle slopes on this side would make admirable practice ground for skiing. Snowdon was unaccountably missing from the landscape, and recollecting loud rumblings in the night we wondered if the Germans had dropped a bomb on it. But the summit peak was only playing hide and seek behind Carnedd Ugain and its sharp point soon peeped out reassuringly as we made towards Y Garn. We glissaded down the snow and peered over into the Devil's Kitchen. Normally there is a sizable waterfall here, but this was now frozen solid and a more awesome, gloomy place one could scarcely imagine. Somewhere I had read that "Several attempts to scale the Devil's Kitchen had ended in disaster" and I could well believe it. Still, what was visible of the finishing traverse at the top seemed fairly clear of ice and we decided to go round and have a look at it from below. The cliffs were festooned with enormous icicles, and with a queer formation that I don't remember ever having seen before; it looked as though water had frozen solid in the act of shooting out fanwise over the edge, forming something like half an open umbrella with extra long spikes and deep-cut bays.

The Devil's Kitchen was blue ice from top to bottom, and we had to cut steps right from the start. Oddly enough it seemed less cold inside the cleft, but how nightmarish it would be to be transfixed by one of the gigantic icicles hanging over our heads. The large jammed boulder gave us some trouble — it was just a huge lump of ice, and in the end we had to use combined tactics. Below the steep crack beside what is normally the waterfall, we paused. At the best of times this is an impressive spot — the guidebook says of the climb: "Severe, owing to its character." On this occasion, though a magnificent sight, it was frightening enough to conjure up the mythical *afanc* (abominable Welshman?) from the cavernous depths of the frozen waterfall. I had climbed it before and knew that the pitches were not really difficult, but nasty little thrills of apprehension kept running up and down my spine. I moved slowly over the ice-covered rocks towards the foot of the crack, and the nearer I got the steeper grew the walls. How cold it all was! Would there be much ice up there? Once I had started, I shinned up as though the Devil had indeed come out of his Kitchen and was at my heels. For some unknown reason I felt impelled to go all out and style went by the board, as my shins and knees showed later. Perched up on the first stance I looked straight down between my legs into the dark cleft below. Charles, who had watched my frenzied antics with some amazement, now came up slowly and deliberately in perfect style despite his rucksack and two ice-axes. I felt I was being silently though nonetheless effectively, reproved, and since some explanation seemed called for, I remarked that I had been afraid of my fingers getting numb. This announcement met with polite, but quite obvious incredulity, and the reply that *his* fingers were beautifully warm, in fact he was altogether too hot. I was now thoroughly warmed up and feeling capable of tackling anything, but there was no need for any heroics; curiously enough the actual pitches were almost free of ice and, barring the cold, were scarcely more difficult than under normal conditions. When we reached the top the sun had gone. Once again we made our way down the now rather worn steps, which we had cut two days before.

The shadows were already deepening as we ran down to Llyn Idwal and Ogwen. On the road to Ty Gwyn I paused time and again to look back at the delicate crests of Tryfan and the Glyders and to the black mass of Y Garn and Foel Goch outlined against the pale, starry sky. Peace reigned over all and some of that peace we took away with us. These were the last days when I could still look forward to telling it all to Jean [Morin].

from A WOMAN'S REACH *1968*

Moses

FRED BECKEY

In the earliest days of Spanish exploration in the West, men dreamt of a mountain of silver, and the Sierra Azul, like so many other myths, was given much currency. This search for the fabulous, which began about 100 years after Columbus, was revived in 1776 when Father Escalante led the first comprehensive traverse of the Colorado Plateau and discovered large sections of what was to become the old Spanish Trail. In this rebirth of the ancient dream of exploration, the cartographer Bernardo de Miera y Pacheco charted the San Buenaventura River, beginning the legend of a water passage out of the Great Basin to the Pacific Ocean, a legend that took half a century to dispel. These explorers found a land of unexpected river canyons and mysteries too awesome to comprehend: "A mighty desert of bare rock, chiselled by ages out of the foundation of the globe." Here, the Colorado River had been cutting its trough for twelve million years.

This is the land of ancient Anasazi Pueblo peoples, ancestors of the Navajos. It is a land where there is a harmony of extremes, both in geology and plant life. The pinion pine and Utah juniper survive on the plateau and the willow and inherited tamarisk thrive along rivers. Verbena, aster, sunflower, penstemon, and princess plume surprise the eye. The land demands particular respect, yet offers unique rewards, addicting trespassers to its treasures. John Wesley Powell, who led the first exploration down the Green and Colorado Rivers in 1869 felt this compelling strangeness when he wrote, "Heights are made higher and the depths deeper by the glamour and witchery of light and shade." On the plateau the party found themselves in the centre of a weird, arid, and ghostly land, a wide cyclorama of barren sandstone "carved into an amazing multitude of towers, buttes, spires, pinnacles . . . all shimmering under a dazzling sun."

The fascination of the desert has overtaken many figures in history. Lawrence of Arabia, and Gertrude Bell, his war-time adviser, fell inescapably before its charm "ringed in bleak bare mountains snow-crowned and furrowed with the deep course of torrents." Likewise, Sven Hedin felt the magnetism of the Takla Makan desert in Central Asia. The Colorado Plateau has a landscape that rings a more familiar chord with the tourist: Arches and Canyonlands National Parks, Monument Basin, Island in the Sky, Land of Standing Rocks, The Needles, Castle Valley, and Fisher Towers. The eroded curiosities of the region, the arches and balanced rocks, are carved from the underlying Carmel formation by wind and water, leaving a cap of harder Entrada. The densest of these Jurassic formations is the Wingate, a reddish buff sandstone vertically seamed by joints extending its full thickness. It is often streaked with a blue-black surface varnish. It is this rock that retains Indian petroglyphs.

A pink skyscraper better than sixty storeys high remained the secret of this dissected plateau. Moab tour guide Lin Ottinger knew it as 'Moses', with a head, eyes, chin, and shoulders bent to resemble in outline the historic desert leader. Anxious to live out the

Manifest Destiny of the rock climber, Eric Bjornstad and I, in 1970, needed little coaxing to follow Lin into hidden Taylor Canyon. When we reached the mythical Green of San Buena-ventura of Miera, we felt the mystery that stirred in a land that spoke of forever. Here were the 'orange coloured' sandstone and 'grandly arched' walls that enlivened Powell's report. Naively over-confident and prodigal with our time, we looked for ancestral relics — arrowheads, chips of chalcedony, perhaps a stone kettle from those who came to the canyons 4,000 years ago.

Moses overwhelmed us. We were somewhat baffled by the 650ft. desert monster, with its massive overhangs on all faces. There were several routes, yet there were no ways . . . We did not even try, but instead spent the best of two days in its shadow on 'Zeus', a tower half its size. Our commitment was sealed: we would return with more time and equipment. Climbing strategy on friable sandstone is a test of perseverance, with an ever-changing wind to enliven the action and bring communication to a frustrating halt. Eyes fill with grit, the mouth is dry. Temperatures are seldom right: either it is bitterly cold or unbearably hot. Every day can distill a life's climbing experience. For some, the reward does not balance the effort.

Our mini-attempt was not good enough the next spring. We arrived with the heat, and the overhanging first pitch on the North Face did me in. Though Moses seemed to mock our failure, we felt an inherited possessiveness toward our discovery. We felt the invisible threat of those who might learn of the tower; we didn't look Colorado climbers in the eye, and trusted only the ravens and hawks.

The third trip was armoured with luck. We chose a spirited group and equally important, the only week of good weather in October 1972. The La Sal Mountains were already whitened with the season's first snowfall, and no longer looked "like blue clouds on the horizon," as they did to the explorers. On the upland there appeared the derelicts of a wet week: cars and a tattered school bus abandoned. Our climbing group was now expanded by the addition of Jim Galvin, Thom Nephew and Greg Markov. Our transport was secure with Ethan Becker and a new jeep, which proved welcome in the quagmire along the Green. Our moral support was complete with the addition of Sara, Karen, Shelley, Chris, and three dogs. In the fall, dusk comes quickly, so the adventurous drive up the canyon was done by headlight. In the morning, Taylor Canyon resembled a boisterous gypsy camp surrounding a lone juniper. With camp attendants as breakfast cooks, the pre-climb ceremonies were limited to racking iron, adjusting new eyes to the shock of Moses, and devising a method of making our food stores dog-proof.

Our game plan developed slowly, due to the complexity and occasional blankness of the climb, the intricate variety of equipment, and a casual yet serious attitude. The grainy surface forced nearly all of the climbing into aid. Rumblings about pushing the deep jam-cracks at 5.9 were repeatedly interrupted by the familiar sound of the bong. One ominous block was happily circumvented by a bolt ladder. We alternated the daily leads in teams of two, setting up solid bolts for the hanging belays and rappels as we proceeded. For a party of five, we were usually well separated, but for the lonely belayer there were relaxed hours sitting in the belay seat, contemplating the exposure and delightful canyon colours.

Two fine days were interrupted by a day of rain. With the comforts of an evening fire at camp, there was little incentive to bivouac on the tower. In two more days – early afternoon the 26th – we sat on the head of Moses. The summit was a bit like a space station reunion, with the real rejoicing awaiting the survival of five long rappels to earth. A stiffening wind brought in a cloud cover even as we were tying the pitons into four large loops of webbing for the traditional 'throw-down'. Raindrops nullified our plans for a victory campfire and wine feast. It was time to load the cars and drive to Moab while the road was still passable. Indeed Moses chased us out, for the next day it snowed.

from ASCENT 1973

Beltane Fire

GEOFF MILBURN

"You're mad Moran! Stark raving mad," howled a voice, as the gale subsided just long enough for the sound to carry up on the wind. Teams had already baled out off The Medlar and The Empire and were purposefully stacking away their gear. As they departed with a last, smug, upward glance, there was Jim hanging one-handed from an evil overhang, looking for all the world like some primitive ape. His hair was blowing in all directions while the contents of his newly-filled chalkbag streamed skywards, liberally coating his grinning face and spotting his glasses prettily in the process. Somehow it seemed eminently appropriate that after the last string of insults Jim should be at grips with Gates of Delirium, until recently one of the hardest Lakeland routes. How on earth had the idiot lured me on to it on such a vile day when the lads were all off to play arrows in the nearest pub? In fact they must be right, "Come down you daft so-and-so, it's not fit for climbing in weather like this." "Not blooming likely, I didn't come all the way up here for nothing." And so there was nothing for it but to huddle up under a little bulge and pray for an early release.

Some comfort was derived from the fact that I had crammed on as many extra layers as I could but how to climb looking like a barrage balloon was a distinct problem. Not that it gave me much to worry about as everyone knows that comfort comes before ethics every time. With stiff little fingers fumbling about here and there I took the groove at a rush and began to lurk under the huge roof where I could chunter away to myself in peace. "If he thinks that I'm traversing downhill at this angle he can think again. I'm not that crazy." The cold sapped enthusiasm away and made me more determined than ever not to remove the substantial runner above my head. After a while the answer came in a flash as I realised that the tatty old sling in the roof would be good for a back rope to keep me in contact with the crag. After some intricate fiddling about with the rope I launched out onto the steep side wall and was soon hanging at full stretch ready to fly. Surprisingly after a move upwards I struck a little bulge with my head and found myself jammed in a back and foot position while standing upright. It was even possible to take both hands off, an utterly ridiculous position which others I understand have also discovered by accident.

Looking slyly sideways and trying to be casual I began to wonder what Jim was attached to as he was leaning out at a funny sort of angle. There didn't even seem to be a stance and we were soon climbing all over each other in a vague attempt to get things sorted out. The wind was having a fine old time whipping the ropes about below the roofs and knotting them up into a web and it took ages to pull it all up onto my knee. The initial adrenalin flow caused by the sensational position soon ebbed away and the cold took over as Jim began to enjoy the intricacies of the pitch. Much later I whipped out the belay slings and headed for the safety of the big groove above. Just to be able to move was a delight but after dropping the peg which I use to tap out little nuts a fierce battle soon started with the sequence of wires. While clipped in at one point I found myself hanging upside down to poke about with a too-bendy threader. The nut had ground in solid somehow and with great reluctance I finally left it behind.

On top of the crag my crime was admitted – very grudgingly – and Jim showed his surprise in no uncertain terms. "That's the first time that I've known you fail in five years. What a let down!" Was I mad, and for minutes on end the air was blue as I gave vent to my feelings. When we sorted out the gear however Jim started to get confused. "Hang on a minute, that's not mine; I've got all mine; and that's not mine either." No wonder I'd had a battle . . . one down suddenly became two up, which is a different ball game altogether. Honour was restored and we crossed the valley to meander up North Crag Eliminate and the rather smart Final Giggle.

from THE CLIMBERS' CLUB JOURNAL *1979/80*

States of the Art

MAX JONES

We arrived in the Gunks excited to climb and full of rumours about this magical climbing arena. The first few days were spent getting used to the rock, and we even managed to pull off Kansas City one morning. Then we had to check out Supercrack – the world's hardest crack (or so every Gunkie told us). We were sure it couldn't be that hard, but you never know, and we wanted to find out first hand if the rumours were true. After all, it had been climbed only twice in four years, and that wasn't due to lack of trying.

Upon first inspection, it doesn't look too hard. I remember telling Mark that I thought we might get it that day. Don't be fooled! After five attempts to complete the first 15ft. I take another look at this thing. It's hard! It's a real bad size and it's very hard to find jams that work. Every time I try something new, and finally I make it to the roof, put in a nut and keep going. The middle section is not too bad, but I can't rest. When I move up into the thin crack, I find my ridiculously taped fingers no longer fit in the crack. Damn! A 20-footer back down to the roof for my mistake. At least now I know it's a safe if gruesome-looking fall.

After that fall, not being in the mood to take another one, I climb from the ground, with less tape, to my high point – this time putting in a nut before my fingers melt out of the crack. I still wonder, will these fingers fit? I grab a nut (watching for lightning) and pull up enough to check. They don't fit. I'm going to have to think of something for tomorrow. All of a sudden this innocent-looking 55ft. of crack has become a very formidable testpiece.

The next day we arrive late in the afternoon so the climb will be in the shade and much cooler. Armed with a new tape job, I climb over the first moves. I'm starting to get those moves memorised and they are finally getting easier – not easy, but easier than desperate. Moving to the top, I struggle to get into the thin section but blow it and come down. I need to climb the bottom quickly so I have strength for the last part.

The next try gets me a little farther before falling off and I just sit there on the rope looking at the remaining five feet of crack below the top buckets wondering if I'll ever get this thing. So close, but so hard. Then down to the ground again, to wait an hour before my next try.

This time the bottom section goes by quickly, I can't believe it, almost effortlessly. I stop to chalk up but have to keep moving to the last section, where I struggle to hang on and get a nut in. I move up to the good holds where I am looking, *looking*, at the top huge incut jug. My foot is sliding on the lichen as I try desperately to find a foothold. There's got to be one. I wait too long and decide to shoot for the hold, but miss. I can't believe it; I fell from the top move and there it is covered by the 'biner and rope — a foothold!

"Going insane . . . yet, I'm laughing in the frozen rain." That Steely Dan song won't stop running through my head, while we walk back to the car in the dark. Maybe tomorrow. I hope I can do the top moves again.

The next day Mark leads Open Cockpit and I have a fun time top-roping it. It's a good route to do for a warm-up. Then the fun is over and it's back to Supercrack. Some friends who witnessed my adventures the day before volunteer to clip the rope into the high point. Who am I to refuse? It takes me half an hour to tape my fingers (I'm getting this down to a science). One more time up this thing.

The bottom goes by effortlessly again and is almost fun. I chalk up and move into the top half. It doesn't give me near the trouble it did the day before and the missed foothold (which I'll never forget) is used as soon as possible. I grab the top jug, mantel, place another nut and climb through easy but still overhanging rock to the no-hands rest on top.

It sure feels good to untie the rope on top of this pillar. That's a lot of work to put into 55ft. of rock. This is a neat place to view a beautiful autumn day. All the trees are changing colours and it's perfect shorts and no-shirt day. An excellent day. The hardest crack in the US? No, but still damn hard.

PHOENIX

"This thing is the hardest thing I ever hope to climb," I say to myself as I begin the 120ft. free rappel to the belay. The top of the crack is all of 1½ inches and just too small to get my hands in to jam. Boy! Mark was close to the top yesterday when he fell off. He had finally made it through the middle section and was going for the top when his arm gave out.

There are no rests on this climb and only a couple of places to stop — sucker rests. The thin crack section is neat, just a finger crack up an overhanging wall with good locks but not much in the way of foot holds. Too bad it starts off so hard. The down-sloping horizontal lower part of the crack is desperate.

Near the end of the rappel, I pull myself into the belay underneath the small corner that starts the pitch. That corner is a hard technical start to a desperate route. The crack opens up only occasionally to allow fingertips. We figured that each section of this pitch — the corner, the horizontal to vertical thincrack and the 1¼-1½ inch section to the top — would be good 5.11 to 5.11 + cruxes on any other route. Too bad there's no rest between them.

Mark glides down the rope and is soon strapped into a comfortable belay waiting for me to climb. It's my turn to go first. Was he thinking the same things I was? That it's our fourth day working on this climb and my hands, at least, could not take much more of this crack? I mention something about not wanting to come back here again and he agrees. Today will have to be the day.

I lead past the now familiar moves, up the corner and the many fixed pins to the horizontal crack. I barely manage to pass that section, and climb only a few feet higher before falling off. Boy, I don't know about this — I did better yesterday.

"Let me down. Have a good one, Mark."

Mark gets ready and is soon machining his way up to and past the horizontal section. He continues up the thin crack, but suddenly falls. He has pulled his shoulder out again. I hope he can still climb this thing — I'm unsure about leading the top part. My hands do not fit into the crack and my mind is about shot from working on this climb for so long.

Yesterday, Mark led to within 15ft. of the top before he burned out trying to place nuts. Some Friends would have been nice. I then climbed to the same point and also fell off. So close! Getting that far was really an achievement considering that the first two days were spent trying to climb the first 60ft. in one push. We finally accomplished that on the third day. It was a great psychological boost to get that far. We might climb this thing after all!

Mark has recovered, is chalking up and getting psyched. He climbs up the fingertip corner that starts the route, to the sequence of moves we've done so many times through the horizontal thin section. Then it's up the thin crack and into the 1¼ inch section to the first stopping place (I hesitate to call it a rest).

He stops to chalk up and shake out each arm, and then continues to move up and clip into nuts left from the previous day's desperate attempt. Passing these he places more nuts, and makes the last moves in the crack to where he has to reach left and around the corner. He hesitates, shoots for the corner, misses once and then gets it, and is soon around the top outside corner. All right! He's done it!

Now I have to get ready. I tighten my boots and swami belt, add a little benzoin to the cuts on my hands to help stifle the bleeding. That hurts! Sorry about this, hands!

I'm getting the bottom part more and more memorised, and work my way up to and then past the crux. I'm climbing better now and didn't mess up any moves. The thin section is not a problem and actually feels easy compared to the crux below (even though it would be like climbing an overhanging Butterballs). It fits my finger size well and I can even get my toes in the crack. Then I arrive at the 1¼ inch section. A tricky size to jam, but finger stacks work well and it's not too bad. I'm climbing smoothly and think my arms might last.

The last 1½ inch section, however, is what I've been fearing. My hands *don't* fit, and every move is very strenuous. Why couldn't my hands be just a little thinner? Shoving them into the crack, trying to get them to fit, hurts. Suddenly I'm nearing the top and I'm almost too tired to unclip from the nuts. I hope that's a hand jam up there. Oops, both feet cut loose and only my left hand is jammed; somehow I manage to hang on. Back on the rock I lunge to the hand jam, and lunge to the left to palm the outside corner above the crack. Another dynamo to the crack around the corner, and I have the top. Finally.

I roll off the climb totally helpless and look up to Mark, who is grinning like a clown. It's over! We *never* have to come back! My hands hang uselessly by my sides, all torn up, and I can barely climb the short easy section up to the belay. "Good work, Mark." We shake hands and they rebel with pain. Sorry about that, hands.

from MOUNTAIN 67 *1980*

Solo on Cloggy

WILFRID NOYCE

It must have been that fascination, overmastering and fatal as was ever the blindness that took Pentheus to his doom among the Bacchae, which led me once to the steepest cliff in Wales. The sense of intimacy that possesses the solitary had become, it may be, an infatuation; more and more I had thought that I might presume, if my love be kind, until it seemed that there was no liberty that I could not take. It was a May morning of 1942, and I was under the precipice of Clogwyn du'r Arddu. I had stepped from bright sun into the slanting shadow of the eastern buttress. I blinked up at it, at the row of vertical cracks that split it. On the right I could see the Curving Crack that Colin Kirkus, I knew, had climbed with Alf Bridge. The day was warm, the rocks dry, and the moss peeled from them under a rubber shoe. I started up the first layback crack; why, I could not tell. There was no sense in trying such a climb. I was tasting simply a physical pleasure – why does the small boy buy an ice cream when he has pennies about him? My legs were arched, feet pressed against the back wall. The rubbers slipped occasionally, ever so slightly. My fingers hooked around the upright crack edge. I was gaining height, slowly. At the top of the first section, 30ft. above the turf, I surveyed future and past: the vertical walls of the buttress and the little ledge on which I stood. A comforting crack split the cliff above me, shaped exactly for the wedging of a human body. But it must be hard; if I could not go on, could I go back? The climber has his lesser Rubicons. I knew that infatuation was upon me; that I could not break this spell of movement, of tense wonder at my physical doing. I must go on, to watch body and mind working in their own right together. Now in self-defence I must give of the best: a poor kind of best, perhaps, if you could catalogue 'bests', but one that would satisfy me for a day. The crack ahead must be a struggle; again, could I get down, was I doomed to crouch like a sheep stranded on its tuft, waiting till I starve or fall? And would it not be a pity so to fall, to end in a moment this bundle of nerve and muscle, of action begun and hope for things incomplete?

I wrestled hotly to the top of the Curving Crack, in a fear and a sure vowing that I could never be guilty of the like rashness again. On the grass above, I lay in the sun. I had done – what? I had done something that only I could tell. Something foolish, something that I must not repeat, but something that I felt still to have been 'worth' the doing. And I could no more simplify the climb into an idiocy than into a conquest; there was more to it than that, as there must be more to any hard effort in which mind and body have combined to give. And yet if it must be set down as the one or the other, idiocy it certainly had been, and conquest never. I had by no fragment, other than the trampled grass or displaced chockstone, altered the life of that cliff. I had been allowed to scramble, a short and precarious hour, over its bare rock. I had no more conquered it than the Lilliputians conquered Gulliver, when they first walked across his chest.

from MOUNTAINS AND MEN *1947*

Three Beginnings

1. JEFF SCHWENN

1970

My father yells at me, "Stay off of those rocks!"

My mother tells me to be careful and that she doesn't want to have to worry, as I head out the door. I tell her that I won't be climbing and that I am just going to take pictures of the other guys. Kris Koprowski, Pete Tovani and I scale a 30ft. wall and christen ourselves the Armadillos.

"Don't worry. I will."

I head out of the door up to Flagstaff Mountain and climb Cookie Jar. I jam up a crack and learn technique . . . through trial and error . . . all of it error . . . dangling. Balancing on friction . . . and lunging. I haul myself up a two-foot overhang. An asthmatic rock rat with chalked lips like a clown, scarred hands, sewing-machine knees . . . (cough). When my asthma gets bad I have to haul to the hospital and get adrenalin shots to help me breathe. There is no danger of my getting a severe attack while on the rocks, because when I am climbing, I produce all the adrenalin I need.

1972

It takes a letter, a phone call, and searching him out, but I meet and go climbing with Pat Ament. He climbs with style and control, never makes a mistake. He expects me to do the same. He coaches me and criticises me when I blunder.

"Looks like it might clear up to our knees," he says, staring upward and disappearing into a cloud.

Before meeting Pat, I hear that he is egotistical. After getting to know him, however, I find out – that he is. But, what is wrong with someone realising he is good at something? Pat has put a lot of work into climbing and has earned the right to think he's great.

T2 (Tower 2) is more than just a climb. It is a process of psyching-up and psyching-up again, of overcoming doubts, and pushing. It involves teamwork and trust. Pat weighs twice what I do, but he trusts me to belay. I trust him not to fall. T2 is 700ft., not counting its zig-zags. From the hike up, the first lead looks blank. A few small flakes and fist-sized ledges are visible from the start. The first 15ft. are an overhang, then it eases off to vertical. A bolt protects the overhang. Pat boosts me up to clip into the bolt for him.

"I'm not proud," he says.

With his rope through the bolt and me on belay, Pat wolfs it in like food and works out and upward. He reaches a foothold, stops and rests, claims his arms are numb. How am I supposed to do it? With asthma.

It is lucky for me when I meet Ament. He is looking for climbing partners and has maybe fifty routes he says he would like to do with me. They are routes he has climbed before and wants to do again. The first route is called Cozyhang, a 200ft. climb on the Dome in Boulder Canyon which I've looked at in awe for two years. The next climb, Evening Stroll, is harder, and then the Brick Wall is twice as hard. I can see I'm in for it. But before I know it, I am doing the Grand Giraffe (an epic), the West Buttress of the Bastille, and the Yellow Spur — three of the best routes in Eldorado Canyon, all rated 5.9 (impossible). Pat talks me up them. I also wriggle up the Umph Slot (5.10), but it isn't really 5.10, because I am able to squeeze through it and Pat has to struggle on the outside.

Three months goes fast when you climb every day and train and get up so many different routes that your brain gets rocky. The most beautiful of all the climbs, the Yellow Spur, is Pat's favourite. We are in our primes on it.

Nobody is happier than Pat when he is on the walls. The route is 600ft. long and exposed. You look between your legs to the tops of the trees and hold on harder than you have to. The summit is a pin-point at the end of a knife-edge ridge and you can see the snow-covered peaks of the high country to the west, the plains to the east, Boulder to the north. A freight train goes through a tunnel in a mountainside to the south. It is warm and a perfect day, and I am feeling happy with myself for sticking it out. I think about Armadillos and laugh. But I better not blow my own head up. Might end up like Ament. He tells me he's going to write a book: "How to win friends and influence people." I thank God for

Ament's influence when I am rappelling off the Maiden and am so scared I almost choke.

T2 is the climax to a wild summer that I never thought would happen. Hope I can make it.

Pat yells, "Off belay. Come on up."

I am able to get past the bolt and up the pitch. The first lead is the hardest of the climb and makes me feel good. The next two pitches seem easy. The fourth lead is long—longer than the first lead and about as hard (5.9−; the first is 5.9+). A yellow wall rises vertically above a grassy ledge called 'The Meadow'. The wall is pierced by a single crack—for fingertips. To reach the bottom of the crack, we climb an inside corner and make a delicate balance traverse left across a blank, 15ft. face. I can tell when Pat is chalking up. Little sprinkles of white powder float down past me. It's snowing. At the end of the fourth pitch, the clouds move in for real and Pat asks me if we should rappel off. No way. I'm not going down after doing the hardest pitches. I tell Pat to relax. His hands are trembling (that's why he uses so much chalk).

My parents like Pat. They have accepted climbing. I have Pat to thank. At first, they wonder about him. He's different, kind of strange, they think. He shows us his climbing slides, plays us a tape of ten songs he has written (a troubadour by trade), and shows us a movie on climbing that he has made. He takes my parents bouldering, goes water skiing and plays chess with me, eats dinner with us every night for two weeks. . . I beat him at chess 24 games to 17. He admits there's bound to be something I'm better at! He takes my parents with us to watch us climb and proves to them that it can be done safely.

He leads the fifth pitch—a long, slippery ramp—and belays below an overhang which is the sixth pitch. The overhang is red and rotten, and we climb with care. Pat lies on a ledge to make a stomach-ache go away. The sun comes through a break in the clouds. We move.

Pat babbles after the last pitch, "Hi. I know my A B C's."

We sit for a while enjoying the scenery, eat some rolls and two oranges, sip water. Some ants crawl around on us. We coil the ropes, shake hands, and hike off.

As fall arrives, several of my friends begin to feel and demonstrate a kind of resentment towards me. Maybe they think I have abandoned them for fame and fortune. Ament is like the Bobby Fischer of climbing and can stir things up. But he is the best friend I have ever had. I forgive my other friends and hope they will be able to forgive me . . . someday. I wish each of them and all the Armadillos could do T2 with Pat. In the end, they might not even be satisfied, but, for sure, they would breathe easier.

2. GWEN MOFFAT

The day after we did the Ordinary we went to Tryfan. I liked the look of the big grey buttress running down towards the lake — it was more mountain-like than the Slabs — and as soon as I was off the ground and starting up the Direct, I knew that this was what I had been waiting for. It was different from yesterday's uneventful progress; this was a series of strange and delightful movements — coming round corners on to unexpected slabs, long sideways strides up little walls, pleasing pulls on the arms using the strength in one's shoulders — and all the time the ground dropping away, a hundred feet, two hundred, and then — nothing, and we were climbing in the cloud. I couldn't see Tom, the rope ran up the rocks and disappeared into the mist.

I loved everything about the Milestone Direct. I don't think I realised that it was wet and cold (for the thaw had set in and the climb streamed with water); I loved the feel of the rock under my hands, rough and satisfying; I loved using the strength of my body to haul myself out of the cracks and chimneys (I had yet to learn that climbing is mostly balance); above all, I loved the intimate feeling of shared adventure between the two of us, alone on a big mountain.

3. DENNIS GRAY

I ran as fast as I could up the steep hill road, arriving breathless at the Cow and Calf; after a rest I began to search for my companions. At the side of the rocks furthest from Ilkley is Hangingstones Quarry, much frequented by rock-climbers, and into this I wandered in my search. There was no sign of the scouts, but a group of climbers stood gazing intently up at the opposite quarry wall. Most small boys are inquisitive and I was no exception. Clutching my bottle of lemonade, haversack on back, I nervously edged up to the crowd to see what held their attention.

A tall, athletic, white-haired man was balanced on what appeared to me a vertical holdless face. Nonchalantly he pulled a handkerchief out of his trouser pocket and blew his nose, to the delight of the watching climbers, and reminded me of a stage acrobat. He began to move upwards, and this was somehow immediately different from a stage show; his agility, grace of movement, control and, above all, the setting high above ground, with no apparent safety devices, sent a thrill through my young body such as I had never before experienced. I had read about mountain climbing but my reaction hitherto had been indifference. One of the group whispered to a newcomer: "It's Dolphin!" as if this would immediately make clear why they were watching. The knot of climbers murmured their approval as the white-haired man reached the top of the rock face, and from the efforts of another of them to follow on a rope thrown down to him, it was obvious that Dolphin must be a gifted climber. The face was only 40ft. high but to me it could have been three times that height. I forgot all about my hopes of meeting my fellow scouts and sat watching for hours. Always Dolphin was the most impressive and I gazed in wonder as he moved up vertical walls and fissures with speed and ease; his mastery held me spellbound. Then suddenly I saw him and some others changing into running shorts, replacing nailed boots with gym shoes, parachute jackets with vests, and before I realised what they were at they had disappeared onto Ilkley Moor.

Although shy, I ventured to ask one of the remaining climbers a few questions about his sport and in particular about the man who had impressed me so much. Good-naturedly he explained some of the techniques involved in rock climbing and told me that I had been watching "Arthur Dolphin, the best rock climber in the area." I thanked my informant, looked around once more for the Woodhouse scouts, then set out across the moor to find my way to Guiseley and a bus home. Walking along I suddenly startled myself with the idea: "I would become a climber like Arthur Dolphin." Up to that moment my ambition, like that of every other small boy at Quarry Mount School, had been to become a cricketer and play for Yorkshire; this was now relegated to second place in my future hopes. My next realisation was equally disturbing — I didn't care about missing the Woodhouse scouts; the unexpected revelation of the sport of climbing had been worth my trouble.

from SWARAMANDAL *1973,* SPACE BELOW MY FEET *1961*
and ROPE BOY *1970*

PART 2

New Found Lands

Generally speaking, the great pioneers of mountaineering have not been the most assiduous of men in recording their exploits, or writing in any way about their driving obsession to break new ground in the mountains. It seems scarcely fair to criticise them for this. We don't require, for example, that Geoffrey Boycott or Vivian Richards should be able to brilliantly re-create the making of their every run. So why expect high literary achievement from mountaineers?

There is in fact occasion for surprise and gratitude that in climbing so many vivid and exciting narratives of first ascents do exist, some of which this section collects together.

They range from Raymond Greene's model expedition account, where he takes us from 100 miles' distance to the summit of Kamet in two and a half pages, to Mick Fowler's terror-inducing eccentricities on the North Cornish sea-cliffs. We end with one of the oddest ascents of all — a climb which never made it beyond the conceptual stage, for all the bright detail of its recall.

Kamet Seen and Conquered

RAYMOND GREENE

The first time we saw Kamet it was a hundred miles away. It was very early in the morning and we were asleep on a verandah at Ranikhet, a little town in the foothills of the Himalayas. Frank Smythe saw it first and woke us. Without getting out of bed we could see a mist beyond the garden. The mist was green with the filtered light of the forests in the valley below. Then came ridge after ridge of rolling pine-covered hills, and at last, apparently hung high in the blue sky above them, the edge of a silver saw. One tooth was bigger than the others – that was Kamet.

We didn't see it again for weeks, because it was always hidden by nearer mountains. Those weeks were filled with delightful wandering through valleys thick with flowers; climbing over high grassy downs and barren ridges; and clambering along the cliffs of deep ravines.

There were nights when our small green tents were pitched in meadows of purple iris, and others when the wind tried to blow them from narrow platforms cut in the hard snow of high mountainsides – until, where the narrow path we had followed turns suddenly northwards and upwards over the edge of India into Tibet, we saw our mountain again. It looked rather forbidding at close quarters, towering nearly 10,000ft. above our heads. On the left a precipice fell very steeply from the summit ridge – an obviously unclimbable place – and on the right the face was covered with a glistening surface of ice up which it would be necessary to cut steps laboriously for days, work too hard at that height where the thinness of the air makes every movement difficult. But between the two there lay steep snow slopes which looked possible. They fell away to a snowy col where a camp could be pitched in a position free from the fear of avalanches. We called it Meade's Col.

The way to the col was guarded by a wall of rock and ice a thousand feet high. It took us several days to find a way up and four camps were pitched between our base and our last camp on the col. As you climb higher, the air grows steadily thinner and your breathing gets faster and more difficult, but you can get used to this by taking time, climbing only about 1,000ft. in a day and then pitching camp and waiting till you have got used to the new altitude. At first the smallest movement makes you exhausted and breathless. It's an effort to do up a bootlace or turn over in your sleeping bag. But gradually strength returns and the next day another 1,000ft. can be climbed almost as easily as the last.

At the camp on the col there was not room for the whole party, so while Smythe, Shipton, Holdsworth and Lewa our sirdar made their successful attempt, we others watched them from the camp below. When our turn came, Beauman, who should have been our leader, was too mountain-sick to start, but Birnie and Kesar Singh, our best porter, and I left the camp at 6.45, as soon as the sun had thawed our frozen tents, and began the slow trudge towards the summit. At this height, 23,000ft. you start tired out. Every step was an effort, and between each step we had to pause for two complete breaths, but we didn't stop, for fear of being unable to start again. So for three hours we toiled slowly upwards – step, breathe, breathe again, step, breathe, breathe again – keeping the rhythm going steadily. The work, of course, falls chiefly on the leader who has to make the steps in the snow, and after three hours I was done. Birnie took the lead, but somehow I couldn't adjust my rhythm to his. I felt sick and exhausted. I decided to stay where I was, and sent on the other two without me.

It was a sunny, windless morning. I took off the climbing rope and lay down in the snow and basked happily. White snowfields and red precipices stretched far away until they merged into the brown upland of Tibet. 250 miles away, the Karakoram mountains lay on the horizon. Looking almost as far away, the little green tents of home were clustered at my feet. I felt happy and comfortable, and I went to sleep.

An hour later I woke up feeling very energetic. The top of the mountain looked very near and glistened invitingly in the sunshine. I told myself that it was too late to make the summit and that I would go on just a little way and meet the others on their return journey. In a little tangle of crevasses I lost their tracks, and the shape of the mountain hid them from view, but I kept near the edge of the great eastern precipice and made good progress.

Three hours passed. Now the slope was steeper, and I had no idea where my companions were. Some 300ft. above me was a white ridge in full sunshine. I thought if I could get this far I would be able to see the top and relieve what was beginning to be a gnawing anxiety for their safety. The way became excessively steep, and the snow dangerous, a shifting powder a few inches deep on hard ice. Once the surface slipped, probably only a few inches but enough to alarm me. Here a serious slip would have meant a fall of some 7,000ft. down the eastern precipice. I felt quite confident about stopping myself, but the others were less experienced and my anxiety grew. I gave a shout and heard a cheerful and unintelligible noise above. Almost at the same moment I saw their tracks. I cut across to them and turned upwards again towards the ridge I had picked as my look-out.

Then suddenly my head rose above the ridge and my eyes, expecting a further snowfield and yet another ridge, saw for one moment nothing. Then casting them down, I saw a sea of white cloud stretching without interruption to the purple horizon. A few yards to my right lay the summit, and coming from it towards me Birnie and Kesar Singh.

from MOMENTS OF BEING *1974*

Day of the Fox

CHRIS BAXTER

This is a tale of intrigue, cunning, shady tactics, and the first ascent of an improbable new route.

The story really started some years ago when, seizing on the none-too-rare opportunity of finding Andrew Thomson partially inebriated, I persuaded him to reveal the whereabouts of a long-forgotten 'secret cliff' he'd unproductively visited years earlier.

Mike Stone and I don't waste time in these matters. We soon tracked down Thomson's cliff in the western Grampians [of Australia]. Two lines, in particular, stood out as being equal to almost any we'd seen. About 180ft. high and in the middle of the crag, they were separated by an impossible and unique silver-grey wall. Being uncommonly modest fellows we named our, or rather Thomson's, discovery 'Mt. Fox'; after two of the oldest and craftiest in the game.

Closer inspection revealed one of the two lines to be choked with earth and grass and the other some grades harder than we cared to contemplate. We then set to work to do the few other lines on this compact little cliff.

Eventually the left-hand one of the two lines was thoroughly cleaned, left for a winter to be washed out, and then battled up over two gruelling days to produce Foxfire (21).

Knowing the right-hand line to be 'beyond the bumbly threshold' we sought to enlist the assistance of one younger, more energetic, more stupid and, above all, more proficient in such matters than ourselves. (A cynic might observe that any climber in the land would qualify on at least three of those counts!) Mike Law ('Claw') seemed the logical choice. Besides, he was dragging us through so many karabiners at Mt. Arapiles on an extended visit there that we wanted the opportunity of watching him suffer for a change.

Even Claw's stubbly orange jaw was seen to slacken a couple of degrees when he was confronted with the most leaning off-width of his experience. To cut a long story short, he failed miserably despite the adoption of shameful ethics; not the least of them being the old foxes forming a human pyramid and using a massive stick to place the first runner for him above the Grade 24 start.

During one of his many retreats to the ground I drew Claw's attention, largely in jest, to a tenuous line of flakes running out one third of the way up the great wall between the two lines.

"It might be impossible," retorted the face-climbing king.

Later that day when I was fulfilling my elected task of abseiling down the off-width to retrieve gear (mine, of course!) I had a good look across the wall. It looked ever so remotely possible and, what was worse, it looked like an old fox might just be able to grovel up it. I shared my secret later with Mike Stone who boggled.

Meanwhile Claw psyched himself up and returned to lead a fearsome little trio up his dreaded off-width to produce Leaner (24) which mysteriously sprouted a bolt in the middle of the crux.

This threesome, Law, Child and Carrigan, has eyes and, above all, ability so we were immediately galvanised into action. At first opportunity we returned and strategically placed protection bolts by abseil on the mind-enfeebling, 180ft. wall. There were two main problems: first, it's obvious and sustained difficulties and, second, the fact that we'd taken Rick White in on the day of the 'dentistry'. Now Rick is a good friend of ours, but has not yet learned the fox-like trait of absolute silence in the face of prying questions from those younger and more devious than himself. It was all very well for him — being a jammer from way back; he had no desire to get on to the wall.

For (im)moral support we let Dave Gairns in on our little secret, swore him to silence and immediately embarked on a training programme.

The first attempt, just before last winter, was little more than a cold and nervous foray to the edge of beyond. Jamming like a man possessed I was quickly up the viciously overhanging crack which marks the start of the one possible weakness we could detect on the wall. Above lay 'the flakes' and, miles up, above them, the first bolt.

The flakes offered me halting progress on side-pulls and lay-aways of surprisingly generous dimensions but with protection that was difficult to arrange.

It seemed like a week had passed before I could stand beside the first bolt runner. The moves up left to the next one were few and relatively easy but there the flakes ended abruptly. Perhaps 40ft. of ripples led up steeply left across to Foxfire. I couldn't see one positive hold worthy of the name. Leaving that bolt for such sustained smoothness was out of the question. I lowered off. The other two came up in turn but arrived at the same conclusion as hastily as I had done.

After a depressing winter we took up climbing again and adopted a vigorous training schedule which merely served to discourage us.

Life for me was made more difficult during this period due to the fact that every time Claw or one of his mates arrived at the door I had to quickly hide my photograph album containing pictures of the wall in my underpants drawer! Meanwhile the Leaner team visited the 'Banana republic'. It was to be some time before the significance of that visit dawned on us.

Each time I ran into Child, Carrigan or Law the questioning about 'the wall' became more intense. Then one night, plying Kim

Carrigan with wine, I extracted from him the rather sordid tale of how Rick had spilled the beans during yet another drinking bout.

I became a veritable Blondin walking a diplomatic tight-rope. On one hand giving the impression that the wall was 'reserved' and that we were training up for it, but on the other making it clear that it wasn't really worth thinking about as it was so unlikely to be climbable: a somewhat ambivalent position! One thing was certain, 'the ferrets' wouldn't continue their uncommon reserve indefinitely.

Finally, one hot December Sunday our little group assembled beneath the wall. Chalk and cameras were more in evidence than courage. Whereas the second pitch contained an obvious blank section it was clear that the first pitch would involve the real technical and mental problems. I offered to lead off, both surprising and relieving the others. What they didn't know was that for weeks that pitch had been costing me sleep and I didn't think I could second it after watching a leader on it.

Mike Stone later commented that he'd gone to Mt. Fox expecting merely to have another play around beside the second bolt. He also said that when he saw the way I got back up to it he was quite sure he was right. If I'd known his thoughts I might have been inclined to agree.

Things didn't look much better than on my last visit to the second bolt. But this time I slipped my mind into 'positive' and started 'dancing across the silver screen' in a little white cloud.

Two moves from the beckoning line of Foxfire, where I knew I could set up a semi-hanging belay, an error caused me to 'barn-door' off the wall. But more by luck than good management I was able to retain contact and arrive at the belay, my chest swollen like a pigeon's.

Being older and craftier than Dave, Mike came up next, belayed from behind. When Dave came up, however, we left a krab on the first bolt and Francine belayed him from behind to avoid the possibility of a big swing.

Traversing back right on to the face Mike led up into the low-angle section of the wall. In the middle of the smoothest part he clipped the bolt I'd placed and made short work of the thin moves immediately above. Dave raved at what he could see from his little perch. Following this remarkable pitch was indeed a treat.

There was no problem about agreeing on a name for our new route, we had referred to it for months as Twentieth Century Fox.

from ROCK 2 *1981*

Botterill's Slab

FRED BOTTERILL

At the foot of the climb we roped up and noticed that the time was 12.15 p.m. The going, over grass ledges, was found fairly easy, until we reached the narrow crack which may be seen from the Progress. The bottom of this was entirely hidden by grass and earth, which when vigorously attacked with the pick, was dislodged in such quantities as to alarm a party coming over Hollow Stones. The removal of some boulders uncovered a large sloping slab which afforded excellent hand and foot holds and enabled the leader to proceed about 15ft. up the narrow crack. Clearly no one had been here before, so we made greater efforts to advance; it was absolutely impossible to do so, however, in the crack, it being only 6 inches wide and about 12 inches deep, and the sides almost as smooth as the inside of a teacup. The leader reluctantly descended to the afore-mentioned slab and examined the projecting face of the crack, which leans away towards Scafell Pike at about the same angle as the crack we had ascended the day before. This seemed equally hopeless, the ledges being all inverted and the slabs too smooth to climb with safety. Traversing about 12ft. outwards to the edge formed by one side of the crack and the face of the crags, I saw that with care we could advance some distance up this nose. Clearing away the moss from little cracks here and there I managed to climb slowly upwards for about 60ft. The holds then dwindled down to little more than finger-end cracks. I looked about me and saw, some 12ft. higher, a little nest about a foot square covered with dried grass. Eight feet higher still was another nest and a traverse leading back to where the crack opened into a respectable chimney. If I could only reach hold of that first nest what remained would be comparatively easy. It seemed to be a more difficult thing than I had ever done but I was anxious to tackle it. Not wishing to part with the axe I seized it between my teeth and with my fingers in the best available cracks I advanced. I cannot tell with certainty how many holds there were; but I distinctly remember that when within 2ft. of the nest I had a good hold with my right hand on the face, and so ventured with my left to tear away the dried grass on the nest. However, the grass removed from the ledge, a nice little resting place was exposed – painfully small, but level and quite safe. I scrambled onto it, but on account of the weight of the rope behind me, it was only with great care and some difficulty that I was able to turn round. At last I could sit down on the nest and look around me.

The view was glorious. I could see Scafell Pike and a party round the cairn. Far below was another group intent on watching our movements, a lady being amongst the party. I once read in a book on etiquette that a gentleman in whatever situation of life should never forget his manners towards the other sex, so I raised my hat, though I wondered if the author had ever dreamed of a situation like mine. I now discovered that our 80ft. of rope had quite run out and that my companions had already attached an additional 60ft. Further, I began to wonder what had become of my axe, and concluded I must unthinkingly have placed it somewhere lower down. There it was, stuck in a little crack about 5ft. below me. Not knowing what was yet to come I felt I must recover it, so I lowered myself until I could reach it with my foot. I succeeded in balancing it on my boot, but in bringing it up it slipped and clattering on the rocks for a few feet took a final leap and stuck point downwards in the Rake's Progress. Standing up again I recommenced the ascent and climbed on to the second nest *à cheval*, from where, after a brief rest, I began the traverse back to the crack. This was sensational but perfectly safe. As usual I started with the wrong foot, and after taking two steps was obliged to go back. The next time I started with the left foot, then came the right, again the left, and lastly a long stride with the right brought me into the chimney. The performance was what might have been called a *pas de quatre*, Complimentary sounds came from my companions below, but without stopping to acknowledge these I pulled myself up 10ft. higher on to a good grass-covered ledge to the right of the crack, smaller but very similar to the Tennis Court Ledge of Moss Ghyll.

"How is it now?" my companions enquired. "Excellent," I replied, "a good belaying pin and just room for three. Do you feel like following?" Without answering me the second man commenced the traverse to the chimney edge while I carefully belayed the rope. Up he came in splendid style and without stopping, taking only a quarter of the time it had taken me. He then untied and we threw down the 140ft. of rope to our third, who soon joined us. We hailed a climbing friend who was watching from the Progress and invited him to join us, but he very generously refused and said he would hover near lest we might not be able to advance further and so require the aid of a rope from above. We next christened our berth 'Coffin Ledge', built a cairn on it and left our names on a card.

Starting off again a long stride with the left foot took the leader back into the crack, and a stiff climb of 20 to 30ft. landed us all into an extraordinary chimney, which though only wide enough to comfortably admit the body sideways ran right into the crag for about 15ft. Like the crack below it leaned to the left at an angle of 70° or so. About 25ft. up, chock-stones and debris formed a roof, and suspended in the middle, some 6ft. below it, were three more chock-stones. When the second man had joined me he exclaimed with astonishment: "What a place! How can we get out?" "Wait a bit," I answered, although I could not then see a way. However, I went as far as I could into the crack and with restricted use of back and knee climbed upwards until the level of the suspended chock-stones was reached; from there a narrow ledge rendered these easily accessible. They were securely wedged and safe to stand upon. The ledge continued along out of the crack until the most outward chock-stone of the roof was within reach. This I seized with both hands, and a steady pull upwards landed me into the Puttrell Chimney of the Keswick Brothers' Climb.

from THE YORKSHIRE RAMBLERS' JOURNAL *1903*

Robbins — On the Plank

PAT AMENT

Two of us stroll up the talus toward the base of an obscure vertical wall; my partner, that brown red-breasted bird of the thrush family — with his stares of coldness to conceal warmth. There is a great discharge of silence which follows a deep cry from my confused stomach. He is noticing everything, the talus stones and ferns, the Longs Peak tundra, Columbines, delicate floral ornamentations, high grasses, and lichen gardens, finding life in even the pores of the granite. Snowfields and nearby Chasm Lake are blinding.

I lead upward on grey rock, ascending with small maraca equipment sounds and tambourine jingles. With a gleam of suggestion reflecting out of Royal's strapped-on glasses, with me checking my grammar, feeling propelled upward in part by his provoking aura below, with sun spilling over him like white water. . ... If he hadn't been a climber he might have lived instead as a mutate from the atomic future, an evil-bearded Cortez of outer solar travel. He stands, a foot forward, his upper half almost leaning backward in defiance, like a fencer. He carries enough passion to subtly electrocute a boulder.

Solid stone, warmth of day, light angling inward from an unobstructed sun, wind blowing, everything steep, curious as it is disorienting. I lead, hanging from pitons which I hope will hold in peculiar cracks which widen inside. Soon I'm on a mossy stance about 100ft. up.

Brown long-sleeve shirt, short-rimmed hat, dark knickers, red knee-socks, boots called Spiders, a carefully combed madness and costume but gentle frowzy sneer, Royal wings up the pitch like a featherweight, and with little conversation ascends 90ft. directly overhead, dangling from wizard blades, tiny hooks, rurps and Chouinard-forged canary toys which support body weight, nothing less, nothing more, because they merely sit, half placed where they should be wholly wedged, balancing where they should be resting. The leader's rope stretches outward through a network of karabiners, whereas the haul line hangs freely away from the wall to indicate perpendicular. In Royal a dangerous little eye traverse is followed by an actual ascent exactly that direction, using small nested pitons tied off at the tips. The friend up there is following an innate integrity which translates into purity of line, leading us where nothing looks to be there to climb. Between us is a science-like stream of mechanical coordinations, with the rope as a medium.

To my astonishment — that quality of amazement which makes the mind gaze — Royal yawns, telling me he's off belay, going to hang right there from a couple of those things, and going to bring me up and see if all will hold so that I can collect and bring him some gear and then belay from there as he leads on. There is too much of life in such a setting for it not to be a story to tell. Here, where all of matter seems to be living, then even the smallest flake has a voice.

I hover in comradeship with a mythical Yosemite climber who is meeting with me in his journey through Colorado and who climbs now under the guise of acclimatisation for a Diamond ascent tomorrow with Layton Kor. It is a special experience to be with this unyielding, competitive form — a man so largely self-created. His is an undeniable flair — and the legends are not the man, only the roaring edges of his sea, while somewhere farther out, far away, there is a great calm. The calm is shattered by a karabiner, by the profundity of a beautiful muted clip. For a few minutes we are personalities without noise, far above a mysterious talus oblivion. A small stone falls, taking seconds to disclose the distance. In a tender way Royal is drifting, looking downward, possibly thinking of his wife Liz.

As I follow the pitch and Royal belays, he pulls from shirt pocket a tiny notepad and pen and calmly records information about the pitch: length of lead, number of pitons, weather, partner. What has he said of me? Royal is then snapping photos, one of me framed between his legs. Then he is a ghostly corona, hanging still like a chairman with a gavel in a cool phantasm. I arrive at the nebulous situation, a right Spider at my head, Royal's toe against the wall, heel in a sling. Here an unbelievable piton has its eye jammed, blade down and not touching rock. I pull up on this piton with all my weight, then notice I can lift it out with a finger. Robbins, face sunburnt. He is covered by a dry perfumed dust like frankincense. He is like a nervous chess piece exposed in the centre of the board. He castles away into a small corner above, leaving the rook in the open place.

Unexpectedly, as he glances down, our eyes meet, two explosions behind blank despondency. These are rurps, one above the other, us courting a steep flat surface below a roof and denying rescue of ourselves by rappel. All of it is aid. We would free climb if there were holds. Eventually, Royal is going free up a finger crack, building up some noticeable space between him and his last aid point – a hook that swings where it hangs. Nothing between the hook and me looks as though it should stop a fall. Much higher he finds a foothold for belaying and anchors to a solid crack.

I follow the pitch, and I rest with my chin for a second on the crook of the hook. I, the tyro, am staring into the filaments of whiskers. Royal, with eminent low voice, says only "Slack," or "OK," if not a witticism barely audible or a pun. With that almost snarl for a smile, he compliments me, saying, "Good boy," which pricks up my ears.

I climb the finger crack above that and try to be smooth, measuring myself alongside Robbins. I am impetuous to make a comparison, but that's how I am at about fifteen years old and Royal on toward thirty. Royal, so irreverently disagreeable, but there are methods to his manners. In truth, he is a bit shy, neither humble nor self-adoring. Philosophical, brilliant, defensive, cut-throat, he is one of the unique ones. I am asked to go on an errand to find the top. Royal, throwing a gear sling onto my shoulder and me feeling the knighthood, I am leading. I must work for what I achieve, Royal inspiring with a clannish omniscience. Soon the top is obtainable by a short interweaving, a free wall causing at one move a near cramp in a leg for us both.

We stand still, breathing hard and thinking momentarily about his climb, a place we went together out by an edge of an obscure darkening buttress. The summit is a high place and a relatively unspectacular pile of huge boulders. It is our first climb together, a new route. The Gang Plank, Royal calls it, for it hangs off the side of the Ship's Prow formation. We coil ropes and stumble down the long tapering deck side of the rock toward Chasm Lake and then beyond to a rock cabin for shelter. The Diamond Wall, so much larger than what we have done, looms darkly far above. A marmot sniffs Royal from a distance. They turn up their noses at one another . . . and are both happy.

from CLIMBING 59 *1980*

Asgard Outing

PAUL NUNN

Dennis, and airy swinging prusiks on lightly frozen ropes for us. of Peterhead Prison, ran quickly through slides gathered during long years as a missionary on Baffin Island. It was a fairy-tale country, remote, ice-bound in half-light for much of the year. The long fjords sliced into granite mountains of unrelenting compactness, while they in turn were half enveloped in great ice mushrooms, ice caps which dominate the geography of the area, make its weather, and spill over the top of many a Yosemite-style wall. I wanted to go.

A 'phone call in May 1972 settled it. Doug Scott, Dennis Hennek from California, Tut Braithwaite and myself were to go. It seemed an excellent scheme, for I had always thought Eric Shipton ought to be right: that little expeditions are more likely to be good expeditions, even at their most extended; and I could think of few places more suitable than Baffin for such an approach. Anyway, the battle of Everest seemed to me to have undermined the very term 'expedition', which now implies multiple forms of exploitation and rigid organisation for which the only compensation for many individual climbers is pretentiousness. The alienation of heart, combined with the extreme graft involved, seems to me to be the complete antithesis of what mountaineering is all about. A small group of climbers, friendly, intimate, motivated but not utterly achievement-orientated, promised to get away from all that.

I was a late arrival. Doug had got some money from the Mount Everest Foundation and Dennis had meticulously ordered food, both in the USA and from the Bay Trading Co. in Baffin; he had also organised most of the equipment. There were no strings: the plane left in a couple of weeks.

We assembled in Hudson Heights near Montreal, where Mrs P. Baird entertained us royally. Dennis proved to be anything but the lean, rock-drilling technocrat that I had half expected. Instead he was a muscular, blond, fun-and-pleasure-loving character who seemed to enjoy the occasional discipline of climbing, and who was prepared to take great pains to do it well. Within a few hours we seemed like a team.

On July 3, we flew to Pangnirtung, a dusty Eskimo settlement across the Cumberland Sound. Blue skies, after a murky journey, boded well.

From the beginning there was a sense of unreality in this land of myth and magic enjoying its brief summer. On July 4, Jok Polliollok and another Eskimo took us by sledge and skiddoo twenty miles down the fjord ice towards the mountains. There was a gala atmosphere, even when a sledge broke under the weight of five people and a boat. The Eskimos played at shooting imaginary seals and we golloped food and brews together when we arrived under the great face of Mt. Overlord. It was a light-hearted and fortunate start, for the sea-ice was late, and we were saved at least two days.

Then we conned one another. None of us had even carried such monstrous loads as we assembled. Food for nearly three weeks, tents, big-wall gear, fuel: the pack frames bent and creaked under the load, and so did we. Somehow, tottering upright, we trekked off from the dump at the fjord head into Weasel Valley's pebble flats. After two days of wandering up these flats and through moraines which disappeared into soaring granite walls and a grey snow-laden sky, we camped to rest for a day by the frozen waste of Summit Lake.

Again the ice was useful. On consecutive days we tramped six miles over the lake-ice, taking half-loads to the Turner Glacier and a camp below Asgard. On July 9, we stamped out tent sites by a glacier lagoon. It was snowing quite heavily, but we were all pleased – the carry was over.

Snow shoes were essential to get far on the glaciers in 1972. Crevasses were deeply covered, making unroped wanderings hazardous, though we sometimes indulged ourselves. It froze for only a short time at night, leaving a weak crust. The camp was idyllic, on the snow at the junction of two glaciers, by the blue lake, with the plumb-vertical walls of Freyr Peak opposite and Asgard behind. Rocks trundled from an outlying minor summit, but we were adequately distant from their path. Moreover, we were well fed and well equipped, and on July 10 the weather began a lasting good spell.

Our first objective, the main cause of our weight crucifixion coming in, was the West Dihedral of Asgard. Doug and I broke a track on the 10th, and dug a trench up deep insecure snow on the lower slopes. The dihedral is a real siren, drawing the eye up its clean-cut features for over 1,500ft. On a sparkling morning, we snow-shoed over the light crust to the base of the face again. Cloud rolled in dazzling furls over the ice cap to the north. Doug and I carried gear, while Tut led up the initial 1,500ft. of snow and mixed ground. It was unsafe and avalanche-prone, with little security. A last lead of over 400ft. led to the dihedral base.

Doug set off up an iced chimney with Dennis seconding, while we cut a large platform. It seemed that the donkey-work was over. For today, tomorrow, maybe the day after, we would swing and dangle, hammer away, and sleep in our hammocks in the relative safety of the vertical. This opinion seemed confirmed when the 400ft. slope avalanched in a sea of slops, although it was modified by ice lumps falling from far above and blowing in a keen wind into the dihedral.

But our confidence was premature, however well-equipped physically and mentally we might have been. Apart from the cold on this side of the mountain, which could have been a problem in a really prolonged attack, the diedre was not a pegging fault but a closed granite joint with aberrant, unlinked cracks. Dennis found himself faced with a painful choice at 200ft. — the first of several long bolt ladders or nothing. The bolting seemed premature, and perhaps ultimately undesirable. In the early hours of July 12 we reached camp after about twenty hours' absence.

Snoozing re-appraisal led to a quick decision. Late on the 12th, Tut and Doug broke tracks to the North-East Ridge of Asgard North Peak. Next day, lightly equipped, we all set off in relentless sun. For me, personally, the route had immense appeal; it was a smooth pillar of slabby and near-perfect granite, about 3,500ft.

high from the glacier. It was to be an alpine-style push with no provision for stopping.

Doug and Dennis led through up the magnificent lower slabs, while for a time Tut and I suffered the divorcing experience of prussiking. Then, about mid-day, we led on. It was a flood of pleasure to me, with corners, jamming cracks, delicate slabs, and a gradual steepening of angle as the upper pillar came nearer. We stopped once for food, and then followed a crack system of escalating difficulty, deeply reminiscent of all the best alpine granite climbs I have experienced. We used few pegs, nut protection being usual. In the late evening, a cold mist flung a grey cloak over us. At midnight, after about ten hours of leading, Tut and I relegated ourselves to the rear for the headwall.

The red granite, compact but split by a crack system, reared up towards the summit. There were four hard pitches for Doug and Dennis, and airy swinging prusiks on lightly frozen ropes for us. Dennis did the all-star lead on a Curbar-style 140ft. crack. It took at least two hours of real struggle and was extremely difficult, especially coming as the penultimate pitch of a hard climb. Doug finished it off up a gritstone jamming crack at Hard VS, straight to the summit. During the sojourns we dozed in our duvets, waiting for the sun to re-appear. At 6 a.m. on July 14, we were on the table-top summit in brilliant sun.

The aftermath was deflating. The glacier lagoon had flooded and the tents were threatened if not awash, fifty-five miles out from Pang. Good weather has its costs. Attempts at a quick descent of the original route were defeated by obnoxious, deep, wet snow, which reduced us to a commando crawl, ludicrous and deadly serious as we sank into crevasses. It was easy to see how people fail to make it under such circumstances. Fortunately the lower glacier was better, and we reached the camp thirty-three hours after departure.

The blue tents were dry but afloat on the packed snow under them. With joyous, tired sploshings they were rescued, and re-erected uphill. Six more hours and they would have been drowned. Two-ton eyelids slumped to sleep, despite the relentless arctic light.

Two days later we began the tramp out. There was more to do, but we were tired and a little self-satisfied. We crossed a col below our route with 70lb sacks, and descended dreadful, deep powder on the Caribou Glacier at less than a mile an hour, tripping occasionally as the snowshoe tips crept under the crust, and finding difficulty in swimming out with the sacks pushing our faces into the morasse. After a snooze at Summit Lake, we continued down to camp in a fine spot below the 4,500ft. face of Thor.

With battered feet and still heavy loads our retreat became a ramble. Time was taken up with peering at flowers and wildlife, and snoozing and eating food remnants.

We took the best part of a week to cover the fifty miles or so to Pang. By then the mosquitoes were coming to life, the pack-ice was breaking rapidly, the arctic summer was weakening enough to allow a little night, the food was eaten and it was time to go.

We had no commitments, except to ourselves, and they were satisfied. Success was aided by fortuitous good weather and a late winter. Dennis's meticulous organisation, and especially the freeze-dried food, made the carry possible. Without air-drops or great expense, we got ourselves from Pang fjord head to Asgard, and back to Pang. We did a dream of a climb, and each led his quota. Almost all the climbing was Very Severe, or harder, so all our egos were satisfied. As an exercise in logistics, and as an intensely personal experience, the expedition was gratifyingly complete. Amazingly, it was a product of motivation which was less 'achievement' – or 'summit-orientated' than most such excursions. Perhaps therein lies its validation.

from MOUNTAIN 26 *1973*

Hetch Hetchy: First Impressions

GALEN ROWELL

For 60 million years the histories of Yosemite and Hetch Hetchy were as one. Both valleys were carved by glaciers at the same time in parallel river canyons. Both were discovered in the mid-nineteenth century by white men and were subsequently included in Yosemite National Park. For the last 10,000th of one percent of the time involved in their creation, their history has diverged – not by the hand of God, but rather by human destiny. Hetch Hetchy was damned and flooded. Almost sixty years have passed since the thirsty mouths of San Francisco became the executioners of its valley floor. It died quickly – a sudden if not merciful death by drowning. Yosemite's valley floor was saved for posterity, but is now dying a slow death by trampling and polluting. The only merciful death involved was that of John Muir, who gave his all to try to save Hetch Hetchy. He died in the same year that construction was begun on the dam. He never had to review his results.

At present Hetch Hetchy is just a reservoir. There are no campgrounds, no businesses, no boating, and the only access is by a winding dead end road. The few visitors to the area usually drive to the end of the road and possibly walk across the dam to gaze at the flooded valley before turning around to go back to the city, or to sardine themselves into Yosemite forty miles away.

While climbers made over 400 routes in Yosemite, no technical climbs were made in Hetch Hetchy. Climbers had told each other legends of half-submerged walls rising out of water and accessible only by boat. Boats are not allowed on the reservoir and swimming becomes rather more difficult when carrying many pounds of hardware.

With this quite dismal knowledge of Hetch Hetchy, Joe Faint and I sought to investigate Hetch Hetchy for ourselves. What we found exceeded our expectations. On the south side of the valley, true to legend, Kolana Rock rose directly out of the murky depths of the reservoir. On the north side was Muir's El Capitan counterpart, known locally as Wapama Rock and flanked by two beautiful waterfalls of Yosemite magnitude. Tueeulala Falls pours over the brow of the cliff and sifts through a 1,000ft. of air before gathering itself together again to cascade toward the reservoir. Wapama Falls consist of two separate falls in a deep and narrow chasm to the east of Wapama Rock. Their total drop is close to 1,500ft. and in volume they are a close second to Vernal and Nevada Falls in Yosemite. The face of Wapama Rock was of very special interest to us. Instead of disappearing into the water, it rose from a level rock bench about a hundred yards wide which continued from the base of the cliff almost all the way to the dam.

In the first days of Spring in 1969 we walked through a heavy thundershower to the base of the wall. We shot several photographs to help in route-finding and beat a hasty retreat back to the dam. It had taken us less than two hours, and even in the grey pallor, we had been impressed by the great beauty of old Hetch Hetchy. John Muir was certainly not exaggerating when he wrote of it rivalling Yosemite.

We had spotted a potential route up the middle of the South Face of Wapama Rock in the same relative position as the Salathé Wall on its Yosemite counterpart. The route would follow the right side of a slab system leading to a ledge about two-thirds of the way up the 1,300ft. face. Above the ledge the cracks were questionable and the angle very steep. In the middle of the thundershower a large part of the upper face was obviously quite dry.

In early April Joe and I drove to Hetch Hetchy, laden with equipment and prepared to spend two bivouacs if necessary. In the first light of dawn we shouldered packs and headed across the dam. Soon we were walking on the level bench, hewn by glaciers out of massive granite and still showing the striated sheen of the ancient polish as the morning sun glanced obliquely from its surface. Frequent cascades poured from the cliffs above, surging through the meadows and wildflowers which carpeted the bench like haphazard throw rugs. The only sign of man's presence on the scene was the thin line of a trail worming its way through the meadow, under the streams and over the undulating granite slabs. The shoreline was not visible unless one walked to the edge and looked purposely downward.

Soon we were hauling bags up a fourth class section at the base of the wall. I climbed an uneventful pitch which was mostly direct aid and sat on a ledge contemplating the wall above against our provisions as Joe cleaned the pitch on jumars. As I looked at the bulging upper headwall I had a sudden urge to recount the bolt supplies. Not finding them in the hauling bag, I yelled to Joe, "Where's the bolt kit? In the pack or in the hauling bag?"

"I didn't pack it. I thought you did!" came the reply.

And so ethics are born. We didn't have the time to siege-climb the wall and we were too lazy to go back for the bolts. Climbing in good style was no longer a matter of restraint or aesthetics. It was the only method of continuing. Joe was soon profiled above me in the morning sun as he ably led a jam crack and continued upward using aid. I cleaned the pitch and ended face to face with him on a small ledge. Not one to use unnecessary words, he beamed me a smile of negative pleasure, i.e. a feeling of relief and complacency generated by knowing someone else will be faced with a problem which very well might have been yours. A long steep jam crack rose above us. Luckily an inobvious crack afforded more adequate protection than Joe had first surmised, and the crack was climbed free with only a minimum of whimpering and thrutching.

Later in the day I watched Joe nail around a small overhang and head for a large alcove which appeared to be the only bivouac spot we could reach before dark. The big ledge was still several hundred feet above and the sun departs early in the beginning of April. As the sun disappeared, Joe yelled, "Off belay!"

I asked him if he was on the ledge and he replied, "There is no ledge; just a steep ramp."

I was beginning to become pessimistic. We had no bolts, hammocks or ledges and the night would be long and cold. Cleaning the pitch as fast as I could, I began to lead above Joe to look for a ledge. I saw one on the face far to my right but it was off route and would require climbing an improbable jam-crack and pendulum to reach. Time was the essence as minute by minute the light dwindled. Nailing higher and higher, I was getting nowhere quickly when I decided to take a chance and pendulum out of the large dihedral to which we were confined. Tension traversing 30ft. to the left, I peered around the corner at the open face and was quite relieved to see a ledge only a few feet above. It was 3ft. wide and seemed so sharply cut into the otherwise unbroken face that one might have suspected that a stone mason had had a part in its construction. After I reached the ledge, Joe prusiked up in the encroaching darkness and sleep came quickly to both of us.

It seemed as if only minutes had passed before the morning light awakened us and Joe went down to recover the iron from the last pitch. I lay alone on the ledge watching the sunrise change the murky shadows across the valley into bold relief. As I looked across at the steep cliffs, I thought to myself that this could just as easily be Yosemite as Hetch Hetchy. Upon looking down, I suddenly realised how different things were. I saw no roads, buildings, or campfire smoke. I heard no motors, shouts or horns honking. I only gazed at a large dark pool of water, rippling quietly in the respective location where thousands of people swarm in Yosemite. I tried to reassure my old beliefs by repeating to myself, "Hetch Hetchy was ruined; Yosemite Valley was saved. Hetch

Hetchy was ruined; Yosemite Valley. . ."

Somehow I just couldn't convince myself as I watched the yellow glow of the morning light creep down the walls and form rainbows in the spray of Wapama Falls. I remember thinking at the time how few areas as accessible as this had escaped the human flood. Reservoirs all over the nation echo with the roars of power boats and people flood the once timbered shores where the water can't reach. But Hetch Hetchy has no level shores. It is flanked by granite walls and man has yet to find a way to convert them into board feet, cubic feet, or legal tender.

My attention was soon returned to the wall where a single crack split the firm but slightly overhanging granite above us. We nailed this to a higher and larger ledge, but still we were not on the big ledge. From the ground only the eye of a climber would be able to spot the big ledge, and yet when we reached it, we were surprised to find it several 100ft. long and up to 20ft. wide. We walked to the east end of the ledge and began climbing the steep headwall. This was the bottom part of the section which had remained dry in the thundershower and we could certainly see why. We even worried about being able to rappel in case our lack of bolts forced us to descend. We spent half a day working through this section, often traversing and changing cracks. The crux of the headwall was an incipient crack which headed in just the proper direction to connect with a crack system leading to the summit. After 30ft. of progress, mostly of tied off pins, I fell and was held by a piton which looked worse than the one which came out. I decided that it was time for a pendulum and after several tries I reached a crack far to my left. From there an overhanging corner finally led into the cracks leading to the summit. Those were climbed free and included several classic jams and laybacks.

Once again the sun was setting but now we were on the summit to enjoy instead of fear the ending of the day. The urgency of the climb was gone, and the view was to be savoured and indelibly imprinted in our memories. We walked over the top of the rock to where the stream flowing over Tueeulala Fall crosses the granite slabs. We washed. We savoured. The wildness of the area was our reward. Nowhere was the hand of man visible. The day is long gone when only nature's grandest sights thrill the heart of man. Wilderness is such a rare commodity that any really untouched place is

per se beautiful. Leaving Hetch Hetchy we were thankful for the
experience just finished and for the discovery that Hetch Hetchy is
not a total ruin after all. The dam which had ruined it in comparison with other wilderness areas fifty years ago, has saved it from
being over-used. We were saddened by the realisation that the antithesis is also true: the ruins of fifty years ago look good today
because many remaining areas are being sadly trampled into high
altitude slums. How wonderful it must have been to see the snowy
Sierra from the coast and to walk through endless wild flowers
across the central valley . . . and to see Hetch Hetchy as John Muir
saw it . . . "standing waist deep in grass and flowers while the great
pines sway dreamily with scarcely perceptible motion. Looking
northward across the valley you see a plain, grey cliff rising
abruptly out of the gardens and groves to a height of 1,800ft., and
in front of it Tueelala's silvery scarf burning with irised
sunfire. . ."

from CLIMBING 1 *1970*

African Escapade

ERIC SHIPTON

Planning a climb is a fascinating occupation. In some respects it is
even more fun than the climb itself, though of course it would lose
most of its charm without the knowledge that the plan would be put
into operation. The imagination is free to wander over the entire
gigantic scene, to dance on the toes of fancy up sunlit rock and
shining silver crest, to shudder in warm security at precipitous icy
gullies and airy crags, to trace link by link the slender chain of
possibilities.

The triangular face between the two main ridges [of Mt. Kenya]
was guarded by a hanging glacier terrace, from which the risk of ice
avalanches precluded any prolonged operations on the steep
polished slopes below. The North-East Ridge was supported by two
massive buttresses, smooth and steep, and divided by a straight,
deep cleft. For all its forbidding grandeur the West Ridge seemed to
offer the best hope of success. It was very long and complicated

and there was much that we could not judge from a distance, many links that had to be taken for granted.

The first thing to do was to get a closer view of the lower part, which might give us an insight into the all-important time factor and the nature of the ice and snow and rock of which the ridge was built. So the next day we set out for the high saddle between the Petit Gendarme and Point Piggot.

We spent a long time cutting steps up the Joseph glacier to a steep snow and ice gully that led to the saddle. Here we had to negotiate a bergschrund. Above this a lot more step-cutting was required, and by the time we reached the saddle we were dismally conscious that we had undertaken a very tough proposition. Nor was the immediate prospect above us in any way reassuring. By now the upper part of the peak was hidden by cloud. The Petit Gendarme frowned down upon us like an ogre that resented our intrusion. It it had been his scalp that we were after we might still have been overawed, but he was only an incident on the great ridge, the first of a long series of obstacles. A direct assault seemed to be out of the question and we must outflank him. This we could only do by climbing diagonally up a very steep slope to the right. Whether this slope was composed of ice or snow we could not tell from where we stood. It was a matter of considerable importance, for if it were ice, cutting steps up it would involve a good day's work to reach the ridge behind the Petit Gendarme. Above and beyond we could see the vertical flanks of the Grand Gendarme thrusting up into the clouds.

We sat down on a rock shelf to reflect, our legs dangling over the Tyndall Glacier several hundred feet below. It was a grand view. Across the way was the great West Face of Batian, so close that we might have been hanging from a balloon before its ice-scarred ramparts. We were about level with the lower of the two hanging glacier terraces; the lace fringe of the upper terrace was just visible through the cloud. These monsters were silent now, which was a pity, for here we had front seats in the dress-circle from which such an avalanche display as we had seen from Two Tarn Col would have been a fine spectacle. To our right the ridge mounted in a series of spires towards Point Piggot, to our left, we averted our eyes; we had learnt as much of the West Ridge as we could digest in one lesson. The stage was set and tomorrow the chosen

How I hated Tilman in the early morning. Not only on that expedition, but through all the years we have been together. He never slept like an ordinary person. Whatever time we agreed to awake, long before that time (how long I never knew) he would slide from his sleeping bag and start stirring his silly porridge over the primus stove. I used gradually to become aware of this irritating noise and would bury my head in silent rage against the preposterous injustice of being woken half an hour too soon. When his filthy brew was ready he would say "Show a leg," or some such imbecile remark. In moments of triumph on the top of a peak I have gone so far as to admit that our presence there was due in large measure to this quality of Tilman's but in the dark hours before dawn such an admission of virtue in my companion has never touched the fringe of my consciousness*.

The next morning was no exception. I remembered that it was my birthday, which seemed to make matters worse. We issued from our lovely warm cave soon after 3 a.m., leaving Masede in full possession, and plodded slowly up the side of the valley in the bright moonlight.

I began to feel a bit more human when we reached the Joseph Glacier. We supplemented the light of the moon with that of a candle lantern and climbed rapidly. Our steps of the previous day, large and comfortable, were still intact. Hours of toil now sped beneath us with an effortless rhythm of hip and ankle joints, as we climbed towards the dawn. Daylight was flooding in upon us as we crossed the bergschrund. Halfway up the gully above, we branched to the left so as to reach the ridge beyond a small but difficult section east of the saddle. In this manoeuvre we were delayed by some difficult climbing on ice-covered rocks, but even so we reached the crest below the Petit Gendarme with the whole day before us. And what a day! Crisp, sparkling, intoxicating. I have never known more complete physical well-being. The western face of Batian caught the full light of the newly-risen sun, and every lovely detail of ice fretwork and powerful granite column was hard and clear.

Though what we could see of the West Ridge towering above us looked no less formidable than before, we were now in a very different frame of mind, and we paused barely a minute. But the

*Tilman describes the climb in *Snow on the Equator*.

slope under the Petit Gendarme soon began to exercise a sobering effect. It turned out to be composed of hard ice covered by a layer, not more than an inch or two thick, of frozen crystalline snow. It was exceedingly steep and ended below in a sheer drop to the Tyndall glacier. While we were both on the slope together a slip on the part of either of us would have been almost impossible to hold, since we were traversing diagonally across it. It was possible, by kicking small toeholds into the hard layer of snow and by sticking the blade of the axe in for a hand rail, to climb up and along the slope with reasonable security. But this security would only remain so long as the snow held firm. The slope was still in shadow, but an hour or so after the sun had climbed above Point Piggot the snow would begin to melt and would no longer offer any hold. The proper procedure would have been to cut steps through the snow into the ice below, but this would have taken nearly all day, and we were still at the very beginning of the climb. This is a common problem in mountaineering, and each case must be judged by the circumstances. We must have a line of retreat in the event of failure higher up, particularly as that event was very probable. Cutting steps down hill, besides being very slow and exhausting, is apt to be a hazardous business when prolonged for many hours on so exposed a slope and without any sort of anchorage. In this case I was fairly confident that we could climb over the top of the Petit Gendarme from behind and rope down its western side. Even if this line of retreat failed, we could always wait until the following morning and come down the slope when it was again frozen. So we decided to risk it and to use the snow layer covering the ice.

Even so it was a long job. In some places, near rock outcrops, the snow was too thin to provide any foothold, and steps had to be cut in the hard blue ice. It took us several hours to regain the crest of the ridge behind the Petit Gendarme. We halted for five minutes to eat some chocolate and look about us. The peak was already covered in cloud. It was obvious that we could not get very far unless things improved, and at first sight there did not seem to be very much chance of that. For a short distance the ridge was fairly easy, but then it rose up like a mighty wave, several hundred feet of vertical and unbroken rock. It was hopeless to think of climbing this direct, and the only chance was to look for a way of turning it on the left. We traversed out on to the North Face and reached a gully that led directly upwards. Here the climbing was more straightforward, and except in a few places we could both move up together. We could never see very far ahead, and had little idea where we were getting to. Suddenly after about an hour and a half we reached the crest of the main ridge again, and were delighted to find that we were standing on top of the Grand Gendarme. This was a very welcome surprise, and our hopes began to revive, until we came to examine the next obstacle.

This appeared to us as a red pinnacle, but it was, in fact, a step in the ridge similar to the Grand Gendarme on a much smaller scale. It was extremely steep and was undercut at its base. This time there was no chance of getting round the obstacle. To the right there was a giddy drop to the hanging glaciers of the West Face; to the left the scoop at the base of the pinnacle ran downwards in a groove towards the centre of the narrowing North Face, overhung by a continuous line of ice-polished slabs.

There was a good ledge below the pinnacle, and by standing on Tilman's shoulders I could just reach two finger holds. Hanging on these, and with a final kick off from Tilman's head, I managed to swing myself up to grasp a hold higher up and also to find some purchase for my feet to relieve the strain on my arms. After an exhausting struggle I established myself above the overhang. Then followed some very delicate work. The wall of the pinnacle was nearly vertical, and the holds were only just large enough to accommodate a boot nail. But the rock was perfect, and at first the holds, though few, were well spaced. Halfway up, however, there was an extremely nasty bit. It involved a long stride from one nail hold to another with nothing but a few rough excrescences for the hands with which to maintain my changing centre of balance. I contemplated this stride for a long time, before cautiously swinging my right foot to the upper hold. It felt so unpleasant that I hastily brought my foot back again for further contemplation. After repeating this faint-hearted operation about half a dozen times, and prompted largely by my increasing distaste for the present position of my left foot which was beginning to hurt, I gradually transferred my weight to the right foot, which to my intense relief did not slip, and by clawing at the face of the rock managed to hoist myself into an upright position.

Fortunately, after this the holds, although still very small, became more profuse. but by now there was a new source of anxiety. The rope between us was clearly not going to be long enough to enable me to reach the top of the pinnacle. It was no use Tilman unroping, for he could not possibly get up the lower overhanging bit without a pull from above. There was a little recess below the top, and I just reached it as the rope came taut between us. In this I wedged myself sufficiently tightly to support his full weight. I hauled up the ice-axes and the rucksacks and sent the end of the rope down again. In spite of my pulling, Tilman had a much more severe struggle than I had experienced. When he had succeeded I climbed quickly to the top of the pinnacle where I got into a really strong position. The rest was easy.

Nothing provides such a strong incentive to struggle on up at all costs as the memory of a really severe pitch below, and from now on we were infused with a pleasant sense of abandon. Time was our chief anxiety, and we hurried upwards as fast as we could. The steps that followed were difficult, but not nearly so bad as the red pinnacle which we had just surmounted. They grew smaller and smaller until at last we reached the junction of the North-East and the West Ridges.

It was an exciting moment as we turned south to look along the final ridge leading to the summit. It is impossible to tell from below how difficult such a ridge is likely to prove. We had seen that it was long and serrated, and that the steepness of the West and North-East Faces on either side of it would oblige us to stick to the crest. Much depended upon the width of this crest. We could not see far along it through the mist, and so the issue remained in doubt. At any rate, the short length of ridge that we could see, though very narrow and broken, was not hopeless. We started clambering along it, sometimes balancing along the top, sometimes sitting astride and sometimes swinging along the crest with our hands while our feet sought purchase on the wall below.

It was a splendid situation, thrust up infinitely high, isolated by the mist from all save this slender crest of granite along which we must find a way, the thrilling knowledge that the mighty West Ridge was below us, mind and muscle set to a high pitch of rhythmic coordination. I have rarely enjoyed anything more. Somewhere down in the grey depths to the left was the great bulge of rock that had defeated us nearly two years before. To the right, below our feet, was a white glow, the upper hanging-glacier terrace of the west face. The rock was superb, as hard and strong as the granite of the Chamonix Aiguilles.

We reached a gap about 30ft. deep, and roped down into it. Our boats had already been effectively burnt, and there was no time to bother about cutting off our retreat still further. One after another pinnacles loomed into view, greatly magnified by the mist. One after another we set about the new problem that each presented, always expecting it to be the last. I soon lost count; the ridge seemed to go on for ever; but we were going with it, and that was the main thing. Surely nothing could stop us now.

At last, in place of the sharp pinnacle we had come to expect, a huge, dark-grey mass loomed ahead of us. A few steps cut in the icy floor of a gully, a breathless scramble up easy rocks, and we were there beside our little cairn on the summit of Batian.

It was half-past four. There was no chance of getting down before nightfall, but no consideration of that sort could stem the flood of my joy and, let it be admitted, relief. I do not know what Tilman thought about it. He did not know the way down the South-East Face. If he imagined it to involve climbing of a standard similar to that which we had just done he must have had some misgivings, though characteristically he expressed none.

There was no view to look at, and so, after swallowing a tin each of some meat essence, we began the descent. The rocks on the south side of Batian were plastered with snow, which delayed us. But we made up time before the Gate of the Mist and the top of Nelion which we crossed without a pause, and plunged down into the gully beyond. In our haste Tilman slipped and lost his ice-axe which vanished out of sight in a single bound. After that we were more careful. It was getting dark as we reached the top of the 60ft. wall above the head of the south ridge, and night had fallen by the time we had pulled the rope after us at the foot of the wall.

It was here that I began to feel very sick. I imagine that the tin of meat essence I had eaten on the summit was bad. But an hour or so later I was sick, and after that I felt more philosophical about it.

The clouds had not cleared at dusk in their customary manner, and it looked as though we should have to stop where we were until the morning. It was already very cold, and the prospect was not welcome. But later, breaks began to appear in the mist, the moon came out and there was enough light to enable us to climb on down slowly. I felt very tired and the phantom moonlight, the shadowy form of ridge and pinnacle, the wisps of silvered mist, the radiant expanse of the Lewis glacier plunging into soundless depths below induced a sense of exquisite fantasy. I experienced that curious feeling, not uncommon in such circumstances, that there was an additional member of the party – three of us instead of two.

It was not very difficult nor even laborious, dropping from ledge to ledge. I remembered every step of the way, and had no difficulty in finding it. We had some trouble in negotiating the chimney where we had found Mackinder's rope, but once below that the rest was easy. When we reached the Lewis Glacier we started plodding up towards the saddle between Point Lanana and Point Thompson. But this demanded more physical effort than we had bargained for, so we altered course and made for the hut by the side of the Skating Lake. Here we huddled over some bits of timber that we managed to ignite, and waited for the dawn. The rest did us good, and we reached the saddle before the sun was up. From there back to our cave in the Mackinder valley was mostly downhill, but it seemed a very long way.

from UPON THAT MOUNTAIN *1943*

Potato Medallist

COLIN KIRKUS

On Snowdon there is a cliff called Clogwyn du'r Arddu. Its name is enough to frighten away many people. It is over 500ft. in height and mostly vertical - quite the most magnificent precipice in England and Wales. Up to 1931 there was only one route on each of the two main buttresses. It was the West Buttress that first attracted me. In 1927, Longland and Pigott and Morley Wood had succeeded in breaking across from the left, to make their magnificent West Buttress Route [Longland's Climb].

My friend, Dr. Graham Macphee, had led me in record time up this climb, and we were sun-bathing by the dark little Llyn du'r

Arddu. Macphee thought he had earned his rest, as indeed he had, but I had other ideas. I had designs on the middle of the West Buttress.

On the upper half of the buttress was a huge slab. If only it could be reached! Below, the rocks were almost vertical. But the main problem was in the first few feet. All the way along the foot of the cliff the rocks overhung. It was a genuine overhang, too; it formed a kind of covered corridor, with a roof that projected in places for 20ft. or more. Nobody had yet succeeded in overcoming this overhang. There seemed to be a faint chance in the middle, where a pile of blocks formed a kind of natural ladder. A well-known climber had tried to climb straight up at this point and had fallen off, luckily without hurting himself. It looked a nasty place, but it seemed to me that, instead of climbing upwards, it might be possible to traverse out to the left, above the overhang. This would lead to a narrow slab, which ran up to the skyline and out of sight. It was impossible to guess what happened after that.

The traverse was very severe. There was one sloping hold where my rubbers would not grip at all, so at last I took them off and managed to get across in my stockinged feet.

I found myself on a tiny grass ledge, looking rather hopelessly up at the grim face above. I had crossed on to a higher part of the cliff and was already about 100ft. above the bottom, with the overhang below me. I felt very small and isolated.

I started up the narrow slab. It was far more difficult than it had looked, and wickedly rotten. I threw down every other hold. A thin ribbon of grass ran all the way up on the right, looking like a long and ragged caterpillar. I thought that even this might be safer than the rock and plunged into it. It wasn't at all a friendly kind of caterpillar; it began to peel off and slide down. I left this moving staircase very hurriedly, and took to the rocks again. I climbed on the extreme edge, where it seemed to be a little firmer. Below my left foot the rocks dropped, sheer and unclimbable, for 200ft.

Macphee called up that I had run out nearly all of the 120ft. line. There was no stance in sight, so I had to stand about uncomfortably while he tied on another 100ft. length. I went on and on, with things looking more and more hopeless. I wondered whether I should ever find a belay.

At last the climbing began to get easier, and I was able to traverse to a sheltered grassy recess on the left. There was a perfect thread-belay, and Macphee soon joined me. It was wonderful to think that no one had ever been here before. It was still more interesting to wonder whether we should ever escape.

I tried the slab immediately above, but did not dare to pass a big loose block, resting on a ledge. A few years later, an optimistic climber was more daring; he succeeded in pulling the block on top of himself, gashing his hand very badly. He had to abseil down, weak and faint from loss of blood. He got back very late, and search-parties were out all night looking for him. By this time he was safely in bed. Some one had made a muddle of things.

We climbed a rib to a little stance. The big slab, for which we were aiming, was away on our right. It was very steep and smooth here; the far side looked much more hopeful. But could we reach it?

I got a long way across, and then stuck. The next move might be possible, by a kind of jump. It would be dangerous, but — well, a new climb was worth a risk. I looked at it a long time. It seemed to grow more and more grim. The exposure was terrifying and I was a long way from my second. I came back.

I managed to find an easier way across, at a lower level; but that meant that I still had the steep part of the slab ahead of me. The corner was a 20ft. wall of literally vertical grass. I made a mad rush at it. I had to climb up more quickly than the grass fell down. It was nasty and dangerous, but I dug in my finger-nails and toes (I was still climbing in stockings) and clutched and scrabbled until I reached the top. I don't know what Macphee thought of all this. He is a safe and careful climber himself. But he is an ideal second. He watches you carefully and says nothing, except to point out a hold now and again. You feel that he trusts you and expects you to get up, and so you jolly well do get up. Also, he is equally famous both as an alpinist and as a rock-climber, so that I new I could not have had a better man to back me up.

The next pitch was still grass, but not quite so steep. The turf split from the slab and curled up. It was rather like standing on a roll of carpet — with the carpet going on unrolling. It was very difficult and unpleasant. But our reward was to come. We had two wonderful airy 100ft. pitches, right up and across the Great Slab, to its top left-hand corner. The rock was warm and very rough, and we felt profoundly happy and exhilarated. All the thrill of conquest was ours. The climbing was just severe, but it was easy after what had gone before and we seemed to glide up without effort.

Macphee said I deserved a kick in the pants or a potato medal, he didn't know which. Why only a potato medal I don't know; I felt I deserved more than that. But it had been a marvellous day. We had done 1,000ft. of rock-climbing, most of it in the very severe class.

from LET'S GO CLIMBING *1941*

Patagonian Virgin

CHRIS BONINGTON

I did not sleep that night, I was too excited, but lay in my sleeping bag thinking endlessly of the climb we were about to do. We had struggled for so long on the flanks of the Central Tower of Paine, had been repulsed so many times, that the peak had become the focal point of all my ambition. Every function of my mind and body was devoted to this one aim to the exclusion of everything else. I think all the other members of the party were keyed up in much the same way; certainly, that night, John Streetly, lying in the tent beside me, seemed as restless as I.

The alarm, long awaited, went at 4 a.m. We had some coffee and set off for the Notch. Don and I went in front to make the route. Barry Page and John Streetly were to follow, carrying the bulk of the food and the bivouac equipment. We reached the Notch at 6 a.m., and quickly climbed the ladders and fixed ropes that had been left a few days before. On the slab, disaster nearly struck us. The rope running down it had been frayed by the constant force of the wind beating it against the rock. It was Don's turn to lead. He gave it a few tugs to test it, but it seemed safe and he started to climb the slab using it as a handrail, with a prusik loop round his wrist. Suddenly, when he was poised on a scrape on the surface of the slab, the rope parted above his hand. He was over 60ft. above me and only the steadiness of his nerve saved him. Somehow he managed to maintain his balance, keep hold of the end of the rope and retie it, all on a 60° slab.

By 8 a.m. we reached the foot of the big groove, and it was my turn to lead. The nature of the climbing now changed. The groove was steep and holdless, broken by roof overhangs, but there were cracks for our pegs. Laden with a jangling cluster of pitons, wooden wedges and karabiners I was soon completely immersed in the climb. It was deceptively easy for the first few feet to the first big roof, where I started using my étriers. I was able to swing out under the roof and tried to pull up over the overhang on a rounded corner to avoid putting in another peg. My leg, thrust out in the étrier at an angle to maintain my balance, slipped as I reached for the hold. Before I had time to think I was dangling in mid-air about 10ft. below; my pitons had held my fall. Angry with myself for my carelessness, I quickly climbed back to the lip of the overhang, hammered in a piton and pulled up. The climbing was intensely enjoyable – free moves interspersed with difficult artificial climbing. Sometimes the cracks were too narrow, at others too wide; after 80ft. there was still no sign of a stance and the rope was beginning to drag, so I brought Don to a position just below me, and carried on. I was beginning to tire and was suffering from hand cramps; my fingers curled round the handle of the peg hammer and I could only straighten them by using my teeth. We had had any amount of training for fell-walking in the previous weeks, but none at all for high-standard rock climbing. At last I reached a narrow ledge after running out all the rope. I had taken five hours to climb 250ft. It was very similar to Chamonix in character, and this long pitch was of the same standard as the East Face of the Capucin or the South-West Pillar of the Dru before, of course, those routes had been pegged.

Don followed up steadily, getting very little support from the rope. By the time he reached me he was cursing and panting. There is nothing more depressing than seconding long, artificial pitches after waiting for hours on restricted stances. He had been a wonderfully patient second, but I could sense his frustration and eagerness to get to the front. We were on a narrow ledge below a square-cut corner of rich, reddish brown granite, which we had named the Red Dièdre. Don raced up it, hammering in a piton, clipping on his étrier, climbing onto the top rung, perhaps doing a free move and then at full reach hammering in another peg. He amply made up for his lack of height with his supreme agility and the strength. In a matter of minutes he was 60ft above me, pulling up over a block overhang. A pause and then a shout – the angle eased off; we should be able to make quick progress.

Meanwhile, the Tower was beginning to resemble a popular, classic route at Chamonix rather than a virgin peak in the 'Uttermost Part of the the Earth'. John Streetly and Barry Page were in the dièdre below us. Below them were five of the Italian expedition who were following up our pegs. On the Notch the rest of our party were sun-bathing and enjoying the spectacle. Excited shouts from the Italians and the ironic cheers of our spectators intermingled. We were worried about John and Barry; they had barely enough karabiners and étriers to make the long run-out to the foot of the Red Dièdre, and Don and I had nearly run out of pitons. To save time they very generously agreed to turn back.

Don and I pressed on. Although we were both tired, it was exhilarating now to climb quickly, uncluttered with a tangle of étriers, hammering in only the odd peg for protection. It was 5.30 p.m. when we reached the Shoulder. Our route now lay on the East Face of the Tower across broken rock covered with snow and ice. At last we came in sight of the summit ridge and what we thought was the top, but it was a false one: beyond it was another gendarme that looked higher and, having reached the top of that, there was yet another, fortunately the last. It was 7.30 p.m. when we reached the top of the Central Tower of Paine. We spent only a few minutes on the top: we were too anxious to get back down onto the Shoulder before it was completely dark. If the weather had broken while we were still on the upper part of the face, we should never have got back without fixed ropes in position, for a high wind would have blown abseil ropes out at an angle of 90° and made climbing completely impossible. We gave a shout, which was heard by the rest of the party, took the summit pictures and quickly started down in the growing dark. Inevitably the ropped jammed in our first abseil. Don climbed back up twice before he managed to free it. We reached the Shoulder just as it got dark and thankfully settled down for the night.

We were warm enough since we had *pieds d'éléphants* as well as duvet jackets, but had only a couple of Mars Bars to eat and, much more serious, nothing to drink. The others had been carrying all the food and the stove. In spite of a savage thirst we were well content, for the weather was settled and we were confident that we should be able to get down the next day.

We started down at 6 a.m. the next morning, abseiling down the upper grooves. At the foot of the Red Dièdre we met the first of the Italians; they had spent an uncomfortable night perched on minute ledges in the groove itself. We muttered greetings but wasted no time; they were keen to get up, we to get down.

We were within sight of safety with only 12ft. separating us from the rest of the party, who were waiting for us with food and drink on the Notch. Don was already down and I was sliding down the last rope when suddenly it snapped. I was falling headlong with no rope to save me. I hit a ledge but bounced off it and rolled, scrabbling at the rock, down a slab. Somehow I managed to stop at the brink of a 500ft. drop and lay shocked and panting on a narrow ledge. I had only sprained my ankle, but it had been a narrow escape.

That same day Derek Walker and Ian Clough climbed the North Tower and the Italians reached the top of the Central. In the following weeks, we made an attempt on another peak in the area, one of the Cuernos, but the rock near its top was both steep and friable, and the party turned back. The Italians attacked the South Tower by its North ridge; it was extremely difficult in its lower parts but eased off higher up and they succeeded in climbing it. Meanwhile, Don Whillans, Ian Clough and Barry Page had gone to the back of the South Tower to attempt the South ridge. This was much longer than they had anticipated, however, and the weather was threatening, so they were forced to turn back.

We had climbed the Central Tower — twenty exhilarating hours on warm, firm rock, trying our bodies and muscles to the utmost, after weeks of frustration, lying in Base Camp and tramping up and down the approaches to the Central Tower. For 2,000ft. climbed, we had walked many hundreds of miles, but that one day of fulfilment had made all the effort worth while.

from THE ALPINE JOURNAL *1963*

Jack of Diamonds

ROYAL ROBBINS

You asked me to reminisce a bit about the first ascent of Jack of Diamonds which Layton Kor and I did in the summer of 1963. I remember that summer fondly. I was doing lots of climbing, was fit, and Liz and I had saved enough money to travel and climb as we pleased. I spent a lot of time around Boulder that year, making the most of the rich lode of climbing opportunities offered by the eastern Rockies. I climbed in Eldorado and Boulder Canyons, fell off Ament Routes on Flagstaff, couldn't get high enough to fall off Gill Routes in the marvellous Split Rocks, scraped skin on the Owls and Sundance, and came to grips with the prince of Colorado walls, the Diamond of Longs Peak.

It's a long but lovely walk up to Chasm Lake. I remember more the loveliness, at this distance, than the length. Embedded in my memory are pictures of the pines and twisted aspen, the fresh stream bubbling downward, the wildflowers, and, up high, the meadows and lakes. It has always been a wonder to me that the Colorado Rockies, which appear so desolate, barren, and dry from a distance, can present to the visitor such an abundance of alps, wildflowers, lakes, and streams.

There were a number of parties camping in and about the stone shelter at Chasm Lake when Liz, Layton and I arrived. We were ambitious to make the second ascent of D-1, because of its reputation as a Yosemite wall in an alpine setting, and also simply because the Rearick-Kamps route was an elegant line up a stunning face. We were doubly ambitious, for we hoped to get up in a day.

I knew there was no one in the country, perhaps in the world, at that moment, with whom I stood a better chance of climbing the Diamond in one day than with Layton Kor. He was fast. Kor, in fact, had never developed the knack of climbing at any speed other than flat out. He was always in a hurry, and climbed every route, even the most trivial, as if he were racing a storm to the summit.

Climbing with Kor, one could not remain unaffected by his tumultuous energy. It was stressful, because to climb with him as an equal required that one function at the limit of one's abilities. Layton was ever alert to a weak moment, and perceiving one, would pounce with the ever-ready phrase, "Maybe I should take this lead?"

Kor was a phenomenon. He was the first climber to break the hegemony which Californians had long enjoyed in Yosemite. Until Kor arrived, it was folk wisdom among Yosemite climbers that *everyone* who came there—no matter how they might star on their home ground—*every* climber on his first visit to Yosemite suffered a decline in his personal estimation of his climbing worth. Yosemite would inevitably take the piss out of the arrogant visitor. This was mostly due to the peculiar nature of Yosemite climbing, which tended toward holdlessness and strenuousness. But Layton wasn't daunted. He astonished us all by his ability to immediately do the harder routes in the Valley, and in record time as well!

I had great respect for Kor, and this would grow during our ascents of the Diamond. But, more than respect, I liked Layton. He was a climber's climber, which is to say, he didn't play to the crowd, and he climbed for the right reasons, that is, to satisfy himself. He wasn't the sort of fellow to step on a piton and later claim a free ascent, because to him that would be utterly pointless. It wasn't what others thought of his climbing, but what *he* thought, that counted.

Layton was certainly highly competitive, and inwardly driven to make an impact upon climbing history. His list of first ascents of technically difficult rock climbs, both free and aid, is perhaps unmatched by any American climber. But Kor was one of the very few highly competitive climbers who never criticised the efforts and achievements of others. He was interested in action, life, joking conversation, and plans for the next climb. In fact, although he never talked about religion, Kor was a sort of natural Christian, generous when others were wrong, and not in the habit of finding fault with his neighbour. There was one exception to this. I once heard Layton express scorn for a Coloradan who had made a tasteless bolt route up one of Kor's favourite sandstone spires in the Utah desert.

During the afternoon of July 12, Layton and I left the shelter cabin and trod the fine brown granite along the south shore of Chasm Lake. We were soon on Mills Glacier and then followed

Lambs Slide to Kieners Traverse, which brought us to North Broadway, and a several hundred foot descent to our bivouac at the base of the Diamond. It was comfortable, and our sleeping bags assured a good night's sleep.

Our ascent went smoothly, except for a ten-foot fall when Kor pulled an aid pin. The icy chute at the top of the wall provided interesting variety to what was otherwise a straightforward, if difficult, technical rock climb. That Rearick and Kamps had climbed this route with only four bolts was evidence not just of their technical competence, but even more of a stern, anti-bolt discipline which had its roots in Yosemite climbing at that time; a discipline which, though occasionally violated, would later prevail in American mountaineering.

According to Bob Culp's prodigious memory, we did D-1 in sixteen hours. Sounds about right. At any rate, we reached the refuge before dark.

After two days' rest, we were back on Broadway, this time by way of the 500ft. North Chimney. This approach was shorter, but not without its dangers. We climbed it unroped with packs, and at times I felt we were engaged in a daring enterprise. There were several unpleasant passages, and at the top a steep section of loose rock. Layton swarmed up it, but I was thwarted by a hold out of reach. Kor, seeing my distress, lowered a vast paw which I gratefully clutched and used to reach safe ground. I excused myself with thoughts of a heavy pack and lack of reach, conveniently forgetting how often shorter climbers than I had managed stretches where I deemed a long arm essential. Hoping to avoid a bivouac, we started even earlier than we had on D-1. I remember Kor swarming up the first pitch, pulling off a great block of loose rock which crashed down the North Chimney.

One of the lovely things about an east face in the high mountains is that the morning sun so quickly takes the night chill from the air. For a while, everything seems warm, secure, and safe. Hard to imagine suffering from the cold in such a place. Quite different from Yosemite, where the breezeless morning sun is an enemy. But mountain weather is ever fickle, partly because we are ever foolish, wanting to believe it is being nice just for us, when it is just one of her inconstant moods.

By noon, the winds were being rude and clouds swirled overhead.

"Don't laugh — it only encourages him."

Now, to lead was a pleasure and to belay a cold hell. Not that either of us fiddled about on the leads. We were competing against each other, yes. After all, each of our lives was given to climbing, and we both wished to excel. In this sense, each of us was an obstacle in the other's path, or so it seemed. In this sense we *were* competing – but our cooperation was far more important. Thus, it is off the mark to say we climbed the Diamond rapidly because we were competing. It is more accurate to say we climbed fast in spite of the running dog of competition which raced with us to the summit.

The East Face of Longs loses its benign aspect when the sun disappears westward. The wind brings numbing cold to fingers and cheeks, and snow whirls about. Discomfort is intensified when one is in a hanging belay, becoming impatient even with the speed of Layton Kor.

I quote from a note about the ascent which appeared in the 1964 *American Alpine Journal*:

> Racing against the setting sun to avoid a bad night in slings, Kor led the last pitch, a long, strenuous jam-crack. On my last reserves I struggled up this final pitch, topped the Diamond, and shook the hand of a great climber.

It was a long walk down. Mile after mile through the night I paced steadily behind Kor, through the Boulder Field – which seemed an enormous area. Kor showed no signs of weakening, and I forced myself to thrust my legs forward, long strides trying to match his. I wouldn't weaken. I would keep up behind this natural force that wouldn't slow down. Aching feet, legs, back. Mind numbed, but there was the light of the shelter; crowded, sordid, smelly, but warm and welcoming. I well remember Liz, but, oddly, I can't recall booze. Ah, I have grown so sophisticated that I can't imagine a climb like that with a walk like that, not being followed by wine, as well as love.

from CLIMB *1977*

Wintering Out

ALAN ROUSE

During the winter of 1975, which I spent in Chamonix, I grew a lot closer to the mountains and the Alps became my spiritual home. The high winds which had plagued the weather of the previous few weeks had subsided and I wanted like hell to climb.

The rarely-climbed North Face of the Pèlerins was conspicuous from the window of the apartment. One could just distinguish a thin line of ice tracing an improbable course between steep rock walls. Tentative probes by French climbers in previous years had highlighted the difficulties we could expect to encounter: dribbles of ice smeared over smooth slabs, immobilised into a gloriously dingy ice chute. The summer route, pioneered by Terray and Rébuffat, provides a *très difficile* rock climb, hindered by water and snow and spiced with occasional stonefall down the gully-like features of the wall. Our recently acquired knowledge of winter climbing would be tested to the full by this extremely technical mixed climb.

Derelict eyeballs greeted the twilight of dawn as we hurriedly packed. Goodbyes and a confusion of unrelated thoughts blurred into slight apprehension as the téléphérique lurched up to the Plan de l'Aiguille. Minutes later we were fumbling with snow shoes and shouldering the huge rucksacks that inevitably accompany a winter ascent. The initial stuttering of movement subsided into a steady plod as we passed from light to shade. Two hours later we shed our snow shoes as the slope steepened towards the start of the climb which lay tucked away near the North Face of the Plan. The seracs teetered ominously above our tracks lending a sense of urgency to our progress. As always in winter the start of the climb was thick with lurking cold. Ready to pounce, it waits patiently until you are committed before making its attack. You cannot see it, or even feel it, but it's there all the same. Noses, deliquescent with dewdrops, peered upwards speculating about nothing in particular. Not much for them in the next few days. Cardboard food and idle phrases provide a poor backdrop to such an inspiring environment.

We paused to don crampons and fiddle with slings, our feelings dominated by a growing awareness and enthusiasm. We raced up easy snow slopes, doubts dispelled by the familiar feeling of crampons biting reassuringly into the ice below. Rab paused to take a belay where the snow petered out and I led through up the steeper mixed terrain. Patch of ice provided secure places for hammer and axe which facilitated the occasional steep rocky steps. The next pitch provided a foretaste of things to come. Three or four off balance moves on nearly vertical ice led to delicate bridging; ice for one crampon and smooth unyielding granite for the other. Speed was dictated by the angle, yet careful precision was needed for security. 160ft. and no sign of a stance. The climb had started in earnest and we knew that from now on maximum effort would be needed to force a conclusion. Rab took a hanging belay and I scrabbled up behind. The next few rope lengths were very trying. At one stage I had to negotiate a vertical arête with ice on each side, nasty and uncompromising, 50ft. above the last runner. My feet skated a little and my arms tensed with effort. Out of balance my sack was pulling me backwards as I struggled up some overhanging bulges. Eventually I passed the last stage of fear and switched onto a kind of automatic. It was as if the subsconscious had decided to kill the fear and devote everything to movement. Thoughts ceased and a determined precision carried me up to easier ground. My unthinking detached view was shattered and I lay on the ice, thoughts jostling for position. After a few minutes, when the strain on my calves became dominant, I set off to look for a secure belay.

The next pitch looked ridiculous and I was glad it was Rab's turn to lead. How climbers like Bonatti and Desmaison continue to lead day after day never ceases to amaze me. I shifted uneasily from one foot to another trying to relax as Rab tackled the ensuing groove. Crampon points became the focal point of my attention as the true angle became apparent. A tunnel of ice two feet wide led up at an angle never less than 70° for at least 80ft. The guidebook description, intended for a summer ascent, mentioned a 5 sup. corner with nine pegs for aid. This was it. Rab led steadily up front-pointing. Runnerless he reached the overhangs blocking the groove so he traversed right and out of sight. A long time passed yet I never asked why. The steady crawl of the rope spoke clearly of the difficulties above. The sky was beginning to darken and I shivered a little at the thought of the inevitable bivouac. I untied from the belay to provide a few extra feet for Rab and eventually he signalled he had found a belay of sorts. I changed from Dachstein mitts to leather gloves and set off up the groove. Reminiscent of the harder sections of Minus Two Gully on Ben Nevis it provided magnificent climbing. The rope above enabled me to fully enjoy the steep heaves and the delicate footwork. I reached the overhangs where a narrow slab of rock slid right to an arête glistening with ice. Below the arête lay an enormous roof festooned with icicles and dribbling with verglas. Above lay gloomy roofs and nightmare grooves leading nowhere. I was separated from the arête by an inch thick layer of ice smeared across the smooth slabs. Six feet of teetering took me across the horizontal band of ice, hands by knees and crouched between the roofs. The bottomless arête provided a superb pitch of the most exposed ice climbing I have ever encountered. With hammers on each side one could lean from side to side to get a new placement, feet perched precariously on the crest. My crampons worked like PAs frictioning on the rock below the ice. I climbed for 70ft. in the gathering gloom and took a perverse pleasure in the grey environment. Then disappointment — no trace of a bivouac ledge and not even a stance as the ice was too thin. My fingers were very cold and I was glad when Rab, interpreting my obvious look of dread each time I glanced upwards, volunteered to lead again. He carried on over ice never less than 70° and belayed. I followed pulling and scraping, carelessly placing hammers and cursing in the half light, technique gone to the winds. The prospect when I arrived was little better than before. We settled down, resigned to a bivouac in slings hanging from dubious nuts in a rotten crack.

6 p.m. and already the cold was intense. 6,000ft. below cars commuted up and down the valley unaware that we were watching with curiousity yet without envy. Rab produced a brew of mint tea whilst I searched in vain for forgotten cigarettes. Next we had alternate attempts at biting a salami until I ended up smashing it against the rock with my ice axe to break pieces off. We sucked the pieces and then pocketed them for a chew later. We dozed until the initial tiredness had worn off and I woke to find all feeling gone from my feet. The slings digging into my thighs had restricted circulation and my feet had become very cold. Fortunately a brew

and a brief spell of restricted movement revitalised them. We had no idea of time as I had long since sold my watch to get funds for climbing. I spent the rest of the night sleeping fitfully and peering around the corner at tomorrow's fare. I didn't like the look of it. An icefall with fluted columns and icicles, it looked decidedly steep for a first lead in the morning.

Fitting crampons and arranging equipment took an hour and a half as we shifted weight from one sling to another, manoeuvring carefully to avoid dropping any piece of vital equipment. I adjusted one strap at a time then returned my hands to the mitts for a few minutes. I was loathe to leave the relative security of our temporary home and only Rab's determined look pushed me out onto the surrounding curtains of ice. I dithered and wasted time looking for non-existent runners. Finally I warmed up a little and fought my way round the bulges to reach a small icefield below an ominously steep corner. Rab followed and attempted the corner. After half an hour of shouting and muttering Rab had only gained 10ft. and retreat seemed to be our only escape. He came back to the stance and we weighed up the possibilities. Very steep holdless rock blocked any rightwards progress. Out to the left lay a thin streak of ice, mind-boggling in its exposure. Rab chose the ice and completed one of the most beautiful ice pitches we have ever had the fortune to climb. Inclined at 65-70° a completely smooth rock slab led up for 150ft. Down its centre ran a sheet of ice two or three inches thick. All in balance but no possibility of any protection. It would be easy a few feet above the ground yet situated here it called for a detachment of mind and a neat execution of carefully planned moves. Each move subtly different and a mistake unthinkable. Rab's slow and measured progress made me glad I was climbing with someone of such a high calibre and experience and not some front-pointing lunatic armed with a few back issues of *Mountain* magazine. In a game where no mistakes are tolerated there is no substitute for hard won experience and judgment. The pitch was finished and seconding it was a mere formality. Immediately above us, easy ground led to the ridge and we sauntered left and right to find the most pleasant way to the top.

from CLIMBER AND RAMBLER *April 1976*

The Mask of Death

PIERRE MAZEAUD

About 3 p.m. we cross the Comici route, not without some regret – it would be so much easier to go that way. But Ignazio brings us back down to earth – we are on a first ascent, so let's forget about the other damn route. Several pitches of similar climbing on hard, grey, juggy limestone bring me to a sharp-edged crack below the yellow overhangs. We assemble on the stance, tie in to the pegs and study the possibilities above, debating which line to take. It is 5 p.m. on Friday July 30. Piussi feels the best of all of us: he fixes the first rope length. An outstanding effort on his part. The pegs seem to bend to his strength of purpose. We take a few photographs and belay him together, one rope each. After a delicate traverse on poor placements he reaches a cave which, he says, would serve admirably as a bivouac. The Civetta is really full of surprises: we are in the middle of an overhanging wall but it looks as if we can avoid spending the night in etriers.

After a 120ft. pitch of extraordinarily difficult aid-climbing, time is really pressing. Roberto follows and cleans the pitch and I jumar up the fixed rope, something I do not enjoy doing. Roberto reckons that it would be impossible for three of us to cram into the cave, so Ignazio sets off again. About 50ft. up he sets up his camp for the night – a narrow ledge with an uninterrupted view and all the water he could ask for: a stream running over his head. Roberto makes things comfortable in the cave for our second bivouac.

The so-called cave turns out to be no more than a hole. It will be difficult to get a good night's sleep. I fix up my hammock while Roberto busies himself with a mass of slings. Then we play at ski-lifts with Ignazio for a while so that he, too, can enjoy the culinary delicacies of his homeland. The entrance to the cave is like a window, opening onto a wonderfully clear evening sky. Sleep comes.

We wake to the sound of Ignazio yelling at us, and to an unpleasant surprise, surely the First Icefield can't be that near! It turns out to be an optical illusion, the wind has changed and is now blowing from the south, making things nearer. In fact, we have two-thirds of the wall under our belts, and expect to reach the top this evening, as planned. Roberto is soon with Ignazio. As last man I have to clean the pitches, the sacks come up next. One more rope length with a large overhang at the start, and we find ourselves at the foot of an inviting chimney down which a waterfall plunges. It has become noticeably warmer, causing the summit cornices to melt. And it has begun to rain too. For the first time visibility is nil, we are trapped in cloud. Roberto whose turn it is to lead today, has little desire to climb these final 1,000ft. soaked to the skin. In his opinion the proper and pleasant place for water is on the Riviera. Ever cautious, he places many pegs, gaining height slowly as the double rope glides out through our hands.

Roberto shouts to me. Water is now pouring down, making verbal communication difficult. Every word is lost in a sea of noise. We can barely hear each other, so rope moves are difficult. I have to climb up through the cascade of water. It seems as though all the water in heaven has been funnelled into this one chimney. For the first time I realise what a job Roberto has had. He still has one more difficult and exposed pitch to do before the end of the difficulties and the exit cracks, he thinks. We climb up to him and at about 11 a.m. on Saturday July 31, with the rain now less intense, we eat our remaining food and drink until we can drink no more. As so often in moments like this, when excitement is at its peak – the wall is surely in the bag now for the final 300ft. look comparatively straightforward – we prolong the halt and ignore any doubts we may have about the weather, which now looks as if it could turn out stormy. Our ropes and rucksacks lie in disarray around us.

At midday, Roberto decides to start up again. If all goes well we'll be at the top in two hours. If all goes well.

Many big routes are completed without incident. This time, however, the Civetta did not want to maintain the tradition. She would not grant that we come here and climb one of the few remaining possibilities on this 3,500ft. wall. It was like a Corneille tragedy, with no hint of intrigue. The dénouement is swift and unexpected. Here, and with only 300ft. to go.

The chimney-crack is blocked by three distinct bulges. It seems easiest to climb the left wall to start with and then up over an overhang to the stance. Roberto sets about the first pitch. Ignazio and I will lead in turn. The climbing is precarious, the rock is very compact and the pegs hard to place. We sent up more gear on the trail rope. He is nearly there.

A sudden flash of lightning. I leap in the air, clutching a karabiner. Am I a better electrical conductor than other people? With a terrible crack the bolt strikes the wall directly above. Ignazio roars with all his might, his voice severe and wrathful, "Watch out." He had not felt the shock. I grab the ropes, thinking that Roberto has been struck. I pull them in easily. An ear-splitting noise makes me look up. Terrified, I see a pillar of rock, about 250ft. high, which the blast has dislodged, hurtling directly towards us. In a split second it is smashed to pieces, a thousand tons of rock explode. . .

Paralysed by terror . . . certain death . . . huge blocks plunge down the chimney . . . with us in the firing line . . . whistling, then the explosion . . . I am no longer frightened, all that remains is the certain feeling that we will die. . . I feel the first blows as the boulders split into a thousand pieces. . . I am hit . . . my helmet burst open . . . I crumple and sway . . . a second blow . . . my head . . . the rock turns scarlet . . . blood . . . my heart stops, I cannot breath . . . my back . . . my legs, everything hurts. . . Ignazio's hand is bleeding, his shoulder badly hurt . . . after what seems an eternity I totter and collapse . . . I tell Piussi, "This is it" . . . the end . . . semi-conscious I hear a voice: "Pierre, try to breathe." I try to follow his advice but fall unconscious on top of a sack. Hardly breathing, I allow myself to give in to awful thoughts: Roberto is dead, I am dying, Ignazio is on his own.

Minutes pass, but seem like an eternity. The stonefall has ceased and it is a miracle that we are still here, still able to feel and breathe. Roberto's shouts pierce the haze – he is still alive, and so are we, I somehow find the energy to concentrate on what he is saying: "Pierre is dead." Here, as in every situation when hope provides a way out, I answer, "No!"

Later on Ignazio tells me that my face was a deathly pale, my lips blue, that my eyes were rolling in their sockets, that he thought: "That is the mask of Death." Gradually, things become clearer, then the terrible shock hits me – the ropes are lying in pieces,

Roberto is hanging from a single peg and all around are tattered rucksacks and shreds of rope. Slowly we tie the pieces together while Roberto, alone and unbelayed, tries to find some shelter from stonefall. The water cascades down, bringing with it the last fragments of loose rock. We wait and wait for Roberto to knot together a rope from all the pieces. When the task is complete we jumar up to him. It seems as if the horror is over. The rain stops and we try to set up a bivouac.

We have cheated death. The last few pitches, although gently overhanging, give us little cause for concern, but we will have to climb carefully and slowly on account of the rope. The bivouac is relatively comfortable and serves as hospital ward and kitchen. We drink something warm and bask in the joy of living, astounded that we are here at all. At last we sleep. During the night a stone hits Roberto and I hear him groan softly.

Morning comes, and with it a new spectacle: four inches of snow. The waterfall is frozen rigid. Biting cold tears through our sodden clothes (later we learn that two climbers had been frozen to death that same night on the Campanile Basso.) Roberto, the only one of us really fit to climb, reckons that it would be impossible to go on in these conditions – the wall would be more difficult and dangerous than in winter. We would be better off waiting a day, or even two if necessary. This enforced inactivity is unbearable. We have nothing to eat, and are out of cigarettes. We drink warm water. And grow weary. We make a wind break from our red bivouac sacks, which will be seen by our friends below. We talk a lot. A time to really get to know each other. A person is a person up here, and the feeling that they really understand me grows stronger. We talk of mountains, of climbing, of memories. Our first ascents, our nights on bivouacs, our friends . . . especially the ones no longer with us. . . The absolute certainty that this wall marks the end of our alpine careers – yesterday's miracle we see as a warning. We are a club with three members who now want only to walk with wife and child, to pick flowers . . . on this we swear an oath . . . an oath which we know we shall never keep, but which we nevertheless take.

More snow. Biting cold pierces us, our wounds hurt. Eventually night falls. Our faces grow brighter. The snow has stopped; it is colder.

Roberto makes his preparations in silence as dawn slowly breaks. We realise just how difficult a decision his is. The last 300ft. are totally iced up now, the roofs look dark and foreboding . . . higher up we can just make out the ledges, the top. It takes Roberto 12 hours to reach the ledges. Half a day to do 300ft. Exhausted I climb up to him; the last few feet are really hard. A thick blanket of snow lies on the ledge, but at the left-hand end is the smiling face of Livio, the hut warden, who has come to meet us with two of our friends.

from ALPINISMUS *1965*

Gentlemen's Relish

H. W. TILMAN

By 6 a.m. we were ready and shortly after we crawled outside, roped up, and started. It was bitterly cold, for the sun had not yet risen over the shoulder of East Nanda Devi and there was a thin wind from the west. What mugs we were to be fooling about on this infernal ridge at that hour of the morning! And what was the use of this ridiculous coil of rope, as stiff as a wire hawser, tying me for better or for worse to that dirty-looking ruffian in front! Such, in truth, were the reflections of at least one of us as we topped a snow boss behind the tent, and the tenuous nature of the ridge in front became glaringly obvious in the chill light of dawn. It was comforting to reflect that my companion in misery had already passed this way, and presently as the demands of the climbing became more insistent, grievances seemed less real, and that life was still worth living was a proposition that might conceivably be entertained.

This difficult ridge was about 300 yards long, and though the general angle appeared slight it rose in a series of abrupt rock and snow steps. On the left was an almost vertical descent to a big ravine, bounded on the far side by terrific grey cliffs that supported the broad snow shelf for which we were making. The right side also fell away steeply, being part of the great rock cirque running round to East Nanda Devi. The narrow ridge we were on formed a sort of causeway between the lower south face and the upper snow shelf.

One very important factor which, more than anything, tended to promote a happier frame of mind was that the soft crumbly rock had at last yielded to a hard rough schistose-quartzite which was a joy to handle; a change which could not fail to please us as mountaineers and, no doubt, to interest my companion as a geologist. That vile rock, schist is, I believe, the technical term, had endangered our heads and failed to support our feet from the foot of the scree to the last bivouac. It was a wonder our burning anathemas had not caused it to undergo a geological change under our very eyes – metamorphosed it, say, into plutonic rocks. But, as has been said by others, there is good in everything, and, on reflection, this very sameness was not without some saving grace because it meant that we were spared an accumulation of rock samples at every camp. A bag of assorted stones had already been left at the Glacier Camp, and I tremble to think what burdens we might have had to carry down the mountain had the rock been as variegated as our geologist, and indeed any right-minded geologist, would naturally desire.

Thanks to the earlier reconnaissance by him and Houston, Odell led over this ridge at a good pace and in an hour and a half we had reached the snow mound which marked the farthest point they had reached. It was a ridge on which we moved one at a time.

In front was a snow slope set at an angle of about 30° and running right up to the foot of the rock wall, perhaps 600 or 700ft. above us. To the west this wide snow terrace extended for nearly a quarter of a mile until it ended beneath that same skyline ridge, which below had formed the western boundary of the broad gully. On our right the shelf quickly steepened and merged into the steep rock face of the ridge between East Nanda Devi and our mountain. We were too close under the summit to see where it lay, but there was little doubt about the line we should take, because from a rapid survey there seemed to be only one place where a lodgement could be effected on the final wall. This was well to the west of our present position, where a snow rib crossed the terrace at right angles and, abutting against the wall, formed as it were a ramp.

We began the long snow trudge at 8 a.m. and even at that early hour and after a cold night the snow was not good and soon became execrable. The sun was now well up. After it had been at work for a bit we were going in over our knees at every step, and in places where the slope was steeper it was not easy to make any upward progress at all. One foot would be lifted and driven hard into the snow and then, on attempting to rise on it, one simply sank down through the snow to the previous level. It was like trying to climb up cotton wool, and a good deal more exhausting, I imagine, than the treadmill. But, like the man on a walking tour in Ireland, who throughout a long day received the same reply of "twenty miles" to his repeated inquiries as to the distance he was from his destination, we could at any rate say, "Thank God, we were holding our own."

The exertion was great and every step made good cost six to eight deep breaths. Our hopes of the summit grew faint, but there was no way but to plug on and see how far we could get. This we did, thinking only of the next step, taking our time, and resting frequently. It was at least some comfort that the track we were ploughing might assist a second party. On top of the hard work and the effect of altitude was the languor induced by a sun which beat down relentlessly on the dazzling snow, searing our lips and sapping the energy of mind and body. As an example of how far this mind-sapping process had gone, I need only mention that it was seriously suggested that we should seek the shade of a convenient rock which we were then near, lie up there until evening, and finish the climb in the dark!

It is noteworthy that whilst we were enjoying, or more correctly enduring, this remarkable spell of sunshine, the foothills south and west of the Basin experienced disastrous floods . . . it was on this day that the Pindar river overflower, sweeping away some houses in the village of Tharali, while on the same day 19 inches of rain fell at the hill station of Mussoorie, west of Ranikhet.

We derived some encouragement from seeing East Nanda Devi sink below us and at 1 p.m., rather to our surprise, we found ourselves on top of the snow rib moving at a snail's pace towards the foot of the rocks. There we had a long rest and tried to force some chocolate down our parched throats by eating snow at the same time. Though neither of us said so, I think both felt that now it would take a lot to stop us. There was a difficult piece of rock to climb; Odell led this and appeared to find it stimulating, but it provoked me to exclaim loudly upon its 'thinness'. Once over that, we were landed fairly on the final slope with the summit ridge a bare 300ft. above us.

Presently we were confronted with the choice of a short but very steep snow gully and a longer but less drastic route to the left. We took the first and found the snow reasonably hard owing to the very steep angle at which it lay. After a severe struggle I drew myself out of it on to a long and gentle sloping corridor, just below and parallel to the summit ridge. I sat down and drove the axe in deep to hold Odell as he finished the gully. He moved up to join me and I had just suggested the corridor as a promising line to take when there was a sudden hiss and, quicker than thought, a slab of snow, about 40 yards long, slid off the corridor and disappeared down the gully, peeling off a foot of snow as it went. At the lower limit of the avalanche, which was where we were sitting, it actually broke away for a depth of a foot all round my axe to which I was holding. At its upper limit, 40 yards up the corridor, it broke away to a depth of three or four feet.

The corridor route had somehow lost its attractiveness, so we finished the climb by the ridge without further adventure, reaching the top at 3 p.m.

The summit is not the exiguous and precarious spot that usually graces the top of so many Himalayan peaks, but a solid snow ridge nearly 200 yards long and 20 yards broad. It is seldom that conditions on top of a high peak allow the climber the time or the opportunity to savour the immediate fruits of victory. Too often, when having first carefully probed the snow to make sure he is not standing on a cornice, the climber straightens up preparatory to savouring the situation to the full, he is met by a perishing wind and the interesting view of a cloud at close quarters, and with a muttered imprecation turns in his tracks and begins the descent. Far otherwise was it now. There were no cornices to worry about and room to unrope and walk about. The air was still, the sun shone, and the view was good if not so extensive as we had hoped.

Odell had brought a thermometer, and no doubt sighed for the hypsometer. From it we found that the air temperature was 20°F but in the absence of wind we could bask gratefully in the friendly rays of our late enemy the sun. It was difficult to realise that we were actually standing on top of the same peak which we had viewed two months ago from Ranikhet, and which had then appeared incredibly remote and inaccessible, and it gave us a curious feeling of exaltation to know that we were above every peak within hundreds of miles on either hand. Dhaulagiri, 1,000ft. higher, and 200 miles away in Nepal, was our nearest rival. I believe we so far forgot ourselves as to shake hands on it.

After the first joy in victory came a feeling of sadness that the mountain had succumbed, that the proud head of the goddess was bowed.

At this late hour of the day there was too much cloud about for any distant views. The Nepal peaks were hidden and all the peaks on the rim, excepting only Trisul, whose majesty even our loftier viewpoint could not diminish. Far to the north through a vista of white cloud the sun was colouring to a warm brown the bare and bleak Tibetan plateau.

After three-quarters of an hour on that superb summit, a brief 45 minutes into which was crowded the worth of many hours of glorious life, we dragged ourselves reluctantly away, taking with us a memory that can never fade and leaving behind 'thoughts beyond the reaches of our souls.'

from THE ASCENT OF NANDA DEVI *1937*

Consolation for a Tragedy?

DAVE ROBERTS

"Someone said, "the best expeditions are uneventful ones." But this does not mean that eventful expeditions can offer no reward. Our expedition was eventful in the worst sense – we had an accident in which Ed Bernd, one of our four, was killed. It happened on the descent, twenty hours after we reached the summit of Mt. Huntington, as Ed started to rappel; we shall never know precisely why it happened. But out of some mixture of loyalty and sorrow – fidelity both to the friend we miss and the climb we are proud of – we refuse to believe that ours was a bad expedition. We refuse to say that it was not worth it, even for Ed. We believe that the intensity of our experience and its occasional moments of piercing happiness justify the risk we could not avoid. Not that they justify Ed's death — nothing can, to those who cared for him; the consolation for them must be the knowledge of his happiness, of which only the other three of us can tell.

A few minutes before midnight on July 30, 1965, as Ed and I were descending to a lower camp, we set up a rappel. He was in position to go first. He put a karabiner through the anchor piton, then clipped our doubled climbing rope through it and got on rappel. We did not have an extra rope to belay with, but I was attached to the fixed rope which in turn was tied to the anchor piton, a precaution in case it pulled. Ed wrapped the rope around his body, leaned back, and flew into space. The rope and karabiner both had come loose; the piton had not budged. Without a chance to stop himself, without even yelling, he fell 4,000ft. to his death.

Apparently the karabiner was the point of failure; either it broke or somehow it came loose. Perhaps the gate had frozen open, and in the dim Alaskan light Ed had not noticed. There is no way of knowing. We were never able even to get to Ed's body.

At the time Matt Hale and Don Jensen were above, camped in a two-man tent out of my shouting range. I managed to descend alone to our lower camp, where I waited two days for them. We had never been able to find a spot on the route large enough to allow all of us to camp together, but there we crowded three in a tent for a last night before completing the descent in terrible snow conditions the next day.

Alaska, one of the last paradises for the mountaineer, is known outside North America for little else but McKinley. But some of its smaller peaks are more incredibly shaped, more difficult; it has its Muztagh Towers and Chacrarajus: the Moose's Tooth, Deborah, countless unnamed spires. And 12,240ft. Huntington, one of the finest and last to be climbed (in May 1964 by an eight-man French expedition under Lionel Terray), still offered three or four superb routes that had not been tried. We picked the West Face, an extremely steep, largely rock, wall, to which we could gain access by a feathery knife-edge ridge that rose from the Tokositna glacier, the last of the glaciers near McKinley to be camped on.

Don Sheldon flew us in on June 29, leaving us in the sudden stillness of the glacial basin with enough food for sixty days and enough gear presumably to get us up our route.

The going was slow. We spent five days hauling loads to a base camp near the face, and two more climbing an ice-fall and digging a snow cave. The feathery ridge turned out to be tough; we had to climb over many snow plumes edged by sharp granite, on the side of the ridge that overlooked a 3,000ft. drop. The friendlier side of it was corniced. To reach the ridge, Matt tunnelled through what was left of a cornice the same day we had watched the rest of it break off.

We put fixed ropes on all our pitches, since we had to carry loads over them. After a few days we began looking for a camp site, but only on July 16 were Matt and Ed finally able to pitch a tent at the top of our 19th pitch, in a wedge-shaped hole of snow and hard ice which they spent five hours chopping.

Often (and this is the curse of the low-altitude Alaskan summer), it was too warm to climb even at night. A pair of climbers never got more than four new pitches placed in a night's effort. We spent long, sociable hours in our cave playing Monopoly, arguing about Ayn Rand, and reliving other climbs. We had done most of ours together: Don and I on two previous Alaskan expeditions, and all of us in the 'Lower 48', especially on weekends with the Harvard Mountaineering Club. We were about equally good technically; as it turned out on Huntington, Don led the hardest free rock, Matt the hardest direct aid, Ed the hardest ice, and I the hardest snow pitch. I enjoyed climbing with the other three as much as I ever had with anyone, because of their individualities; Ed's jovial spontaneity, Don's solidness and devotion, Matt's quiet intensity.

But for all the fun the climbing was, for all the pleasure of clean rough granite, we were not getting anywhere. We had so far always climbed in pairs; after July 16 we also camped in pairs. Matt and Ed, with four days' food, got established in the tent, which they had pitoned to a protecting rock wall, just before a storm hit; Don and I stayed below in the cave. For three days none of us could budge. At last Don and I forced our way up to the others, scraping the ice off the fixed ropes, and Don stayed with Ed while Matt went down with me. On July 20 Don led our 25th pitch, the first of the real face, a fierce pitch about which he said to me later, "When we saw it I was sure it's require aid. But I got up there, and there were these beautiful holds. . ." Ed led the long exposed pitch above, his

crampons scraping steep slabs and knocking ice chunks down on
Don. This was the most difficult climbing we had met, evidently a
preview of things to come.

Two days later Don and Ed had just repaired their defective
stove when Matt and I showed up. They were not very glad to see
us, since it meant switching, going out supperless into the cold. But
they gallantly left us their warming chicken stew.

At this point Matt and I were pretty pessimistic. Two new pitches
did not seem much gain for four days, and when it took Matt and
me six hours to get light loads to the top of them on our first effort,
we saw nothing to justify the enthusiasm Don and Ed had
expressed at their progress. We only sensed that our chances were
shrinking.

But the next day, the second clear one in a row, we got quickly
past the old pitches and put in seven new ones. The first was a steep
ice-filled chimney that required aid past a chockstone; the last was a
50ft. ceiling in which Matt found a series of cracks he could
nail nicely up. Suddenly we were at 11,000ft., and the summit
seemed within reach. Descending late in the night, we passed Ed
and Don, who were coming up in the gloom. "Tremendous, guys,
we saw you way up there!"

They pitched our other tent that night, then carried it up to just
below the ceiling the next day, following Matt and me as we carried
food and equipment for them. We left them that night knowing we
might not see them until after they had reached the summit. Matt
and I thought it quite possible that they had our only chance of
reaching the top. But any success would be enough; we had done
our part.

For Ed's third time, they laboriously chopped out a platform in
the ice. Again, they secured the tent to rock pitons above. It was a
beautiful site; the door opened on the distant hulks of Foraker and
Hunter above the door-mat of the Tokositna. They had to pitch the
tent narrow, or it would have overhung the edge of the platform.

The next day they only had time to put a fixed line of stirrup-
loops over the ceiling. But on July 29, our 31st day, they got an
early start. The weather was still perfect; none of us could believe
it, and I often looked uneasily south for the sign of a storm. With
only a minimum of hardware Don and Ed led pitch after steep
pitch. Don solved the last rock problem, twice using aid from

small, shaky pitons far above any protection.

Ed led up a short, steep fluting, and emerged on the summit ice-field. Soaring, sweeping in the afternoon light at an angle of 50° toward the summit, it seemed as featureless and open as a desert. They alternated leads on the slope, but the sun had warmed it dangerously. Around 5 p.m. they stopped on a rock ledge, the highest on the mountain, to wait for night and better snow. They pitched Don's tiny bivouac tent and crowded inside.

Matt and I meanwhile were bringing up the last of the hardware from the lower camp. We got to the higher one quickly and found Don and Ed had left it. We knew they were short on pitons, so we climbed the ceiling and followed their steps and fixed lines. We could help safeguard their descent by improving the protection, and if we felt strong, perhaps. . .

We were amazed at their pitches. With so few pitons on such steep snow, ice and rock, they had climbed marvellously. It was getting late, but there was not the slightest breath of wind, and we continued.

Late that evening we popped onto the summit ice-field and caught up with Don and Ed. As the sun faded behind McKinley, we ate some candy bars and hooked up as a rope of four. Don led in the growing darkness. The snow was still not good, and ice lay a few inches beneath. Once he had to belay from a rock piton driven in ice. A little after midnight, in the eerie starlight, we reached the summit ridge. We were almost there: yet it had taken the French four and a half hours on this last stretch, the only part our route had in common with theirs.

As the first light sprang from the tundra beyond McKinley, I took the lead. We faced two short, vertical, fluted walls. Attacking them very high, almost on the cornice, I found they were made of airy, soft snow. After a lot of excavation and some delicate pull-ups on an axe and a picket, I was over them. Carefully we belayed each other up the fluted steps. Extremely tired, for we had been going seventeen hours straight, we climbed the last few pitches. The world seemed to hang in a held breath, perfect, still, a world of glacial snow and soaring rock and, out to the limitless horizon, the hazy blue of the vast tundra; ours, ours only for that hour as we stood together on the summit. Nothing could last thus suspended; we were bound to die, Ed in only twenty hours; but if time for us had ever stopped to let the savage splendour of the earth declare its time-lessness, it was then.

from THE ALPINE JOURNAL *1966*

Dangerous Dancing

ALEX MACINTYRE

After our failure on the Walker's flank, three weeks of bad weather passed, and ideas changed. Terry King turned up, and Gordon Smith came back from Leysin. They directed their considerable charms towards the Croz Direct. I wanted to do the Dru Couloir and teamed up with Nick Colton, an 'aristocrat' from Manchester and one of the scruffiest people on God's earth. Once, having just had a vision in which he had cleaned the Fissure Nominé, he threw away all our hardware except for an ice-screw and a couple of bugaboos (ever lost eighteen krabs and twelve pegs at one go?). That night, two 'enlightened' persons perched themselves on top of the Petit Dru, to freeze in the teeth of a north-easterly and study a starlit and by then plastered Jorasses North Wall. Visions of Armageddon faded, and around midnight we cracked. We decided to go back for another try.

Which indeed we did, though we nearly didn't because I left my head-torch behind and so dedicate this affair to the congenial Froggy who lent me his, and to the half-roll of Sellotape with which I repaired it. 10.30 p.m. on August 6, 1976, found two little lads at the foot of the Walker Spur. This time we had decided to beat the 'schrund with a short left cross. Water was still running, but the face was quiet and the night clear. To start the spur, we took the left-hand rock alternative (the initial ice-slope did not exist) and followed this as far as the main ice-slope that cuts into the buttress on the right. Then it was softly, softly rightwards, to slip between the upper 'schrund and the rocks above, out on to the ice-field for a tense tip-toe affair, like ants going the wrong way up a bowling alley, with not a sound uttered lest we bring the house down. We hung left to avoid being anywhere below the mouth of the Japanese

Gully—vulnerable, so vulnerable. A roar: hearts in boots, we froze in fear, but it was only a plane passing low from the south.

2.30 a.m.: we hung back on our ice screws, sorting the gear, roping up, peering and wondering, because it looked steep up there. At least, it looked steep as far as we could see, which was as far as you can throw a head-torch. There was no moon and it was dark in the couloir.

There followed five pitches in a grand Scottish illusion: steep, bulging, demanding, all engrossing, totally rewarding. Up through a spindrift flow, in the teeth of a biting wind. Belays for sitting, but not for falling. Few runners—no time—fantastic stuff. We emerged with the daylight on to the ice-field separating the two rock-bands. Around us, ropes darted in and out of the ice like frozen umbilical cords. I counted footage, but thought in cash. We rescued a couple of shiny krabs and took a hefty swing at a little blue sack, but its coffin was hard and rubbery and it would have taken an hour to release, so we left it with parting tears. It was no place to linger: a sensational, exposed, vulnerable, 50° platform in a vertical sea, a mean place to quit in trouble.

Above, fixed ropes ran up a broad shallow gully of compact looking rock, but we were hungry for ice and, a little to the left, there seemed to be a connection with the runnel above. It looked a little like The Curtain on Ben Nevis, but the first 50ft. or so turned out to be unconsolidated powder, so we took to the steep and deceptive pile of rubble on the right. It was loose, a fact to which Nick swore blind as he sailed past for a sixty-footer on to a hapless second.

"Just hold tight and I'll monkey up the rope."

He did, and reached the top of the pitch for a belay. There followed a full and interesting run-out, on the border between ice and rock, and finally we were through the second barrier, with 1,000ft. of sensational climbing behind us. Then it was away up the cold, blue runnel that broadens out into the second ice-field. We front-pointed. Audoubert understands:

> Now begins that very special ice dance, a rhythmic ballet in four movements, a mixture of barbaric and primitive gestures and classical movement. The character before his mirror of ice makes precise steps with his front points, like a lead dancer rehearsing. In this special ballet pirouettes are forbidden. The emphasis on the

curve of his calves and the strength of his ankles equals the fierce, attacking look on his face. The best dancer, like the best toreador, strikes only once.

It was a long haul. Away to our right we could pick out more ropes, relics of the mammoth Japanese siege. Somewhere round here Lachenal and Terray passed by, but I think it must have been in pretty bad visibility. We heard voices but saw no one. The ice was hard and, after three years' wear, my poor Chouinards (God bless him!) let my toes know there was no more curve left. What had appeared to be three pitches up the ice extended to five, and we regained the rocks with creaking calves.

The final head-wall is about 800ft. In it, a well-defined gully system curls up and left in behind the Red Tower, to join the Walker Spur about two pitches below the summit. For about 400ft. it is backed by a thin ice weep. But this wouldn't take the gear, so we kept to the right wall. It was mean stuff: deceptive, awkward, and inevitably loose. And this was no time for mistakes, for we were tired now. It seemed a long way from that 9.0 a.m. rise the day before. In the northerly wind, the rock was bitterly cold. Above, sunlit walls beckoned, but progress was slow and any thoughts we had dared to entertain of reaching the heat receded to the summit. Incredibly, we had seen no stones all day, but Nick made up for that by burrowing away through the rocks above. In places the second is nastily exposed. I took a slate on the leg, with much wailing and gnashing of teeth. Nick solved the problems of getting back into the gully bed by falling off. . .

"What's happening?"

"Nowt – just fallen off."

. . . and finally we arrived at the summit of a dream, a couple of pitches down and desperate for a brew.

We charged on up but then there were these two little ledges just asking to be sat upon, so much more comfortable than the cold, wet snow on the other side and so much more convenient. So we sat down, just five minutes short, to dine on cheese and ham butties, with coffee by the gallon. Rare moments: we were asleep before the night came.

Next morning we woke late. The weather had closed in and it was doubly bitter. The stove worked, but the theory didn't. 20 minutes could only provide water on the rocks. We dozed over this cold brew until shouts from below drew us out of our lethargy. Two Japs appeared, fresh as daisies, despite their fourth bivi. They were the first party up the Walker for weeks. We chewed hurriedly at laces and gloves and raced them to the summit. They had come thousands of miles to climb this hill. It was like Christmas on top of the Walker.

Oh yes, I nearly forgot:

"And they all lived happily ever after."

from MOUNTAIN 53 *1977*

Taxation no Tyranny

JIM PERRIN

I am not a good psychologist and do not know by what springs fear works in us. Yesterday, for example, on a steep little piece of rock in Llanberis, there it was . . . I'll tell you how it came about. Martin [Crook], who is young and headstrong, and I had gone out on a warm Sunday to try a new route. It was on Castell Cidwm, and to be quite frank we got nowhere on it. It seemed to us scarcely feasible for there was not a hold we would have defined as such in view. Also, the day was one of those when you get up late and the car breaks down and your EBs, still wet from yesterday's sweat, slip on as easily as an elephant down a mousehole. It was a day of the aching muscle and the wrong decision, the ill omen and the throbbing toe. I was even frightened walking along the grass terrace at the foot of Cidwm to our projected route. Fear elicits from me the intensest desire to get my backside on the ground. I have sidled thus quite happily across the steepest grass in Wales when on my feet there would have been only a good whirling, toppling dose of vertigo. Some day some kindly and inspired equipment manufacturer will invent the pantseat crampon, and usher in the era of the first backward ascents. But this is the merest rubbish. We ran away from Cidwm.

He said, "What shall we do now?" with the day half gone. "Where's near, and what have we not done?" said I. At a certain stage in a climber's life he enters the phase where everything which he has not done, he has not done for very good reason. Either that the most intense effort of fitness only will carry him through, or evil reputation adheres, or at best, the route has never caught his eye. I cannot tell you which of these reasons covers yesterday's choice. But he, this youth, Martin, has decided to do Spectrum and I had to tag along. "No hardship," you may say, "Not hard at all." And it may be so, but last year I watched someone fail upon it, and therein lies the point. By subtle illogic I had convinced myself of its unattainability. In my imagination it had become a feat, something in the order of tumbling into bed with Charlotte Rampling, Shirley Williams and Marjorie Allen all at the same time. Which would economise on your vocal chords, but could leave your performance in some doubt.

Where was my theme? Oh yes; the point is, I had seen someone fail at a particular point on this route, and was convinced therefore that it was beyond me. So strange an emotion is apprehension. We arrived at its foot and Martin, too eagerly for my taste, volunteered to lead the first pitch. In an anxiety situation, you make the evidence fit. Instead of realising that the pushy young bastard was actually grabbing the supposed hard pitch, leaving the easier top pitch for his grandad, I thought the opposite. When he fell off his pitch, twice, with all the aplomb of youth, I suggested he should come down and let me do it, for I could see what he had not seen and treacherously, competitively, miserly, was not prepared to tell him so. But he would not, and was spurred on, and said, "Watch the rope whilst I jump," which he did. And when I came up I used my secret hold and could reach what he could not reach, so that it fell easily to hand. A tactical point you might think, but not so, for it confirmed my point of view. I gathered his gear and quaked, and set off up a thin crack. "Oh," I said to myself, "You have climbed so little these last few years. You are fat and lack finesse." So this thin crack, where all should be ease and pleasure, was fretful tribulation to me. I put in a runner, and then another, and stood up a little, and explored it tentatively, became rather engrossed, stretched inquiringly after a hold and when it slid beneath my fingers pulled on it, though it was less than it appeared, and slubbered a foot over a piece of slimy blankness till it stuck in a groove, and the net result of all these manoeuvrings was that I was caught with my runners 20ft. below, an overhang at eye level, and little choice but to carry on—which I did, and then I was 30ft. from a runner, and frightened, and not relaxed. So there followed a period of squirmings and contortions and the dropping of karabiners and fumbling with ropes and similar ineptitudes at the end of which a point of security emerged, and a smile re-emerged, and fear went to hide itself again a while.

I moved up to a ledge. Ledges are hard to leave. I recognised this one. The poor man I had watched last year struggled to leave it for an hour or more before he came down. Chalk marks went off right into the gully. Again, I totted up the evidence. Looking round the corner the sun shone in my eye and I could see nothing. So I groped, and could feel nothing, and I dabbed with my feet and they would stay on nothing. "Where does it go?" I wondered. "Can it really go out there where it is so blank and steep?" Such rhetoric is good: it makes you put on more runners. I leered down at Martin and told him how frightened I was, hoping that beneath the assumed quaver in my voice he wouldn't detect the shrill, dry undertone of fear. He merely told me that I was a cowardly old fart, which I knew anyway. Now a little more groping revealed a large, sharp hold, and the next thing I knew I was up it. Then the rope jammed, so quite blasé by now I put a tape on a flat spike and climbed back down to free it. Nothing so easy as a known quantity, which is all to labour a point about the duplicity of apprehensiveness.

I shall tell you another story or two. At Easter I was in Pembroke. It was the time when a far-back Sandhurst-type complained to Dave Cook that the plate was full of people-who-didn't-know-how-to-do-as-they-were-damned-well-told, and to me that these bally-climbers who came on the bally-tank-ranges were bally-irresponsible and might bally-well-damage the archaeological remains, which I suppose has something to do with blowing up one's credibility. To come to the point, Littlejohn collared me, probably mistaking me for Friar Tuck, and carried me off to do a route with him. Or rather, to hold his rope, which I did with utmost unctuous competence, and when he put a runner above his head I thought to store up riches in heaven, or rather a tight rope in the near future, by holding the rope, subtly but distinctly, tight. But instead he shouted at me and told me not to cheat, and I quaked with fear. When he had been on it an hour or more he arrived at the top, and this not without some difficulty, and then he was all smiles and told me, great ironist, that it should be called The Pleasure Dome. No-one seemed to be crossing the water from the direction of Porlock, so I climbed it, in a state of near-panic. Some people I have known climbed like this all the time. It fills you with good resolutions about getting fit and climbing more and the like, all of which hurt. The best one-liner I've ever heard in this area was from Warren Harding, who told me, without leaving his preference in any doubt, that he had either "gotta climb a whole lot more, or just a little bit less."

When I had climbed just a little bit more, I wound up the machine called pioneering instinct, and focussed it on a slippery little crack sidling through the first belt of overhangs on Mewsford Point, which I think Pat must have wanted to do, because he half-suggested that it had already been done, which made me suspicious. So I had a weekend in Derbyshire, where strong arms grow and, since it was still vacation-time co-opted Jim Curran and drove down to Pembroke on the Monday. We called in at Pat's on the way, to check on the truth of this route rumoured to be in the vicinity. And actually enough it turned out to be nowhere in the vicinity, and Jim and I were all glee, and Pat said we were bastards because he had to go up to the Lakes to do some guiding, and anyway this route would be too hard for me. Next day we slept late, abseiled in, and looked at it. Mewsford is a big, complex, and quite wonderful cliff. At the top is a band of shaly degeneracy, and at its base is a narrow channel between the cliff and a tilted slab of rock, which clears at low tide, but through which the water races furiously from half-tide onwards. My little crack was just what it seemed to be: an easy entry to what lay above, overhanging, but on big firm holds. Forty feet up I took a belay and brought up Jim. As I watched him tie on, the zeal of the convert rose in me. All the slapdash habits of ropework which had sufficed for years were now repugnant to me. But I kept silent and tried covertly to adjust a few things, then set to work on my pitch. There were sundry traversings left and right and soon the one way and the one way only became apparent, and it was hard. "How long," I wondered, "since I did a 5c pitch on this end of the rope?" No answer from the mists of time. I vented my terror on Jim. I lectured and wheedled and nagged; I gave him my Sticht place and fiddled with his belay and he, most long-suffering of men, grew distinctly irritable and told me how long he'd been climbing and so on. The more he protested, the more finicky I became, and the sun beat down upon us. When I'd got everything to my liking, it was not to his, and he complained, and I complained, and the sun baked as the sea crept in. The route was not getting done and Jim was saying Hail Marys, so finally I tried this smooth little groove, and came down, and tried again and wobbled up for a few feet, got frightened, fixed a runner, moved on, got elated, climbed fast over a bulge with big holds, found myself miles from a runner with no prospect of another, climbed on to where I could fix four or five, worried about how much rope was left, and ground to a halt beneath the collapsible top. There were wafer-like flakes of some loosely-compounded aggregate. There were monstrous blocks of pure, incomprehensible detachment and poise. I pulled dragging rope through, and shuffled breathlessly past. What I threw off by now plopped into deep water. I reached the top with just enough rope to sit on the edge without a belay. And Jim leant heavily on the rope. This, I thought, is a *volte-face*. As soon as I could, I crawled over to secure myself to a military flagpost. Jim came up, and it was all apology and exultation. We waggled our toes in the sun and lost an abseil rope in the sea, but it didn't matter. A week or two later I watched a razorbill wavecutting erratically out over the wide sea which stretches to America.

On it flew, dipping, veering, finally lost to view somewhere out on the rough, cloud-dappled plain of waters. "Yes," I thought, "it is a joke, of sorts, or the work of a cosmic joker, who gives to each of us his battle, to each his clamorous victory."

from THE CLIMBERS' CLUB JOURNAL *1979/80*

Henna Horror

MICK FOWLER

Five weeks later both Mike [Morrison] and myself were established at my previous high point above the lower overhangs. A distinctive rope groove in the rock reminded me of our previous epic whilst a solitary cloud which we had been studying with great concern was discharging its contents over Henna whilst apparently everywhere else stayed perfectly dry! An epic descent seemed even less appealing than previously (with or without stakes!) so an optimistic wait wedged across the fault line ensued.

Preparations this time were considerably more detailed than previously and exposed themselves to the public eye in the form of two home-made stakes and a sack full of bivouac equipment. The former we judged to be useful if a retreat should be necessary above the first overhanging band and the latter seemed advisable judging by our slow progress on the previous attempt.

For the first time at Henna luck was with us; the cloud dispersed, sun emerged and the soggy rock quickly dried. Resuming climbing we were pleased to find that the next pitch, although it provided us with two difficult bulges, was easier angled and not so sustained as the previous ground — we felt in high spirits to gain 100ft. so quickly. Above us though the second band of overhangs was getting closer, a massive block with its top forming an obvious ledge split the continuation of the fault line, two alternatives presented themselves: to our left a steep, sandy fault line led directly to the top of the block whilst to our right compact, blocky rock led to a rightwards slanting groove from which a possible traverse line led left onto the top of the block.

Owing to the necessity of a short descent to attempt the left hand line we immediately decided on the right hand possibility. Poor ice screw belays did little to encourage rapid progress but solid rock if technically difficult and with little protection, allowed steady movement to the point where the traverse line led leftwards towards the next stance. From close up this could be seen to be uncomfortably sloping with some horrendous precariously poised blocks at the start. Unfortunately a short overhanging wall separated the groove from the start of the ledge line and forced a wild swing leftwards into a strenuous position uncomfortably close to the blocks. Tentative probes and further prods with the terrordactyl confirmed that the blocks were in fact at least as unstable as they looked – levering them off however was distinctly out of the question with Mike belayed directly in the line of fire and voicing a healthy lack of enthusiasm for block-clearing activities. Some challenging contortions had the rather surprising effect of establishing me on the end of the ledge intimately entwined with the blocks. The only possible solution to this uncalled for intimacy appeared to lay in picking them up and throwing them as far away as possible, however being curled around them in the first place this obviously posed a severe technical problem! Having lovingly manoeuvred myself into an acceptable position I tried to pick up the biggest block – unfortunately the result was not quite what was anticipated – a crack promptly appeared down its centre and my efforts to prevent the pieces falling on Mike resulted in a very squashed finger for me and a nastily dented helmet for Mike. A joint decision was promptly made that the blocks should remain *in situ*: if at all possible. Careful climbing and rope management persuaded the blocks that their present position was best suited to their requirements as a desperately sloping hand-traverse led to the stance on top of the huge block to my left. A spike belay, the first on the route, presented itself as a welcome gift and gave a much needed feeling of security. Mike followed quickly, the encumbrance of the sack forcing him to trundle the offending blocks, and we were soon in a position to compare injuries. Continuous battering from small shale slivers had left interesting – evenly spaced cuts over his hands whilst my finger nail was turning a harsh shade of blue after its incident on the previous pitch. Fortunately the sun was now shining and in high spirits we ignored injuries and contemplated the next pitch.

From below the initial section, at least, looked reasonable – a shallow, sandy chimney led up to large overhangs which it seemed possible to outflank on the left or right. However, once engrossed it immediately became apparent that first impressions can be distinctly misleading – the walls of the chimney were sufficiently unstable to prevent the use of orthodox techniques and progress was only possible by exerting a lateral force on the walls at all times. Being too V-shaped for chimneying it provided a very absorbing cross between a mantelshelfing and bridging exercise, fortunately protected by a good ice-screw. At the overhang matters took a turn for the worse, the possibilities noted from below looked at the best frightening and at the worst thoroughly impossible, the death potential looked excellent. For a long time I remained motionless. Up to the left overhangs could be seen to appear with a disconcerting frequency whilst to the right an overhanging rib abutted against the main overhang, its only redeeming feature being one uncomfortable-looking projecting handhold. How it managed to remain on the cliff and not join its friends over 400ft. below in the sea was a worrying mystery; however, it seemed just possible that it might last long enough to permit a swinging movement out onto a small grass ledge ten feet higher—anything looked better than the left-hand alternative so the route finding decision was made. Down below Mike was showing understandable concern at the lack of progress, not to mention the fact that (yet again!) he was in the direct line of fire. As he pointed out retreat from here seemed an horrendous proposition involving the loss of many brain cells as well as much equipment. The realisation that the future of our precious equipment was at stake prompted renewed efforts culminating in a particularly uncontrollable swing on the offending hold which, much to my relief, resulted in my being established safely on the ledge. We had hoped that the overhang would provide the final obstacle but half an hour later I had to admit that the slightly off-vertical ground ahead was nastily devoid of holds and frighteningly constructed of outward sloping shale slivers. Only 15ft. up to the left a wide crack offered probable runner placements but the moves in between seemed impossible—I envisaged the epic potential of a retreat and searched even more studiously for runner places — nothing worthwhile could be found and it became increasingly clear that either it was done without protection or it wasn't done at all. In frustration I started up yet again; sloping footholds and fragile layaways were the order of the day—passing my previous highpoint the moves seemed irreversible and I could not help but realise that retreat was impossible without a long serious fall. With the crack almost in reach the holds thinned out even more—progress only seemed possible by balancing up on a particularly suspect sloping hold at waist level. The prospect seemed appalling but the lack of alternatives, combined with failing strength, prevented any further consideration. . . Heart in mouth my weight was transferred and I straightened up; the crack was now in reach but the best jamming position was still too high . . . stretching higher I could feel the footholds move, my leg began to shake . . . the hold moved more . . . panic took over and I lurched into the crack, dust flew up from the back; the chick above was sick over me, but a runner was placed and suddenly the panic was over, everything seemed under control again. The chick settled down deep in the crack, the dust settled and ten feet higher I removed a seagull from the secluded niche and thankfully belayed.

Watching Mike seconding the pitch it struck me how out of place the sack containing the bivouac gear appeared on a south-west British sea cliff, however, Mike seemed quite at home with it as he joined me once more. Above us things were finally looking more amenable – a short steep wall separated us from a slanting grassy ramp apparently leading to the top – but we were learning not to be optimistic, most shale climbing appears about two grades easier than it actually is! Remarkably the pitch above seemed to be an exception to the rule; the cliff appeared to be succumbing at last – the initial wall proved desperate as anticipated but beyond this reasonable climbing led to within ten feet of the top. Excitement mounting I climbed the final easy wall to emerge on the cliff top path amidst the calm and tranquil scene of grazing sheep and families out for leisurely weekend strolls. The humans regarded us with a pitiful indifference, the sheep with curiosity; both no doubt resented this intrusion into their privacy – I felt like belaying to them, explaining it all to them, telling them just how I came to be standing on the edge of a Cornish cliff carrying an ice-axe and ice-screws, pegs, hammer, nuts, helmet etc.

A tug on the ropes reminded me that an impatient Mike was still installed 70ft. below and doubtless keen to 'escape' the cliff. I belayed and Mike arrived quickly – the sheep ran away, the humans disappeared; we were left with our own thoughts – we didn't really care – they probably wouldn't want to understand. Anyway we had an appointment with the landlord at Morwenstow – just to ensure that his line wasn't identical to ours!

from MOUNTAIN 75 *1980*

Boredom and the Big Numbers

REINHARD KARL

"No more 8,000 metre peaks!" I said to myself after Everest. The calculation, three months for a one-week climb to the summit, wasn't on. I had a good deal of difficulty getting used to being in Heidelberg again—I was totally drained. I needed a couple of months before I felt that I was really there again. I think it was not so much the rarefied air which had made me so depressed and unhappy, but rather the three months' solitude. Although I had been in company with others, it had always been as a solitary individual. The mountain, which I felt I had to climb, and which had so strongly impressed itself on my consciousness, had strengthened this feeling of being alone with the mountains, and everything against me. I was glad that Heidelberg lies so far away from the mountains. But it is astonishing how short the time-span is between "No more big peaks" and a new mountain goal. Come the winter, everything appears positive again—up there, over 8,000 metres high, to change into a breathless superman—that must be really something. Still, time to enjoy lazy evenings watching television from a reclining chair, beer glass in hand. When I hear news of disasters, I feel glad to be at home in a warm room, but from March on, when occasional glimpses of the sun are here again, then the only thing I want to do is to get away.

A chance to go with Hans Schell to the 8,035 metre Gasherbrum 2 in the Karakoram crops up. It will be expensive: every metre of its height will cost more than a mark. When I meet the other expedition members at Frankfurt airport, the negative side of Everest suddenly comes to mind again: the waiting, the weary time-wasting at the camps, the apathetic gasping for breath, the emptiness of the mind at high-altitude, the arguments with climbing friends who, like me, had only one goal in their mind: to reach the summit. The unwritten law reads, "the expedition is a team, but a team with only one purpose – to let me reach the summit. The expedition is only successful for me, if I stand on the summit." The line between self-interest and the common good is easily overstepped. All that and much more suddenly come to mind. Why can't I have ordinary holidays with my wife, like so many other millions. At the sea or somewhere else. Too late now, but I shall make up for it.

The others, meanwhile, are ready to go and are as excited as little children. Kurt wants to climb his fifth eight-thousander, Hans his third, Hilmer his second. Karl had already climbed to 7,000 metres on Hidden Peak before becoming ill. Now he wants to know if he can make it. The others: Walter, Gerald, Wolf, Alfred and Ernst, they all want to know what it is like to climb above the magic 8,000 metre mark. 8,000 is a big number — it signifies.

According to numbers our expedition was large, but only according to the numbers. Thanks to Hans' parsimony we were no 'dinosaur' expedition, but rather a 'hungry wolf' one. We had to budget carefully with the money since we hadn't any sponsors and Pakistan isn't Nepal: the porters, like everything else are much more expensive. We paid everything out of our own pocket, and that increased the pressure to accomplish our aims. We were a poor-man's expedition. By contrast, with us into the Baltoro region went the giant French K2 expedition. With its 1,500 porters it was a major national undertaking.

As we moved off into the wilderness our half-starved troop with its few porters and scanty equipment, was regarded by the French as a mountain-trekking group. But I was glad not to be a member of their strictly organised mountain commando unit and in the final analysis my feeling was justified. Almost all of us got to the summit. Despite the bad weather, the French tricolour remained drooping at the base camp.

At first glance it seems enticing to travel among foreign people, and climb mountains. As everyone knows, travel broadens the mind, but when you intend to climb a high mountain then you are no longer a tourist and not receptive to those things which interest others. You are possessed by the mountain and see everything in terms of getting to the base camp as fast as possible. The unfamiliar cities and villages are seen as obstacles en route. And towards the foreign people, or rather the natives, you take an employer's attitude: you require a service, pay good money for it, and know it. In lands where, with the exception of time, everything is in short supply, the restlessness of civilisation's neurotics is unintelligible to the native people you meet; educated people who can reel off a complete account of the economic geography and political happenings of recent years in the guest country, who speak to the ancient people there as if to their students or employers.

Yet there are a few simple rules which enable you to get on with any person without knowledge of his language, even at the end of the world near the border of China. Treat the person as a person, not as a substitute for a donkey or a beast of burden, which because you are paying it your good money has to carry loads that you yourself would never agree to carry.

It also seems questionable whether or not the tourists, who aimlessly wander around to study the culture or whatever, learn very much from it, for the contrast between an educated Western traveller and a Nepali or Balti is too great. It is really coloured television in a foreign language that is unveiled to the open-mouthed observer. As for friendships the basic requirements are lacking. As a climber, although hurried by the egotistical desire to be able to say "I have climbed an eight-thousander," you perhaps take in a lot more about the people and the country. After all, you live there for months, and money or social status don't count for much in the mountains.

The route into the Baltoro region is long and hard: a fortnight's walk through desert-like mountains and over glacial moraine. Endless glacial moraine without paths—"one step forward, two steps back." The poverty of the mountain villages is great. A plastic bag or an empty gas cartridge are treasures that improve the quality of daily life. The people mainly live in self sufficient farming communities; load-carrying is the only way of obtaining cash. Nevertheless, there are more important things to them than pride in money, in contrast to Europe where to a great extent people will do anything for money. Earlier there were frequent porter-strikes in Pakistan: one word out of place and the proudly impecunious porters threw down onto the glacier the 20 kgs. of junk required for the mountain-heroes' self-realisation.

There have been many expedition-organisers who have not properly read the handbook *How to handle subordinates* and who have retreated unsuccessfully from the wildest mountains in the world. Today the government has stretched out its thin arm even here, and controls by thumbprint the agreed contracts between the illiterate and the mountain heroes. First impressions are that the people here are content, a long way from demarcation disputes and civilised schizophrenia. Their integrated life-style with possession of land, labour, house, wife and animals has been going on for thousands of years. Some people use the term 'meaningful happy existence' for this drudgery of day-to-day living and survival, but to those for whom there is only the opportunity for subsistence, the term 'happiness' or 'meaningful existence' is completely empty.

The religion of the Baltis is Islam and even today hands are chopped off for stealing. However, for the Baltis' sake they do not stick to the letter of the law in this matter. By which, I don't want to say that there are more thieves among the Balti than among us but when there is such a low standard of living and godlike beings come along with vast amounts of material goods for the completely senseless purpose of climbing one of the uncountable mountains, then it is understandable that occasionally they suffer from sticky fingers.

The Braldu Valley which leads to the Baltoro Glacier is a hard region and the people are equally hard and what they eat is even harder: Chapatis with 25% sand in the flour. When I think about the chapatis I still get indigestion. Nowhere has the old saying, "A man is what he eats" appeared more appropriate to me. The men are like the chapatis: as hard as nails. I've always believed that I was pretty hard myself and that I could put up with as much hardship as other people. In comparison to these people, however, I am an effeminate, pampered dandy, who, by chance, happens to have climbed a few mountains. I had always regarded tramps as the real bivouac kings, sleeping on park benches covered only by newspapers, but here I saw people running over the scree-sprinkled glacier ice carrying 30 kg. packs. When, however, a porter who looked about fifty, asked me how old I was and I indicated on my fingers that I was thirty-two, it came as a shock to me to learn that he was younger than me.

The last village is called Askole — a pathetic collection of huts. A few kids gesticulate that they want sweets. There are a few dogs and hens but no women: not even the old women or those with goitres are to be seen: it is a male society. The policeman checks our papers, the last policeman we shall see. Here just about everything ends. When there isn't a policeman anymore, then there is nothing:

only mountains, rocks, snow and ice. We pass through the village without taking particular notice of anything. We do not even remark on the bed, the only bed, which has been erected in the middle of the village in our honour. How I shall look forward, later on, to being back here again.

If only there was a highway to China!
Two days later at the river, we meet the giant French tape-worm with its Napoleon, Yannick Seigneur and his 1,500-strong army. A month earlier this tributary of the Braldu could be waded; now it is a raging torrent whose far bank of which cannot be reached without a bridge. The French build a rope-bridge. Although it takes each man only one minute to cross the river, almost three days are needed before all their porters and their loads are on the other side. It looks as if Alexander the Great is retreating.

Urdukas is the last patch of green along the glacier. The last plants and flowers are there. To us it appears as if we are taking leave from life itself. Opposite this viewpoint, which no tourist office could have set up better, stand the Trango Towers, the Uli Biaho Tower and the Payu Peaks looking like Lego-constructions – incredibly beautiful six-thousanders. They are reckoned to be the Yosemite of the future and when photos of the dream towers are examined while reclining on the sofa, that may well seem to be the case. In comparison El Capitan is only a children's climbing frame for daydreamers. To get to the foot of El Cap it is only a five-minute walk from the car. The Yosemite Valley is a land of milk and honey for climbers: the weather is always fine, the climbing has a dreamlike quality. When you have had enough you abseil off, that's it: ice cream, beer, and restaurants are all waiting for you. To get to the nightmare mountains of the Baltoro you have to walk for a week and the climbing is correspondingly serious: climbing and fun take leave from each other. What counts here are the summit and food. But if ever there were to be a highway built to China, it would be a different story.

From now on the route is completely on moraine; past the grandoise Masherbrum to the even more grandoise view from Concordia. On the left K2, 4,000 metres above the valley, dominating it with a harmony that takes your breath away. The quietness of the mountains rendering you speechless. I shout something; no sound, no answer. Only the wind whispers something to the mountains. Mt. Everest is the highest of mountains, but what does that mean? K2 is without doubt the king, at least when seen from Concordia. Broad Peak, to the right of it, is only a pile of scree that happens to be 8,000 metres high. Mitre Peak and Gasherbrum 4, just under 8,000, and therefore uninteresting, light up in the evening sun. Numbers still have their meaning and power here.

After another two days we reach our Base Camp at the foot of Hidden Peak. Our mountain, Gasherbrum 2, is just a minute point. It is the most distant of the whole group. It is good to be back in the mountains again in this a beautiful place with its superb view. Rocks, mountains, snow and ice: what more do we desire?

I have never seen the mountains as they appear on slides
Me? I do not want to have any more diarrhoea, but no fairy godmother comes to fulfil my wish. Moreover, I feel as if I had been born with a rucksack on my back. Continual carrying and setting up camps; we are climbing the mountain without sherpas. It sounds good, doesn't it? When I look at the slides back home in my living room the mountains appear beautiful, simply unbelievable. But I have only seen the beauty of mountains on slides. Never have I seen their beauty in the flesh as I have seen it on the slides. On the slides the mountains resemble a moon landscape. I have never been on the moon but I've seen the slides of it. . . There is a 'frog-perspective' and a 'rucksack-perspective', from both of which everything looks less imposing. When one has diarrhoea on top of that then the mountains look more like giants. . .

At 7,000 metres our luck with the weather comes to an end. Over a metre of new snow falls. We wait in the tents. Above and around us the mountain, nothing but snow and ice. Below at Base Camp there are still stones and it is good to sit on stones. Nearby is another expedition – a Japanese one. Unfortunately they speak hardly any German. For months they have been skirting all the Karakoram glaciers: Chogolungma, Hispar, Biafo, Baltoro and the Siachen. When you look at a map and see how far that is: every glacier over 70 kilometres long, everywhere only glacial moraine winding through desolate mountains, then you can imagine that after such a journey a person cannot be normal any more (if he ever was in the first place). It is like writing a Ph.D. about Sisyphus and

Tantalus. The liaison officer wasn't normal at the start, but now he is about to go completely mad. We call him Captain Homesick. But we all feel homesick. The Japanese have a good piece of equipment with them which we don't have: a well-read copy of *Playboy* in Japanese. Not that the naked women interest us. All that has died out with the altitude. No, it is the advertising: cars, food, parties, records, music, a city, streets, cinemas, supermarkets, televisions; that is what interests us. We dream of the normal things in life. Fayyaz, our liaison officer, Captain Homesick and myself play with stones and dream of Rawalpindi. There life begins again.

We are up here and you are down below
The weather is still bad. Nevertheless, Hilmar, Karl and myself want to try to get to the top. It is incredibly tiring to make progress in the deep snow. Still, in driving snow we manage to set up the last camp at 7,500 metres. As a result of the trail-breaking we are pretty well done for. Hilmar has a cough caused by the altitude which has almost deprived him of his voice. He can only whisper, but he still feels strong. Karl is more or less OK although he is a bit worried about the altitude. I have a stomach and intestinal complaint. The chapatis have ruined my stomach and every time I try to eat anything I bring it up again. We know that in the sort of shape we are in, tomorrow will be our last chance to make the summit, and then only if the weather is on our side. It is maddening; so long spent hanging about on the mountain, and then everything hurrying on a single day. We speak to Hans in Base Camp using the walkie-talkie. Sometimes technology is also a curse. He wants us to wait for him. He doesn't understand. We tell him that we are up here and have to give it a go. He doesn't want to understand. "But an expedition is only successful when I have been to the top." This terrible truth divides us now. We tell Hans, "We are up here now and you are down below. We have to have a go now."

It is a bad feeling to go for the summit against the wishes of the others. Now we are really alone. In the morning the three of us cook in the minute tent and get ready. It is snowing lightly and the wind sweeps over the snow. Disheartened, we begin the ascent. After half an hour we realise the futility of it and go back down. "That is it, the summit is out for us. Just our bad luck with the weather." I get stomach cramp and my breakfast comes up again.

We sit in the tent and wait to go down. The tears run down my face. I don't know why, whether from the pain in the stomach or the pain in my soul. We will never come back here again. What bad luck! Why isn't the weather good today? No I simply cannot give up. Everything in me resists, I will not lose. I look out of the tent, the weather has improved a little. The others are stoically packing their rucksacks. "Look lads we have to give it another go. Later we won't have the strength to manage it, we must have a go now."

"OK, if you think so." We try again. The traverse to the right is like a ski slope. But it is almost 8,000 metres high. Originally I had wanted to try climbing straight up the rock pillar to the summit on my own: it is much more direct, but today we have only got one chance, together or not at all. The final slope is steep and exhausting. Hilmar gives up, "We won't reach the summit today," he says despondently. Karl is already dropping behind. OK, I'll go first as far as the saddle. I manage it although I have just about had it. I get another spasm of sickness, but my stomach has been empty for a long time now; only bile comes out. "Lads, the snow isn't deep any longer; we'll make it." Hilmar comes up and Karl too. Hilmar goes first, but after 100 metres we are in deep snow again. "No, I can't continue, we won't make the summit today," Hilmar whispers. The rarified air has robbed him of the rest of his voice. I hear myself answering him, "I'll break trail until 3 o'clock, and wherever we are then we'll turn around." I really can't continue. Why dig a ditch up the steep slope simply in order to get higher. There is only snow up there too; why do it? The secret is to be found in the words, "I have climbed Gasherbrum 2." If I turn around now, then I won't have managed it, and everything will have been pointless. You might not understand it, but that is the way it is.

It is easier when you are completely exhausted, to make a trail for two hours than to continue making a trail until you cannot go on. At five minutes to three the summit silence is broken by a racking cough. I have won. I am up. That is it, there is nothing to see, because I am in the clouds. My watch says three o'clock. Hilmar arrives and then Karl. We are happy because we have managed it. We are above at the top and a long way away from the normal world. As far as the view goes we could be on top of a mountain in the Allgau, but as I said the secret is in the sentence, "I have climbed Gasherbrum 2.''

That isn't the last wish

When you are on top of the mountain, then you immediately wish that you were down at the bottom again. When you are down the bottom again, you say the following: I want to walk along a path again, and want to be together with people again, and you want to be in a city, and I want to be home and I want to be together with my wife. That isn't the last wish, it is the first, but it is the last in order of realisation. While we are on the glacier, we run out of food. For the last two days we stagger over the glacier completely exhausted. In hallucinations brought on by hunger, I dream that I am going through a supermarket with a shopping bag and from the thousands of goods on sale picking exactly those that I most like. Then I get into my car and drive off. It must feel good to have an ignition key again, to sit in a car and to drive where you want — not to have to walk any further. We meet two porters, who are walking back from another expedition. ''My God, they've something for us to eat, they'll really give us something.'' They make a fire straight away and bake chapatis for us on the stone-slabs. It always seemed to me that chapatis were training for eating stones, but now they are much better than stones. Our life-savers cannot bake them fast enough for us.

I shall never forget our entry into Askole. It is a profound feeling to walk along a path again and to return to a human settlement. The people come out and welcome us in a friendly way. The mayor, who has been to Mecca, comes and invites us to his house. He greets us formally.

We laugh. Suddenly we become like animals. We see a tin of food. ''How much'' — we only see the tin. ''20 rupees'', ''OK''. Greedily we open the tin. There is cheese in it. In less than a minute it is empty. ''More?'' He has eight tins. On top of that he has a large jar of jam and many eggs and a goat and lots of chapatis and hens. Our hunger is satisfied but not our longing for home. On to Skardu, the first city, the first beer. Then Frankfurt airport — it always bowls me over. There you know you are back in Germany: perfection in concrete.

In photographs the Karakoram looks enticingly beautiful but I know that the reality is other than the appearance. At night in dreams the reality occasionally visits me. Why do I still want to climb although I know it is such a difficult struggle? Perhaps the difficult struggle is an integral part of the ascent and because it is so exhausting it remains deeply engraved in the memory. The elation on the other hand is like the descent. Quickly and easily you are back down again and it is forgotten.

from ERLEBNIS BERG: ZEIT ZUM ATMEN (MOUNTAIN EXPERIENCE: TIME TO BREATHE) *1980*

Imagined Heights

HUDSON STUCK

Three years later Doctor Cook organised an expedition for a second attempt upon the mountain. In May 1906, accompanied by Professor Herschel Parker, Mr. Belmore Browne, a topographer named Porter, who made some valuable maps, and packers, the party landed at the head of Cook's Inlet and penetrated by motor-boat and by pack-train into the Sushitna country, south of the range. Failing to cross the range at the head of the Yentna, they spent some time in explorations along the Kahilitna River, and, finding no avenue of approach to the heights of the mountain, the party returned to Cook's Inlet and broke up.

With only one companion, a packer named Edward Barrille, Cook returned in the launch up the Chulitna River to the Tokositna late in August. "We had already changed our mind as to the impossibility of climbing the mountain," he writes. Ascending a glacier which the Tokositna River drains, named by Cook the Ruth Glacier, they reached the amphitheatre at the glacier head. From this point, "up and up to the heaven-scraped granite of the top," Doctor Cook grows grandiloquent and vague, for at this point his true narrative ends.

The claims that Doctor Cook made upon his return are well known, but it is quite impossible to follow his course from the description given in his book, *To the Top of the Continent*. This much may be said: from the summit of the mountain, on a clear day, it seemed evident that no ascent was possible from the south side of the range at all. That was the judgment of all four members of our party. Doctor Cook talks about "The heaven-scraped granite of the top" and "the dazzling whiteness of the frosted granite blocks," and prints a photograph of the top showing granite slabs. There is no rock of any kind on the South (the higher) Peak above 19,000ft. The last 1,500ft. of the mountain is all permanent snow and ice; nor is the conformation of the summit in the least like the photograph printed as the "top of Mt. McKinley." In his account of the view from the summit he speaks of "the ice-blink caused by the extensive glacial sheets north of the Saint Elias group," which would surely be out of the range of any possible vision, but does not mention at all the master sight that bursts upon the eye when the summit is actually gained – the great mass of 'Denali's Wife', or Mt. Foraker, filling all the middle distance. We were all agreed that no one who had ever stood on the top of Denali in clear weather could fail to mention the sudden splendid sight of this great mountain.

But it is not worth while to pursue the subject further. The present writer feels confident that any man who climbs to the top of Denali, and then reads Doctor Cook's account of his ascent, will not need Edward Barrille's affidavit to convince him that Cook's narrative is untrue. Indignation is, however, swallowed up in pity when one thinks upon the really excellent pioneering and exploring work done by this man, and realises that the immediate success of the imposition about the ascent of Denali doubtless led to the more audacious imposition about the discovery of the North Pole – and that to his discredit and downfall.

from THE ASCENT OF DENALI *1914*

PART 3

The Moral?
It's the Travelling

. . . said Jean-Luc Godard, when asked for the meaning of his film *Weekend*.

It has always struck me that the infrequent heights of those drearily-interminable expedition narratives were reached not in accounts of the climbs themselves, but in the little anecdotes and incidental details of the approach marches, the dynamics of group-enterprise, the suspicious hints of scandal.

In the following are offered up for your delectation my particular favourites for the travel-compendium. If the climbing intrudes here and there amongst these alternative delights, never mind — even the hopeful traveller must sometimes arrive at his destination.

And should the climbing pall, there is always the delicate eroticism of *But I Never Returned . . .*, Lito Tejada-Flores' unrequited romanticism in *Crooked Road to the Far North*, the outrageous bawdy of Peter Livesey's *Travels with a Donkey*, or Anderl Heckmair giving his simple man's view of the nubile Leni Riefenstahl and an encounter with Hitler.

So, like the needy traveller in Johnson's *Vanity of Human Wishes*, let's walk the wild heath and sing our toil away.

Once in a While

G. F. DUTTON

Ski-ing is a vice few of us can altogether avoid. I had succumbed to temptation several times, once even tasted a polythene-wrapped package course under sardonic Continental instruction. The Apprentice, well-trained by early glissades in vibrams down Twisting Gully, took to it readily. Goggle-hats and numbers fitted in well when he felt too tired for climbing or when the particular bird-in-hand leaned agreeably towards après-ski complaisance. Obviously our ski-tracks did not often cross. Moreover, the Doctor's performance on boards, though darkly hinted at, remained unknown to us.

One weekend, however, we did, more or less, ski together. The Apprentice's girlfriend and his mini-van had both suffered mechanical failure at the last moment. Snow was flour on marble; good for ski-ing, shocking for gullies. He came to my door on the Saturday morning, disconsolately magnificent in heliographic steel-and-plastic boots, and carrying the glittering balance of a hundred pounds sterling on his shoulder. Such splendour in distress moved me to pity, though I preferred the kind of sartorial ostentation more usually displayed by The Weasels – rusted ironware and egg-hardened rags. Could I, would I, join him? But I had no car that weekend, either. . . We thought of the Doctor, our traditional transport in emergency. We rang him up.

"Where were you off to? Glen Scree? Ha, so was I. Excellent snow I believe. Jolly good idea. Like to see how you fellows ski. You can't have been at it very long. . ." So he met us with his old Mercedes and we strapped our planks aloft, beside a long leather canoe-like object.

At Glen Scree the fair was in full swing. We took down our skis. The Doctor unlaced the canoe and drew out a pair of huge sledge-runners, turned up fully a foot at each solid hickory toe. He laid them massively down, then extracted two long bamboo poles, ending in plate-sized wattle baskets. A large shapeless rucksack appeared on his back. As he wore his regular poacher-pocketed

251

climbing tweeds, fishing hat, gaiters and clinkered boots he struck uncommon silence into the chromatic throng about us. Shouldering his burden and scattering lesser fry, he strode off. We had agreed to go on to the plateau, although the Apprentice, dreaming of effort-less thousands of feet of Jaguar (a curiously revolting Grade 2 descent), remained reluctant. I followed. The Apprentice roared at us over the juke-boxes.

"You're not climbing up? What's the lift for?"

The Doctor smiled back benignly across an open sea of mouths.

"We can't waste time on a lift. We're late already. I told you, you should have brought your skins." He turned, causing a travelling ripple of ducking, and marched on. I hurried after him.

When the crowd had thinned sufficiently for us to see the snow beneath us, we stopped and put on skins. The Doctor produced from his rucksack two 7ft. lengths of genuine seal skin. "Damned fine animal it must have been," he said reverently as he buckled the harness. "Never let me down in twenty-five years. Tore out a big chunk on a tin the first time we did the Haute Route, and lemmings ate a bit that Lapland trip; but there's always enough left for patch-ing." He pulled the last thong tight and stepped aboard into great hinged and bolt-headed bindings. A pause to press his pipe; then he clanked away elk-like and I shuffled after, in unyielding con-temporary footgear. No wonder the Apprentice—who would be clamped irreversibly flat to aluminium and fibreglass—preferred the chairlift.

Hoots followed us from the queue where that metallescent youth was indulging in ignoble gibes.

"Can't think how he can waste good ski-ing time—never mind money—on those antiquated sack-elevators," remarked the Doctor, plunging upwards through a Gate. A local Beer Trophy was being run, and I scuttled alongside, ears burning.

True enough, we were quite a way up before the Apprentice reached the end of the queue. Then he whisked above us, attempt-ing to spear the Doctor's hat with a flash of Japanese chrome steel. "I'll get a couple of runs in while I'm waiting for you," he shouted. Waggling his glitter in triumph, he vanished into the blue. I heaved along grimly, exiguous on icy rubble. The Doctor, well ahead, elaborated on the superior rhythm of climbing in skins. "Now even with trikes your feet would be slipping about in a place like this.

Effortless with skins.'' Push. Slide. Push. Slither. Slide. Push.

We climbed higher. We stopped once to reassemble a gentleman in an ankle-length cagoule and a label. My companion felt him all over, pronounced him fit as a fiddle, slapped him on the back and returned him to his erratic and billowing descent. He did not get far. ''Carrying too much sail,'' observed the Doctor. Push. Slide. Push.

Nearly there. Above us an individual appeared at great speed, bent in a stiff right-angle. We paused. Ski-sticks and expression fixed unwaveringly ahead, legs wide apart, he charged past us to the enemy below. Appropriately, he was capped with a Balaclava. Our respectful resumption was momentarily interrupted by the trajectory of his Instructor, bewailing the errant lamb—''Benzeneez, benzeneez''—cursing fluently in Austro-Glaswegian. The rest of the flock clutched each other on the pebble-dash wall above. We agreed the slopes were busy enough for the time of year. Slither. Push. Slide. Push.

The air rarefied and I became aware of a great silence. We had topped the corrie. The upper station of the lift lay just visible on our left. No sign of the Apprentice. ''He's probably gone down again for his run,'' I remarked, not without envy.

''We can't wait all day. If he doesn't come by the time I've finished waxing, he's obviously funked it,'' said the Doctor. ''Seems to admit he needs more practice. Though I'm not at all sure we haven't beaten him. Those things are so slow.''

We had in fact beaten him, as we discovered later. At that moment, and for the next three hours, the Apprentice, blue as his boots, was dangling 30ft. above icy scree in a cold iron chair, consoled by a boisterous north wind. The drive sprocket had jammed. The papers made a lot of it the next day.

Meanwhile, the Doctor applied a glistening tar-like concoction, smelling of Andalsnes boat-yards, to his considerable square-footage. He rubbed each hull energetically with a slab of cork, explaining the eminent practicability of this composition. ''Your plastic soles'll be ripped to pieces on any really interesting bit of ground. All I need do is give another rub—just like this—and be as smooth as ever. Sure you don't want some? I declined, but my apprehensions, always alert in the Doctor's company, shifted uneasily.

No Apprentice. "The lad's not coming. Playing at Sliders. Even a lift can't take as long as this. Let's go." And the Doctor poled off bonily across diamonded whiteness.

There was an uncanny lack of orange peel. There were no other tracks. The sun shone out of a cloudless sky. Miles of glistering plateau. The Doctor was moved to song, not one of his several accomplishments. I cruised behind, lulled by the more agreeable purr of powder smooth plastic. Bliss.

Yes, it was a good day, although, being early January, a short one. I steered him away from the worst stretches of dragon's teeth ("nothing like rough stuff to test your technique!"). I followed gratefully his tracks, twin country lanes, through fathoms of drift. I skidded, marvelling, above his flagship manoeuvrings on steep ice (gold would not have tempted me beneath them — nor within range of his poles, wielded with true Bannockburn fervour). I drank unashamedly his ice-cold wine and tea at our farthest point. "Nothing like it; cools you and warms you at the same time. Just the thing for today. I bet he's slogging beer right now, hogging the fleshpots between runs. Must have done tens of thousands of feet — but he's young, and needs the practice. Takes a long time to learn how to ski."

We sailed leisurely back. At times, I clattered frantically and expensively across windsawn patches of granite and heather; the Doctor did not appear to notice them, being occupied with his pipe, which was not drawing well that day ("this damned north wind"). At times, too, I narrowly escaped engulfment by the craters his baskets left among the polished windslab.

His falls, for — mercifully — he too had falls, were collapses worthy of such imperial progress. When the powder clouds had blown away, crossed limbs and hickory stood magnificent in ruin against the landscape. A grunt, then Ozymandias himself creaked and elevated out of the depths, raising himself with impossible flexions of hinge, leather and tendon. He would dust himself down, search for his pipe, and explain at length how, given that precise conjunction of dynamics and meteorology such a fall in such a direction in such snow was quite inevitable; almost, it seemed, praiseworthy. After which, climbing over the rim of his late demonstration, he would punt away, apparently satisfied. He was, however, notably more cautious for fully three minutes after each fall, and later in the day I detected a slight limp and a recurrent reindeer-like clang as if some weight-bearing machinery had come adrift in his bindings; but there seemed more than enough to spare and our speed remained respectably high on the Amundsen scale.

At last we returned to our starting point, not far from the top station. The Doctor cast anchor with both sticks, fiddled a chain or two and sprang lightly ashore. Puffing his pipe, he raised seven feet of hickory and examined below waterline, to the wonder of a small crash-hatted, green-goggled urchin, Number 10.

"Hm, not bad. Picked up very few stones this time. Excellent wax. Pity I've almost finished the last barrel. Comes in drums now; not half so good." Then he suddenly straightened up and dropped his timber, pinning beneath it the fluorescent ski-lets of Number 10. "There he is! Just coming off the lift. For the nth time, I'd say. Look how he's staggering. Punch-drunk, these fellows." The Apprentice indeed slid drunkenly towards us, skis crossed, eyes staring. He had in fact just been released from his three-hour dangle at minus five. He could not speak.

The Doctor picked up his ski, reassuringly patted the liberated Number 10, and climbed back into the cockpit. He put away his pipe and prodded the still speechless Apprentice with a monstrous basket (I was fascinated by the curved iron hook beneath it). He beamed invitingly.

"Come on, now—a race down, eh? Give us ten yards' start; remember you've been practicing all day, and we're stiff."

He sculled furiously off, leaving black streaks on the snow.

A couple of wee smashers, preening nearby, tittered.

My leader of a hundred icy cruxes, the Apprentice, is nothing if not game. He rumbled some improbable liquid-nitrogen oath, rolled eyes to the sky, and hurled himself stiffly down. I followed, circumspectly. It was, after all, Jaguar.

There is a small rock island near the middle of Jaguar. The Doctor, leaning back contemplatively in a shower of ice, rode his sticks like an experienced cavalry general; a tug at the reins, and he was carried off safely leftwards, out of the fray. The Apprentice, bombing down inert and frozen, remembered too late. Jaguar struck — hard. He somersaulted several yards and continued, mercifully beyond teeth and claws, on his back, head foremost. Eventually he came to rest, against a pair of spectators. The Doctor, completing his 100 metre flourish, sallied in on one knee, bent in a pensive Telemark. He slowed gracefully to a halt; rose, and leaned, sticks beneath chin. He looked down, Wellington from his horse. The spectators held gloved hands in silence.

"Well, well. You fellows just do too much Downhill for one day. You should take time off, sit around a bit. Chair and a nice cold beer in the sun for an hour or two. That's what I'd do if I had to stay and practice here. Not race up and down like this. You get careless. Lose control. Must keep control on a mountain, you know; otherwise, even ski-ing can become dangerous." He and the sun gleamed together, through gold-rimmed Polaroids.

The Apprentice glared up weakly. His crash hat was dented. Small blue fragments lay about him on the snow.

In the bar we grew mellow. The Apprentice was gratefully welcoming back his various joints. "Oh, ski-ing's good fun once in a while," said the Doctor, raising his Glen Rauchle, "but not a patch on glissading. Glissading's straightforward. Don't need all these contraptions. But mind you, one thing you do need" — he tipped back reminiscently — "you do need a good long axe."

from THE SCOTTISH MOUNTAINEERING CLUB
JOURNAL *1976*

10 Tobin Sorenson crosses the difficult Kor Traverse during the third ascent of the Eiger Direct in September 1976. *Photo: Alex MacIntyre*

11 A fatal accident in the mountains.

12 Phil Burke solos Mongoose, Tremadog, North Wales. *Photo: John Stevens*

13 (overleaf) Kalanka and Changabang (Garhwal, India) at sunset.
Photo: Joe Tasker

14 The North Face of Latok 1 above the Choktoi Glacier, in the Karakoram, offers challenge for 'super-alpinists' in the eighties. The rib on the right defeated attempts by American and British parties in 1978 and 1982. *Photo: Dave Potts*

15 (right) The steep slopes leading to the North Ridge of Kanchenjunga – a route first climbed by a four-man Anglo-French group in 1979. *Photo: Doug Scott*

16 (overleaf) Morning sun picks out the sandstone flutings of The Titan in the Fisher Towers, Utah. This 900ft. column was first climbed by a route up the right edge in 1962 by a party led by Layton Kor. There have been two further routes: Sundevil Chimney (right of the sun/shadow line) and the West Face. *Photo: Craig Martinson*

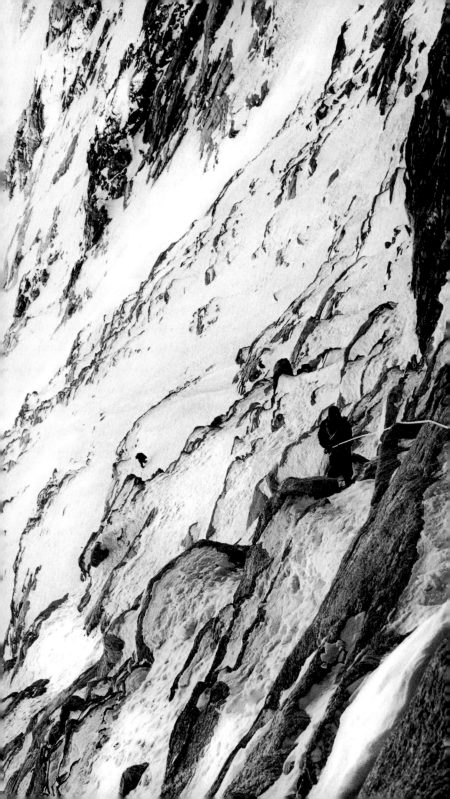

Uninvited Guests

H. W. TILMAN

Early in the morning, before the clouds rolled up, Tensing and I climbed on to the moraine to see where we were. Not far away the glacier terminated and its waters drained south-east into a deep gorge. Beyond we could make out the dark cleft of the main valley, to all appearances an even deeper gorge, where, the rivers still running high, we could count upon meeting all sorts of trouble. Southwards from the kharka a well-defined path apparently followed the ridge lying parallel to the main valley to the Panch Pokhari. We were not long in making up our minds which way to go. Apart from our wish to see the sacred lakes, the path was a temptation which we did not try to resist. If the main valley could not be reached from above, why should we not enter it from below from the nearest village? According to the map there was a village called Tempathang on the east side of the valley close to a bridge; whence, from our experience of the Langtang and the Ganesh, we might expect to find a track to some high alp in the heart of the Jugal Himal.

Accordingly we packed up and began a march which was to last until nightfall. On we went, crossing a succession of small streams and sharp ridges, past many deserted kharkas, until at midday in thick mist we emerged upon a wide down. In the distance we could hear dogs barking. Just as a soldier cannot do wrong by marching towards the sound of the guns, so that traveller in unknown country cannot do better than march towards the sound of dogs, sheep, cattle, or any other token of human habitation. Unfortunately we neglected this rule and in our eagerness to reach the valley took a well-marked path leading downhill through straight-growing juniper trees and bamboo. After dropping very steeply for about a thousand feet, the path, evidently one used by shepherds cutting wood, petered out; and having wasted an hour over this, the first of several attempts to reach the valley, we resumed the march along the proper path in heavy rain.

About 2 p.m. we came to an occupied kharka where two loud-voiced Tamangs received us with less warmth than we thought our due. Having parted grudgingly with some curds they informed us in a hearty bawl that Panch Pokhari was "not far away" — ominous words of encouragement, I thought, from men obviously anxious to see our backs. A little later we accosted a half-naked shrimp of a man who surprised us less by giving the same answer than by the extraordinary energy with which he gave it. I have often admired (for a short time at any rate) the loud, virile way in which Frenchmen and other Continentals converse, but these goatherds of the Panch Pokhari ridge seemed to be all descendants of Stentor who, I am told, had the voice of fifty men. At the next kharka, where there was a sodden, fireless hovel, I myself thought to galvanise the listless inmates with a hearty roar. Nobody took any notice except Tensing who was so startled that he hastily offered me a cold potato he had brought from Langtang. Indeed it was time for us to be settling down somewhere for a meal and to pass the night, and had not these men assured us in a powerful bellow that the lakes were now "quite near" we should have stopped there, miserable though it was.

At dusk my drooping spirits were cheered by the sight of an old moss-grown chorten, and very faintly out of the mist and gathering dark came the bleating of sheep. When Tensing, who was far behind, had caught up I got him to try what he could do in the bellowing line; and upon getting a reply we headed into the mist away from the path, trusting that those behind would hear and act upon this long-range exchange. At last we came to a lake and by it a long matting shelter. Wading through a sea of sheep we went inside. No one got up to offer us a place by the meagre fire and no one offered to mend it until Tensing took the matter into his own hands and threw on an armful of logs. Even the uninvited guest is sometimes critical of his welcome; the shepherds of these parts, I reflected, are merely loud-spoken, churlish skinflints, all cry and little wool. But it has since occurred to me that if a couple of dripping strangers burst in about supper time to claim the best seats by the fire, at the same time heaving on a bucket of coal, my welcome to them might be cool. Yet the fact that both Tensing and I were disappointed by our welcome is a measure of the hospitality expected and nearly always received at the rough, kindly hands of Himalayan peasants and shepherds. Happy the countries where the

people are so uncivilised that hospitality is not a virtue but second
nature; the better for being accorded spontaneously, without the
careful preparations we are often obliged to make when entertaining; the screwing of the host's mind to the requisite sticking point
of geniality—and in due season the long premeditated revenge.
Tensing's liberality with their firewood and the number of socks I
peeled off made an impression. Perhaps it occurred to them that
they might be entertaining angels unawares, so they presently got
out their milk and butter and offered it at fully commensurate
prices. But after such a long, wet day, seated in front of a blazing
fire of which we had now pretty well taken possession, drinking hot
tea, we could afford to ignore the rain hissing down pitilessly upon
the wretched sheep outside.

from NEPAL HIMALAYA *1952*

Hitler and Leni

ANDERL HECKMAIR

One morning in Bayrischzell I found a telegram from my friend
Hans Steger in Bolzano. For many years he had been the best and
also the best-known rock climber in the Sudtirol, and had now
become a qualified guide. The telegram said that Leni Riefenstahl
wanted to climb with him, but he had an engagement with the King
of Belgium. "You take her. Rendezvous Wolkenstein today."
Everyone knew about Leni Riefenstahl from Arnold Fanck's
mountain and ski films, and she had produced and starred in a fine
mountain film of her own, *Das Blaue Licht*. It was also well known
that she belonged to Hitler's most intimate circle. Party leaders
often had film stars among their friends and followers, but in her
case the rumour was that she was one of Hitler's closest friends, if
not more. That she was a star did not trouble me in the slightest,
but the connection with Hitler gave me food for thought. Up until
then I had no contacts with governmental or party big-shots. No
matter. Naturally it did not occur to me to turn down such an offer.
I travelled to Wolkenstein and asked at the hotel for Miss

Riefenstahl. Immediately I was treated with exquisite politeness. It is quite remarkable the bowing and scraping and dashing to and fro occasioned by names and money.

My future client had gone out for the day with a climber I knew well, Xaver Krayse from Kaufbeuren who, however, was not a professional guide. After a few hours she appeared looking radiant and more beautiful than I had imagined her to be in reality. Her feminine charms and untroubled naturalness soon dissolved my inner reservations. Whatever her relations with Hitler might be she was obviously a fabulous woman, and her years spent in the company of Arnold Fanck's casts of outstanding climbers and skiers seemed to have taught her not to play the star or the capricious diva among mountaineers. What she was worth as a climber herself I would soon find out.

When we discussed the routes we might do I suggested the West Ridge of the First Sella Tower as a training climb, knowing full well that there was a pitch of Grade 5 on it. If she had trouble there, she could find another guide and I would go home. I was arrogant in those days and interested in nothing but the difficult stuff.

To my vast surprise, and I may say to my pleasure also, she had no difficulty on the crux pitch. Indeed, she positively danced up it. Knowing little about women, I would never have believed it of such a delicate-looking creature. When she explained that before going into films she had been a ballet dancer I began to understand why her movements were so graceful and sure. Thereupon we undertook a series of harder and harder climbs, including the Schleier-kante, which we knocked off in two and a half hours as a party of three. This success made me presumptuous, and for our next climb I suggested the Guglia di Brenta, not just the ordinary route but the Preuss route.

As we walked up from Madonna di Campiglio to the Brentei Hut we got to talking about her film *Das Blaue Licht* which she had shot in this district. Hitler had been so impressed by it that he had commissioned her to make the films of the National Socialist Party Meeting and the Olympic Games.

Before I had set out from home my brother had drawn my attention to these matters and had drummed into my head that I should on no account let on that I knew next to nothing about her and had never seen one of her films. That was bad advice. At every bend in the path she kept asking if I could remember the scene she had shot there, until like a fool I confessed that I had never even heard of the film. That offended her and she went into a sulk. Just wait till tomorrow, I thought to myself, and I'll cut you down to size so that you forget your own film. In fact she was to be cut down much smaller than I intended, and that was my fault again, because after the experience on the Schleierkante I had simply overestimated her ability.

I fixed our time of departure at 10 a.m. sharp. We wandered gently up to the Tosa hut, had an agreeable midday rest, and reached the foot of the route by 2 p.m. I was reckoning on three hours up and one down, so that there was plenty of time even though we were a party of three. However, this was adding up the bill without the tip. I was feeling my oats, and right at the beginning decided there was no point in following the ledges across the Bergerwand when a convenient corner led straight up towards the Preusswand. Unfortunately, this corner turned out to be much harder than it looked. Half-way up Leni suggested: "It would be a bit easier out there on the left." I was of the opposite opinion, but experience gave in to inexperience, a thing that should never happen in the mountains. The somewhat easier rock led around to a good stance on the East Face, but there everything came to an end. So back to the corner. I took some tension on the rope, then climbed free to the top of the corner and gave the word to follow. That was easy enough to say. Leni peered around the edge, took one look at the smooth wall and overhangs in the corner, and refused to move another step. In this she was fully within her rights. I called down that I would abseil back so that we could return to the hut. At this she grew angry and insisted on continuing up, but not at this particular place. In reality we had no choice; there was not enough time to go any farther. At this point, however, she made the mistake of informing me that she had engaged me as her guide and that I must do as she said. In a sense she was right, but not in these circumstances. There was nothing for it but to go down so that she could find another guide who would do as she told him.

I kept the belay rope over my shoulder while I hammered in a ring piton for the abseil. Suddenly, without any warning, there came a violent tug and Leni pendulumed across into the corner. I therefore hauled in the rope with all my strength and before long she was standing in front of me, her eyes red with weeping. Xaver followed, grinning with embarrassment. Only now were we at the foot of the Preuss route proper. Normally people allow four hours for this, and it was 5 p.m. already.

"The sensible thing would be to turn back."

"No, I want to go on."

All right by me. Up we go then. I turned and started climbing without further delay. Even today the route cannot be described as easy, and it kept us busy until 8 p.m., by which time it was dusk. Whether a bivouac was inevitable or not did not bother me in the slightest, but out of the west, a black wall of cloud was bearing down on us flickering with blue lightning. It was essential to get off the summit with all possible speed. I found a niche between two blocks on the North Face.

"Right, this is where we bivouac. Now it remains to be seen how we survive the storm."

"But you don't expect me to spend the entire night here?" sobbed Leni. "I mustn't catch cold, I'm not well. . ."

The rest of her words were drowned in a terrifying crash of thunder. Hail poured over us, while the lightning flashed and glimmered incessantly in the black cloud.

"This is unpleasant. Let's get down farther."

Going on implied abseiling, hammering in pegs by the harsh glare of the lightning. Xaver had to descend unbelayed on the two 40 metre ropes in the pitch darkness. Leni could only be belayed on a thin cord for the first 25 metres. The shower of hail had turned into a cloudburst. We abseiled on all night, arriving exactly where we had left the sacks at the bottom of the climb. It was either pure chance or sixth sense, as most of the time I had no idea where we were.

It was far too dark to follow the route back to the Tosa hut, but in the gully running down to the coomb below a faint light shimmered off the ice. Nothing much could happen to us now, and by cutting our way step by step down the gully we at least kept moving. The weather had relented a little, but cloud came up from the valley, enveloping us in a Stygian gloom compounded of fog and darkness. Luckily we had just got off the ice. Although we had no torches, we could at least move forward in a sitting position. For me there was nothing new in that. Leni and Xaver did not care for it, but wanted even less to bivouac. We missed the little track leading through the coomb and found ourselves in a wilderness of blocks the size of tables or even houses. After I had tumbled over one of these I found my readiness for self-sacrifice exhausted, so I stretched out and announced that I was going to sleep until it got light. In a moment I was snoring. Xaver had to spend the rest of the night comforting and rubbing Leni to keep her warm. As soon as day broke they wakened me; despite the wetness and cold I felt fresh and fully revived. By climbing back up again we soon found the track, up which the hut warden and his wife in a state of great concern were already coming to look for us.

After we had had three days of rest at the hut, Leni Riefenstahl's friends gave a banquet for us at the Hotel Greif in Bolzano. There were heated discussions over the table concerning modern mountaineering techniques. The subject of the Eiger was brought up. One of the older men looked deep into my eyes and said: "Heckmair is the man who will climb the Eigerwand." I was taken aback, having believed that nobody knew anything of my intentions. However, his confidence did me good, as in view of my failure and defeat on the Grandes Jorasses I was not at all sure of myself.

It was now September, and Leni had to attend the Party Meeting at Nuremberg as Hitler's guest of honour. As she wanted to convert me, she insisted on my coming too. Afterwards I was to accompany her to Berlin, where everything I needed would be placed at my disposal at the national stadium so that I could keep in training. For an offer like that it was even worth attending a Party Meeting; what harm could it do anyway if one regards the whole thing with disapproval?

At Nuremberg we were lodged at the Gauleiter's house. Everything was costly and hyper-refined except the Gauleiter himself. So that was the face of National Socialism! Hitler himself was staying at the Deutscher Hof Hotel. Naturally, the whole place was hermetically sealed off, but Leni had a special pass that opened all doors. We went to the hotel for afternoon tea. Leni took up a position where the Führer could not help but see us when he came in. It worked perfectly. He went straight towards her with outstretched arms and complimented her on her appearance. We were invited to sit at his table in a neighbouring room. Thus I found myself sitting beside Leni in immediate proximity to Hitler and could study his face at leisure. I make no claim at all to being a profound connoisseur of men, but I could find absolutely nothing so extraordinary about him.

Leni told Hitler about her experiences in the mountains but he seemed neither impressed nor enthusiastic. Instead, his brow drew down and he growled: "How can you risk your life so lightly when I have entrusted you with so great a mission?" She answered that for this very reason she had employed a guide to see to it that her life was in no danger. Now, for the first time, he looked straight at me and I came into the conversation. Far from being stupid, the questions he put to me were very much to the point, although it was clear that he had not the faintest idea about mountaineering. What interested him was the "why" of it all—what one would feel and experience on a severe climb as opposed to a simple walk in the mountains. Without any intention of embarrassing me he bored his way relentlessly into every aspect of the subject. In all this my own person interested him not a straw. It was the phenomenon that absorbed him, and apparently he had never before discussed it with a mountaineer.

Thus the meal went by. Outside darkness had fallen and a torchlight parade began to march past. The Führer's adjutant—I do not know if it was Bormann—came up behind him and murmured that it was time to go out on to the balcony. As we got to our feet Hitler asked me another question which called for a lengthy answer; nobody dared to interrupt us, and so it was that I accompanied him out on to the balcony, still talking, there to find myself in my grey suit amid all the uniformed Party dignitaries. Below us the crowd clamoured its unceasing cry of "Heil." The torchlight procession came to a halt. Hitler saluted it with stiffly outstretched arm, something rigid in his gaze as though staring into the distance. For the first time in my life I raised my hand in the Hitler salute. My situation as an anonymous, unpolitical and unbelieving climber standing beside the fanatically acclaimed leader struck me as so grotesque that I felt like laughing out loud. The march past lasted two hours, and throughout this time I stood at his elbow. As the umpteenth thousand marcher paraded past us yelling I thought of the loneliness of the mountains and of the hordes of humanity below. Naturally I came to no conclusion; I simply found the whole thing remarkable, disturbing, somehow inexplicable.

The following day I stood beside Leni Riefenstahl on the tribune of honour watching the parades and the march past of Party members, wondering how people could be herded around like that and why they let it happen. One could not help admiring the organisation, yet I felt a kind of shudder in my soul. I understood that something was in motion that was going to sweep everything away with it, but where to I could not tell.

from MY LIFE AS A MOUNTAINEER *1975*

An Excursion in Scotland

ROYAL ROBBINS

When Chouinard returned to the States from his visit to Scotland, he said he had been treated like a king. He spoke highly of the manly, hardy race from the northern part of the British Isles. I wondered if I would be received the same way. Everyone likes Chouinard.

Impressions . . . legends . . . the Scots figure early in the consciousness of Americans — the edifying parables of Robert the Bruce; the great hero, Wallace; Macbeth, a rough but good man gone wrong . . . an evil woman led him astray . . . one mustn't get in with bad company; and the other characters in that play — Duncan, who was all good, the smooth-cheeked princes, they were Scots too.

When I met the reality I understood more deeply the legends. I visited Scotland while on a lecture tour down in England. It wasn't really a lecture tour. I showed some slides and a movie, and said a few interpretative words. Not really lecturing. I remember the reception at the Alpine Club: exceedingly polite, exceedingly unenthusiastic. One can't blame them. It was mostly the old guard, the conservatives who disdain pitons. And what I offered was mostly American ironmongery, and some monkey tricks on big rock walls, hardly *grande alpinisme*. They must have felt like spectators at a zoo.

Tom Patey was the cause of our trip north. He telephoned us while my wife, Liz, and I were in the Lake District, and turned his considerable powers of persuasion to the task of convincing us of the propriety of making what we considered an impossible trip. Patey was enthusiastic. He would come down from Ullapool if we would come up from the Lakes. Meet us half-way. The time was late afternoon; with a lecture awaiting us just two days away, we found Tom's logic less than cogent. His enthusiasm, however, was so infectious as to be virulent. We caught the bug.

Late that same night we motored north along winding, narrow roads. I was occasionally startled into wakefulness when the car careered around a particularly bad curve. Liz was driving. I remember little except waking up amid amber lights. They were eerie, those long rows of amber lights in the black, wet, Glaswegian night. It seemed not a gay city.

I stumbled into a phone booth and called the number we had been given. Tom came out and led us to Mary Stewart's home in the country. In the morning we awakened to a life which one occasionally reads about in books, but rarely sees in reality, at least in the sedate American sort of reality to which we were accustomed. There were about half a dozen children, robust youngsters, beaming with superb health. Their frontier dress gave a hint of their wild free-spirited nature. The older ones cared for the younger, the strong for the weak. And there were the animals. Mary loves animals. There were dogs and cats of various aspect, goats, a horse, and . . . a lamb. Behind the house were 200 cats in cages, which Mary used, alas, for research.

Scattered about the house were individuals of widely varying sorts, folk-singers, do-wells and ne'er-do-wells, even a climber or two. All had come to Mary Stewart's for a bit of comfort and relaxation, and to escape the cares of the world.

Patey insisted we go to Glencoe. I felt more like sitting around Mary's place, taking it all in, but resistance was futile against such a tornado of energy. I can't remember when I first met Tom, but I had long admired him as one of those rare persons who have so much life that it rubs off on those around them. We had recently been involved together in a television stunt on the Anglesey sea cliffs in North Wales.

Tom drove north like he had only a few hours to live, and didn't want to waste a second. He talked continuously, telling Liz and me of this adventure and that, and relating pithy anecdotes of various climbing personalities, and other stories as well—doctor tales of marvellous complications which arise as a result of vaginitis. I couldn't help but suspect that Doctor Patey embellished the stories a bit, added a bit of Ullapool colour, as it were. But we didn't mind. As the car rattled north, Tom told us how proud of it he was. It was a red Czechoslovakian crate, and the wonder was, to us, that it ran at all. Patey says he's not mechanically adapted. If true, that car was a fine companion, as it seemed the most ill-adapted mechanical contrivance to which I had ever dared trust my life. But it got us there, and somehow got us back.

As we approached Glencoe, Tom pointed out various areas of climbing interest, and indicated several couloirs from which acquaintances had been avalanched. We bounced to a stop on a gravel lot. Before us stood the Buachaille. In front of it, much closer, was a white building, the SMC hut. As we strolled by it, toward the mountain, Patey, ever anecdotal, told us how naughty Dougal Haston had estranged the leadership of the SMC by painting the interior livid colours because he was bored by its drabness.

We were on our way to the Rannoch Wall, to do Agag's Groove, an easy Very Difficult route, which shows, damn it, how times change. The weather looked terrible, but Tom assured us he thought it would only rain. Only rain? I thought of the white, warm, Yosemite granite, and of the endlessly blue skies of the California summer days. Only rain? But clearly it rained a lot in Glencoe. Every footfall squeeged into the turf. We seemed to be walking on a gigantic sponge. The rock face was a long time getting closer. These hills are bigger than I thought, I thought. It's no wonder that in the winter, with the short days and the fearful Scottish ice climbs—of which we have heard, even in California— it's no wonder the epics occur, and that the stories find their way 6,000 miles to the West Coast. But this was to be a fun rock climb, and Tom would take good care of us.

The route was pleasant, but undistinguished—just the sort I wanted. Liz and I roped up at the bottom, while Tom soloed ahead, to show the way. He kept close by, relating how one climber had fallen off here, another there. I can remember little of the route, except that it was enjoyable and just hard enough, considering we used no pegs. I was faced with a series of problems, none fearful, each of which had possibly several solutions, but only one elegant one which, when I found it, gave a feeling of pleasure, when my body moved up—a feeling akin to the thrill of solving a chess problem with just the right balance of simplicity and complexity. That is to say, the possibilities were, or appeared to be, complex, but the solution, when found, was beautifully simple. Such climbing, abundant in the British Isles, is comparatively rare in my country. One needs a steep wall which is rough, textured with small ledges, knobs, holes, jam-cracks, rugosities, bulges, shelves, flakes, horns, corners, ripples and overhangs, so the climber has something of a choice of whether to pull, push, wedge, cling, bridge, straddle, or fall off. In the States, the free-climbing problems, though sometimes very hard, tend to be simpler in terms of intellectual problem-solving. This is particularly true of Yosemite. There, the smoothness of the rock limits the possible ways one can get up a given section of rock. The holds which a cunning mind might ferret out on a British crag often just don't exist in the Valley. I have observed that British visitors to the Valley fare no better than the locals on such walls as the North Face of Sentinel Rock, which is 1,500ft. of slippery jam-cracks. And even Don Whillans had to sweat on the super-smooth Crack of Despair. But on the Crack of Doom, regarded by Yosemite veterans as just as hard, he found a very Whillanesque solution, an ingenious but straightforward combination which enabled him to pop up a section where I, for one, passed half an hour in intense struggle and finally overcame by dint of brute force and determination. While I am not the cleverest of American climbers, I believe this episode to be typical. And I believe it is at least partly a result of where the emphasis is placed in one's home training ground. In America, stress is on strength, gymnastic ability, and technique, in the sense of making movements (liebacks, jam-cracks, etc.). "Working things out" is less important partly because of the type of rock we have, and partly because we use a lot of free-climbing protection (mostly pitons). With good protection, a leader can afford to go all-out whether he has worked out a solution or not. If his security is middling, then judgment and cunning become reliable assets.

Anyway, Agag's Groove made no exorbitant demands upon my physical capacity, but what with those long, pitonless runouts, to err might be human, but it would also be fatal. Yet it was refreshing to climb with just a rope, sans paraphernalia. And I was feeling a bit northwallish clinging to the cold rock which a drizzle was now wetting. Liz came up happily, without apparent effort. It was her sort of climbing, if not our sort of weather.

When we reached the top, the yellow rays of the lowering sun were bursting through new rents in the clouds and lighting the vast moor to the east. My first moor. A moor at last. I had long heard of the great Scottish moors, and here was one for real. It, and the surrounding mountains seemed eerily desolate, and brought to my mind Jack London's tales of the Alaskan tundra. Patey had earlier described a frightful massacre that had occurred here. It seemed a fitting place for dark deeds and heroism.

The descent was a trifle dangerous, with the wet rock, and the lichen, moss, and grass which occasionally covered it. Tom saw us safely off the crag, and then, bursting with energy, ran cross-country to fetch the Red Blitz to meet us at the end of our more direct descent. We walked straight down and passed what I presumed was a climbers' hut. Some men were in front and one shouted something incomprehensible. But I sensed it was shouted not to us, but at us. Anxious to avoid a situation in which I might be called upon to do something honourable, I light-stepped it, with Liz on my heels, from stone to stone quickly across a creek and reach the safety of the far side. And if you think that's easy, try it.

Later, Tom told us we were lucky they hadn't stoned us while we were crossing the creek. And at another time, another place, Davy Agnew, upon hearing me relate the story, told me exactly the same. Creagh Dhu boys, they were, and tough as they come. Jim McCarthy of Manhattan, no patsy himself, had first told me of this fabulous group, and described them, much to my astonishment, as such a rough bunch that they made the New York Vulgarians look like cream puffs in comparison. I didn't really believe this, at first. But now I have heard so many stories that I no longer doubt. Some of the best stories came from Agnew. Davy and I worked together as fellow ski-instructors in the Leysin American School, in Switzerland. And as I write this, we are again co-performers in the production of a ski movie. Davy is a burly, strong, smiling man with a generous spirit. He skies like the wind, does back-flips off the balconies of Swiss chalets, drinks with his friends, and is capable of slowly breaking the fingers, one by one, of a man who, in a fight, has grabbed him where he shouldn't. So, when Davy tells me of his mates in the Creagh Dhu who are really tough, I listen with awe.

As we drove pell-mell and lickety-split back toward Glasgow, Tom told us of Joe Brown's first trip to climb Ben Nevis in the winter, and of how happy the Scottish climbers were when the Human Fly fell several hundred feet down an icy couloir, and all this related in the spirit of good-natured, healthy, competition.

That night I showed the Yosemite climbing film which I had brought for my lectures to a small group in Mary's home. To give the right impression, I presented it professionally; that is, I lectured and played music on a tape while the film wound out its 40 minutes. By the time it was half-way through, I felt a pompous ass treating that small group as an audience, and my embarrassed voice dribbled off into occasional self-conscious interjections. Later, the party improved as the drink flowed and Patey sang his wonderful songs. Brian Robertson was there. I had first met Brian after the Dru Direct caper that John Harlin and I had cut. Brian had been on the regular Dru West Face route at the time and had taken some pictures of us, which he later tried to sell to John. I confess I remember feeling slightly superior to this commercialism, not realising that a poor American climber was affluent compared to a poor Scottish one. I'm less uptight now. (Anyone want to buy some pictures?) Despite Tom's repeated refusals, Brian kept urging him to sing 'John's Song', a Harlin-deflating ditty in the Patey manner. Considering that John had just died on the Eiger in circumstances prophetically described by Tom's song, and that I, a former friend of John's was sitting in the room, I thought Brian's repeated insistence a piece of marvellous Scottish *sang froid* in the face of that grinning, expectant gloater waiting out there in the darkness for all of us. Finally Brian sang it himself, but rather diffidently, as if he must. I met Brian again in that haunt of the egoists, Yosemite Valley. He came to the Valley camera in hand, with modest ambitions and without fanfare; that is to say, with a sensible attitude, and proceeded to enjoy himself, to do good climbs, and to win the respect of the hypercritical, snobbish Yosemite climbers. I remember Brian on the Camp 4 boulders: he was at first stopped by their peculiarly rounded and smooth character, but he kept at them with the dogged persistence of the famous Scottish spider, and was soon doing the hard ones.

Next morning, although a bit haggard, we drove south feeling proud and happy to have fitted so much living into so little time. We did not realise then that we had forgotten the lecture film, nor that when I had recorded the singing I had erased the music I used to accompany the film. . . Mary Stewart saved us in the nick of time—but that is another story. As far as we knew, we were living happily ever after.

from THE SCOTTISH MOUNTAINEERING CLUB
JOURNAL *1969*

The Mountain Tourists

SIR LESLIE STEPHEN

On sitting down to supper, I discovered a large wound in my ankle. On exhibiting this to a medical friend next morning, he asked for my clasp-knife. Extracting from it a very blunt and rusty lancet, and observing that it would probably hurt me very much, he quietly took hold of my leg, and, as it appeared to me, drove the aforesaid lancet right through my ankle with a pleasant grin. He then recommended me to lie down on the sofa, and keep my foot higher than my head. I obeyed his directions, and remained in this attitude (which is rather commodious than elegant) for eight consecutive days of glorious summer weather. I had the pleasure (through a telescope) of seeing my friends one day on the Wetterhorn and another on the Eiger. I read through the whole literature of the village, consisting of an odd number of the *Illustrated*, half a Bell's Life, and Tennyson's *Princess*, about a dozen times, and occasionally induced two faithful companions to trot me round the house in a *chaise à porteurs*.

I studied with a philosophic eye the nature of that offensive variety of the genus of primates, the common tourist. His main specialities, as it seems to me from many observations, are, first and chiefly, a rooted aversion to mountain scenery; secondly, a total incapacity to live without *The Times*; and thirdly, a deeply-seated conviction that foreigners generally are members of a secret society intended to extort money on false pretences. The cause of his travelling is wrapped in mystery. Sometimes I have regarded him as a missionary intended to show by example the delights of a British Sunday. Never, at least, does he shine with such obvious complacency as when, armed with an assortment of hymn books and bibles, he evicts all the inferior races from the dining-room of an hotel. Perhaps he is doing penance for sharp practices at home; and offers himself up for a time to be the victim of the despised native, as a trifling expiation of his offences. This view is confirmed by the spirit in which he visits the better-known places of pilgrimage. He likes a panoramic view in proportion to the number of peaks which he can count, which, I take it, is a method of telling his beads; he is doomed to see a certain number of objects, and the more he can take in at one dose, the better. Further, he comforts himself for his sufferings under sublime scenery by enjoying those conundrums in stone—if they may be so called—which are to be found even in the mountains. A rock that imitates the shape of the Duke of Wellington's nose gives him unspeakable delight; and he is very fond of a place near Grindelwald where St. Martin is supposed to have thrust his staff through one hill and marked the opposite slope by sitting down with extreme vigour.

Some kind of lingering fetish worship is probably to be traced in these curious observances. Although the presence of this species is very annoying, I do not think myself justified in advocating any scheme for their extirpation, such as leaving arsenic about, as is done by some intelligent colonists in parallel cases, or by tempting them into dangerous parts of the mountains. I should be perfectly satisfied if they could be confined to a few penal settlements in the less beautiful valleys. Or, at least, let some few favoured places be set apart for a race who certainly are as disagreeable to other persons as others can be to them—I mean the genuine enthusiasts, or climbing monomaniacs.

Milder sentiments returned as my health improved.

from THE PLAYGROUND OF EUROPE *1871*

Notes From a Fund-Raising Brochure

(NON FICTION)

You are Cordially Invited to go on the 19—
— Expedition.

The world's —nd highest mountain is only a few
rope lengths short of Mt. Everest, but to a mountaineer—
is more difficult and challenging than Everest.
The — — Expedition needs
your financial help to make the summit.
It also needs your positive thoughts.
The team members would like to take some
part of you with us—your name—to the top of —
in August, 19—. To share with you and
thousands like you the agony and joy of the climb.
What we envision is a human chain of
cooperation that will stretch its energy from
America to Pakistan, up the Baltoro Glacier,
and then up, up —ft. to the —nd highest
point in the world.
Come with us to the top of—

. . . A microfilm of the list of names will be
placed in a pack on the summit.
. . . The 19— — Expedition is united in their
determination to put someone on the summit of —, perhaps
only two, perhaps more. But twelve alone cannot climb —.
If they are successful, those thousands of names in that
pack on the summit will share in the joy of
standing atop the world's — nd highest mountain.
"The courage of mountain climbers is not
blind, inexplicable, meaningless; it is courage
with ability, brains, tenacity of purpose."
    — Robert F. Kennedy
See back cover for information on how to
join the — climbing team.

Alaska: Journey by Land

GALEN ROWELL

He was walking down the road in a drizzle, a few miles from
Watson Lake in the Yukon. An ageless Indian. Maybe fifty; more
like thirty. We couldn't tell and it made no difference; he put out his
thumb and we stopped. Now there were five of us plus a thousand
pounds of gear in the Chevelle station wagon. It wallowed around
curves like a water bed on roller skates and bounced over chuck-
holes with the shock of a steel ball rolling down stairs.

The Indian was quiet and oblivious, eyes focused at infinity. His
twisted Asian face seemed incongruous above western cowboy
clothing. His nose had been broken, and when he turned my
direction it still pointed at 10 o'clock. We asked him questions and
he answered in a guttural, barely intelligible monotone. What did
he do? Worked in a motel part-time and lived off the land.
Trapping, shooting game. Suddenly the dam opened and information poured forth, almost too predictably. Many brothers. Hard
winters on the trap lines. Constant referrals to boozing. All the
stereotypes of the Northern Indians. We began to wonder, was this
all for our benefit? Was he just telling us what we wanted to hear,
guarding his private life in a last vestige of dignity? Or was he for
real?

We asked him his game. He looked at me intently, "Just call me
the Black-Haired Yukon Kid."

We took the Kid to the bar of his choice in town. It smelled of
beer and piss. An imaginary Mason-Dixon line separated the
Indians and the Whites. Ours was the only integrated table. The
Kid was on edge. Conversation flowed, but not in a stream. Rather,
it resembled a canal system with locks that ended abruptly before a
change to a different level. He didn't tell stories, he dropped fragments, and unlike a skilled politician, he made no attempt to tie
them together.

Realising the window of his soul was closed to us, we began to
talk about our trip. Halfway up the Alaska Highway. 600 miles
through the dirt and 600 more to the border. We talked about

glaciers, wildlife and all the things we expected to see in Alaska. Our palms sweated when we talked about climbing; each of us was unsure how we would perform on 5,000ft. of granite in the Alaska Range in May.

The Kid was drunk. Something roared up inside of him and he yelled at us. Screamed. Bellowed. Just as quickly his anger subsided and he began to sing a weird improvisation of primitive sounds and modern jazz. He sang of his family and his mother and just as suddenly he stopped. It wasn't embarrassment. Maybe pride and anger for having given us an inch of his soul. The window closed; he clammed up for good. Communication dwindled to awkward tense stares. We gulped our beers and left him sitting there.

We were back on the highway at 6 a.m. When passing cars we kept our windows rolled tight and heater fan on high to prevent dust from sifting through every nook and cranny. Trucks were a different matter. At the beginning of the highway, near Dawson Creek, a passing truck had unleashed a rock that hit our windshield like a bullet. It was the first of seven breaks. But the dust was more dangerous.

Winnebagos and Aristocrats, crammed with American geriatrics, crawled along the road at 30 m.p.h. — pathetic products of the Affluent Society whose only touch with the environment was an occasional forage for food, gas or souvenirs. But the truckers drove the road at 60 to 70, leaving a wake of dust and gravel that defies the imagination until you try to pass one. Fifty miles from Whitehorse we were cruising at a comfortable 65, raising an opaque cloud behind us. Wisps of dust, at first barely noticeable, began to appear on the road in front of us, like cirrus streamers before a storm. Soon, thick dust surrounded us on all sides, pierced only by the bouncing tail-lights of a charter bus, glowing an eerie maroon through the murk. We followed them for miles, I couldn't decide whether to pass, to stop and wait, or to hang behind in the dusty pall. The bus was travelling a consistent 60 m.p.h. and would be much more difficult to pass than the shorter, slower houses-on-wheels. I made up my mind to pass after I chugged behind the bus at 20 m.p.h. as it climbed out of a ravine. When a half-mile straightaway appeared, I pulled out to pass and found myself going 75 to get around the accelerating bus. Gravel from its tyres rattled off the station wagon like machine gun fire. Forward vision was totally obscured when we came abreast of the wheels. I determined my position on the road only by watching the side of the bus. Suddenly the strafing ceased, vision returned, dust began to settle in the car. We breathed a sigh of relief. But the dusty wisps continued on the road in front of us. A minute later we encountered another set of maroon tail-lights in another murky cloud. The passing scene repeated itself, but to our horror we were behind a third tour bus. The view through the windshield was a continuing explosion, and the rear-view mirror was filled with the front of the second bus. Smog and the Manhattan rush hour seemed pale by comparison.

In Whitehorse we replaced our third tyre. All three steel-corded radials had burst in about the same place on the sidewalls, while a rayon tyre rolled along just fine. We would never know why. It was like the story of the plastic Jesus still standing upright on the dashboard of a demolished car.

Whitehorse is on the railroad, the highway and the Yukon River. It is the transportation and tourist centre as well as the capital of the Yukon. Winnebagos and clicking shutters surround dead hulks of old sternwheelers, beached near the middle of the city. Neon and Mounties and Pavement.

The Alaska Highway was built across Canada by the U.S. Army Corps of Engineers as a military objective during World War II. After Pearl Harbour, the Pentagon boys decided that having the Japanese in the Aleutian Islands without a supply road to Alaska was not a good thing. So they told the Corps to get with it. Nothing beats hard work and American dollars, so tens of thousands of people and dollars were sent to the North along with a suitable number of bulldozers. The effort began in March 1942, with crews working from both ends toward the middle. On September 2, 1942 the bulldozers met at Contact Creek, in the Yukon near Watson Lake. Never before had so many bulldozed so far so quickly — 1,200 miles in less than six months. Even the Alaska pipeline is unlikely to beat the 1942 speed record.

Unlike more habitable places — such as Southern California – the Yukon has not been quickly populated in the wake of the road builders. Even today, the entire population of the Yukon is only 18,000 in a land larger than California. A boom may be coming, however. Mineral exploration has tripled in the past five years.

Two new national parks will bring in more tourists, but only in the summer. A record temperature of −81°F was recorded in the town of Snag in 1946.

Near Whitehorse we visited the Yukon Game Farm, which advertised 'Wild Animals of the Yukon in Their Natural Setting'. For two bucks we drove our cart past some sickly Dall sheep and caged predators. A golden eagle tried to flap its wings in a cage the size of a closet made of cyclone fence. A wolverine slobbered and grunted on a half-chewed piece of plywood inside a similar enclosure.

We imagined how a family might tour the farm. Mom and Dad would gaze through dusty windows, commenting ecstatically at 'real' wildlife, while sitting in the rear of the mobile home, the children might possibly view a scene closer to reality by watching "Wild Kingdom" on Whitehorse TV.

A hundred miles past Whitehorse we reached the shore of Kluane Lake, over 75 miles long at the foot of the St. Elias Mountains. The big peaks were hidden from view by a front range of mountains under 10,000ft. Even so, the monotony of the relentless boreal forest was broken by views of glaciers, green fell fields and the giant, still-frozen lake. At the lake's inlet, white dust clouds blew across the flood plains. The dust was glacial milk, but it gave the place the impression of an alkaline desert.

We were on the edge of Kluane National Park, second largest in the western hemisphere. We talked to one of the two park wardens and found out that the entire population of the park at that time, including tourists, was probably less than ten. There are no roads and no facilities in the park. More than half of its 8,500 square miles lie under ice. Mt. Logan, Canada's highest peak, rises to nearly 20,000ft. in a remote section of the park. When it was first ascended in 1925, the party spent seventy days installing supply caches over 130 miles of the route in winter, because the terrain was too rough to pass with pack animals in summer. When horses could go no further, they guided dog teams over the snow-covered ice fields in 50-below-zero weather. We felt pretty insignificant complaining about the dust and the chips in the windshield.

At the edge of the lake, a sign next to the highway proclaimed 'Sheep Mountain'. It was a beautiful setting. Sun, wind, ice, green hillsides and white Dall sheep. But here, in a land where the human population was less than one person for every ten square miles, the sheep were adversely affected by people in many ways. As the sun and the temperature dropped on a May afternoon we were not alone scrambling on the hillsides for a closer view. Many tourists stop at the sign, and the area is mentioned in most travel guides. The sheep's normal predators, wolves, bears, eagles, were greatly reduced by hunting and trapping. Gradually the sheep lost much of their fear of the approach of large mammals, developed over eons of time when life hung on the thread of seeing and escaping enemies without being seen themselves. They have little use for their powerful telephoto vision, often likened to 6x binoculars. A chink was missing from their boldness, and they lay on the hillsides like bundles of inanimate white wool, moving only when I approached them very closely. I might have had stunning photographs except for the fact that some self-centred biologist had hung collars on many of the animals. The old ram with huge horns wore the latest in wide natural leather, while an adolescent yearling was attired in a day-glo pink. I could not explain why I found the collars such a flagrant affront to my senses. I have not felt that way about tags on the ears of camp-ground bears in National Parks. It is more like the hatred I would have if I visited New Guinea and found the tribesmen primitive except for Sears Roebuck tennis shoes—an unnecessary, degrading intrusion of the modern world into the last strongholds of wildness. I wondered why the study of wildlife is so often pushed so far that it robs the very wildness it seeks to comprehend.

After hours on the hillsides we squeezed into the car and drove along the lake. We had travelled more than a thousand miles on the dirt, and it began to seem like home. We now expected dust and rumbles under the car. The road is perhaps the best unpaved highway in the world, carefully maintained by large crews that constantly repair the frost-buckling, chuck holes and wash-outs.

The original course of the road was not intended for modern tourists and truckers. Quite the opposite. It was purposely twisting and winding to safeguard military convoys from aerial gunfire. Even across flatlands the highway meanders. Many of the winding sections are being slowly replaced with modern straight roads and wide right-of-ways. Pavement is one step closer.

The dirt road—almost continuous for 1,200 miles except for small sections through towns — was something we originally dreaded. We thought to ourselves how easy and pleasurable our journey might be if those miles were only paved.

We drove through the long hours of subarctic twilight. After midnight we reached the Alaskan border. The USA and asphalt roads beckoned on the other side of the customs building. A small, but determined customs agent searched our car, sure that our youth, laughter and long hair meant illegal drugs. He looked serious, dedicated and definitely unhappy when his search was fruitless. Like big-game trophies on a hunter's walls, the waiting room was adorned with drug-oriented spoils: elaborate pipes, bags, bottles, etc., mounted in locked glass cases.

We rolled out on pavement. The end of the dirt and dust. But the road was worse! More curves. Poor banking. Harder to drive. Frost-buckled pavement caused us to hit more bumps in the first five miles than on all the miles of dirt. The bumps were severe and unpredictable; but the worst thing about the pavement was insidious. We sensed it but could not express it. An element was gone from the Alaska Highway mystique. Finally, after an hour of winding through the mountains next to double yellow lines, someone said what we all felt, "It doesn't seem like wilderness anymore. It's just like any other paved road in any other mountains."

After a long day on asphalt, we reached the end of the drive. Talkeetna, Alaska. Fifty-three people, two airstrips, hundreds of dogs, uncounted drunken Eskimos and two bush pilots who refused to speak to each other. It was truly the Last Frontier. We watched two young men in buckskins walk through town, carrying rifles and knives. Ever-present Winnebagos occasionally rolled past, turned around at the deadend, and rolled out again. Grotesque, dusty, myopic eyes of our times, unable to focus at one point longer than the time required to stick a decal onto a window. Behind the first row of houses a man dressed totally in leather negotiated with a bush pilot to be airlifted, with his dog team and canoe, to a very remote lake. He talked only about one-way terms; no mention was made of coming out.

'GOLD GOLD GOLD GOLD ALASKA IS THE PLACE TO GO!'

I found this inscription on a men's room wall in a Winnemucca casino, but in Alaska I saw the other side of the coin. Rising gold prices have brought would-be prospectors back to the North. On the airstrip a man with tomorrow in his eyes thrust a chunk of rusty metamorphic rock in my hand. "Gold," he said simply. "It assays at over $200 a ton, but I've got to fly it out. I'd be rich if only there was a road." That night he was dead drunk in the Fairview Inn.

At ten in the morning the main street looked like a typical western town in the 1950's. Two-lane road. Dirt shoulders. Neon yet to come. Outside the Fairview sat two young men—one wearing Levi's, a sweatshirt and a crewcut; the other with a Hell's Angels style vest, cowboy hat and gun belt. Rattling the doorknob of the closed tavern was a wizened, almost blind Eskimo, leaning heavily on his cane. Age, booze and twenty hours of daylight had obscured his awareness of time.

At the corner of the building a chattering group of Japanese, wearing double-boots and bright parkas, busily crammed equipment into the rear of a brand new van. In the distance, far beyond the railroad, the river and the spruce forests, the Alaska Range loomed above the horizon. A 40-minute plane ride would transmute us into an ice-age scenario. Like a shabby time-warp in a cheap movie, we would find ourselves in a primeval, uninhabited land, staring alternately at unclimbed, un-named mountains and at our mound of tents, skis, beer, freeze-dried food, paperbacks and week-old newspapers. We had arrived.

from MOUNTAIN GAZETTE 17 *1974*

Travels With a Donkey

PETE LIVESEY

BOOM—a plume of water shot 50ft. into the air. Kelly beamed all over his face. BOOM—the second depth charge went off. Kelly's beam turned black as the expected trout failed to surface.

"Not enough gelignite," explained Kelly as he rummaged through the back of the transit for his two cardboard boxes containing a hundredweight of high explosive.

The third explosion of atomic proportions was curtailed however, as the brush around us swayed and parted revealing a large and heavily armed portion of the Greek Army completely surrounding our strategic position on the bridge.

I suppose, in retrospect, they had a good reason to capture us; it was probably a mite thoughtless of Kelly to start dropping bombs off a crucial bridge in the military border area between right-wing Greece and lefter-than-left Albania.

The other problem was that Kelly was a bandit and looked more like a bandit than most bandits. A week earlier he had disappeared into the dusty, crumbling heart of Ioannina, a mountain-backed military town in northern Greece, with five bottles of whisky. Several hours later he returned grinning all over his bandit-ridden face with a large cardboard box full of gelignite under each arm, forged permission to enter the military zone in his teeth and two full bottles of whisky still in his pockets.

Again the whisky came to Kelly's rescue, though I suspect the cavalry commander was still unconvinced that everyone in Britain fishes that way.

Several hours later we were high in the Timfi d'Oros range at the drivable limit of our van, which I thought was pushing it a bit, but then it wasn't really our van (Kelly had hired it in Salford for the day, three weeks earlier, to move his granny's effects from Dukinfield to New Mills).

I actually suspect it was the first time a vehicle larger than a bull donkey had been sighted in the tiny cluster of huts that was Upper Papignon.

Here Kelly produced a sawn-off shotgun; he had vowed back in New Mills that its sole purpose was to shoot the choughs that flew about the top of the pothole we were to descend, loosening rocks on those below. Now, however, he used it effectively to round up all the village donkey drivers so that we could get our ton of gear transported up the mountain.

It's a strange thing about donkey drivers that what fits exactly on one man's twelve donkeys will also fit perfectly well on another man's two donkeys, which are of course cheaper.

With a kind of friendly prodding action with his shotgun Kelly put me in charge of donkey management because of my previous experience. (I should perhaps mention here that the experience in question consisted of having a father who had once owned a donkey for a few months before it drank the half gallon of bright blue paint that he'd put in its field, with which to paint the fence.)

We hired and paid a Greek who promised us eight stout donkeys for the trip. The following morning he arrived with four things that resembled tatty Alsatians and a fifth animal with one ear and a splint on its back leg.

The Greek proceeded to load the animals with me supervising while the others went off to get drunk. The technique was quite simple—load the animals up with mountains of gear until their legs buckled and they collapsed, then remove one item of equipment and kick the donkey as hard as possible in its knackers to raise it to its feet again. It was barely possible to see the donkey beneath the mounds of ropes, ladders and recently ex-army tents but off they staggered, driven forwards by a sharp 'thwack' on their private parts with a specially designed 'donkey thwacker' that all hill Greeks carry.

The donkeys collapsed at regular intervals up the hill, sometimes never to rise again, until the donkey man stopped at the halfway stage, surveyed the hillside strewn with gear, dynamite and dead donkeys and said that enough was enough, that was as far as he went.

The rest of the expedition was boring—carry all the gear up a mountain, carry it all down a hole, bring it out again, carry it down the mountain and so on: exactly the kind of boring repetitive stuff you read in expedition books. It was on the way back that my interest in the world about was rekindled, I suppose.

She was in the van when we got back from the orchard we had found miles from anywhere as we crossed the Pindus Mountains. We all piled into the back, trousers and shirts spilling oranges and peaches everywhere, and were screaming off down the road before we had even noticed the beautiful, diminutive sunburnt girl sitting amongst our gear.

"Who the fuck are you?" snarled Kelly graciously.

"Elizabeth," was the gentle reply, then as an afterthought, "and I like screwing." She smiled a beckoning Californian smile at everyone but me, about whom she was obviously reserving judgement. Kelly's black eyes bulged as she unwrapped her only luggage, a sort of coloured tea-towel containing a full two-pound block of hashish.

The expedition drifted aimlessly and happily homeward along an undetermined and certainly illogical route as the block of happiness diminished.

Somewhere in southern Yugoslavia occurred the 'Kelly and the Giant Melon' incident. Admittedly I don't remember too much about it, although I do recall being a central character; I was still rather dazed from lack of blood and the shock of seeing Kelly auctioning two pints of my rhesus positive in the streets of Thessaloniki to pay for my share of the petrol.

The van screeched to a halt, the dust and daze subsiding to reveal a large field containing a large central melon.

"Get it," said Kelly. As I staggered towards the melon the field got bigger and bigger and the melon began to grow. Even before I'd reached the giant, the peasants in bullock carts were beginning to take an interest in our activities. Once there the first thing that was immediately obvious was that I couldn't even lift the thing. I beckoned for help but by the time we were struggling across the field fumbling with a melon nearly a yard wide the peasants were after us. More help! Kelly came and we ran for the vehicle, heaving the giant into the back as the show made a flying getaway.

An hour later we stopped to eat the prize; the knife wouldn't cut it and a saw only managed to win a small piece. It tasted awful but we were determined to eat it. Then Frank, the *Daily Express* man who was exceptionally clever, came back from the front for a look at the yellow giant.

"It's not a melon," he screamed with delight, "it's a bleeding pumpkin!" Somewhere in the middle of a road in southern Yugoslavia there probably still lies 98% of a giant, uneatable pumpkin.

By the time Austria came I began to ponder why I wasn't getting my share of Elizabeth and why Kelly was getting more than his. It wasn't that she ignored me, she just observed with a strange look from a distance.

One night the team visited a disco in Spittall; I couldn't go because they'd spent all my blood money on petrol, so I stopped behind in the van. A few minutes later the girl returned with a bottle for me. She edged hesitantly closer, letting her shift slide off.

"I'd like to screw a queer." Who was I to argue? It transpired that Kelly, after he'd had his turn, had told her not to bother with me because I was homosexual and consequently wasn't interested in women. At last I had the laugh.

Four years later I found myself in a similar situation, living 11,000ft. up in the Zagros mountains of Persia amongst the Kurds (spelt with a K, not a t). Again we were caving and I was penniless, but we had a leader who was the antithesis of Kelly; Judson was such a low-profile leader that most of us never met him until the expedition was half over.

I had been in the advance party dumped by bus in the desert town of Kermanshah, a genuine dust bowl hell-hole. The rest of the party were to follow when the food and other survival gear arrived by Land Rover.

Our problem in the advance party of four was quite simple; we had to get half-a-ton of caving gear from Kermanshah across 20 miles of desert to a Kurdish settlement, hire donkeys to get the gear to the cave entrance at 11,000ft. and ladder up the cave. Without food or money.

The first problem seemed a bit daunting how to get the gear across the desert to the Kurds' donkeys? A promised helicopter, as expected, failed to arrive. Standing on the central island of a short dual carriageway leading out of the town, Glyn, the expedition poet from Dukinfield (I know, that's what I thought) had a brainwave. He just held out his hand and a taxi stopped.

We pointed at the four of us, the half ton of gear, then at the desert. The taxi driver beamed in Arabic and began dementedly throwing our gear into the taxi then persuaded us to climb in after it. We had just over 9p between us; we thought it only fair to show this to the driver first, then just wait and see how far down the road to the desert this would take us.

Minutes later we were at the roadhead with ten miles of pure desert between us and the Kurds' tents. Instead of stopping our beaming driver careered off the road into the desert with dust, sand and sagebrush flying everywhere. That taxi went in a dead straight line for ten miles over sand, dry streambeds, rocks, camel skeletons and the like to drop us at the Kurdish encampment. Off went Abdul in a cloud of dust with his 9p, beaming all over his face.

The donkeys were there, dozens of them all controlled by one impudent little twelve-year-old Kurd and his younger sister. He was very efficient, leading all the donkeys up the crag-littered mountain flank on his own after tying them all together. He tied a short rope from one donkey on to the tail of the next one and so on. This Whymper-like arrangement was to have disastrous consequences later.

This little Kurd tried to swap his sister for my Swiss Army knife, then when that didn't work he upped his offer to his sister and a donkey. I didn't go much for that either so he stole it from me.

Well, the caving ended uneventfully with little of interest happening, apart from a ten-foot-long mountain leopard jumping over John and Colin as it passed them going the opposite way on a knife-edge limestone ridge at night (what either party were doing there at that time is a complete mystery to me).

The donkeys returned for the trip down, were loaded up and tied together. At the very top of the steep south flank of the mountain the donkey Kurd decided to take a short cut across a smooth limestone slab. One donkey fell and another six went with it, donkeys and our gear strewing themselves down over hundreds of feet of hillside. The Great Donkey Disaster left much of our gear and several dead donkeys on that hillside for ever, but the Kurds kept beaming all over their faces.

Returning to Kermanshah there only remained the most dangerous part of the expedition for me, the final meal out and booze up. It was here that Caver X made his first series of attempts to murder me. (I should explain here that he was not without motive, I did owe him £5.36 for the expedition insurance cover).

Mister X took the expedition to a desert village mealhouse in the

Land Rover and we ate and got plastered. This in itself was quite dangerous—to drink at all in these orthodox Moslem areas was risking being stormed by the Arabs, though we felt fairly safe in numbers.

Having taken us out there Mister X decided he wasn't taking me back, but would leave me to the glaring Arabs around. I didn't fancy this so when the Land Rover set off I jumped on to the roof rack.

Halfway back I couldn't resist hanging down over the windscreen and peering in at Mister X. He was furious and immediately drove off the road into a forest of low trees in an attempt to sweep me off the roof; too drunk to argue, I got off, only to grab the towing ball on the back as I saw how close the Arabs were getting. You should try hanging on a greasy ball with your backside bouncing off the desert in the middle of nowhere, being chased by hordes of stone-throwing Arabs.

I survived, but I nearly succumbed in another assassination attempt a week later. I was sure I was in dire need of antibiotics; X, however, had padlocked the medicine chest to induce me to die. Having broken-in in the dark, I gobbled half a bottle of painkillers by mistake.

I don't think they did me any permanent damage.

from CRAGS 21 *1979*

The Soloist's Diary

JEFF LONG

". . . not to imply that I wish to specify the degree of pain and passion with which I die, nor the actual manner of death, nor even its approximate instant. But to control my death's quality . . . to have mattered, one mute perception spanning the ages which this remote tirade against the rock has paradoxically rendered eternal, wrought in its own inconceivably lonely vast body.

Today: performed a most elegant movement. It was yesterday, I think, that I threw away all but twenty feet of rope.

Sound is the most tenuous of things: untouchable, deceiving, hiding in shadows, cohering its damp tracks with echo, cacophony, history hanging on its subtle dark pallor or harmonies, a night which ridicules vision. So too I have trouble these days in hearing beauty. It is years now. All the rock is as it appears: a barrenness ending in human things with warped and mangled flesh, pale veins and tendons utterly void of strength. My nostalgia is infinite. My heritage of vacuum in the rich sombre architecture of nature. My desire an impossible return.

Long ago I spoke with other wretched ones. One swore he remembered starting from waves, another from the desert. Still others mentioned primeval forests, rice terraces, lagoons; and another, a remarkable figure, yelled to me ages ago from across a crack that he had been born on the wall and was trying to find his mother somewhere high above him. I arrived by crude error and, forever, here. . ."

I can vaguely remember starting to climb. Reduced to myths, I suffer on the rock. Various amnesias blot the tissue of my memory and deprive me of a heritage, making me into a creature of the rock. By climbing an infinite height we have created an infinite depth and our pasts have become doubtful.

But still . . . still it seems as if there was once a period of beginning, a time when the dead climbers seemed grotesque as they hung from the crack or became bones upon small ledges. Years of dedicated horror have eaten that innocence away. The ground is no longer visible, nor its image, and even the horizon is obscured by dense low mists. There are no sides to the wall. There is no summit, which is our first dilemma.

We climb because it's what we did. For a long time now we've persuaded ourselves of our humanness by fluctuating and challenging the rock with our stifled personalities and raging diversions. There have been seasons of religious intent and seasons of ennui, and of hatred. Our eyes flashed those days of flux, but the days are different now. Everything seems ancient. The days are indistinguishable from the rock and our eyes have nearly mineralised. We no longer take pride nor find pleasure in pretending. We no longer change. We simply climb.

So there was a world I knew. It consisted of the rock and the sky upon my back, of my strength, of Aaron and Gareth, of the cold nights, and water bottles and pitons, ropes, hammocks and fading things. They recede more and more. Within me I feel a far-belowness. There are caverns in me that are marvellously daubed with thick, phosphorescent pigments and rich echoes, places that hide me from the wall and this gagging subjection. It is a sheer journey, a mercy of myself to myself. My mind, receptacle of images, is at once a holy strife. Half-formed characters grope their way into shimmering position. Many present moments but only one past, a darkened sanctuary.

In the mist there was nothing to see, only ashen forms a few yards distant. Unjointed shadows that faintly resembled things of the normal world existed down there. What seemed like a tree swimming before us was sometimes a tree; at others it was a thin strand of erect rock; sometimes it was nothing. Even the trees were without roots, free to wander. The outer world had disappeared. We were submerged, the brief scents, cool trees and wet rock . . . without form. Only our touch was above suspicion in that place.

We edged cautiously through the forest, our huge packs looming up in perpetually slow light, with grey tails of mist gliding behind, attached to our thick, veined shoulders. Those wafting tails of mist were true ghosts, I suppose, dismal and pathetic remnants from earlier ages in nature. We felt this. They were no terrifying apparitions at all, just impotent little driftings without more purpose than to absorb all echoes, all definite perception, and all our thoughts. Everywhere we were relentlessly hung, pursuing, and pursued.

We came across a tree with a patch of its bark shaved away. In the polished oval of wood there was carved a deliberate figure, a calligraphic revelation, a single character that seemed simple, but was incomprehensible. I found it; it was one of the first nights. There it was suddenly, an impression, a solemn insolvent word deep in the mute forest, but as to whether there was meaning in it? Yes, I think so; but from that fossil I knew then and ever will, nothing. It was not to be the last of such scriptures.

It was a forest of petrified wood. Even the cold trees, their green needles hanging in a semblance of life, seemed forever frozen and empty of life. Petrified. Every tree stood faintly, fog-moistened and brown in the greyness. Each tree was a grotesque climax of the gloom of that place, and in a similar way the spectral birds with their dimly flashing colours increased rather than diminished the loneliness of that land. When the slight sound of their beating wings came plummeting between the trees, we weren't raised out of the silence but only reminded of it and sunk deeper into its glaze.

Two ancient climbers were there, all rotted from aging and from the eternalness of apathy that was the fog. We were passing through the forest when suddenly we came upon them, two bent little figures squatting dwarfishly over a tiny birth of orange flame that was licking meekly at their world. There was no noise, not even spitting or crackling from the little fire. We watched them in silence, in astonishment, not knowing at all what they were. (Later we would know that they had descended while there was still a way back, an equally fatal course to take). Both of them were clothed in rags; each had draped long scraps of old cloth over the shoulders of their parkas, shredded and emptied of feathers, vacant and flat. Both were wearing pants heavy with mud and holes, and both were barefoot in the cold, their feet flattened, cracked like baked mud.

Standing there apart from them and their flame, I had to struggle to keep from choking, and my mouth was slack and whistling hollowly with my ruptured panting. I could hardly force air into my lungs, and I was hard at forcing it back out again. It was them and their fire; something in the separate baseness of it strangled me. There they crouched with their tangled hair wet, matted in heavy clenching nests upon their shoulders. They weren't talking. They were just crouching intensely over the flame, absorbing its meaning, squatting under, within; possessed by the mist.

We withdrew silently and went far around their little circle with its handful of contemplated flame, away from the primality of their neanderthal scene, away from the awfulness of their underworldness and their abysmal degeneration, and especially away from the fact of our similarity.

Gareth came to camp with a human bone nestled gingerly in his open hands. We followed him to a broken hut built of granite and rotted pine. In its shadows lay a thin skeleton half buried, a layer of dirt covering its legs. Something in the hasty nature of its covering imparted an air of breathlessness to the scene, as though near death the man had hurriedly dipped himself into the shallow grave. We stood about looking at it for a few minutes, then Aaron and Gareth drifted away. I stayed waiting, while the earthen skull stared sightlessly into the depths of the wasted ceiling. I was filled, for the few moments I contemplated the hollow sockets, with something beyond myself, but soon, discerning no message, I left the sepulchral shadows and re-entered the mist. Night came. We had no idea where the rock wall began. We'd searched for days in the mist, groundbound. Now we ate our rice, carrots, onions, drank our tea. And sat by the fire.

Mosquitos, the lips and arms of succubi, their opaque wings humming, sang at me in the darkness, luring me from my veil of smoke. But I wouldn't leave the fire. Feeling the black air on my cold back, I knew somehow that if I so much as closed my eyes to the light of the fire, the night would devour me. I could do nothing but cling to the fire. Out there was some character of the void and seemingly I was the only one of the group to sense it. I said nothing to warn Aaron and Gareth; instead I hugged the flames with my worried brow, afraid, protecting the others with my fear. I heard popping, clattering noises and whirled about to face the night. I grabbed a thick stick and mumbled hoarsely, but there was nothing. Later in the night, when the others slept, something touched my shoulder. I was instantly alert. But again it was nothing. My horror: It was far worse being touched by nothing than by something. The nothing offered no substance, no resistant solidity to belie oblivion. I can remember that. I was new to voidness then.

We found the wall and soon after the preliminary crack. A queer beach spread out before the wall. We thought at first we'd come upon the site of some massacre or a gruesome sacrificial field. There were men lying everywhere, not in any dense abundance, but randomly scattered all about. Some were more recently dead and were only partially eaten and decomposed; others were only bone or shadow. The remains lay positioned so that we were unnerved at times when one or the other of us suddenly tripped over the hidden bones of an unexpected body. There was no predicting where to set our feet. Grass and brush were everywhere; the bodies were anywhere. We were, as children, stunned. It was my first exposure to dead bodies, and it was a grisly first. The limbs twisted in terrible directions, skulls were bashed and empty, parts missing. Tropical birds and ravens had long before settled on them and had picked away their eyes. Animals had since died and had been buried, so to speak, on the dead compost of the skeletal piles. This too I remember, how the animals fed upon and died upon a single substance.

Lying everywhere were weathered pieces of manila, nylon, refuse, words.

We should have known. They were fallen climbers. We looked up and acknowledged the rock. It was above us irregularly, and hardly visible for the mist. Gareth drew a circle in the air and pointed upward; Aaron secretively scratched a figure into the dirt. This terrible deadliness was a new dimension to climbing for all of us. In climbing we'd always known an elusive risk, but such rampant danger? We'd assumed a dignified nonchalance before in the presence of rock. Here though was a graveness. There are victims of accident and there are victims of something more (something of themselves). These were like so many mites shaken off an animal. Other occasions would arise in my future, occasions for my will, but by the time those sediments and springs of seeming freedom initiated balance, or ties to the earth (in apparition), I would long since have been swallowed by my choice, and circumstances would never again permit a contradiction of this. Naively I opted for the wall as I treaded its beach of grass and lost ones.

We groped about at the base of the rock wall, seeking out the proper crack to begin climbing. We knew of it but had no method of finding it. It was in fact merely a climber's tale that had fertilised our venture. The vague rumour of an unclimbable wall . . . but we could see nothing for the mist. Nevertheless, from the root of the abruptly rising rock, we could sense that it was a huge wall, and too that it was occupied. From the base it was an empty slab, no sight or sound coming down, yet we could easily feel its population. We put our hands to the rock and knew that somewhere above us were other climbers touching its glabrous angles.

For two days we wandered along the base of the wall, searching for the primary crack, craning our heads back to stare upward into the mist and to imagine the great wall. Amidst the scree, the congestion of dead shattered things slowly grew. That afternoon we were touching the crack. It was horrible. There was a cozy simplicity then, sanctioned by such a mass above us, an unseen thing. There was no drama in the beginning. We were unsure of everything and had set no regimen for the ascent. We inserted our pins into the crack and ascended. And there upon the rock was the vision of the outside. Everywhere were dead climbers and climbers' things. Ropes hung from hanging bodies. The sky was rock.

Scarcely above the thickest of the mists appeared immense, inverted platforms of granite that blocked our sight upward and looked impassable. We had never encountered anything like it before. The entire wall just changed directions and flattened out as an endless ceiling, a panoply. That they are territorial gates which allow progression but no descent is possibly the greatest factor that traps us here on the wall, but something more prevents us from even attempting to retrace our path to reach the ground again. We took several months to sew our way across the ceilings, and can never retreat. The roofs composed an agglomeration of hundreds of down-vaulting rotten bulges and overhanging crumbling dihedrals requiring innumerable fixed anchors. Had we been able to see through the mist before starting, we would have witnessed this catastrophe of nature: a flat, horizontal wall thousands of yards above the ground, extending along a parallel over the forest for miles, with nothing to suggest that the entire colossus shouldn't topple as a mountain in itself to earth. Its confusion is indescribable; my accounts have often times been discounted by Aaron, and his by Gareth, for we each formed perspectives and fears of the overhangs, none the same, none even consistent within themselves.

There were, hanging from the rock, thousands of geometries which we had to skirt, but there were so many and they were so varied. Forms seemed to recur as we wove about beneath baffling plates of rock, doubting our paramnesias. The filaments of colour, the membranes that laced the ceiling like wafers, were static, but their effect was disturbingly animate. As we negotiated the stone roofs, we were closed upon by the rock. As soon as the last man had finished cleaning the pitch, we would look back in the direction from which we'd come and would know we were lost backwards, that we could only move by ascending, by going outward. We had come out of a myth, an elder earth, and felt wrongly, fatefully, about it from the instant we were suspended.

Then one early grey dawn we could see the ending of the roofs, and we perceived a summit awaiting us over the rim. Before the ground below disappeared, I was struck by a last real vertigo while surmounting what we thought to be the last of a seventy-day wall-roof. I was on the pitch leading. I manteled onto a long and wide cup of amber flakes, but as I did so I was confronted by two tiny, insane things. They were crack animals such as we ate, but something in their extrafamiliarity was abnormal. One opened its beak and shrilled at me, its black tongue lapping vilely. I backed away, one hand on the wall for balance. Wildly they sprung about, in a frenzy at my trespass. They were just crack animals, no larger than my hand, smaller than many I've killed, yet they had me backed against the rock. I went to my knees and began swatting at them, swinging my free hand at them with a fierceness to balance my fright. But they came on anyway. Their insistence was all the more intimidating; I'd never before had a crack animal chasing me, always they only hid. They pattered about in little circles, striving to drive me off their world. By chance I tapped one with my fingers and the creature was lifted up and across the lip of the basin. It shrilled feebly, then sank away. The other paid no heed and that one too, as light as a pebble, was caught with a swipe of my hand. It fell and I watched. And for the first time, still spastic from their miniature aggressions, I realised something of what was meant by my height. The yawning panorama had absorbed them valuelessly.

Suddenly I understood what danger I was in. Hitherto believing I had escaped by climbing apart from the world, I was reprimanded with sickness for having diluted a truth; there can be no escape from the ground, it would say, that womb, that voracious pit all spread out below in mocking. I froze and dizzied, became faint and desperate for solidity. I wanted the reassuring pressure of something firm against my body. I wanted total security of compassion in matter. I fell onto my belly, but as I lay prostrate it seemed my back might somehow betray me, perhaps fall and pull me with it. I clutched deeper and unhappier into the slight turf of the basin, then carefully, very slowly, I rolled onto my back. Crossing my arms over my chest, I cautiously looked into the sky, but it was all empty, depthless too, full of content (its blueness) but barren even of cloud, a formless form. I lay pinned hysterically on a platform in the thin mist, a last dream before the rock became the sky and the earth disappeared behind me and under my body, in both directions and backwards. I closed my eyes and lay miserably on my back, throbbing with wild intuitions of the hungry earth and the hungry sky absorbing me into its granitic eternity. We began coming upon decaying parchment fragments like chronicled flotsam on the rock. Folded or tucked into old haul bags, or tied within pieces of plastic that hung from the wall, we usually found these mementos in some isolated spot, rarely in the company of other journals. The dead men presumably preferred it that way.

Later we found several pairs of men wrapped in homosexual postures . . . tender deaths. And there were some signs of brutality, as in the case of one climber who'd been thrashed with a hammer. And brawls, verbal destruction, even two lynchings, all strung as twilights of inconsummate longing upon the rearing, unspeaking rock. Several of the journals mentioned tales that a certain climber, upon reaching 'a summit plateau', kept on climbing, hanging slings and karabiners on tree limbs, playing out his few remaining meters of rope through ascenders as he crawled immortally over rocks and tree roots that carpeted his horizontal stone. At times he grew desperate as he manoeuvred upon the ground; at times he was confident of his safety. He slowly perished that way, carrying the wall with him.

Toward the bottom many complained of banshee whispers. But gradually the individual ascents, each one toward the lassitude of varying degree, forced upon them all the realisation that much of what was thought to be external (ghosts and screams) was in fact internal. However, it was hardly a soothing realisation. Each

climber had become an isolate, a centred organism with its own
pantheon of unsharable, internal phenomena, accumulating a
private transparency, echoes reshaping a convulsing and writhing
world, effecting interior disasters (or salvations) whereby the
climber would untie and return quickly to the blurred ocean and the
soft humus below.

We continued on up the headwall. The months of progress over it
were like research through vague tombs, daily efforts to recapture a
past figure's deeds and character in some prehistoric network.
Gareth began assembling biographies, Aaron began compiling a
grammar of linguistic cores. We read of men, of the signs they had
used to appease their restlessness, and then we destroyed their
diaries and the scraps of the wall's history have long since blown
away.

Except for the idea and reminders of our solo climber. Nearly
every journal we read included two separate passages regarding this
gentle creature. Everyone on the wall seems to have acknowledged
him at some point. His story is like a branch.

Crudely put, he began as a beginner. Some of the journals swear
this climber had never climbed before. Apparently he just
approached the wall, then simply banged his way up the rock, a
process variously interrupted for food, rest and night. His style was
comically inadequate, as testified to by journal italics. He was slow
and an early doom was predicted for him by the many climbers who
continually passed him. He was described as friendly and im-
peccable. Several climbers urged him to retreat from the wall. He
didn't. One party had to revive him from a coma brought on by
exposure after a short fall. They stayed with him on a ledge for two
days, urging him to get off the wall, and then climbed on. He
followed slowly. In time he crossed the first great overhang and was
thereby committed for the rest of his life to climbing the rock wall.
His history becomes a blank for some time until a record of terrifying notice about his transformation. Perhaps he had found some
hidden couloir with its own crack system and meditated there. It's
not unlikely that he came into contact with the legendary Taoist
climbers, or the yamabushies. I don't know. No one knows. The
next mention is of his ease and his beautiful style, and awed
descriptions of his smooth speed. He was said to have climbed

naked, even on cold days when everyone else was suffering in their down jackets; one or two journals spoke of him climbing without the use of hands. One climber swears to have seen him ascending without touching the rock at all.

There are tales of cryptic chanting and foodlessness. Some say he required no water but fed instead upon sunlight and his own saliva. One passage speculates with rather extreme detail and rhetorical treatment on the possibility that the soloist reached a top. The fragment is abstract but painstakingly defines the soloist lodged in a landscape of ascension "serenely reflected." After hopeless deliberation I considered it highly probable that the summit had indeed been reached by the soloist. I stared up the wall to its governing horizon of rock and sky and was pleadingly thrilled. If the summit truly existed, and if the soloist had reached it, then obviously there was a chance that we too would find it. It had a tremendous impact on our morale and pace. We covered large stretches of rock each day for many weeks, believing we could almost see it, but soon enough our excitement was played through and the tedium we had grown used to again resumed. We slowed our pace, climbed more methodically, hauled the foodsacks and water, the hammock, winter gear, our pens and paper. Little by little our new-found energy was sapped and expended. In its place we were left with a transient faith. That was enough, to believe there was a summit. . . Years seemed to have seeped into my core . . . the delirium of pastness, an impetus beyond memory.

Many climbers were left abandoned when their partners died, and for a while they'd carry on. Not as well, but at least for a while. We found traces of one climber who had taken off horizontally, knowing his suicide, seeking desperately perhaps an edge or corner to the wall. His packet of notes described the pathetic ambition; we know nothing about the actual attempt. He questioned the value of upward ascent and bravely, we thought, separated from the vertical flux. He left the traffic of the wall and became alone twice over; first he was cast into hermitage by his partner's death (a sliced rope, we read), and then he tossed away all hope of reaching anywhere on the regular route, climbing sideways, wandering across the face. The cracks were few, though, and doubtful. His notes could have been anything: diversions, a dirge, dreams, a hoax. We wondered if he ever reached an edge to the wall. And as we wondered, we too began to sense the ritually fatal power of our dreams.

We climbed and found no summit. In winter it was too cold to climb so we settled on a huge forklike outcrop. Each winter morning we would wake coldly and everything around would be frozen. The lichen would be frosted, and the thin bed of water made into streaked glass. I later learned how to concentrate on the particles of sunlight and fire myself with their semblance of heat. We had nothing to burn. So we emerged from our bags and gathered close together to talk. To make warmth, or at least collectively to forget the cold.

But silence came. One bitter morning something happened. We gathered, shivering, standing in a tight circle, our hands tucked in the bellies of our sweaters, and we tried to talk. But terrible day, terrible sun . . . my first word became a white vapour, a netherness. Our winter breaths were marked by clouds of frost, a common fact of winter, one about which we'd never before cared. Until this day. "Gareth," I said. And there Gareth hung, there he vanished in a puff of frost. We started, then gaped as it hung and drifted a little higher, finally evaporating. Before our very eyes the word withered. We all heard me say the word, each of us understood what I meant by it, but suddenly, breached by our space, it was emptied of inertia, of its semantic value. It was no longer the same, it was humiliated by the vaster elements, condemned to limbo. (Aaron later added the phenomenon to his grammar.)

We were astonished. We blinked.

"Gareth," I said. This time we tracked the punctured cloud anxiously. The breath of frost rose again, but again it came apart. Our eyes deepened. The word *was* for a moment, but then it wasn't. It went nowhere. It was inaudible music, a particular cadenza which was for us an artifact, an instant of locality beneath the compromise of matter. The whole affair is almost not worth mentioning, but . . . you see?

Strange. As we got higher and left below us the mist, and eventually the clouds too, and as the sun was less and less filtered, colours disintegrated. I can't make distinctions between particular colours anymore. There is the sky colour, no matter what colour. And the rock is constantly the colour of rock. Even we climbers and our multi-hued gear have lost colour.

One day we would be in a gigantic chimney-crack, or again we'd find ourselves coaxing holds from an incipient groove, or squatting upon a ledge or hanging lazily beneath small, shading overhangs. But it was all the same rock, and only our experiences and perceptions fluctuated. After a while it seems the world froze and that the flux we sensed was merely internal and practically unreal. For a moment time has fallen asleep. At some other point we were born. Now, solidified like rock, time is ethereal and volatile as the sky. We climbed upon time as though it were mineral, and as we did we breathed it and our bodies exhibited time's marks. Our greyed hair dozed in lengths.

We had long since escaped the pit, when suddenly it stirred and rose up after us. Some of the very old journals we'd collected had records of the mist ascending the wall. Those earlier men had described demons and angels that flew about within it, hunting, haunting climbers. The mist, it was recorded, was filled with musics and scents, and now and then the sound of heavy objects fluttering down through thick air, or banshee screams of other climbers. They described peculiar agonies and frequent suicides. Gareth and Aaron and I meticulously read the accounts, but none of us could understand why the mist should be of such consequence. It seemed to us that the tracts concerning the mist were more like fairytales that wearied climbers had invented for their survival.

But the day came when the wet smoke rose. Serenely it rose up, fathomless, extending for miles up into us, swirling about our ankles and knees, then drifting on high above, swallowing us on our wall. In it were the brilliant wet colours we'd known below, and there the agony began, for the vivid colours wrought memories we'd forgotten. Images flooded and exhausted us. After the first desperate days we became more and more vacant, and climbing was at last impossible. We found a large, flat tower of rock and made our camp there and for a long time hovered in our opiate, the mist, engulfed in the past, moist nostalgias; its rich texture even softened the callouses on my hands, ruining them. When I touched the rock they shredded like springtime fingertips. Aching, limbs would collapse not just from weariness, but from emptiness.

In the morning we would wake and excitedly begin chattering to one another, trying urgently to relate each valuable detail of our night's dreams. The excited lesions of speech would quickly fall away as we collected ourselves in sad dissipation and sat closer together, one by one describing our nocturnal utopias. It was private territory and we each knew it would be a violation of the dreamer's sacred cosmos if we dared offer a word of interpretation. Instead we'd nod ambiguously and wait several minutes before the next would set in with a dream, eager to spin it out.

Frequently, by the time our dreams had been told, half the day was gone. Though the sun was layered with heavy mist, we could still discern its relative position by its lighter aura in the murky sky; thus we could mark our days. After the dream-telling was done, we would retire to separate parts of the ledge, maybe to exercise on the rock or to sleep, but usually just to sit and remember. And later, when the sun was going down for the night, and the menonic afternoon was expended, we were visited by spirits. Those which other climbers had called demons and angels came to hover by and talk to us individually. We each had a personal conclave that hung by us; as mine was invisible to Aaron and Gareth, so theirs were to me. They were pit phantoms come to convince us to return to where we'd risen from. Mother phantoms came, and various succubi, and old friends showed their tender concern for me. Even philosophers and poets would come up to talk with me. They appealed to my passions and my reason, arguing and cajoling, debating, kissing my head. I sat hunched up, my eyes squeezed tight, listening and sometimes crying a little, envisioning past loves and duties, recalling ideals I'd once championed. They were sweet echoes, but I felt a need to deny them all. What of the future, I would ask the phantoms, and they would flicker hesitantly before ignoring my words. My firmness would dissolve and I'd remember all the good things, all the fine pasts, just by sitting there against the wall, sighing. At last I flailed my arms against the phantoms when they demanded I dance in the air with them. My knuckles began bleeding where I'd knocked them violently against the wall.

I stared at my blood and many things rushed into place. Rough hair, nails broken, hominidal fears at night, and hungers, yes, the bloodness being the great hunger. I licked my knuckles clean and watched as more of my own blood welled up. I began lapping the scrapes, drinking of myself. Hunger seeped through me, and when the phantoms circled again I croaked at them to leave me. Look at me now, I warned them. They re-formed out beyond the ledge. You rest, they whispered, we'll leave. But I knew they'd return. Dreams and seasons have no evolution.

I glanced about. There were Gareth and Aaron, one lying in his bag, the other sitting in a corner smiling. I wanted to scream to them of the danger. Instead I went to Aaron, shook him gently and pointed to the wall. His eyes were glazed in distance and his smile seemed permanent, but he nodded his head and murmured assent . . . tomorrow, tomorrow we'll climb. When I shook Gareth he struck at me, weeping.

So with pieces of sling and old rope I lashed him fast to the wall. He didn't mind much. He struggled, but not with meaning. He was too possessed by the mist.

And next day, early in the morning I shoved and pushed Aaron awake. I was frightened that he might continue his depthless smiling, so I beat him. That morning we began our escape.

The first day we ascended only a short distance, but most importantly we began bleeding again and feeling ourselves as bodies and not as dreams. Each afternoon we'd return to the mist-enclosed ledge. Gareth recovered day by day, but still tended to collapse into reverie, so we kept him tied to prevent his suicide. We climbed each day, surrounded by the mist, shoving our way through its melancholia, fixing ropes for the coming day when Gareth could sanely join us.

I sat on a ledge for a long time, the rope draped around my waist and piled at my feet in loose coils as Aaron led above. Somewhere far below me Gareth was waiting for us to come sliding down to him with food. But I came awake instantly. Something about the rope insisted an end to my stupor. No words had been spoken, no warning, but I was suddenly alert to a tension burning down from above. Maybe the rope conducted the tension, maybe it was the air that was adhesive and saturated with urgency. And suddenly it came in an eruption of space. The rope's tension collapsed on itself as I clenched it anxiously. One moment there was tautness and demand streaking down into my hands; in the next I was left holding a limp substance, useless and without strength. Aaron was falling. The stillness woven deeply in the fibres leapt and the rope jumped fiercely; my palms screeched, taming the motion, searing, stopping the serpentine speed into sluggishness and final stasis of smelt flesh and inertia. I heard a distant slap high above me. Aaron had finished falling. The rope began pulling insistently at my waist, weighted on its far end. I set against it and wrapped it about my thigh, wondering why and how long the fall had been. In a minute there was the grappling sensation of lessening pressure, followed by a vibrating tug, and then a relaxation of the invisible pressure pulsing through the cord. Finally the hard pull eased, its tautness properly restored, fluid rather than enmeshed in the drastic sleekness of weight. I began working in the slackness as Aaron revived himself and started up the crack again.

From somewhere I remembered how immediately before the fall, the air had been warm, the sun directly above me. But I was beginning to shiver with the coldness, and the sun was low by the time the rope released itself once again. Another crashing. This time the slap came two times quickly as I held the fall, then sounded twice more just before I felt his total weight pulling violently against my waist. This, I could feel, had not been a good fall.

I waited for Aaron to call something down, but he didn't. He said nothing, just his weight. Invisible, existent only by the proof of the rope, he revived himself again. I could feel the rope jerking and releasing as he tried to pull himself into a prehensile position. Again I forced pain away from my burned hands, oblivious to the chill about my throat, demanding the same patience that dominated our life on the wall. I waited. Finally Aaron found a hold and the rope became unweighted again. I waited more. And while I lurked in my shadow (the pre-night), I heard what I had never dared to hear, an end to hope. It came like a small, dry bat through the fog; a groan, a tiny, bleached noise, muffled, half-sheltered by its shock, smothering. It was a memory, stars blowing hilted, stars in their cobalt flood of fear and aloneness infecting me in the night. An acute hum. I hit out, thrusting in every direction at the frightening blindness, and by chance my hand struck the rock. The spell snapped; there was rock, and my consciousness was restored, transfigured. My eyes came open. I could feel the rope again, and bit by bit I let the rope slide through my hands, running it as smoothly as my braking palms would allow. I worked him down through the mist gradually. Our sun was pallored, buried in the universe, already hinting at its usual bile black. One knew simply that one was; if he heard voices, or groans, he was conscious, and nothing more, of another, less verifiable existence. Aaron didn't answer. I continued letting out the rope.

At last I could hear his feet scraping weakly at the rock as he tried vainly to keep his balance against the arcing wall. And his hands kept slinging against the opaque, moonless stone. I continued lowering him. Finally his slumped body materialised, all wet and dark. On his head was blackness, a frigid blue shimmering, and his sleeves were also wet and bloody. I pulled him onto the ledge and laid him out. The mist became verglas and illuminated his epileptic form. The grey cold was at its margin. Drained by the night, I knelt and manipulated him down an overhang toward insomnial Gareth.

For the fallen one, days were spent in the heap of his drugged, lacerated half-corpse. But soon enough he could drag himself about, and would lie gazing out into the mist, numb with his private thoughts. He slept, pampering his scabbed face even in his sleep, careful not to touch a large bald patch where his scalp had ripped. On a few fingers the nails were pulled off, while on the rest, the cuticles had burst and bled, and his knuckles were flayed. A few times we had to kick him hard before he'd come awake from his delirium. But Aaron never really recovered from his fall, for though his wounds healed they were poisoned by the mist, and he was skittish and impacted with nightmares. One day the mist began to recede. Just like that, and we again became indistinguishable from the rock, and knew then we had risen slightly further.

We found a female mummy. She left no diary or notes. She was dried and desiccated after many years from hanging upon the wall. Tucked in her nylon hammock, she was well-covered with a thin silvery poncho that had at one time been painstakingly sewn as a lid to the hammock, but had long since been partly opened to reveal this precious corpse. Her hair was still long and beautiful, golden and soft. Short phrases of poetry were inscribed in the stone, and a multitude of names covered the rock above her head and chest, wreaths and bouquets of remembered loves that were immortalised here and dedicated to this one. How many had passed this way, brutal and hardened by the elements, and lifted the torn flap to witness her? Had there been even an intimation of company? But no, instead, each moving fragment of a body on this glossy wall, dissuaded by worn faith and weariness, persists death-like to its own final isolation, there to be devoured by loneliness and gravity. For a moment, peering reverently at the body of this dusty and lofty female, I was gorged with her delicate process, her every grace. The fine woman. And the rock pushed at me with its slickness and with its fine-flaked, deep, deep sterility . . . but the woman, she never pushed toward death; instead to her own vanities, her clutching thighs, her fertility and population. I am her child, but what labours must I undergo to forget her. Some would challenge the contradiction on sheer principle and insist that consistency either is or is not valid. I never suffered as I poised between the rock and the female, but I can never eliminate that possession which was their harmony.

Another season of nailing and bouldering above our ledges transpired and we entered a weird, vertical plateau, still believing in the soloist and the escape he represented. Artistic exercises suddenly flooded the rock. There were carvings, bas-reliefs, etchings, poetic and philosophic engravings, statuettes and figurines. Curiously they all seemed confined to a particular zone, its area covering roughly three hundred square feet. It began and ended with no reason, its perimeter was not dictated by an encroachment of bad rock nor was it lined with cracks. It just ended, top, bottom and sides, by common aesthetic agreement. Climbers had religiously fixed pitons and bolts throughout the zone so that those hapless ones who followed would not accidently chip or scar the art pieces while climbing through. All we had to do was snap our etriers onto the provided pins and we could easily ascend the vertical museum. We spent some two months in the region, rappelling and wandering about the abutments and fineries, returning to our hammocks each night to await the day when we could again resume our discoveries.

Everything was carved out of the wall rock. Pitons and drills had been skilfully wielded by the sculptors and masons, and the work had been beautifully polished by the wind. Some of the pieces were fragile, subject to destruction but at least temporarily surviving the elements.

All of the pieces, whether poetry or sculpture, reflected the medium of rock and the unavoidable reason for climbing forever. Everything was immediately apparent to us. But where had all the energy for this work arisen? Some of the pieces were overtly human creations and consisted of major rock workings, with heavy chiselling methods, while others were less forceful. These last works were milder compromises between natural design and human interpretation. Of these, some works were simple mineral patterns that were emphasised and highlighted by chip-out around the borders. The most gentle of the manrock compromises were what we called the shadow creations. These offered grave difficulties to the understanding. Upon first glance they seemed just misshapen knobs, chicken heads, crystals jutting abnormally from the surface of the wall, but after some time we discerned that at certain moments, the sun cast from these knobs particular and significant shadows which would stray sinuously across the granite entablatures surrounding them. The shadows were ephemeral, of course, and the work was only complete for a few minutes each day, but they were the most precious and abundant of works in all the zone. The more I became familiar with the shadow creations, the more I discovered in them. To my amazement I found that some of the knobs had been so carved as to give off a shadow pattern of one sort in the morning and an antithetical pattern in the afternoon. But then one day our hearts nearly burst when we recognised our own shadows. The rock, the immovable sun were devouring us in our introspection. Naively we had conceived of our immersion as a source of invention; it was our last intelligible clue.

In the mornings, with the first rays of sun, we would begin climbing. While Gareth and Aaron started up the crack, I would pack the sleeping bags and hammocks, rig the sacks for easy hauling, then jumar to where the others were waiting or climbing. I'd haul up the gear, fix it to the pins, and wait. Or climb, then wait. Or wait, then climb. The three of us could cover ten or twelve pitches in a period. We made leisure into a doctrine, trying not to sweat because water was so precious, breathing as regularly as we could, following the rhythm of our bodies religiously, and surviving by being conscious of that process of survival. When we came to what looked to be a sure death pitch, we would clamour for the lead, anxious to contradict our lethargy. But even death pitches lost their possibility and we'd sometimes hang for days, becalmed at one point and lacking all desire to do anything. We'd hum to ourselves all day as we lay, tightly pressed against the rock, in our hammocks, noting our passive miseries, sucking on pebbles, staring blankly at our hands or the similar sky. But these spells would grow heavy with their own unique tedium and soon enough we'd begin climbing again just because it was something else to do. Seasons passed.

A winter was approaching. Still we were nowhere. Still following the primary crack, many pitches beneath us and no top, only the dull sky overhead and beneath us; no deviation from the grievous music that would rattle our afternoons.

And then, the first instance in over a year, curled and dead, self-buried beneath a shelf of rock and loose stones, lay a naked, still shimmering climber. I mantled frantically up onto the miniature pedestal and caught sight of his body, and after fixing the rope for the others to follow, I unburied him. His flesh was cold, yet it was still pliable, and when I caught his hand it was limp and flexible. The fingers would bend or straighten when I worked them, as would all his joints, and with a start I noticed that there wasn't the slightest sign of discoloration or rotting. A saint, canonised? Some monk of the mount who had overextended himself? The corpse was not only intact, it was also undead. It smelled sweetly, like pine, and though it was dry it seemed fresh, even unctuous. And yet it was a dead thing. It didn't breathe nor could it move. It was affixed in a limbo midway between deadness and life. It was *ready* to move; it was flexible and unrigid, but it was unable to actually initiate the movement it seemed to contain. It was a wonderment, but at second thought it was a terrible thing, a boneless, cold mass. It had bones, and was in every way a human body, but because of its preservation it seemed empty. It showed no sign of escape. Most terrible of all, when Aaron and I dragged it from its recess and pulled one of its eyelids open we discovered it was lacking an iris and pupil. It looked as though the eyeball was pure, white marble, unveined and with a dull sheen to it. I could, I swear, even see the tiny crystals in its surface. But neither Aaron nor I would touch the eye.

And Gareth was behind us, gasping and snarling, tossing and wrenching his ruined wild head. I looked to Aaron for help, but he had pendulumed to an adjoining belay area, frightened immediately by what we both must have accented in our ancient suspicion, the finality of Gareth's despair. All that night I was left on the ledge with Gareth and his madness. Aaron stood desperate, waiting sombrely and shivering only some yards across and below. Gareth kept his head-shaking on and refused to answer his name, keeping his clasped fists in primal hidden postures of innocence and disbelief. Man, I said. What man? But he only shook his head and wept on, snarling; so I tucked the unthinkable damp corpse back beneath its covering of rock and snapped myself into a piece of anchored sling lest my peril in Gareth's presence be realised this night.

Then I walked to the limit of the sling and reached my hand out to Gareth and pulled him to me and hugged his tense head against my shoulder for our first contact in years. With this motion he groaned once and, weeping, gave over his fists to me quietly and at last. It was the journal, a mere few paragraphs of language, but it was the solo climber's own journal and at that we all three were cast irrecoverably into infinity.

from ASCENT *1974*

Confusions of an Odium Meeter

ROBIN SMITH

Thirsty First: Snaked and lathered up from the Deep South. Wet outside. Sneaked Frazer's chicken from under his nose. He knows. Frazer's chicken. Frazer's foul but fowl is fair. We are the three whiches. Food goes missing and all know its one of which (but not which one of) three. Who'd go missing here? May as well get lost. Bloody boots. Iron in their soles, rough on the heels. Giggled at Elizabeth: "We must drink to Pris." Seen at not-ours end of pantry. Scene. Found lot of odium (Ours is Bare). Gave Hughes (singing songs) water bucket; went to his head, foul. Went to bed. Fights. (Put out songs; Hughes put out).

Thirst: Now sated. Many sored but few rises. Wet inside. Fraser the Tee-total whole-meal rich-tea twice-cooked two-bit deep-fry basket rose, phrasing, smelling of soap and tea rose totally vertical but thorny as a green horned toad so dessicatedly croaking that he

would have been twice as much by the horizontal ones if they could have ris and would have got his chips and croaked and kicked the bucket that was going in his sleeping-bag beside him. Also was he one of a prickly pear, two-biters-in-the-night. (His complement bit at we three whiches for abusing her Primus, but Fraser had her first. More odium.) The other leg of the Jeans was eating a ginger nut. There were too two cling peaches like an order to command-oes: "Move in together in the dark and lie lo on landing and keep a grip and spread out in the morning." I spread down stairs after noon and sat and got a cold looking at the sun on Ben Attishow. *Second*: — wind. Back on our feets (of harms) Harma Virul-enceque Canis. In the grip of odium. 3 Addicts we, foil to double, treble, trouble, multiply (sic), 8 times 4 are 32. Hate times for our thirty-two. We dog them. Are now each feeling still-a-bit-Grey-but-like-a-Dash-Hound. And so to the races. We fan our sickened wind of whispering fiction, spirit of competition, stir the pygmies and Amazons onto the Clownic Ridge. Go dog go. The whiches leap into BRM sticks and brm along the Ridge. The rest just sticks, we knew they would, it's no ill wind that bodes no glue; honking behind, like geese, with salt (25 Odium) on their tails. We go by saddle horse-shoe and all. The rest go bare-back, each fails even to end the Ride, id est. Blow home on the dying wind — oh, panefully. Even the ill hills have their phil. Go doggo, collapse into pits for feats on our backs for days and daze.
Third: Stirred.
Fourth, Fifth, Sixth, Seventh, Eighth . . .?
Some or other day is ris. I wonder where the bodies is. Gone with the wind. Caught even Strork slipping out of the corner of an eye. Migrated. Maybe I grated, they got cheesed off. Welched. Rabbited. Thus I have but now am won, am self undone, am left so lo, odium winds up, runs down, nothing to hate, nothing to rob, nothing bewares, no wind in my sales, have got windead, panting for odium, allodium exhausted, mine run dry, must get out or I will die.
Nine . . . Teen Squared Sun Sets To Wait.

from ROBIN SMITH HOLOGRAPH IN THE HADDEN-WOODBURN MEMORIAL HUT LOG BOOK *c.1960*

Rawalpindi to Rawtenstall

DON WHILLANS

On September 24, 1961 I was ready to start the 7,000 mile journey by motor-bike from Rawalpindi to the UK [after the Trivor expedition]. After ten days' preparation I had got the necessary visa for Iran, and what was even more vital, some money. I was at last ready to leave the peace and quiet of Colonel Goodwin's house, and face six weeks of hard, hot and dusty driving through eight different countries. I said farewell to the Goodwins, and to the one remaining expedition member, Geoff Smith, and with good luck wishes ringing in my ears drove out on to the road to Peshawar, my first objective, 105 miles away.

I have first to make a call on an RAF pilot I had met on the journey out by boat. He was stationed at Risalpar, a place just short of Peshawar. After three hours' drive, a signpost indicated a right turn, four miles to Risalpar. I soon found the camp and was directed to his quarters. Unable to attract any attention, I went to the bungalow next door, and an extremely attractive Pakistani girl informed me he had left for the weekend, and gone to Rawalpindi. After talking for some time she said that if I did not want to continue that day to Peshawar I would be quite welcome to stay the night with them. I did not take long to make up my mind. If I continued, I should probably end up at the Afghan border after dark and have no place to sleep. Later in the afternoon, her husband, a squadron leader in the Pakistan Air Force, returned, and fitted me out in more suitable dress for a drink in the mess.

In the evening conversation drifted to my plans for the journey home. I received many pitying glances from the company, as they began to fill me up with stories of murder and robbery in Afghanistan. The appearance of a missionary, much to my relief, put an end to the topic; and it came as no surprise to me later, as I had already discovered what a small world it is, to find that he lived only eight miles from my own home.

I retired to bed slightly uneasy, already imagining myself going flat out up the Khyber Pass, with bullets singing past my ears.

Next morning after a good breakfast, I loaded my belongings on the bike, and said good-bye to my hosts.

I was determined to spend the next night on Afghan soil. After I left Peshawar, the hills, through which the Khyber Pass goes, soon appeared through the heat-haze of midday. As I approached the Pass, I thought of all the violence this place had seen, though it seemed fairly peaceable today. It wasn't long before I was stopped at a road block, with a couple of guards loaded down with bandoliers of bullets, to discourage any awkward customers from forcing a way through.

I was directed to a small hut at the side of the road and produced my passport.

"You have no frontier stamp," I was informed. It seemed one had to report to the police at the last town and obtain a stamp on the passport in order to cross the frontier.

I drove back to Peshawar, and soon found the police station, closed! This seemed to be unusual, the police station closed, so after a careful search round the building, I discovered a side door open and a miserable-looking fellow seated behind a desk. I produced the passport, and he disappeared into the chief office. One hour later I was heading back to the Khyber, a friendly nod at the road block, and I was entering the Pass on a good asphalt road, a thing I had hardly expected. Keeping a wary eye for snipers I stopped to take photographs and look at the badges of the many regiments cut into the rock. After passing several tribesmen with rifles walking along the road and not being shot at, I soon felt quite happy.

On arrival at the far end of the Pass I was halted at the Pakistan border. After a long business with papers I rolled up to the Afghan border 100 yards away. First they wanted the certificate of inoculation against cholera, as it seemed there was an epidemic on. After this the passport, *carnet* etc. Everything seemed to have gone off all right, when I noticed a clerk looking very intently at my visa stamp. I guessed what was wrong: it had expired.

A few minutes later I was back on my way to Peshawar to book in at a hotel and wait for the Afghan Consulate to open office in the morning. By 9.30 next morning I had completed my calls on the Consulate and C.I.D. and was once more driving through the Pass, which by now seemed almost as familiar as the Llanberis Pass in

Wales. This time everything went smoothly and in no time I was humming down the road towards Kabul, the capital of Afghanistan 180 miles away, very confident of reaching it before nightfall. For the first fifty miles to Jalalabad there is a super highway, and stories of Russian and American roads being built all over the country came to mind. Then came the rude awakening; this super highway was replaced by what I would call a farm track. What I did not know, as I began picking my way through the pot-holes and boulders, was that it was going to take me something like three and a half weeks' tough driving to reach the 'farm'. By 5 o'clock I had crashed the bike once, bent the footrest, and toppled it down a sand bank trying to avoid a lorry. I looked like someone out of a flour mill, and had a terrific thirst. I unpacked the primus stove and made two huge brews of tea, then fell asleep on the ground sheet.

I woke early, and continued towards Kabul through a very impressive gorge, through which the engineers were building a reasonable road, but unfortunately they hadn't made a lot of progress to date. I arrived in Kabul around 9.30, and stopped to watch the traders in the market. The best thing to do seemed to be to go to the British Embassy, where I would be able to get the information I required.

The Consul proved to be an extremely nice chap, and his assistant immediately offered me some breakfast, a wash, and a couple of bottles of beer to set me in the right spirits.

After breakfast I inquired about road conditions etc., and it seemed that I had arrived at the right time. The road I wished to travel on to Kandahar had just been opened that day; it had been closed because of the cholera epidemic. After the routine report to the police, I cashed some cheques in the bazaar and booked in at a reasonable hotel. By the time I had cleaned up in the shower, had a meal and the customary sleep in the afternoon, I discovered that I should be reporting to the Embassy for some more beer with the nice Consul.

After a very pleasant evening drinking and talking, I left the Embassy and discovered that the lights on the bike had failed. Having decided to accept the penalty for drunken driving without lights, I jumped on the machine and wove a course through the city back to my hotel and a clean bed.

After completing all necessary matters, like filling up with petrol and also the gallon can that I carried, I left Kabul wishing that I could have stayed longer. As the road might have closed again it was imperative to leave at the earliest opportunity. This was the first really long stage of the journey, being 340 miles with no cities in between. I drove all day, being stopped at several road blocks and asked for my cholera certificate. The tightness of the regulations regarding travel during an epidemic was beginning to cause me a little worry, for several reasons. First, cholera inoculation needed two jabs and I had had only one; then, the certificate had almost expired; and lastly, I might catch cholera. Anyway luck held and by nightfall I had reached the halfway stage. After a cup of tea and half a melon, a gift from a wagon driver, I bedded down on the sand just off the roadside, only to be awakened by the intense cold during the night.

The next day I expected to reach Kandahar, though I knew I would be in for an extremely hard day. I was not disappointed; for a solid ten hours I bounced along the track trying to stay upright, sometimes in sand, at others in rocks or gravel. Just before darkness I had only eight miles to go when I had the feeling something had happened to the steering. A quick look revealed a broken rear mudguard. Far too much weight, something would have to go. It was too late to start to rearrange the packing, so another night was spent in a dry river bed, the only disturbance being caused by some animal rushing past my head just after I turned in. The glimpse I had made me think it was a dog, or could it have been a wolf? Not being sure if there were wolves in Afghanistan I fell asleep still wondering.

After cocoa and a juggle with the kit I wobbled into Kandahar in the early hours. Several essential jobs required attention, so I decided to spend a couple of days in this city. After a clean-up in the hotel I took the bike down to a welder in the bazaar and had the mudguard repaired, then bought oil for the oil change now due, and returned to the hotel. In the meantime, two girls had arrived at the hotel, one from Oldham, some ten miles from where I live, and a girl from New Zealand, travelling together back to England. We combined cooking arrangements and I enjoyed several good meals. Hotels in these countries do not object to cooking in the bedroom. Two bottles of beer arrived, one each for the girls from a chap down the corridor who appeared concerned for them, though I think he became even more concerned when I downed both bottles before he could say knife.

The following day I spent on routine maintenance of the bike and visits to various offices for stamps in the passport or on the certificate. During the evening several motor-cycle dealers arrived, and began offering to buy the bike. Unfortunately there were too many technical snags, otherwise I would have sold the machine, their offers were very high and would have bought me a new machine with some to spare.

The next stage of 235 miles was reputedly the toughest, and so it proved to be, not that the road became any worse, but extremely hot and desolate; only towards evening, when nearing Farrah, did I see the odd village. There is one stopping place called Dilaram where one can buy petrol in tins if one is running short. Just as the sun began setting I pulled off the road and made camp for the night some ten miles from Farrah.

A call in the bank next day proved unfruitful, they refused to cash a travellers' cheque. Stopping only long enough to buy a packet of cigarettes I pressed on to Herat, arriving around 4.30. I searched out a hotel and within minutes of my arrival had been invited to dine with a Swiss couple in the evening. He, it seemed, was a geologist, and had been in Afghanistan for several years. He asked if I had come through Dilaram, and told me he met the famous Peter Townsend there, while he was making his round-the-world trip. Also in the hotel were two English lads travelling back from Calcutta and later my two ex-girlfriends from Kandahar arrived by bus.

The following day I carried out the usual routine of bank and garages in preparation for departure next morning.

I left early in anticipation of trouble at the frontier. I had been warned not to take food that had been opened as this would be thrown away by the Iranians at the border because of the cholera. The track became very sandy in places and I had great difficulty in crossing several troughs of sand. Midday saw my arrival at the frontier, the place seemed deserted. I eventually found the officers in charge asleep. They quickly clipped the necessary stamps etc, and returned to their cots. A mile up the road I encountered the Iranian border post. They threw away my water and several bits of food, and checked my cholera slip for the last time, then I was heading for Kalla Islam, the frontier town. Here I encountered a whole host of people from the hotel in Herat. The last bus for the day had gone, so they were spending the night in a shed which was the town's hotel. I decided to stay the night and have a chat with English-speaking people for a change, and spent the evening drinking Coca Cola with an American who told me about the angry scene on the bus after one of the English girls discovered her camera had been stolen. Just when heads were about to roll a man cycled up and handed the camera over. How he came to have the camera in his possession was still a mystery.

On the journey from Kalla Islam I encountered my first bad 'corrugations' which in no time broke the mudguard again. My English friends passed me later in the day on the bus, waving, then disappeared in a cloud of dust, and that was the last I saw of them. I arrived in Meshed mid-afternoon, and after deciding one hotel was too expensive I tried the usual trick of picking on a knowing-looking youngster and repeating "hotel". I was then taken through the town, and finished up at the same hotel. Tired out, I booked in, and after a shower and clean-up I had the mudguard welded; then set off to look round the famous 'Blue Mosque' and the bazaar.

Next day I picked up a student guide and made a tour of the city, buying several souvenirs, and a watch for £1 which I thought might just last the trip. It did, just! At Boulogne it packed up.

From Meshed to Teheran is 576 miles of horrible road; I expected to take three days for this leg of the journey. It did in fact take me four, and during these four days in the saddle many incidents occurred, some amusing, some not. At my first stop the entire police force arrived at my hotel in dribs and drabs until finally the chief himself arrived to see this stranger in the town. I was at first rather angry with all the town in my bedroom, particularly as I had the front wheel off the bike trying to repair a puncture. Later it became so comical during my interrogation, that I found it impossible to keep a straight face. Many severe glances were directed at me, which only added to my amusement. Finally with a stiff bow I was handed back my passport and the room was emptied.

The following midday found me seated by the roadside in a particularly deserted stretch with another puncture. Deciding that it was useless to use the same rubber solution again, I thought I would sit it out until someone arrived. Nightfall saw the wheel back on with the puncture repaired. Exhausted after my struggle all day in the sun, I slept at the scene of the mishap.

Deciding that the spare jerry-can of petrol was no longer necessary I threw it away, a good find for some wanderer. Pulling in at a small town for bread, I was immediately pounced on by the local bobby and while I was being once more interrogated, managed to have the mudguard welded again. At Damghan, my overnight stop in a cheap hotel, I traded a tin trunk for a decent job on my punctured tyre.

Ten solid hours driving brought me to Teheran on the first stretch of tarmac road for weeks. The ride from Meshed had taken its toll of me. I looked a very sorry sight, dirty, unshaven, face badly cracked with weeks of exposure to the sun, and extremely sore. Deciding on a fresh start, I called the inevitable stray over and was guided to an expensive-looking hotel. The apartment was luxurious, own bathroom and telephone and all the trimmings. After a good bath and a huge meal I passed into oblivion between spotless white sheets.

Next morning, feeling much fitter, but around three pounds poorer, I visited the British Consulate to learn the dos and don'ts for leaving Iran. After taking the camera for repair, I visited a park to watch some tennis, quite a change in this part of the world. Nobody seems interested in wasting energy on sports of any kind.

From Teheran 100 miles of tarmac road were a marvellous change after the 'track'. However, all good things come to an end, earlier than usual around these parts, and soon the track reappeared. While I was having a 'Coke' in a transport café a GB Land Rover pulled in, the occupants being an Australian and an Englishman heading for England.

I put my kit in the Land Rover and we drove along together until nightfall, then camped in the desert for the night.

Leaving the two lads to repair the three flat tyres they had inherited overnight, I pushed on to the next town to await them and do some shopping. Whilst I was waiting for them, the London-Bombay bus pulled in, spilling a crowd of young people out and filling the village with the sound of Cockney voices. Talking to one fellow I asked him how he came to be going to India. "Well I just got fed up, so I got on the bus at Hampstead Heath." "Got a job out here?'' I asked, reminding him there is no dole in India. "No. I'll look around for a couple of weeks before I start work.'' A few minutes later they were gone, leaving me scratching my head.

Meanwhile, the lads were having the patches vulcanised at a garage down the street. While strolling around, one particular 'nosy parker' who spoke a very few words of English began to annoy me. A fight looked like developing from the show I gave him, when I was informed that he was the chief of police, in civvies. After this I decided to leave town and drive slowly to allow the others to catch up. A mile from the town I stopped by a stream to swill the dust off the bike. About an hour later I saw the Land Rover approaching at a fast rate. I asked what the hurry was and they told me they had to make a run for it for refusing to pay the price asked by the garage man.

Later in the evening we arrived in Tabriz. A few inquiries soon had us installed in a reasonable hotel for the night. Next morning I said farewell to the boys, who wished to press on with all speed. The day was spent in collecting exit permits and in changing money, also maintenance of the bike. The rear mudguard needed welding again. On the way to the welder's shop I had a head-on collision with a cyclist. In view of the threatening crowd, and the fact that I had been going up a one-way street, I had to pay up a pound and try to look happy.

The next day I expected to reach the borders of Turkey. I left at seven and drove steadily until midday when I caught up with two more Australians in a van. Over a thick slice of bread and jam we decided to press hard for the border, as we were all rather fed up with Iran and Iranians. The scene at the border post made us think of a hotel in Paris, quite luxurious and full of tourists. The fabulous cars made us think civilisation had arrived.

True to form, trouble arrived in the shape of the passport officer, who went a little too far and began pushing people about. Unfortunately for him, none of us was in any mood, after a hard day, to be pushed about. He found himself in the unusual position of being an Iranian surrounded by a threatening crowd, and as this had never happened before he quickly disappeared into his office. It was too late to cross the frontier, so after a meal in the Tourist Hotel we slept in the yard on camp-beds.

Strangely enough it was our sparring partner from the previous evening who got us away one of the first in the morning. As soon as one entered Turkey there was a magnificent view of Mt. Ararat, 16,900ft. Seeing a snow-capped mountain after so much desert made me feel almost at home again. Although the roads were still unmetalled, there was a very marked improvement; also noticeable at once was the appearance of neat fields, and road signs. The most startling thing of all was that people were working. It was also nice to discover that the children didn't play the game of 'Stone the Motor-cyclist' as in Afghanistan and Iran.

A few miles into Turkey we came across our old friends from Tabriz. Over breakfast the idea of climbing Mt. Ararat was discussed, but after I submitted my estimate as to how long this would take from where we were, the subject was not mentioned again.

Expecting to meet up again at the next town we each departed separately, but it was the last I saw of either of them. That night I slept for the first time on grass by a lovely clear river with enough water in to completely submerge oneself.

During the course of the three-day drive to Ankara I went through the towns of Erzurum, Erzincan, Sivas and Kayseri; the country in parts became mountainous, with good scenery. My first encounter with rain occurred on the way to Kayseri, causing high jinks on the muddy road surface.

Ankara for me meant that I had successfully made the trip home and the rest was just a formality. I had been told by a couple travelling the other way that from Ankara to England one followed a tarmac road all the way. Having decided to spend a couple of days in Istanbul instead of Ankara I was soon using the power so long stifled in the bike. Whilst in Istanbul I went into a shop to change a rather large note into something small to pay a rascal of a hotel-keeper who was trying to cheat me. When the owner of the shop arrived he began to tell me how he had lived in London and for several years in Leeds, where he had attended the university. He took me in hand, and fixed me up in his uncle's hotel, then took me out to dine in a very smart restaurant where I had the best meal I'd eaten for over six months. As I was staying in the fairly rough quarter of the city, a café proprietor insisted that I leave my bike in the restaurant which enabled me to sleep easier, although it meant rising at six in time to pull it out before opening time.

After locating the Consulate and obtaining the Yugoslav visa I left Istanbul and headed for Bulgaria wondering what an Iron Curtain country would be like. I arrived at the border in the early morning and was refused entry on account of having no visa. I had been misinformed at the Consulate, and had to return to the border town of Edirne and obtain one from the Consulate there.

On entering Bulgaria I noticed at once how neat and orderly everything was, tree-lined roads with all the stones along the roadside painted white, all dead leaves swept into piles, an absence of advertisements. In fact it was like an army camp. People with whom I had contact were very polite and efficient, they almost seemed afraid to be anything else. Driving along these roads was in fact quite pleasant, mostly farming country on each side. One of the large towns, Plovdiv, seemed very plain; I can barely remember it at all. Unfortunately before I arrived at my hoped-for destination, Sofia, I had a back-wheel puncture: a nail which I had noticed embedded in the tyre in Iran eventually burst it. With the help of a passing motor-cyclist I was soon on my way to Sofia. This town I liked very much, clean with several very nice buildings, one in particular with a gold-coloured roof. An obvious foreigner walking around with a camera seems to give every policeman the idea that he's just found himself a spy. After several hours wandering and a meal I drove off to the Yugoslav frontier some thirty miles away.

This frontier crossing proved to be the stormiest of the whole trip. A huge fat Italian, obviously very wealthy, had all his money spread on the table, Canadian dollars, American dollars, and several heaps of other currency, all being meticulously counted by the officer. Unable to understand a word of what was being said, I guessed that there was a great danger of his losing the money, as he seemed about to blubber any second. Standing by the gate the customs officer gave me back my *carnet* and passport, then asked if I had any money. Thinking he intended to change my money, as did the fellow on my entry, I handed him about £3 10s. in leva. When no money came forth I asked him about it. All he said was "Confiscate" and as far as I could see, to him that was the end of the business. Roused to fighting fury by this cool cheek, I started a riot which finished with the guard running from the gate with fixed bayonet, and myself cursing the officer and telling him if he touched me with it, I'd shove it up his waistcoat. Quite surprised that anyone should dare to say anything at all in this country, he wrote out an official form for me to draw the money from the *Banc de Bulgarie* in Erchard. Sure that no such bank existed, I drove into Yugoslavia still seething with rage. Ten minutes later a passing car flung a stone straight through my headlamp.

My first experience of a town in Yugoslavia put me on my guard against policemen. I was fined 10/- on the spot for a miserable parking offence. Determined the 'Big Brother' should get no more money for his next rocket from me, I drove very warily. The ride to Belgrade, some of the way on the 'Autoput', was quite pleasant, though not of any particular interest. Along the 'Autoput' which connects Belgrade and Zagreb, I was travelling fairly slowly, looking for a good spot to sleep the night. I was surprised by a man in uniform waving me down. Thinking quickly, I knew that I was breaking no laws, so I stopped, with the engine ticking over. It was a policeman. "You are travelling too fast, comrade," he said in bad English. I shook my head and said "Autoput." He then made a sign which I knew at once: money. Shoving the bike into gear, I let out the clutch and drove off with him grabbing at my shoulders. With a good hefty hand-off I was rid of him, and motored down the road for a couple of hours at a steady 75 m.p.h.

A second 'Autoput' from Zagreb goes to Liubliana and here the countryside takes an almost Swiss look, small chalets and churches on the mountainside. Within a short time after leaving Liubliana I arrived at the Italian border, expecting both trouble from the customs and sunshine. I got neither. Almost casually I passed through the formalities, to be greeted by torrential rain which continued almost all the way from Trieste to Manchester. Three days later, after terrible weather and damp nights in hayricks, I landed in Dover after a very rough Channel crossing to be greeted by the report: 'Floods all over the country.'

A night in a transport café, a puncture on the M1, and at midnight in teeming rain I stood outside the house I had left six months ago. A few pebbles at the bedroom window soon had Audrey, my wife, down to greet me with a pint of tea and a big fire. The date was Friday, November 4.

from TO THE UNKNOWN MOUNTAIN *1962*

Crooked Road to the Far North

LITO TEJADA-FLORES

At a beer garden in Berkeley, putting down a pint with my old friend, Chris Jones, the subject of summer climbing trips came up, and that's how I got back on the road . . . Chris had planned a mini-expedition to the Devil's Thumb, a redoubtable granite spire in South-eastern Alaska, with two Salt Lake City climbers, George and Jeff Lowe. Something has come up, Jeff couldn't go. Did I want to come? Sure.

The juke box was blaring out Elton John, the air warm with summer and tasty with pizza smells, students and freaks and half-naked chicks swirled around us, through the open patio, the pop-corn machine was spitting and the avant-garde cinema beside us disgorged its Fellini-eyed crowd into the night . . . Not exactly an atmosphere for reflection but perhaps 'up there' would be more real than 'down here'. Sure. We left La Val's drunk and enthu-siastic. Chris and George would drive most of the way, via Salt Lake and Canada, as far as Prince Rupert. I would go by bus to Seattle, then ferryboat to Petersburg, Alaska, and meet them there. We'd fly into our mountain, air-drop our gear, and climb it, even if it took us a month.

We were laughing and joking and it wasn't really too clear just what I was getting into. (On a last-minute practice climb before leaving I discovered how out of shape I was, and a real anxiety about the climb began to build up inside me.) But one thing was sure: before I knew it, I'd be travelling again, stepping out, in the grip of strange currents again, and it felt good.

Early in the morning in Seattle, bleary-eyed and loaded down with ragged old duffle bags, I find my way down to Pier 48. False front of wood and plastic, giant Indian totem designs, yellow and blue Alaska Marine Highway signs. Right away, I've got a problem: the list of walk-on passengers is full, closed. No, we don't make reservations but all these folks came in yesterday; first time it's ever; we'll put your name on the stand-by list; yes, we'll know around three or four this afternoon. A helluva note. Only one boat

319

a week from Seattle, and my friends up there waiting. Screwed. Well, what can I do but trust my Karma, again and always? Leave my pack and bags at the feet of a giant stuffed Kodiak bear in the waiting room, and go out to see Seattle.

After an endless walk in cowboy boots, I decide to eat lunch at The Prague, a gallery/restaurant in a waterfront district of run-down brick buildings, slowly being remodelled into a funky, posh shopping area. I know it's overpriced but I shrug my shoulders: there won't be anything like this up north.

Lunch is good: watermelon and fruit, cold meat and cheese, a mysterious central European soup to go with the tangled images on the wall. It's 2 o'clock. Time to say goodbye to Kafka and Klee, Teleman and Bach on the stereo, time to say goodbye to Prague and Seattle and, somehow, get on that boat to Alaska.

Back in the ferry terminal, the situation has deteriorated: there are now some ninety frustrated, confused people on the stand-by list (and a few really angry ones). Their story is the same: we tele-phoned from Tucson; drove all the way from LA; no plane till Wednesday; they promised; I told my husband, planned this trip for three months; they'll tell us at four, no, at five . . .

In the middle of this displaced-persons atmosphere is a lovely slender girl, tallish, in faded jeans and a big, loose Levi jacket. How do we begin talking? An unimportant, impersonal remark addressed at random to the milling crowd. A minute later she is saying, with a smile: Want to hitch-hike north with me if we don't get on? Inside me a small voice is already shouting yes, yes! I am surprised at myself. She has a little child and an enormous duffle bag. We compare luggage, miles, laugh at the impossibility of it. Don't worry, we'll get on! . . . A long conversation begins. Something else has begun.

Her daughter's name is Ajila: a lovely smiling face, a snub turned-up nose, short blond pigtails. She sits between us on the high ticket counter and draws with a ball-point pen on application blanks for Master Charge cards . . . We exchange names, fascinat-ing bits of information that unfold and unfold: Kathleen, unlike her daughter, has dark, wavy hair pulled way back, a pale oval face with only two spots of colour on her cheeks, prominent without being really high-boned. A tiny gold dot in a pierced nostril makes me think of gypsies, central Europe, far away places. She is

beautiful without being beautiful. She doesn't sparkle, she glows.
But she's real, she's tired, has real problems, a real mixed-up past,
her own crooked road leading her north. She's going to Ketchikan
to meet her old man, they'll travel, work, she's not sure, maybe
she'll wind up working as a nurse as she did in Crescent City . . .
Her dreams are close to the surface: she talks about going to South
America someday, adopting a lot of kids . . . Ajila? It's an Arabic
name, her father studied Arabic, no someone else, she married him
to keep him out of the Army.

Around us people fester and complain. Behind the counter, the
harassed clerks with their gold and blue *Alaska Host* pins pretend
not to notice the people on the other side. But eventually the
purser's list arrives with ninety-six places: room for everyone, I
think. My own name is third on the list. I buy my ticket and stagger
to the gangplank under my enormous bags.

The MV *Malaspina* is so big that its levels, decks and passage-
ways seem, at first, a labyrinth. I lug my dufflebags in relays to
the solarium on the top rear deck of the big blue and white
boat. This is home. What next? Look for Kathleen, of course. I
meet her at the top of the stairway from the car deck; her bags are
down there, so we go down again and I carry them up on the deck.
We're still amazed at having got on board at all. And we sit
down, out of breath, and stare at Seattle, rising up the hill behind
the waterfront in grey tiers of freeways and office buildings, a grey
city under a cloudy sky. It looks like rain.

We relax, the three of us, on a wooden box-seat full of life
preservers, peeling oranges while Kathleen makes cheese sandwiches from the food left in her old carpet bag. A bushy-whiskered,
prophet-like figure of a man walks by (prospector? recluse?
hermit?) dressed in Army fatigue pants and an old brown sweat
shirt. Are you hungry? Would you like some? Kathleen knows,
offers, dispenses, smiles. Strange easy-going vibes are all around
her, all around us.

Paul is, indeed, an old recluse with a philosophical bent, going
up to Wrangell to "work in the woods." He takes me down to the
deck below to show me a part of the ship he has 'captured',
hanging a large blue and orange tarp across a corner of the covered
walkway. Beneath it are his incredibly worn-looking possessions
and his pride and joy, a big black iron pot. He pulls two beers from

a paper bag. One for your wife. No, she's only my friend. A strange rush of emotion that will be explained later, or never.

When we get back to the solarium, the ship is just casting off; silently, imperceptibly at first, the long wharves slide away from us, gathering momentum as the whole panorama of Seattle distorts, expands, recedes . . . It takes a long time to lose the city astern, but already we're in a new space. The North is already more real, our day-to-day lives already half-forgotten. Under threatening skies we enter another world.

The solarium is full of backpackers, young people, freaks. Kelty packs and down sleeping bags are everywhere. Paul spreads a hundred-year-old hand-embroidered quilt on a kind of raised dais, like a legendary bearded pasha out of the Arabian Nights. Down inside the boat, there is a second scramble for the remaining staterooms. The other walk-on passengers, those of a certain age, or a certain life-style, will be spending the night stiffly upright in airplane-type lounge chairs. They don't look very comfortable, or very happy. . .

The evening is forever. Already the northern latitude gives us more daylight than we're used to. It's a late, long twilight, the lamps are on, Kathleen and Ajila are tucked under a forest-green sleeping bag. I lie on my stomach on a deck chair beside her, and we talk, ask, answer, tell: What kind of women do you get involved with? A funny question, women like you. (My words surprise me, the feeling doesn't).

Our talk takes us back to our other lives, takes us forward to the edge of the far North, the edge of our own dreams. We surprise each other by talking of death, finding that we've both met it, thought about it, made a temporary truce with it. Kathleen has put a degree of order into a confused life. She talks of her "life plan," a good one if slightly impossible, as anything must be that makes sense. She asks me questions that stop my standard answers cold. Her face is full of possible answers. Her beauty is as hard to understand as my reasons for taking this trip, or wanting to climb that mountain. I fall asleep beside her with an open heart.

The next day was long and lazy, monotonously beautiful, and at the same time full of a quiet excitement that had nothing to do with the scenery—the low forested hills sliding by on either side, the stark rocky inlets, isolated homesteads, tiny lighthouses, lonely channel markers on a lost spit of granite, sudden waterfalls cascading out of the clouds into the inky blue of the strait.

We walked and read, and even ventured into the high-priced world of the ship's cafeteria for coffee and hot chocolate for Ajila. We met our fellow-vagabonds on the rear deck, and talked about their trips, and their scenes. The real landscape of people and faces began to take shape. There were climbing boots to grease and free hot showers to enjoy, and the lazy quiet flow of water on every side to pace us through the day. In the evening I wrote a small poem for Kathleen and gave it to her:

> Frontiers are places so beautiful,
> and so empty, that men
> have to fill them with dreams.
> Frontier women, too, have
> calm deep faces that
> make men dream . . .
> It's good to know that
> both still exist,
> and that you're
> one.

Her smiles went through me like knives. Wherever she went on board, the air would ripple around her. I enjoyed watching her random movement on our deckside world: finding her and losing her, smiling, exchanging private glances, watching her disappear around a bulkhead, spotting her through a window, noticing how other people were attracted into her orbit, coming up to her to offer their smiles, their gifts, listening to Ajila play with the other kids on board, only smiling when I noticed that her mother wasn't really as beautiful as she seemed to be . . . Her beauty was beneath and behind beauty. I was in love with a gentle dark-haired puzzle in faded blue jeans.

Everyone in the solarium that evening looked hungry. In any case, no one could afford to eat in the cafeteria, much less the dining room. The prices were unbelievable. Someone, I think one of the kids on a bicycle trip from Seattle, suggested pooling our food for a community dinner. (Some hadn't thought to go shopping before our departure, and others, caught in the 'stand-by list', hadn't had time.) It was a huge success, a feast, not a dinner. Food appeared from everywhere: bread, cheese, sardines, celery, fruit, peanut butter, cold meats, cookies . . . I bought some Rainier beer and Jay, the neuro-psychologist whose daughter played with Ajila, contributed some wine. We were already drunk without it. Serious bearded faces, young hairless ones, homely girls beginning to look pretty because they were having such a good time. Paul was there, beaming like a prophet; and the art-school teacher from the east coast who had sketched Kathleen resting against her duffle bag; two teenaged boys from Maine who looked as if they hadn't eaten for days; pint-sized touselheaded Ray, a diminutive chain-smoking 16-year-old whose dad was a steward on the ferry, on his way back to Alaska after a year in an 'institution' for some adolescent craziness, smiling and stuffing his face like the rest of us. Ajila was kneeling at her mother's side. Incongruously, older 'straight' people were drawn into the warm circle of our picnic on the floating bank of this endless winding ocean highway.

After dinner we borrowed the ship's vacuum for our crumbs, then played charades till midnight, laughing, jumping up, crying out, losing track again and again, still drunk with each other, coming down slowly, slowly, like the long pale northern evening, reluctant to give up the last light in the sky, or in each other's faces. . .

Fatigue finally triumphed. The kids were already asleep. Ajila was a blond Moslem angel under her green nylon sleeping bag. Lounge chairs were pulled out flat to sleep on. Kathleen and I headed below decks for a midnight drink in the ship's bar. A perfect day, perfect evening. I wanted to stretch it out, talk to her until the words dried up, until there was nothing left to say — knowing that in a life you hardly begin, that one more evening wasn't even time to begin. . .

In the bar we talked, drank Scotch because neither of us could think of anything else to order, listened to a guy in the booth across the way thump out a bluegrass polka on his banjo, laughed when two of the cyclists from Washington, brother and sister, started to dance crazily up and down the narrow aisle. Out of breath from dancing, Mike came over to sit with us: his hair sticking out in all directions, his chambrey shirt pulled out, his thick smiling lips covered with fever blisters (beautiful people, we learn, don't have to be too beautiful). And out of the blue, he delivered a crazy, moving, totally disarming speech about Kathleen and me, about having watched us on the ship, about the way we stayed together without grabbing onto each other, about watching the way Kathleen treated her little girl with such respect, letting her choose what to do next, what clothes to wear in the morning . . . And going on to talk about himself, his efforts to find himself, not to be possessive with girlfriends, with people . . . And he said a lot more, but what moved us was how he said it. Letting the barrier between himself, his ego and his words become eggshell-thin, exposing himself in a strange trusting way to talk to us like that, so that we learned more from where the words were coming than from the words themselves. At any rate, we blushed when he talked about the two of us, but he was right: our bond in the present was so real we hadn't even begun to hold onto each other for an imaginary tomorrow. Even the bar was closing, we left.

There you are. Happiness, desire, perfection. Where, if not inside you? Who, if not us now? When, if not here now? We fell asleep, warm on the cold deck, arms outside our sleeping bags, hands clasped.

Reborn under dazzling blue skies. They stole the clouds during the night. Nothing to do. A million things to do. Time rushes forward out of control. Before we can adjust, Ketchikan is swimming into view like a postcard of some far Norwegian village. The dark blue water is full of pale white jelly-fish. At the railing, Ajila has a tearful moment, imagining that we'll have to swim ashore. No, it's not like that at all. Minutes later I'm carrying their duffle bag downstairs and across the ramp to Ketchikan. Farewell is a little picnic on the rocky bank, a few words, Ajila crying out: Oh, mommy, you kissed him! and an incredible knot of emotions in my stomach. Kathleen's old man, the fellow she's been living with for two years, should be arriving on the afternoon ferry from the north, and the three of them will have to begin the business of making a new life. All my concern, my good wishes, for her, for them, seem superfluous; of course, it will work.

Back on board, I remember my Solzhenitsyn novel, *Cancer Ward*, that she was reading, find it in my pack and manage to run ashore at the very last minute to give it to her. An extra farewell, stolen kisses. Kathleen and Ajila running out to the dock's end as the *Malaspina* pulls slowly away. My eyes are full of tears. I've just lived through something unbelievable. Paul is standing beside me at the rail. Whatever he is saying seems to make sense, with such a long grey beard he must have lived through all this too . . . The knot in my stomach starts to untie itself, we're still moving north.

from MOUNTAIN GAZETTE 15 *1973*

Your Lovely Hills Are Very Dangerous

KEVIN FITZGERALD

There cannot be more than half-a-dozen real hard men, perhaps youthful aspirants to the Alpine Climbing Group, who have made the journey, on foot and by road, from the beginnings of Llanberis Pass to Beddgelert. To the best of my knowledge I am the only man living who has made this appallingly dangerous journey on two occasions. Of the second, on which I had a companion, I have already written in another place, but my solitary attempt has remained unchronicled. I now set out, below, what I recall of my experience in the spring of 1951. I was not able to make notes at the time, but the facts are essentially as I record them here.

About 10 o'clock one morning towards the end of March 1951, or it may have been 1950, I was sitting in the bar (since remodelled and renamed the Smoke Room), of that small hotel at the foot of Llanberis Pass which is known to all travellers in those parts. I was sipping a whisky and soda, having just finished reading a most excellent article on the climbing situation in Wales in the 1940s called *Return to Arfon*. On the table in front of me was a big blue-coloured volume, *Rock Climbing in the English Lake District*, by a man called O. G. Jones. Some people from a place called Keswick had taken some old-fashioned photographs to illustrate the work and I was finding it of interest. My presence in that hotel at that time of year was due to an obligation I was under to write a book of fiction containing a gang fight in Wales, preferably on the face of a steep rock climb.

My thoughts had no connection with Beddgelert and were indeed focused upon the measurements of the bar. It had just occurred to me that a determined man, sitting where I had positioned myself, could hardly miss the landlord with a shot from a .32 Mauser pistol, *if* the landlord happened to be standing at the cash register. At that moment the door of the bar opened and the landlord's wife came in to join me. She was not in those days much given to conversation, being endlessly busy about the house. "I've come to have a little chat with you," she said, "It's nearly 11 o'clock."

"So late," I said, emptying my glass, "I was sitting here thinking."

"Not thinking," she said, "Drinking."

"So I was," I said, holding up my glass, "I must have another of these."

"That's what I want to talk about," she said. "You drank a bottle and a half of Scotch last night in this very room, and here you are doing it again, or in a fair way to doing it again, before lunch. You should go out more, into our lovely hills."

"I did that from this very hotel, just after Christmas," I reminded her, "and I was ill for weeks. Your lovely hills are very dangerous."

I stood up, all the same, and returned the red Journal of the Fell and Rock Climbing Club of the English Lake District to the corner bookshelf in the bar which, in those days, had twenty or thirty of the Journals, but not one of them with anything quite so good as *Return to Arfon*. I didn't know what any of it meant. It was just interesting to read. The author was a man called A. B. Hargreaves, and I didn't know him either. I put *Rock Climbing in The English Lake District* under my arm. It had just come into my head that my hero might well be reading it in his bath when a villain, still uninvited, thrust a gun through his bathroom window. The essence of thriller writing is that heroes, preferably unarmed, should invariably outsmart relentless thugs with guns in either hand. It seemed to me, as I weighed it in my hand, that *Rock Climbing in the English Lake District* was at least throwable.

"I'll get hold of my packed lunch and go," I said. I tried to sound a little hurt, a trifle wounded: I've always found that difficult. The landlord's wife picked up her broom and duster. "Don't forget to take off those red slippers," she said.

There was a packet of sandwiches lying on the hall table bearing the legend, "Mr. Fitzgerald, no cheese." As cheese makes me frightfully ill, I knew what would be inside the grease-proof paper, but I shoved the packet into the little knapsack I used for carrying books, put aside 'Rock Climbing in the English Lake District' while I was putting on my shoes, and walked out into the icy conditions of a Welsh spring morning.

A man with a coiled rope over his shoulder was standing motionless in the driving rain. He was wearing scarlet stockings, and what appeared to be velvet knickerbockers. There was a look of total despair on his face. "Have you seen Marcus?" he asked me.

"There was a man in the bar last night they were calling Marcus," I said. "He was trying to read the 'Tractatus' of Wittgenstein, but they kept interrupting him."

"Sounds like him," said the despairing man, "I was to meet him here at half past ten."

"And you've been standing here in the rain all this time? Come in at once and have something to drink."

To the look of despair he added a look of real horror.

"I am a member of the Alpine and of the Climbers' Clubs," he said, "I never drink in the middle of the day. We try to keep ourselves reasonably fit." I bowed, silently. It seemed to be the only thing to do.

"You'd have seen Marcus at breakfast, if he'd been there, wouldn't you, don't you think?" the despairing man said, almost to himself. It was clear to me from his constructions that he, at least, had not, spent the previous evening reading the 'Tractatus', or even the 'Philosophical Investigations' of Herr Wittgenstein, but it was my turn for the look of despair and horror.

"I never eat breakfast," I said, "I'm never well enough."

That man seemed not to like being with me. "I think I'll go inside," he said, and I stood alone with my problem in the heart of Welsh Wales. I could see no way round it; I would have to go for a walk of some kind. It had been on the tip of the despairing man's tongue to ask me to go climbing with him. I had only saved myself with my inspiration about breakfast. I embarked upon my journey.

I still had no thought of Beddgelert. I don't suppose that I had, in those days, even heard of it as more than 'a place'. But there was, as there still is, in a much altered form, a High Road and a Low Road for part of the way in which I was, merely by chance, going. I stood at the junction (there was no gateway then), took a pull at my pocket flask and considered matters. A blonde woman in Scandinavian costume who was standing beside me began to sing 'Solveig's Song' from Peer Gynt. As I turned to seek her advice she disappeared. There was a lot of loose gravel on the Low Road, and a little bird with a white rump was hopping about. It frightened me rather, and I set out along the High Road.

There was very little traffic on that road in those days, and it had not been straightened out anywhere. But there was a blinding flash every five or six minutes as a motor bicycle or motor car skidded upon me round unsuspected corners. There was an Admiral of the Fleet in full dress uniform walking beside me, making a rather curious clanking noise with his sword. I asked him if he thought our situation dangerous, but he didn't reply. I asked him if he would like a sip out of my flask, but he had vanished.

Some time later I reached a Post Office in a place they told me was called Nantgwynant. I enquired for licensed premises and was told that Beddgelert was my first hope, but that "they might be closed by the time you get there'. I sat down by the roadside and opened my sandwich packet. Everything was made from cheese and onions. One of the misty people all round me said something that sounded like "lucus a non lucendo," but I didn't know what he or she meant and just threw the sandwiches away and emptied my flask. It seemed wasteful in my desperate circumstances to pour a libation for the gods, and I did not. I struggled towards Beddgelert.

It was a long journey, but I thought I could do it. I remembered dreamily that the night before someone had been talking about a man called Carr who used to stay in Beddgelert and run over Snowdon every morning, with a bicycle on his shoulders, on his way to a mountain called Tryfan. "It's quicker that way," he is alleged to have said. I supposed that was why I was without conscious design, now on the way to Beddgelert, and moreover, with an empty flask. I began to recite aloud the Love Song of J. Alfred Prufrock, but when I came to the bit about measuring out my life with coffee spoons an Australian Aboriginal, who kept throwing a boomerang across my head, and snatching at it with his left hand as it came back, asked me to shut up. "You need concentration for what I'm trying to do," he said.

I made for the public house where Mr. Borrow was said to have spent a night or two on one of his missionary journeys, reaching it as the rain stopped. You could say I was wet. They told me the bar was closed, and that, at that time of year they seldom bothered to open it during the week until 'going on seven'. The barmaid was knitting a strange looking tube from a huge ball of grey wool. "Nice not to see climbers," she said, "If you and I were locked in the snug no one would know, isn't it?"

"Not a soul," I said. We drank a bottle of gin together in the snug and quite soon the Australian went away and I was alone with her. Just before six o'clock I asked her if she thought a determined man with a .32 Mauser pistol could blow the lock off the snug door. "You had better be getting back, isn't it?" she said. We embraced, a brother and sister in extremis. Perhaps there was a cousinly touch to the final kiss as she slipped a half-bottle into my pocket and kept the change.

"Don't let them put you into one of those places, bach," she said, "I've a book to finish," I told her, stiffly, and set off on my return journey. "You're going to find this bit difficult, cobber," the Australian said. He'd been waiting for me outside, together with a man from a circus who had a herd of camels with him. I put my face towards Nantgwynant.

I woke up just before it was fully dark. I think I had rested, with a book, because, as I opened my eyes, a little man in a pink hat closed 'Esmond' for me and dropped it into my book bag. As I reached the hotel the guests were just coming out from dinner and the landlord's wife called out to me, "Oh, there you are: You're just in time if you hurry up and change. You look ever so much better."

In those days I preferred dining alone, and I gave any loitering diners all the time they needed. There was never a crowd in the early fifties, just a few climbers. When I reached the dining room the Wittgenstein man was sitting by himself reading, and absent-mindedly picking at a plate of Welsh mutton.

"Do you happen to know any German?" he asked me, "I'm trying to re-write and re-translate a rather bad piece for the Alpine Journal."

"I did once, long ago," I told him, "But where the number two bus used to stop they've set up a kind of jungle with orang-utangs hung on the trees." I must have spoken all Kästner's piece from *Emil* in German because I heard myself saying, "Orang-Utans hingen in den zweigen,'' and the Wittgenstein man stood up and held out his hand.

"Please don't bother," he said, "my name is Marcus, and I'm a doctor. What you need is a nice long rest."

I go to that hotel rather a lot, now, and the other night a woman guest said, "Don't you ever drink anything except tonic water?" "Oh, yes," I told her, "at Christmas time and Easter I quite often have a bitter lemon, or something like that. You see I'm a member of the Alpine Club, and the Climbers' Club, and we have to try to keep fit." Then I went up to bed. There was a book up there waiting for me called 'Rock Climbing in the English Lake District' and I was longing to read it for the twentieth time, and to look again at the lovely photographs, taken by the Abraham Brothers of Keswick eighty years ago.

from MOUNTAIN LIFE *May 1974*

Himalayan Hopefuls

GREG CHILD

Delhi. A crazy quilt of humanity baking on the plains of northern India. The air so hot and thick it smothers. Sitting on a pavement outside the airport, waiting for our transport, we watch the chaotic traffic and jostling crowds that spread for miles in every direction. Plagued by beggars and rupee shark salesmen who would sell you their sister, I close my eyes and picture the cool mountains to our north.

That things run altogether differently in India becomes quickly apparent. I know of no restaurant in the West where you could order a drink at three in the morning, roll out your bedsheet on the floor for the night, then crawl out from under the table next morning and order breakfast.

My daydream of mountains is interrupted by a small Indian boy who seats himself between Whillans and me and begins a conversation in perfect English.

"Are you an expedition to the mountains?" he enquires.

"Aye," replies Whillans.

"But are you not too fat to be climbing mountains?"

"Perhaps," returns Don in his Lancashire drawl, eyeballing the kid. "But by the time we're finished I'll be skinny and they'll be non-existent."

Our expedition was a small one and a mixed bag in terms of its members. Doug Scott, Don Whillans and Colin Downer had come from England. Doug, after some dozen expeditions to the Himalayas had the game wired and Don is a legendary figure of British climbing. From France came Georges Bettembourg, a guide from Chamonix who had been on several of the world's highest peaks. From New Zealand came Merv English and from America Steve Sustad. Rick White and myself were Australian. In Uttarkashi we were joined by our liaison officer, Colonel Balwant Sandhu who had been to the summit of Changabang with Doug in 1974.

Our permit was unusual in that we had no restrictions on any peaks in the area and could climb whatever we chose. This 'blanket permit' was issued by virtue of an agreement to impart some knowledge to Indian climbers in the area. So with no specific goal till we chose one, there was nothing to worry about on the approach.

As we travelled north by bus towards Uttarkashi and Gangotri the tempo of life slowed. The dusty haze of the plains lifted in the clear air of the hills, and as the bus swayed steadily round hairpin bends the landscape became greener, with steep hillsides terraced into farms and small villages. And below us flowed the broad grey Ganges, as it carved its path toward the Bay of Bengal.

After crossing the Gangotri Glacier and walking along its bank for a day with our thirty porters, we came to Tapovan, a grassy meadow where we established Base Camp at 14,000ft. We were not alone at Tapovan. In the nearby moraine lived three yogis, who inhabited hobbit-like dwellings elaborately tunnelled into the hillside. One, who had spent many seasons there, seemed curious about our interest in climbing mountains. "First travel, then struggle . . . then calm . . . very good," he concluded.

Base Camp was nestled between the imposing walls and ridges of the Bhagirathi Peaks, and Shivling rising directly from the meadow. The mountains of this area are mainly composed of compact granite, forming fang-like towers and huge faces. In 1947 the Swiss explored the area and climbed Satopanth (23,213ft.), and Kedarnath (22,770ft.), the highest points in the area. Although

Shivling was climbed in 1961 by the Indians, from the Merugi glacier, little else was done till recent years due to the restricted nature of the Gangotri, a restriction imposed after the Chinese invasion of neighbouring Punjab State some years ago. The area has now been reopened, and since 1979 several Western expeditions and at least ten Japanese parties have climbed most of the remaining untrodden summits.

The next two weeks were spent acclimatising around Base Camp, climbing on nearby crags and boulders and investigating the valleys to choose our route. Having moved from our homes at sea-level to the altitude of Base Camp, we all felt, in varying degrees, the effects of altitude. Symptoms such as shortness of breath, headaches, and nausea were noticed even by those who had been high before. To lessen the rigours of altitude we gained height slowly, levelling off at plateaus of 12,000ft. and 14,000ft. and spending a few days there to let our bodies acclimatise to the rarified atmosphere. The difference betwen slow and rapid altitude gain is roughly the difference between taking a stroll and running headfirst into a brick wall. Probably the greatest object lesson in support of slow acclimatisation lies in the Chinese invasion of India in 1962. After the Chinese filtered into Punjab over high Tibetan passes and occupied border towns, the Indians responded by rushing thousands of troops to areas at 12,000ft. to 15,000ft. The Indians suffered massive losses due to pulmonary oedema and other altitude sicknesses. The Chinese on the other hand had spent much time at altitude preparing the invasion and were fit and well.

By late May we were physically ready to go high and had decided on our route. Attracted by the Matterhorn-like symmetry and striking beauty of Shivling, we chose her as our peak. And the mountain is female, for Shiva, her namesake, is a female deity.

Doug, Georges, Rick and I decided to try the unclimbed East Pillar, while the others would climb the mountain by the original route. The Japanese had last year climbed the North Pillar over some forty-seven days, fixing ropes the entire way. On the East Pillar we planned to move alpine style; moving constantly and without fixed ropes, finding bivouacs as we went, and relying on the supplies we carried on our backs.

June 3: we set out from Base Camp and retraced our footsteps to the beginning of the long knife-edged ridge that leads to the pillar.

After descending in a storm a few days before, I'd begun to feel comfortable with the view of Shivling from Tapovan, but now I found myself again trudging one foot at a time up steep snow to our tents: and having reached them, saddling a 60lb pack and humping it along the ridge, the pack swaying in close harmony to the rhythmic deep breathing of 17,000ft. accompanied by the steady bass line of double boots thudding on snow-covered granite. To say that my body was a living protest to what was happening to it was to say the very least, as each day for three days we moved in this fashion, over and around pinnacles and sidling around blade-like crests with dizzying exposure on either side. That is, when I wasn't lying on my back with a pack strapped to it, gasping like a fish out of water, my chest thrust upwards to the sky, as if in some high-altitude hallucinatory misconception that such a position would attract more oxygen to my lungs.

And the tent, ah yes the tent, ha ha: a little incident with our two-man tent and a cartridge of gas. Boom, a fireball in our living room, an exit at speed into a night of snow, the smell of singed hair and melted nylon mingling with rising steam. Yes, I know that you're not supposed to blow your tent up on a mountain, but this is our debut here. The outer skin of the tent is unscathed but the inner evaporated, disintegrated. There's not even any wreckage left. But we make do.

Day four, and the ridge butts into the pillar. As Rick and I were feeling a little more acclimatised, we led the sharply-fractured wall to a short snow ridge beneath a 1,000ft. orange prow. With our ice-axes we excavated two platforms for the tents, an everyday ritual that seemed to have two things in common throughout the climb; firstly, there was never enough room on which to fit the whole tent and someone had to sleep perched over an abyss. Secondly, the digging was almost always done during an afternoon snowstorm. The weather we found fairly predictable; warm, clear days with afternoon storms that cleared by night.

On the fifth day we followed long and continuous cracks that snaked their way to a vanishing point far up the prow. In places the cracks were perfect hand- or fist-width but at one point we came upon a crack that widened to an awkward and glass-smooth six-inch fissure choked with ice. Puzzling out one move at a time I inched up its 30ft. slowly. A boot jammed into the crack, a handhold chopped into the ice and a desperate swing of my alpine hammer till the pick bit and let me pull on to a ledge. It was too late to continue up the wall and there was no ledge for a bivvy, so we fixed our five ropes to this section and abseiled to the camp below for another night. We returned next morning to this point, hauling our packs, and crossed a broad snowfield to gain the next rock step and a ledge. All we felt like doing was getting in our tents and sleeping, but we first had to spend time melting snow for tea and soup to replace the moisture our bodies had lost.

Once more the face above appeared to lack a suitable bivy site that could be reached in a day, so we ran out our rope and used this ledge again, our seventh bivouac. Georges led off on a narrow slab covered in powder snow. To either side of him there was a drop of 4,000ft. of thin air to fluted icefields. His crampons scrattled shrilly at the rock beneath the snow for 60ft. before he found a crack to hammer a pin into. The face above was in constant shadow and vertical. Two freezing pitches later we returned to camp, numb and exhausted.

Cramming into one tent for dinner, cold limbs were rubbed warm and conversation made us forget our position. It was more like being invited to dinner at the neighbours than being on a mountain. When the hour came to stumble across crisp snow to our tent it was hard to believe that we were in fact over 20,000ft. above sea level.

"Think you can make it home all right?" asked Doug.

"Hmm . . . better call us a taxi, I'm not sure of the neighbourhood."

Over the next two days we continued up the steep wall towards the prominent tower in front of the headwall. The rock was becoming increasingly iced up and our line began to blank out 100ft. short of the tower. Rick led up, placed a pin then lowered off it and swung left into an evil icy chimney that gained the tower. Another bivy, our ninth, and we ate the last of our solid food. Only a few packets of soup and some oats were left. Not even any scraps to throw to the choughs that flew with us.

The predictable weather also changed. An eerie fog engulfed us as we climbed the ridge the next day, a still silence put my body further into a waking dream. The shroud lifted to reveal a vivid pink and blue sunset behind Nandi Devi, Kamet and the Garwhal mountains. We seemed to stand level with the summits of the Bhagirathis, and with our own summit in sight, felt that an end to this long climb might be near. But the clear skies belied the storm that struck that night and kept us deep within our sleeping bags all next day. We lay silent, sleeping or brooding to ourselves over the prospect of descending the forty-five pitches in storm. Our main concern was that the storm, fiercer and colder than the afternoon squalls, blew not from the north but from the south-west, the direction of the monsoon. Pundits had warned of an early monsoon this year but could it be here so early? With limited food and fuel we were in no position to dally in a storm.

"What does Don Juan say?" shouted Doug across the void between our tents. I picked up Castaneda's *Teachings of Don Juan*. Opening it at random I read:

"He says to find a path with heart and follow it to the end."

"Does our path have heart?"

"It's the only one we've got."

On the eleventh morning our path could be clearly seen, plastered in fresh snow, but sunny and windless. We moved again.

Slow moving along a delicate corniced ridge interspersed with 200ft. towers we have to chop down, and man- (and woman-)sized stacks of whipped-cream-snow to get over before reaching the final obstacle, the 1,000ft. headwall. The climbing turned to mainly direct aid. It became clear that we would need another bivvy, so while two climbed, the other two chopped out a space for one tent. Lying like four sardines in too small a can we slept well though hungry, with the knowledge that all our decisions were now made for us. So close to the top, we had little choice but to reach the summit and descend the other side of the mountain. For us the easiest way down was up.

With a cold south-west wind howling next day to remind us of the approaching monsoon, we set off. A stew of clouds bubbled behind Kedarnath and the air filled with spindrift. 60° ice, then a series of grooves led to the summit ridge. Georges waded through soft snow above, dumping bucket loads of the stuff on to we three below, who crouched like cold monks in Goretex with hoods drawn and heads bent.

But the mountain held on to us for another night, forcing us to bivy on a terrace a mere 40ft below the summit. Too tired to be frustrated, too cold to sleep, I just dreamed of the hot plains below.

The last day, the thirteenth: we crawled over the wind-thrashed summit cornice and stood on a bald dome of ice. Whether all the pain or suffering of a long climb justifies the final goal seemed irrelevant as we stood there in the wind. We had done what we set out to do and could only laugh and embrace each other.

Then down the icy dome, front points biting into the hard ice, belaying down the steep slope. The Merugi Glacier seemed so close, Base Camp so near. And then an understatement. An understatement so keen and precise that I could find no reply but to dig my ice-axe into the snow and wish that I'd untied a moment before.

"Here I come," said Rick as he slid past in a flurry of snow. Nothing to do. Just wait for the back-wrenching jolt — ugh — cartwheeling like a rag doll, umph, face first into the slope, cold crystals stabbing into my cheek, a crevasse out of the corner of my eye, airborne over it, urgh, wind forced out of me as I land head-first into a flat bowl 600ft. from where I stood. Then quiet; no wind, no voices, nothing. Finally I heard the hiss of disturbed snow sliding down the slope and looked around. Rick was moving his legs and arms. I could do the same. We could even stand up. Georges and Doug appeared, puffing loudly, agape as we walked towards them. They too could only find understatements.

Delhi again. I'm hobbling about with frostnipped feet, dodging the deadly traffic and rupee sharks. A fat character sits at the helm of a three-wheeler taxi curling his greasy moustache, eyeing the crowd with the eye of a predator. In his sweat-stained safari suit he looks like a villain from an old Bogart film; a gun-runner or white slaver. Peter Lorre on a bad day. His eyes zero in on me.

"Psst . . . you want sell?"

"Me? Sell what?"

"Cigarettes, whisky. . . ."

"No. Sorry."

"Then," he leans forward, revealing the grandeur of his black-ened, betel-nut-stained teeth, "you want buy?"

I walk away swimming in the dripping heat. I've never been so hot. It's too much. I wish I were up in the mountains, a cool breeze blowing off a glacier on to my face. . . .

from WILD 3 *1982*

But I Never Returned . . .
(A Thirties Idyll)

RAYMOND GREENE

We camped that night, July 3, near the Rongbuk Monastery and the next day set out on the fourteen-mile march to Chodzong [after the 1933 Everest expedition]. The Rongbuk Valley, which on the way up had seemed the dreariest on earth, had greatly changed. Instead of a biting wind and flurries of snow there was a light warm rain, laying at last the intolerable Tibetan dust. The desert had begun to blossom in small bright tufts between the stones, islands of sedum, purple vetch and pale blue iris. The hills along the valley, on our upward way black and dismal, were brown and yellow and in the distance brightest purple. Chodzong had had little grass when we passed that way before. Now the valley floor was brightest emerald interspersed with yellow buttercups, pink primulas and scented violets.

The invalid contingent had not arrived from the base hospital at Tashidzom to which I had sent them. I wanted badly to see the Kharta Valley but instead Ruttledge and I set out to examine the situation, leaving the others to go over the Doya La to Kharta. After about two miles we came to what had been a trickle on our upward journey but was now a raging torrent that we crossed with difficulty. Below the ford the valley became very fertile and we rode through fields of flowering mustard towards pale brown hills over which snow peaks showed pale blue beneath lowering clouds. The rain fell steadily.

About five miles from Tashidzom we were met by the local squire, riding a gorgeously caparisoned mule and proudly wearing the green Homburg hat that we had given him on our upward journey. At first (for speech between us was impossible) we thought that this was an example of the great courtesy we had learned to expect from Tibetan gentlemen. But no; hearing on the local grape-vine that our party was bound for Kharta, he was hoping to catch us at Chodzong to extract payment for grain supplied to our ponies while we were 'up the hill'. The history of these ponies quartered at Tashidzom while we were in the high camps, had been a sad one. Knowing from previous experience that the oriental thinks no

338

shame to add to his income at the expense of a horse's stomach, my first act when I went down to Base Camp had been to summon all the ponies from Tashidzom for examination. They were skeletons, and on making inquiries I found that the ration ordered for them was about half of what I thought necessary. I doubled the ration and sent them down again. Thereafter they not only resorted to short rations again but amply lined the pockets of Nerbu, our chief seis, a revolting old man whose dishonesty was equalled only by his inefficiency. Birnie, arriving at Tashidzom three weeks before, had taken all in hand, but the condition of the ponies was still very poor and Smijth-Windham's was so weak that it could carry him no more.

About a mile from Tashidzom we were met by Birnie in a delightful grove of willows, as peaceful a camping ground as we could hope to find. Violets grew thickly in the grass and scented the whole scene. Most of the invalids had largely recovered and were, I decided, fit to take the road to Gangtok. I wanted to stay awhile in the warm green world, but I had to get them away. We left the route of our upward journey and followed the main valley of the Dzakar Chu, which flows east and south towards the end of the Kharta Valley where it flows into the Phung Chu. We moved slowly, for McLean was feeling very weak and our guide did not know the way. Five miles from Tashidzom we had to call a halt at a large farm. The farmer and his family, including three pretty daughters who had never before seen a white man, came out and regarded us with huge amusement. One of the daughters particularly took my fancy. Taller and slimmer than most Tibetan girls, she had a more Aryan face, a tip-tilted nose and a lovely figure. One small firm grimy breast occasionally peeped through the folds of her still dirtier robe. She showed in her amusement at our quaint appearance a row of perfect teeth unusual in Tibet. Later I told Karma Paul about her and he immediately offered to go back and fetch her for me. "But, Paul, supposing she would come, what would happen on my return to England?" "Sahib, it is simple. You give her a few rupees and her travelling expenses home." "But she would never then be able to marry in her own village." "You are wrong, Sahib. She would have great honour." However, we left it at that.

My invalids were doing well except Wood-Johnson and McLean.

Wood-Johnson's gastric ulcer was not healing and McLean was too ill to be of any assistance to me. We continued our pleasant way and on July 9 rejoined the main party at the end of the Kharta Valley.

Natural laziness, medical responsibility, a feeling that nothing now mattered much, combined to end my diary. I am left only with vignettes of memory.

Of the day when Jack Longland and I, stark naked, raced our ponies across a great green plain, and, forgetting our state, into a village of which the inhabitants had never seen a white man, least of all a nude one.

Of the night when George Wood-Johnson's gastric ulcer threatened to perforate and I spent the night beside him with the immediate prospect of acting, in Willy McLean's state of incapacity, as anaesthetist and surgeon both.

Of the border between Tibet and India where the wind was bitter and strong and with our packing cases we built a long wall to protect the tents. The natives came in the night and stole the top layer of cases, which included almost all my zoological specimens, all except the few still in my rucksack collected on the previous day. Karma Paul and I went to the nearest village, paraded the villagers, and told them that if the boxes were not found their children would die of smallpox. They wailed and fell on their knees, screaming for mercy. The boxes were not found. I do not know whether they got smallpox.

Of our arrival at the beginning of the road to Gangtok where I knew that the responsibility would drop from my shoulders and I put my heels into my horse's flanks and galloped into town to the kind and competent Doctor Henriques who immediately sent out an ambulance. We dined that night with the King and his charming Tibetan Queen.

Of a weekend with Sir Malcolm Hailey, the Governor of the United Provinces and his delightfully unconventional Italian wife. Rumour said that he had been offered the Governorship on condition that she was sent home; that he refused; and that he got the job just the same. One day when I was having a morning cocktail in the ADC's room she entered in a girl guide's uniform and a state of high dudgeon. "I," she cried, "have troubled myself to get all the badges I can, shooting, first aid, everything, even good conduct.

And now they say that officers must not wear badges. Ha, but see, I fox them." She lifted her skirt, and there they were, neatly sewn on to her bloomers.

Of the day when I called on my cousin Roland Raymond, a medical officer in the Royal Air Force. I found I was billed to play hockey for the Army against the RAF. Never having played hockey I was released, but with difficulty. I remember a hectic drive to the playing field on the pillion of Roland's powerful motor-cycle, but not much else till a mob of somewhat mimsy officers took me to the station and attempted to install me in the private compartment of the Military Secretary. Foiled in this effort they decided to debag the General, but I dissuaded them from this and attempted entry into another compartment. They then lifted me into a horizontal position, held me there till the train began to move, and propelled me head-first through the happily open window, landing me, still horizontal, on the lap of the astonished inhabitants. This I gathered afterwards, was the traditional farewell of the Royal Air Force in India reserved for its more distinguished guests.

Of lunch with the Viceroy, the Marquess of Willingdon and his fury at the Everest Flight. This journalistic effort had as its moving spirits Colonels Blacker and Etherton, a couple of most entertaining adventurers, who, when the latter was British Consul-General in Turkestan, had succeeded, according to Lord Willingdon, in selling to the Standard Oil Company the non-existent oil rights in Turkestan, which were of course not theirs to sell.

Of the night in Bombay that I always think of as a whiff of chrysanthemum. The Japanese House, easily recognised by the lantern that hung in the cherry tree at the gate and floodlit the clean white walls, was quiet and peaceful after the filth and horror of Grant Road. The old lady who owned it, gnarled and twisted like a bonsai, was voluble and lucid in a wild mixture of languages, Urdu, Japanese, English and a smattering of anything convenient. She showed us into a large room two-thirds of the floor of which were covered by an immense divan, on which after, of course, removing our shoes, we gratefully reclined while three charming girls in national dress, all comely but one of exceptional beauty, with the fragile loveliness of the geisha of dreams, knelt at our feet and kept our glasses filled with Bass. Occasionally, assured that our immense thirst was temporarily allayed, they would slip off the divan on to the floor and divert us with little tinkling songs sung in their little tinkling voices.

> *Tora chini, tora char,*
> *Velly fine gentlemen yes you are!*
> *Queen Victoria rule de lan'.*
> *Queen Victoria velly fine man.*

At last they were allowed by the old lady, who kept a most careful eye on what went on, to sit beside us. Emboldened by Bass I put my arm round the waist of the most beautiful of the trio. She stiffened but made no effort to escape. I talked to her soothingly in English, of which she didn't understand a word, and she gradually relaxed and lay close within the crook of my left arm with one hand in mine, and occasionally even took a sip from my glass. Sleep overcame me.

When I awoke Keiko was still there, very close and fast asleep. I kissed her very gently on the forehead and she half awoke and snuggled still more closely. I cannot remember how long we lay there, but suddenly I realised that we were alone and that dawn was creeping into the room. I kissed Keiko again and she fully awoke, gave me one embarrassed glance and fled. I slid down the divan, put on my shoes and made for the door. The others were all under the cherry tree. I was horrified to realise that Bonham, who was a little drunk and whose conversation in fluent Urdu was sometimes difficult to follow, was attempting to buy Keiko, not for himself but for me. "My friend," I heard him say, "is extremely rich. A little matter of a few thousand rupees is nothing to him. Surely just for a night that would be a good profit." The old lady, far from being shocked, was rocking with laughter, refusing every offer. Frank departed to some unknown destination. The old lady pushed Bonham with unerring instinct into a house across the road in which he wished to make what we would now call bioavailability studies, from which he did not emerge for many hours. Me she detained. Drawing me into the kitchen she attacked with admirable directness.

"Do you love Keiko? She is 16 but she is still a virgin."

"Madam, I can recognise innocence when I see it," I said (pompously), "I can respect it."

"But do you love my little granddaughter?"

"I think she is a charming girl."

"I would like her to marry you. She can sing and play and cook and will make a good wife. Also she loves you and so do I. You would make her happy."

"Honourable grandmother, I am honoured and very touched. Never has so much honour been done me. But it is impossible."

"Why?"

"Because I leave for England in a few days."

"She can be ready to go with you."

"But she will not be happy in England. She doesn't know the language; she will be lonely without friends; the climate is cold and damp."

"As to the first, she will soon learn; she will not be lonely with you there; our climate is too hot and either too dry or too wet."

"Nevertheless, after so short a friendship I cannot agree, tempting though your proposal is."

"When will you be back again?"

"Perhaps next year."

"I shall keep her for you."

"No, you must not do that. I cannot be sure that I can return."

"I know that you will return."

But I never returned.

from MOMENTS OF BEING *1974*

PART 4

Cast List

If you will forgive the truism, achievements, performances, and records, are only the symptoms of sport—the causes are entirely based on the personalities involved. There is no way of proving that the characters of climbing are more interesting than those more public figures of football, motor-racing, tennis, or any other such footling pastime, but my suspicion is that this probably used to be the case.

In this section are gathered together scurrilous interviews, attempted character-assassinations, eulogies, balanced portrayals of the most scholarly nature, weighty word-exchanges on alpine history, and also two of my favourites in this book—Don Lauria's *Letters from Herbert* and the Paul Ross interview—both of them outrageously honest and delightful pieces straight out of climbing's social history. The latter in particular will perhaps tell you more about the spirit and nature of climbing than anything else ever to have appeared in print. *In vino veritas* was never more truly exemplified.

Climbers

JAMES MORRIS

There is no denying that in externals climbers have changed.
Innocents who go to mountaineering inns anticipating a fragrance
of dons, pipe tobacco and leather map-cases, may expect to be dis-
illusioned, as they sidle their way through the babel of rude
language, the blodges of large pink thighs, the clutter of nylon
ropes, bottles and miscellaneous spiky things that are the pre-
requisites of modern alpinism. It is a long time, I think, since a
classicist read his *Religio Medici* over the Gentleman's Relish,
before setting off with his friend, the incumbent of Brambletree
Magna, on another demanding ascent.

But in deeper essentials the sport is very resilient – by which I
mean that it remains to the outsider perfectly inexplicable, and
indeed rather ludicrous. In the century odd since men started to
climb for pleasure, nobody has really succeeded in explaining what
the pleasure is, and climbers have remained from that day to this
testily on the defensive. Like any other comical minority they take
their foibles seriously, seeking to prove that if a pastime cannot
logically be fun, then it must have meaning – like the man Kinglake
quoted in *Eothen*, who habitually retreated when a joke fell flat to
the assertion that anyway it was *true*.

So the fact that it is all perfectly useless has given mountaineering
its nimbus of mysticism – enshrined once and for all in Mallory's
ultimate bathos, "because it's there". Climbing is not, like tennis
or water-skiing, an absolute occupation. You absolutely must hit a
ball with a racket to play tennis, just as there is no substitute in kind
for a pair of water-skis: but in most instances you can reach the
summit of a mountain, or the top of a rock face, by some easier
means than climbing. Mountaineers are accordingly obsessed by
the reason why. They anticipate the question every time, with
skimble-skamble stuff (for there is a good deal of Welshness to
their attitudes) about challenge, solitude and vision.

I don't know how the piton modernists explain their sport, which
seems to consist of choosing the hardest possible place to climb,

and then making it artifically easier: for to tell you the truth, fighting shy as I do of too many beards and bulging muscles, I have never summoned up the nerve to ask—expecting to be rebuffed with some modernist oath, or throatily laughed at. But I have a very strong feeling that the rationale, such as it is, has not much progressed, and that the vicar of Brambletree Magna would soon feel himself at home if deposited among the spilt beer and potato crisps of his successors. A fence separates climbers from the rest of the world, and there on the other side of it, old or young, earthy or urbane, down the decades they happily exchange the jargon of their beloved and arcane cult.

from THE BOOK OF MODERN MOUNTAINEERING *1968*

Letters from Herbert

DON LAURIA

The envelope was wrinkled, as if the postman had carried it in his hip pocket all the way from Coarsegold. It had been addressed to me, but a line was stricken through "Don," and "Anna" Lauria was the addressee. The scrawl was unmistakable . . . a letter from T. M. Herbert:

"Dearest,
We must never let the clod know how close we are. Okay, now here's the plan; you and the kids will come up with Don next weekend. We will, of course, be together almost all the time, however, I will pretend that I am all hot to go climbing with him (or as we would say, 'IT'). Now there are places to slide around in the snow near Rixon's Pinnacle for the kids and Squaw while I entertain the clod. Later on we'll have drinks and music *and* I will do an impersonation of someone who is dumb and ugly—you won't believe it! So cancel all rinky dink Brownie and Cub Scout goodies and order all those brats to prepare for a weekend with HERBERT!
See you next weekend,
T. M. Valentino

PS Have you thought of a way to break the news about our overnight snow-caving to IT?''

Letters from Herbert arrived frequently during the spring months of Yosemite's transitional years—1967 through 1975. I saved them, because they reflect T. M.'s personality, his humour. I will not apologise for T. M.'s choice of words, because those who know him realise that to edit Herbert is to mute Beethoven—you lose the essence. His letters are collector items—gems. His humour is scathing yet harmless; coarse, yet witty. He uses vulgarity in a way that defies abhorrence—instead, one is unabashedly amused. His lack of propriety (or rather his ignorance of propriety) occurs only among his peers . . . those whom he cannot offend.

T. M. is really quite shy outside of his milieu. The following are excerpts from assorted letters:

(on his physical prowess) ''. . . I now weigh 103½lb. and yet I can still lift the front end of a D-9 tractor. And also I can hold a full lever on the high bar with my wee-wee.''

(on having a good time) ''. . . If climbing at Joshua Tree is out—how about a get-together at your place—we can get drunk and really tear the place up—break windows and furniture and leave the place in flames. . .''

(on remembering climbing routes) ''. . . Some guy wrote me about that Baja Rock. Shit! I can easily remember my name and age, but things like what route we did—no way . . . maybe what model and year car I have . . . would he accept that . . . do you think?''

(on getting it together) ''. . . Then Friday morning we cut out to Ventura and climb somewhere Saturday for thousands of heroic glorious feet . . . Then Saturday night we drink and take powerful artificial drug stimulants and cruise the boulevard for young girls—you will pose as my uncle who is driving. We will stash your old lady and kids. . . Our old bag wives will pose as our mothers. . .''

(on family living) ''. . . Can you come to the Valley over Easter vacation? Or are your kids gonna play jacks. . . And your wife is probably entering the local knitting contest. . . Are you a man or a mouse? Order all those dip-shits into the car and tell them to head for the Valley, where your wife and I have special hideaways while you stay home and spray the aphids and pull crab grass. . ."

(on his favourite candy bar) ". . . How do you think that during the war the Germans persuaded informers to give information? Money, love, jewels? No . . . ABBA ZABAS!"

(on becoming more masculine) ". . . Now why don't you quit hanging around with those pacifistic, long-haired queers down there—come up and we'll kick shit out of a couple of bars. The ones where the shit stompers hang out. Then head over to Hornitos an' take on some dupes on the pool table. Then a bunch of clawing scratching women will be fightin' for us. . ."

Herbert was so frustrated by his inability to arouse a written response from me that he often sent a multiple-choice reply for my convenience. Here is a sampling, shortened for lack of space:

"Don,
I'm doing some correspondence psychology work; could you fill out this form so's I can see what kind of weird perverted mother-fucker you really are? Check appropriate boxes:
"( ) I'm fairly well adjusted.
"( ) Well, I'm not so adjusted as I'd like.
"( ) Oh, I'm all ———ed up.
"( ) Creepin green Chinese crud, I've got a sabre up my ass!
"( ) None of the above.
"( ) Some of the above.
"( ) Every other one of the above.
"( ) I'll kill anyone or anything that even looks at me. . .
"( ) I wanna ——— a sheep, an a cow, an a dog . . . and a big clawing Bengal Tiger. . ."

The following note was received in the aftermath of a bawdy, outrageous party held in 'old' Camp 4. Joy Herron and Mick Burke were dancing to a blaring Stones album in my campsite when the rangers arrived. Tourists peered from the surrounding Winnebagos, unable to hide their disgust. Herbert gathered his family and fled into the night, leaving his lantern and stove on my table. Two days later, in Los Angeles, I received:
"Don,
We came back to Camp 4 about 8.15 a.m., but you had

already gone. You should have seen us sneak in—we parked our car many tables away and whisked our stove and stuff off as we walked by. Many evil eyes were upon us—so I had to disguise myself—when you next see me I will be in the form of a larger sugar pine.

See you, T.M."

from CLIMBING *1980*

Lock Up Your Daughters

LAURA AND GUY WATERMAN

The climbers' record of environmental concern is far from perfect, despite all we've said so far. There are still a hard core of piton-drivers and a somewhat larger minority that hold it acceptable to drive a piton if no nut placement can be found. Some still drive bolts (horrors): Recent new routes in Yosemite Valley involved as many as 21, 70 and 85 new bolts. (It must be conceded that these routes couldn't have been made without this aid, but Yosemite with its huge walls of sheer granite is not a typical situation.) The ethic is far better established at some places (e.g., the Shawangunks) than others (e.g., New Hampshire climbing areas). One serious flaw in the climbers' professed desire to leave the environment unmarked is the popularity of chalk as a medium for drying sweaty hands, which marks up the holds on the cliffs in a terrible way.

Nevertheless, the over-all picture remains a favourable one. In no other field of outdoor activity that we can think of has a group of recreationists so swiftly and so completely lived up to its responsibility to safeguard the environment from the adverse effects of its own actions.

In describing these trends, we have seriously erred if we've given you a picture of climbers as stuffy do-gooders, soberly and pompously standing up for law and order, motherhood, and the American Way. Good grief, no! Climbers are scruffy, bearded, sloppy, dirty, and foul-mouthed, and their devotion to most of society's laws falls somewhere between that of highway robbers and bank embezzlers.

Highly individualistic, they regard themselves as alienated from society's strictures, sometimes even conceiving of climbing as a way of achieving a freedom that is denied elsewhere to them. Some of them are tolerably well behaved, but others violate social mores at every turn. They change clothes on the highway, swear in public places, and wind up most Saturday nights drunk or stoned. Furthermore, they smell.

You wouldn't want them in your living room. But they'll take good care of the most fragile of mountain environments. You can't trust them with your daughter. But you can trust them with the outdoors, more than any other single group.

from BACKWOODS ETHICS *1980*

Three Obituaries:

1. *Glacier Pilot—Don Sheldon 1922-1975*

JIM SHARP

He drove up to meet the train in an old jeep, eased himself out of it and limped up to the platform. "Now boys," he grinned, "just lay your gear in there easy, easy . . . easy does it."

Sheldon is dead. I can't believe it. He flew like he was immortal, on the fine feathered edge of perfection, very close to an aerodynamic abyss. He liked it there. He was good enough to be comfortable there—relaxed, free and easy, yeah, easy. I always thought the 'E' in Sheldon's name was for easy. He was always saying it, especially loading airplanes. You see, an airplane is built pretty lightly, especially in the doors. Your average passenger is used to the doors on the Family-Fordor-Behemoth that weigh in at 175 apiece and swing on eight inches of hinged steel. If Sheldon didn't say "easy" at least ten times each loading, hell, he wouldn't have any doors left on his airplanes. Climbers don't know their own strength.

Sheldon had a good life. He wore out thirty-two airplanes doing the finest kind of flying there is, mountain flying. He worked thirty-four years for the best boss a man can have, himself. His expertise and wisdom launched most of the significant climbs in Alaska. His bravery and resourcefulness saved many lives. His life glistened.

Our expedition, like most others bound for McKinley, spent a couple of days at Sheldon's hangar waiting for the weather to clear. I spent all that time walking around the village airstrip at Talkeetna watching Sheldon fly. If he was light, he'd break ground, get a little airspeed and then rack the airplane around in a nice, tight 70° bank over the rolling waters of the Big Sue. It looked like great fun.

On the day we flew into the mountain the wind was blowing pretty hard. There were some good-sized plumes coming off the cornices on 'One Shot' Pass. Ol' Sheldon paralleled the ridge at first, found a good patch of air without any downers and zapped right across. He'd been there before.

So we flew down toward the south-east fork of the Kahiltna. The peaks were plumed all around us, but it was calm down on the glacier. I dropped spruce boughs out the right window on a low pass. They fell in a straight line and helped Sheldon plumb that white abyss. He banked around in the Kahiltna, dropped twenty degrees of flaps and set her down flawlessly in the deep powder. We unloaded the airplane, moved our gear out of the path of the stabiliser, slogged out to the wing tips and rocked them while Sheldon gunned the engine. The airplane surged away slowly, disappeared in a cloud of snow and rose, a small silver speck 'way down-glacier. Three times the silver-winged Cessna returned, slipped softly down on the snow and took off again. Black rock, blue skies, dazzling snow and shimmering aluminium. Goddamn, it was a beautiful sight.

Five years later I went back to Talkeetna. Times had changed. Sheldon looked old. The winter before he'd fought hard for his life. He'd just barely pulled through. Cancer. Goddamn cancer.

One day I helped Sheldon change the plugs and drain the oil on his floatplane. First we puttered around the hangar getting everything together . . . ol' Sheldon limping around in these real baggy white overalls, with a wool shirt two sizes too big, and his sock hat. Roberta had fixed him some fruit juices, which we managed to spill on the floor of the pick-up on the way out to Talkeetna Lake.

It was a beautiful sunny day. Sheldon had a list a mile long of people to take places and people to pick up, but we managed to while away the whole day out there, talking and working on the plane. I asked him flying questions.

"Don, how do you come into a short strip—slow, with a lot of power, behind the power curve?"

"Nope, you want to have plenty of airspeed . . . I can remember almost spinning in a 15° bank. I was coming in with a load . . . had five big men and gear, must have been 1,500lb. I put the nose down and added power . . . recovered just before I hit the trees."

"Say Don, how short a strip can you get a 180 into?"

"Too short and you don't have any business being there."

During lunch Sheldon told a funny story. It seems that Hans Moser was up on McKinley making a ski-ing film. Somebody got hurt up close to Windy Corner and Sheldon had to land at the 14,000ft. level to pick him up. Just after he landed a big storm came in and buried the airplane in snow. The next day it cleared and the Moser crew spent the whole day packing out a 2,000ft. runway.

"Well, I was paying so much attention to the take-off that I didn't notice this cloud bank had moved in . . . I got off okay, then — whop! — there was this cloud bank. Now the valley is tight in there and I knew that if I got into it I wouldn't get out. So I set her back down and went sliding across those ice holes . . . it took us another whole day giving her full throttle, and with all of those guys pushing the wings, before we got her up the slope again."

In the afternoon Don and I took out the old spark plugs on his floatplane. They had only about 140 hours on them, but the electrodes looked like footballs because of the high power settings float-flying requires. Sheldon was a slow and methodical mechanic. He insisted on changing every plug himself. "I can keep track of them that way," he explained. I had to loosen them for him, though. He'd lost strength.

I was in Talkeetna to film some of Sheldon's flying. There was a group of climbers waiting to be flown in for a late-season attempt on Mt. Foraker. The weather was bad on the mountain for days, but finally it cleared. I gassed up the camera plane at Sheldon's pumps. We had a little chalk-talk before we took off.

"Now don't dry-dock her in there," warned Sheldon. "Don't get too low and slow. The glacier comes up pretty fast." Sheldon took off. I waited a minute for the dust to settle and then followed. We flew in tight formation, 10 to 15ft. apart. We kept in touch on the radio.

"Sharp-Charlie, 64-Tango, how do you read?"

"Loud and clear."

"Over there on the right, in the clearing, see the moose? I saw the biggest one ever there four years back, great place for moose. See that mine over there on the ridge, about your three o'clock? Lot of gold came out of there . . . no more gold left, but the view of McKinley from there is something else. I've flown photographers from all over the world in there. It's a dandy. Say, see that lake down there, pretty little lake, you should see the . . . most beautiful you ever want to see. . ." Sheldon rapped a blue streak. We were on 122.9, interplane flight frequency. While Sheldon was catching his breath another pilot's voice came over the headphones. "Hey, Mac, did you hear that travelogue? That guy must be in heaven."

I flew on behind Sheldon through 'One Shot' Pass and down to the south-east fork of the Kahiltna. I remembered what he said. I came in close behind him, dropped a notch of flap, filmed the landing, added full power, turned gingerly to one side of the canyon and then made a gradual turn out of the fork. I picked up some speed, buzzed Sheldon for fun, climbed back up-glacier and did lazy, buzzard circles in the sky while the climbers unloaded the airplane.

I radioed Sheldon: "64-Tango, I want to come in behind you and film the take-off. I'll give you a slow count."

"Roger, Sharp-Charlie, standing by on the slow count."

I jockeyed around to get in position up-glacier and started the slow count—"ten, nine, eight, seven, six, five. . ." Sheldon took off. I poured on the power and roared down the glacier, but I was too late. I pressed the mike button and said, "Hey, Don, you jumped the gun. I missed the take-off."

"Oh raspberries," replied Sheldon.

from MOUNTAIN GAZETTE 31 *1975*

2. I'm Alive – How Can He Be Dead? Jörg Lehne

DIETRICH HASSE

I don't know whether I just lack a certain imaginative power: no matter how hard I try, I cannot picture Jörg Lehne, my close friend of many years. For a brief, fleeting moment I can manage it. I want to sharpen the picture, but feel unable to do so. Typical movements, gestures and phrases occur to me but as soon as I concentrate on them they fade away. All that remains is an all too crude memory of the time when our paths crossed, of his conversations and his adventures. Vivid, but at best fleeting glimpses of things that happened: but only momentary, incomplete, fragmentary yet through them I know that Jörg, my close ally for so many years, was closer to me than anyone else.

From the point of view of character we were in many respects contrasting rather than closely alike. Nevertheless, although in the twelve years that we were friends we enjoyed needling each other, we never once quarrelled or had a clash of opinion. Our mutual rapport had grown so deep that I simply felt that my friend was ever present. Whether consciously or unconsciously he always had a place in my thoughts. If I had not seen him for a few days, I felt as if there was something missing in my life.

Sometimes it grieved me that Jörg found it so difficult to unburden himself to other people. He could be as happy as a young boy, but when we were sitting together, as we so often did out in the mountains, on a bivouac or, more often, at home, Jörg always seemed wrapped up in his own thoughts. Even with me he didn't really try to overcome this reluctance to say what was on his mind.

Jörg always lived for the present: this he took to astonishing lengths. Anything out of the ordinary had a magical power of attraction over him; the ultimate experience, in every walk of life. This was behind his great successes, both in climbing and in his career. He was incapable of being orthodox. His high level of intelligence and swift power of perception, unshakeable optimism and physical strength, his tolerance and generosity, his obstinacy and unfailing reliability in seeing through what he had begun, were all the hallmark of his character. If he believed in what he was doing, he did it. Few could match his stamina, not least in all-night drinking bouts.

His cheerlessness in the mornings surpassed even mine. On occasions I would wait for him for hours on end, and when he finally appeared (usually from his place of work) he was always disorganised, staggering around bleary-eyed, with crampon holes in his duvet and his Alpine Club subscriptions unpaid; he never possessed a rope right up until the time he climbed the Eiger Direct.

He didn't give a damn about anything which did not concern him directly. In later years that led to a certain mature wisdom with regard to climbing. His job, which occupied him for five or six days a week, came first, but this meant that he entered all the more into informed debate about climbing when the claims made on his time were not so great.

I always felt so safe with Jörg on the other end of the rope – even though he remarked on my fanatical safety-consciousness somewhat sarcastically instead of sharing it – but whereas that was true on the routes, I sometimes sat trembling with fear in his car. I was well aware that he had remarkable reactions and knew that he was a good driver, but he was too reckless for most people's nerves and we knew him as 'the lunatic'. But in the mountains?

In 1962, we had already climbed together several times in the Eastern Alps, we set off for the first time in the direction of the Walker Spur. In 1963, after another futile wait for the weather to improve, we buried the bottle of champagne, which was to have been cracked on that fateful bivouac, in the Montenvers campsite. The plan was to walk up to the Grandes Jorasses, bivouac at the start of the difficulties and go for the summit the following day. We dug the champagne out undamaged in 1964, but the weather again denied us. Things were no better in 1965 when Jörg had to leave for business reasons. Thus four seasons had been practically wasted. Full of remorse, we again turned our attention to the Eastern Alps and the Dolomites where we hoped the weather was more stable.

Differing weekend and holiday arrangements meant that to a certain extent we each pursued separate projects: for Jörg there was, amongst other things, the Eiger Direct, in the winter of 1966, the Schwarze Wand in the Wettersteingebirge (1967) and attempts on the North Face of the Droites in March 1968. Our plan for the Walker Spur was still there but no little more than a pipe-dream. Jörg repeatedly referred to it as his last great alpine ambition. In the summer of 1969, when I was away on an expedition to the Bolivian Andes, it seemed as if his chance had finally come. Jörg drove to Chamonix with Karl Golikow, an experienced partner on several hard routes over the years. Montenvers — Mer de Glace — Leschaux Glacier — Grandes Jorasses. The last lap. From July 24 to 25, 1969: bivouac on the Walker Spur; 1.30 a.m.: stonefall . . . a grotesque nightmare.

On the occasion of the death in 1962 on Nanga Parbat, of Siegfried Löw, Jörg Lehne recalled in the obituary of his friend, with whom he had shared his first climbing days, the bivouac that they had had on the North-East Face of the Piz Badile. He wrote:

Experiences such as the one we had on the North-East Face of the Piz Badile either move one to vow never again to set foot on the mountains, or they bind the chains even more tightly. They may, furthermore, destroy a climbing friendship or seal the bond.

Afterwards one who has experienced death in the mountains knows that it no longer holds any fear for him. Not every climber could, or should, possess the presentiment of death that Leo Maduschka possessed and thus he clings too much to life; there is no wall, no mountain in the world that is worth a single limb, let alone life itself. I am well aware of the contradictions inherent in such a view every time I am on a difficult route. Life is the experience of climbing, life in all its forms, magnified, intensified. Death is never further from that momentary experience than when one is struggling on the crux of a route. Nevertheless, climbing is dangerous; it is just as foolish to cheat death as it is to glorify it. Man's sense of self-preservation and his determination are powerful defences against death. Yet in certain situations one's thoughts turn to death as something inevitable and intimate and the body awaits its fate passively.

So his own death was to be. One piercing blow from a rock and he was at peace.

1962 had claimed Siegi Löw and also — and there can be no doubt that the two were connected — saw Jörg's most serious loss of form, and the only one that really had a deep effect on him. Our retreat from the Philipp-Flamm Route on the North-West of the Civetta was its nadir. Five years later, in August 1967, we were once more climbing on this, the greatest of the walls in the Dolomites and this time we eventually won through. A storm forced us, together with Yvette and Michel Vaucher, into a soaking wet, icy bivouac and although Jörg was poorer by one big toe after his adventures on the Eiger, he was as strong as ever. That same year we had to abandon our attempt on the first ascent of the Burel-South-West Face because of the weather and the fact that Jörg's holidays were unfortunately drawing to an end.

1968 brought even worse weather conditions. When Jörg ran into us in the Dolomites everything looked so cold and miserable that the mere mention of Capri fired his enthusiasm. A lover of on-the-spot decisions, the 1000-kilometre drive down to Sorrento was nothing to him in view of the promise of sun-drenched limestone cliffs above the Tyrrhenian Sea. From time to time he complained of an occasional stomach disorder which, combined with phthisis brought on by too much work, laid him low. Soon he was up and about again and neither the punctured airbed on the rough pebble beach nor a sleepless night spent standing up in a dripping wet beach cabin could dampen his enthusiasm. We had rarely seen him in such a carefree and boisterous mood as in those days in Capri. And once more he amazed me — just where did he get his continual fitness from when he lived such an exhausting life? Together with Georg Haider and Hans Heinrich, we were fortunate enough to put up some superb and difficult new routes on the island.

At Easter 1969, shortly before I left for South America, we went on one of our last climbing trips together, to the Danube Valley. We had our eyes on routes like the Dachsteinkante, 'Rossi', 'Robert-Klemm' and others and also hoped to do the Weite Schritt ('The Stride') which involved a leap across a wide gully. One stands at the top of a pinnacle and has to get across to the wall opposite. Below is space, especially since both sides are overhanging. If one uses the rope it presents no problem, but I wanted to do it without any aid. Jörg was already laughing and predicted at the beginning that I, the 'arch bungler' wouldn't make it. In actual fact I fell down the gully. The rope came tight halfway down. How amusing for my friends! I can still hear them laughing fit to burst, and above them all Jörg's wicked quip: "Well, if you weren't so fat. . .!" Naturally I also had to buy the round for falling off. It was rare that we didn't indulge in some kind of light-hearted ribbing, and one of us usually had to play the fall-guy, usually me. I didn't mind in the least. But joking apart, to talk seriously about climbing, the greatest irony is that he is no longer with me. Who knows for how long? For in this hectic world the chances of dying are great.

Jörg is dead. That much is certain, but I cannot comprehend it. I felt no sorrow, nor do I now. I am incapable of believing it, for I feel his presence now as keenly as in all the years before. If my thoughts turn to him I see only a companion full of the joys of life, cheerful and reckless but at the same time for ever mindful of what was expected of him. I am alive, so how can he be dead? My thoughts are confused: I am awake—and am frightened of awakening.

from ALPINISMUS *1970*

3. *Who Was Oscar Eckenstein?*

DAVID DEAN

In the past twenty months we have had a number of Library talks. Their subjects, and their approach to their subjects, have been most varied; but one thing they have all had in common. All have been designed to call attention to some aspect of the Library's resources.

Today we are doing something rather different. This talk will not only, I hope, rescue from comparative oblivion an interesting character, but will also demonstrate some of the ramifications into which a routine library enquiry may devolve.

It started like this. Mr. Whitting came in one day last autumn and asked, "Who was Oscar Eckenstein?" It will be remembered that Mr. Whitting gave a Library talk last year on Sir Richard Burton, the Arabist and traveller. Well, shortly before the last war, a most valuable—indeed a unique—collection of books and documents by and relating to Burton was presented to the Royal Asiatic Society. This collection, a truly remarkable one, containing not only the different editions but the differing issues of editions of the same work, had originally been the property of Eckenstein. Owing to difficulties during and after the war the collection remained unexamined until 1958, when Mr. Whitting catalogued it. From this work, two queries at once arose. Who was O. E., and why, and how, had he acquired a collection of this calibre? The numerous lives of Burton contain no mention of any connection between the two men, nor indeed did it seem likely that they ever met. Burton died in 1890, aged 69, when Eckenstein was 31; and during the previous 18 years Burton had been consul at Trieste (1872-90). Thus, though a meeting would have been possible—physically speaking—between the two men, in view of Eckenstein's youth it seemed improbable that even if one had taken place, it would have had any very compelling impact on him. It does, however, appear from Penzer's bibliography of Burton, published in 1923, that Eckenstein had assisted him with valuable source material.

It was at this point that enquiries were begun. From correspondence in the Royal Asiatic Society collection it seemed probable that Eckenstein had died some time between 1921 and 1939; so the obvious sources, *Who was Who* and the obituary notices in *The Times*, were examined first, without success. Reference to Somerset House elicited the date of Eckenstein's death in 1921.

After a few more checks of this kind, the enquiry rather hung fire; and it is more than likely that we still would not be able to answer the question put to us if the Library had not purchased last winter an agreeable travel book called, *A Short Walk in the Hindu Kush*, by Eric Newby. Newby is a young man who took a rather random decision a few years ago to go off to the Hindu Kush with a Foreign Office friend. He had never been on a mountain before; and solicitous friends took the pair of them down to Wales for some quick practice before they set out. I was glancing over the book when my attention was suddenly caught by this passage:

> After a large, old-fashioned tea at the inn with crumpets and hard boiled eggs, we were taken off to climb the *Eckenstein Boulder*. Oscar Eckenstein was a renowned climber at the end of the nineteenth century, whose principal claim to fame was that he had been the first man in this or any other country to study the technique of holds and balance on rock. He had spent his formative years crawling over the boulder that now bore his name. Although it was quite small, about the size of a delivery van, his boulder was said to apparently embody all the fundamental problems that are such a joy to mountaineers and were proving such a nightmare to us.

Here was a new lead. It seemed likely that if Eckenstein was distinguished enough to have given his name to this boulder, his death ought to be recorded in the pages of *The Alpine Journal*. The Journal in fact produced very little about Eckenstein, for reasons which later became clear, but I did find, in an article called 'Classic Cols', by J. P. Farrar, in the 1923 volume, the following passage:

> I went to see (E) as he lay dying, one summer day two years ago, at the little hill town of Oving. His lungs had gone, he could only gasp; but his eye was as clear as ever, as dauntless as it had ever been in disadvantages of race, often of poverty, dying a brave man – wrapped up to the very end in his beloved mountains.

This incidentally illustrates quite neatly the dangers of pre-supposition in an enquiry of this kind. The whole tone of that passage is very strongly directed towards mountains, and I assumed Oving to be some wind-grieved spot in a remote Swiss canton. In fact, of course, as I later found, it lies five miles north-west of Aylesbury at a height of 478ft. above sea level.

A recent work, *Mountaineering in Britain*, by R. W. Clark and E. C. Pyatt, filled in the picture a little. From it we learned that Eckenstein was the inventor of the Eckenstein crampon, and helped "to formulate the new balance technique of climbing which was ultimately to revolutionise the standards of rock work . . . (he was) a queer character, a railway engineer who applied to the problems of climbing difficult rocks and principles of stress and strain which he utilised in his work." Among the illustrations in this book were two group photographs which included a sturdy, pipe-smoking, sombre, bearded figure identified as Eckenstein.

After a quick, and fruitless, check in the obituaries of the *Proceedings of the Institution of Civil Engineers*, and, for good measure, in those of the Royal Geographical Society, search was made of other books on British climbers, and we learned that Eckenstein had climbed in the Karakorams and in Mexico with Aleister Crowley. Perhaps the Himalayan connection, or the Crowley connection, would provide a link with Burton, for though we were by now well on the trail of Eckenstein as a mountaineer, we had yet to shed any light on our original problem.

We tackled Crowley first. Crowley was a curious, distasteful, extravagant man, a gifted dabbler (or plunger) in the occult, with a single-minded enthusiasm for diabolism. A substantial aid to our search came when we examined *The Great Beast*, by John Symonds (1951). This told us, among other things, that Eckenstein, who was 17 years older than Crowley and, like him asthmatic, had first met Crowley at Wasdale Head, when Crowley was 23. Eckenstein was already distinguished as a climber, for he had been on Sir William Martin Conway's Karakoram expedition in 1892. Incidentally, both Conway and Eckenstein himself left accounts of the expedition. Symonds says that neither mentions the other in his book, for they discovered that they disliked each other, and Eckenstein left the party and wandered back home. The dislike was there all right, but it is far from the case that neither mentions the other. In Conway's *Climbing and Exploration in the Karakoram-Himalayas* (1894) he speaks frequently, though guardedly, of Eckenstein, indicating that Eckenstein was so continuously unwell that as leader of the party he decided that it was useless for him to continue, and sent him back to London.

For his part, in *The Karakorams and Kashmir: an account of a journey* (1896) Eckenstein nowhere expresses open contempt for Conway; but it is not hard to find behind his references the profound disapproval of a tough, austere, unorthodox Alpinist for a darling of the Alpine Club. He is irritated by what he thought a failure of nerve on Conway's part while they are crossing a rope bridge. At one stage the party divides up; Eckenstein reaches the rendezvous before Conway, but, he says, unfortunately Conway "had specially asked me not to do any of the several expeditions I could have made at this time, as he did not want anything of importance done in his absence; so I had to be content to wait till he arrived" (pp. 195 ff). A week later, Conway having arrived, "we had a sort of general meeting, at which it was arranged that I should leave the expedition. There had been a good deal of friction from time to time, and as we had now been some two-and-a-half months in the mountains without making a single ascent of importance, having only crossed two previously known passes, I was not anxious to go on, and accordingly we agreed to separate." Perhaps Eckenstein's view of this *mountaineering* expedition is suggested in the sub-title of his book—"an account of a *journey*."

It is not a good book. Competent, pedestrian, not very informative, it does throw a little light on its author. He is courageous, an expert mountaineer, physically tough (e.g. his bathe, in company with a small icefloe, in a glacier lake); he is irascible and doesn't suffer fools gladly, he has a sense of humour, and a strong affection for the native. No interest in literature, thought or religion emerges from the book. Indeed, the only literary judgment of Eckenstein's that I have anywhere come across is the unsupported statement of a biographer of Crowley that Eckenstein found Crowley's lyric *Rosa Mundi* the greatest lyric in the English language, though he thought it "too sacred" to publish; it should, he felt, be found among Crowley's papers after his death. Crowley in fact dissented from this judgment, at least from that part of it which estimated the poem's relative sacredness; for he duly published it. (Ref. to Cammell: *Aleister Crowley*. Richards Press, 1951).

To return to Symonds's biography of Crowley; he tells how, soon after their Cumberland meeting, Eckenstein and Crowley climbed widely in Mexico, living, according (typically) to Crowley, on canned food and champagne, and breaking several world records. Then, Eckenstein returned to London to organise an expedition to K2, of which he was to be leader and Crowley second-in-command. They set out in 1902; but in Rawalpindi Eckenstein was detained on, it was said, the personal orders of the Viceroy (who was Curzon), and refused entry into Kashmir. There were rumours that he was a Prussian spy, on account of his name; but three weeks later he rejoined the party. He had been down to Delhi and seen Curzon himself to demand a reason for his detention; but apparently Curzon never told him, for he still professed ignorance. I shall have a little more to say about this episode in a minute. The expedition got to nearly 22,000ft., when misfortune and bad weather drove them down again, though not before Crowley had inexplicably threatened Guy Knowles, the third Englishman in the party, with a huge revolver and had had to be forcibly disarmed, nor before Crowley and Eckenstein had clashed over Crowley's insistence on "carrying my library with me. . . Milton and the rest." (There is a lot of Crowley in the incident; unquestionably a competent climber, he was, as unquestionably, a doggedly persistent *poseur*.)

But the biggest lead from Symonds's book came when I learned that Eckenstein had stayed at Crowley's house at Boleskine, near Loch Ness, with Gerald Kelly, whose sister Crowley had married. Accordingly I wrote to Sir Gerald Kelly asking for help; and he was good enough, though he was only just out of hospital, to ask Mr. Whitting and myself along for a talk about Eckenstein. He received us in bed, and was silent at first as he listened to us sketching in the story and the problem. Then, as I mentioned the Alpine Club, he spoke for the first time. "They quarrelled; Eckenstein and the Alpine Club quarrelled," and he began to talk, slowly and deliberately, soon ranging ever more widely, over Burton, over Gertrude Bell, over Lawrence and over Sir Ronald Storrs. He talked of Crowley: "I had met him in a book shop in Cambridge. I liked him; we made each other laugh; but he was a *poseur*, a great pretender to scholarship and languages. His magic I thought was all bunkum (and so did Eckenstein), but he was, I understand, wonderful on mountains. And that is where Eckenstein came in. He and Crowley went off to Mexico and climbed mountains. At this time Crowley had plenty of money while Eckenstein was poor. I think he lived in lodgings and was a sort of engineer, though not, I think, a very successful one. I admired him for his obvious integrity. He was a very good influence on Crowley; he was a superb climber; Crowley thought him the greatest of all. They were both adventurous and unorthodox mountaineers and they regarded the Alpine Club rather as the best people, the 'intellectuals', regard the Royal Academy! In himself I think Eckenstein was rather a dull man—I never came across anything to suggest that he had any interest in Burton—and certainly no one ever left his rooms chuckling and thinking of what fun they'd had after a visit to him.''

Two small glosses at this point. A relative of Eckenstein's whom I met later told me that Eckenstein certainly lived, not in lodgings but with his mother in South Hampstead from 1893 until his marriage twenty-five later. Further, he could not justifiably be called a poor man. He was a member of the National Liberal Club; drew a regular salary from his employers, the International Railway Congress Association; was always able to travel abroad when he wanted to, and my informant, in the fourteen years that he knew him well never came across any suggestion that he was hard up. My informant suggested the reason for the misunderstanding: Eckenstein cared nothing about style in externals, and, in consequence, as he always travelled first class, it became a family joke that the contrast between appearance and mode of transport led him to be regarded, when he travelled overseas, as an eccentric millionaire of the 'mad Englishman' variety.

As we thanked Sir Gerald and apologised for taking up his time, he waved our apologies aside. "Not at all. I find it most interesting, the idea of someone's finding anything about old Eckenstein that could possibly interest them.''

Two or three days later I heard again from Sir Gerald: ''Crowley was a rather strange character, but fundamentally very conventional. As undergraduates he and I were friends and we were, I think, fond of each other—he was certainly a delightful companion—but later on in his life he wrote his confessions and took care to write everything he could that he thought would offend and wound me. Fortunately for me it only made me giggle! A good deal of it is nonsense, and some of it is bombastic lies, but he was a genuine and admiring friend of Eckenstein, and it would be worthwhile for you to read this book. Even though I should not execute a mouse on his evidence, I feel you ought to read this fantastic document. Would it be possible for you to call here and let me lend it to you. . .?"

Sir Gerald was kindness itself when I went to borrow this (indeed) fantastic document. More reminiscences, of Yeats, of Maugham, of Eckenstein himself—including the memory of finding Eckenstein absorbed, at his London home, in Kirkwood's *Schoolgirl Problem*, a complex mathematical problem concerning a girls' school, so that Sir Gerald had to stand nervously in the hall as the puzzle was spread out all over the house. I duly bore away the two volumes of the *Confessions*, along with some notes that Sir Gerald had made for me, calling attention to some of the more laughable misstatements in the book, and pointing out, for instance, as a gloss on the passage where Crowley lays claim to an altogether remarkable popularity in Paris, that "Crowley was widely unknown in the Montparnasse quarter. His French was poor. He was, for the most part, I fancy, *disliked* by the few whom he met."

I shall have something to say about the *Confessions*, ludicrous rubbish though some of them are, as they contain quite a lot about Eckenstein. But before I do that, I want to say a word about my further enquiries into the mysterious barring of Eckenstein from Kashmir.

An examination of records at the India Office filled in some details, but did not solve the mystery, which indeed remains unsolved. I found a letter from Eckenstein applying for a permit to enter Kashmir, and an answer from the India Office that permits were not necessary, "so far as this Office is aware." In the *Friends of India* for May 1, 1902, was a report of the Eckenstein party's embarking on "the most ambitious climbing feat ever attempted—to reach the summit of Mt. Everest," then another column three weeks later concerning "a hitch over Mr. Eckenstein's pass. . . What exactly happened no one seems to know, but it is certain Mr. Eckenstein returned to the plains, interviewed the highest authorities (waylaying one great man, it is said, in the mail train on his way from Calcutta to Simla), and succeeded in getting the matter put right and his pass satisfactorily visa-ed" (May 22, 1902). No official report of the incident could be traced; and no mention of it appears in the India Office Collection of Lord Curzon's private correspondence with Lord Hamilton, the then Secretary of State for India.

At this point I turned to Crowley's *Confessions*. His account tells of how the D.C. came to their camp beyond Rawalpindi and announced that Eckenstein was not to be allowed to enter Kashmir. Then was he arrested? Eckenstein asked. "Heaven forbid," said the D.C. and Eckenstein chased all round northern India, finally cornering Curzon who (says Crowley) "saved his face by authorising Eckenstein to rejoin the party on guarantees for his good conduct subscribed by Knowles (the third English member of the party) and myself." Eckenstein "insistently professed himself in utter ignorance" of the reasons for the incident: "We could not but connect it with Eckenstein's quarrel with Conway in 1893. We pumped the bigwigs of Kashmir, and we sifted the rumours of the Bazaar, but beyond learning that Eckenstein was a Prussian spy and a cold-blooded murderer, we obtained little information of importance. Eckenstein was the noblest man I have ever known. His integrity was absolute, and his sympathetic understanding of the native character supreme. I remain unrepentant that the incident was the result of the unmanly jealousy and petty intrigues of the insects who envied him, complicated by official muddle" (*op. cit.* 2, 129-31).

Some little time after reading this, I was fortunate enough to meet, through the good offices of Sir Gerald Kelly, Mr. Guy Knowles, who had actually been present at the Kashmir episode in 1902, and his view of it, though more temperately expressed, inclined towards that of Crowley, in other words, that Conway, by this time President of the Alpine Club, interposed to put obstacles in Eckenstein's way, and that Curzon, added Mr. Knowles, did not relent until faced with a threat to expose the whole story to the *Daily Telegraph*.

"The greatness of (Eckenstein's) spirit," says Crowley, "was not inferior to that of such giants as Rodin; he was an artist no less than if he has actually produced any monument to his mind. Only his constant man-handling by spasmodic asthma prevented him from matching his genius by master-pieces. As it is, there is an immense amount in his life mysterious and extraordinary beyond anything I have known. For instance, during a number of years he was the object of repeated murderous attacks which he could only explain on the hypothesis that he was being mistaken for somebody else." (And there follows an account of one such incident; *ib.*, 1, 210-15).

"His business in life was mathematics and science, and his one pleasure mountaineering. He was probably the best all-round man in England, but his achievements were little known because of his almost fanatical objection to publicity. . . He hated self-advertising quacks like the principal members of the Alpine Club with an intensity which, legitimate as it was, was almost overdone. His detestation of every kind of humbug and false pretence was an over-mastering passion. . ." (*ib.*, 1, 202-3). "Like Byron, Shelley, Swinburne, Tennyson, I left the University (Crowley goes on) without taking a degree. It has been better so; I have accepted no honour from her; she has had much from me. . . I felt that my career was already marked out for me. Sir Richard Burton was my hero and Eckenstein his modern representative, so far as my external life was concerned" (*ib.*, 1, 233). With this conjunction of the names Burton and Eckenstein it looked as though the search might be nearing its end, especially when I read the dedication to Vol. 2 of the *Confessions*: "To three immortal memories. Richard Francis Burton, the perfect pioneer of spiritual and physical adventure; Oscar Eckenstein, who trained me to follow the trail; Allan Bennet, who did what he could." But alas; it was to prove a mere tantalising glimpse!

Eckenstein "openly jeered at (Crowley) for wasting my time on such rubbish" (as magic). In Mexico one evening "I told Eckenstein my troubles, as I had done often enough before with no result beyond an insult or a sneer. . . At the end of my outburst, (he) turned on me and gave me the worst quarter-of-an-hour of my life. He summed up my Magical situation, and told me that my troubles were due to my inability to control my thoughts. He said, "Give up your Magic, with all its romantic fascinations and deceitful delights. Promise to do this for a time, and I will teach you how to master your mind." He spoke with the absolute authority which comes from profound and perfect knowledge. And, as I sat and listened, I found my faith fixed by the force of facts. I wondered and worshipped . . . I agreed at once to his proposals, and he taught me the principles of concentration. I was to practise visualising simple objects; and when I had succeeded in keeping these fairly steady, to try moving objects, such as a pendulum. . . (Then he) put the brake on. One must not overstrain the mind. . .'' (*ib.*, 2, 22-4).

This then was the first glimpse of any intellectual or spiritual interests on Eckenstein's part, and indeed the last, unless one excepts Crowley's account of his desire, not otherwise substantiated, to spend the autumn and winter of life "in Kashmir meditating upon the mysteries which appealed to his sublime spirit" (*ib.*, 1, 210).

I went to see Mr. Guy Knowles, who had been with Eckenstein and Crowley in Kashmir. It was a house full of treasures; a Degas bronze, two Rodins, ten Whistlers, and a magnificent Guardi sketch—Mr. Knowles told me that he had been with his father in the 1880s when he had bought the Guardi and a Titian sketch for 12s. 6d. a-piece. Mr. Knowles, whose father used to shoot snipe on Chelsea marshes and whose great-aunt Carrie danced at the Waterloo Ball, was the source of some entertaining personal detail about Eckenstein, including the fact that he was a special constable in the 1914-18 war; but apart from recalling that he bought *Burtoniana* wherever he came across any, he could throw no light on Eckenstein's passion for Burton.

Incidentally, I never found any corroboration of the "repeated murderous attacks" mentioned by Crowley from anyone who had known Eckenstein. Guy Knowles's reaction was typical. He laughed and said, "That sounds just like one of Aleister's stories."

He did, however, give me the address of Eckenstein's greatnephew, who in due course referred me to his uncle, who later emerged as a man who had for years been fascinated by the Arctic. Eckenstein's nephew filled in the picture admirably.

Eckenstein was born in Canonbury in 1859, educated at University College School and studied chemistry in London and Bonn. He married in 1918 and died at Oving, in 1921. An excellent gymnast in his youth, he also played the bagpipes. He smoked Rutter's Mitcham shag unceasingly, and, as a keen amateur carpenter and mechanic had a bed which pulled up on ropes when not in use. My informant was aware of his excellent library, but, once more, could throw no light on the reasons for his urge to collect Burton.

So there the quest for Eckenstein in effect ended, a long way from its starting point, but not a great deal nearer to answering the initial question. And yet—perhaps his nephew himself provided the clue. No, he could give no *reason* for Eckenstein's absorption in Burton; but, after all, take his own case. He had never even seen an iceberg, but nonetheless for many years he had been passionately interested in the Arctic. Could it be that some tiny and long forgotten incident had randomly brought Burton to Eckenstein's notice, and that, in the uncle's case as in the nephew's, the appetite had imperceptibly grown by what it fed on?

from THE ALPINE JOURNAL *1960*

Two Eiger Failures:

1. A Short Walk with Whillans

TOM PATEY

"Did you spot that great long streak of blood on the road over from Chamonix? Twenty yards long, I'd say."

The speaker was Don Whillans. We were seated in the little inn at Alpiglen and Don's aggressive profile was framed against an awe-inspiring backdrop of the Eiger Nordwand. I reflected that the conversation had become attuned to the environment.

"Probably some unfortunate animal," I ventured without much conviction.

Whillans' eyes narrowed. "Human blood," he said. "Remember—lass? (appealing to his wife Audrey) I told you to stop the car for a better look. Really turned her stomach, it did. Just when she was getting over the funeral."

I felt an urge to inquire whose funeral they had attended. There had been several. Every time we went up on the Montenvers train we passed a corpse going down. I let the question go. It seemed irrelevant, possibly even irreverent.

"Ay, it's a good life," he mused, "providing you don't weaken."

"What happens if you do?"

"They bury you," he growled, and finished his pint.

Don has that rarest of gifts, the ability to condense a whole paragraph into a single, terse, uncompromising sentence. But there are also occasions when he can become almost lyrical in a macabre sort of way. It depends on the environment.

We occupied a window table in the inn. There were several other tables, and hunched round each of these were groups of shadowy men draped in black cagoules — lean-jawed, grim, uncommunicative characters who spoke in guttural monosyllables and gazed steadfastly towards the window. You only had to glimpse their earnest faces to realise that these men were Eiger Candidates — martyrs for the 'Mordwand'.

"Look at that big black bastard up there," Whillans chuckled dryly, gesturing with his thumb. "Just waiting to get its claws into you. And think of all the young lads who've sat just where you're sitting now, and come back all tied up in sacks. It makes you think."

It certainly did. I was beginning to wish I had stayed at Chamonix, funerals or no funerals.

"Take that young blonde over there," he pointed towards the sturdy Aryan barmaid, who had just replenished his glass. "I wonder how many dead men she's danced with? All the same," he concluded after a minute's reflection, "t'wouldn't be a bad way to spend your last night."

I licked my lips nervously. Don's philosophic discourses are not for the faint-hearted.

One of the Eiger candidates detached himself from a neighbouring group and approached us with obvious intent. He was redhaired, small, and compact, and he looked like a Neanderthal man. This likeness derived from his hunched shoulders, and the way he craned his head forwards like a man who had been struck repeatedly on the crown by a heavy hammer, and through time developed a protective over-growth of skull. His name proved to be Eckhart, and he was a German. Most of them still are.

The odd thing about him was his laugh. It was an uncanny hollow quality. He laughed quite a lot without generating a great deal of warmth, and he wore a twisted grin which seemed to be permanently frozen onto his face. Even Whillans was moved.

"You — going — up?" he inquired.

"Nein," said Eckhart. "Nix gutt! . . . You wait here little time, I think . . . Now there is much vatter." He turned up his coat collar ruefully and laughed. "Many, many stein fall . . . All day, all night . . . Stein, stein." He tapped his head significantly and laughed uproariously. "Two nights we wait at Tod Bivouac." He repeated the name as if relishing its sinister undertones. ("It means Dead Man," I said to Whillans in a hushed whisper.) "Always it is nix gutt . . . Vatter, stein . . . Stein, vatter . . . so we go down. It is very funny."

We nodded sympathetically. It was all a huge joke.

"Our two Kameraden, they go on. They are saying at the telescopes, one man he has fallen 50 metres. Me? I do not believe this." (Loud and prolonged laughter from the company.)

"You have looked through the telescope?" I inquired anxiously.

"Nein," he grinned, "Not necessary . . . tonight they gain summit . . . tomorrow they descend. And now we will have another beer."

Eckhart was 19. He had already accounted for the North Face of the Matterhorn as a training climb and he intended to camp at the foot of the Eigerwand until the right conditions prevailed. If necessary, he could wait until October. Like most of his countrymen he was nothing if not thorough, and finding his bivouac-tent did not measure up to his expectations he had hitch-hiked all the way back to Münich to secure another one. As a result of this, he had missed the settled spell of weather that had allowed several rivals to complete the route, including the second successful British team, Baillie and Haston, and also the lone Swiss climber, Darbellay, who had thus made the first solo ascent.

"Made of the right stuff, that youngster," observed Don.

"If you ask me I think he was trying to scare us off," I suggested. "Psychological warfare that's all it is."

"Wait till we get on the face tomorrow," said Whillans. "We'll hear your piece then."

Shortly after noon the next day we left Audrey behind at Alpiglen, and the two of us set off up the green meadows which girdle the foot of the Eigerwand. Before leaving, Don had disposed of his Last Will and Testament. "You've got the car-key lass, and you know where to find the house-key. That's all you need to know. Ta, for now."

Audrey smiled wanly. She had my profound sympathy.

The heat was oppressive, the atmosphere heavy with menace. How many Münich Bergsteigers had trod this very turf on their upward path never to return to their native Klettergarten? I was humming Wagner's 'Valkyrie' theme music as we reached the lowest rocks of the Face.

Then a most unexpected thing happened. From an alcove in the wall emerged a very ordinary Swiss tourist, followed by his very ordinary wife, five small children and a poodle dog. I stopped humming immediately. I had read of tearful farewells with wives and sweethearts calling plaintively, but this was ridiculous. What an undignified send-off! The five children accompanied us up the first snow slope scrambling happily in our wake, and prodding our rucksacks with inquisitive fingers. "Go away," said Whillans irritably, but ineffectively. We were quite relieved when, ultimately, they were recalled to base and we stopped playing Pied Pipers. The dog held on a bit longer until some well-directed stones sent it on its way. "Charming, I must say," remarked Don. I wondered whether Hermann Buhl would have given up on the spot—a most irregular start to an Eiger epic and probably a bad omen.

We started climbing up the left side of the Shattered Pillar, a variant of the normal route which had been perfected by Don in the course of several earlier attempts. He was well on his way to becoming the Grand Old Man of Grindelwald, though not through any fault of his own. This was his fourth attempt at the climb and on every previous occasion he had been turned back by bad weather or by having to rescue his rivals. As a result of this he must have spent more hours on the Face than any other British climber.

Don's preparations for the Eiger—meticulous in every other respect—had not included unnecessary physical exertion. While I dragged my weary muscles from Breuil to Zermatt via the Matterhorn he whiled away the days at Chamonix sunbathing at the Plage until opening time. At the Bar Nationale he nightly sank five or six pints of 'heavy', smoked forty cigarettes, persuaded other layabouts to feed the juke box with their last few francs and amassed a considerable reputation as an exponent of 'Baby Foot', the table football game which is the national sport in France. One day the heat had been sufficiently intense to cause a rush of blood to the head because he had walked four miles up to the Montenvers following the railway track, and had acquired such enormous blisters that he had to make the return journey by train. He was nevertheless just as fit as he wanted to be, or indeed needed to be.

First impressions of the Eigerwand belied its evil reputation. This was good climbing rock with excellent friction and lots of small incuts. We climbed unroped, making height rapidly. In fact I was just starting to enjoy myself, when I found the boot. . .

"Somebody's left a boot here," I shouted to Don.

He pricked up his ears. "Look and see if there's a foot in it," he said.

I had picked it up: I put it down again hurriedly.

"Ha! Here's something else—a torn rucksack," he hissed. "And here's his waterbottle—squashed flat."

I had lost my new-found enthusiasm and decided to ignore future foreign bodies. (I even ignored the pun.)

"You might as well start getting used to them now," advised Whillans. "This is where they usually glance off, before they hit the bottom."

He's a cheery character I thought to myself. To Don, a spade is just a spade—a simple trenching tool used by gravediggers.

At the top of the Pillar we donned our safety helmets. "One thing to remember on the Eiger," said Don, "never look up, or you may need a plastic surgeon."

His advice seemed superfluous that evening, as we did not hear a single ricochet. We climbed on up, past the Second Pillar and roped up for the traverse across to the Difficult Crack. At this late hour the Crack was streaming with water so we decided to bivouac while we were still dry. There was an excellent bivouac cave near the foot of the crack.

"I'll have one of your cigarettes," said Don. "I've only brought Gauloises." This was a statement of fact, not a question. There is something about Don's proverbial bluntness that arouses one's admiration. Of such stuff are generals made. We had a short discussion about bivouacking, but eventually I had to agree with his arguments and occupy the outer berth. It would be less likely to induce claustrophobia, or so I gathered.

I was even more aware of the sudden fall in temperature. My ultra-warm Terray duvet failed by a single critical inch to meet the convertible bivy-rucksack which I had borrowed from Joe Brown. It had been designed, so the manufacturers announced, to Joe's personal specifications, and as far as I could judge, to his personal dimensions as well.

Insidiously and from nowhere it seemed, a mighty thunderstorm built up in the valley less than a mile away. Flashes of lightning lit up the whole Face and grey tentacles of mist crept out of the dusk threatening to envelop our lofty eyrie.

"The girl in the Tourist Office said that a ridge of high pressure occupying the whole of central Europe would last for at least another three days."

"Charming," growled Whillans. "I could give you a better forecast without raising my head."

"We should be singing Bavarian drinking songs to keep our spirits up," I suggested. "How about some Austrian yodelling."

"They're too fond of dipping in glacier streams . . . that's what does it," he muttered sleepily.

"Does what?"

"Makes them yodel. All the same, these bloody Austrians."

The day dawned clear. For once it seemed that a miracle had happened and a major thunderstorm had cleared the Eiger, without lodging on the Face. Don remained inscrutable and cautious as ever. Although we were sheltered from any prevailing wind we would have no advance warning of the weather, as our horizons were limited by the Face itself.

There was still a trickle of water coming down the Difficult Crack as Don launched himself stiffly at the first obstacle. Because of our uncertainty about the weather and an argument about who should make breakfast, we had started late. It was 6.30 a.m. and we would have to hurry. He made a bad start by clipping both strands of the double rope to each of the three pitons he found in position. The rope jammed continuously and this was even more disconcerting for me, when I followed carrying both rucksacks. Hanging down the middle of the pitch was an old frayed rope, said to have been abandoned by Mlle Loulou Boulaz, and this kept getting entangled with the ice-axes. By the time I had joined Don at this stance I was breathing heavily and more than usually irritated. We used the excuse to unrope and get back into normal rhythm before tackling the Hinterstoisser. It was easy to find the route hereabouts: you merely followed the pitons. They were planted everywhere with rotting rope loops (apparently used for abseils) attached to most of them. It is a significant insight into human psychology that nobody ever stops to remove superfluous pegs on the Eiger. If nothing else they help to alleviate the sense of utter isolation that fills this vast Face, but they also act as constant reminders of man's ultimate destiny and the pageant of history written into the rock. Other reminders were there in plenty — gloves, socks, ropes, crampons and boots. None of them appeared to have been abandoned with the owners' consent.

The Hinterstoisser Traverse, despite the illustrations of pre-war heroes traversing "a la Dülfer," is nothing to get excited about. With two fixed ropes of unknown vintage as an emergency handrail, you can walk across it in three minutes. Stripped of scaffolding, it would probably qualify as Severe by contemporary British standards. The fixed ropes continued without a break as far as the Swallow's Nest — another bivouac site hallowed by tradition. Thus far I could well have been climbing the Italian Ridge of the Matterhorn.

We skirted the First Ice Field on the right, scrambling up easy rubble where we had expected to find black ice. It was certainly abnormally warm, but if the weather held we had definite grounds for assuming that we could complete the climb in one day — our original intention. The Ice Hose which breaches the rocky barrier between the First and Second Ice Fields no longer merited the name because the ice had all gone. It seemed to offer an easy alley but Don preferred to stick to known alternatives and advanced upon an improbable-looking wall some distance across to the left. By the time I had confirmed our position on Hiebèler's route description, he had completed the pitch and was shouting for me to come on. He was well into his stride, but still did not seem to share my optimism.

His doubts were well-founded. Ten minutes later, we were crossing the waterworn slabs leading on to the Second Ice Field when we saw the first falling stones. To be exact we did not see the stones, but merely the puff of smoke each one left behind at the point of impact. They did not come bouncing down the cliff with a noisy clatter as stones usually do. In fact they were only audible after they had gone past — WROUFF! — a nasty sort of sound halfway between a suck and a blow.

"It's the small ones that make that sort of noise," explained Whillans, "wait till you hear the really big ones!"

The blue-print for a successful Eiger ascent seems to involve being at the right place at the right time. According to our calculations the Face should have been immune to stonefall at this hour of the morning.

Unfortunately the Eiger makes it own rules. An enormous black cloud had taken shape out of what ought to have been a clear blue sky, and had come to rest on the Summit Ice Field. It reminded me of a gigantic black vulture spreading its wings before dropping like lightning on unsuspecting prey.

Down there at the foot of the Second Ice Field, it was suddenly very cold and lonely. Away across to the left was the Ramp; a possible hideaway to sit out the storm. It seemed little more than a stone's throw, but I knew as well as Don did, that we had almost 1,500ft. of steep snow-ice to cross before we could get any sort of shelter from stones.

There was no question of finding adequate cover in the immediate vicinity. On either side of us steep ice slopes, peppered with fallen debris, dropped away into the void. Simultaneously with Whillans' arrival at the stance the first flash of lightning struck the White Spider.

"That settles it," said he, clipping the spare rope through my belay karabiner.

"What's going on?" I demanded, finding it hard to credit that such a crucial decision could be reached on the spur of the moment.

"I'm going down," he said, "that's what's going on."

"Wait a minute! Let's discuss the whole situation calmly." I stretched out one hand to flick the ash off my cigarette. Then a most unusual thing happened. There was a higher pitched "WROUFF" than usual and the end of my cigarette disappeared! It was the sort of subtle touch that Hollywood film directors dream about.

"I see what you mean," I said. "I'm going down too."

I cannot recall coming off a climb so quickly. As a result of a long acquaintance Don knew the location of every abseil point and this enabled us to bypass the complete section of the climb which includes the Hinterstoisser Traverse and the Chimney leading up to the Swallow's Nest. To do this, you merely rappel directly downwards from the last abseil point above the Swallow's Nest and so reach a key piton at the top of the wall overlooking the start of the Hinterstoisser Traverse. From here a straightforward rappel of 140ft. goes vertically down the wall to the large ledge at the start of the Traverse. If Hinterstoisser had realised that he would probably not now have a Traverse named after him, and the Eigerwand would not enjoy one half of its present notoriety. The idea of a 'Point of No Return' always captures the imagination, and until very recent times, it was still the fashion to abandon a fixed rope at the Hinterstoisser in order to safeguard a possible retreat.

The unrelenting bombardment, which had kept us hopping from one abseil to the next like demented fleas, began to slacken off as we came into the lee of the 'Rote Fluh'. The weather had obviously broken down completely and it was raining heavily. We followed separate ways down the easy lower section of the Face, sending down volleys of loose scree in front of us. Every now and again we heard strange noises, like a series of muffled yelps, but since we appeared to have the mountain to ourselves, this did not provoke comment. Whillans had just disappeared round a nearby corner when I heard a loud ejaculation.

"God Almighty," he said (or words to that effect) "Japs! Come and see for yourself!"

Sure enough, there they were. Two identical little men in identical climbing uniforms, sitting side by side underneath an overhang. They had been crouching there for an hour, waiting for the bombardment to slacken. I estimated that we must have scored several near misses.

"You – Japs?" grunted Don. It seemed an unnecessary question.

"Yes, yes," they grinned happily, displaying a full set of teeth. "We are Japanese."

"Going – up?" queried Whillans. He pointed meaningfully at the grey holocaust sweeping down from the White Spider.

"Yes, yes," they chorused in unison. "Up. Always upwards.

First Japanese Ascent."

"You-may-be-going-up-Mate," said Whillans, giving every syllable unnecessary emphasis, "but-a-lot-'igher-than-you-think!"

They did not know what to make of this, so they wrung his hand several times, and thanked him profusely for the advice.

"'Appy little pair!" said Don. "I don't imagine we'll ever see them again."

He was mistaken. They came back seven days later after several feet of new snow had fallen. They had survived a full-scale Eiger blizzard and had reached our highest point on the Second Ice Field, if they did not receive a medal for valour they had certainly earned one. They were the forerunners of the climbing élite of Japan, whose members now climb Mount Everest for the purpose of skiing back down again.

We got back to the Alpiglen in time for late lunch. The telescope stood forlorn and deserted in the rain. The Eiger had retired into its misty oblivion, as Don Whillans retired to his favourite corner seat by the window.

from THE SCOTTISH MOUNTAINEERING CLUB
JOURNAL *1963*

2. *Under Starter's Orders*

JOHN BARRY

Luxuriating I was, just lying there in a rare burst of sunshine about halfway through what I reckoned was a well-earned rest day. After all – against my better judgment mind you – we had just ticked off a brand new route on the North Face of the Gletscherhorn. And fairly respectable it was too, some 2,000ft. of steepish ice, grade 4/5 Scottish-like and all the hard bits led by the Captain, who just happened to be on the sharp end when we ran out of easy ground. Still, just desserts, since he had spotted the line in the first place – as if the usual route at *très difficile* – wasn't enough.

So there I was planning a touch of personal administration, a few pints or two when up bounces the Captain, bursting with all usual vigour which past painful experience would normally have led me to regard with a deep suspicion. But here we were, a rest day and a new route under our belts. Surely even he would be happy with that!

It was 11 o'clock and I was contemplating breakfast:

"Just got the weather forecast from the heliport," he chirped.

"One or two eggs?" I replied, mind still on the food I was about to savage.

"Reckon we should crack straight up today," enthused he, "Plan B." Plan B! The full horror of its implications scrambled my two eggs and any vestige of coherent thought:

"Plan — bloody — B," I whimpered in anger/anguish, "that's the bloody Eiger."

"S'right," cut in the Captain, and with the convoluted logic of a man who doesn't recognise a rest day when he sees one, he proceeded to turn night into day, black into white and a dream into reality. He proved beyond doubt, at least to his own satisfaction, that the time to spring Plan B was upon us.

I knew better than to argue and started to pack. Carefully we laid our gear out over an acre of ground. We'd planned this day for years and our kit was carefully prepared. I had cut the route description from a book to save weight and covered it in polythene to keep it dry. A large photograph we had taken from Heinrich Harrer's 'White Spider' to show the route more clearly was similarly protected. He was to take the stove and the fuel, I, a cooking pot and a bivouac bag. The rest we shared equally — or so he still thinks. Packing the sacks very carefully we tested for weight and, deciding they were too heavy, unpacked and thought again. Out went half a day's grub and a spoon, a few ounces saved, and the process repeated until we were convinced we could go no lighter. The sacks still weighed too heavy by far, but they included the ropes, which would seem lighter when worn, and clothes that will eventually end up about us — still weighing the same but feeling less.

The train ride to Kleine Scheidegg was a curious affair. Hundreds of passengers crowded onto this little toyland train, and none of them Swiss. About fifty per cent American, fifty per cent Japanese, each armed with a camera more expensive than anything you ever imagined and sophisticated beyond their touristy technical expertise. An immaculate conductor waved us imperiously, and with scarcely concealed disgust, to a far corner which we were to share with a dog who had apparently disgraced himself. There we crouched on our sacks, the object of a great deal of almond-eyed curiosity, assailed by a dozen daft transatlantic questions and captured on a thousand centimetres of celluloid.

The Captain was disrespectful enough to suggest that it was my legs that excited this curiosity; I countered that it was probably the way he had to cross his ruckstrap straps so that the load just teetered on non-existent shoulders. For sure, it was ironic that in this land of mountains we were rendered oddities by virtue of our mountaineering attire.

The short ride to the Eigergletscher station was quieter, most of the tourists regarding the Scheidegg as the edge of the known world and anything beyond, even though it was rail-roaded, cafe'd and pastured, as Columbus-only terrain. Our repartée slunk into silence and, for me at any rate, contemplation. Nothing I had read about this face had lessened my respect for the seriousness of the undertaking, nor my admiration for those that had climbed it well. Toni Kurz intruded, and hard as I tried to dismiss him with rationalisations about the superiority of our equipment and clothing, and the fact that the route was now well-known, it was difficult to dispel belly trepidation with cold logic. From any perspective it remained 6,000 steep feet from bottom.

You'll remember Toni Kurz and his three mates and how, in an early attempt on the face back in 1936, they had died of exhaustion in their retreat from the Second Ice Field. And how, after his three mates had perished, Toni Kurz fought for his life days and nights until, literally within a hand's grasp of his rescuers, he too had no more to give and died. I think I was nervous. I *was* nervous. But as the train stopped, so did the reveries and though the fears yet lurked, action lent them boldness.

A short level walk around the buttress below the West Face brought us in half an hour below the North Face—this the longest, best-documented, worst-represented, wrongly-feared face in the Alps—perhaps in the whole mountaineering world.

It's an extraordinary setting. No long hut walk the day before, no glacier approach, indeed no glacier; the Kleine Scheidegg, Tokyo and New York visible the while and there rising straight out of cattle-clanging pastures, this huge ugly face; a piece of gigantic stage scenery. Not a pretty sight; no classic sweep of sculptured rock or pleasing rock architecture, while even the ice was pock-marked by stonefall and looked second-hand.

Looking up into the Stygian gloom I shuddered, for the top half of the face was shrouded in cloud, descending cloud at that. "What happened to your perfect weather, mate?" "Oh it'll clear up, just a drop of afternoon cloud." It started to rain.

We found what seemed to be the start, decided the rope was unnecessary at this stage, and began. The first pitch was a struggle, with sacks, up some steepish cracks. Half-way up I regretted the decision not to rope up, but a couple of grunts and a snarl or two led to easier ground. The easy ground led uncertainly upwards through the cloud, which happily cleared from time to time just long enough for us to recognise the odd landmark.

The guidebook description mentioned two pitches where difficulties might be encountered, but we were unable to find them and soloed on up until we recognised a steep traverse that led rightwards to the 'wet cave' and the 'difficult crack'. Here melted water Niagara'd down the face, so after roping-up we doned our waterproofs in the vain hope that we might escape a soaking. Carelessly, I left my sleeves and neck open as we both waited for the other to take the lead.

Rather unchivalrously, I thought, the Captain reminded me of my idle boasting about the steepness and strenuousness of some recent routes I claimed to have done. "Much like this I imagine," he said with mock innocence. What could I say? I led off rather quicker than was entirely safe to try to escape the deluge, but not as quick as that water, which poured into neck and sleeve. In no time I was soaked, sopping. Belaying in the comparative shelter of the 'wet cave', I took in the rope as the Captain sprinted across— faster with the security of the rope, and drier with his sleeves and neck secured— a wise virgin.

Immediately above rose the 'difficult crack'. Having seen photographs of it and read so much about it, I almost felt that I'd already climbed it a dozen times. Technically it's about 'Severe', I suppose, but with heavy sack and in a waterfall it made me puff a bit. I ran out 150ft. of rope and belayed just below the Hinterstoisser traverse. Somewhere left of here Toni Kurz had fought that great fight.

Out came the stove and both tea and soul were warmed. A couple of pegs in the roof of the cave and a stock-take and a sort out. I was drenched right down to my socks and was already missing some of that spare gear I had ditched to save weight. And worse. The weather was not good, even the Captain was admitting it — rain, avalanches and stonefall were difficult to ignore. Still, the big decision could be left until the morrow.

We addressed ourselves to the preparation of a meal with the undivided attention of men with absolutely nothing else to do. We wolfed the lot, soup and all, and washed it down with a gallon of tea, the sweetest smiling tea you ever saw.

It was not until about 11 p.m. that we began to make preparations for the night. As bivy sites go the cave wasn't too bad. There was just enough room for both of us to half-lie dry, full-lie wet — and if it's damp it's at least sheltered from stonefall, which makes it as good as home on the Eiger.

In his near-dry gear the Captain snored as an innocent man should, like three pigs. I shivered the night away and gazed longingly at the twinkling lights of Grindelwald thousands of feet below. It was a long night — they always are — and the water trickled all through it, which meant no freeze higher up and stonefall all the next day, which counselled retreat.

A wet, storm-laden day dawned. There was really no decision to be made, and yet we held a counsel of war. I was in poor shape after a miserable night — I would have been prepared to finish the climb in that condition, but to start it? And what with the weather and all, down we went — after all, it would still be here next year.

Ten abseils and two hours later we were at the foot of the face, and looking up in a mixture of anger and relief. Anger that we have been thwarted, relief that we had been able to retreat in good order and were safely back at the bottom.

For the umpteenth time we justified the decision to retreat to ourselves, and wandering back I reflected that there was something in the old military tenet "time spent in reconnaissance is seldom wasted." We now knew the line to the Swallows Nest, that would save time next go. We knew too to take care to keep dry and to wear waterproof leggings as well as jackets for the first few thousand feet — and on the last abseil we had found an easier first few feet. But more important than any of these we had stepped on the face and had dispelled the mystic and much of the fear; it no longer held us in its thrall.

And back we went the very next year. We saw it then on a sunny day and climbed it in another two—and I'll remember them forever.

from SPORT AND LEISURE *October 1980*

The Eyeglass

TOM LONGSTAFF

I took the steamer down Kootenay Lake, and to spare the deck and ease my feet I wore moccasins: I had on an Indian buckskin shirt belted over the top of a pair of untearable canvas trousers, and a ragged red beard. On the boat were two army officers returning from a shooting and fishing trip. One of them I recognised so I began talking shop. He seemed rather surprised at my temerity, though perfectly polite. Seeing that he didn't recognise me I used his name. He called up his good-looking yellow-moustached brother cavalry officer and said, "This chap was at Eton with me." "Good God," said his friend, and in his horror his eyeglass dropped to the deck and was smashed to smithereens.

from THIS MY VOYAGE *1950*

Le Grand Melchior

RONALD CLARK

Every craft, every sport, every profession, produces its legends. Melchior Anderegg was one of these. There was nothing told about him, one feels, which might not have been true, nothing which a man so remarkable might not have achieved. He was the perfect guide, the man whose list of ascents was equalled only by that of

Christian Almer, the man who was known, quite literally, from one end of the Alps to the other.

It was Whymper who asked in his *Scrambles*: "Who is Melchior Anderegg?" and then replied in words which showed that even the reserved conqueror of the Matterhorn was somewhat over-awed by the name of Melchior. "Those who ask the question cannot have been in Alpine Switzerland, where the name of Melchior is as well-known as the name of Napoleon," he said. "Melchior, too, is an emperor in his way, and a very prince among guides. His empire is among the 'eternal snows', his sceptre is an ice-axe." It was, perhaps, not surprising that Whymper, the inventor of so much mountaineering equipment, the organiser of victory, should have his favourite ice-axe built to the same speci-fications as that of Melchior Anderegg.

In his attitude of mind, as well as in his achievements, Melchior was a laboratory specimen of the guide, produced by both heredity and environment. Together with Christian Almer he had, as the editor of *The Alpine Journal* puts it, "dominated the Alpine world" from 1860 to 1880. "So long as mountaineering counts for anything in the minds of men, so long will the names of these two men stand out as essentially emblematic of that professional skill and of those virtues that are, not without some show of justice, commonly ascribed to the ideal guide of the High Alps."

Yet Melchior's background was almost identical with that of nearly all men who became guides. Its one outstanding feature was, as with so many other things in his life, its approach to the ideal. He did not only help his father to tend cattle: he did not only teach himself wood-carving so well that his work was exhibited in London galleries; he carried out, in addition, all those other activities which one would expect of the embryo Alpine guide, and he carried them out supremely well. He hunted chamois early in life and his first experience of rock and ice work was in the little Oberland valley containing Zaun, the hamlet near Meiringen; and he became not only a wrestler but the champion wrestler of all the valley.

He had been born at Zaun in 1828 and, as is the case with so many guides, we know few details of his early years. Although the Laueners, the Melchiors, and the Almers became quite literally household words among a small circle of men, the details of their lives went largely unrecorded: however strong the comradeship of the mountainside, the guides came from a social strata different from that of their employers and it was not an age in which biographical immortality reached down to that lower strata. Melchior's earlier years, we may fairly imagine, were not very different from those of most other village boys in Switzerland at the time, and not so very different from those of village boys there today. He helped in the harvesting, in timber-cutting, in cattle-tending, in all those activities of the peasant which are so governed by the changing seasons: he developed, therefore, that instinctive reaction to slight changes in the weather which are almost imperceptible to those whose living does not depend on noticing them. He would probably follow his father after chamois in his early 'teens, and from his youngest days he would begin to develop that sureness of foot which comes not instinctively but from constant, year-long contact between foot and rock in the normal occupations of one's life.

He grew up thus, quietly, with little contact with the world beyond his native valley, and it would have seemed easy to forecast his life. There would be the inheritance of his father's small property, an early marriage, hard labouring work: a few rare and great occasions when he and his wife would go as far as Interlaken, and perhaps even a journey to the great city of Zurich, a whole fifty miles away. With its serene middle age, it would be a life good and complete, although circumscribed by the peaks at the head of the valley, the village church, the far-away town where the valley opened out to the world beyond: the life seen "steadily and whole," as Arnold puts it, but a life which would, as it turned out, hardly have satisfied the enquiring mind of Melchior Anderegg.

It was not to turn out like this. At the age of twenty Melchior left his father's house for the little inn on the Grimsel. We are told by some of his contemporaries that he went there as a servant; by Mr. Mathews, one of his most constant employers, that he went to assist his cousin, Johann Frutiger, in the management of the inn. Whatever the exact details, he quickly found that his experience as a chamois-hunter, his interest in the Oberland mountains, and his knowledge of how passes led from one valley to another, qualified him as a guide. His first expeditions are unknown, for the fuehrerbuch with which he started was stolen in the fifties by a man who for a short period impersonated him and traded on the reputation he had even then gained.

His first client, he remembered in later years, was an Englishman named Robert Fowler, but it was not until 1859, when he obtained a new fuehrerbuch, that he began to keep regular records of his work. The first entry in this second book is by Frank Walker: the last, dated September 10, 1872, by a M. Albert Millot of Paris who states that "any recommendation of Melchior Anderegg is unnecessary."

The real start of Melchior's Alpine career might be said to date from 1855, when he first met Thomas Hinchliff who was later to introduce him to Stephen, thus bringing him on to the centre of the Alpine stage and allowing him to show the stuff of which he was made. Hinchliff, who wished to cross the Strahlegg from the Grimsel to Grindelwald, had enquired of the inn-keeper for a guide, and the following morning after breakfast he was introduced to Melchior and another man named Johann Hockler, both of whom he considered very promising-looking fellows. Melchior, aged 28, was already a fine figure of a man, tall and big-muscled, his square-bearded face surmounted by a mop of jet-black hair and his steady eyes shining from beneath dark upstanding eyebrows which gave his face an almost Mephistophelian air. Hinchliff had agreed to start at four in the afternoon and after a morning stroll over the Rhone Glacier he returned to the inn. "Here," he says, "we found our two guides making various preparations for the start, and bustling about with veils twisted round their hats, which showed clearly enough that they had got something of an expedition in view. A good guide can turn his hand to a great many things, and Melchior soon showed a taste for cobblery by putting some right good hob-nails with rather pointed ends into the gaps made in our shoes by the last week's walking." When they left, Melchior carried a knapsack in which the food was stored and on top of which was strapped the rope; in his hand he carried what appears to have been the older, longer version of the alpenstock which had not yet been outdated. The second guide bore the cellar, a large tin vessel fitted with straps so that it could be carried on the shoulders like a knapsack.

It was an uneventful journey to the hut, where Hinchliff notes that the guides slept in one compartment and the travellers in another, and it was followed by an equally uneventful ascent of the Strahlegg the following morning. The mere fact that Hinchliff makes so little comment is perhaps in itself something of a tribute to Melchior. The traveller's observations were reserved for the summit of the pass and in a few lines he summons up the spirit of the place far better than most mountain writers of the period. "It was about 10 o'clock," he says. "Not a cloud marred the face of the heavens, and not a sound broke the solemn silence that reigned about us, except for the occasional fall of avalanches at the back of the Mönch or Eiger, while the air was so perfectly still that a lucifer was not blown out, even in this exposed situation."

It was one of Hinchliff's first glacier expeditions, and he was thoroughly pleased with it, not least because of the small sums asked by the two guides, 30 francs each and a tip, a reasonable sum considering that they had to return to the Grimsel. It was natural that Hinchliff should remember the journey with pleasure, but one cannot help feeling that there was more to it than that: that he had found Melchior a pleasant companion and that some real comradeship had sprung up between the two men. One feels this when reading Hinchliff's account of the expedition and it is confirmed by his account of the incident at the Schwarenbach Hotel a few weeks later.

He called in at the hotel, then the only habitation between Kandersteg and Leukerbad, and found a party of travellers crowded in a little room inspecting the wooden figures of chamois and chalets which hotels even then sold to summer visitors. Turning the little models, explaining them, giving their cost and probably indulging in encouraging descriptions of how well they were made and how well they would look in some fine house in Paris, Berne, or London, was the man who carved them, wearing a green baize apron strapped over his working clothes. "At first I noticed the profile only of this man, but thought I knew something about it," says Hinchliff. "In another moment, he happened to turn his full face towards me and whom should I see in the person of this carver of graven images, but our old guide over the Strahlegg, Melchior Anderegg?" The enthusiasm of the two men who had crossed the mountains together suddenly blazed up in the little room among the carefully dressed tourists. "I greatly disconcerted and surprised his customers by rushing at him with a 'How d'ye do?' in German

and a hearty shake of the hand which he returned with interest,''
says Hinchliff. ''We were really delighted to see one another again:
but after exchanging a few words I told him to proceed with his
business and talk to me afterwards.''

Shortly before this meeting, and since he had last met Hinchliff,
Melchior had received a good offer to become carver-in-ordinary at
the Schwarenbach and had accepted the offer quickly, settling
down in the place and finding that he could combine guiding with a
profitable side-line in wood-carving. This was, throughout the
whole of his life, one of his main loves, and into it he put not
merely mechanical competency but a genuine attempt to express
himself. He had taught himself carving by the time he was 18 and
even in a community where the fashioning of wooden images was
almost part of the daily round, his skill was noticed. Yet for years
he never carved human figures, so bound was he by the humble and
conventional demands of his work. Then one day an Englishman
with whom he was climbing asked him to carry out some carving.
They were resting on the lower slopes of the Wetterhorn and
Melchior began to suggest subjects. ''Would you like a chamois,
Herr?'' he asked. ''No, Melk, I won't have anything to say to a
chamois,'' his employer said. ''Perhaps you would prefer a cow?''
it was suggested. ''Well, do you know, Melchior, I hate cows in
wood rather more than I hate chamois in the same material,'' he
was told. Melchior hesitated, then asked a little doubtfully:
''Would you like a chalet with rocks?'' ''No, Melk, I won't have a
chamois, a cow, or a chalet; but I will tell you what I will have – a
portrait of yourself, carved by yourself, in wood, and about, let us
say, about two feet high.'' Melchior was astonished and dismayed.
''I couldn't do it,'' he said. ''I have never carved a figure and I
don't know at all how to set to work.'' Within a few months the
figure had not only been completed but was on exhibition in the
Dudley Gallery, London.

Throughout the whole of his life, there came a constant procession of little objects from the implements he wielded so successfully, not only chamois and chalets and cows, but in later years
almost anything that a customer might require. On one occasion he
was sent two photographs of Landseer's famous picture of the
fighting stags; within a few months the carved fighting stags had
been sent to England.

His carving could easily be combined with his work as guide but Melchior's wrestling activities were apt to create difficulties, as in 1864 when Stephen, Crauford Gove, and Macdonald all delayed their departure from Lauterbrunnen so that Melchior could enter the ring as the champion of the Hasli men.

The contest was held on the 'neutral' grass slopes of the Wengern Alp, outside the upper inn, and Stephen, Macdonald, and Grove joined the local crowd that gathered around the magnificent arena. "A sheep was to be the prize," says Macdonald, "and after many inferior combatants had wrestled, the results giving the advantage slightly to the eastern faction, Melchior and his opponent entered the ring. The latter, favourite and chosen representative of Lauterbrunnen, was a younger and stouter man than Melchior, and had I not well-known the strength of the latter, and received repeated assurances of his great skill, I should have looked upon him as over-matched. A handkerchief is now tied firmly around each of the combatant's legs, half-way between the knee and the hip. After shaking hands, they grasp each other by this artificial hold, and dropping down on the right knee, each tries to turn his adversary over on his back. According to the laws of this kind of wrestling, the best of three falls decides the contest. In the first fall, Melchior, after a long struggle and, as I thought, while slipping downhill, is rolled, more than thrown, on his right shoulder, his antagonist coming down heavily on him. Though much bruised, he goes in pluckily for the second round, in which he succeeds in throwing his opponent fairly and quickly full on to his back. When the Lauterbrunnen hero, whose name I forget, rises from the grass it is ascertained that neither man is quite fit to resume the fray." Melchior's badly-sprained shoulder was swelling so fast, in fact, that a local man had to be engaged to help in their next expedition, the passage of the Rottalsattel.

The future fame of the man for whom a whole party would politely wait was unguessed at, however, when he once again met Hinchliff over the carved chamois of the Schwarenbach in the summer of 1856. Hinchliff engaged him immediately for the ascent of the Altels and that second journey appears to have confirmed his earlier impression. It was Melchior therefore, whom Hinchliff recommended, a few years later, to Leslie Stephen, the eminent Victorian whom we have already met, the man who "walked from

Alp to Alp like a pair of one-inch compasses over a large-sized map.'' A man of Melchior's calibre would, almost inevitably, have been noticed but it is, one feels, from the two meetings with Hinchliff that the great career really springs; from the year 1859, when Melchior met Stephen on the first ascent of the Rimpfisch-horn, the future could be clearly seen. It was in that year that Melchior made his first really great expedition – the ascent of Mont Blanc by the Bosses — an expedition which he carried out after the careful planning of Hudson, who wrote of Melchior when it was over: "For difficulties, the best guide I have ever met."

Melchior had the unusual advantage of a journey far beyond his own country early in his career, for in 1861 Stephen invited him to England. It is difficult, perhaps, to define exactly what advantages, other than social ones, a journey of this kind would give to a man whose profession was carried out on the glacier, the rock rib, and the snow-slope. Yet one quality which can be seen in most of the great guides is their overwhelming curiosity in all things and their ability to learn from what they saw. Whenever they came to London—and many of them did, though few as early in their careers as Melchior Anderegg—they seem to have drawn as much experience as they were able from this contact with a new and more complicated world. Melchior was no exception. Among the most remarkable incidents of his first visit to England was the famous occasion when he brought into the grubby heart of London the quality of the mountain path-finder.

He had arrived at London Bridge station during an exceptionally thick fog and had been met by Stephen and Hinchliff. The trio went on foot to Hinchliff's rooms in Lincoln's Inn Fields, feeling their way cautiously through the foggy streets in which even the flaring gaslights made little impression. A day or two later they all found themselves again at London Bridge station having returned from a visit to Woolwich.

"Now, Melchior," said Hinchliff jokingly, "you will lead us back home."

Melchior, the man who had never before known a town larger than Interlaken, accepted the situation, looked about, and then led the way to Lincoln's Inn Fields, pausing only once, at the foot of Chancery Lane, when he appeared to be examining landmarks which had been invisible to the other two men when they had previously passed the spot together.

Melchior was fascinated with London, in spite of the fogs, in spite of the confusing bustle, and it was his remark about the superiority of a view of London chimney-tops over the view from Mont Blanc that inspired Stephen's chapters on 'The Old School' and 'The New School' in the first edition of 'The Playground of Europe'. "A highly intelligent Swiss guide once gazed with me upon the dreary expanse of chimney-pots through which the South-Western railway escapes from this dingy metropolis," Stephen wrote. "I remarked with an appropriate sigh: 'That is not so fine a view as we have seen together from the top of Mont Blanc'. 'Ah, sir', was the pathetic reply, 'it is far finer'."

Melchior had a busy time in the capital visiting his friends — it would be incongruous to call them his employers — being shown the sights and even being taken down one of those coal-pits of whose existence he had previously been only dimly aware. "I can see him now," wrote Mathews nearly a quarter of a century later, "clad in a miner's jacket, holding a dip candle stuck into a lump of clay, and watching colliers at work with the grave earnestness which is his distinguishing characteristic."

Lady Stephen recorded in her dairy that she was "very much pleased" with Melchior and while he was a heavy man who even in later years could throw an opponent with the swing of the born wrestler, he had a gentleness, a certain kindliness of heart, and an unfailing courtesy that made him a favourite among the few women climbers of the period. "He was my guide for forty-two years," Mathews once said, "and I never heard him use an expression to which the gentlest woman might not have listened."

Notable among the early woman climbers to whom he acted as guide was Lucy Walker, the first Englishwoman to climb regularly in the Alps. For twenty years, from 1859 until 1879, Melchior was employed by her, as well as by the other members of the Walker family, whenever they visited the Alps.

There were others less competent who felt that under the guidance of 'le grand Melchior' they could carry out even the more difficult expeditions, and Stephen once asked Melchior how he managed to get a certain lady under his care across crevasses. "Well," was the reply, "I first go myself: then I pull a piece of sugar candy out of my pocket. I hold it towards her and say:

'Come, come, come,' and over she comes at once."

He had first met the Walkers in 1859. Miss Walker had wished to ascend the Altels and her father had told her that the only man for the job was Melchior Anderegg. Arriving at the Schwarenbach, she asked a porter where she could find the famous guide. Drawing himself up to his full height, he replied: "Ich bin der Anderegg." At this time his English was still poor and as he was not used to travelling with a family party he asked his friends how he should address each of its members. He was advised to use the terms which English people normally used, to listen and repeat what he heard. On the first day of his engagement the Walkers were therefore surprised to hear themselves being addressed by the serious-faced Melchior as 'pa-pa,' 'Lucy', and 'Horace', a fact which the family remembered for the rest of their long association with him.

It was on his return from London in the spring of 1861 that Melchior's career really began to open out. He was already a competent guide, he was already known to most of the leading amateurs, and he had worked with many of them. All this, however, was also true of at least a dozen other men, and the speed with which Melchior's reputation grew was due to something more. Just as he had known, by some inner sensitivity, how to find his way through the foggy streets of London, so could he divine, by a method perhaps not clear even to himself, the chinks in the armour of those great Alpine problems which intrigued the amateurs of the day. Melchior could see, with the simplicity of genius, the way in which a difficult mountain might be tackled, and one feels that it was not so much instinct as imagination, a fine queer quality, the stuff almost of another world, which was added to his mechanical competence on rock, snow, and ice. This competence was in itself of an extraordinary quality, and almost every amateur who climbed with Melchior noted his superb craftsmanship, his 'thoroughness' one of them called it, without which all his imagination would have been of little use.

To these two qualities, imagination and craftsmanship, he brought another that could easily be dismissed with the one word 'caution'. It was not merely, however, that he was careful: it was his whole approach to the mountains which made him 'a safe man': he knew that above the higher alps one entered a region where man lived on sufferance, and where the fairest day might end suddenly in a grim battle for existence. An emperor he might be, but he kept a sense of proportion about the matter.

It is regarding Melchior's prudence that one of the most famous of all stories about guides has been told. As reported for more than fifty years it tells how he had reached a dangerous spot with one of the finest amateur climbers of the day. Both guide and employer inspected the situation. "It goes," said the amateur, seeing that the place could be passed. "Yes, it goes," replied Melchior, "but I'm not going." That was the story as first told by C. E. Mathews in *The Alpine Journal*, retold in similar form in the *Pioneers*, and then handed down into Alpine history. It is only recently that Doctor Stevens has pointed out that the correct and rather different version of the incident was told in one of Sir Edward Davidson's papers published in *The Alpine Journal* after his death. The incident occurred when Melchior, together with Davidson, Mathews, and F. Morshead, were standing on the top of the Dent Blanche in 1876. They began to discuss the problem of climbing the Zmutt ridge of the Matterhorn, most of whose length they could see. It was then that Melchior uttered his famous: "It goes, but I'm not going." Thinking of the falling stones, he added: "Anyone who wants to go that way must have a head of iron. That is something for Herr Middlemore"—the reference being to Thomas Middlemore whose first passage of the Col des Grandes Jorasses, led by Hans Jaun, had brought down upon him the criticism of many AC members due to the climb's unavoidable dangers.

The truth of Melchior's legendary 'ich gehe nicht' is not, therefore, quite what two generations of climbers have imagined, since there is considerable difference between being stopped by a single but practicable pitch on a climb and rejecting a new and obviously dangerous route; yet the mere fact that the story lasted so long in its original form is an indication of Melchior's caution. It was true, as a friend said, that he left nothing to the valour of ignorance.

His record during the two golden decades of the sixties and 'seventies can only be fully appreciated by studying the climbing records of the time. If there is, in the climbing career of any great amateur of the period, any one particular feat which attracts, any great ascent in which one feels some particular interest, Melchior is more often than not found to have had a hand in the business. One feels, as Mathews once wrote, that "it is difficult to set down undoubted facts about such a guide as Melchior Anderegg and yet to avoid altogether the charge of exaggeration." The Walkers, Stephen, Tuckett, Kennedy, and Moore are the great names with which he is most regularly connected but almost every leading climber of the period employed him. When they could secure him, that is, for Melchior was invariably booked up for at least a year ahead so great were the demands for his services. His old friends always had first call on these. "If his services at any particular time were not required by Stephen or Walker or Morshead or myself," wrote Mathews, "then, and then only, was he open to fresh engagements."

In 1864 Melchior married Marguerite Metzener, the girl who at that time was in charge of the wood-carving in the hotel at the foot of the Rhone Glacier. He settled in his native village and was soon bringing up a constantly increasing family that finally consisted of eight sons and four daughters. The eldest of his sons, also named Melchior, was trained as a guide but lacked his father's great strength, and finally became a wood-carver; his second son, Andreas, inherited much of his father's ability and flourished as a guide.

There was one expedition in Melchior's life which deserves special notice, not only because it was a fine mountaineering feat but because the record of it which has survived gives such a full feeling of the splendid age in which he lived and of which he was a part. It was the first ascent of Monte Disgrazia in 1862, and the story of the climb, written by Edward Shirley Kennedy and startng on page one of the first issue of *The Alpine Journal* might have been a symbol. For that narrative, prosy though it is in parts, perhaps a little overloaded with Victorian excrescences of style, still interprets far better than most similar records the expansive leisurely way in which the Alpine pioneers and their guides went about the business of climbing. It is, of its kind, a classic period piece, a laboratory specimen of climbing literature, and it is right that Melchior, who more than any other guide typified that age, should be pictured in it. The opening phrases are not, one feels at first, from a climbing narrative at all, but surely from some colourful romance of battery and barricade. "As the chimes of midnight were clanging from the Campanile at Sondrio, a carriage

rolled heavily into the courtyard of the Hotel della Maddalena.''
That is how it starts, before revealing that the party consisted of
Kennedy, the Rev. Isaac Taylor, Stephen, Melchior Anderegg, and
Thomas Cox, Kennedy's servant, who accompanied his master on
more than one mountaineering expedition. The first attempt on the
peak failed and the party returned to that swarming hotel where so
many people offered advice that it was never discovered ''whether
the landlord were a knot of men, or a parcel of women, or a crowd
of children, or an Italian bagman who took especial interest in the
welfare of the house, or a combination of all these motley groups.''
There, in the suffocating Italian heat, the party grew dispirited and
it appeared that the attempt would fail. Then Kennedy discovered
that a pleasant carriage drive to a 'Grand Ancient Italian Bathing
Establishment' would outflank the mountain and bring them to a
point from which it could better be attacked.

''Two hours later we sallied out from the courtyard in a couple
of cars,'' he says, ''amid the tramping of seeds, the cracking of
whips, and the shouts of the hangers-on of the hotel. In the first
carriage were Stephen and I, driven by the head waiter, who
appeared in person, as *fils aîné de la maison*, and whose mother
turned out to be one of the 140 persons of distinction who were
imbibing nitrogenous salts at the bathing establishment. In the
second carriage were Melchior and Cox, driven by a boy in blue,
who had been specially impressed for the occasion. The head-waiter
was pleased with the prospect of seeing his parent, the boy in blue
was delighted with his holiday, and we four were in high spirits at
the prospect of another chance of attacking the Disgrazia.
Altogether we were a very cheerful not to say an uproarious
party.''

That was how the great day started. And, after Melchior had
carved his way through the difficulties, and landed the party
successfully on the much-coveted peak, it ended in the same high
spirits, with Stephen and Kennedy in one carriage trying to ''get up
an Olympic chariot race with Melchior and Cox'' in the second.
''We reached Sondrio at half past ten,'' says Kennedy. ''Supper,
champagne and success put us at peace with all the world, and we
found ourselves, somewhere about midnight, once more in bed. We
had thus made a day of 24 hours, but whether it was the same day,
or the next day, or the day after that day, or the same week or the

next week, that that day ended, is one of those things which no fellow could tell.''

That was the spirit of the age in which Melchior worked and he, as much as any man, not only took part in it but helped to create it. For Melchior was not only a great guide but he also made great guides. He inspired them and taught them and was held by many other men in his profession much as the marshals held Napoleon or the staff officers of the Eighth and Second Armies held Montgomery in a later age. His cousin Jakob, after a typical but foolish act — he had led his party through a dangerous passage almost for a bet — turned to one of his employers with the words: ''Don't tell Melchior.''

Melchior was, in fact, the headmaster of that great school of Oberland guides to which belonged such men as Hans Jaun, Andrea Maurer, von Bergen, and a dozen others without whose work mountaineering would never have developed as successfully as it did. The exceptional men were never numerous enough to satisfy the demands of the growing body of climbers during the sixties and the seventies, while the vast majority of guides were neither capable enough nor enterprising enough to plan and execute fresh expeditions. It is difficult in fact to see who could have filled the positions later occupied by the pupils of the masters, the men who while not in the class of Melchior or Christian Almer were yet incomparably more competent than the average glacier guide.

Jaun, more than most of his contemporaries, almost revered the qualities of Melchior, under whom he had blossomed out as a guide. Mathews tells of how on one occasion, when Melchior was leading in a position of great difficulty, he called Jaun's attention not only to the confidence which Melchior showed in the position, but to his wonderful grace and ease of movement. ''Yes,'' Jaun replied, ''but he is the king of guides.'' So in fact he was, the man to whom other guides came for advice, the Solomon dispensing wisdom and, at the same time, the man of action, the supreme technician.

While helping to enforce the rules and regulations of the Oberland guides system, Melchior had little patience with those of other regions, particularly if they had been framed, as had those of Pontresina for instance, with an eye to exacting from the traveller the maximum amount of money for the minimum amount of service. There was one famous occasion when he was visiting the area with Mathews and Morshead, who wished to ascend the Bernina. They had thought it better to employ in addition to Melchior a local man who happened to be the chief guide in the district; the man not only demanded a stupendous fee for the ascent but insisted that another guide, a friend of his, should be hired on the same terms. Melchior, called in for advice, pointed out that he, alone, could quite adequately cope with the ascent and proceeded to do so.

He was, perhaps, the most sought-after guide in the whole of the Alps, and even in old age continued to receive numerous offers of work. Most of these he declined, being comparatively well off. He could never refuse old friends, however, and we find him, at the age of sixty-nine, visiting the Eastern Alps with the Walkers again.

The party was taking an off day when Lucy Walker—herself then sixty-one —"quietly stole off with Melchior and paid a visit to the Staubach Hut, the journey to and from which according to Baedeker takes more than four hours."

Before his retirement from regular guiding, which came in 1893, Melchior made a second visit to Britain, this time as the guest of William Mathews, with whom he stayed first in London and later at Mathews' cottage near Machynlleth.

While with Mathews there occurred one of those little incidents which explain so well the difference between the Alps and the British hills. Mathews took Melchior on the ascent of Snowdon, going from Pen-y-Gwyrd to the summit of Crib Goch and then around the Horseshoe, over Y Wyddfa and Lliwedd. Mathews led, through deep, soft snow, and at one point, where he hesitated for a few minutes, Melchior went to the front, offering to lead.

"No," said Mathews, "I am guide today and you are Herr."

"On reaching the summit of Crib Goch, there was the peak of Snowdon on our left, a great white cone rising into a blue sky," says Mathews. "Melchior, whose knowledge of Swiss distance is faultless, at once said: 'We must go back: we cannot climb the final peak in less than five or six hours'. 'Oh yes', I said, 'we shall be there in an hour'. 'That sir', was his reply, 'is quite impossible'." In five minutes more than the hour they were both on the summit.

It was on this visit to Britain that Melchior was presented to the Alpine Club, being introduced to the members at the general meeting on April 10, 1888. Six years later, on his retirement from active guiding, he was honoured at the Winter Dinner held in the Whitehall Rooms. With Douglas Freshfield in the chair, 260 members and their guests sitting down to dinner, and guests that included Viscount Cobham, the Dean of Westminster, and Professor Maitland, it was a distinguished gathering to pay tribute to the man who had started his working life as a porter at the Grimsel.

He lived for another 18 years, playing an increasing part in the village affairs of Meiringen, taking a keen interest in the development of the wooden causeway through the Aar Gorge, which is still such an attraction to casual visitors, and coming down from his house at Zaun to explain its intricacies to special friends.

from THE EARLY ALPINE GUIDES *1949*

Arnold Küpfer

CLAUDE BENSON

"Dear Master of John's, you can enlighten me: with your marvellous memory you will have retained the name of that chivalrous and gentle guide who conducted us up the Schulthorn . . . that model of courtesy and consideration—whose name I have often endeavoured to recall but without success."

To which the M of J said gruffly: "I suppose you mean Arnold Küpfer."

"That was the name!" cried the Master of Trinity in an ecstasy. "Thank you a thousand times for recalling a name which brings back to me some of the best and sweetest days of my life—happy hours when guided by that chivalrous Arnold Küpfer we took the wings of the morning on the Alpine ridges." He presently withdrew. Someone said to the Master of John's, "Was Küpfer really so delightful a guide? I never even heard of him."

"Neither have I," said the M of J. "I invented the name. I could not have Butler going on like that."

from THE LISTENER

Tenzing Norgay

MICHAEL TOBIAS

There is the nearly-pathetic anachronism of his coming-of-age, a culture shock he has gracefully manoeuvred. Ever since he led Hillary to the top of Everest he had been shuffled around the globe as guest of one alpine club after another, called upon to re-hash the old epic, to smile. His teeth are those of a twenty-year-old. This Tenzing attributes to the salt he has rubbed on them since childhood. For eighteen years he tended yaks in Khumbu, during a time when Nepal was as sealed and alluring as is Pemakod today. Born in 1914, Tenzing was reared in the shadows of Everest, the mountain which Sherpas say is "too tall even for birds to fly over." It was Tenzing's dream to climb it. And on the seventh expedition he did. By then he'd already moved to Darjeeling looking for work. He still resides there, overlooking Kangchenjunga, an admitted alien in both Nepal and India, between two worlds.

For all of his mountainy humour, there is some bitterness in Tenzing. The Indian Government, explorers' clubs, tour agencies, the press, other Indian mountaineers, tea and airline companies — the list goes on — have all exploited his *joie de vivre*, an innocence which Tenzing has, admittedly, learned to exploit. He seems troubled whilst reflecting on the burden of his good luck. A Tibetan Stein Erickson, neither reading nor writing, he conceals bewilderment with a charm that Eric Shipton first noticed back in 1936 when he hired Tenzing to porter in place of other more qualified Sherpas.

He wears a white sports car cap, a red wind-jacket, woollen knickers, a Norwegian pullover. Huge sunglasses give him the slight seriousness of a World War I fighter pilot. Like most Sherpas he is stout, thick-footed, somewhat bow-legged, barrel-chested, with a reddish throat thinly latticed by wrinkles acquired on a myriad of glaciers. His eyes are dark and mottled with colour. In jeans from Italy he looks, somehow, emaciated.

Tenzing speaks a random English with the effeminate, Sir Edmond Backhouse kind of inflection of a Mandarin or French montagnard. His timidity can be unnerving; and his raucous, immediate affability seems to survive from the gentleness of Cro-Magnon times. He laughs at the slightest provocation, out-of-control like Polynesian old-timers, like children who haven't been forced to read books, take dancing lessons or not say "shit". Once I asked him what the funniest event in his life had been and he frowned for long minutes pondering. Finally he said "Krushchev!" "Krushchev?" I asked. "Yah. A man with a thousand chickens in his stomach!" Tenzing cried, curled over in hysterics.

Tenzing believes he could climb Everest until he's seventy. After that, maybe not. "Mountains give little trouble to older men once they are used to them," he says. For the past two decades, as director of the Himalayan Mountaineering Institute abase Kabru in Sikkim, with headquarters in Darjeeling, he has seen more high altitude action than nearly any mountaineer. To say that high altitude peoples are more fit than ourselves is something of a wild understatement. It is no secret that the cardio-vascular respiratory, and skeletal systems are greatly benefited by thin air and rough terrain. At eighty-four Tenzing's grandmother made the difficult two-week trek from Thami to Darjeeling. Tenzing himself has a robustness which one simply does not witness in lowlanders. He breathes an energy that seems to defy entropy.

As legendary a figure throughout Asia as Mohandas Gandhi, dogs know instinctively to come begging for food from Tenzing. Seeing two caged yaks in a New York zoo he whispered words of an old Tibetan breviary and relates that the yaks turned anxiously. Tenzing is also turned, toward the hearty folklore of his haunting grounds which is fast disappearing. The Sherpas have all gone down to Katmandu looking for trekking business. Meanwhile the language of the Sherpa, the farms of their upbringing, their whole way of life is sadly on the plunge. Tenzing can't help but blame himself in part and this is his peculiarly Western tragedy. Still he is a hero. Children happily assail him on the street. His large home in Darjeeling abounds with medals and gifts and worldly letters which he can't read. Letters from kings and astronauts.

Tenzing manages to flirt, playfully, with his double-bind. His children speak five and six languages. His third wife, Daku, is a beauty. He earns a scant livelihood as retired adviser to the HMI and as an uncertain tour leader for the Mountain Travel-type

Golden oldies — Tenzing and Hillary

organisations. The tourist influx, however, is a primary concern of Tenzing who, like the rest of us, suffers from that ineluctable ·paradox of loving mountains too much, while needing money. He sees Bhutan as the last possibility for medieval mountain preservation. Though even Bhutan is beginning to sniff the dollars, to the extent that when Tenzing and I journeyed there together in 1975, as leaders of a tour, the price per head was something on the order of $160 a day. Grossingers' can cost that much, or Caesar's Palace. Needless to say Bhutan is worth it. But is the price worth itself? Tenzing doesn't think so. Nor do I. But what does someone do about it? In the meantime, the Rumteks and Thyangboches suffer irreparably.

Tenzing walks like a mystic. I followed him for a month, peeing in the deodar when he did, running when he did, taking the similar course through boulder fields and snowdrifts. He was like a Himalayan Tarahumard. The man has tracked a good 10,000 miles of ultimate wilderness. The Zen 10,000. My hope was to assimilate something of his keen spirit, of his easy breathing exuberance which lends him to the spirit of brown bears and oxygenless days alike.

Nothing. I was locked into my particular way of handling steepness, of looking straight ahead and down, of meeting villagers. There was nothing peripheral to my approach, whereas his gaze was tiger-like, all over the place. He possessed rare perspective no doubt deriving from his unusual purgatory of experience and allegiances. Not an enviable place to be, as his own restlessness is borne out in his autobiography. "There I was, torn, ignorant, wanting the left and the right." Tenzing seemed capable of commanding the kind of ancient perception students of cross-culture are wont to search out. V. S. Naipaul, on a learned level, examines such a plight when he treats the modern, unassimilable Indian.

Perhaps it is the quality of mountains, the nurturing of intelligence year in and year out beneath their gleam which has endowed Tenzing with the hapless ability to confront his duality. He manages; and there is no one who will not be caught up in the splendour of his typical embrace, a homecoming of hugs, some instant of affability from the primeval past, with a *coup de grâce*; a feverishness proclaiming impossible juxtaposition. Tenzing pulls it off, with his trans-etiquette, his modesty.

He does not sit still. After twenty-five major climbing trips he is more gung ho than ever before. He discusses his climbing feats with the calm, the unheroics of a tailor or an elevator operator.

I don't think he's ever hammered in a piton. I can't imagine him bothering. I doubt if he takes rock-climbing very seriously. It's the snow that captivates him, the big mountains. His peaks are those of the Vedas, the Sutras, the Old Testament. If there is true ecology in the world it is in the fact that Tenzing climbed Everest first, and surely foremost. Tensing is indispensable to that mountain. Their greatness lies in one another, somehow. I remember being snow-bound with the old Sherpa in his tent, along the ridge to Sandakphu. It was a blizzardly night. His kids were all over him, goosing, in frenzied frolic. I was lying there cold, out of phase with the life around me, nervous for my little comforts and wondering, was there anything in the world for which I was as indispensable. I doubted it then, and I still can't say.

from CLIMBING 49 *1978*

Sahibs and Sherpas

MIKE THOMPSON

"Towards the head of these Dales was found a perfect Republic of Shepherds and Agriculturalists. . ." (William Wordsworth, *A Guide through the District of the Lakes*.)

Recently, while watching a Bonington lecture (Over Yet Another Horizon), I began to tot up his tally of Himalayan expeditions to date: Annapurna II, Nuptse, Annapurna South Face, Everest '72, Brammah, Changabang, Everest '75, The Ogre . . . K2: an impressive list that is made even more impressive by its remarkably high success rate. The only failures being Everest '72 and K2. Historians, I suspect, would agree that already it represents one of the finest personal achievements (perhaps the finest) in Himalayan mountaineering. And yet, despite their unanimity, they would be wrong. Relying upon written records, they would have overlooked the fact that, as well as German, Polish, French, Swiss, Austrian, Italian, American, Japanese, and British climbers, some Nepalese have also been active in the Himalayas. I do not know which Sherpa would turn out to have the most impressive record, but I do know that any Sherpa with only nine expeditions to his credit would not even rate a mention.

One February evening last year I was sitting by the fire in Pemba Tarkay's house in the village of Phortse, a day's walk from Everest Base Camp. His older children are now grown up and away from home and so the company comprised just Pemba Tarkay, his wife, his youngest son who is only three years old, Ginger Warburton, a British climber/cameraman, and myself. Since he has now retired, more or less, the conversation soon shifted from the health of his yaks downstairs to reminiscences about his climbing days. When I tried to find out how many expeditions he had been on, he and his wife laughed and said that, as it happened, just a few nights before they had been trying to work that out themselves. They were not sure of the exact total but it was somewhere around 24; and what a 24! The list includes: Makalu, Taweche, Ama Dablam, Kangtega, Everest, Tamserku, Everest again, Annapurna South Face, Everest again, Glacier Dome . . . Everest yet again.

The next morning, just as we were leaving the village, we met an enormous pile of hay descending, apparently unaided, from one of the high pastures. As it drew near the mystery was solved; its prime mover was not levitation but another mountaineering grandad, Mingma Tsering, who I had not seen since Annapurna South Face eight years before. Minutes later we were sat around his fire, dishes of hot potatoes in front of us and mugs of *chang* in our hands. Neither he nor his wife had any very clear recollection of how many expeditions he had been on, but there was one thing he did know: he was going on another one in a few days' time. A message had arrived a week or two before, from Colonel Jimmy Roberts of Mountain Travel, asking him to go to Kathmandu to join an expedition to, Mingma thought, Annapurna I with the American women. As it turned out, he had got it wrong. It was a German expedition to Dhaulagiri—the American Ladies' Expedition was not until after the monsoon—and we could imagine him musing how much Annapurna had changed since the last time he was on it, and how hairy and guttural American ladies were. (In fact he went on both, reaching the top of Annapurna without oxygen.)

Communication between Katmandu and Phortse is not instantaneous. Letters are sent by plane to Lukla and then carried up to Namche and left at Pasang Kami's shop. Every Sunday there is a market in Namche and anyone from Phortse who goes to it collects the letters and takes them back with him the next day. As often as not, the messages are verbal and Pemba Tarkay had a lot of fun announcing his retirement by sending the reply: "Tell Jimmy Roberts he'll have to come and ask my wife whether I can go to Dhaulagiri or not."

My purpose in relating these anecdotes is not to denigrate Bonington's achievement but to pin-point the difficulties we all face when we try to evaluate mountaineering achievements across cultural boundaries. Perhaps, by confronting these difficulties, I may be able to redress the balance a little in favour of the Sherpas.

One way of looking at Sherpa mountaineering is to see it as just another kind of trading activity. The Khumbu Sherpas have always traded and, indeed, they moved into their remote homeland in order to take advantage of the trading opportunities that it offered. Once established in their high valley, they were able to link the grain-producing areas of the Middle Ranges, that lay a week or so's journey down the Dudh Kosi, with the wool-producing plateau of Tibet, that lay on the other side of a 20,000ft. pass—the Nangpa La. Once this primary trade was established, the varied and sophisticated products of India to the south and of China and Mongolia to the north could also be tapped. All this happened a few hundred years ago and came to an end, temporarily, with the Chinese occupation of Tibet in the 1950's.

Trans-Himalayan trade is a risky business, both physically and financially, and the Sherpas conducted it on a somewhat easy-come-easy-go individualistic basis. Some families, especially those based in the well-sited village of Namche, became very rich, others remained quite poor. If the financial risks were too great or the physical risks too daunting, the Khumba Sherpa could always reduce his level of involvement, or even pull out of trading altogether for a while and fall back on his potato fields and his yak herd. In this way, trading was essentially the entrepreneurial froth on top of the Sherpa's subsistence *chang*. Man, they have always felt, does not live by spuds alone; and their individualistic, exuberant, risk-taking, reward-enjoying trade has formed the basis for a cheerful, convivial, easy-going, open, and hospitable life-style that has endeared them to generations of Western mountaineers.

Sherpas are great opportunists and, as Himalayan mountaineering developed, they took to it like ducks to water. The duration of an expedition is similar to that of a trading trip, the risks involved are comparable (but more physical than financial); there is the opportunity for adventure (including amorous adventure), the prospect of congenial company, and the lure of high financial reward—good pay and, even more important, very worthwhile swag.

In other words, expeditions are attractive to Sherpas for very much the same sort of reasons that they are attractive to Western mountaineers. Admittedly, financial reward comes to the Westerner in a rather more circuitous and unreliable manner than that in which the Rupee notes are counted out into the sweaty Sherpa palm, and of course he can look forward to all sorts of less tangible rewards—fame, prestige, autobiography-writing, and even perhaps co-option onto a BMC Committee—but, when it comes to swag, Westerner and Sherpa are indistinguishable. In recent years Sherpas have mounted mini-expeditions into the Western Cwm in order to bring down all the abandoned equipment they were, regrettably, unable to carry down the mountain at the end of the main expedition. I well remember Mick Burke, who was the last one down the South Face of Annapurna, clanking his way into Base Camp, like some diminutive and horseless crusader, completely sheathed in alloy karabiners.

Should one emphasise these similarities between Sherpas and Westerners or should one emphasise their undoubted differences? After all, though they may be united by a shared willingness to take large personal risks and by a common passion for swag, they are very much set apart by culture. One is the product of advanced Western industrial society, the other a remnant of a rural and technologically backward society that has changed little since the Middle Ages; one is a lax and almost heathen product of secular Christianity, the other a devout and committed upholder of the Buddhist way of life; one speaks a dialect of English, the other a dialect of Tibetan.

Being an anthropologist by trade, I was very much predisposed to emphasise the differences and, for a long time, I felt that the similarity that I observed between the Sherpas and the elite Western climbers they accompanied was based on nothing more than a shared addiction to hot sweet tea, Gauloise cigarettes, and chips; but gradually the obscuring mists of cultural difference began to clear and I came around to the realisation that it was much more than this: that their behaviour, their attitudes, and their cheerful acceptance of appalling risks were identical because their situations, within societies separated by 6,000 miles of land and sea and by thousands of years of history, were identical. As I came around to this position I became increasingly sceptical about the usefulness of my trade when it comes to making comparisons between Sahibs and Sherpas.

Anthropology, especially pop anthropology, all too easily succumbs to the Little Furry Animal Syndrome: the "Oh dear! Isn't it terrible the way the wonderful traditions and way of life of these marvellous simple people are being destroyed by contact with Western civilisation' reaction. In the Sherpa case such a reaction is grotesquely patronising and quite irrelevant for there is little likelihood that the thousands of tourists who each year trek up to (and sometimes die at) the Everest Base Camp will be diverted and little chance that, if the Everest National Park (such is now the official status of Khumbu) became a Sherpa Sanctuary, the Sherpas would stay inside it contentedly breeding their yaks, spinning their prayer-wheels and circumambulating their *chortens*. For the fact is that the Sherpas, despite their remote and romantic homeland, have always been a cosmopolitan lot.

On the way to Everest in 1975, halfway along the two-week walk to Base Camp (during the monsoon there are no flights to Lukla), we met a Lama and his retinue of fifteen porters. He was the Rimpoche – (Abbott, literally 'precious one') of Trakshindu Monastery on his way to take up a six months' visiting professorship at Berkeley. Such to-ings and fro-ings in the Himalayas are as old as Sherpa society itself; modern technology simply serves to bring California nearer than Lhasa used to be. So, rather than bewailing the loss of an Eden the Sherpas never had, we should try to understand the changes that have been wrought, and will be wrought, by the fortuitous arrival, so soon after the Chinese put an end to the trade with Tibet, of the Western (and Japanese) tourist.

This analogy between Sherpa trade and Sherpa mountaineering, though helpful in many ways, does overlook one crucial difference: wool and grain are inanimate, tourists (usually) are animate. The volume of trade passing through Khumbu was largely in control of the Sherpas themselves. If a lot of individual Sherpas wanted to trade extensively, the volume of trade increased, and if for some reason or other individuals felt like cutting down a bit, the volume of trade decreased. Grain and wool only flowed if Sherpas wanted them to flow, but the tourists come whether the Sherpas want them to or not; and in just a few years their flow has increased from a tiny trickle to a raging torrent. When the Sherpas depended upon trade for their involvement with the wider world, the form that their cosmopolitanism took was of their own choosing. Pemba Tarkay and Mingma Tsering, happily living among their families, their fields, and their animals and going off every now and then on a profitable mountaineering adventure, typify this Sherpa-controlled cosmopolitanism (Sherpa women too, I should mention, are free to go off on business ventures and many do). Basically self-sufficient and able to decide how and to what extent they should become involved with others, they are in that admirable human state—'very together'. But, as the flow of tourists increases, so it becomes more and more difficult to get it, and keep it, together.

The path from Lukla to Everest Base Camp is part of the Grand Tour of The World Traveller and is strewn with freaks in a profusion so rich as to rival that of the alpine flowers along the way. Some are religious maniacs of an ego-focused intensity so powerful as to bore the hind leg off any yak unwise enough to stray into their self-indulgent path. Others, wholly obsessed with avoiding hepatitis/getting the maximum exchange rate on the Pakistan black market for their Afghanis/watching out for rip-offs/getting the cheapest fare for the Katmandu-Bangkok leg, cannot spare a single moment to absorb the people and the landscape through which they are passing and might as well have stayed in the Greyhound Station in Milwaukee. Still others are shrewd, sensitive, threadbare, and entertaining travellers whose casual wayside company is pure delight. One wide-eyed itinerant Alaskan who we bumped into on several occasions was, it became clear, determined to be astonished by everything. His response to even the most mundane pieces of information, such as that Ginger had got a blister on his heel, was a breathless "WOW!" and we became curious to know what would happen if we managed to impart to him something just a little more momentous.

The opportunity presented itself when, near the end of our visit, we spotted him through the pot-smoke and the chang-haze of the Buddha Lodge at Lukla. As I developed my theory that the Grand Tour this dedicated traveller was embarked upon had, like its eighteenth-century counterpart, become so stereotyped, so hackneyed, and so predictable as to be no longer capable of giving any novel insights or unexpected delights and that the only useful purpose it could serve was to open one's eyes to the disregarded variety and richness of the despised country and society from which one had set out, I was rewarded with a succession of WOWs of ever-increasing intensity. "Yes," agreed Ginger finally, "There's nothing like travel for narrowing the mind." Anxiously, we both looked at our Alaskan friend. Would he explode, or emit a WOW audible only to passing bats? Neither — he was struck dumb — and in the ensuing silence I pondered the significance of Ginger's *coup de grâce*. If trampling through the Sherpa's homeland does this to us, what does it do to them?

It is a great pity that the vast majority of the visitors to Khumbu now fly straight into Lukla from Katmandu. Quite apart from the undoubted advantage that, if they had to walk all the way most of them wouldn't get there, they miss out completely on one of the most remarkable experiences that this journey affords: the striking contrast between the Buddhist Sherpas and their Hindu neighbours. It is one of those rare and vivid contrasts that are experienced through the stomach:

> Anyone who has travelled in rural Nepal has experienced the difference in the attitudes of Buddhist and Hindu communities. In the former it is easy to gain entrance to houses and offers of hospitality are usually freely forthcoming while in Hindu villages no stranger is admitted and even his attempts to purchase victuals often meet with difficulty.

To arrive by foot in Sherpa country is to gain some insight into what it was like for the Israelites to reach the Promised Land. Though Khumbu may not overflow with milk and honey, *chang*, chips, *chaypa*, tea, and *tsampa* issue in a steady stream from every wayside shack between Tragdobug and Gorak Shep.

As the flow of tourists increases, and as trekking agencies proliferate to satisfy their needs, so more and more Sherpas, in order to get any sort of share in the action, find that they have to move away from Katmandu and spend more and more time in Katmandu: Katmandu is where the tourists arrive and it is where the agencies spring up. As they make this transition they move out of the free and easy atmosphere of home into a Hindu world dominated by group controls: land is controlled by joint families, the nature of the relationship between any two individuals is specified by the positions within the caste hierarchy of the groups to which each belongs: all is ordered, prescribed, and regulated, not with a view to securing a maximum level of individual economic advantage, but in order to maintain the separation and the purity of social groups. The Sherpa arriving in Katmandu to seek his fortune finds himself incorporated into this alien world in a rather lowly position. The omnivorous diet and the easy-going egalitarianism, that would serve him so well on his trading trips and his climbing expeditions, ensure that this despicable and polluting cow-eater is fitted in at the very bottom of the caste hierarchy. Three possibilities exist for him. He can try, by ignoring his new social environment, to rise serenely above it; he can sink beneath its surface: or he can decide that it is all too heavy a scene and return to his potatoes and his yaks in Khumbu. Increasingly it is an either/or predicament. To stay 'together' he has to return to Khumbu but, if he does that, he has to give up any hope of getting a worthwhile slice of the tourist cake. The traditional option, enjoyed by Pemba Tarkay and Mimgma Tsering, of having one's tourist cake and eating it in Khumbu is becoming less and less available.

The new Sherpa entrepreneurs, who have done so well out of mountaineering and tourism, often come from the less important families. Since mountaineering was quite well developed before the trade with Tibet came to a sudden end, the important families have to some extent missed out and it is those who, having little to lose to start with, were prepared to take the big risks who are now (provided they are still alive) building hotels, visiting Buckingham Palace, sending their children to private schools in Darjeeling, and driving around Katmandu in long-wheelbase Land Rovers. Pemba Tarkay and Mimgma Tsering poke some gentle fun at these wheeling and dealing businessmen as they rush back and forth between their hotels and shops in Namche and their trekking interests in Katmandu. Perhaps the most convincing evidence for the existence of these three clearly separate options that confront the present-day Sherpa is provided by the different ways in which his time and space can be organised.

The 'together' Sherpa is usually encountered in Khumbu and, though his time is clearly valuable, he has it unobtrusively organised and is able to act the considerate and attentive host. On his occasional visits to Katmandu, a casual call or a chance meeting in the street may be followed by a pleasant evening at a Tibetan restaurant: The Om, The Utse, or The An An; no hustling for work, no respectful bullshit, no talking business—just an easy-going friendly occasion with some good gossip and a few sly digs at Pasang Kami (who was sirdar on Annapurna South Face and has since made good in Namche and Katmandu) and Kelvin Kent (who was Base Camp manager on Annapurna South Face and on Everest '72 and has since made good in Colorado). Sherpas that take up the other two options are readily distinguishable; some are almost impossible to get hold of, the others are almost impossible to get rid of. The latter tend to hang around the compounds of trekking agencies on the off-chance that they may get some work or else they will, off their own bat, perform various unnecessary services for you in order that you may become obligated to them in some way. The former have so many irons in so many widely-dispersed fires that their time is always in short supply. I had, for instance, hoped to meet up with Per Temba (who was sirdar on the 1975 Everest Expedition and is now, among other things, a group leader with Mountain Travel) at his parents' house in Khumjung but this was not to be. In the seventeen days it took me to visit Khumbu and walk back to Katmandu, Per Temba had had a trip there, one to Pokhara, and had been to Delhi and to Bombay as well.

It is in the contrast and tension between the frantic entrepreneurial option and the cool, 'together' option but, it seems to me, the close similarity between Sherpas and Sahibs is located. There is no finer Sahib example of the entrepreneurial pole than Chris Bonington. At the time that the South-West Face of Everest suddenly became available he was already involved in the early planning stages of a live Eiger broadcast. Despite the massive inroads that they made upon his time, he kept both options open and eventually was faced with an agonising dilemma. Since they were scheduled to take place at the same time, he could not go on both of them. Clearly, Everest was the more important, yet its outcome was less certain and what is more the Eiger broadcast, unlike Everest, would go on with or without him. The prospect that, if he went to Everest, *somebody else* would cavort across the television screens of Europe was almost too much for him to bear, and it was only after he had tried, unsuccessfully, to have the Eiger programme rescheduled that he was forced to accept, grudgingly, that even he could not manage to be in two places at once.

This slightly malicious 'Bonington story' is just the sort of tale that would be relished by Pemba Tarkay. Indeed, it is very similar to those that he himself recounts about 'all those businessmen in Namche'. And, of course, British mountaineering too has its Pemba Tarkays—those little slit-eyed Mancunians who seem to spend their lives fishing and playing darts yet, somehow, always manage to be in the right place at the right time.

The Western climber who visits Nepal is likely to spend most of his time in the company of Sherpas who have taken up one or other of these two options and he may remain blissfully unaware of the existence of those who have chosen, or have been forced to accept, the third. Last year some Sherpas (on a 'safe' tourist trek not a 'dangerous' mountaineering expedition) were caught in a storm on the Thorong La—the pass that links Manang with Muktinath. The well-equipped clients and the well-equipped Sherpas survived but several of the local (non-Sherpa) porters, who had only cotton clothing and were carrying heavy loads, died. Some Americans also happened to be crossing the pass and they did all they could, and tried to get the Sherpas to help the exhausted porters. One porter who had collapsed in the snow had just been left there and they tried to persuade the Sherpas to go back up to help him. They refused, saying, "He is not a member of the party." This 'collective-survival' response—drawing a protective boundary line around 'Sherpas' or 'the party' and then saying to hell with anyone outside it—is typical of this third option. It is an option that more and more Sherpas are taking up. Why?

Like Hindu castes, the ever-proliferating trekking agencies too seem to have sorted themselves out into a hierarchy. At the bottom of the pile come the rip-off merchants in Pokhara who promise to organise a trek, ask for an advance to buy equipment and food, and then just disappear. At the top of the pile is Mountain Travel, closely followed by Annapurna Trekking, International Treks and Tours, Manaslu Trekking, Trans-Himalayan, and the Sherpa Cooperative. Between them, these firms take about 70 per cent of the market.

In Britain, it is the large and long-established organisations that tend to become stodgy and traditional whilst enterprise and innovation flourish among the upstart newcomers. In Nepal, it is the other way round. The agencies near the top of the pile, though their bread-and-butter is the lavishly-equipped and staffed standard tourist trek, also provided the much more varied, specialised, and demanding services required by television teams, ornithologists, rafters, botanists, canoeists, hang-gliders, and above all, mountaineers. It is in the optimistic, competitive, expensive, and initiative-encouraging milieu of these up-market organisations, with good rates of pay and handsome retainers for big-name Sherpas, that the Khumbu equivalent of Dick Whittington is most likely to be able to turn a blind eye to the daily preoccupations of the Hindu world. But increasingly the chances are that, arriving penniless in Katmandu, he will fetch up somewhere very different.

In the agencies lower down the hierarchy, costs are pared and a sirdar will be offered a fixed figure for the complete organisation of a trek—the unspoken assumption being that, if he can do it for less, he can pocket the difference. This is the start of the system of fiddles. Once the trekking agency gives tacit approval to the sirdar's 'legitimate perks' the same unmentioned principle works its way right through the system: the cook (second-in-command) gives a backhander to the sirdar, collects backhanders from the cookboys, and does a lucrative little deal with the various shopkeepers in return for false invoices. Porters, in return for employment, have to give a proportion of their wages back to the sirdar (the going rate in 1978 was whispered to be Rs 2 per porter per day—one eighth of his pay). The result is a facade within which cheery smiling Sherpas take all responsibility out of your hands, and an incredibly cumbersome and over-staffed *bandobast* totally dedicated (apparently) to the comfort of the Sahib and poised ready to satisfy his every whim. In fact, it is no such thing. It exists primarily to satisfy its own ends which, because they are defined entirely in terms of fiddles, have always to be kept hidden. As the managing director of one trekking agency said to me: "As long as the clients are well fed and are happy with the trek, and as long as we get our profit, then everything's fine." In such a setting, innovation becomes virtually impossible. Since, behind its obsequious facade, the whole system is stabilised by an elaborate framework of differentials – differential rights to fiddles – any tiny change that might seem desirable in the interest of economy or efficiency is almost certain to result, somewhere along the line, in someone's legitimate perk becoming too large or too small.

The Sherpas that the élite Western climber is likely to meet are of his own kind – big-name Sherpas or promising up-and-coming young lads retained by one of the specialist agencies. These are the Sherpas who have been able to take the big-risk and big-reward option and rise serenely above the restrictive social environment of Katmandu. But the naturalist, the fell-walker, the adventurous tourist, or the ordinary club climber, who after years of saving finally signs on for a package trek to Everest, will probably meet Sherpas who have taken the fiddles option: "Let us pamper you with legendary Sherpa hospitality and efficiency during your travels in the world's mightiest mountain range," pleads one trekking agency's brochure. If he is well fed and has good weather, if the scenery and the rigours of the journey match up to his expectations, and if the Sherpas keep smiling, he will leave Nepal a satisfied man. Only if he happens to be caught in a storm on a high pass may he get a glimpse of what lies behind that efficient, pampering, smiling facade. In that rare eventuality, his life's dream may well turn into a nightmare.

In substituting animate tourists for inanimate trade goods, the Sherpas have laid themselves open to an insidious variety of cultural imperialism. As tourism increases so, inevitably, most of that increase takes place towards the package end of the market. At the same time, mountaineers, who whatever else they may do to the Sherpas are at least prepared to meet them half-way, constitute a diminishing proportion of the total tourist flow; and anyway they are now tending to dispense with the services of Sherpas on the

17 Joe Tasker, Pete Boardman and Dick Renshaw at 26,000ft on the North East Ridge of Everest in 1982. The attempt ended in disaster. Renshaw retired ill, and Tasker and Boardman continued, never to return: they disappeared while attempting to pass the distant, mist-shrouded towers. *Photo: Chris Bonington*

18 19 20 21 Views of the West Ridge of Everest, first climbed in 1979 by a goslav expedition. The route took a direct line from the Lho La, crossing the 1963 American route and climbing the upper pyramid well to the right of the Horbein Couloir. Ice caves are used for the Lho La camp (as in the 1982 Spanish attempt – p left). The avalanche-threatened slopes of the West Shoulder (top centre) lead to asier angled slopes (left) and then the characteristic sloping terraces and cliffs of the final pyramid (above). *Photos: J. Altadill* (top left) *and Stane Belak*

22 23 24 25 The West Face of Makalu – four views taken during the three-man Anglo-Polish attempt in 1981. The climbers tackled the face in alpine-style, involving long periods of unroped climbing. They were defeated by sustained technical difficulties above 25,500ft on the upper headwall. *Photos: Alex MacIntyre*

26 27 28 Reinhold Messner's solo ascents of Nanga Parbat and Everest in 1980 and 1982, brought to a climax his long campaign to ascend the world's major peaks in the purest possible style. The photos show the camp on the Diamir Face and the summit of Nanga Parbat (this page) and approaching the summit of Everest (opposite page) to complete an ascent of the North Ridge – the route that defeated all the pre-war expeditions. Both climbs were made without oxygen.

29 K2 retains its reputation as a difficult mountain and many expeditions have been defeated on its ridges. American climbers, after a series of ill-fated attempts spanning forty years, finally climbed the mountain in 1978 by a route linking the North East Ridge (right) with the upper part of the Abruzzi Ridge (left).

30 Pete Boardman climbing old ladders in House's Chimney, on the Abruzzi Ridge, during an attempt in 1980. *Photo: Joe Tasker*

grounds of economy and mountaineering aesthetics. This is the awful paradox of mass tourism: the more we insist that a country and its inhabitants remain the same, the more we change them. The Khumbu of Shipton and of Hillary, like Wordsworth's Grasmere, now exists not as a place but only as a state of mind.

But Sahibs and Sherpas have always met one another in the mental, rather than the physical, Khumbu – that is why they are so similar:

> The mind that ocean where each kind
> Does straight its own resemblance find;
>
> (Andrew Marvell, *The Garden*)
>
> *from* MOUNTAIN 68 *1979*

Alpine Fleas

T. G. BONNEY

Mr. W. Mathews and myself, accompanied by Jean Baptiste Croz and his brother Michael Auguste (one of Mr. Tuckett's guides), arrived at Claude Giraud's auberge in Ville Val Louise on the evening of August 24. Unhappily it was Sunday, and the *Selle* was filled with peasants, who made those demoniacal noises by which hilarity is ordinarily expressed in the French Alps. Not easily shall I forget one gaunt old fellow, who, for an hour or two, kept up an almost incessant clamour, something like the howl of a broken-down foxhound troubled with asthma, and drove us to the verge of desperation. I suppose it was a song, but nothing could be inferred from the changeless expression of his face, except, perhaps, that his wine did not agree with him. The landlord, however, was very attentive, and his cuisine, for Dauphiné, commendable. Hunger appeased, we fled from the noise to the open air, and, looking up to the bright stars, were surprised to see, a little above the Great Bear, the pale misty light of a large comet. An hour or so passed pleasantly in watching and speculating on this unexpected sight, and then, rather loath, we turned into a long narrow room at the back of the house, in which were two beds. They *looked* inviting; but I draw a veil over the horrors of that night. I did think I knew something about fleas, but I found there were experiences beyond any that I had hitherto reached. Let me not, however, seem to take away the landlord's character. I am sure that he does his best to entertain travellers, but at present he has so few of the better class that he cannot afford to reserve a room for them. He told us that, not many days before, he had been obliged to let an "individu très-malpropre" occupy my bed, and that though, after the man's departure, he and his wife had had a 'chasse', and caught 'beaucoup de puces et de punaises', till they thought they had cleared the covers, some must have been left. From the anxiety he displayed to satisfy our wants, I believe that in a few years, with proper encouragement, he will make his auberge all that need be desired.

from OUTLINE SKETCHES IN THE HIGH ALPS OF
DAUPHINÉ *1865*

The Llanberis Movement

JOHN CLEARE AND ROBIN COLLOMB

The matutinal spirit of conventional rock-climbing, occasioned by a walk of an hour or two, sometimes more, to a high north-facing crag, vanished with the advent of Anglesey. Visitors get there at midday or early afternoon, when the sun is highest and the sea breezes are voluptuous. They merely have to stroll across grass bands for a few minutes to the cliff tops. However, in the heroic days (only five years ago!) the stroll was replaced by a scramble to beat other parties in the 'rat race' to collect new climbs. Open competition flourished between climbers on these cliffs. Subterfuge in passing on information, laying false trails, inventing non-existent routes on horrible pieces of rock were common ploys pressed into service by rival parties. One contestant held a pack at bay by clinging to the first pitch of a potential new route for three hours, moving slowly up and down 30ft. of rock, unable to get higher, until an overdue companion arrived to take up the lead. A performance reminiscent of Brown on Resolution (no, not the Llanberis one) deserves to be reported in a better set of circumstances. Though pundits in the Welsh school, championed in the publicity field by Ken Wilson who had focused attention on Anglesey in a blaze of photographic light, denounced such behaviour, it was accountable in most cases to and symptomatic of the dissipation ruling among an amorphous group of climbers living in the Llanberis district, or attributable to other climbers deeply influenced by association with the Llanberis movement. The extremes of conduct witnessed on these cliffs have no parallel in British climbing history. This disaffected group of people formed for the first time in a mountain area a commune of a type not unfamiliar nowadays in large cities with overcrowding and work problems, and young people rebelling against social order and the establishment. In their fundamental desire to escape from the claustrophobic cities, from nine-to-five jobs and attendant responsibilities, and live in the mountains, they became in time estranged by a veneer of poverty and aimless purpose in life from the surroundings they admired and wished to preserve.

Anglesey happened notably because the potential for big routes was drying up on Clogwyn du'r Arddu. This most famous of all post-war British climbing grounds had dominated ambitions of greater and lesser climbers for a long time. Technical achievements on the steep blank walls of Cloggy progressively reached new heights through the fifties and sixties, spurred on by the masterful performances of Joe Brown. Finally Cloggy became the only cliff in the country to have an entire book published about it. Some time before this event a lassitude in purpose had descended over elements in the Llanberis 'movement'. Climbers were heard complaining openly of boredom. They preferred the hard and insecure living of keeping up with competitors in some new trend or development with general recognition. Approval in this sense could be an example set by one climber. Following a fashion, sheep-like, and keeping in step with rapid changes as in pop music, are afflictions in modern mountaineering caused by closer alignment with normal society. In the mountains it is increasingly difficult to escape the subtle pressures that publicity and advertising exercise on attitudes and actions. In the psychiatrist's paradise of Llanberis and Deiniolen, development had become patchy, the consumption of beer rose in bars now commandeered and degraded by unruly climbers, and energies were expended in various unsavoury directions commonly pointing to a catch-phrase of the age; the permissive society. Previously, and on a much smaller scale, misfits in mountaineering had generally acted with stylish discretion but the scene now was thoroughly squalid. Drugs were circulating and the police were making inquiries about a multitude of misdemeanours and attempting to catch the culprits.

Against this disquieting background the sea cliffs of Anglesey entered the public domain with a loud fanfare of trumpets in 1966-67.

from SEA CLIFF CLIMBING IN BRITAIN *1973*

A large percentage of people met on climbs are quite normal.

Reflections of a Broken-Down Climber

WARREN HARDING

"Climbing would be a great, truly wonderful thing if it weren't for all that damn climbing." – John Ohrenschall

As I sit on the veranda of my quarters at T. M. Herbert's *Rock of Ages Home for Old Climbers*, enjoying my Graham crackers and warm milk, I think about the past eighteen years . . . my rise and fall as a rock-climber . . . what a fine person I used to be . . . where did I go wrong?

Finally I realise what's wrong with me . . . why I'm rather oblivious to many of the things around me. It's simply that I've spent too many nights and days dangling from Yosemite's granite walls. My once-keen analytical mind has become so dulled by endless hours of baking in the hot sun, thrashing about in tight chimneys, pulling at impossibly heavy loads, freezing my ass off on long, cold nights in various examples of the 'ideal bivouac gear', so that now my mental state is comparable to that of a Peruvian Indian, well stoked on coca leaves. . .

I've been at it too long . . . thought that when I'd cleverly run in front of a rapidly moving truck (September 1969) I'd be spared any further indignities (i.e. climbing). But my badly-smashed right leg recovered sufficiently to allow me to pursue this ridiculous activity.

A couple of years ago I had met a rather unsavoury character name of Dean 'Wizard' Caldwell (Wizard?). As our acquaintance dragged on, I discovered that we had much in common. For one thing we were both rather lazy . . . an important quality of the serious climber. We talked much of past glories and future plans. But for the most part didn't actually do anything. Grandiosity of our plans seemed to be directly proportional to the amount of booze we would consume at a sitting. One night, completely taken by Demon Rum, we decided we would climb El Capitan's Wall of the Early Morning Light . . . The Big Motha' Climb!

421

We knew it was quite safe to indulge in such talk since neither of us was capable of climbing anything . . . Dean had some badly torn ligaments, result of stumbling over a tree stump while walking to the potty room in Camp 12. My right leg was still pretty bad . . . weak knee would barely bend. Tried a new climb, east edge of Royal Arches, only got out about 40ft. We adopted the name of 'March of Dimes Climbing Team'.

Fall—beginning to get worried now . . . physical condition has sufficiently improved; we can stall no longer. Began carrying loads up to base camp; cloak of secrecy surrounding our activities . . . 'great hairy giants' were all around waiting to annihilate any trespassers on 'their route'. Fearfully Wizard and Batso skulked around the valley. Difficult to be discreet carrying things like 12 gallons of water, big sacks of food, bivy gear, six hauling bags and the like. Eventually got things sorted out and bagged up. Led and fixed the first two pitches.

Then, of course, the weather turned bad . . . sitting it out at Dave Hanna's place we were shocked to learn that the dreaded Royal Robbins had suddenly appeared in the valley . . . what now? Would he come charging up the wall . . . just plough us under? Desperately, we moved out.

Almost predictably, rain started falling as we reached top of the first pitch where our five hauling bags were hanging. . . So in mid-afternoon we set up our first bivouac. . . Bat tents with plastic tube tents over them. It soon became obvious that we had vastly under-estimated the time that this venture would take us. Fortunately we had also greatly *overestimated* the amount of food and water required for a day's sustenance. We had figured twelve days stretch-able to fifteen days. (Turned out to be 'stretchable' to twenty-six days).

End of second week . . . things looked different—very bad! We'd been on a rock wall longer than anybody else ever had (at least in Yosemite) . . . last two days in a wretched state of *soggification*. As the fifteenth day dragged on, still raining, we realised we were in a very critical position. We were only about halfway up . . . at the bottom of the Dihedrals, where our hopes of finding a good crack had come to nothing.

Our mental and physical condition had somewhat deteriorated

from the effects of the soaking rainstorm, the general wear and tear of bashing our way up 1,500ft. of the hardest climbing we'd ever experienced.

Dave Hanna and Pete Thompson came up to the base of the wall. . . Bull-horn voices from below informed us that the weather forecast was not very encouraging: clearing tomorrow, but another storm on its way. . .

We pondered the situation as the rain continued through the day and into the night. Realised it could take another ten days to go the rest of the way. Carefully inventoried the rest of our remaining food. We'd have to radically reduce our rations if we were to stretch them out to even come close to finishing the climb.

But the thought of giving up the climb seemed simply unacceptable. It wasn't at all hard for us to make up our minds to press on . . . somehow try to make it. Another factor . . . the thought of trying to descend the 1,500ft. of mostly overhanging wall with our gear made us retch!

Next morning we informed Dave and Pete of our decision to continue. They seemed to feel we were insane but. . .

Weather cleared . . . a day to get dried out and reorganised, then come to grips with the Dihedrals. Only took us five days to get up this delightful area . . . lots of A4 nailing, bolting, riveting up overhanging bulges. On about the twentieth day we heard unfamiliar shouts from below. The shouter identified himself as T. M. Herbert.

"Hi T.M. – Good to see ya! What're you up to?"

"We've come to rescue you!"

" . . . . . . Whaaaaat?"

About this time Dean (leading) noticed ropes being lowered over the rim about 800ft. above. A great deal of shouting ensued. Most of our – uh – 'rhetoric' would be unprintable in all but the most 'advanced' periodicals. We did make it quite clear that we were fine, had the situation well in hand, were not about to be rescued. Fortunately those in charge of the rescue operation elected to suspend the effort, thereby sparing everyone some rather bizarre scenes: rescuers landing on Timothy Tower to find 'exhausted' climbing team enjoying a fine mini-feast of salami, cheese, bread and an entire bottle of Cabernet Sauvignon (Christian Brothers, of course) all in a beautiful moonlit setting. Dialogue. Good evening!

What can we do for you?"

"We've come to rescue you!"

"Really? Come now, get hold of yourselves—have some wine. . ." The action could have gone anywhere from there . . . a quiet intelligent conversation with the would-be rescue team returning in the morning via their fixed ropes. Or had the rescue team been over-zealous, a wild insane piton hammer fight might have followed. For we were very determined not to be hauled off our climb. We'd put too damn much into it to give up now! The hard part was behind us.

We were still feeling quite strong in spite of being on very slim rations for the past week. Perhaps our minds were becoming a bit fuzzy, though . . . had dark, cloudy visions of the National Park Service being influenced by envious, money-hungry climbers who would like nothing better than to fill their pockets with $$$ while removing two clowns from a climb they didn't deserve to be on. The wall would remain (with all the hard work done) in a virginal state, awaiting a team of super climbers who could do it in real style. . .

So onward and upward!. . .

Finally there was Dean battling his way up what we hoped would be the last pitch. But as he came to the end of the climbing rope, still about 60ft. below the rim, the day too came to an end! Frustrating—disappointing to be so near and yet have to wait until the next day, but no use taking a chance of blowing it now. . .

Next morning I was totally unprepared for what I saw as I floundered up the last overhang onto the ledge at the rim . . . a veritable army of newsmen, friends, would-be rescuers (and a beautiful girl, Beryl Knauth). As I anchored myself to the ledge, I suddenly felt an overwhelming feeling of emotional release—sort of came 'unglued' for a moment. Pulling myself together, I joined the happy carnival atmosphere that prevailed at the summit: batteries of camera snouts trained on us, gorging ourselves on all the food and champagne! All sorts of friends and well-wishers, ecstatic kisses and embraces—what a marvellous little orgy! Only thing lacking was a Mexican mariachi band!

But if I could have foreseen what would happen in the next few months I might have been tempted to say, "Oh, screw it all!" and bail off the top—well not really! With all the bullshit there were a lot of good things.

But there were ominous cluckings from certain pious experts about the degenerative effect on climbing of all the publicity attendant on such a climb. It would tend to attract hoards of unworthy persons to the rock walls and mountains—got to reserve all this for us 'good guys'. Keep the masses out! Maintain the esoteric image of climbing, raise the standards, etc., etc. . .

It comes to mind that climbing is rather commercialised, certainly highly publicised, in Britain. Has this resulted in total deterioration of British climbers and climbing areas? It's my impression that it has not! Apparently Britain's relatively small climbing area is quite heavily used. Is the countryside becoming one huge garbage dump? I've been told by those who have been there that it definitely is not. Why? Could it be that the people, even though they are large in numbers, have come to know and love their mountains and desire to take care of them?

Elitists will argue that it is necessary to discourage the masses from mountain areas. No doubt this would work quite well in a feudal system where a small nobility had complete control of the peasantry. But such is not the case—theoretically, at least, this country operates as a democracy. . . All, worthy or not, have equal right to the public lands. Again, theoretically, the use and preservation of our mountain areas would seem to depend on the vote of the masses. How, then, can we expect the support of the average citizen in conservation if he is told the mountains are too good for him, that they should be reserved for a minority of self-styled 'good guys?'

Perhaps the hope of the 'Valley Christians' lies in some form of regimentation patterned after the meticulous system of climber control so magnificently conceived and employed by the Soviets. Apparently well-structured training programmes are carried out—screw-offs quickly weeded out!—examinations and ratings given, climbs assigned only to the properly qualified—everyone kept in his place!!

But this is digressing . . . back to what's important: climbing.

Why did we climb the Wall of the Early Morning Light as, how, and where we did? . . . I had always felt that the route should follow the right-leaning cracks in the lower section—traverse into the Dihedrals, then roughly straight up. This was not prompted by *Comician* ideals, but rather by some undefinable aesthetic attraction this particular area held for me. As with some other routes — Leaning Tower, Half Dome South Face — I was not concerned about how many bolts it might take. It was simply that it appealed to me and I wanted very much to climb it!

With the storms — three in all — food shortage, and, most significant of all, the rescue fiasco, the whole thing, reflected by the press, captured the imagination of the public. Oddly enough, the 'high adventure' magazines, *True, Argosy*, etc., showed only the mildest interest . . . maybe it was just a glorified flagpole-sitting exhibition after all.

But whatever it was (the real climbers knew!) there definitely was general interest. An exciting, fun-filled whirl-wind tour of public appearances followed our return to the valley. Fame and fortune were ours! — though I did seem to be getting quite a bit more of one than the other; like my share of the proceeds — $1,500 for four months' work. It didn't exactly seem like a 'get rich quick' scheme. Anyway, at least there was great professional satisfaction: I had advanced from my lowly status of unemployed construction worker to the enviable position of unemployed TV star!

The emotional and monetary aspects of something like the aftermath of the Wall of the Early Morning Light are little short of amazing! Whether they like it or not, the principals involved suddenly become a business organisation (or perhaps, a disorganisation!). Some personalities can change significantly, others don't. Warm friendship and camaraderie can be replaced by cold contempt and suspicion. Happy laughter can turn to nervous, polite chuckles.

But we all know each other better now . . . for whatever that's worth. I still believe that it's entirely possible to work with the various commercial aspects of climbing without destroying the flavour.

Do I really want to, though? What is this climbing trip all about, anyway? Does it really matter if a particular climb is done in any particular 'style?' Is there one 'true code of ethics' that is admirably suited to all climbers? There are those who profess to have the real answer. In other fields, so did Jesus Christ, Karl Marx and Adolf Hitler!

I have often been asked why I seldom, if ever, write my views on all this ethics business. In thinking about it, I realise I really don't give a damn. If all or most other climbers feel a need for the comfort and shelter of structured thinking—if there are those who feel a need to establish and promulgate these principles and lead the masses to a better 1984-ish life, fine with me! I still feel inclined to do my own thinking. As long as the VC don't get their own secret police and employ Spanish Inquisition methods, I won't worry about being imprisoned, stretched on a rack, forced to confess my sins, and then burned at the stake as a heretic. Rather, to the self-appointed Gurus, I say: Bugger off, baby, bugger off!!

As I observed earlier, I'm entirely fed up with all this crap about bolts, bat-hooks, press releases, commercialism, etc., etc. . . . . At a trade show in Chicago, Dean and I received the electrifying news (rumour?) that R. R. and Don Lauria had just completed the second ascent of the Wall of the Early Morning Light, and had chopped out all the bolts and rivets; all this in only six days!!

Naturally many people at the show asked our reaction to this. At

the time, the best we could come up with were weak little attempts at humour: "Oh, well—they're just faster than us. Chopping bolts? Whatever's fair, etc., etc."

But the questions still came, especially upon returning to Yosemite Valley.

"Well, Harding, how does this grab you? What do you think about the bolt-chopping thing?" Frankly, I hardly knew what to say, or think. For one thing, it didn't seem worthwhile to go to all the trouble of finding out what had really happened. . .

Still, some people thought that I should be concerned about all this—shocked, offended perhaps. Fact is, I don't give a rat's ass what Royal did with the route, or what he thought he accomplished by whatever it was he did. I guess my only interest in the matter would be the possibility of some clinical insight into the rather murky channels of R. R.'s mind.

Perhaps he is confusing climbing ethics with some fine (obscure?) point of prostitution morality . . . like, perhaps, a 100-bolt climb, e.g. Tis-sa-ack (or a $100-a-night call girl) is very proper; but a 300-bolt climb (or a $300-a-night call girl) is gross, immoral, or whatever. Or maybe Royal has gone the way of Carrie Nation—substituting hammer and chisel for hatchet! And then again, maybe it's got something to do with rivets—I don't know. In a way, I feel sorry for Royal (a veritable Alpine Elmer Gantry) with all these problems, bearing the responsibility of keeping rock-climbing the 'heavy', complex thing it must be. . . .(?)

Many years ago, when I first started climbing, it really seemed like fun. I truly enjoyed busting my ass trying to somehow get up something like Lost Arrow Chimney . . . or picking out a new route . . . but always feeling good about it. But suddenly it just seems like a drag. Maybe I should have stuck with sports car driving. . .

Perhaps this turned-off feeling will pass; the relaxed atmosphere in the foothill location of *Rock of Ages* is conducive to mending the soul. It's good to be in such fine company . . . Al Steck and Steve Roper sitting at a table playing checkers, mind and vision too dim to cope with the rigours of chess . . . Chuck Pratt wiling away the hours conducting some imaginary symphony orchestra. Truly beautiful to see Earth Mothers, Jan and Beryl, bustling about in their long pioneer gowns, looking after the old fellows. . .

The sun is slowly sinking, another day is drawing to a close. All the old climbers are putting away their toys and games, soon will be drifting off to their quarters to await the cheery call to dinner. Perhaps some of the more daring will have a small glass of Red Mountain.

I remain in my chair a bit longer—I try to probe further back through the years . . . before the Wall of the Early Morning Light . . . but it all seems like, "I've seen this movie before" . . . always the good guys vs. bad guys. Maybe I should have played cowboys and Indians; only trouble is, I'd surely have been an Indian!

from ASCENT *1971*

Brick-Edge Cruiser

ALEX MACINTYRE

"Going anywhere this summer?" enquired the brick-edge cruiser. A question well put. The whimpering white chalk haze which might just conceivably have been going somewhere this time hit the deck again.

"Dhaulagiri," said I.

"Where's that?" asked the youth, now revolving effortlessly around a finger nail before poising, purring.

Again, a good question. In Nepal judging by the postmark on the card. At least it had been when I first met it courtesy of the Reprint Society's rendering of Herzog's classic, *Annapurna*, via my Mum's bookshelf.

"Near Annapurna."

The instant look of non-recognition spoke for itself. I qualified the statement, broadened the base.

"In the Himalayas."

The lad switched into a perfect crucifix from opposing finger locks. Orgasmic eyes eyed bulging muscles until the pump gave. A neat one arm pull up landed him on the balcony. He looked down with disdain.

"Near Bolton is it?" he said, heading for the weights.

from MOUNTAIN 77 *1981*

True-Born Englishmen

CLAUD SCHUSTER

I turn now to four men who were still in their full vigour when I began to climb, Charles Wollaston, William Pickford (Lord Sterndale), Edward Davidson, and Edward Broome. To each I am indebted for many happy days and hours both in the Alps and at home. Of Charles Wollaston I have written elsewhere. Of each of the others I will try to preserve some traits which may have escaped their biographers in *The Alpine Journal*, distinguished as those biographers are. Broome was born in 1845, Pickford in 1848, Davidson in 1853. Broome died at Zermatt in 1920, Pickford and Davidson in the summer of 1923. They came of different stocks and had different upbringings and different outlooks on life. Except inasmuch as Pickford and Davidson were both barristers, both King's or Queen's Counsel and both Benchers of the Inner Temple, their careers lay widely apart, though towards the end association at the Bench and in the Parliament Chamber drew these two together and a common interest in the Alps and in the Alpine Club made a tie between the three. All three were men unusual in bodily powers, in strength of character, in powers of mind and of very striking physical appearance. Each might have been chosen by one who took pride in the Englishman, as a physical and a spiritual being to represent the race. If they could have been fused in one the resulting composite might have stood for all the world to mark the type.

I do not know where or when I first met Edward Broome. I am sure that, whenever it was, I was more than a little frightened of him. His portrait in *The Alpine Journal* hardly does him justice. He looks there too grave, too sedate, too trim. I like to think of him as tempestuous, animated, his eye twinkling with an amusement which denied the fury of his speech. To be with him was to be infected with his enthusiasm, carried away with the raciness of his talk, terrified by the probable audacity of his next speech or act. He was made for adventure, seeking ever new worlds to discover, to enjoy with his friends, to revel in. But his pleasure in action was not

430

the whole man. He had a vivid sense of style. He knew and loved English verse. And his habit, when he had worn out his guests with a long tramp over the Worcestershire hills, and they were drowsy round the fire, was to sit at the organ in his drawing-room and use his fine voice in music of the oratorio type. He was indeed an artist by temperament, with the appearance and the appetite of a conquistador, in the environment of a carpet manufacturer. Not that he despised his surroundings or his trade. When he came up to London and swept a friend off to lunch he was as pleased at a good morning spent in buying wool as if he had once more climbed the Marmolata from Alleghe. He loved the contest and the storm, the clash of will as much as the silent battle with nature.

He was said to be a difficult man, and his bursts of violent invective and his fine command of the more direct forms of English expression required a peculiar audience. But it was impossible to quarrel with him. The visions which abide are of Broome in a fine mist on some Welsh hill, or some Cornish moor, his beard dripping with rain, somewhat weary (for he was nearing his seventieth year) declaiming passionately in the manner and with much of the language of a Hebrew prophet on the stupidity of those who did not agree with him as to the way; or Broome, when he had passed that era, leading his party, in spite of protest, up one of the Lliwedd gullies over rocks slippery with wet; and perhaps still more characteristic (though I did not see it) of Broome returning from Switzerland in August 1914, turned out of his carriage to make room for French troops joining the colours, and whistling the Wacht am Rhein to show the independence of a free-born Englishman. But these angers and petulancies were of the moment. They melted by the evening fire. The man remained, and all through, his brain kept its quickness and resource. His marvellous performance on the Nordend at the age of sixty-six, his wonderful traverse of the Charmoz at seventy-four, were not undertaken on the spur of the moment. They had been thought out calmly in the preceding winters. Once too often at the last he matched himself against the mountain and that more desperate foe—old age. But even this final audacity followed deliberate reflection. He said good-bye to his friends before he started for his last journey gaily, but as one who would never see them any more. We laughed at his premonitions, while at the same time we counselled prudence. He laughed at us, not as despising the counsel, and went the way which he had chosen.

> The world may like, for all I care
> The gentler voice, the cooler head.

There was about Edward Broome a vital energy, a glow of courage, hope and affection which warmed and inspired and set him in the hearts of his friends beside that 'dear passionate Teucer.'

In the autumn of 1893, when I paid my first visit to Zermatt, Pickford was staying at the Monte Rosa and Davidson at the Riffelalp. The three of us, though all in separate parties, spent a stormy night that September in the Matterhorn hut. Fourteen years later I again met Pickford at Zermatt and going thence to Chamonix with him, celebrated with befitting pomp and revelry his farewell to the high Alps. Five years later again I made with Davidson an ascent of the Riffelhorn, which was his 250th, and my ninth. And the association thus begun and thus intermittently renewed in the Alps was maintained with both men, with Davidson in London, with Pickford on the Northern Circuit and in the work of the Courts, as well as in his perfect hospitality at King Sterndale and in long tramps in Derbyshire dales and Border straths.

Pickford was not a pioneer. Probably he never made a new ascent or a new route. His memory endures as a man to whom mountaineering, like other activities of life, served as a setting.

He died in an August vacation after a full day's exercise and in the apparent fulness of health and vigour. Those who had parted from him at the end of the previous sittings found it impossible to believe the news that he was dead. He was to many the embodiment of splendid manhood, the physical type of Englishman that we all delight in – tall, broad-shouldered, mighty in sinew, calm in manner, and with an unruffled serenity; he diffused a golden feeling of sunshine, not languorous but with something of the bite of those Alpine sunrisings and down-settings which he loved, or of those high dales in which he lived. But he was much more than this; fearless and clear-eyed as he was both in the greater and the lesser issues of life, neither shirking nor struggling, he possessed a strength and a sweetness which corresponded to his magnificent appearance.

He came of a tough northern stock whose roots struck deep into the commerce of England. The great wagons of his forebears battled over the windswept road from Manchester to Ashbourne, drawn by great horses; and the love of the horse and the dog and the open air remained with him until his death. As a boy he followed the hounds through those grim fastnesses, and in later life he learnt the dales anew, preserving, long after the allotted years of man, an exceptional eye for country and a firm love of walking for walking's sake. In early middle life he had been a keen and a successful mountaineer. His great weight, and perhaps a due sense of the proportionate values of things, forbade him to attain to the very first rank. But he was a master of the craft as it was practised in his time, steady on snow or ice, and sure-footed on rocks to a degree surprising in so big a man. No wiser, no more considerate companion ever girt on a rope; no one knew so well how to make cheerful the gloomy hours of apprehension that precede or the glorious hours of fruition that follow a great expedition.

Edward Davidson was of Scottish extraction, though of English birth. He was educated at Balliol, where he took a first in Natural Science, and was called to the Bar in 1879. He must early have attracted the attention of those whose attention was worth attracting, for from 1881 he, according to his own account, "assisted the Law Officers in their official work," which means, I think, that he devilled for Herschell. He must have been an ideal devil. His handwriting was beautiful. He arranged facts logically and stated them clearly. He was most laborious, most careful, and his mind seemed to take delight in the drudgery of detail. He had a retentive and accurate memory. He possessed in addition an outward appearance which is not often found in combination with these qualities. His features were regular, his movements those of a natural athlete and his manners correct and, when he chose, charming – a certain stiffness and reserve being relieved on occasion by an engaging smile. Thus endowed he speedily made way. He became a master in the procedure of the Attorney General's Office and a high priest of the mysteries alike of an English Information and of a *Nolle Prosequi*. He was appointed Junior Counsel to the Board of Trade in Bankruptcy, and then in Company matters. When Sir Farrer Herschell became Lord Chancellor on the formation of Mr. Gladstone's short administration in

1886, he appointed Davidson to be his Secretary of Commissions. And in the same year Davidson accepted the position of Legal Adviser to the Foreign Office, which he was destined to occupy for thirty-two years.

As he was in his official life, so was Davidson as a mountaineer. He began early, but not early enough to belong to the first generation. He devoted his great physical powers to the accomplishment of great expeditions. Being possessed of exceptional sureness of foot and exceptional powers of endurance, he was soon recognised as one of the leading amateurs of his time. He gave great attention to the preparations for his expeditions, both by training his body and by exercising his mind. Everything was thought out beforehand and recorded afterwards, and the smallest deviation from accuracy in any contemporary reference to his exploits or to any mountaineering event in which he took an interest provoked a correspondence which was saved from weariness by his abundant knowledge, by the lucidity and directness of his style and by the elegance of his script. Such a man, so circumstanced, is subject to the temptation of becoming a little rigid, touchy or pedantic; and Davidson did not wholly escape these censures. He had an imperial air and he did not make friends easily. But to those whom he chose as friends he was generous and loyal. His climbing partnerships survived until they were broken by death. His courtesy to those who were younger than himself never dropped into condescension. And when, in later life, he realised the high esteem and indeed affection in which he was held in the Alpine world, he enlarged his circle and became a most encouraging adviser and most genial companion.

My last sight of him in the Alps was at Zermatt in the August of 1912. He had not completed his sixtieth year, and his appearance gave no indication of the advance of age. I was, however, surprised and distressed at the slowness of his pace on the path up to the Riffelalp. A few days later we ascended the Riffelhorn in a large and imposing company of amateurs and guides. We took the route straight up from the lake. Davidson climbed somewhat slowly, though with complete confidence. But, looking at him, and observing the way in which the guides looked at him, I became a little uneasy at the thought of the descent. The sky-line route, chosen for the purpose, is easy enough. But the frequent passage of nailed boots have polished the rocks like glass and a slip by an unroped man might be fatal. Someone produced a rope from the recesses of a sack and suggested its application as a matter of course. Davidson rejected the idea with contumely. An absurd discussion ensued in which every argument for its use, except the true one, was put forward and refuted. At last someone whispered to Davidson that the rope was really required for the sake of ***, whose feelings would be hurt if this were mentioned openly. Then he consented and we descended. I hope and believe that to his last hour he remained unaware of the pious fraud.

Such are the foibles of the great. They did not diminish our feeling for him while he lived, or our sense, when the end came, that there had gone from us one of the best men who ever put on a rope or debated a vexed question of Alpine topography.

from MEN, WOMEN AND MOUNTAINS *1931*

Pratt

PAT AMENT

Tom Higgins and I are at the base of El Cap, set on doing a 400ft. exfoliation crack called The Slack, a Chuck Pratt masterpiece. This will be a vendetta climb, since we have failed on it before.

After two rope lengths, the flaring section of the crack is in sight. Memories of previous vain motions flash back at us.

It can't be that hard. Pratt did it years ago . . . on first try. Bridwell hauling me up it my first attempt at it. Oh well, Chuck hauled Robbins.

I lead. Pratt. Plastic Man . . . or Poe. I grunt and gasp, swing into a layback . . . Kor on the Bastille Crack . . . I mantel on a ledge above the crux. Higgins follows. Following this one is just as hard. Having the rope in front of you is tricky. You can grab it. Sometimes coming second is harder than leading. You don't have the adrenalin flowing. You have to match the leader's show, but Tom makes it, and we shake hands, grinning at each other as if we hadn't seen each other for awhile.

"I'm tired of being social director of Camp 4," I hear Pratt say to someone pestering him for information. I see Pratt juggling wine bottles at Church Bowl, the clearing east of the lodge. Royal tells tales of Pratt's bouldering drunk, in the dark, in army boots, nobody able to come close. Descriptions of Pratt: a "tragic figure . . ." or ". . . born in the wrong time . . .," yet no climber is more respected or liked in Yosemite. Inimitable, enigmatic. He is hard to figure out and doesn't want to be figured out. "Actions speak for themselves," he says. We hike in the night in the Valley floor. On climbs such as The Slack, one is able to sense the workings of Pratt's mind.

Divergence of contemporary judgments on him. With those he loves, who see him in repose, he is gentle, affectionate, and obliging. He is devoted. Others, who happen to meet him in moments of excitement, find him irritable, arrogant, self-centred, sombre, rebellious and go as far as to accuse him of lack of principle or conscience.

His sensitiveness to the beauty and purity to be found in nature, his writing, an account of the South Face of Mount Watkins . . . The View From Deadhorse Point . . . At times, one gets the feeling that Pratt's imagination has taken him away from this earth and the material world into a lonely, personal flight to meditate on ultimate cause and a last climb.

His silence, for some, throws a sullen cloud over his disposition. But, he is truly modest. A cat inclined to fits of laughter, to party, or to vanish for weeks. A weird and wily storyteller . . . "Nothing worse than a hungry bear," he says. He walks wires. He has nightmares. A soul afflicted with a susceptibility to the effects of beer. The attraction toward it, he does not resist. I have memories of delirious shouts in the Yosemite dark . . . shouts coming from a short, bald-headed man with a beard.

Fighting to keep his genius clear, to reveal the elements that give the true depth and intensity to the total sheen or dismal glow. . .

He is a soul with feverish dreams to which he applies a faculty of shaping plausible fabrics out of impalpable materials, with objectivity and spontaneity.

He takes, in my mind, a prominent place among universally great men.

Our first big climb together: the North Wall of Sentinel Rock, Pratt's eleventh time up the 1,600ft. face, my second. As he begins the overhang, the fourth pitch of the route, I hear him say softly to himself, "Grown men." We finish the sixteenth pitch in a light, blessing rain.

from SWARAMANDAL *1973*

A Superiority Complex

E. L. STRUTT

We yield to no one in admiration for the German overseas parties led by Rickmers, Bauer, Borchers, Merkl, and others. The modesty of these parties have been excelled only by their skill; moreover — to quote this *Journal* — "They have left invariably the best possible impressions behind them," in the regions explored and visited. But for the present-day German mountaineer in the Alps, wonder replaces admiration. There is no lack of skill — on rocks at any rate — but judgment and even an elementary knowledge of the ethics of mountaineering are often conspicuously absent. In these pages it has been too frequently our task to relate some unjustifiable exploit and, in the same number, to record the inevitable disaster accruing to the perpetrator. While regretting the folly of it all, we mourn the loss of promising lives.

So much for the actors; but for those apostles appointed as propagandists and chroniclers, not to say financiers, of youthful German scrambling, our feelings are very different. The symptoms of disease existing in the German press show no signs of diminution. The most recent and unhealthy example will be found in the D. & Œ.A.V. *Mitteilungen* of June last. Depressed conditions and morale may warrant the statement that ". . . Our [German] mountaineers have in recent times been successful beyond compare . . ."; but with the immediately following sentence — "their exploits, contrasted with those of other nations, stand without question on an overwhelming pinnacle . . ." — is not merely self-glorification carried to an absurd pitch, but is also far beyond the bounds of actual fact. We brush aside the question of good taste.

After remarking that other mountaineers, "notably English and

Swiss," had completed the exploration of the Alps "by the easiest routes," the article goes on to state: ". . . For instance, allusion need only be made to the first conquests of the most difficult rock and ice walls in Valais, to the first ascents of great faces and ridges in the Oberland, and of similar performances on the more famous Mont Blanc arêtes – all accomplished by German parties. Also by winter and ski explorations our nationals have a large share in the conquest of the great glaciers of the Western Alps, for there, in the nineteenth century, they accomplished the first high ski tours and are in consequence without doubt the first [sic] pioneers of high altitude ski-running."

By statements such as these the writer displays his complete ignorance of the rudiments of Alpine History. He quotes the eastern face of the Monte Rosa massif as an example, but the Dufourspitze was first climbed by a non-German caravan, while the first guideless party was Austrian. The first ascent of the Nordend was by an Italian party and, as regards the Signalkuppe, its conquerors were French. The first winter ascent of the Matterhorn was by an Italian, of the Dom by a party containing no German components, while the remaining great peaks fell, almost without exception, to the Swiss. Excepting the unjustifiable but wonderful conquest of the Matterhorn's North Face and foolish variations of the Dent d'Hérens and Dent Blanche by guideless if misguided amateurs, Germany, in Valais, has played the smallest part.

Let us turn to the Oberland. The northern faces of Finster-aarhorn, the Fiescherwand, Eiger, Mönch, and Jungfrau fell to Swiss parties, the Scheidegg face of Wetterhorn to another nationality; the northern slopes of Lauterbrunnen-Breithorn, Breit-lauihorn and the reasonable North Face route of Grosshorn, again were conquered by Swiss, while the great passes overhanging Lauterbrunnen – nearly as high and quite as difficult as their adjacent peaks – fell, mostly in early times, to pioneer parties of quite another origin. The same is the case with the most famous ridges of Gspaltenhorn, Schreckhorn and Lauteraarhorn and, we need only add, an Austrian party stormed the South Face of Bietschhorn. As for winter work, to save tedium, we will but quote Schreckhorn, Mönch, and Jungfrau by an American long before the days of either ski or lifts.

Now for Mont Blanc: the intermediate routes from the Col de

Bionnassay to the Col de la Brenva did not fall to Germans, save for the tiny portion between the Col de Péteret and the head of the Couloir Eccles. The North Face of the Aiguille de Géant was conquered by Austrians and, since we should quote like the *Mitteilungen*, none but 1919-1933 'new atrocities', these have been the deeds of French, Swiss, and Italian parties. One other nation has played a part and that nation is certainly not Germany. At the risk of being as fulsome as our contemporary, we will add that Mont Blanc was first conquered in winter by a lady who acquired by her subsequent marriage French nationality, while the Aiguille Verte surrendered to a Swiss mountaineer. But the Péteret peaks *did* fall in winter to a worthy German party—one pebble on the beach.

Our contemporary's knowledge does not extend apparently to the Bernina—where a solitary peak rewarded a (much-beguided) German—or to the Graians and Dauphiné. In the latter's history Austria has played a small but brilliant part; America the greatest of all. Its winter history belongs to France alone, a befitting fate for perhaps the finest of all Alpine ranges. As claimed in the *Mitteilungen*, the Caucasian Ushba may or may not be a 'German' mountain, but its North Peak, now considered the highest, was scaled long before the earliest German visits.

Enough: sufficient has been said to refute the *Mitteilungen's* all-embracing claims. We need not appeal to Alaska, Canada, New Zealand or Kenya-Ruwenzori. German mountaineers need no such 'artificial aids' to enhance their fame, far less to boost their present courage. But one more specimen of propaganda must be exhibited as demonstrating the last word in unconscious humour: ". . . It is an ancient English custom to climb in the Alps with professional guides; the German mountaineer finds as a rule his own way, he cuts his own steps and trudges through deep snow relying on his own steam. Owing to these traditions we are still more prepared than the English for the struggle with the eight-thousanders. . ." Yet, in the struggle for the said eight-thousander *peaks*, German mountaineers have not hesitated—in some cases ruthlessly—to avail themselves of the devoted services of British Empire porters to "trudge through deep snow" carrying superhuman loads, for the glory of another country than their own.

This is what the nation that has played some part in mountaineering history, that was the pioneer of guideless climbing, that despises gladiatorial displays, but that still possesses some sense of proportion and of the ludicrous, is called upon to smile at but endure!

from THE ALPINE JOURNAL *1935*

Ross Talks . . .

PAUL ROSS*

What are your feelings about interviews? This seems to be the standard question to begin one.

There is little flattering about being interviewed, but it gives you a chance to piss people off, and that's good for the climbing world. I do feel that there's a tendency in interviews and in British climbing to disregard what really happened in the past. I don't want to be one of these old fogies talking about the past, but the past is the future because people keep bringing it up. They say, "He did this, we did that," but they often overlook something by seeing it through modern eyes. For instance, in my day people used to solo routes, but it's forgotten when a route is soloed now. People seem to be bringing in all these 'new eras' without knowing exactly what came before.

You have often been criticised for your over-use of pegs. Do you feel, in light of what you've just said, that perhaps some of your routes can be done with a feeling of greater security today, using modern protection, than you had, using pegs?

As far as security is concerned, it's relative.
Obviously you can't kill yourself now unless you're an asshole, or unless you do something wrong. I do things wrong now and again and nearly kill myself. There's so much protection now. But if you'd thought that in twenty years' time the Editor of *Mountain* was going to play hell with ya, you wouldn't have done some routes with pegs, they would have been done without.

---

*Responding to questions from the Editor of the Leeds University M.C. Journal.

How was it that you began climbing?

Well, I was sixteen and gripped up about birds, eggs, nests, and stuff. I was born in Gateshead, a really scruffy city, and lived there till I was twelve. When I came out to the Lake District, stuff like Skiddaw looked like Everest. A bloke took me up Castle Head when I was eleven, a little bump of rock, about a ten-minute walk, and I was really gripped. Eventually I made that, and thought one of these days I'll be able to climb Skiddaw. Coming from the city, that's the way I felt, but when you think about it no guy from the country can climb usually.

Were you in a gang in Gateshead?

Yes, we called ourselves the Windsor Avenue Gang. We were a small gang and relied on agility to escape. If you went out of your area, you got chased all over the place. The way our gang stabilised itself against these other groups was to evolve superior weapons. The one lethal one we developed was made with darning needles. We'd stuff them down split canes and leave about four inches of needle sticking out, then tape it and fire it from bows. When the other gangs found out we had these lethal weapons, they never bothered us. None were ever fired in anger, though, which is just as well.

Who did you start climbing with? Did you start your own club?

Well, as I was saying, me and these other guys got gripped up about birds' nests. We heard that jackdaws nest on Shepherds Crag, so we thought we'd go and try to get at them. Four of us went down there one day, walked up to the cliff and saw all these nail marks on Brown Slabs. We thought, "we'll wander up here," and we went up one after the other. As one took his foot off the other put his hand on and the four of us went up it like that. There were some old blokes on the left, Fell and Frock people, and they played holy shit with us! We didn't know what they were talking about, and we thought, "this is great," so we all climbed back down again one after the other. We went looking for other marks and found some more on Little Chamonix. They went up Little Chamonix and forked into 'Crescendo' and I went and finished up Little Chamonix. Within a week I was really gripped with rock-climbing.

When was this?

This was in 1953. I started asking around, George Fisher and
people like that, whether I could join a mountaineering club and go
rock-climbing, but like anybody else, they were into their own
climbing at the time, so I bought a rope off George. It was six years
old, like a dead mouse. You didn't think about a rope breaking or
anything. As long as it was long and looked like one, it was near
enough. We bought a guide book and the four of us would tie onto
this 120ft. rope. The others wouldn't lead, so I did all the leading,
but your second was usually climbing with you at the same time.
You'd only be able to go about 30ft. and the only way we knew
how to belay was to tie an overhand knot and put it over a spike. If
you didn't come up with a spike, that was it. "Okay, Frank, start
climbing" and off he'd go. Eventually you'd reach a ledge and get
a belay on, but by that time the last guy had no rope at all. We used
to sack haul. We never dreamt of leaving our sacks at the bottom,
and we would sack haul our army framed packs up through V.
Diff. chimneys and the last guy would end up with these four
packs, clinging onto a little ledge. It was always Frank, and we'd
shout down, "we're going to leave ya," after we'd hauled up the
sacks. Half the time we never belayed. I fell off once with a big
block and hit the ground. My partner was belaying without a spike
and he just let go of the rope when it started burning.

*When did your climbing become more than just a thing to do,
something for its own sake?*

Well, I think everyone starts off with a hero. I had a hero called
Günther Franz. He was Austrian, and I admired him because he
was the best climber in the area at that time. He worked felling trees
and was apparently the strongest guy who had ever worked in the
forestry, really big. I thought that if you worked felling trees it
would make you strong for climbing, so really liking climbing, and
doing things by impulse as I always have, I dropped out of school
and went to work in the woods. Günther was the first person to
actually take me climbing, but I hadn't been there long before he
went to work for the Outward Bound. A couple of months later he
was chopped on Central Buttress. I was so mad with the rock for
killing my hero, that I became obsessed, and was determined to

solo Central Buttress twenty-three times, whatever his age was. Of course I never did. I did the climb several times, though not in anger. I'd become more proficient by then. At first, though, I wanted to smash it. You get like that when you're sixteen.

Is it true that in your youth you were devoutly religious to the extent that you prayed before you did a hard climb?

Oh, sure. That was a tremendous help. Every time you got to a crux, you didn't have just yourself to rely on. You just said a quick five Hail Marys and off you went, you never thought twice.

When was it that you began to do new routes?

Actually, the first person ever to take me up a VS, the big breakthrough then, was Mike Thompson. That was Innominate Crack and I went back and led it quite reasonably. Then some lads in Keswick told me they were trying to get up a route on Black Crag and failing. So I went along, I was seventeen then, and got up it. That was Super Direct on Troutdale Pinnacle. That was my first new route and I liked the idea of new routes from then on. They're much more interesting. The thing about routes which other people have done is that you're obliged to do them, because if they can do them, so can you. At that time I was climbing well, so it didn't matter who they were, they had arms and legs the same as me.

But weren't you in an isolated area, and one of the few climbers in that area?

I knew that if I wanted to bother my ass to go to Wales, I could get up the routes at that time. When I climbed with Whillans I realised he was just a regular climber, I mean, he's tremendous as a rock-climber, but the odd times I climbed with him I saw he was completely human. He got gripped, and backed off things, which was absolutely dreadful. I could see that he was human, and if that's supposed to be the best in Wales I knew that whatever he had done I could get up without a shadow of a doubt AT THAT TIME.

Nobody can prove this wrong because I'm too old now. But I'm quite convinced that if I gave up smoking and drinking and started doing press-ups and drinking orange juice, I still could, but who wants to give up all that shit?

You still do OK, it seems to me . . .

Well, when I push myself now, it's because I've never backed off a climb in my own mind. It's quite possible that someone could say, "OK go do that one," and I wouldn't be able to get up it . . . unless they gave me an enormous amount of money, then I'd really start doing press-ups and orange juice tricks. I haven't done that yet, but one day I'm going to have to just to get up V. Diff's!

Let's go back to the good old days. When was your next breakthrough in climbing?

I was eighteen at the time and had just done CB. I'd done one or two new routes, Cenotaph on Kern Knotts in one run out without any protection, etc. A guy I was knocking around with called Robin Scott introduced me to Peter Greenwood, who at the time was considered the best climber in the Lakes. The following weekend we went out and did the fifth ascent of Do Not and I led through and found it easy. I thought that was a fluke because it was considered the hardest climb in the Lakes after Kipling Groove. We did that the following day, and I didn't ask to lead through because I'd thought it a fluke when I found Do Not easy. So Greenwood led me up that and I came down and was so elated that I'd found it easy, that I set off up the ledges to solo it. Greenwood shouted at me, "where are you going?" and I said, "I'd like to solo it." "Come back down," he said. I daren't disobey him, because he had a big heavy group. "What's up?" I said. "That's Arthur's route and if you solo it, you'll ruin it." So that was that. He had a tremendous respect for Dolphin.

Was Dolphin still alive at the time?

No, he'd been killed about a year before. I think Greenwood climbed better than Dolphin. He did the second ascent of Deer Bield Buttress in the rain, the third ascent of KG without the peg, he led the crux pitch of Hell's Groove, he led the crux pitch of Sword of Damocles, and these are Dolphin's top routes. Well, Greenwood told me to come down and I didn't question it at all. I didn't understand that sort of thing but I didn't have any intellect. I still haven't any now.

Was it a shock to discover that climbing had rules?

Possibly, this sort of surprised me. Greenwood confessed to me,
"I don't give a damn about you killing yourself, but I don't want
you to screw Arthur's routes up."

How did you get on with him after that?

Greenwood and I teamed up. He was a complete climbing bum.
We were climbing in black gym shoes at this time which we bought
at Woolworths for half a crown. We pottered around and did new
routes and it was much more interesting than doing the stuff that
was already there. We did Hell's Groove with incredible hangovers,
but it wasn't interesting. New routes were more challenging, as they
say in America.

*Were you aware while you were climbing in Britain that you would
end up with a bad name?*

Of my eighty new routes in Britain, what they criticise is about
three of them. The Horror for one, and bloody If. We did If as a
totally provocative route, up an incredible piece of rock. I find it
very rewarding to climb the most impressive part of the cliff, like
the Ghost on Cannon Mountain which goes up these big white,
smooth, smooth, smooth streaks coming down an immense gap of
rock between 'lines', and it was the same with If. Greenwood
provoked me into it. I got Geoff Oliver interested in turn and he
tried it twice before I did it. He was a little bit that way, trying to
provoke people, but he never pulled it off, he was a nice guy.

*What would you say were the best rock climbs you did in Britain,
the ones which made you feel your climbing was at a peak?*

At the time, I don't think I realised anything was particularly
outstanding. I'd have hard times on some climbs which stood out in
my mind. I had a little trouble getting up Post Mortem. Whillans
and Greenwood had tried it the previous week and Whillans fell off
it. Greenwood told me about this really good line, then Lockey and
I went up and did it. We had quite a lot of trouble on that. Post
Mortem's not one of the routes they complain about. When we did
new routes in those days we weren't thinking about what some
assholes and the professional writers would be saying about these

routes in ten or twenty years' time. We were just enjoying ourselves. People told us that Falcon Crag would never be climbed on again because it was a rotten cliff and whoever would want to climb there? We climbed there for fun, we never dreamt that people would complain about the 'ethics' of these routes later. At that time, any peg we put in, we'd mention whether it did us any good or not, any runner or peg. You had to mention everything and there wasn't any great onus the way there is today that leads to cheating and omissions. We were doing a lot of these climbs with tremendous hangovers. On Bludgeon it started to rain on the top pitch. I thought, screw it, I'll just get up the thing, and you never thought what people would say later.

You were in a group called the Crag Rats weren't you?

Yes. That's the term the Borrowdale farmers used to describe climbers. They thought we were all crazy buggers and we did some crazy things. None of the guys in the forestry where I worked thought I'd live past thirty. Most of us drove motor bikes. . .

Did you ever have the horrendous crashes, so famous in climbing lore?

Many times. My finest crash was in Langdale. I had an incredible bike, no front brake and screwed up looking but it would do a 100 miles an hour. I managed to hit a flock of sheep whilst doing 70 with a girl on the back. The farmer claimed the girl killed one of the sheep as she flew through the air. That seems a bit exaggerated, but he stuck to it in court. That was a tremendous crash and my last. So many people seemed to be getting killed at that time in car crashes and motor-cycle accidents that it seemed a very unhonourable way to die. I mean, anybody can do it on a motor bike, so I thought I'd get rid of mine.

Bikes and climbing were variations on the same theme, then?

Yes, at the time they were. Greenwood drove one. I admire him. He's a guy who just stopped climbing and took off into business. Greenwood was a great climber. As I said, I reckon Greenwood was better than Dolphin. The thing is, Greenwood was a bad guy, like Allan what do you call him, can't do anything wrong. It doesn't matter how many pitons they use or how much cheating they do. A good guy will always beat a bad guy at climbing no matter how good the bad guy is! Greenwood was a bad guy. They called me the climbing teddyboy and he was a bit like that. If you look into the history of climbing in the Lakes and see how Dolphin did his routes . . . I'm not saying that Dolphin wasn't a good climber, he was a great climber, but Greenwood was better. Look at KG which Dolphin top-roped: Greenwood did the third ascent and missed out the peg. He didn't knock in a peg like Brown did. That was a really shitty thing in those days, to knock in a peg on a route like that whether it had been done top roped or not beforehand.

They say Brown did it in very bad conditions . . .

That's just a bloody folk tale. You wouldn't go on a route that was supposed to be the hardest in the Lakes in bad conditions. I never heard he did it in bad conditions. The thing is, Brown can't do anything wrong 'cause he's one of the good guys. But he's obviously a tremendous climber.

In British climbing what made the good guys and what made the bad guys? Was it just the limelight and the undercurrent?

Quite frankly, I don't know . . . The good guys are the ones who went fishing, and the bad guys are the ones who went dancing. Brown didn't like dancing much so he went fishing. A nice, quiet sort of guy, and what can you say about a guy who goes fishing. Now Whillans, he was almost as good a dancer as I was (that will piss him off). Whillans thought he was the best rock 'n' roller. We had many a good dance together. Actually we used to practise together. We'd do these throws and things which the women wouldn't do, and nearly killed ourselves. We always thought we'd meet a woman one day who would do throws. It was more dangerous than climbing. Whillans wasn't a bad dancer come to think of it. He was a much better dancer then, than he was a climber.

You've climbed with another controversial figure, Chris Bonington, I believe.

I first met Bonington on the Bonatti pillar. He was in the army at the time. I don't know whether Bonington is a good guy or not. He's something else. The only thing that keeps him totally from being a good guy is his commercialism; I admire his business savvy. He's the only one in Britain apart from those who own equipment shops who makes a living out of climbing.

You've done a fair amount in the Alps

Well, I went out there six times if that's what you mean. I did the Bonatti in my second season. I had to be persuaded to go out there the first time, but I really liked it when I got there. I was nineteen my first season. I hadn't a clue about the Alps. I met Morty Smith out there and we got together to do the West Face of the Dru. I had a pair of Timpson boots, an army camouflage parka and a pair of school trousers I'd made into breeches. We got above the Fissure Vignes and a big storm came which killed about twenty people. We had a bit of an horrendous time. I'd read about the West Face in a book and thought that that was the Alps. We had stonefall in the couloir every ten minutes and we didn't have any hard hats. I thought that was just part of the game. It would frighten me to death now.

Moving from escapes from death to the pursuit of happiness, what do you think of the comment in Mountain 30 which implies that the British still hold the edge over the Americans on the social scene?

Perhaps, but I really think its been on the decline since the early 60's. The Padarn is probably the best they have left and that's O.K. only as long as its the boys you're after. The American scene is quite the reverse, thank goodness.

Seems Mountain needs either a special gossip editor or a team to hunt down errata! That stuff about Barber learning how to drink when he went to England is about the same as saying Jonah taught the Whale to swim.

What are your feelings about other climbing literature, autobiographies, the twenty-years-after sort of thing?

Twenty years after. What a good title. There's only one climbing book left to be written and that's the climbing book where you tell all. What will eventually happen is that some climbers will become so very, very good, that people will threaten to bring out books about them. The only books that will sell will be exposés.

Portnoy's Complaints in climbing? Do you think it will become that decadent?

Except for the writing, it's past it. It's already been there. To try to give this a modicum of seriousness, don't you feel that those who harp on ethics in climbing often try to set up their local heroes as crusaders, and the black knights of the surrounding kingdoms are immediately suspect, decadent, or bad guys as you might say?

That's just the point. These people are the 'clean up' men of climbing. It's like the curb on pornography. They'll let it go just so far without letting it get out of hand.

Do you think that climbing with Americans and in America has changed any of your ideas about climbing?

It's really the reason I came to America, it broadened my outlook. At first it gave me a liberation. Climbing was just in a beginning stage in this area [New Hampshire]. I don't think I've changed my attitudes, though. People seemed to climb here for fun rather than competition, at least not a noticeable competition compared to what I was used to.

It was a joke here?

Yes, but in the past year-and-a-half it's accelerated. When I first came here it was much like Borrowdale twenty years ago, an unthreatened area, with scope, and only a few people doing new routes, so you could say, "We'll do them tomorrow." The people here were the same "do them tomorrow." There was no one to come and rip your routes off.

But you and Joe Cote had a race not so long ago. You did a route called "The British are coming," and Joe named his "Don't fire till you see the whites of their eyes"

Get this right. Joe jumared up my ropes to finish his route! That was the summit of developing competition between us. It got to such a stage by pure accident. We were racing each other up for a particular groove. The summit in this case was stacked-up beer cans. This was our big showdown. We were going up the cliff side by side passing beer to one another. Joe would get a little ahead and manage to get across with a beer for me. Then he'd weaken a bit and I'd make any excuse and get ahead. The outcome was unimportant, competition can go on which stimulates climbing. In a way it's an extension of which I was saying about the liberation in climbing here. Most British climbers don't consider themselves purists when it comes to drink. It's a sort of a British 'tradition' (I suppose that will make people cringe). As soon as a British climber arrives here, people think, "Here's a good climber who can really drink." I don't think they still do. You get drunk odd times and go climbing, but to actually take drink up on a climb is one better.

On big walls it's got to be different!

I disagree. In Yosemite you've got more luxuries than you have in any other mountain area in the world. You drive up to El Cap in your car, get out your roast turkey and your beer, and Coca Cola for those who don't drink, and stuff it all in big bags. It's going to knock the hell out of your hauling, but when you get on the ledges, it's great.

Is this what the American civilisation has to offer? We are naturally a 'Take-Out' nation, that is, we don't have pubs. Buying your beer at the corner store and taking it home, I suppose it's an obvious extension to take beer to the cliff as part of your daily routine

That's about it, but it's something new. The British climber never conceived of this.

What would happen to all the good guys in England if you loaded them on a boat, say the Mayflower? . . .

That's the only boat they'd get on mind. . .

Landing in Yosemite? . . .

If you could reverse history, you'd have got all of them on the Mayflower and look what they've done to this country with their ethical ways. . . What were you saying about a boat load?

If they'd gone to Yosemite? . . .

Oh, right. I always think for those guys the actual driving of a piton would be far too sexual for them. That's the main problem really with them lads. They couldn't handle it.

I don't know if you should explain that one or if a Freudian psychologist should but I won't even ask, I'll just quote it

There's your sex in climbing zip zip!

Yes, I was going to ask you about that, but I no longer need to. You give your next answer then I'll ask a question for it

My next answer is . . . this is a bit dated, but only just. If I'd gone to Yosemite when I'd been climbing in Borrowdale, I would have got into trouble, especially if I wanted to get up an aid route. Hell, they called me the mad pegger but they don't know what pegs are. The pegging out here is so different. The people who criticise Harding and Maestri haven't done the routes. Say Maestri's route on whatever it is, that hill in South America. If anybody else got up the route . . . I'm not saying anything about the British team, I know they had bad weather and wet socks and things, but if they'd got up that route and come down and said, "what a heap of shit that route was," then I'd think, "what a heap of shit that route is." But if they criticise these routes without having done them. . . Robbins changed his mind about Harding's route after he'd done it. I'll accept the criticism of my routes when people have done them. But nobody should say, "That's a shit route because it's got a bolt in it"; they should do them first. Otherwise they're just going on somebody else's opinion or some fairy story in their head.

My question for that one is, what sort of a climber would President Nixon make?

Don't take all this seriously lads. I'm just trying my best to freak you out.

Ever try to analyse why you climb, Paul?

Because it's hair. No I don't know. Why do I climb? It's all moods I suppose. Plus when you get obsessed you have to climb. Once I did three new routes on three consecutive days. It was a good laugh. I just wanted to see Joe's face when he came up the next weekend and asked, "Did you do anything this week?" "Ya, we did three.'' I climb better when I'm depressed. When you're in a good mood, why bother to go climbing? I can easily be distracted when I'm having a good time. Whillans used to call me holiday bollocks for that reason.

Can anything in climbing be taken seriously?

Well, I suppose I once took climbing seriously.

Is that when you prayed before you went climbing?

No, I did that because I thought if I fell off, I'd kill myself. If it was Saturday, I'd get really upset because we had to get to the dance. I actually nearly fell off a climb one Saturday. I was sure I was going to go, positive! I'd done the route before. It was the first new route I'd ever done, Triple Direct on Black Crag, and like a daft bugger I went up the crack the wrong way round just for fun, and I thought I wouldn't get up it. I was up about 40ft. with nothing in and shouted down "COMING!" My second shouted up, "Don't COME. You'll kill us both!" All he was belayed on was a ¼″ line, one loop around a spike. And he was probably right, but that wasn't the British thing to say, you should say, "I've got you." That would bring your confidence back, vaguely, and you could clear your mind and try to climb your way out of it. But he said, "You'll kill us," and I thought, "Bloody hell, it's Saturday." That was the first thing that came to me, "I'm going to miss the dance." Even if I survived the fall, I wasn't going to be in any shape to dance. I was in a flurry of fright because he was convinced we were going and I was going to miss the dance, so I managed to grab something, but it was more by good luck than good judgment. I seemed to be in situations like that quite a lot. And sometimes when I put these extra pitons in, I didn't realise they were extra at all, but subconsciously, it was Saturday. Sunday, I wasn't too bothered, because I had a hangover, and the bird had gone home.

If you had a chance, would you go on an expedition?

I suppose some of it would be OK, especially going through Katmandu. It would be good to get that far and sprain your ankle and sit there looking at all the flowers. I'm a devout botanist. I like flowers. But there are so many failures on these things. I'd be really pissed off if we didn't get to the top. If I'd flogged me ass off with a big pack for a hundred miles, and scratched around in a lot of snow and couldn't get up! I'd be pissed with all that work. Whillans uses it to dry out, but I couldn't think of a good excuse. I don't want to dry out.

What's the funniest thing about climbing?

I think it's all pretty funny. I like to watch people's reactions after I do a climb. I suppose it's warped sense of humour. It's a good sport, but I don't know, is it?

from LEEDS UNIVERSITY MOUNTAIN CLUB JOURNAL *1973*

New Breed

KIM CARRIGAN

Up and away! "There were years of middle-class living in outer suburbia, as well as a fairly traditional, conservative education through the Public School system. A five-year sentence at Sydney Grammar School was spent by mostly living and dreaming climbing. I started when I was fourteen, mainly through sitting next to Mike Law and reading the inevitable climbing literature perched precariously on his knee, beyond the prying eyes of supposedly strict disciplinarians. This same subversiveness carried on to our climbing after several trips with the school-based Endeavour Club prompted letters home urging parental control stopping us leading above Grade 12."

Climbing to the top. For some years Carrigan was just another leading Australian climber, then he really took off. This was due to a combination of a number of things. "Spending 1977 in America made me aware of the seemingly impossible standards that could be achieved through training and discipline. At this time, for me, this consisted mainly of pull-ups and traversing on the walls of stone buildings. However, when I returned, I lived in Sydney for a while, which was really retrogressive as all new routes required either massive bolting (for protection) or boldness, neither of which I was interested in then. So I moved to Melbourne and the potential of

Mt. Arapiles totally enthused me. No matter how hard I climbed, there were always so many lines which were so obviously possible, if only one were a little fitter or stronger."

"*The cost is high* in many ways, yet the satisfaction makes it worth it. The biggest cost is in time. I usually climb six out of seven days a week at the moment, as I did nearly all last year in America. If I don't climb this much, I train. My body has come to expect to be worked hard; I feel guilty if I don't. Usually if I don't train for a few weeks I get unfit fairly quickly, but it doesn't take long to regain my previous best. This only happens when I'm injured or forced to work. Another cost is in injury. Over the last three years I've damaged nine flexor tendons in my fingers and torn my shoulder badly through over-training. Injury is so frustrating, especially finger tendons, as they usually take a few weeks of not climbing to repair and then a couple more weeks to re-strengthen."

"*Every little bit counts* if you want to be at the top. Certainly diet is pretty important to me, being a vegetarian. In fact, cooking is probably my next favourite pastime, along with eating that is. Mostly my diet consists of nuts, grains, fruit, vegetables and dairy products, although since I've been in Britain potato chips seem to be taking over to my utter disgust, so maybe it's all psychological. Physical conditioning is obviously of paramount importance. To climb the desperates these days, you must be super fit rather than especially strong. Mostly, the hard routes that inspire me now are the ultra-sustained 'pumps' and the nasty scarey horrors, both needing control and confidence. I train by either climbing, or a combination of traversing, swimming, running, weight-training and climbing a caving ladder set up at about 50°-60° that one ape-swings up, on the under side. To keep my head in shape I do unroped climbing at grade 16-20, which helps with control on the bolder routes. I usually do a lot of eating and try to forget about the route until I actually touch rock."

"*Climbing has so much more to offer* than any mere sport. It combines the need to be an athlete, both fit and technically proficient, the mental strength to do very difficult moves in, at times, very dangerous situations, the creativity to solve problems whilst operating under intense pressure as well as the aesthetic enjoyment of being out and about 'on the hill'. Also, every route is a different experience which tends to fend off the boredom."

His hardest climbs. "I suppose a few of the hardies at Mt. Arapiles would have to count: routes like Yesterday (grade 28), Denim (27), and Picking Winners (27) are fairly solid although all were heavily sieged. I was pleased with Intranscience (24) because of the style in which I did it: on sight (without prior acquaintance) and no falls; also, it was one of my first routes of this type and marked a big change in my ethical awareness. I was also pleased with some of my ascents in 'The Gunks' of New York, like Gravities Rainbow (27/28), Scarey Area (27), and Supercrack (29) which were all in the best style of the time. Lately I've been doing a lot of modern limestone routes in Britain, in a style that I was pleased with, such as Psychic Threshold (27), at Great Orme, Pinkginsane (26) at Avon Gorge, and Cave Route (28/29) at Gordale Scar in Yorkshire. Psychic Threshold and Pinkginsane were both first free ascents, and Cave Route a second."

"*Competition is a big motivation.* I have a pretty strong will to succeed, and it gives me the necessary boot. I'm as good as any of the top *climbers* in Britain and the USA judging from what I've seen in my travels and the routes that I've done, but there are many people who climb better on short boulder problems: probably the reason why I never bother to boulder. I'd probably not climb at all unless I was successful. Some of the Californian crack-climbing specialists are definitely more practised at that than I am, although I hope to remedy that at some time in the future."

"*Being the best* is not, in itself, especially important to me, but to make money in this game you have to be well-known and it seems a pity to put in so much effort if for a little more you can get paid. It's a lot easier than shovelling superphosphate in a factory."

"*The hardest climbs* demand loads of discipline, a reasonable amount of technical ability and a strong determination to win. They're certainly not accessible to everyone."

Falling. "On well-protected routes it allows you to push beyond your limit. A lot of technically desperate routes get done this way, but on the bold routes, it can mean death. Climbing has now gone the full circle. In modern climbing, the old maxim 'the leader must never fall' is being revived."

"*Ten years from now* I hope I'm doing something different. I'd go round the bend if I did this for another decade!"

from WILD 2 *1981*

A Word for Whymper: a Reply to Sir Arnold Lunn

D. F. O. DANGAR and T. S. BLAKENEY

The following two articles are examples of the extreme levels of 'scholarship' that are sometimes focussed on old alpine controversies by luminaries of the Alpine Club. In addition an interesting picture emerges of the preoccupations and prejudices of the 'traditional' climbing world.

A recent book by Sir Arnold Lunn, *Matterhorn Centenary*, has afforded him the opportunity for a reiteration of his well-known adverse criticisms of Whymper. For many years Lunn has used his talents to voice his dislike or his distrust of Whymper: it would scarcely be worthwhile to attempt an exhaustive scrutiny of his former books, in order to see how often he had said the same things, but readers of *Matterhorn Centenary* will certainly find much of the work in the pages of *Mountain Jubilee* (1943), *Switzerland and the English* (1944), *Zermatt and the Valais* (1955), and *A Century of Mountaineering* (1957). It seems reasonable, therefore, to ask whether this repetition is due to the whole subject of Whymper, and of the first ascent of the Matterhorn in particular, being exhausted; or to Lunn's views being definitive and consequently not susceptible of change; or to those views being governed by a prejudice that prevents him from doing justice to his subject?

Mr Ronald Clark has recently shown (*The Day the Rope Broke*) that we cannot say that nothing new is to be found about the Matterhorn catastrophe, so our first alternative will not stand; Lunn himself would appear to adopt the second alternative and to hold, as he has expressed it, that as a historian he is bound by what A. H. Clough once called "the mere 'it was'." Undoubtedly, any historian is bound by facts, but in our view Lunn has so distorted the facts in his presentation of them as to develop a "mere it wasn't" in too many of his references to Whymper, both in relation to the Matterhorn and in a wider application. In fact, one cannot

456

avoid an uneasy feeling that Lunn has used the prestige that he rightly enjoys, as an interpreter of Anglo-Swiss relationships, to foster and propagate error as regards Whymper.

This accusation, which clearly must be justified, comprises both specific charges of inaccuracy on particular points, and a general disposition on Lunn's part to run down Whymper by use of petty charges that, collectively, would damage his reputation. In the handling of these charges Lunn, as it seems to us, drops the historian for the journalist, and fails to distinguish between gossip and evidence.

The leap on the Ecrins:
For Lunn to continue to charge Whymper with inventing this, and the deep notch on the arête that had caused the leap (p. 41) is, we submit, a gross instance of a false accusation made in the face of evidence that is overwhelmingly on the side of Whymper's statement. And Lunn is specially vulnerable in the matter, for the subject was examined carefully by the late Lord Schuster in his book, *Postscript to Adventure*, in the chapter entitled, 'One Word More,' which bore a sub-title, 'An Open Letter to Mr. Arnold Lunn.' This volume was published in the New Alpine Library, of which Lunn himself was general editor. He has, therefore, a double reason for not forgetting Schuster's criticisms.

In view of Schuster's thorough examination of the matter, it is not necessary here to do more than summarise the case. In *Scrambles*, Whymper wrote an account of the descent after the first ascent of the Ecrins, illustrating it by a drawing of Christian Almer making a spectacular leap over a gap in the West Ridge. After Almer's death, W. A. B. Coolidge wrote that Almer had told him no such leap took place. In further support of this, it has been pointed out that A. W. Moore in *The Alps in 1864* did not refer to the leap; and it was alleged that no one else has ever found the gap in the ridge. It is also suggested that the Alpine Club's subsequent election of Coolidge to Honorary Membership was tacit support for his statements against Whymper.

Against these propositions we set the following, which may be studied more fully in Whymper's 'Letter Addressed to the Members of the Alpine Club', and in Schuster's book, already mentioned.

1. That Almer's denial of the story depends wholly on a statement by Coolidge, who was a violent and quarrelsome partisan, who constantly made foes of other people. Coolidge's asseverations on controversial matters always need scrutiny and checking; he fought with member after member of the Club—Whymper, Davidson, Freshfield, Farrar, Montagnier—and with various Committees of the Alpine Club, to say nothing of foreign climbers and clubs. To accept Coolidge's insinuations unverified is almost enough of itself to rule out Sir Arnold Lunn as a historian.

2. that Ulrich Almer, Christian's son, testified that his father had, after the Ecrins climb, told him of a remarkable jump he had had to make.

3. that Peter Almer, another son, also remembered his father speaking of making this jump.

4. that Ulrich Almer, when descending the West Ridge of the Ecrins with his father and Coolidge, in 1870, was shown by Christian where the jump was made.

5. that Monsieur Guillemin, when descending the ridge in 1886, wrote that his party were interested to see the place of Almer's famous leap (*Annuaire du CAF*, 1886, p. 38).

6. that Whymper, on learning of Coolidge's statement, not only challenged it, but wrote to Horace Walker, who had been on the climb with him, and the latter answered that he clearly remembered the leap, which had certainly taken place, and it was 'cheek' on the part of Coolidge, who had not been present, to question it.

7. that Walker had spoken soon after the climb to a friend of his, mentioning the leap, and the friend had reminded him of the fact.

8. that Ulrich Almer, when informed of his father's 'denial' of the leap, said that "if ever the remark was made at all to Coolidge, it was probably only intended to mean that the leap was not quite like the drawing."

9. that the tacit accusation, that Whymper invented the whole matter, since the jump was not mentioned by Moore, is met by the fact that Moore on his side mentioned events on the climb not referred to by Whymper. And in any case Whymper said he had, before he ever printed *Scrambles*, visited Moore

and shown him the proofs of the story, plus illustration, and Moore never raised any objection, then or later.

In the face of all this, we think that Coolidge's story is virtually disproved. Schuster discusses the whole question very judicially, and until Sir Arnold Lunn can upset Schuster's arguments, he ought to stop retailing Coolidge's fallacies. Coolidge himself did not stand to his statement; when Whymper challenged him by calling for a special general meeting of the AC, to debate the matter, Coolidge threw in his hand by resigning from the Club. Throughout the affair, Coolidge's behaviour was contemptible, nor can one think it out of character for him to misconstrue what Almer said, as Ulrich Almer evidently realised. Yet this is the man whom Lunn chooses to follow, and he does so, we contend, simply out of his unreasonable prejudice against Whymper.

As for the action of the Committee of the Alpine Club over the Ecrins controversy, at their meeting of December 11, 1899, they recorded their view that precedent showed that "except in matters arising out of the relation of members to one another as members of the Club, or in connexion with any of the publications of the Club," the Committee could not interfere in personal matters.

Any suggestion that the Club's later election of Coolidge to Honorary Membership was meant to indicate that they sided with Coolidge, rather than with Whymper, is baseless. Coolidge had resigned from the editorship of Ball's *Guide* by a letter received and accepted at the Committee meeting of January 23, 1900; and at the General Meeting of the Club on February 6 following, a statement was read out explaining that on account of his difference with Whymper, Coolidge had resigned from the Club and from the editorship of Ball. "Mr. Coolidge has twice before resigned from the editorship of the *Guide*, but has been induced to resume it. On the present occasion the Committee have felt that they could not make a third attempt to renew a connexion so liable to interruption."

This reads as though the Committee were at last tired of Coolidge's tantrums; they were certainly taking up no stand on his side. But, nearly five years later, on December 6, 1904, the then Committee chose Coolidge to be an Honorary Member of the Club. Earlier that year they had chosen Doctor H. Dubi as an Honorary Member; seeing that Dubi was a distinguished Alpine historian, it is reasonable to suppose that the Committee thought it only fitting that Coolidge, an even more notable historian, should be similarly invited. But the Committee that chose Coolidge as Honorary Member was utterly different from that which had been confronted with the 'Ecrins leap' row; new President, new Vice-Presidents, new Honorary Secretary—indeed, of those present in Committee on January 23, 1900, only A. L. Mumm was also present on December 6, 1904. Clearly, the Almer trouble had long since faded out and could have had no weight with the new Committee.

'*A bit of a Swell*'. A favourite, and too-often repeated, titbit of Coolidge gossip that Lunn likes to relate is that, after the descent from the Ecrins, A. W. Moore chose to bivouac and to let Whymper go on ahead with Croz, because Moore was 'a bit of a swell', and disliked Whymper's uncouth company. Here again, it strikes us as essentially unhistorical to repeat such silly little pieces of gossip, especially when coming from such a malicious source as Coolidge, without, at the least, trying to find corroboration for the tale, and without employing a sense of proportion and a little 'nous' in estimating it.

The party split up because, darkness having fallen, Moore, who was very short-sighted, would have found it almost impossible to make a long descent without a lantern or light of any description. Moore and Almer had just had an unpleasant experience in descending the moraine of the Glacier Noir ("I never was in such peril," wrote Moore), and he and Horace Walker had given up hope of reaching a roof for the night and were searching for a suitable bivouac site.

Is there, in fact, any reason for thinking that Moore was a 'swell'? The implication is that Moore was a gentleman of considerable social standing, and Whymper was not. Moore, in fact, came from a respectable but not distinguished family of Anglo-Irish origins, of the landed gentry type; this is hardly what the nineteenth century called a 'swell'. Nor was his position in life, in 1864, especially notable; aged twenty-three, he was a clerk in the Financial Department of the India Office. The Whympers were an armigerous Suffolk family, resident there since at least the mid-seventeenth century. They owned at one time Glevering Hall, one of those small manor houses that are so common in East Anglia.

Like the Moore family, the Whympers were not especially notable, but there was certainly nothing against them. As in many another prolific family, the sons tended to follow the usual professions available to them, of Army, Navy, Church and Medicine; but Nathaniel Whymper (1787-1861), the grandfather of Edward, established a brewery at Ipswich. At that time, the best-known member of the Whymper family was Sir William Whymper (1785-1850), first cousin to Nathaniel, and a notable physician in his day. After serving throughout the Peninsular War, he became surgeon-major to the Coldstream Guards and physician to the Duke of Cambridge.

Josiah Whymper, Edward's father, did not take to the brewing industry, but determined to make a career with his artistic talents. About 1829 he established in Lambeth what was to become a flourishing business as a wood-engraver. When, later, he made his home at Haslemere, he entered readily into the society of the place, which included the Tennysons and the famous surgeon, Sir Jonathan Hutchinson, to name no more.

Josiah's sons were to show themselves to be men of strong, original minds, who made their way in the world successfully. Charles, the artist, was well-known and respected; Henry, who went out to India quite young, proved to be a man of enterprise as manager of the Murree Breweries. He fostered plans for extending the railway to the Murree Hills; gave generously to famine relief in 1878-79, and, though under fifty when he died, had received the C.I.E. for public services. It is, indeed, rather laughable to read the Coolidge-Lunn rigmarole of how Edward Whymper was socially unsuitable for the tastes of a youthful clerk in the India Office, while Henry Whymper was thought fit to be the host at Murree of two Viceroys of India (Mayo in 1869 and Ripon in 1883). And a letter (holograph) from Lord Dufferin in April 1888, is extant, in which the Viceroy affably and at some length regrets that he has had to abandon a visit to Henry Whymper because of danger from cholera.

Finally, it may be noted that both Josiah and Edward Whymper won places in the *Dictionary of National Biography*: A. W. Moore did not.

What evidence is there of Moore adopting a superior attitude towards Whymper, as Coolidge implies? Perhaps the nearest to it is a reference in Whymper's diary of June 30, 1864, when Moore and Walker managed to engage the two last two places in 'the courier' going to Bourg St. Maurice, leaving Whymper and Croz, who had arrived later, behind them. "No room for Croz and myself, for which they appeared rather glad," wrote Whymper. Yet anyone who has travelled with a companion or companions will know how easily a temporary irritation against another person can arise, and as quickly disappear. To build on such occurrences is very unwise. Thus, Whymper records in his diary how Croz was in the sulks throughout the first ascent of the Aiguille de Trélatête on July 12, 1864; again, he wrote to Reilly (June 20, 1865) saying that "Croz has become awfully humptious, not to say fractious." But no one can read Whymper without recognising how sincerely he appreciated Croz and how deeply he felt his death on the Matterhorn. Their differences had disappeared and did not, on the lines of Coolidge-Lunn reasoning, reflect a lasting outlook on one another.

As for Moore and Whymper, their relationship was probably not particularly close—indeed, Whymper does not seem to have made any close climbing friends—and no doubt Moore was on closer terms with Horace Walker. When Adams Reilly joined Whymper in Chamonix in 1864, Moore went off on his own to team up with Morshead, just as Walker went off to join his father and sister. But Moore rejoined Whymper later on for the Moming Pass, just as he rejoined Walker later in the Oberland. The Moming Pass was, indeed, Moore's idea and he specifically asked Whymper to join him on the expedition (*The Alps in 1864* pp. 259-60). By itself, this almost disposes of Coolidge's allegation that Moore could not stand Whymper's company.

There is nothing written about Moore that leads one to think he was a snob, as Coolidge suggests. On the contrary, his death evoked very warm tributes, Whymper, at the AC meeting of March 1, 1887, not only endorsing what others had said of Moore, with whom he had been friends since 1861, but himself proposing that the condolences of the Club be sent to Moore's family. The tributes elsewhere in the *AJ* by Coolidge and Horace Walker, or by Freshfield in the *Proceedings of the RGS (New Series*, ix, 200-1) all bear testimony to Moore's kindly nature, which made him an admirable travelling companion.

Two men who might, with more justice than in the case of

Moore, be called 'swells', were Sir Edward Davidson and D. W. Freshfield. With the first-named, particularly, the entrée, as Farrar says was not easy. Yet Davidson corresponded for years with Whymper over the latter's guide-books, and took much trouble on his behalf; there is no suggestion of his giving Whymper the 'brush-off'. And Freshfield, a somewhat Olympian figure, wrote the obituary notices of Whymper in *The Alpine Journal*, the *Geographical Journal*, and *DNB*. If these two did not disdain Whymper, it is likely that Moore would do so?

Altogether, Coolidge's 'bit of a swell' story seems to us quite worthless as a serious criticism of Whymper.

Whymper and Hudson. In his constant efforts to belittle Whymper, Lunn decries his skill as a mountaineer as compared with Hudson. He bases himself on an absurdity of Coolidge, that Whymper's fame arose from Hudson having been killed, so there was no one to share the distinction of having made the first ascent of the Matterhorn. Whymper, remarks Lunn, "knew that he had attached himself to Hudson's expedition, and must have known that Hudson was a more experienced mountaineer."

This statement certainly cannot pass unchallenged. It simply is not true that Whymper tacked himself on to Hudson; they chose the same route independently. And in 1865 Whymper had a much wider and more varied experience of climbing that Hudson had. The latter's fame rested (apart from his prowess as a walker) principally on his having been a pioneer of guideless climbing. His actual record of peaks, however, was a short one and very largely restricted to snow mountains, with Mont Blanc in first place. Prior to the Matterhorn, Hudson's record is as under—completed ascents are shown in inverted commas:

1853 (January): Ascent of the 'Dôle' (5,505ft. near Geneva).

(March): Several attempts on the Aiguille du Gouter (guideless), with local chamois hunters. Hudson, solo, nearly completed the ascent of the Aiguille).

1855 'Klein Matterhorn' and 'Breithorn'; guideless. 'Monte Rosa'; first ascent (guided).

Mont Blanc; attempt via the Col du Midi (Sir J. H. Ramsay's route a week earlier). During this expedition one member of the party—perhaps Hudson—made the ascent of 'Mont Blanc du Tacul'.

'Mont Blanc'; first guideless ascent of the mountain, and the first ascent from St. Gervais.

1856 'Théodule Pass' crossed.

1858 Mont Blanc; attempt by the Bosses route. (A so-called guide and some porters accompanied the party, but for practical purposes this was guideless.)

'Mönchjoch'; first completed passage; guided.

1859 'Monte Rosa'; guided.

'Mont Blanc'; first ascent via the Bosses route; guided.

1861 Col de Miage reached in an attempt on the Dome du Gouter; guided.

1862 Visited Zermatt on his honeymoon; no climbing recorded.

1865 'Aiguille Verte'; second ascent and first by the Moine Ridge; guided.

'Mont Blanc' from Chamonix; guided.

In the foregoing list, the Dôle (1853) might almost be ignored, but, giving Hudson the benefit of the doubt over Mont Blanc de Tacul (1855) and crediting it to him, he has barely a dozen completed expeditions in eight seasons. Farrar's remark that Hudson had twelve or thirteen years of mountaineering experience is not correct, therefore, and the experience had been almost wholly on snow mountains, some of an easy nature, and mostly with guides.

Hudson's big year was 1855, though even here, and in fairness to earlier climbers, it must be noted that the first ascent of Monte Rosa had been virtually achieved some years before, by Ulrich's guides in 1848, by the Schlagintweits in 1851 and by the Smyth party in 1854. They all climbed the Ostspitze, from which the Dufourspitze is 'an easy scramble of but a few minutes'. And until 1865 (the Verte) Hudson had not made a single reputable rock climb.

Hudson's general reliability as a climber was, in fact, based largely on his activities on two mountains, Mont Blanc and Monte Rosa. Although in 1865 these were still held in higher estimation than today, their prestige was already somewhat reduced. F. Morshead had deflated Mont Blanc by climbing it alone and in a single day in 1864, as a protest against the large posse of guides usually taken, whilst Tyndall had ascended Monte Rosa alone as far back as 1858.

Whymper, by comparison, and prior to the Matterhorn ascent,

had in six seasons attained a list of thirty serious peaks or passes completely (in order not to weight the scales too much against Hudson, we will disregard some further fourteen minor passes crossed by Whymper); and there were a number of noteworthy attempts, not merely on the Matterhorn but also on Monte Viso (1861), Dent d'Hérens (1863) and Ebnefluhjoch (1865). Thus, in a shorter period Whymper had nearly three times as long a record of ascents as Hudson, and of a much more varied nature. Except for his two guideless attempts on the Matterhorn, Whymper had travelled with guides. His list is too long to be shown fully here, but, to take a selection, he made ascents of such peaks as the Pelvoux, Monte Rosa, Grand Tournalin, Aiguilles de la Sausse (South Peak), Barre des Ecrins, Mont Dolent, Aiguille de Trélatête, Aiguille d'Argentière, Grand Cornier, Dent Blanche, Grandes Jorasses (West Peak) and Ruinette, most of them 'firsts'. In addition, he made first crossings of several passes, some of them of extreme difficulty for those days, and not reckoned easy today: Breuiljoch, Col des Aiguilles d'Arves, Brèche de la Meije, Col de la Pilatte, Col de Triolet, Moming Pass, Col Dolent, Col de Talèfre; to say nothing of lesser passes not crossed for the first time.

On any estimate, Whymper's record is far more impressive than Hudson's. Not that the latter's technical ability, by the standards of those days, is in question; T. S. Kennedy, Leslie Stephen, and Whymper himself all bear testimony to it. But there is no need to exaggerate; as noted above, Hudson's climbs had been almost entirely on snow peaks, so when one finds Farrar writing of Hudson as "almost the sole great master and exponent" of new principles of rock-climbing(!), one can only wish that he had not allowed his enthusiasm to outstrip his judgment.

Although Lunn chooses to call it "an uninformed verdict" to describe Whymper as the greatest mountaineer of his age, there must have been few, if any, in 1865 who had an equal record. But readers can judge for themselves, from the data given above, which of the two men, Hudson and Whymper, was the more experienced climber. In our view, Whymper's record and experience was easily the most extensive of the three principal amateurs on the Matterhorn, and both Hudson and Douglas should have been glad of such an accession of strength to the party.

Whymper's Drawings. Lunn's mistaken contention, that

Whymper's part in the illustrations to *Scrambles* was limited to the provision of the 'slight memoranda' referred to in the preface to the book, has been adequately dealt with by Professor Graham Brown, who pointed out, as only one example, that the very accurate view of the summit of the Col Dolent could only have been drawn in detail by Whymper himself. There are more than 100 illustrations in *Scrambles* and Whymper lists nine artists who drew them on wood, the leading individual James Mahoney (not 'Mahonney' as Lunn – p.74 – calls him), being responsible for about fifty. (On a quick look over the illustrations, we have only been able to identify about half this number.) But as none of these artists employed by the Whympers (Josiah and Edward Whymper did the engraving) accompanied Edward to the Alps, clearly they must have been dependent on his own drawings except in the cases (twenty-two of them) where photographs were used. No matter whether Whymper referred to them as "slight memoranda" or "designs", the fact remains that they were his original drawings, and the preparation of the illustrations for the book took up no small part of Whymper's time during six years. By all means let Mahoney, Cyrus Johnson and the other craftsmen be given credit for their work, but why try and belittle Whymper's basic contribution to the pictures?

But really one can scarcely any longer be surprised by anything Lunn writes in his campaign against Whymper; it is hardly an exaggeration to say that he appears ready to impugn Whymper's veracity on everything he wrote about the events of July 13 to 15, 1865. The 'fog bow' is a case in point; this Lunn says Whymper imagined. Whymper himself is quite open about it and admits that it has been suggested "that the crosses are incorrectly figured in the illustration and that they were probably formed by the intersection of other circles or ellipses . . . I think this suggestion is very likely correct; but I have preferred to follow my original memorandum."

There is no reason for thinking that Whymper did not see some kind of optical phenomenon akin to those with which all of us are familiar in rainbows, fog bows and (more rarely) the Brocken Spectre. That he over-dramatised it in his drawing in *Scrambles* is no doubt the case. Lunn claims that it 'must' also have been seen from the Gornergrat and other viewpoints; but this would be looking at it from a totally different angle as compared with

Whymper. It is essential to bear in mind that a fog bow (to employ Whymper's term) is personal to the observer, just like a reflection in a mirror. If, therefore, conditions looking from the Gornergrat away from the sun were not suitable for a fog bow, observers would not have seen one. The fog bow seen by Whymper was not a thing suspended in space over the Lyskamm for all to see. If observers on the Gornergrat had seen a fog bow, its axis would be a line passing well north of the Lyskamm.

In short, the fact that observers on other mountains did not see a fog bow is no proof that Whymper could not have done so.

The Italian climbers on July 17 appear to have seen the Brocken Spectre whilst descending, between 6.30 and 7 p.m., at about 14,000ft. so both they and Whymper saw a similar type of phenomenon at much the same height and same time of day. Miss Brevoort and Coolidge, in 1871, saw a fog bow from the same position as Whymper had (*Annuare du CAF* 1882, 24); Lunn expresses no doubts about these observers, for he seems only concerned to doubt the truthfulness of Whymper.

Whymper's Knowledge of French. Lunn claims (p. 65) to have shown that Whymper's knowledge of French was almost non-existent and that Taugwalder soon had probably no more than a rudimentary knowledge of the French patois spoken in the Val Tournanche. In fact, Lunn has 'shown' (i.e. proved) nothing; in *AJ* 55 p.293 he sought to make out a case on these lines, and now he asserts that his case (which consists largely of assumptions) is a fact. Thus is false history made.

So far as Whymper is concerned, Lunn's opinion is based on a single entry in his diary, made three weeks after his first arrival in Switzerland (August 14, 1860), where he says that, "In the best French I could muster I asked if I had the honour of speaking to Monsieur le Curé Imseng of Saas." Lunn omits to mention that Whymper then went on to talk to the Curé ("I told him how much I had heard of him and how glad I was to see him"; Smythe, *Edward Whymper*, p. 86), and so is able to claim that Whymper's knowledge of French was only adequate for the simplest of questions. He also asserts that there is no evidence that Whymper learnt French between 1860 and 1865.

Apart from visiting the Valais in 1860, Whymper went on to Courmayeur, to Chamonix, to the Vaudois, to Grenoble and the

Dauphiné mountains, to Monte Viso—does Lunn really believe that he could get about in those days, in areas some of which were almost unknown to English travellers, without some acquaintance with the local languages? How many of us might not use the phrase, "In the best French I could muster. . .", and yet be able to converse adequately, even though not an expert? As we have pointed out elsewhere (*AJ* 61 p. 502), a man could not travel for several seasons with guides and not have some skill in ordinary conversation in their languages. How could Whymper and Croz, in 1864, after the descent from the Ecrins, sit up half the night "recounting wonderful stories," if they had not a language in common? Croz, we know, spoke no English or German, but only French. To any unprejudiced person, it will be clear that Whymper even in 1860 had a working acquaintance with French, and by 1865 it must have increased.

In later life it is known that Whymper spoke French tolerably well. Walter Dollfuss (*Neue Zürcher Zeitung*, July 14, 1965) meeting Whymper at St. Niklaus in 1906, says he spoke good French but with a strong English accent; Emil Gos (*Les Alpes*, 1965, p. 143) says almost exactly the same—well enough, but with a strong accent. Admittedly, this was long after the accident, but since foreign languages are learned more easily in youth than in old age, there is far more to suggest that Whymper's French in 1865 was at least passable than there is to support Lunn's sweeping statement that it was almost non-existent. So far as we can tell from the printed Official Enquiry into the Matterhorn accident, Whymper was questioned in French, the language in which the report is written; the questioning of the guides is declared to be translated from German into French, but nothing is said of Whymper's questioning having been translated.

Lunn is on no better ground in his remarks about Young Peter's knowledge of French. Taugwalder had done his military service in the French-speaking Canton of Vaud, and as both Farrar (*AJ* 33 p. 247) and Ronald Clark (*The Day the Rope Broke*, p. 106) observe, Young Peter must have acquired a fair knowledge of French. It is pretty obvious that it was because he and Croz had a language in common that Young Taugwalder was chosen to go along, on July 13, 1865, with Croz, after camp was pitched, to reconnoitre the route ahead. Or does Lunn think the two men, away for about three hours, could only communicate by signs?

Lunn, ever ready to accuse Whymper of something, has thrown out suggestions that Whymper invented things in order to give picturesque detail to his story in *Scrambles*. The "sharp-eyed lad," who, Whymper says, saw and reported an avalanche fall from the Matterhorn shortly after 3 p.m. on July 14, 1865, is a case in point. Because he was not mentioned by Whymper in his letter to *The Times*, Lunn (*Zermatt and the Valais*, p. 39; *A Century of Mountaineering*, p. 56) hints that he was a myth invented by Whymper, since he only made his first appearance in *Scrambles*. As we have pointed out before now (*AJ* 70 p.159), this boy is a fact, not a fancy; nor does he first make his appearance in *Scrambles*. Four years before Whymper's book appeared, Charles Long had written about him in *Echo des Alpes* for 1867, and Seiler told the Rev. H. Downton in July 1865 that the lad had seen "what he described as an avalanche" (Ronald Clark, *The Day the Rope Broke*, p. 174). Does Lunn never read anything about the Matterhorn accident except what he has himself written? Charles Gos's *Le Cervin*, which reprints (vol. 1, p. 99) Long's testimony, has been out for nearly twenty years, so Lunn should know of it. The boy's identity is known, too; he was a son of old Peter Taugwalder.

On the same pages of his books referred to above, Lunn also accuses Whymper of greatly exaggerating the interest with which the natives followed the climb, and says that half the guests in the Monte Rosa Hotel refused to leave the luncheon table when Seiler announced that there were men on the Matterhorn, "and continued placidly eating." Well, Lunn, for all the confidence with which he writes, was not present, whereas Joseph McCormick, who was there, says that "every person at the table immediately got up, and went out to see them" (*A Sad Holiday*, p. 13). Or again, if Lunn would only read Gos's *Le Cervin*, he would find (vol. 1, pp. 100-1) first-hand evidence of great excitement being shown; Charles Long entirely supports McCormick and entirely demolishes Lunn's tale.

Lunn relies on a remark of Herr Lehner, that an old lady who was a girl in 1865 said that people who heard the news of men being seen on the top of the Matterhorn showed no interest. Who was the old lady? How long after the accident was it that she was questioned? Lunn ignores such points, but we suggest that the accounts of those who recorded their impressions at the time are likely to be much more accurate than a chance remark of an old woman years after the event. 'Old Men Forget'; so do old women; and not only forget, but even imagine things. What stuff this is, for anyone to trot out as history! Miss Brevoort, who with Coolidge visited Zermatt in September, 1865, recorded in her diary a conversation she had with the maid, who had been at the Monte Rosa Hotel on July 14. The girl "described the excitement in Zermatt the day they reached the top. No one went anywhere. All stood abt. with glasses watching the haughty mtn. . ." (Ronald Clark, *An Eccentric in the Alps*, p. 21). Even allowing for exaggeration, Miss Brevoort's maid is substantially in agreement with McCormick and with Long, and not at all with Herr Lehner's old lady.

As for Whymper exaggerating the interest taken, Lunn does not quote chapter and verse for this, nor can he. For Whymper in fact makes little reference in *Scrambles* to the local interest; he said that the victory flag was seen from Zermatt and the Riffel, but this is the truth, not exaggeration at all.

The Matterhorn Accident. We have dealt with this already (*AJ* 61 p. 494; 70, pp. 26 and 159) and see no reason to alter our views in any substantial degree. Fundamentally, we think that Whymper's narrative holds good; he said much the same, though at different lengths, in his letter to von Fellenberg (*AJ* 70 23), in his letter to *The Times* (August 8, 1865), and in *Scrambles*. And in all essentials, what he says agrees with McCormick's letter to *The Times* of July 22, and with *A Sad Holiday*. Naturally, at different times Whymper emphasised some aspects a little more than on other occasions; naturally, too, by the time he wrote *Scrambles* he was able to amplify earlier statements. Naturally, again, in his old age he became forgetful, as in the remark he recorded as having been made by Croz, about preferring to go up (or, it may be, down) with Whymper alone rather than with the others in the party (*AJ* 55 p. 294). Lunn can hardly hold it against Whymper that his memory at times misled him. In which of us does this not occur? Lunn himself records a piece of forgetfulness on his own part (dealing with the 'Whymper-cut-the-rope-himself' story), so Whymper's error (an 'up' for a 'down', or vice versa) is not especially culpable.

It is quite understandable that there was some confusion over the remarks made by the Taugwalders (Young Peter principally, it would seem) on the way down after the accident. All three men had had a harrowing experience and were likely to say more than they meant, and in the stress of the moment to misunderstand what the other said. On the matter of the accusations against Old Peter, of either cutting the rope, or of deliberately using a weak one, Whymper disposed of the first so thoroughly that it only needs now to be ridiculed, if mentioned at all. We have pointed out how these remarks originated among the inhabitants of Zermatt, and how it suggests that Old Peter was not highly thought of there. Lunn tries categorically to deny that any of the locals ever said anything of the sort (p. 67), but as he quotes (p. 142) the late Bernard Biner to the effect that Taugwalder aroused jealousy among the other guides, some of whom were very unpleasant about him, Lunn's case is authoritatively denied, whilst our contention is supported. Lunn will hardly convince people of the camaraderie of Zermatt residents to the extent of believing that in 1865 no back-biting could have taken place; much more recent events than the Matterhorn catastrophe could be adduced to show the contrary. Moreover, if Whymper's charges had really roused such resentment in Zermatt, it is remarkable that it took about three-quarters of a century before anyone got up to defend the Taugwalders.

On the second count, Whymper's use of the phrase "ugly look" in connexion with the use of the weak rope (when there was ample good rope available) may be regretted, since it has occasioned so much heart burning. Yet in fact the term was not inaccurate; there is a sense in which it did have an ugly look, but this is not to say that Whymper was saying in effect that there had been dirty work done. He was stating how the matter looked.

Lunn notes more than once how Otto Furrer on one occasion said that he (Lunn) was the first person to defend Taugwalder, and how Lunn deprecated the praise, since Leslie Stephen had done so first. Yet, as we have before now pointed out (AJ 70 p. 160), Stephen's defence was a very lame one; to defend a guide's misdeed on the plea that it was not deliberate but merely habitual carelessness, is a very qualified extenuation.

We think we have shown (AJ 70 pp. 31-32) that Old Peter's reputation was not wrecked by Whymper; on the contrary, 1866 was one of Taugwalder's better years of climbing and had he only shown more enterprise he could undoubtedly have 'cashed in' on the Matterhorn ascent. Since *Scrambles* only appeared in 1871, it could not have damaged Taugwalder before that date. For the rest, the world had to be content with the letter to *The Times* (except for the few people who had read the *Bollettino del CAI* for 1865) and Whymper said nothing there seriously to damage Taugwalder's reputation. If he refers to the guides' broken morale immediately following the accident, he also says that "the guides did their duty manfully" and exonerates them from all blame.

The Victorians, vis-à-vis guides, were in rather the same position as mountaineers today in relation to Himalayan or Karakoram porters. They tended to be more outspoken than at a later date, when guides had become more sober and more educated; no doubt, in years hence mountaineers will speak less freely of Himalayan porters. There were from early days guides like old Melchior Anderegg or Christian Almer or Auguste Balmat, who were welcome in any gathering. Equally, there were rougher diamonds like Peter Bohren. As the latter type died out, so did the heavy Victorian criticism of faults. Still, even fifty years ago, as G. D. Abraham's books show, there were rough specimens about, and Geoffrey Young writes of actually having to pay off on the mountain-side a shouting, unnerved guide. That Whymper found the Taugwalders unnerved and upset emotionally by the catastrophe they had all witnessed, is not only convincing about the two men themselves (and Young Peter in his own narrative admits to it), but likely from what we know of other contemporary guides, and such instances as we mention in *AJ* 70 p. 31, note 8). Nor must it be forgotten that in 1862 on the Dent Blanche Old Peter had lost his nerve to such an extent that what would have been the first ascent had to be abandoned. He was unable to proceed.

A story that Lunn seems to wish to accept as true is the yarn that Whymper had himself cut the rope, at the time when he and Croz were preparing to race to the summit of the Matterhorn. This tale was referred to in our foreword to Young Peter Taugwalder's narrative of the first ascent of the mountain (*AJ* 61 p. 485), and was introduced as an illustration of the strange tales that have got about, and we observed that "probably few people today believe these stories." Lunn, because the tale would tell against Whymper, appears to be one of the few. Hearsay stuff of this sort cannot be accepted; it came to one of us from G. E. Howard, who had had it from A. E. W. Mason, who said he heard it said by Whymper after a very good dinner, where the wine had flowed freely. Almost anything might be said or thought to be said in such circumstances; we would need to know, before taking it seriously, how sober the diners were, Mason as much as Whymper. Did Mason hear Whymper aright? Did he recount what he heard aright?

Considering the utter needlessness of cutting the rope on this occasion — it would be much simpler to loosen the knot than to have to grope for a knife and then cut the rope — and considering the improbability of Hudson standing by silently, and not objecting to the cutting taking place, we submit that, unless it can be well authenticated, to accept this story is simply absurd.

Turning to more general aspects of Whymper's character, it is necessary to see him in relation to his times, especially in the 1840's and '50's, when he was growing up.

Whymper had to leave school at the age of fourteen, as the family finances were heavily burdened. He was duly apprenticed to his father. But if anyone thinks that this means that he was uneducated, the notion is absurd. Lunn (p. 38) insinuates this, but anyone who has looked at Whymper's early, boyish diaries (Smythe prints many extracts from them in his biography) or his school essays, let alone his later writings, will recognise, unless hopeless bias prevents him, that Whymper had a very acute, meticulous intelligence, and could write as good English as anyone. No one indeed can look at the well-known pictures, either of the young Whymper of 1865, or in 1910, and not recognise a decidedly intelligent face; Schuster in *AJ* 52 p. 150 (for it is undoubtedly he who wrote that unsigned review of Smythe's biography) extols the sensitive, spiritual face of the young man. Lunn would appear (p. 74) to think poorly of Whymper's literary ability; certainly one can find banal passages, but in this Whymper would seem to have been following a practice that was all too common among Victorian writers, of apostrophising or soliloquising in a style quite out of fashion today. One has only to turn to the writings of men such as Trollope, or Dickens (the latter a particularly irksome example), to see it; and Gilbert takes it off in *The Mikado*, when Ko-Ko starts, "Oh matrimony! . . ." is interrupted, an exclaims, "can't you see I'm soliloquising?"

Whymper must be viewed against the background of the age he belonged to; opinions will naturally vary somewhat about his writing; to us, it seems that he wrote with great clarity and precision. The description of the view from the Matterhorn may be, as Lunn has claimed, largely a catalogue of names, yet it has a certain dignity about it, and Lunn at any rate should be glad that there was a general absence in Whymper's writings of the sort of 'purple passages' that so often spoiled the writings of Whymper's biographer.

Finally, in estimating Whymper's intelligence, Lunn might well reflect on the fact that although Whymper was not a trained scientist, he was so much one by instinct that he had the unusual compliment paid him after his death of having, as a supplement to the more formal obituary in *The Alpine Journal*, a special note by Professor Bonney on 'The Scientific Work of Edward Whymper', in which he receives high praise.

A further suggestion that Whymper was ill-educated lies in the statement in Smythe's biography (p. 315) that towards the end of his life Whymper tended to drop his 'H's. Lunn, needless to say, seizes on this. Smythe says that Whymper sought to correct the fault by getting his nephew, Robert Whymper, to attend his lectures and snap his fingers when an H was dropped. Somehow, the notion of being able to get a relative to follow one around, attending lectures for so fanciful a purpose, strains one's credulity, and we have been told by one of Whymper's great-nephews that members of the family regard the tale as simply an instance of a habit, well known in the family's circles, of making whimsical criticisms of one another. But, assuming it is true, surely Lunn should ask himself how it was that an experienced lecturer of many years' standing, like Whymper, who had addressed numerous fashionable audiences, had never, so far as we know, been found out in the fault of dropping his H's? Smythe's allegation only refers to the later years, and he tells us earlier (pp. 310, 313) that Whymper had been troubled with failing sight, and with attacks of faintness. Surely, it will occur to anyone that, if the habit of dropping H's had suddenly arisen, it may well have had some specific cause, such as a slight stroke or something of that nature, that could cause a slurring of speech. Lunn's case against Whymper is weak indeed, if he has to bolster it up with stuff like this.

Whymper was understood to have died of a cerebral haemorrhage, so there is no improbability that some earlier and milder attack may not have occurred.

Another of Lunn's gambits is to relate how he was introduced to Whymper at an Alpine Club lecture in 1908; how Whymper, instead of being surrounded by a crowd, was standing alone; and how Whymper only made a few remarks to him about ski-ing. Whilst we are all of us naturally affected by first impressions of people, Lunn's experience of life must have taught him that first impressions often need correction. Some men are good mixers, some are not. Whymper clearly was of the latter type; a reserved, taciturn man, an introvert. Members of the Club who remember C. G. Bruce will agree that he was the very opposite, an extrovert if ever there was one, a tremendous mixer, always in the centre of things, jovial in manner and speech, and with a penchant for Rabelaisian stories (*AJ* 45 p. 334; 52 p. 105). Other AC members have represented every gradation between a Bruce and a Whymper; Collie, a notably impressive personality, was seemingly less reserved than Whymper; Farrar was less boisterous than Bruce. If Lunn is trying to imply that Whymper was "out of things" in the AC for reasons of social status, he must do better than this. Whymper was a formidable figure, with, as Lunn has to admit, the aura of greatness about him; there would be nothing incongruous in his being aloof and part of the reason at least was likely to be a shyness on the part of the other Club members at accosting him. This is no unusual thing where powerful personalities are concerned; Gladstone records how as a young man he steeled himself to speak to Wellington, only to be nonplussed by a brief "Ha!" The youthful Lunn seems to have fared better at Whymper's hands, and indeed on his own showing there was little time for any talk before the lecture began.

A rather trivial dig at Whymper is Lunn's statement that Josef Knubel said once that he was not liked in the Zermatt valley. In view of Lunn's remarks, often made, that Swiss peasants do not easily reveal their minds and tend very readily to say what their interrogator wants to hear (a characteristic not at all confined to the Swiss), one would like to know whether Knubel had sensed Lunn's dislike of Whymper and was saying what would please him to hear. In any case, did Whymper ever go out of his way to seek popularity? His descendants will tell you that old Uncle Edward was always regarded as a rather awesome figure. Yet, as Smythe notes (op. cit. p. 311), his diary records many examples of kindness and generosity, not least to children, and Frau Otto Furrer could tell Lunn today how she looks back to the occasion when her father took her, as a small girl, to be introduced to Whymper, and how he delighted her by the gift of a coral necklace, which she regularly wore to church every Sunday when in her best clothes. No doubt, Whymper was a severe and autocratic employer of guides, and not popular accordingly; but the other side of the medal must be shown also: there is no need to list acts of kindliness, but equally there is no point in going on repeating chance remarks by Knubel or anyone else, as though these were a definitive verdict on Whymper's character.

A regular entry in Lunn's gibes at Whymper is the latter's supposed remark, "What would Zermatt be without me?" and the rejoinder of Seiler's daughter. "And what would Whymper be but for the Matterhorn? It was really rather a feeble sort of reply, for Whymper's reputation as a mountaineer was firmly established by a number of noteworthy ascents outside of the Zermatt valley, and his later reputation depended more on his work in Greenland and the Andes than on his subsequent few Alpine climbs. But his notoriety on account of the Matterhorn was inescapable and there can be little doubt that the tremendous drama of the first ascent contributed not a little to making Zermatt the outstanding climbing centre it was to become, eclipsing even Chamonix and Grindelwald. Add to this that Whymper's guide-book to the valley, *Zermatt and the Matterhorn*, went through many editions (as did his Chamonix book), and we can see that Whymper did bring fame to Zermatt.

In any case, how can we be sure whether the remark was made by Whymper seriously or jokingly? The very fact that the Seiler hotels boarded Whymper free, though certainly generous and creditable to them (but is Whymper the only person who has been treated liberally by Swiss hotels?), is in itself a recognition that he had contributed much to Zermatt's distinction.

Whymper's marriage was known to be unhappy, and broke up, and this alone would have driven him in on himself. A similar withdrawal into himself had happened years before, after the Matterhorn accident. That event undoubtedly hit him hard at the time; he as, after all, only twenty-five and although remarkably mature in some respects, still it must have been a great shock. Contrary to some of Lunn's insinuations, Whymper behaved creditably at the time, though this is not to say that he did not make mistakes, as anyone else might. But, upset and harassed as he was, he immediately, on his return to Zermatt, busied himself in every possible way to get the bodies recovered, the two other survivors, the Taugwalders, not lifting a finger in the matter. He was involved in much publicity; in an official enquiry (and he found time to put down certain questions with a view to clearing up rumours about old Taugwalder and the weak rope); he had to pay the two surviving guides (though not, strictly, employed by him); he had to see to the fund for Croz's widow, and he took, later on, much care over a suitable memorial to the man who had been, despite occasional differences, undoubtedly his favourite guide. In the midst of all this, he went off to search for the body of W. K. Wilson, killed on the Riffelhorn.

Little wonder if, after it was all over, he decided, as he expressed it in later years (*The Graphic*, October 6, 1894), in future to travel alone. No doubt it would have been better for him not to have retired into himself; could he have married happily soon afterwards it might have made a world of difference to him. As it was, he tended to become solitary and crusty, when what he needed was the humanising influence of a happy home life.

In brief, Lunn's attempt to decry Whymper on the score of various selected oddities, even unpleasantnesses of character, is invalid, as invalid as it would be to choose only kindly actions and build up from that. Most men and women have one or two characteristics more fully pronounced than others, but all human history shows how dangerous it is to say of any individual that this or that is 'out of character', or impossible to believe. Generous men can suddenly do a mean action; truthful ones fall for some pointless lie; honest men be found shop-lifting; cruel men perform a kindness.

In Whymper's case, his reserve probably arose from a natural disposition that way, and from his early life. His alpine diaries of 1863-65 show that he had some sense of the ridiculous, but the Matterhorn accident certainly dealt him a blow, and whereas he might otherwise have come out of his shell, he was driven back into

it. "Ever afterwards I have travelled alone." And, characteristically, he died alone. When one compares the advantages given to
young explorers today, it really is astonishing that Whymper,
starting as a relatively poor boy, managed, quite apart from his
meteoric Alpine career, to run his two Greenland journeys and his
Andean expedition, and to become a well-known lecturer and
writer. If he had his faults and failings, this is no more than one
would expect: nobody wants to make him out to be a saintly
character. But Sir Arnold Lunn's habit of petty denigration seems
to us quite unworthy, and is generally baseless, and it is time that
his attacks were brought to an end.

from THE ALPINE JOURNAL *1966*

Whymper Again

SIR ARNOLD LUNN

I read with great interest and some little profit 'A Word for
Whymper: A Reply to Sir Arnold Lunn' in the last issue of the *AJ*.
Messrs. D. F. O. Dangar and T. S. Blakeney, hereinafter referred
to as 'my critics', make some good points and if *Matterhorn
Centenary* is reprinted I will make one or two minor corrections. If
their object was to represent Whymper in the most and myself in
the least favourable light, they were wise to omit everything I said
in Whymper's praise and to ignore instead of quoting and con-
ceding those of my criticisms which they could not answer.

I started with a strong prejudice in Whymper's favour. Of his
famous book I wrote in *The Mountains of Youth* that it "was the
first book which I laboriously spelt out for myself, and even today
there are few books which I can re-read with greater pleasure than
Whymper's great classic."

In *A Century of Mountaineering* I wrote (p. 61): "At its best
Whymper's writing has a simplicity and directness which recalls the
Greeks. There is indeed something of Greek simplicity and Greek
irony in the story of the Matterhorn triumph and tragedy."

In *Matterhorn Centenary* I wrote (p. 72): "Many eminent
mountaineers have contributed to the history of the Matterhorn by

forcing new routes up its cliffs, but the Matterhorn remains Whymper's mountain, partly perhaps because he himself had something of the indomitable character of that great peak with the result that we tend, as Geoffrey Winthrop Young rightly says, to identify him in our memory with the greatness of the Matterhorn . . . (p. 75). At its best Whymper's writing has a simplicity and directness which in his description of the Matterhorn tragedy challenges comparison with Thucydides.''

It is characteristic of my critics that they misrepresent a very sincere tribute as a denigration. They suggest that I implied, in their words not mine, that ''Whymper was 'out of things' in the AC for reasons of social status.'' What I actually wrote was in terms of warm praise of Whymper for being ''serenely unconscious of the social gulf'' between him and so many members of the AC. ''He gate-crashed,'' I wrote, ''into their society without realising the existence of any barriers. . . Whymper had at least one characteristic of greatness, superb self-confidence. He was uninterested in and therefore uninfluenced by class distinctions.''

I am attacked for the ''mistaken contention that Whymper's part in the illustrations to *Scrambles* was limited to the provision of the 'slight memoranda' referred to in the preface.'' Whymper had expressed his indebtedness to James Mahoney ''for the care and fidelity with which he followed my slight memoranda and for the spirit he put into his admirable designs'' and I do not think the attempts which have been made to explain away this explicit statement are particularly convincing. Anyhow I do not see why I should be attacked for assuming that Whymper meant what he wrote.

My criticisms of Whymper are that he had an inadequate sense of truth and that his attitude to other mountaineers was in certain cases, described below, worse than uncharitable. It is that which worries me, not his tendency to invent picturesque details. In *Scrambles* he records his descent of the Gorner glacier with a long dramatic description of nerving himself for a jump over a crevasse: ''First retreating as far as possible, I ran forward with all my might, took the leap, barely reached the other side, and fell awkwardly on my knees. Almost at the same moment a shower of stones fell on the spot from which I had jumped.'' We possess what he wrote about the same expedition in his dairy. ''It took me three-quarters of an hour to get down 350ft. I should think. Once on the glacier, moving was pretty easy, though the crevasses at the side rendered getting on it a work of time to a novice." Not a word about the dramatic jump.

Again he represents Carrel as saying on his return from the attempt on the Matterhorn which coincided with Whymper's victory, "The old legends are true—there are spirits on the top of the Matterhorn. We saw them ourselves—they hurled stones at us." But Carrel did not mistake Whymper for a demon. He recognised him by his white trousers and sadly reported the British victory. My critics admit that Whymper "overdramatised the fog-bow" seen on the descent from the first ascent of the Matterhorn, the fog-bow which provided the frontispiece to *Scrambles*. Why are they so reluctant to admit that the picture of the Ecrins gap was also over-dramatised? If this gap ever existed, what has happened to it? Why did it not become as famous as the Mummery Crack? Why did not subsequent parties photograph or at least sketch the Whymper gap? I do not claim to have made an exhaustive search of all Alpine periodicals but I have yet to find an account of the Ecrins which specifically mentions this gap. Can my critics provide a reference to such an account? I have consulted the GHM *Guide du Massif des Ecrins* in the AC library and there is no reference to this gap in the text. It would, I suggest, be an excellent plan if the AC committee induced two or three of our members to photograph this famous gap and provide an exact description for the *AJ*.

It is consistent with my critics' intention to represent me in the worst possible light to imply that I endorsed everything which Coolidge said against Whymper, but was it fair to repeat Coolidge's story that "Moore was a bit of a swell and Whymper grated on him" without quoting my comment, "His gloss on a certain incident described by Whymper in *Scrambles* was characteristic of Coolidge's feline malice?" How could my critics possibly imply after this that I agreed with Coolidge's view of the relations between Moore and Whymper?

Had my critics written to me after my earlier books in which most of my criticisms were published I should have been grateful, and corrected in *Matterhorn Centenary* the few points on which their criticisms are sound, and this with all the greater pleasure because of my great debt to *Scrambles*.

Again and again in their article my critics, as we shall see, either misquote some source or give a definite twist to facts. "It took," they wrote, "about three-quarters of a century before anybody got up to defend the Taugwalders." They are writing of the Zermatters, and the implication is that the Zermatters only after my article appeared, rushed to the Taugwalders' defence. Berglers in point of fact avoid controversy with tourists. Guides have often been attacked or criticised in the *AJ* but I do not remember any letter in the *AJ* from Berglers protesting against such attacks. When my defence of the Taugwalders appeared in the *AJ* Otto Furrer thanked me and conveyed the impression that some such reply to Whymper's monstrously unjust attack had been expected—for we still have a reputation for a sense of justice—and that my defence was better late than never.

Frank Smythe, whose boyhood hero Whymper had been, had put the best construction on Whymper's attacks on the Taugwalders in his life of Whymper but, after reading my article in the *AJ*, came down on the side of the Taugwalders and, in his preface to the new edition of Whymper's book on the Andes described the suggestion that the weak rope was deliberately selected as a "vile insinuation without any valid foundation." Do my critics agree that the insinuation was indeed vile, and if they do agree why should they be so anxious to denigrate poor Taugwalder, even to the extent of misquoting Leslie Stephen to attribute to him an attack on the Taugwalders which he never made? Stephen is alleged to have accused Taugwalder of "habitual carelessness." Here is what Leslie Stephen actually wrote: "Knowing the carelessness too often displayed on such occasions, the confidence which guides will show in weak ropes, and the probable state of excitement of the whole party, which would easily account for such an oversight, I think that the hypothesis of deliberate intention on Taugwalder's part is in the highest degree improbable; and there is not a particle of direct evidence in its favour. The presumption would be that Croz was almost equally responsible; and, at any rate, such accusations should have some more tangible ground than a vague possibility."

My critics describe this defence of the Taugwalders as "a very lame one." Could anti-Taugwalder prejudice go further? Nothing could be less lame than this decisive exposure of Whymper's "vile insinuation.'' Anybody less prejudiced than my critics would not need to be told that there is a world of difference between accusing a guide of deliberately putting a weak rope between him and his client, almost the worst crime which a guide could commit, and mere carelessness—''To defend a guide's misdeed on the plea,'' write my critics, ''that it was not deliberate but merely habitual carelessness is a very qualified extenuation.'' Stephen wrote nothing even faintly tolerant of the interpretation that he was accusing Taugwalder of ''habitual carelessness.'' What he did write was clearly intended to clear Taugwalder of sole responsibility. ''Croz was almost equally responsible,'' and the oversight could easily be accounted for by ''the probable state of excitement of the whole party.''

Herr C. Egger, author of many scholarly articles on mountaineering history, argued in *Die Alpen*, July 1940, that Whymper wished to deflect attention from himself to his guides in order to diminish his responsibility for the accident. After all he was one of the two amateur leaders of the party.

I quoted Knubel's remarks that Whymper was not liked in the valley, and Knubel was certainly not the only Zermatter to say this. Characteristic of my critics' controversial methods is the following comment. ''In view of Lunn's remarks, often made, that Swiss peasants do not easily reveal their minds and tend very readily to say what their interrogator wants to hear (a characteristic not at all confined to the Swiss), one would like to know whether Knübel had sensed Lunn's dislike of Whymper and was saying what would please him to hear.''

Mountain people have sometimes let a climber believe he was making a first ascent of a peak which had, in fact, been already climbed. Wills, for instance, thought that he was making the first ascent of the Wetterhorn and other instances could be cited of visitors being left under similar innocent illusions, but it is insensitive to equate the casual relations of Berglers with visitors to their valley with that close friendship between a guide and an amateur with whom he has climbed season after season. I look back on my friendship with Knubel as one of the best things that the mountains have given me. In our long talks I learned much from him about the mountain people and the mountain way of life. Knubel was a man of outstanding integrity. I am unruffled by my critics' personal attacks on me, but their petty denigration of Knubel, represented as a man who would tell a lie about Whymper to please me, has, I admit, nettled me.

My critics have paid a tribute to my contribution to Anglo-Swiss relations, and it was these relations which explain my original involvement in this controversy. It seemed to me un-English to bring the vilest of accusations against a guide without, as Stephen said, "a particle of direct evidence in its favour." I was sorry that it was so long before any member of the AC dissociated himself from these charges and that only one prominent member of the Club said what so badly needed to be said, and then only in *Macmillan's Magazine*. Hence my article in the *AJ*.

It seems to be impossible for my critics to defend Whymper without putting the worse construction on everything which the Taugwalders did. A pity, for their reputation in their own valley was good. Berglers do not readily subscribe to erect monuments to fellow Berglers, but a monument was erected to the Taugwalders on the instigation of Abbé Julen. "We wished to make it known," the Abbé said to me, "that we knew they had done their duty."

This somewhat acrimonious controversy will have been worth-while if it helps to clarify an important chapter in alpine history. I am sure my critics are as anxious as I am to write as historians and not as partisans briefed to defend Whymper or the Taugwalders. My critics have convinced me that Whymper's mountaineering record was far finer that Hudson's, that his knowledge of the French language was greater than I thought, and that on one or two other minor details I was wrong, i.e. that the "sharp-eyed boy" who reported an avalanche on the Matterhorn at the time of the accident was not one of Whymper's picturesque inventions, and that there was far more interest at Zermatt when the party was reported on the summit than I had been led to believe.

I am sure I am not unduly sanguine in my confidence that my critics agree with me.

1. that there is not a particle of evidence to support Whymper's insinuation that a weak rope had been deliberately put between Taugwalder and Douglas, and

2. that this vile insinuation should never have been made.

My own prejudices, or rather postjudices, against Whymper are provoked by his very unpleasant attitude to three mountaineers. My critics have tried to belittle his attack on Taugwalder, but they wisely ignore two other cases which I mentioned of Whymper's denigration of other mountaineers. Perhaps they could reassure me that their view does not differ from mine on

3. Whymper's statement to the Secretary of the AC that he spent a miserable night on the Matterhorn after the accident, fearing that the Taugwalders might murder him;

4. on the fact that Whymper, according to Graham Brown writing as editor of the AJ, "allowed his bitterness against Hudson to appear in an unfair attack";

5. on the following summary of an article in *AJ* 57 (pp. 339-40), which seems to me far more damaging to Whymper than any of Coolidge's attacks and which certainly had a far greater influence in prejudicing me against Whymper than anything which Coolidge wrote or said.

　　The Alpine Club has been presented with Whymper's own copy of Mummery's *My Climbs in the Alps and Caucasus*. Against Freshfield's tribute quoted in the preface: "his untimely death is a grievous loss to the Club," Whymper wrote, "I do not agree." In *The Sphere*, January 30, 1909, Whymper reviewed the book and described it as a "vicious" book. A memorandum pasted inside the volume shows that in the event of the review provoking comment he intended to try and belittle Mummery by quoting "my times across Col Dolent against his across the Col des Courtes, and my times on the Aig. Verte against his times." He then speculates on the condition in which Mummery's body is likely to be should traces of it be found. "It will be," he says, "in the shape of a dislocated skeleton, one bone here and another there. . . The stomach and heart will be nowhere." Mrs. Mummery, be it noted, was alive when this review appeared. He concludes his review by postulating that in certain important matters Mummery was insane.

　　It is perhaps not surprising that my critics make no comment on my quotation of this passage, the writer of which by the way was T. S. Blakeney. I am rash enough to hope that in spite of our many differences of opinion about Whymper we agree in our views about Whymper's review of Mummery's book. It is pleasant to end a controversial article on a note of cordial agreement.

from THE ALPINE JOURNAL *1966*

PART 5

Contingencies, Castastrophes, Death

For all that modern climbing has grown increasingly well-safeguarded as standards have risen, the element of risk remains and will always be courted by those practising at the highest standards. The accounts included in this section act as grim reminders of the likely consequence of error, the unpredictability of the mountain environment, or the heartfelt relief of the near-miss.

A Crevasse on the Ecrins

GEOFFREY WINTHROP YOUNG

In a year hitherto unique for its fine circumstances, before we had had time to discover the new forms of danger which such circumstances can produce, our party began its serious climbing by an attempt upon the South Buttress of Les Ecrins, then unclimbed. We slept out beside the Glacier du Vallon de la Pilatte, through a thunderstorm which may have been intended for a danger-signal. In the early half-light we started up the furrowed snow-slopes below the face of Les Ecrins. It is a névé upon which all authority informed us that no crevasses had ever been detected. We halted where the slopes steepened, to fix our ice-claws. In the course of some previous days of pass-wandering between the Meije and the Ecrins, a competition in ice-glissading down narrow couloirs with Laurent Croux and Knubel had left me the reminder of a bandaged left hand. The others therefore were well ahead by the time I had fixed the claws and started in pursuit.

The surface was of that corrugated, old-snow kind which is of all the most reassuring. I had the claw-marks of five hardened veterans to guide me; and the automatic glances which we throw by instinct to right and left upon all snow, to detect the remoter shadows that give warning of the proximity of a crevasse, revealed to me only an unwavering respectability. And then my foot went cleanly through. I flung myself forward with my axe instinctively held fore and aft. My second foot followed. The little circle of world-crust which I commanded sank without a murmur; and I dropped upright through space.

It was certainly not alarming: hardly even unpleasant. As I am convinced happens in these accidents where no chance of action upon self-behalf remains, my consciousness was at once shocked into an observant detachment. "So it's your turn, after all; the inconceivable is happening to you too!" it commented protestingly. "Well, of course you'll be killed; people are by these things! But, equally of course, you being me, and I still I, you can't be!" Over all, there was a superficial, part-gratifying part-agonising

487

excitement as to the event; and, under all, a flame-like intensifying of the essential Ego, of the individual vital principle, subduing for the second into its single assertion of self all sensation and all eternity. They are both stages familiar likewise from our memories of the first spinning and of the later deepening of unconsciousness under anaesthetic.

I stopped. The axe had jammed, head and spike, across the ice walls; and my right armpit locked over its shaft, rigidly. Simultaneously, the soft snow which had fallen with me packed softly against my chest and back, and helped to support my weight. I kicked tentatively. My feet moved freely in space, between widening walls; and the movement released a little of the packed snow, which swished and hissed down into a silence that betrayed no bottom. I looked up through semi-darkness. Some 15ft. above me stretched a wide and flat roof, vanishing in gloom to right and left. Its underside was glazed and stuccoed with small icicles. I guessed at once that in a normal year this lid would be carrying a depth of snow above it which could conceal any signs of a crevasse underneath, supposing one to have existed. But this year the snow had thawed away above, and perhaps the ice had opened wider beneath; until nothing was left but a skim of harmless-looking old-snow, resting upon a level roofing of ice, ready to break at a touch, but neither sagging nor shadowing perceptibly above. Under the lid the inner walls of the crevasse first bulged, and then receded on their descent, something like the inside of an hour-glass. I, or rather the axe, had jammed in the narrow neck. The falling snow, arrested by my obstruction, had therefore been able to pack helpfully on the ice-bulges, under my chest and shoulders. Right in the middle of the stalactite roof was the neat hole of light through which I had fallen.

As a schoolboy, clambering once upon the roof of the cloisters, I had fallen, or rather bounced, through a skylight. Looking up then from the pavement 12ft. below I had been amazed to see that only one pane was gone from the skylight, and that I had shot through a single small square of frame. It looked so improbable that my shoulders could have come through it longways, or my head crossways, that I had had to go up it once again, and make a second try. But I had failed entirely that time to squeeze through it, lacking probably the limp abandon of an involuntary swoop. When

I now looked up at the snow hole, this forgotten incident, and all its attendant emotions, returned with ludicrous point. The hole was at about the same height above me, and it looked just as impossible that I should ever have passed through it.

It was not to be expected that the rest of the party could continue the climb without noticing the shortage of numbers: Josef had always eyes in the back of his head for my whereabouts. At the same time my feeling now was fear of their return. They would see the hole, and make for it; and as the crevasse was undefined above, they would not learn until too late of the huge extent of brittle ice-vaulting which surrounded the hole. The fear was not solely unselfish; for I was not uncomfortable, and I had no wish to be driven like a cork through the safety neck of my ice-bottle by any fresh downfall. If I called aloud, they might think I was hurt, and hurry back incautiously. If I did not call, they might be still more alarmed, and in any case remain unwarned until too late. So I tried to tune my shouts from the depths to a note of casual cheerfulness, counting thirty between each, in the hope that the slow rhythm would issue upon them soothingly.

A waiting time has rarely seemed so short. I had hardly time to work my injured hand into the warmth of my pocket, before I heard voices, shouted my warning, and felt the swish of a rope on my head. The noose was ready — they were a prompt party — I slipped it under my left arm, and then very cautiously over my right shoulder, until I could get my right arm through it without surrendering my arm-lock on the axe. A second noose came down; and I twisted that round my left arm. Then I pushed the packed snow down past me into depth, and swung clear between the walls.

But the ropes, with my weight on them, grooved deeply back into the roof bordering the skylight. A lot more crust and snow had to be carefully cut away from round them, and I was deluged in the process. At last the ropes ran free enough to allow the men to lift me a few inches. I loosened the axe from its sturdy jam, and nicked a foothold on either bulging wall. As I moved up, up went the slack. But above the bottleneck the walls were too far apart to allow me to straddle across on my opposite nicks. So I turned, and chipped them up the one undercut wall immediately under the ropes, pulling myself up by the noose round my left arm, with the shoulder-noose steadily shortening up in support. The lines formed by the descending ice walls of a great crevasse, glistering down into darkness, are some of the most terrible in nature, even to look down upon. But when we are down among them – the all-enclosing, timeless, and deathly-cold impression they can give us is overmuch that of a tomb. It seemed all the more a smiling world to return to above, of sunshine and pleased faces. I took a further small comfort from the chance that I had never been driven to use my bandaged hand, for all the mountain guile. Since the fault was my own, the end fortunate, and no one else involved except to his credit, I was not really sorry to have had the experience. It cleared up for me a number of technical points, of procedure, which had been much debated among us in connection with like accidents.

from ON HIGH HILLS *1927*

'Sir, I refute it thus'

SIR DOUGLAS BUSK

Noetzlin was a distinguished physicist, much immersed in the technicalities of his and allied sciences. Alain de Chatellus recalls an entertaining incident in an earlier year. He and Noetzlin were descending with Armand from a traverse of all three peaks of the Aiguille de Blaitiere: At that time the theories of de Broglie and Heisenberg on the calculation of probabilities were much in vogue in learned circles. Noetzlin endeavoured to explain to Armand that it was not theoretically impossible for a stone to fall up to the top instead of down to the bottom of a mountain. "I don't know if that is true," replied Armand, "but we should nevertheless keep our eyes open, because the folk behind us are certainly not familiar with the theory."

from ARMAND CHARLET *1975*

On the Edge

SUE GELLER

"Hey! The haul-line is stuck. I can't move. Can you free the rope?"

"No. It's blown around the corner and become snagged. I'll have to rappel down to free it. You'd better come back down."

Fortunately I was only 15ft. above the belay, so descending to the ledge was easily accomplished. Upon arriving at the small stance, I found Coral already setting up the rappel, muttering angrily to herself about wasting time and energy. I agreed: we both should have known better than to leave the haul-line and the lead rope hanging down with a stiff breeze blowing.

A feeling of haste and annoyance developed as we finished rigging the rappel. After all, we still had three hard pitches to go and we wanted to get on with the climb while we were still psyched up for the difficult climbing ahead and before the afternoon thunderstorms developed. Having to fuss with tangled ropes seemed an unjust intrusion into our carefully laid plans.

Coral busily tied the rope into the anchors, and told me she would rappel, free the rope, and then climb back up with a top belay from me. I was just standing around, feeling confused by the speed of events, but I got the general drift of the plan. I figured I could get sorted out and improve my tie-in after Coral left on the rappel. Meanwhile, I did what I was told. I had climbed all summer with Coral and knew her to be a competent, safe climber. I trusted her judgment implicitly.

Coral was still talking when it happened. She checked her brake system, leaned out on the rope and fell.

For me, all of existence condensed into a few seconds which lasted an eternity, a vertical space which enclosed only two ropes and a falling body. I had time to calmly think, "Her brake system failed but she's tied into the end of the rope and will be caught by that. But will she hit that ramp below first?" Coral's eyes, astonishment and disbelief reflected in them, briefly met mine, and then quickly receded. Even as I thought of it, she reached out and

491

grabbed the haul-line in front of her and tried to hold on. I could see no noticeable slowing of her rate of fall and doubted her ability to stop such a fall with only her hands. I accepted the fact that she would soon be dead, for I had belatedly realised that it was not the brake system which had failed, but the anchor. The rappel rope had come free from the karabiner and she and the rope were falling together. A quick glance at the anchors verified this, and I looked back down the wall, expecting to see her falling free onto the ramp far below, meanwhile planning how I could get to her quickly, dreading the sight I would find there. I felt intense guilt that I had allowed this mistake to occur and was now absolutely helpless to correct it.

But no! She was still hanging on to the haul-line and was even slowing down. Stopping.

At this point, my mind shifted gears and the rest of the world returned to existence. It now seemed only natural that, while falling, someone should be able to grab a 9mm rope, slide 50ft. down it on a vertical wall, and stop. My thoughts automatically turned to retreat . . . how to manage it safely, how to deal with the emotional shock we had received. "I almost died!" Coral cried after she stopped, and that was the only time that day either of us voiced our mutual thought.

Coral's hands were badly burned, but before they stiffened up into unusable claws, she was able to undo the now useless lead rope from her rappel system and clip into the haul-line. She then swung around the corner to a lower belay stance and clipped in.

I stood on my own ledge, unable to see Coral, praying she was together enough not to make a mistake. I was shaking and it required several minutes of deep-breathing to calm body and mind, for my job was just beginning and I knew I had to be thinking clearly. I had to rappel down to Coral on the haul-line, administer first aid if needed, and figure out how to get us both back down five pitches. Because my attention was focused on solving this logistical problem, and because of the feeling of responsibility for Coral's safety, I was able to push the preceding few minutes out of my mind. There were other things to worry about.

The retreat was full of anxiety for me. In my agitated state I was fearful of making a mistake and killing us both. Coral first tried to rappel with a belay, but it quickly became obvious that she could not handle the rappel rope because her hands were so painful and useless. I, therefore, lowered her to the next belay ledge and rappelled down after her. We followed this procedure all the way down. Fortunately, we were on an established route and the anchors were already set up. We were on the ground within an hour, and walked over to a group of spectators who were watching some climbers on another route and begged a ride to the hospital. We were safe.

It was not until the next day that I fully realised how close to a tragedy the incident had been, how close to dying one of my best friends had come, how easily it could happen to any one of my friends or even myself. I had always felt immune to this sort of self-caused accident because I was very conservative and safety-conscious in my climbing philosophy and practice. Obviously, this immunity did not exist and I had to deal with a heightened awareness of my own mortality. It was several weeks before the image of Coral's surprised face faded from my memory, but, almost a year later, I still have periodic flashes of unreasonable anxiety when rappelling or setting up a hanging belay. I have come to accept these feelings as a reminder of my fallibility and I am even more committed to controlling as many elements of a climb as possible.

Why do these accidents happen? We had trained hard for this climb and were in good physical shape. Yet, on that particular day, we each had doubts about doing the climb which we did not mention because of our feeling of commitment to each other. These doubts were brought on by problems outside our climbing lives but which intruded radically upon our climbing mentalities. If, when faced with something new and challenging, we always give in to self-doubts, nothing would ever be accomplished. Yet, it is important to understand one's emotional self and to recognise the times when small doubts or upsets become big enough to warrant a re-evaluation of plans. Because of this incident, I listen more closely to my inner feelings and am not as hesitant to say "Not today".

Coral's hands have since healed with only faint scars, but I'm not sure if our emotional scars will ever completely heal. Is climbing worth it? I still climb; Coral does not, although the fall is only part of her reasons for retirement. And, while I hope to never have to undergo such an experience again, I feel that because of this incident, I have reached a better understanding within myself about why I climb. I feel a deeper personal commitment to climbing, as though a higher level of participation had been reached, and I try to enjoy more deeply the companionship of my partners and the time we share on a climb, for I now realise I might not have another time with them . . . one of us might not be here tomorrow.

from MOUNTAIN 72 *1980*

Othon Bron

JANET ADAM SMITH

Othon had been up at the Col du Géant for several days; about July 15 he had come rushing down to Courmayeur, because he had dreamt that Horace was dead.

On July 24 he did the Géant three times, meeting the second and third parties at the foot of the rock. That night he told his brother, now guardian of the Torino, that he wanted to settle his account; and next morning he started for the Montenvers with two young Italians. One was a young student of nineteen from Rome, the other was about twenty-four; neither had done much climbing before. There was some new snow on the Glacier du Géant, and the going was fairly tricky; twice Othon went into small crevasses up to his waist. They were near the séracs when he stopped and lit a pipe, saying there was just one more stretch, and the worst would be over. Almost immediately he stepped on to a snow-bridge (tested already with his axe), and it broke; he sprang for the further side, just failed to reach it (he had a heavy sack), and fell; his two clients tightened the rope, but while Othon was still swinging it was cut by a blade of ice in the crevasse itself. He fell 40 metres. The two young men called for help; the Requin hut wasn't far off. For over an hour Othon lay there conscious, talking; the two men did not like to go near the lip of the crevasse, so they could not hear what he said, though at one moment it sounded as if he were praying. Men arrived from the hut; the first was a porter from Courmayeur. Othon heard his voice— "C'est toi, Henri?" — and asked him to take his pocket-book and watch to his wife. He told them not to try to lift him. "Tu souffres, Othon?" "Je souffre." As they were bringing him up, he died.

from MOUNTAIN HOLIDAYS *1946*

The Beginning of a New Life

FREDI RÖLLI

Early morning, Tuesday August 14. Turning over restlessly in my sleeping bag, I know I shan't get back to sleep. In my mind I am already climbing. I can see every detail, each move, each hold. Just lying there doing nothing is driving me mad, what's the point? So I give up my warm sleeping bag in exchange for a pair of cold, stiff gym shoes.

I start off really relaxed, walking then running through the woods, weaving through and under the trees, running faster, then slower. Jumping between and over tree trunks, small streams and ant hills. It is so good to feel the warm blood rising slowly up to my head, to feel my heart pounding beneath my chest and the wind cooling my face which is warm and sweaty from running. I am tired so I sit down on the soft ground and feed myself on a few of the berries which grown in profusion here.

I am on my feet again, looking up, awe-inspired at Mont Blanc, the Aiguille du Midi, the Tour Ronde – and over towards the Aiguille Verte studying their features. By the pale light of the moon everything appears, as though from another world. What I'd give right now to be walking in to do a route, any route, rather than waiting here. I am really keyed-up and feeling in great shape.

I can't understand my friends; they are still lying asleep in the tent. Such beautiful weather, it couldn't be better for climbing, and they can sleep on as though it's a certainty that it will stay fine. I've only to think back over the last two weeks. Brrr! When it rained for four days without a break (how depressing!). You get wet feet even in the tent. Even worse when you're lying in your sleeping bag and the water comes in threatening to drown you while you lie there!

The stars disappear slowly as the night makes way for the new day. What will it bring, I wonder? Only yesterday the streets were full of foul-smelling cans and my ears were buzzing from the various noises. Now, the snow on the highest peaks is gradually taking on a red colour, eveything is quiet, beautifully still. Now and again I can hear something rustle, on the ground or high up in the

496

trees. A bird perhaps, or a squirrel. Occasionally in the distance the sound of a car or a motorbike starting up. Somewhere a dog is woken up, he in turn wakes his master, he wants a game. In the grey light of dawn a few men are on their way to work.

What are my friends doing? The scene inside the tent is disappointing; they are still sleeping. In the next tent two climbers are busy clearing away their cooking utensils. They must be in a hurry because a little while later they are walking quickly towards Chamonix. How I envy them and the other people who are already climbing. If only we were!

At last now that the sun is shining in the valley Jung and Toni open their sleepy eyes. They, unlike me, are not in a hurry. Wearily they wash and dress themselves. Breakfast must obviously be properly savoured. I am so excited I don't eat a thing.

Two months and nothing else to do but climb. Two months' holiday; for the first time I can do what I enjoy. My first time in Chamonix. I can hardly wait to experience for myself the famous routes put up by climbers like Cassin, Rebuffat, and Comici. I always listened excitedly when the hard men talked of their routes on Mont Blanc; poring over maps and studying the guide, sometimes through to the early hours of the morning. Then I could hardly wait, and now here I am. Ideally I'd like to set off straight away, immediately. Every minute that we remain in the valley seems to me a terrible waste.

Half-an-hour later we're organised and ready to go. We queue for the lift tickets at the Aiguille du Midi téléphérique. We are standing way back in the depressingly long queue, more precisely right at the back! Is everything conspiring against me today? Waiting, waiting, and still more waiting, I am practically going out of my mind. The tourists piss me off, all in their Sunday best, with camera, the women made up as though they were going dancing rather than up into the mountains. I share some of these feelings with my fellow sufferers; they feel the same way. Standing around makes you hungry. Jung and Toni have bought a couple of French sticks, some meat and cheese. So the waiting around is slightly more bearable. I can now at least control my anger.

At last after an hour-and-a-half we're standing at the ticket window. We are in luck; now we each have a lift ticket but still have to wait till our numbers are called. I've never had to stand and wait

around like this before, not for anything. When, after another two
hours doing nothing, we start swinging up towards the Aiguille du
Midi, my enthusiasm for climbing has almost died, I'd rather spend
the day wandering around the area here. We leave the cable car at
the mid-station as we want to pitch the tents on the Plan de
l'Aiguille.

Tomorrow we want to try the French pillar, which means an
early start. So today we don't want to be climbing too late. After
much hesitation we decide on the NNE Ridge of the Aiguille de
l'M, about which Rebuffat says in his book, *The 100 finest routes
in the Mont Blanc Massif*, "this route is therefore an excellent test-
climb both for the novice, who can try out his competence in
techniques for different types of climbing, and for the more
experienced climber who, at the beginning of a season wants to get
back into practice, and assess his own fitness." For us, no doubt,
an interesting way to fill in an afternoon. I would actually have
preferred to climb one of the routes on the North Face. But when
there are four of you, you can't just think of yourself. So settle for
the Aiguille de l'M.

Something is wrong; just a couple of hours ago I thought nothing
could stop me. I felt I was in good shape for the big routes, that I'd
be able to power up them. Now I must watch out so I don't trip
over before we get to the start of the route. It's as though I
suddenly had two left feet, and I want to climb steep mountains!

Once at the start of the route all thoughts, except those of
climbing, disappear. When I see the ridge, reminiscent of the
Badile, I am in my element again. I tie onto the rope and
immediately feel more relaxed. Have I got everything? Quickly I
check that I am tied on properly, that I have everything I need in
the sack, another couple of slings from the sack and we are ready to
go.

Toni is already climbing the first pitch, belayed from above by
Ernst. Mm, that should make a good photo, "Hey Toni, wait a
sec." Lens cap off, focus . . . click. "OK Toni you can climb
again now!" Another quick shot of the Aiguille Verte.

Jung wants to lead the first pitch, so I set up a belay. While he is
climbing I watch his every move, particularly when he has to look
for holds. I can hardly wait for him to belay before I start climbing.
His call, "When you're ready," comes as a relief.

The rock is warm to the touch and it's good to feel the rough granite under my fingers. The first few moves are stiff and unco-ordinated. But soon I develop a rhythm and am climbing as though in a trance. The sun makes everything pleasantly warm, the rock, the air and my whole body, especially my face. Now and again a cool breeze blows over the ridge. The climbing and the situation, each perfect, combine to bring me complete peace of mind. True the rock is a bit polished in places, the route is done pretty often, but you don't have to choose the easiest line, you can go for the line up untouched rock.

The second pitch, which I lead, is technically not so interesting, not as steep and presents no real difficulties. I run the rope out quickly and take a stance.

The next pitch is better, good crack-climbing and I have to use all the holds or I'll run out of strength. Above the cracks there is an excellent resting place where Jung is already belayed.

We exchange a few words and I lead on past, I climb up a couple of metres and for some strange reason look down at Jung, something about the belay doesn't seem right. I climb back down. Ah ha! the belay is OK for a downward pull, but if the tension came from above he'd be pulled off the stance. So I change the belay although Jung doesn't quite understand the point. How this will affect later events we don't yet know.

I start climbing again, the first few metres are easy, then the wall steepens and the holds thin out. Up past three peg runners and the angle eases off considerably, a few metres of easy climbing and it is time for another runner, but where? The rock looks pretty blank up here. I don't want to climb back down. Wait! There's a crack, I might get a peg in. Shit! The crack's blind. A nut might go in, a small one. I don't like it but there's nothing else. Standing on small holds I continue climbing. . . .

I wake up and open my eyes. It's dark, suddenly it occurs to me as my first coherent thought, I've fallen! Instinctively I know what has happened, although I can't remember anything about why I fell or about the actual fall itself; but I can't explain my presence in this strange room in any other way. I fall asleep again, for how long I can't tell. I've lost all sense of time and space.

When I wake up again I feel desperately thirsty, as though I've crossed the desert without any water. My throat and mouth are both dead dry and I feel as though I am suffocating. Now and then a thick gooey slime comes up from my throat, it makes me sick just thinking about it. I want to call or scream for something to drink, but I can muster no more than a whimper. At last the nurse arrives, "Can you get something to drink please?" She doesn't understand! Of course, we are in France—I must for better or worse try and speak French; I think she has understood me—what, I am not allowed anything to drink? Yes, but why not? I am thirsty, desperately thirsty. I am just not allowed to, end of matter. I fall asleep again. I wake up, having no idea how long I've been asleep. My shoulders are hurting and my whole body has gone to sleep so I call the nurse once more, "Would you move my legs, there is no feeling in them." Has she understood, I wonder. "I don't know why you've behaving like this, you haven't lost anything!" But my legs! and my arms, I can't move them, help me please!" "Relax and go back to sleep." She switches out the light and leaves the room. It's quiet now and the breathing of the other patients is the only noise to be heard.

As I lie there, it suddenly hits me like a thunderbolt. I realise I am paralysed; yes, paralysed. I cannot yet imagine what it means to be paralysed. Luckily I don't have much time to think about it before I fall asleep again.

Nurses come and go, their wooden clogs clattering on the floor, they alter something on my bed. Men in white coats appear, they talk amongst themselves occasionally chewing on their pencils. Perhaps they recommend something to the nurses. Then, frowning, they leave the room.

What's that? I recognise those voices. Ah! there they are; Toni, Jung and Ernst standing at the door. "Hi! Come on in," but before they can answer someone wearing a white apron has chased them away. They are sure to come back, and with that thought I fall asleep.

Strange; when I was last awake I was in a different room, wasn't I? The noise; somebody is drilling into my skull! The bright lights and all these people in white coats. Where am I? What are they doing? "Lie very still, you are in Grenoble," a voice answers me in broken German. "You have broken you neck, we have to drill two small holes so we can attach some clamps to keep your head in the right position, tomorrow you will be flying to Basel."

"Yes but I live in Zürich and all my friends are in Zürich!" "You must understand in Basel they can do more for you."

So I've broken my neck, I am paralysed. That's why I can't feel my legs or my arms nor move at all. What happened, why did I fall? It wasn't hard. I wonder, will the paralysis be only temporary? It must be, otherwise I'll never climb again. What I've heard before about paralysis caused by spinal injuries makes me feel very pessimistic; they are mostly long term. Then I'll no longer be able to go into the mountains with my friends. In future I shall have to forgo those beautiful days in the mountains. Now I can only dream of the ski trips over virgin snow, and the high mountains. What about the bivouacs? Mournfully I think back on those lovely hours spent high up in the mountains. The thick steaming soup which Hans would cook, or the *fondue* with Leo, when we were still kids. And earlier still, with my parents, when we walked from Engelberg over the Jochpass to the Melchsee and were stormed on and had to spend the night in a hay barn, without any warm clothes or hot tea. While I am absorbed in memories of past exploits, I fall asleep again.

Someone wakes me up: "The people from Switzerland are here, we are going to take you to the airport in an ambulance, where there is a plane waiting to take you to Basel. Doctor Brucker and Doctor Steinmann are introduced to me. It works wonders on me just to hear and speak Swiss-German again. I feel things aren't half as bad now. In Switzerland maybe they will work a miracle and bring my limbs back to life.

"We will be flying to Switzerland in a jet," says one of the doctors. Although I am very excited, I fall asleep on the way to the airport. I didn't want to miss the take-off under any circumstances but it can't have been too long ago because as the pilot banks the aircraft I catch a glimpse of Mont Blanc. I would so much like to have stood on that summit but now that must always remain a dream, like all the other routes I wanted to do. My friends will go into the mountains without me, I will have to let them go off ski-ing and for trips into the woods without me. I remember how I used to wander amongst the trees and the plants, photographing the flowers, in spring when they are just emerging from the buds and later in Summer when they are in full bloom and the bees are flying from one to another. Sometimes I'd lie in wait for animals with the telephoto at the ready. I remember spending a whole afternoon stalking a lone bird, without getting a single decent picture out of it.

What about the musical evenings and will I be able to talk to people any more? Those times when we played all evening and the audience kept asking for more. All that, gone for ever. That can't be true?

The view from the window takes my mind away from these sad thoughts. The bright blue sky makes me screw up my eyes. I want to look out, I move my head just a little and Doctor Buckart warns me, "Don't move your head! You must lie perfectly still or you will lose the little that you can still move." But so that I can see the country that we are flying over the pilot banks the plane over a little. Now that we are flying level again I catch sight of a commercial aircraft from Swissair flying above us.

"In a few minutes we arrive in Basel," announces the pilot a while later. "From the airport an Allouette III will fly us to the paraplegic centre." My first time in a hospital and one in a strange city at that. All too soon we arrive in Basel—Millhausen; the pilot lands the aircraft gently. The flight, the excitement was all a bit too much and before the aircraft has come to a halt I am already asleep.

From this moment on I am certain of one thing—I will make it—I will cope with the new situation—I want to live! Somehow there will be something left for which it is worth living.

The Death of Gary Ullin

ROBERT W. CRAIG

Carrying [on Pic Lenin] in the now deep snow was increasingly tiring and the morning of July 23 was unusually warm. We floundered up to our waists in places. This was the nastiest work of the expedition thus far. We gasped moving up with our loads and intermittently seemed to drowse in our steps. We could not recall ever being more uncomfortable from heat and a kind of lassitude at such a modest altitude. At last a fairly steep rise, giving way to a gentle slope whose snow alternatively held us up then collapsed, and we could see we were almost at the foot of the ice-slope.

We considered the alternatives for the Campsite and all simultaneously agreed on a spot under the bulge of two ancient collapsed seracs. We were somewhat to the left of the main ice face and probings of the slope around the tent platform area indicated settled, stable snow. We dug the platform to accommodate our two tents.

Gary Ullin and I found ourselves in the spacious Bauer Himalayan, and in the smaller tent were John Roskelley and John Marts.

The cached loads were brought up from a short distance below in a single carry by Gary while the rest of us dug in and set up the camp. I never ceased to be impressed with Gary's quiet, constant strength. We were all terrifically excited to be where we were.

Later in the morning of July 23 at Camp 4 the air became even more oppressive. Huge cumulo-nimbus thunderheads boiled up from the Alai Valley all the way east into the desolate brown distance of South West China. Even at 16,700ft. the air seemed heavy. We had dug a spacious tent platform, with our minds on the gathering squall line (it had begun then to seem like more than a characteristic summer thunder shower), and our bodies reacting to the lassitude brought on by the still heat in that momentary, glowing, glacial oven.

The platform was on a slope of perhaps 35°. We had probed the slope above and to the sides of the platform to determine snow stability. There had been perhaps twelve to fifteen inches of snow in the past two days of afternoon squalls. We had, in fact, climbed up and down through some of that on our relays. There were no sloughing slides even as we broke through to our waists on our way up from Camp 3. All in all, because of that and the lack of any slides from above the snow seemed quite stable at Camp 4. However, when we were in our respective tents a few minutes after 12.00 noon we heard a thundering boom from the direction of the big hanging glacier on the north-west shoulder of Peak 19.

Gary was closest to the side of the tent on which the avalanche let go, and looking out the partly opened vestibule, he could see the huge mass breaking off the ice cliffs. He shouted, "Holy Christ, you won't believe it!"

By the time I got onto my knees and peered over Gary's shoulder, there were still sizeable pieces breaking off the face of the ice-cliff, but the main mass had pulverised into a huge blend of ice blocks and dust and, gathering more material in the form of seracs and surface snow, it was churning and roaring down through the ice-fall on the upper west side of the North Face and billowing directly toward our tent, though somewhat on the right diagonal.

It was an enormous thing, travelling at great speed with a sustained grinding, roaring, as all the ice pulverised in the kinetic energy of its stupendous force.

The avalanche kept coming and coming, and all this was happening in the course of thirty to forty seconds. In such a situation even catastrophe becomes a subject for reflection and fascination. There was nothing we could do, no place to go. By this time Roskelley and Marts had their heads out and were looking up and back, spellbound yet very scared. Just as the billowing cloud of snow came up and over our tents, we realised the main body of the avalanche had turned off to the left down the main North Face. We finally heard it roar out below onto the moraines we had traversed days before. The snow and ice dust settled on our tents for another fifteen or twenty seconds.

We were shaken. We didn't, at that point, really know how far away it had turned down the face, for it was snowing hard again and we were not particularly inclined to go out on that slope and find out.

It was lunchtime and we were assembled to eat in the Bauer.

Lunch was not complicated, but since we had perspired a lot carrying up and making camp, we decided a fairly salty soup and some Dutch cheese plus a lot of Wyler's lemonade were in order.

Between 12.30 and 1.00 p.m. I kicked the tent wall because the snow load in the midday storm was building. As I did so, the whole mountain began to shake and oscillate. Although we didn't immediately acknowledge it, we knew were were in a big earthquake. We had read of the earthquakes in Uzbekistan and Kirghizia which had destroyed villages throughout history, but this one was here with us, real, and if we had been greatly frightened and upset by the avalanche, moments before, now we were all genuinely fearful.

After I kicked the tent wall, Ullin quietly, but with feeling, said, "Jesus, what is this?" I couldn't say anything; I couldn't believe what was happening, and I think we all honestly suspected the whole mountain might fall and take us with it. We simply stared back at each other. There was a feeling that at any moment our whole camp might go tumbling down the ice cliffs just below us. It was a moment of unspoken terror. While it lasted (perhaps five or six seconds), I had the sensation of being suspended in air with the surface oscillating underneath.

Strangely, the earthquake did not bring the mountain down on us, though we heard large avalanches in the distance through the snowstorm. It was at that same moment our friends on Krylenko Pass were in serious trouble. We did speculate about what might be happening to them and were later relieved that in the evening radio transmission there was no sign of emergency.

The afternoon passed slowly with intermittent but heavy snow showers. The cloud masses during infrequent breaks appeared more ominous than they had in the morning heat. We got out during the pauses in the storm and checked the slopes around camp for stability, but could find nothing out of order. The surface snow and older layers all seemed quite stable. Camp 4 had nonetheless become a very spooky place. Gary, our most inventive and frequent dinner chef, decided we had had enough trauma for the day and that it was appropriate that we have a special meal that evening.

We had a lot of food at Camp 4 on July 23. Our relays had been heavy and we were in an exceptionally strong position in terms of equipment and rations. Our food was roughly half Russian and half American.

Dinner on the night of July 23 was one of these mixed affairs with red caviar for a starter, followed by Astro eggs and then a steak-and-a-half per man, served with green peas and almonds. By the time we got to the frozen strawberries, we weren't sure we could get through that sumptuous dessert. We decided a chess game was in order. Gary and I were black and Marts and Roskelley white. Marts turned out to be a very formidable opponent and Ullin and I were quickly dispatched.

We were unusually sleepy and barely able to stay awake for the 9.00 p.m. radio transmission. The snow continued to fall heavily and we realised we were no longer in a series of intermittent squalls: we were in a real storm.

Thunder had been rolling around the horizons towards China all afternoon and evening, and at midnight we heard Roskelley shout something about, "There's a war going on over there." As we awakened, we became aware of an enormous lightning storm to the north and east of us. The Chinese and the Russians? The storm which had held us seemed to have pulled back to the west; the storm born in China seemed to be advancing as a black wall, moving westward down the Alai Valley toward our section of the Pamirs. As it moved toward us, thunder was as continuous as the flashes and getting disturbingly close. When it had reached an estimated five miles distance an hour or so later, it suddenly veered to the north and east. We slept uneasily into the morning.

It continued to snow into mid-morning on the 24th and then became warm again, clearing, and we got a glimpse of the Achik Tash Valley and Base Camp and the main Alai Valley. Everything was thoroughly covered with snow, all the way down into the Alai Valley, perhaps as low as 9,500ft. We piled out of our tents happily, thinking we could reorganise our equipment left outside, dig a snow cave for safe storage and possible emergency shelter, and prepare our loads, technical gear, and ropes for the summit attempt on July 25.

During all the preceding days of snow, the final ice slope had remained largely free of any surface build-up, and we had been very hopeful that we could pretty much front-point directly up it to the rock bands near the top. By the morning of the 24th, we were disappointed to notice that the face was not completely sloughing its new snow. Now it was snowing again late in the afternoon of the

24th. If much more fell on that face, we would have to wait another day. We briefly considered digging the snow cave out sufficiently to provide a bomb-proof shelter in which to wait out the weather, but gave it up in favour of conserving energy for the climb. Also staying in the tents we could keep a much closer watch on the weather and on the slopes.

We felt the camp was doubly secure. We had re-pitched the tents following the snow build-ups, had stored the substantial supplies of food and climbing gear in the snow cave, and made up our packs for the summit climb in the morning. We were not optimistic about conditions for an early morning departure. It was snowing steadily with little wind.

I first awakened at about midnight. It is an old fly fisherman's and mountaineer's habit to be able to awaken virtually at will at all hours of the night and early morning in pursuit of God knows what, but early on that morning it was snowing hard, and I felt a dull sense of apprehension as I went back to sleep. The snow was not letting up and there were 3,000ft. of blue ice above us. I awakened later, noting the time to be about 1 a.m., got partly out of my sleeping bag, opened the tunnel entrance of the tent, and looked out. Still snowing—another six to eight inches of new snow since dinner.

I wakened Gary, described the situation, and said, "We've got to forget it, Gary. We're not going to go up today; we're just going to have to hope the storm eases up so we can get off this mountain."

Gary sighed, obviously disappointed, and said, "Well, let's check it again at 2.30 or 3 a.m. I sure wish we could get the hell out of here! This place gives me the creeps. We can't stay on this face in this storm much longer."

The storm made it relatively warm in the tent that night. As I returned to sleep, I kept my right arm outside the sleeping bag. I was sleeping on my left side, facing toward the uphill side of the slope, Gary for the first time was sleeping with his head at the same end of the tent, and he, too, slept on his left side closest to the uphill side of the tent. His head was well up into the tent corner, as we had stored all the food, cooking gear, stove, and fuel bottles in the opposite end; his knickers and down sweater served as a pillow. Gary tended to sleep rather soundly, as did Marts. Roskelley and I slept fairly lightly.

We must both have slept very soundly during the next thirty to forty-five minutes, for the next thing I remembered was a kind of hissing in my ears, a shout from the other tent, a kind of popping as the tent collapsed over Gary and me, and the building up of an enormous weight on my body as the avalanche engulfed our tent platform.

My first thought was that we were definitely in an avalanche and it was carrying us down the slope and into the cravasses below. That was followed almost immediately by the realisation that we simply were buried in the tent and that I could not move. My right arm was across my face, and the avalanche had rolled me partially onto my back. I was totally, frighteningly, immobilised and under enormous pressure. "You are going to die. . ." was the only thought at first.

It was incredibly still. The only sound I could detect apart from my racing heartbeat was an occasional soft 'thump' as the snow of the avalanche settled and set up into what seemed concrete hardness. I had an air pocket of perhaps four or five inches in front of my face, created by my free right arm outside the sleeping bag. My first reaction was a tremendous sensation of claustrophobia and a feeling of "This is ridiculous . . . it's not supposed to end this way, but this seems to be it! Somehow, this is not the dream of the airliner crashing . . . this is the crash . . . and you are in it!"

I began calling out to Gary who should, after all, have been no more than two feet away. There was no sound. I tried again and again, saying, "Gary, if you are there, make some sound against the tent with your hands." Nothing. Perhaps he was alive but pinned so as to be unable to move. Then why no voice sound? This was very bad.

I could move my right arm a little but any movement made me gasp and use more air than I suspected I should. It was becoming evident that with as much snow as seemed to be covering us, there had to be a limited supply of air in the envelope of the tent. Judging by the small pocket created by my arm, there was perhaps thirty minutes worth. How can you calculate that sort of thing when you have no way of knowing the total dimensions of the remaining air space? My estimate of thirty minutes almost immediately seemed ridiculous—I could have an hour or minutes for all I knew.

I could almost taste panic; the thought of making a desperate effort to push the snow off us, even though I might black out in the process, was tempting. From another part of my mind there seemed to be an insistent, quiet voice that said, "Calm down, boy, you can get out of this mess, but you have got to stay cool!" If I could hold on, perhaps the two Johns if they had survived would be able to get free and dig Gary and me out. If they hadn't survived the avalanche—well, that was one of the things I was not going to consider. But Gary? What had happened to him? The thought that he had not survived the avalanche was almost inconceivable. Still, there wasn't the slightest sound and he couldn't be more than two feet away.

I decided that my only hope was to try to achieve something like a state of "Zen suspension," or perhaps the lowered tension and breathing levels claimed by adherents of various forms of meditation. Whatever it was and however it was done, I needed to find out in a hurry.

I called again to Gary. I pleaded with him to answer, but realised I was gasping again and slowly forced myself to reduce my rate and depth of breathing. As I tried not to focus on our predicament. I could not avoid thinking of my life, my children, Carol, my family, and friends. It was hard to separate sleep and dream from the sudden overwhelming fact of the avalanche. There was the vague sense that I had heard a shout as the snow came over the tent. Could Roskelley or Marts have been trying to warn us? Could the slide have carried their smaller, lighter tent down the mountain? Don't even think about that. The thought process was quite random. A thought in one direction and then another. There was no sense of serenity—just a dull nagging sense of futility, but an equal sense of stubbornness that I had to stay alive, to find a way out.

I reflected that all in all I had been very lucky in my life and that if this was to be the end of it I could accept the fact. Almost simultaneously I chided myself for allowing such resignation to take over. I felt a flicker of anger at the circumstances after all the work and effort to put the expedition together. How had we gone wrong? We had sited the camp prudently and constantly checked for avalanche danger. Should we have gone off to the North-East Ridge that afternoon before? No. No one had even given it a thought. Had there been another earthquake or an aftershock triggering a slide on an otherwise stable slope? We would never know.

I had reduced my breathing and my sense of complete conscious-ness, but I felt I hadn't completely lost my sense of time and I estimated we had been buried perhaps fifteen to twenty minutes. The thought of so much time and no sound of Marts and Roskelley and no movement or sign from Gary aroused a new sense of con-sciousness: I might be the only one left. The thought of being conscious of my death, of slipping away bit by bit, dying without some kind of effort to escape, was equally difficult to accept, and despite the danger of consuming my remaining oxygen too rapily, I decided to hang it all on trying in some way to cut my way out.

I had begun to doubt that the others had survived the avalanche. I could move my right arm back and forth in the shell I had created over my face. I managed to press my right arm ahead to the point of reaching into my pants pocket and slowly extricating my knife. Then I had to push my elbow enough to insert my arm under the flap of my sleeping bag and thread my right hand down to my immobilised left hand. I managed this strange manoeuvre somehow and, holding the knife in my left hand I was able to pull out the large blade with my right fingers and then move it up through the bag within the narrow shell created by my right arm and into a cutting position.

It suddenly dawned on me that if the snow was solidly set up by the avalanche, to cut my way out through God knows how much depth above would mean the immediate sacrifice of what little air space remained to me. What to do with all that snow? I had reached the most despairing moment of that sombre night, for I had really begun to doubt that the two Johns had survived, and now there was little or no practical hope of getting out on my own. I thought for a brief moment of willing myself to sleep. Struggle was obviously useless; my last exertions with the knife convinced me the air pocket was rapidly going stale. I felt pressure suddenly against my feet; a muffled voice was calling, "Gary, Bob, are you okay?" and I thought, "Good Lord, we're going to get out!" More digging and I felt fresh air coming in along the right side of the sleeping bag and I could hear more clearly John Roskelley yelling for us to answer; I could feel the frantic digging in the snow at the foot of the tent. What an incredible feeling of freedom where there had been, moments before, so little hope!

I screamed, "I'm okay, get Gary; I can't hear him! Get Gary; he's on your right!"

Roskelley replied, "Okay, Bob. You're going to be all right: we'll get Gary right now."

I heard John Marts in a muffled voice say, "Oh, Jesus! Gary's really in deep."

Roskelley said, "Dig, John, but don't freeze your hands." Marts had no gloves and was digging with his sweater covering his hands but not very adequately. As they dug on Gary's side of the collapsed tent, I felt the pressure on my left side gradually lessen and I could more clearly hear the labours and efforts of Marts and Roskelley as they got closer to Gary. They had his side of the tent fairly well uncovered and my right arm began to feel free enough to move in the new space. There was a brief debate about cutting the tent fabric. I reached out with my right arm, only inches, and touched Gary. There was no movement or response. He was very still. The back of his head and his neck felt very cold. Then I could feel and hear both Johns cutting through the tent and reaching in to extract Gary. They got hold of his arms and torso, but couldn't seem to free his upper body His head was wedged deeply in the upper right corner of the tent; the snow outside the tent seemed to have compacted around his neck and head, and they couldn't dislodge him entirely. I reached across and pulled his head by the hair to free it from the snow that encased the collapsed tent surrounding his face. It came free and the neck seemed somehow distressingly limp as they pulled Gary's body through the split in the tent. What this suggested did not occur to us at that moment: his neck may have been broken by the force of the avalanche. It had now been so long; Gary was clearly unconscious. When they had pulled Gary's body from the tent John Marts began mouth-to-mouth resuscitation, pumping violently into Gary's lungs. This went on for 10 to 15 minutes, Marts furiously breathing into Gary, trying to ignite some spark of life.

He cried out, "It's just no use, the goddamn air in his lungs is stale! He's dead!"

I felt the two Johns pull Gary's body further out from the uphill side of the tent and then resume digging in the centre and right of my body. The immense weight of the snow seemed gone. I was saved; it was at the worst a bad dream. But Gary was dead and the sudden sadness was overwhelming. The brutal fact of Gary's death mixed with the agony of those long minutes of burial left little more than numbness. I wanted to weep and I simply wanted to be out of the tent.

Roskelley seemed to sense the situation from my perspective and shouted, "For Christ's sakes, John, let's cut the goddamned tent; Bob is still alive in there!"

I was just about to suggest exiting through the hole cut for Gary, which would have been the most logical move, when Roskelley, who had cleared the last snow from over my head, cut a slit in the fabric above my head. As he did so we all heard an eerie terrifying sound. From above and seemingly some distance away, a strangely metallic, whining, grinding rumble bore down upon us and almost simultaneously I heard both Johns cry out in dismay, "Oh, no! Look out; here it comes!"

And then, in unquestionably the most despairing and hopeless moment of my life, I was buried again, snow flooding in through the slit in the tent as I lay facing up on my back, my right arm again partially covering my face, but not so effectively for this time the air pocket seemed smaller and the weight of snow seemed if anything heavier.

I thought, "My God, this is really it!" Somebody really wants me up there. The others must have been carried down in that slide. There is no way I can get out of this one!"

I felt more deeply buried than before and the left side of my chest ached as if I had cracked some of my ribs. Snow was now inside the tent and enveloped my face, but somehow, my right arm and hand had been in position to create an air pocket again.

The sense of despair and hopelessness seemed complete. Hadn't we lost enough? Gary was dead, we had all been buried once, and now this! It was so desperate and ridiculous that amusement almost flickered across my mind.

It had really been only a matter of seconds, then I heard the muffled voice of Roskelley calling, "Bob, are you okay? We'll get you out, Big Daddy."

Probably forty seconds to a minute had gone by since the second avalanche came down. Near-death and resurrection twice within thirty minutes.

Marts and Roskelley had nearly uncovered all the snow over me the first time, cut a slit in the tent, and were about to help me crawl out, when they heard the second avalanche. Rather than trying to jump out to the side or simply trying to brace themselves against the downward flow, they had jumped into the hole left when they removed Gary's body, then backed up into the avalanche.

They couldn't have gained more than one or two feet, if that, but they caused the snow of the avalanche to flow around their bodies. It wasn't a large slide, depositing no more than two to three feet of snow on me, but they avoided being swept off their feet and into the system of crevasses below.

They quickly dug me out, and I crawled through the previously cut slit in the tent out into the wreckage of our camp. Roskelley and Marts hugged me. I was suddenly aware I was only in my thermal underwear and socks.

It was snowing hard and I couldn't see any sign of the others' tent. I had found my flashlight at the head of my sleeping bag and I moved the beam over what had been camp. It was now only an irregular mound of avalanche debris with a small portion of tent showing where I had escaped. Gary's body had been buried again in the second avalanche. Save for the disordered lumps that marked the violence of the past hour and a quarter, the campsite looked very much as we had first found it. Roskelley was anxious to get away from camp and to a safer site. The situation was clearly desperate. We had nothing left . . . our tents were gone, all our equipment and clothing buried. The storm seemed to have intensified, the whole mountain sounded as if it were avalanching. It had grown bitterly cold.

Marts moved out, following Roskelley up and to the right towards the bergschrund formation we had planned to pass on our way to the final ice slope of the north face. It seemed the only place left to us with any kind of protection from the steam of slides sloughing off the ice face. I remained in the wreckage for a few moments as the others started up the slope. John Marts was stunned; he had no gloves and no boots and he said he thought his hands and feet were freezing. Before leaving the campsite, I reached back into the slit and dragged out my sleeping bag as well as my knickers. I pulled my heavy down parka out and, in rummaging around at the head of my bed, uncovered the Russian radio we had been keeping warm under our clothes, and the spare batteries for the set. Knowing that Marts and I were without boots and had no chance without them, I rummaged further, finding Gary's boots and mine. Fortunately, we had left the supergaiters on our boots which made them easier to drag along behind.

Dragging the sleeping bag and the two pairs of climbing boots and following up the rapidly filling-in tracks of Marts and Roskelley, my progress was very slow along the 300ft. toward the schrund. My feet were rapidly turning numb, covered only by a pair of medium weight socks, but there was no time or place to stop and pull on my boots. As I climbed, I kept telling myself. "This is not happening, the avalanche was a dream, after all. I read about all this somewhere before."

Above I could hear Roskelley digging desperately into the base of the schrund. Marts joined him while I was part way up the slope. By the time I reached them, Roskelley had scooped out a shallow ledge in the granular old snow at the schrund's base, with a low sloping roof overhead. I gave Marts my mitts to dig with. . .

from STORM AND SORROW IN THE HIGH PAMIRS *1977*

A Few Moments*

MERV ENGLISH

It was beautiful up here. It must have struck us both about the same time, for the conversation slowly stopped. We were just staring at the mile after mile of peaks. All of it was completely new to us both. A gentle curiosity to see it all from close quarters comes, but I spoil the silence by asking Ken how we raise money for half a dozen trips. He doesn't have the answers and chatters on as he climbs to the end of his rope. Phrases like "this has been the best climbing of my life" and "tomorrow we're going to get there" were flowing out of him. Half of me was still occupied with the surroundings, so it took a moment or two to realise he was very happy and almost tranquil. Perhaps that should have been a warning, for the day before all four of us seemed driven by a nervous tension. Maybe it was just the oppressive closed-in atmosphere the lower part of the climb had, or perhaps a strong drive had built up over the months of planning and was now finding a release. Whatever it was had settled and the cold, determined, detached look had gone from Ken's face.

About the time he reaches the end of the rope there's a thunderous boom, followed by a continuing roar. I stare in total disbelief at the ice blocks, massive ones, curling through the air directly above us. As they get closer they break up. This can't be happening. There is a yell from below and I leap off the small rock spike and try to hide behind it. Out of the corner of my eye I can see Ken lie against the ice, clutching his axe. As the blocks start coming over me, I still can't believe it. Several big ones hit my back and the pain brings reality. The blocks are scraping the outside of my helmet, jolting my head, each one worse than the last. They bounce off my back and then continue their violent path. The suddenness of the violence is terrifying. "You're not gong to survive this," goes through the head, but I cut the thought out almost before I've finished thinking it. There's an enormous jolt on the rope which

*During an attempt to climb the West Face of Ama Dablam by English, Ken Hyslop, Pete Hillary and Geoff Gabites.

515

I'm holding Pete on. As I struggle to hold him, a very big block hits a shoulder-blade. I can't hold the rope anymore. The pressure pulling me down and the pummelling is enormous. I wonder if the body can endure any more. Harnesses and slings are cutting into my body. Skin is tearing and limbs seem to be being squeezed off. The whole world slips suddenly. My hand is through the Karabiner clipped into a small hexentric, the cord has to be cut. After an inch, or maybe two, the world stops again on a sling over the rock spike. From somewhere way down inside, the primeval fight starts rising. I manage to get the hand out of the krab and over the sling to protect it. I start struggling against the pressure pulling me down. It's almost an anger. The pressure eases. Then it stops.

There is absolute and complete silence. My body is no longer in the hammer mill. Snow fills my glasses. I struggle to get upright and a message of pain is coming through from a leg. I don't really feel it though. The mind is trying to take in so many things and is in a world of its own. With no help from me it works through each fact. I take the glasses off to clean them and call out to Ken. He doesn't answer and I don't look. I know he'll be gone. I seem to be in three pieces. A body which is trying to tell a brain that it is hurting. A brain that is preoccupied, trying to cope with the facts and understand them. The third part is just existing, it's life itself. The brain goes on doing things automatically on its own. It checks the belay. Sees my watch in the folds of clothing. The strap's broken. An aching body is brought into action to put the watch into a pocket, I don't know why, but the brain has some reason. It starts a check of the body. A hip is sore. A hand rubs the hip and finds a broken holster and an ice axe gone. That holster was made of ¼ inch thick leather. Reality is slowly coming back. The brain is trying to bring the three parts together into a functioning being again. The process is slow, as if the brain knows it can't take too much at once. The pain is making itself felt and the check of the body continues. A leg is next and somehow the rope has hitched around it and a pack hanging on the belay. The rope disappears below a rock bulge 40ft. lower. I try to lift the rope to free the leg, but there is an enormous weight on it. With a shock I remember the other two and call out to Pete. There is no answer. Geoff is no longer on his belay stance either. As the total aloneness starts to come, the brain skilfully takes over again. Ideas begin to flow; go down the face or push the last bit to the ridge and hopefully find the old American fixed rope. All energies are concentrating on working out how much gear is left. The brain seems to understand that the only way to stay alive is to keep thinking. In the distance there is an intrusion and it takes a moment to register. It's someone screaming.

I call Pete's name and Geoff answers. The screaming has been replaced with the pitiful, heart-tearing moaning of great pain. Pete calls out and I realise my struggle with the rope is causing the pain. It takes a few moments to set the belay up, so I lean out enough to satisfy the overpowering need to see the others. They are hanging on the end of the 45-metre rope, somehow tangled together. Where the rope disappears over the bulge, the sheath is gone completely and there seems to be a few strands of the core sticking out as well. I warn them about it. We exchange a few words, telling each other what state we're in. I only half listen after a few sentences, the first thing is to get free and get down to them. A wave of nausea clouds in and I realise I'm probably a bit concussed. A Scoutmaster from years ago is giving a lecture on the signs and symptoms of concussion. He's standing in front of a small blackboard, addressing the troop – "recovery may be accompanied by nausea and vomiting." It's a very vivid picture. The brain seizes the word "recovery" from his statement. There's hope about that word, the condition must be improving, but keep an eye on it. End of problem and on with the next. Time has no relevance; it's solving each problem as it comes up that is important. Back struggling with the rope and one jumar, trying to lift the others enough to free the caught leg. The voices from below are saying hurry up, but also abusing me for jerking the rope and causing more pain. Brutally I yell down that it can't be helped and I'll be as quick as I can. Sentiment is of little value in a chess game. The coldness of the mind shocks me.

I jumar down the tight rope to the others, it is in a hideous condition and one cut is extremely bad. There is nothing that can be done about it at present, so there is no point in worrying. Pete's hand is at totally the wrong angle. He is talking about his injuries. From the waist down he has no feeling. His chest hurts badly. Geoff is holding one of his own arms. These are facts, this is reality. I accept it without emotion. My internal conversations have gone and the cold acceptance no longer shocks me. If you think about the wrong things then you will not survive. The second rope disappears below a bulge. It is in a worse condition than the first. A little later I climb down it, towards Ken, towards more facts.

Three days later, as the helicopter flies over a crevasse, Ken's grave beneath the face, I start weeping.

from MOUNTAIN 72 *1980*

Nanda Devi Unsoeld

WILLI UNSOELD

Following their magnificent summit success [on Nanda Devi] on September 1, Lou Reichardt, John Roskelley and Jim States descended to Camp 3 the following day. The second summit party of Pete Lev, Andy Harvard and my daughter Devi Unsoeld had been slated to occupy Camp 4 that day, but an ominous black cloud which settled slowly around the summit block persuaded them to take another rest day. As it turned out, the cloud lifted in the afternoon and the day became fine, making it easy for the summiters to descend to Camp 3.

This reunion of our entire expedition was the first we had had since early in the climb, and it was a happy time as we congratulated our successful team members on their outstanding summit effort and heard their account of the difficulties they had overcome above Camp 4. Morale was extremely high. The weather seemed to be improving steadily and two more summit parties were poised for immediate attempts. Rascal (John Roskelley) and Jim both expressed worry about Andy's persistent cough and Devi's current diarrhoea and flare-up of an inguinal hernia which had shown up originally on the second day of the approach march. However, Andy had been coughing during the whole trip and Devi had never been slowed by either diarrhoea or hernia while carrying between the lower camps. Our situation seemed so ideal that within the next three days both Rascal and Lou headed for Base Camp — Rascal intending to await our return from the summit and

Lou to head out to try to make it back home to join his wife, Kathy, in time for the birth of their first child.

On September 3 then, the second summit team headed for Camp 4 while our third unit, consisting of John Evans, Nirmal, Kiran and me, trailed along to carry another tent and extra food to cache. With seven climbers trying to use the fixed ropes at once, the waits were too long and so we four turned back from the top of the third pitch. As we rappelled down the buttress and watched our second team slowly working their way upward, we marvelled at the kind of climbing which Rascal had performed while leading this stretch, going from 5.8 or 5.9 to direct aid and back, and in crampons.

At 7 p.m. Pete radioed that he had just arrived at Camp 4 after leaving Devi and Andy behind in order to steam ahead to get the camp ready and water going. At eleven o'clock we got word that Andy had pulled in and that Devi was on the last pitch. It took her until midnight to haul up over the final lip to Camp 4. It had been a long, slow day for her. The next day was brilliantly clear, but the summit party was not in condition to take advantage of it.

On September 5 our back-up party of four moved early to join Pete's group for a joint summit try the next day. We set 3 p.m. as the deadline by which we would have to reach the Sugar Delight Snowfield or else turn back. Picking up the cached food and gear increased our packs to dangerous proportions. Kiran and I did not reach the snowfield until around four o'clock and Evans and Nirmal were still a pitch below. The snowfall was increasing and so we were forced to drop our loads where we were and retreat, despite Kiran's protests. As it was, we didn't reach Camp 3 until 9 p.m. and all four of us were dragging from the effort.

September 6 dawned clear and bright, and since I felt remarkably strong despite our previous day's exertion, I decided to go all-out and join the party at Camp 4 for a summit attempt. They had radioed that Pete had made a reconnaissance yesterday to halfway to the summit before turning back in the bad weather. Kiran and Nirmal were too tired to make another effort so soon, and Evans was wiped out by an illness which later turned out to be the onset of hepatitis.

The familiar ground flowed smoothly past under my jumars until I reached the snowfield. I was elated to see that to the mid-point it had taken only two-and-three-quarter hours actual jumar time.

There I added more food and a tent from the cache and put on my crampons for the traverse into the gully (called 'Spindrift Alley' by the first party). My pack was very heavy now, but I found the beauty and boldness of the route totally exhilarating. The 400ft. of the gully were a ghastly slog with no certain footing in the depth of sugar snow which had accumulated. The final pitch to the lip at Camp 4 was 200ft. of vertical going with occasional small traverses to attempt to keep the rope away from the nastier rock teeth which protruded from the wall. It was a definite relief to heave myself over the snow lip at the top.

September 7 was a pure blizzard at Camp 4 and none of us moved from the tent. It was a day full of liquids and the easy talk which fills rest days at high altitudes. Devi was feeling better, but was still quite weak when measured against the energy output required for the summit try. It was decided that she should wait at Camp 4 while the rest of us made our try and then descend with us the same day to Camp 3.

However, that night was a bad one for Devi. Her stomach generated gas in such quantities that she simply could not sleep and spent most of the night sitting up to belch it forth. By morning she was extremely tired. Because of the high winds and continuing snow, we decided to head down at noon and wait for better weather in the relative comfort of Camp 3. Pete, Andy and Devi had now been at 24,000ft. for nearly five days. We were packed for departure when at 11.45 a.m. Devi was suddenly stricken. She had time only to say with great calm, "I am going to die," before she lapsed into unconsciousness. We tried mouth-to-mouth resuscitation, but with no sign of success. Within fifteen minutes I felt her lips growing cold against mine and I knew that we had lost her. We continued our efforts to revive her for another half hour without result. As the enormity of our loss slowly sank in, the three of us could only cling to one another for comfort while tears coursed down our beards.

from THE AMERICAN ALPINE JOURNAL *1977*

Earthquake

H. ADAMS CARTER

On Sunday May 31, 1970 at 3.23 pm. an earthquake of 7.8 magnitude on the Richter scale struck northern Peru. Its epicentre was in the Pacific at 9° 12′ South latitude and 78° 48′ West longitude about nine miles south-west of Chimbote. The focus is calculated at a depth of some twenty-five miles beneath the sea. Damage was heaviest in the coastal towns and inland in the Callejón de Huaylas, as the valley of the Río Santa is known where it separates the Cordillera Blanca from the Cordillera Negra. In terms of deaths, this was the worst disaster ever to strike the Western Hemisphere. Some 70,000 people were killed. In the Santa valley's large. city, Huaraz, over half of the inhabitants, some 20,000 people, died and about ninety per cent of the town was destroyed. Miraculously, apparently none of the mountain porters of the Cordillera Blanca, most of whom live in Huaraz, were killed when the highly unstable adobe-brick houses toppled. Houses of these sun-baked clay and straw bricks with tile roofs supported by wooden beams offer little earthquake resistance. Most of the villages, many of which like Huaraz were up to ninety per cent destroyed, were built on deep, poorly compacted, alluvial deposits with high water tables, which tend to magnify the intensity of the shaking. The earthquake began with gentle swaying, followed by hard shaking which lasted for about a minute. There were pronounced side-to-side movements. Adobe buildings began to fall after about fifteen seconds of hard shaking. In the whole region an estimated 1,000,000 people were left homeless. Rockfall on steep slopes also accounted for many deaths and injuries. Strong tremors continued in the region for weeks.

An avalanche fell off the 2,500ft. high, nearly vertical West Face of Huascarán Norte: some 10 to 15 million cubic metres of rock, carrying with it some 3,000,000 cubic metres of ice. The pressure caused by the impact of its fall caused an increasing proportion of the ice to turn to water. This mixture of ice, water, mud, moraine and rock hurtled down across Glacier 511 and down the valley

towards Ranrahirca, travelling at a speed of nearly 200 miles per
hour. (It took some three minutes to cover the nine miles to
Ranrahirca and drop the 13,000ft.) The track was the same as that
of the avalanche which wiped out Ranrahirca and its 3,000
inhabitants in 1962, but this time it was much larger and had a
higher proportion of rock and lesser one of ice. A portion of the
avalanche swept uphill some 650 vertical feet from the river bed
and spilled over a hill into Yungay. Although a mere trickle when
compared to the main part which devastated Ranrahirca, it
snatched away some 18,000 inhabitants of Yungay, and buried
them under 35 to 50ft. of debris. Only 241 people who managed to
get to the high ground of the cemetery were saved. The two
branches of the avalanche rejoined and swept on down the main
Santa valley in a wave some 50 to 65ft. high. None of the mountain
lakes spilled, as was at first incorrectly reported by the press.

Another completely unrelated avalanche crashed off the
northern slopes of Huascarán Norte. This plunged down onto the
neck of land between the upper and lower Llanganuco lakes.
Tragically it was just this spot where the Czech expedition had
placed its Base Camp. One of their number had been killed a few
days before while descending from Huandoy. The remaining
thirteen Czechs and the Chilean, who was accompanying them,
were buried under tons of moraine and ice. All that was found were
a couple of sleeping bags, a jacket and a box or two floating on the
lake.

from THE AMERICAN ALPINE CLUB JOURNAL *1971*

A Mountain Vision

FRANK SMYTHE

My strangest experience happened in the Highlands. I was walking
over the hills from Morvich on Loch Duich to Glen Glomach and
the Falls of Glomach. It was a bright sunny day, and there was
nothing in the least sinister about the vista of cloud-chequered hills
and the distant blue of the sea. In crossing the ridge before
dropping down to Glen Glomach I passed for a short distance

through a grassy defile. There was nothing outwardly sinister about this pass and the sun shone warmly into it, yet when I entered it I at once encountered—that is the only word to express it—an atmosphere of evil. Something terrible had once happened at that spot, and time had failed to dissipate the atmosphere created by it. I was interested in my reaction to the place, and as it was as good as any for lunch decided to halt there and see whether I could make anything of it. Ghosts and ham sandwiches are scarcely companions, but after lunch, when my pipe was well alight, I surrendered myself to contemplation of my environment. As I reclined, drowsily smoking, the atmosphere of the defile seemed to press upon me with an even greater force than before. I did my best to keep my mind unoccupied with anything, to make myself receptive and allow imagination a free rein, and this is what I saw, or, as the sceptical reader will say with perfect justification, what I imagined I saw.

A score or more of ragged people, men, women and children, were straggling through the defile. They appeared very weary, as though they had come a long way. The pitiful procession was in the midst of the defile when all of a sudden from either side concealed men leapt to their feet and, brandishing spears, axes and clubs, rushed down with wild yells on the unfortunates beneath. There was a short fierce struggle, then a horrible massacre. Not one man, woman or child was left alive; the defile was choked with corpses.

I got out of the place as quickly as I could. Screams seemed to din in my ears as I hastened down the broad heather slopes into Glen Glomach. I am not a superstitious person, but it seemed to me that I was vouchsafed a backward glimpse into a blood-stained page of Highland history. I know nothing about the history of that part of Scotland and should be grateful for any information throwing light on what I still believe was a genuine psychical experience.

from THE MOUNTAIN VISION *1941*

Salt-Water Cure

PAT LITTLEJOHN

"I think I'm going to be sick."

Keith [Darbyshire] took one look at me, saw I wasn't joking and pulled over on to the grass verge. I tumbled out of the door of the mini on to my knees and disgorged the beery froth which was all that remained of the previous day's sustenance.

The scene had a strong element of deja-vu. We had been driving along this same stretch of road (near Blackwater on the A30 in Cornwall) in the grip of another monumental hangover three or four months previously. Then, we had devised and effected a cure, the 'salt-water cure', which consisted of having a long gruelling day on a sea-cliff involving a thorough wetting. The hangover would be forgotten in the first couple of hours and the body purged of all impurities by dusk, ready for the next evening's intake. Carn Gowla had provided the setting then, and it seemed no mere coincidence that this cliff should be so close when the salt-water cure was again urgently needed.

We had no sooner remarked on this than Keith began babbling about suitable objectives. We had never been secretive about new lines but he confessed there was a superb one on America Buttress which he had never told me about. He had seen it from an abseil rope—an immaculate corner rising straight out of the sea to the ledge beneath the groove of Escapist, the perfect and natural first pitch. By the time we arrived at the clifftop I was almost enthusiastic, and very surprised to find that sea conditions were favourable for reaching the foot of the crag. In view of the number of foiled attempts to make the first sea-level approach to America Buttress, despite careful planning with tide tables and weather forecasts, today's conditions seemed too good to be true. But on descending we discovered that despite the exceptionally low tide there was quite an energetic swell thrashing around the boulders and sloping ledges at the cliff base.

Helped by familiarity we quickly sorted out the short tyrolean and crossed boulders to the foot of America, beyond which the low-tide shelf dipped slightly and continued to the recessed chimney of The Mausoleum. I was halfway along the shelf when a foot-high wave swept across it without warning, soaking me to the knees. This was annoying, particularly as Keith had seen it coming and scuttled back to higher ground. Fearful of bigger waves to follow I rejoined him, and when several large waves arrived we decided to put the rope on. From the shelter of the chimney we had to negotiate another low section to gain the corner. By now it was obvious that the tide was coming in fast and the sea was showing signs of hostility. Keith took advantage of a calmer patch and disappeared around the corner to fix a belay at the base of the line. Five minutes later the rope was taken in and I followed, getting a second wetting in the process. Rather than the usual amusement at my plight, Keith's expression betrayed anxiety. A glance at our proposed route told me why. The 'immaculate corner crack' ended after 40ft., and the line became an overhanging groove with a peg-width crack at its back. Memory had proved fickle.

At that point I suppose we could have got back. It would have been tricky and we would have got very wet, but there were no insuperable obstacles. But as so frequently in the past, my blind optimism conspired with Keith's recklessness to banish all thoughts of retreat. By the time we had belayed higher in the corner and organised the ropes the sea had cut off all possibility of escape.

My progress up the corner crack was slow and ungainly, with the rock curiously damp to the touch and my PAs squelching and oozing water on to every foothold. When the real difficulties began it was obvious that something would have to be done about my skidding feet, so I lowered back down to a resting place, rolled up my soaking jeans, took off my PAs and wrung out my socks. I was just drying the boots in my shirt when Keith yelled up, for Christ's sake get a move on as he was getting wet.

Back at my highpoint I had just placed a runner when there was a great slap of spray beneath my feet. I looked down into a foaming turmoil of water just as Keith emerged from it, spluttering and cursing. Within seconds he was hit by a second wave and I clung to the runner as he disappeared under another barrage of spray. After that the waves resumed normal proportions but Keith was quite emphatic that he wanted the belay moved higher. Fifteen minutes later he was belayed at the 'resting place' and I was ready again.

Out at sea, the weather was bright and blustery, but on our north-facing cliff we saw no sun, and only suffered the wind. With his soaking clothes Keith would soon be getting chilled, and our only thought was to get off the crag as quickly as possible. The only way off was upwards – the traverse had been submerged long ago and to swim out would be suicidal. Anyway, there was nowhere to swim to – the crags plunged sheer into the sea for a mile in either direction, and the swell would make it impossible to land anywhere but a beach.

I seemed to be climbing myself into a cul-de-sac. The rock was smeared with salt spray and the crack getting thinner and more impending all the time. Eventually I clipped into the highest sling I could place and hung there.

"Hey, Keith. It's not going to go."

He was silent for a while.

"Can't you just peg up it?"

"I didn't bring any pegs."

For some months I'd had an ethical bee in my bonnet about carrying pegs. It now seemed very foolish.

"You didn't bring any, did you?"

He had, just one, a blade peg for removing nuts. I thanked God that my fanaticism hadn't prevented me from carrying a hammer for gardening.

The problem was, how to get up 15ft. of blank groove with one peg. I teetered up for a move and poked it into the crack at my fullest reach. I couldn't hold the position long enough to hammer it so I moved back down to the sling, praying that the peg wouldn't drop out. After a rest I moved back up and gave it the crucial first tap, then two or three more before the strain was too great and I collapsed back into the sling. Next time I hammered it home with the strength of desperation and clipped in, exhausted. I had no idea what to do next – the crack was too thin for any nut and the rock too slick with moisture for any chance of free climbing. To add even greater urgency to the situation Keith was starting to get wet even on higher stance, and although he never complained I could see him shivering with cold. I made several doomed attempts to move up from the peg then eventually slumped back into the slings, angry, frustrated, and quite demoralised. It was time to face up to the fact that we weren't going to get out.

It was imperative by now that Keith should move up higher still. The larger, 'seventh' waves were exploding into the corner with alarming force. If anything as big as the two freak waves we had experienced earlier should appear Keith would be lifted off the rock, and the single nut belay would be plucked out. Once again I took in the streaming wet ropes and kept them tight as Keith climbed to the next runner to make a hanging belay. We were now sitting in slings, 25ft. apart, and with one runner between us. From his position Keith had as good or even better a view of the problem as I had:

"Any chance of getting out to the right arête?"

I craned back. There were some flat holds on the arête, but the prospect of launching out on to them was daunting. There would certainly be desperate or even impossible difficulties above and our situation was critical enough without risking a long fall. But there was no other alternative. Tucked out of sight, on a remote sea-cliff, inaccessible from above or below, we were beyond help or rescue. We might have risked exposure and waited nine hours for the next low tide, but there was no guarantee that the sea-level traverse would be passable even then.

Keith held me in tension from the peg as I stretched towards the flat holds. When I had grasped them with both hands he slackened off and I swung right around the arête. I was astonished to find myself on easy ground. The far side of the rib forming our overhanging groove was almost a slab. I gave a whoop of elation then yelled for slack and headed up to the belay of Escapist. Keith was so numb with cold that he had great difficulty following even with a very tight rope, but now that our predicament was no longer serious I was beginning to feel affection for the cliff again. Particularly as it had granted us such an unexpected reprieve. We were now belayed on the farthest right hand corner of the huge wedge-shaped slab which cuts across the buttress, and towering above us to the left was the dark, impending bastion taken by America.

Although we were still in shadow the entire seascape was bathed in sunshine and speckled with white horses whipped up by the fierce wind. The only remaining obstacle was the Hard Very Severe groove of Escapist, pioneered by Keith five months previously, and before long we were back at our rucksacks in the lush heather at the top of the crag. We had been on the route for five hours.

I couldn't help laughing at Keith as we walked back along the top of the cliff to the van. There was not a cloud in the sky yet he was clad in his full waterproof suit with the hood drawn tight, slowly thawing out. The holidaymakers parked nearby looked at us as if we were from another planet. We trundled homewards and it wasn't until we reached a favourite pub on the northern edge of Dartmoor that we remembered what had sparked off the day's events. The salt-water cure had worked again.

(*Previously unpublished*)

Five into Eight Won't Go

GEORGES BETTEMBOURG

The next morning we* dawned at 4 a.m. and toiled up the cwm in the dark. Because I had lost my pack above the scree terrace, I carried up another sleeping bag and additional gear which the others already had stashed away at Camp 3. My pack was heavy. At the foot of the fixed ropes, we found that we were two jumars short. Ang Phurba had forgotten to bring the jumars we had reminded him many times not to forget. We had eight between the five of us. Two of us would have to jumar up with only one. Ang Phurba would have to have two and Doug would get two because of his frostbitten hands. Who else would get two? Peter, Joe, or me?

Both Peter and Joe were quick to point out that they had already climbed up once with one jumar. Hence they deserved the extra jumar. I had already volunteered more than my share in many ways and decided to stand my ground, for a change. I noted that while they were moving up the rope with one jumar, I was leading on the North Col where I had done three carries to the upper section of the face that same day after having led the hardest pitch on the entire face. In addition, I now carried a heavier pack to replace my lost equipment and sleeping bag. Peter remarked that it was not their fault that I had lost my pack during the storm and Joe said he had carried up my sleeping bag the day I led the difficult chimney pitch with nothing on my back, which I corrected, noting that I had

*Pete Boardman, Joe Tasker, Doug Scott, Ang Phurba and the author.

carried two coils of rope across my shoulders. Besides, I had not carried a pack on my back because it had been necessary to fix up the last section with great haste in order to make the North Col before dark—that I not only had led the hardest pitch and made three carries, but that while he was gently coming up with one jumar, I had also dug a platform and installed the tent in a storm. Peter remarked that while I was climbing the difficult pitch I had loosened a rock which had broken his wrist. This entitled him to the two jumars. But if he had broken his wrist, he wouldn't have been present two days later, climbing up 3,000ft. of rope. Tempers were flaring and nerves were on end. The mountain was taking its toll.

I have never approved of the heavyweight mentality which goads one climber to weasel an advantage over the others. A sensible approach to the jumar problem was for each of us to treat our companions as equals and to resolve the difficulty by drawing straws, which is what I finally suggested. I won the two jumars and moved up the face.

from THE WHITE DEATH *1981*

Shuffling Off This Mortal Coil

GEOFFREY WINTHROP YOUNG

. . . to the mountains, the deep love of his life, he answered even with poetry. No passing was ever more happily timed than his. Upon the slopes of the Pizzo Bianco he had just looked round, and said, "I always thought this to be the most beautiful place in the world, and now I know it." And he died in that moment of perfected vision.

from THE INFLUENCE OF MOUNTAINS UPON THE DEVELOPMENT OF THE HUMAN INTELLIGENCE *1957*

Prisoner of War

W. H. MURRAY

Mountaineering in Scotland was the product of three years in prison camps. It was hammered out in Czechoslovakia and Germany. The first year, under the Abruzzi mountains of Italy, saw only a preliminary stoking of fires.

One of Rommel's panzer divisions had scooped me up from the desert in June 1942. The first year at Chieti had nearly wasted away before I shed lethargy. My imagination took fire at last from two slow-burning matches. The first was my daily view of the Gran Sasso's snow cap. It kept mountains alive in my mind. The second was the recurring thought of a German tank commander, whose capture of me held an element of comedy that Samivel, the cartoonist, might have enjoyed. I had seen nothing funny at the time.

My battalion of Highland Light Infantry had been whittled down in battle to fifty men. My brigade in the headlong retreat to Alamein was left astride the coast road south of Mersa Matruh to stop the 15th Panzer Division. Their tanks came in after sunset twenty abreast. Our two-pounder guns hit them on the nose at point-blank range. Their armour bloomed red where the shells glanced off in showers of sparks. The tanks staggered, but came on. They machine-gunned the ground for five minutes till all was still. Then the crews climbed out to deal with any survivors. I was one of the lucky few. I rose to my feet and was faced by a young tank commander. He waved a machine-pistol at me. He and it shook. He had been rattled about in his tank like a pea in a tin can, not knowing what hit him. He was just as raw-nerved as I. In his position, with crying need to release tension, I could imagine myself squeezing the trigger. I held my breath while he took quick stock. To my astonishment, he forced a wry smile and asked in English, "Are you not feeling the cold?" The question was not daft. The desert is very cold at night if one is still wearing shirt and shorts, but not till then did I notice it. I replied, "Cold as a mountain top." He looked at me, and his eyes brightened. "Do you mean – you climb mountains?"

He was a mountaineer. We both relaxed. He stuffed his gun away. After a few quick words – the Alps, Scotland, rock and ice – he could not do enough for me. "When did you eat?" he asked. I reckoned, "Two days ago." He led me over to his tank and produced bully beef, biscuits, beer, chocolate, and an army greatcoat, all British. "Take them," he grinned. "Loot from Tobruk." We shared the beer and toasted "Mountains."

An hour later, he and his tanks clanked away, heading for Cairo (he hoped). I was left to the less tender care of Italian infantry. I often wondered about that climber, whose name I never heard. He had come unbroken from the Russian front. I wondered whether he survived El Alamein. The wondering kindled my urge to write, but that was stultified by want of paper. The urge became compulsive. The clincher was my receipt from the Red Cross of Shakespeare's *Complete Works*, printed on thin India paper. As I took this in my hand, I could not help reflecting what excellent toilet paper it would make, thus freeing my ration of Italian toilet roll for use as writing paper. I felt confident that William Shakespeare would approve. I sat down to work that very day, but the page stayed blank.

I had no doubt what I should write. I should write about good climbs, and these only. My zest for mountains was felt and expressed on hard routes, on rock, snow and ice, and not only in walking the hills. I wanted to share the experience. That was the first compulsion (others grew later). Mackenzie, Dunn, MacAlpine and I had teamed up in 1936, when the time was ripe for progress. Almost nothing had been done on ice, or on snow and ice bound rock, for twenty years. We had taken to the long ridges and buttresses on Nevis and Glencoe. Planning in advance was needed to catch the right weather-cycles and take the rocks under snow and ice of the right quality and quantity. Our aim was to climb the routes not when easy but hard, and sometimes with massive accumulations of ice. We made mistakes, and our first attempt on Garrick's Shelf on the Buachaille was one. I had taken the lead high up when I landed on a run of verglassed slabs at dusk, just when the worst blizzard in twenty years was breaking. We took fourteen hours to get down in the dark. We turned this defeat to good account – always thereafter we carried pitons and karabiners and maybe a sling to secure retreat. We never drove a piton as direct aid, but occasionally did for belays. Another lesson we learned was the practicality of climbing by torchlight if the winter route was known. Thereafter we devised head-torches, and proved them invaluable on the longer Nevis climbs when conditions would otherwise have stopped an ascent.

Apart from head-torches, the main equipment changes were the slater's hammer and long ropes. The normal ice-axe had a 33-inch shaft. The wrist strain of prolonged, one-handed cutting above the head was severe, and a slater's pick with a 14-inch shaft eased it greatly – the climbing time on a pitch could be almost halved. I reckoned that the ten shillings I paid to an ironmonger for my first pick was the best-spent money I ever laid down on a counter. I have rarely enjoyed anything in life more than cutting up a long, high-angled ice-pitch where the balance was delicate. The craft used had to vary with the quality of the ice: white, green, blue, black, brittle, and watery, each had a quirk of its own, which had to be learned until one could tell them apart at a glance and cut accordingly. We still used the adze of the long axe to cut handholds on white ice, for that was faster.

No climbers carried crampons on Scottish hills; they were not reckoned worth their weight, for the tricouni-clinker nailing gave a non-slip grip on hard snow, allowed much neater footwork than crampons on snow and ice-bound rock, and allowed too an occasional 'miracle' to be pulled off on thin brittle ice that ought to have peeled. I used to call such moves levitation for want of a better word – nothing so crude as a step up, but rather a float up, with no weight placed anywhere so far as humanly possible. It worked if you hit top form, and got Mackenzie and me up some nasty places on Garrick's Shelf, Deep-Cut Chimney, and the like.

Hardly more than a dozen climbers in Scotland were involved in such work. The rest had little notion, and most none at all, of what Scottish rock could offer in winter. Many had the idea that our climbs were 'unjustifiable' (then a fashionable word for damning hard moves and routes). A few, when I first produced my slater's pick with its 14-inch shaft, had called me a *poseur*, for they had no conception of its use. I wanted to dispel ignorance of the rich harvest available on winter rock, and to propagate the fierce joys of fetching it in — I say 'fierce' in deference to Scottish weather.

Such were my limited thoughts when I first put pen to toilet paper in Italy. Without diary, maps, or books to refresh memory, I feared I should lack detail of the climbs, which could not be spun out to chapter-length. I was right, but the daily concentration of mind in trying to remember, continued day after day for weeks, gave at last a most astonishing result. Memory began to yield up what it held more and more freely, until it came in a flood. Every detail of experience was suddenly there, and in full colour. Nothing had been forgotten. I discovered that memory safely holds all experience in minutest detail, and that what fails (from disuse) is the ability to pull the record out of its pigeonhole.

The deprivation of reference material became a gain. Every climb had to be re-lived, which in writing terms means re-created. I have since believed that the main reason for the dullness of many an expedition book is the author's too easy access to diaries and printed matter. These allow him to write without re-living—a trap all the more easy to fall into when time is short and distractions many. The book, then, was going well when the Allies invaded Sicily late in 1943. The Germans dropped parachute troops on Chieti. We were herded into cattle-trucks and trundled over the Brenner pass to a concentration camp in Bavaria. The place (Moosburg) was infested with fleas and bugs, and packed with 20,000 starving Poles and Russians. They fought over any black bread we passed to them. Writing was impossible for the next two months. I had no paper.

We were moved at last to a camp in Czechoslovakia, Oflag VIII F at Mahrisch Trubau. I fell foul of the Gestapo on arrival. In a personal search they found my MS. The fact that I was secreting it on my person, not carrying it openly, aroused their worst suspicions. (A coded record of things seen in Germany?). I was photographed, finger-printed, interrogated. When I said what it was, and that I carried it under my shirt only for safer transport, they dropped their eyes to the desk and believed not a word. These were the first men I'd met who could put a shiver up my spine. They looked hard-eyed of course, but not mean or nasty, for that implies an element of humanity. I had not before appreciated how much good there is in the common criminal. The Gestapo agent was a man from whom all good had been wrung out, and the result was an animated corpse. My flesh crept. Not till then did I understand why this war had to be fought. I had known only Rommel's Afrika Korps, and they had my respect. The tank commander had won more than that from me. War, I had felt, was a bloody lunacy. Now I knew that this one had been inescapable.

They had to let me go, but I never saw the MS again. Its loss hit me hard at the time, yet proved another blessing in disguise. At Mahrisch Trubau I began afresh, this time screwed to a new frame of mind by worsening conditions.

The thousand bomber raids were unleashed on Germany. We were living on frosted turnips and potatoes—often only their peelings—a starvation diet of 800 calories a day. The guards dared no longer turn their Alsatians into the compound at night, for they went straight into the pot, and the skins would be hung over the fence before morning. Stray cats went the same way. The Russians were on Rumania's frontier. We had reports that the SS were under orders to machine-gun camp inmates on Russia's path of advance. We agreed that no escapes should now be allowed. Our escapers were invariably caught by the Gestapo, truncheoned, incinerated, and the ashes returned to the camp of origin. The tunnels we'd made had to be freed from the searches that escapes entailed, and so kept for emergencies. I no longer believed I'd climb mountains again, but felt blindly determined to get the truth about them on to paper. I no longer wanted to write just of hard climbs, or to enlighten anyone. I was writing because I must, all humbug shed off, and with it all understatement of difficulty, all exaggeration of danger, all reticence about feeling. The whole mountain scene was vivid in mind and detail. I now had good paper, had learned how to ignore distractions, and could write fast. I had in mind to say what I'd found of beauty, effort, fun, and delight. I would try for the truth only, and while knowing it could never be said, still I would try.

I finished the first draft on my birthday in March 1944. It was the day of the war's greatest air raid. 4,000 planes had bombed Frankfurt. The fall of Rome and invasion of Normandy followed. We knew all this, for the engineers had built a wireless set and we published the BBC bulletins daily. When the Russians burst through Rumania that summer we were evacuated to Germany, and imprisoned in a former Luftwaffe barracks in a wood near Brunswick.

I returned to the MS again and again at Brunswick, trying to get it right. My main anxiety was at first the Gestapo. They had still to be dodged, for their searches went on. They were maddened by our daily publication of the BBC News, to which their own people were not allowed to listen. They searched everywhere but the right place. The set was plugged into the power line vertically under the electrified barbed-wire fence. The tunnel entrance was right out in the open compound, where they never thoroughly looked (the trap door was invisible). Random interrogations continued, but I would not again be caught with the MS on my body.

A greater risk was soon bomb-blast. The British and American armies were through France, and the Russians in Hungary. Day and night, the Allied air fleets were overhead. During these last nine months we saw neither sky by day nor stars by night – all was obscured by a vast pall of dust and smoke rising off the burning cities all around. Brunswick, Magdeburg, Hanover, and most others were engulfed. One daylight raid wiped out our German garrison, but we were unaware of it. Stupefied, we could see nothing through the wall of flaming trees round the barracks. I carried the MS under my tunic at all times, for the Gestapo menace had gone. They were off to more congenial tasks. A big purge was on following the attempt by Rommel and others to kill Hitler. Each time a general surrendered on the Russian front, public notice was given that vengeance had been taken on his family and friends.

Earlier reports of the SS machine-gunning prisoners in eastern camps were confirmed. We knew it could happen here at any time. Our twelve new tunnels running under the perimeter wire were kept strictly unused. There had to be a last-minute chance of mass escape – supposing we were strong enough to make it. We had been given too little food for too long. TB was rife. My finger-nails were corrugated from vitamin-lack, and my hair thinning. I could no longer walk around the camp without feeling dizzy, nor climb stairs without palpitation of the heart. Hopes of survival had dimmed a bit. Day and night we dreamed of food; otherwise not once over the last year had I felt imprisoned. I lived on mountains and had the freedom of them. I waited on the machine-gunners without concern. Most of us had found our own ways of doing this. But we did prepare ourselves.

At the end, the American 9th Army beat the SS to the gates. I remember still my first ration of one chocolate-bar—the swift run of heat through the body as if from neat whisky. In May 1945, I returned from the freedom of prisons to the chains of civilised society. Dent took the book. They asked for changes where I'd expressed myself too openly. I could see their point, but refused. The book had to be as it was, written from the heart of the holocaust, and not as if written on home ground.

from MOUNTAIN 67 *1979*

War Ironies

ARMAND CHARLET*

"After Italy entered the war we had the pleasure of opening fire from the Col Infranchissable on a group of Italian machine gunners going to the Dôme hut. But the next day it was we who were machine-gunned by an enemy post on the Col de Trélatête. We retired to the Aiguille Béranger out of range. One of my men had the heel of his ski pierced by a bullet. It was the Italian mountaineer Gervasutti who commanded the Italian troops on the other side. At the same time two of my Italian friends, René Chabod and Evariste Croux, held the Col du Géant for the Italians, while Edouard Frendo, who knew them both well, had his command post facing them at the Réquin hut. It was an intriguing situation."

from ARMAND CHARLET *1975*

---

*As related to Sir Douglas Busk

The Pity of War

LIONEL TERRAY

I was lucky enough to be spared the butchery on Mont Froid; but to make up for this I was involved, albeit from some way off, in the second attack on the Pointe de Clairy, which was also exceedingly hard-fought. The Pointe throws down a long, spiky, but not particularly steep ridge to the Col de Sollières. The Germans were firmly installed at several places along this ridge, so that to become fully master of the situation it was necessary to deal with all these as well as the summit itself. The attack was commanded by Lieutenant Edouard Frendo, who a few months later made the second ascent of the Walker Spur on the Grandes Jorasses. His force consisted of three sections from the 11th Battalion the Chasseurs Alpins, the 3rd Scouting Section from the 15th, and also on the extreme left, a combat group from the 1st Company of the same battalion, under my command.

The lie of the land was against us. The three platoons from the 11th had to crampon up a steep open snow slope which led to the ridge, without any shelter until they reached it. Similarly the section from the 15th, which was to attack the summit, had to crampon up a steep couloir containing no cover at all. During the night these four sections, entirely made up of sure-footed mountaineers, climbed so silently that they were not noticed by the sentries until they had almost reached the crest, where they charged with such skill and dash that they won a foothold among the rocks.

Unhappily only one enemy pocket of resistance was overcome by this first assault, and all along the spine of the ridge the Germans remained in their chosen positions, protected by stone walls and well supplied with ammunition. The job of my own group, on the left, was simply to cover the ground over which the enemy might have effected a flanking movement and so taken our men from the rear. Thus we played only a small part in the proceedings, and I contented myself with keeping my men under cover of some rocks from which we were able to fire on a few German attempts to send reinforcements from the Tura fort.

From my position I had a ring-side view of the battlefield. Both sides were putting down a heavy barrage, and I would go so far as to say that the French were probably deploying up to eighty or so field-guns of various calibres, and the Germans about the same. The reader can imagine the racket produced by some hundred and fifty cannon all trained on an area of a few hundred square yards. It was like hell on earth. Up till then I had not had much to do with artillery, and I don't mind admitting I was terrified. Without knowing a lot about these matters, it seemed to me that on both sides the object of the bombardment was to reduce points of resistance on the ridge and to make their reinforcement impossible: but, whatever its cause, the shooting was remarkably inaccurate, and I was unable to see that it had any effect at all on the course of the fighting. Shells landed all over the place, and some of the French ones, intended no doubt for the other side of the mountain or at least for the summit, went off only a few yards from where I was lying. The deafening sound of the explosions, and the disagreeable feeling of being at the mercy of blind forces, threw me into a state of confusion such as I had never know in my life.

During all this time the Scouts of the 11th and the 15th were fighting heroically on the ridge, trying to dislodge the Germans from their strongpoints. Several were killed, others gravely wounded. Jacques Boell tells vividly of their plight:

"It was impossible to evacuate the wounded, so that they were forced to save themselves by sliding down the hard snow-slopes into the Combe de Mont Froid. By lying down in deep furrows in the snow they were able to get most of the way under cover from the enemy snipers, who, whether out of humanity or being too busy elsewhere, did not in fact pay them much attention. Their sufferings can be imagined as they slipped and sprawled in the snow, losing blood and in certain cases even limbs that had been half sliced off by machine-gun fire. At the bottom of this agonising descent the victims fortunately found stretcher-bearers, led up under enemy fire by the Chaplains of the engaged battalions."

But despite all the courage and sacrifice of our troops, the enemy remained in command of the Pointe de Clairy and the greater part of the Arête de Sollières. It was becoming obvious that we would not only fail to dislodge him, but that as our men ran short of ammunition there would be a serious risk of counter-attack, which might be fatal. Faced with this desperate situation Lt.-Col. Le Ray, who was in touch with Frendo by radio, gave the order to retire in spite of the obvious dangers attaching to the descent of a snow slope under enemy fire.

This Battle of the Pointe de Clairy, in which I took part more as a spectator than as a fighting man, made a profound impression on me, and I went back down to the valley through the peaceful forests full of disgust. Spring was beginning to burgeon. Creamy snowdrops speckled the ground, and the air was full of odours evoking peace and love. As I descended through this poetic landscape I realised that the hell I had just left, in which so many men had meaninglessly lost their lives, could never again have anything in common with the naïvely sporting game I had played through the winter months. The whole abomination of war was suddenly and overwhelmingly apparent to me.

Faced with the foolhardiness of some young (frequently German) climbers, quite a lot of French mountaineers are apt to say: "It's not playing the game: climbing isn't war." Yet it must be admitted that for many people it *is* a way of satisfying the primaeval aggressive instincts which find so little outlet in modern life. I am one of these myself. If I had been born in another age I would probably have been a soldier or a buccaneer, and it may be, therefore, that climbing has been for me a kind of fighting. For five months fighting had even seemed a new kind of mountain challenge; but all that had nothing in common with the sort of warfare I had just witnessed in which man, far from raising himself above the material by his physical and moral virtues, was reduced to the level of a beast hunted by blind forces of iron and fire. No, climbing is not war: because war is no longer anything but an immense murder.

from CONQUISTADORS OF THE USELESS *1961*

A Breach of Faith

ROB TAYLOR

The heat . . . now as I slowly emerge from my deep morphia-induced euphoria, the incredible heat returns, so oppressive I find myself sucking for breath in this leaden jungle air, seemingly devoid of oxygen. As reality returns I am aware of the steady streams of perspiration from my naked, filthy body soaking the straw mattress upon which I lie. Once again it has come alive with the rustling and buzzing of countless lice and fleas. Soon my mind is released from the drug, or more rightly in this case, imprisoned in reality. The pain increases in my left leg as I gaze at my blackened toes and distended gaping ankle oozing great masses of green slime, jolting me into consciousness. What may well have passed as a bad dream, is in fact a living hell. It all comes back now as I lie in Kilimanjaro Christian Medical Centre Hospital in Moshi, Tanzania. The peak, the face, Henry, mistakes, the accident, misjudgments, feelings of anguish, anxiety, regret, remorse, pain, abandonment . . . all welling up to fill my very soul. Moans and wishes for death remain unanswered. Eventually a squat, sombre Bantu nurse arrives none too cheerfully with relief, two ampoules of morphine. Grudgingly she gives me my jab and as I stare through the open slat windows, I can see a distant Kilimanjaro quickly being enveloped by the swirling morning mists. The morphine rushes over me like the swell of a pounding Pacific breaker, and I am enveloped and swept away back to Kilimanjaro's Breach Wall, back to relive my experience on this face for the thousandth time.

January 12 Ahead looms the summit block Kilimanjaro and the Breach Wall, a study in contrast with alternating hanging white ice-fields and black pumice cliff festooned with the most incredible and unlikely looking icicles. One of which, at the 18,500ft. level, is the key to the Breach Wall and would prove the main factor in determining Henry's and my success or failure on the face. No photograph can truly catch the awesome immensity of this side of Kilimanjaro, as its great width, approximately twice that of the

Brenva Face on Mt. Blanc, destroys one's perception of the 7,000ft. vertical rise to an altitude of 19,000ft. The fog and mist appears, as if from nowhere, engulfing the entire wall in a matter of minutes and with it our possibility of approach this day. At only 10 a.m., Henry and I are already firmly ensconced in the Barranco Bivouac, a round, sardine-can-shaped affair at the 13,000ft. level, finished for the day as the first rain comes slattering across the tin roof. The remainder of this day is simply a series of endless brews spent by the two of us in deep but separate contemplation; Henry absorbed in an old copy of a November issue of *Newsweek* and I reading the hut register. As I scanned the faded pages wrapped in the remnants of an old Digestive Biscuit box, one name in particular jumped out at me, Dave Knowles. As if the gulf of time had suddenly been swallowed up, I now pictured Dave stomping his way across the barrancos through the wind and pouring rain, like some half-crazed scarecrow, on his solitary journey to be the first to circumvent Kilimanjaro so many years before. The thought alone made me howl with laughter but my musing quickly turned to sorrow as I now envisioned that dark day in August 1974, when Dave's blood ran red on the Eiger and one of my closest friends was taken from me.

We were off before dawn the following morning and were soon plodding along our way under cold, clear skies across the lower reaches of the Window Buttress toward the snout of the Heim Glacier, which we reached in roughly three hours. As I settled down on the edge of the ice to change from my shorts, which I had worn on the approach through the jungles, into my pile clothing and Goretex, I suddenly realised what was missing. In contrast to all the other glaciers I had ever seen before, there was not a drop of water to be found at the snout of the Heim. It certainly gave one an insight as to the porosity of pumice. While we soloed up the lower reaches of the Heim, rapidly gaining height, we could see far below us the quickly mounding cumulus clouds ascending up the mountain valleys like some raging torrent defying gravity. It was quite obvious as the mist overtook us by 10 a.m. that this was to be the present weather pattern on Kili and one could expect only three clear hours per day for climbing. Quite unexpected, however, was the snow condition and the effect the fog had on it. Even in the cold early morning, the snow was of a consistency I had never seen before; a firm, frozen surface, yet integrally and internally, completely rotten. When stressed, this made for easy but insecure and unreliable cramponing. When the mist enveloped this surface, instead of preserving its doubtful integrity and protecting it from the sun it turned, to coin a Russian word, into Kasha or porridge and provided about as much security. Henry and I roped up as we blindly groped our way through the final headwall ice cliffs of the Heim Glacier, reaching the Silver Saddle at noon. I was not at all happy about conditions and when I expressed my concern to Henry he said that I was much too worrisome and paranoid to be in the mountains. After being reminded of this several times, I began to wonder if this might be true.

With the visibility now down to 20ft. we set about trying to find out exactly where the Silver Saddle bivouac was located. After some minutes of aimless wandering I located a small rock promontory, which turned out to be the summit peak of the Window Buttress and immediately below this, two likely looking bivy sites. Unsatisfied with my find, Henry went off in search of a proper place to spend the night. However, he shortly returned luckless and just as we settled in, all hell broke loose in the skies above us. Lying in my bivy sack, I began to have second thoughts about Henry's comprehension of the present conditions on the mountain; and the consequences which might befall us by pushing it. His carefree, nonchalant attitude made me wonder if he realised the severity of our position. With these thoughts in mind, I drifted off into a restless sleep.

The morning of Saturday, January 14 once again dawned clear and cold and as we brewed up, still in our pits, there loomed out of the darkness behind us the main Breach ice-field and icicle. As the sun rose crimson over the plains of Africa, we set out soloing from the Silver Saddle, slowly making a rising diagonal traverse onto the main ice-field. As the angle increased and the face became pure water-ice, we roped up but continued to move together, the leader placing protection and the second removing it as we climbed. From the immense, grouped, streaked, and pitted appearance of the ice-field's surface, it was apparent that at times this would be a very dangerous place to be. The day became unusually warm and stifling as the equatorial sun rose overhead; and as we arrived at the base of the icicle just short of noon, great spouts of water were pouring off the summit crater, streaming into space.

To me, climbing, especially alpine climbing, is not simply the acquisition of technical expertise to overcome a series of difficulties during an ascent. But even more important, the ability to assess a given situation, make the proper judgment and take the correct action accordingly. Little did I know, this day would be a severe test of my convictions, and my failure to uphold them would nearly kill me. As I gazed up at the dripping, rotting mass stretching 300 vertical feet to the top of the Breach Wall my immediate reaction was awe and then recoil. It was quite obvious to me this Breach Icicle just wasn't in 'nick' at the present, and besides, to go on it now in the heat of the afternoon would be suicidal. This I said to Henry in so many words, and added that I felt we ought to bivouac and attempt it around three or four the next morning. Although to be honest, even by waiting I didn't give us much chance of success because of the deplorable conditions. Immediately Henry countered, that under no circumstances was he going to sit around for eighteen hours and wait, now that we were so close to success, adding that it would give us a greater chance tomorrow should we fail to knock it off today.

Knocking heads was nothing new on this trip. In the past, Henry's and my relationship had been solely of the working variety. That is, we made a good team and climbed well together but beyond this we had little else in common. Our personalities, outlooks and in fact our entire beings, are just too contradictory to allow any type of close friendship. Our different natures had fortunately never intruded on our climbing, but now at the most inopportune time, our working relationship just wasn't working. After several minutes of silent stalemate, I conceded. As I prepared to set out, up the icicle, I stated one last time for the record that although I would give it a go; I was 100% against it.

Man often tends to justify his questionable actions with the most insane and nebulous rationalisations imaginable. I was no exception. Although I felt under present conditions, particularly at this high altitude, that a fall was a very real possiblity, I simply justified my course of actions by thinking that I would over-protect each pitch, thus remaining in complete control of the situation.

The ice on the icicle was the worst I had ever encountered. The surface was composed to a depth of three feet, foot upon foot of fragile latticed-striations of rotted ice crystals, and collapsed with the slightest touch; it needed to be cleared away for each tenuous placement. At a point approximately 20ft. above Henry, I placed a bomb-proof ice screw deep in the bed ice of the icicle and climbed past it until it was within two feet of my right boot. As the ice degenerated at this point to where it would no longer hold my tools, I anchored them in slightly better ice to my extreme left. Then I attempted a lay-back move off a projecting ice pedestal across to them. In the midst of this, the pedestal snapped off on me and I flew back into space. By rights, with protection so close at hand, this should have been a very short controlled fall, but it was of a very sudden nature catching Henry unaware, allowing slippage in the rope before he held me. This, with the extra stretch in the rope, resulted in my smashing feet first into a sloping ledge at the base of the icicle before the tension of the rope caught me up. Dazed, I was slowly revolving, hanging horizontally in space, staring from below, up at Henry on the belay ledge. As I became aware for the first time of pain in my left foot, I stared down in horror; instead of seeing the top of my red and blue supergaiter, I saw only the 12 points of my Chouinard crampons and boot sole, the arch of which was touching my inner calf. To say that I momentarily freaked out would be an understatement, and my declaration to Henry was met only by a stare of blank incredulity and, "are you sure it's broken?" I assured him it was. In a matter of seconds his look changed from disbelief, to disappointment, to annoyance. Meanwhile, the only thought which ran through my head was, please God, don't let it be compound.

Shortly after, Henry concluded that our best course of action would be for him to lead the icicle and for me to jumar behind. This way we would complete the route and he could traverse the summit dome going down the tourist route for help after leaving me on top of the face. I told him I was going nowhere but down, much to his dislike. I could blame no one but myself for this accident because of my lack of assertiveness, but I wasn't about to let it finish me off now. My reasons for opting for descent were quite simple. First and foremost as far as I was concerned, the icicle wasn't climbable or at least not safely on this day. Secondly, the possibility of shock due to injury is always greater with increased altitude, and lastly, there have been many examples of people lost

31 Climbers collecting garbage from the foot of the North West Face of Half Dome in Yosemite Valley, California. Refuse pollution is now a serious problem in mountains and climbing areas on both sides of the Atlantic. *Photo: Ron Partridge*

33 34 The evocative Swiss location (top photo) for 'Five Days in Summer' with which veteran film-maker and mountaineer Fred Zinneman finally realised his ambition to make a major feature film based on mountaineering. The three main characters – played by Lambert Wilson, Betsy Brantley and Sean Connery (above) – interreact in a classic romantic triangle ending in poignant tragedy.
Photos: The Ladd Company

32 (left) Gustav Diessl and Leni Riefenstahl in Arnold Fanck's thirties epic 'The White Hell of Piz Palü' – the best known of an earlier genre of mountain feature films.

35 (above) Naomi Uemura receives the 'International Award for Valour in Sport'. Uemura was one of a number of mountaineers who were drawn into this spurious event organised by a London gambling club. The event ceased when the club was raided and lost its licence in the late seventies.
Photo: Julie Tullis

36 (left) The antithesis of the florid adulation of the Valour Award was the irreverent style of the British magazine Crags (also now defunct). Here Livesey, Fawcett, Bonington and others are lampooned in a typical entry.
Photomontage: Courtesy of High magazine

*Some of the
writers whose
work appears
in this book*

37 Greg Child

38 Reinhold Messner

39 Don Whillans and Chris Bonington
(in 1962, leaving for the Paine Expedition.)

40 Galen Rowell

41 Anne Sauvy-Wilkinson

42 Pierre Mazeaud

43 Max Jones and Mark Hudon

44 H. W. Tilman

45 Rick Sylvester

46 D. F. O. Dangar and
T. S. Blakeney

47 Alex MacIntyre

48 Jim Bridwell

49 Anderl Heckmair

50 Mick Fowler

51 Ivan Ghirardini

52 Claud Schuster

53 Willi and Nanda Devi Unsoeld

54 Kim Carrigan

55 Doug Scott

56 Kevin Fitzgerald

57 G. F. Dutton

58 Michael Roberts, Othon Bron
and Janet Adam Smith

59 Dave Roberts

for days in the mist on the thousands of acres of snow which make up Kili's summit. In taking into account the present weather conditions, this certainly was a distinct possibility and so I forced the issue for descent.

From our vantage point, perched on 70° ice, at the base of the final Breach Buttress we could see, from the incredible amount of debris falling onto the ice-field below, that an attempt to retreat across it now would mean certain death. So as anxious as I was to get lower, there was little choice this day but to stop and bivy. Henry led off rightwards on a horizontal traverse for several hundred feet to an excellent ice ledge, tucked away safely beneath the final overhanging rock cliffs of the Breach Wall which afforded excellent protection from rock and ice fall. Following Henry proved not only to be very strenuous because of my useless left leg, but was further complicated by the loss of two tools in the fall. I surprisingly found however I could manipulate quite well and make excellent time utilising my left knee as a substitute foot, cutting a small hold for it each step I took by balancing on the front points of my right crampon. All the while I was constantly pondering the extent of my injuries. I had little time to wait, for as soon as I arrived in our hollow I immediately set about gingerly loosening my supergaiter and boot laces sufficiently to allow me to probe with my fingers the distorted area beneath my three pairs of socks. Under no circumstances did I want to remove my boot as I realised in the present state I would never be able to get it back on. I almost retched as my searching fingers located the greasy, protruding end of the fibula where my ankle should have been. I quickly yanked out my blood-covered hand and stared in disbelief as drop by drop it stained the ice beside me. Suddenly the overwhelming severity and hopelessness of the situation struck me. I realised that this time I would die. There was no escape. We were now at over 18,000ft. and nearly fifty miles away from the nearest hospital and long before I could hope to reach any proper medical assistance, I knew gangrene and infection would take its toll, making me beg for death. With this sudden realisation it was all I could do to fight off the insidious sweeping haze of shock and prevent it from totally overcoming me. And yet, as bad as things appeared I saw the choices quite clearly. Shock was immediate death, whereas in fighting, at least I had a chance, however slim it might be. As I leaned against the uneven, coarse brown pumice, I searched my brain for some hint or clue I may have forgotten which would help me decide whether or not to reduce the fracture. The options were obvious: either leave it and splint it where it lay and have no foot by morning, just a dead, black mass, waiting to be cut off; or reduce the fracture and chance knicking an artery with the fibula and die in a pool of my own blood in a matter of minutes. I opted for a reduction and instructed Henry how to pull traction on my boot. Eventually the fibula popped back into place and we promptly splinted it under tension with an ice hammer shaft, some crampon parts and an old hip belt from one of the packs.

Although I carried with me several strong pain medications, I have been warned as to strange effects they may have at this altitude and so I stuck with aspirin. For the first time I had forgotten to take with me any type of antibiotics which I so desperately needed now. After a small amount of soup and fruit juice I sank into a deep sleep, my heavily splinted leg taking on the apparition in my dreams of some nagging old lady. . . .

January 15 We were away from the bivouac at dawn and began retracing our steps on the long, downsloping diagonal retreat back across the Breach Ice Field, still cloaked in deep blue shadow to the Silver Saddle already bathed in the sun's first light. I rigged up a harness of slings around my splinted ankle and attached this to the back of my Whillan's Sit harness. I found that this constant tension not only greatly relieved the pain of my ankle but also gave me a good deal of added stability which minimised further damage to it. Rope length after rope length we descended leaving one screw as an anchor for each rappel. Henry always going first to set up tension on the rope at the bottom, to facilitate my almost horizontal passage across. After a number of different trial manoeuvres such as hopping feet first, kneeling, I found head first downhill lying on my right side, proved to be the fastest and least painful on the descent. By the time I arrived at the right-hand edge of the ice-field after several final pendulums, I was in a state of complete exhaustion. Never before had I experienced the necessity of such a total output of effort for such an extended period of time. As the last remnants of my strength ebbed away, I collapsed in an easy-angled snow above the Silver Saddle and realised as I looked down that blood was saturating the outside surface of my supergaiter. So intense had my concentration been, I hadn't even noticed the blood working its way through the three pairs of socks, boot and gaiter. Shortly thereafter, we arrived on the Silver Saddle in the usual sea of pea-soup mist and once again we were left with little choice but to bivouac. The sporadic roar and rumble of the Heim's headwall ice-cliffs breaking off and strafing the lower face was all the persuasion needed as we settled down for another night.

I feel that during the course of an alpine climb, the relationship of partners should be one of total commitment, trust and reliance. It is undoubtedly true that I could never have managed to survive the descent on the face if it wasn't for Henry's physical assistance. For this I am immensely grateful. However, it became very obvious to me during the descent that I was nothing but a burden to him and the only bond between us was the 50 metres of climbing rope. I had the impression of a cold aloofness that he retained and his involvement was purely on the level that might be likened to dealing with the business at hand, which was in this case getting down the face. And although from my point of view, the compassion and supportive insight I desperately needed from him was solely lacking at this time, no one could have been more efficient in executing our retreat.

The sun was already up and shining brightly on the Silver Saddle on the morning of January 16 as I slowly shook off the deep peaceful sleep which provided so much comfort, protection and escape from the existing pain and nagging doubts. Full reality returned to my dull and deadened senses over a brew of warm fruit juice. As I unzipped my pit, once again anxiety flooded my brain, catching a faint but distinct odour, similar to that of an over-ripe, rotting pear. It lasted but several seconds and then vanished in the cold, fresh morning air as I wildly beckoned Henry over. But it returned with an ever-increasing intensity as the day progressed.

Because of the multiple ice cliffs and bergschrunds which comprised the Heim, negotiating this section proved to be by far the most dangerous and difficult. This was aggravated by the fact that we no longer had any ice screws left and had to rely solely on boot-axe belays for security. For me it also proved to be most excruciatingly painful. The lowering down from the overhanging walls caused incredible jolting to my ankle which was again soon spilling blood from my supergaiter onto the snow. After what seemed an eternity we arrived at the easy-angled ice at approximately 17,000ft. near the snout of the Heim just as the mist swallowed us up and it began to snow. After so many days in verticality, it was wonderful now to be on ground you couldn't fall off of. But it also became immediately obvious that along with the loss of steepness came the loss of my mobility. Now I could only grovel on my chest a few metres at a time. There was little choice in the matter, I couldn't walk and Henry certainly couldn't carry me, so it was agreed that Henry would leave me and go to the Horombo Hut located at the same elevation approximately six hours away where we knew there would be people and a radio and he could make a call for help. Before departing he made the tremendous effort of carrying me on his back from the snout of the Heim down across the pumice moraine to a sheltered ledge 500ft. below on the lee side of several large boulders.

As I settled back into my pit and bivy sack, Henry readied himself for departure, packing into his sack which he would take: his own gear and my exposed film and camera. Once again, we rehashed plans and decided he would follow the Horombo trail to the hut and I could expect help later that night or at first light. Although he was not certain he would be able to return with the rescue party because he planned to run most of the way and might be too exhausted, he assured me he would take care of everything at the hospital, seeing me through the extensive surgery it was obvious I would need, and remain until I had sufficiently recovered.

I stared down across the mounded pumice moraines mottled with white a long while and thought to myself, "I am alive, I've made it, finally my ordeal is nearly over" . . . little did I realise as I watched Henry's blue clad figure slowly vanish below into a curtain of heavily falling snow, that this would be the last time I would see him for two months and that in reality my ordeal was only just beginning. . . .

Postscript:

I wasn't rescued that night or even on the following night but eventually the third day, the Norwegian alpinist, Odd Eliassen and four rangers arrived. Henry has since said he decided not to go to the hut with the radio six hours away but chose to go down the mountain instead. a Trip that took thirty-six hours.

In my weakened state, I could never have survived the succeeding two days off the mountain if it had not been for Odd's constant encouragement and selfless giving which kept me going. The first day was spent crawling and hopping down the lower Window Buttress, and the second, being carried accross the Shira Plateau. By the time I arrived at the KCMC hospital near midnight on January 19, Henry had already departed from Moshi, Tanzania, for his return trip to the US to attend a sports convention. At this point, with my ankle and foot gangrenous and severe infection deeply entrenched in my system, once again the question arose whether I would live or die. Emergency surgery was immediately performed by a Swedish missionary doctor. It is not possible to express in words my feeling of total abandonment when I regained consciousness and the full realisation hit me that Henry had not even waited to see me.

After further surgery and a two-week stay in KCMC, I was transferred back to the United States for a two-month period of hospitalisation.

I still have my leg. Sitting now in the warm summer sun I must wait to see how much use I will have of my ankle. To this day, Henry is adamant that every decision made and action taken was the right one. I know some of mine were not.

Time has allowed me the opportunity for a great deal of introspection and self-analysis. I have found an experience such as this, painful as it may be, offers a wealth of insight and wisdom, if one doesn't get too hung up on the "If only's." One must recognise mistakes and poor judgment in order to profit by them and realign oneself, or he is doomed to repeat them in the future. I think I have . . . for there is no success like failure.

from MOUNTAIN 63 *1978*

Henry Barber Replies

After the publication of the previous article, the editor of *Climbing* interviewed Henry Barber to get his side of the story. This is the relevant part of that conversation.

Travelling, then, is what you attribute your growth in climbing to?

Sure, you go more places, and you accumulate more experience from which to draw in later situations. Even a trip such as the one with Rob Taylor in Africa wouldn't make me shy away from going into an unfamiliar situation. I mean, I'd already been in that sort of predicament when you piece together all the climbs that I've done. The sum of the parts leads to a whole. Granted, I'm not terribly excited about returning to Africa. It wasn't an especially easy place to go and get something done. It's an exaggerated continent. But I don't have any regrets that I went. Each time that you go some place new or go up on another climb, the experience means something different. You interpret an experience in any one of a thousand ways. If you can appreciate that, you're going to be able to perform an act in a better way than you did before. This kind of an appreciation for certain instances is what saved Rob Taylor's life up on Mt. Kilimanjaro.

How do you feel about the experience, in light of the articles that Rob Taylor has published?

I don't really care to say that much because there's been so much press about it already. I haven't read the articles at this time and am making a point not to. From the people who have read about it, who don't know anything about what went on up there, I understand that I lack compassion. Well, you have to separate your priorities. The fact is that there was a job to do there; he's down and he's alive. That's a cold way of looking at it, but it's true. He's here. And why's that? Because somebody had a better soloing ability and a better sense of what to do than anybody else, in that particular situation. I feel that enough has been said against me, and in that light I'd rather say nothing than negate various 'charges' that have been levelled at me.

Could you briefly go over the problems that you see as making up the whole incident?

Look, it all comes down to a guy who's under extreme duress. There don't exist very many situations that create much more physical and psychological problems than a guy falling and breaking his ankle at 18,000ft. And the guy didn't just break his ankle. He mangled it. And he had to get through the jungle, not to mention 4,000ft. of 45° to 55° ice, traversing, mind you. Furthermore, we only had six or seven ice screws. Now, if Rob had been a weak individual, he would have gone into shock from the word go. But he didn't. He never went into shock during the whole descent.

About all I could say about the situation is that under the circumstances, he performed brilliantly. No normal person could have ever kept things together like he did.

What about your decision to leave when you knew he was at the hospital? I think that this is the point of all the debate

It's an awful lot like the Messner problem, when they said he left his brother to die. The guy did the best he was capable of, and that's the simple fact of the matter.

I made a mistake and left Rob in Africa, but I left only when I knew he was at the hospital. One of the Norwegians who went up to get Rob had his wife call me and tell me that he was down.

We had made that decision on the mountain, that I would go back to the States on account of several factors. Rob had told me on the mountain that he didn't see it as necessary for me to stick around. I told him that I'd see him when he got down. I didn't see him, but I made damn sure that he was safe before I went anywhere. The thing boils down to the fact that I made a wrong decision. But I did what I had planned to do, and now I'm paying for it. But I don't think that I should have to pay for it in an inordinate way, especially after making so many good decisions in the days previous to leaving. I would never do it again, but that doesn't erase the past. I don't feel guilty, though, because of the nature of so many critical decisions I had to make while getting off the thing.

What about the decision that Rob mentioned in his article about

you picking a different way to go out than you had come in and
spending a day-and-a-half to get help?

The situation there developed as a result that we didn't have a
map, and I didn't even want to look at a map. We got most of our
information from a guy named Iain Allen. My point is that if I was
looking at maps all the time, I wouldn't be out there in the first
place. I'm speaking about self-reliance. The problem was that we'd
heard about two guys walking between two huts near our route in a
day. After attempting to do just that on the way out, I would have
to say that not even Bill Toomey would have made that trip in six
hours. Well, I figured that I'll try that way to avoid a leopard's
den. There was no way that I wanted to go by that thing. So what I
ended up doing was trotting through the jungle for over thirty
hours to get to the park gate. I figured that I wasn't even going to
deal with any Africans in this instance, so I went directly to two
Norwegians who were there who, in turn, effected the rescue. At
that point, I was close to not being able to walk. My feet had been
wet in boots that were very stiff, and had swollen. I put my feet in a
bath tub when I was finished with the rescue people, and I
immediately passed out from the pain. There wasn't much way I
was going to be able to go up and help get Rob.

So you have no regrets, as to your actions in the matter, save for
leaving when you did?

I did the best I could. I don't think that I lacked in compassion to
the extent that it's been hinted. It's a very intense thing to rappel
for two days with a guy who's in extreme pain. There's a distinct
feeling one must have for preservation of the self, in order that
things could be done in a rational manner, so that actions on the
part of others could be effected. It's a job that has to be done in a
businesslike manner.

It sounds as if you feel that your talents in particular contributed to
Rob's surviving the six days after he was hurt

Put it this way. I don't think that more than just a handful of
American climbers could have helped him more than I did. Maybe
one of the Lowes could have. I don't know. But I think that the
whole thing has begun to stink in that there were insinuations that I

forced Rob into leading the ice pillar. Well, that's foolish. If you're in the type of climbing that we were doing, you don't let yourself get forced into a dangerous situation. At that level, every decision becomes internalised to the point where you have to look very hard and see if you feel a hundred per cent sure about going up on something. And the main point of the whole discussion is that Rob knows his ice-climbing. He's a far better ice-climber than I will ever be. He made a mistake, either in the actual process of climbing, or in the initial decision-making process, and that's a clear-cut, very cold thing that can never be negated. Everything stems from this.

I think that what Rob was getting at in his article was that he felt affected by your personality as far as going or not going was concerned

Besides the fact that I've never pushed anyone to do anything, I think that the question that you're posing is unanswerable. Rob is the only person who can answer as to whether he felt pushed or not. A mistake was made. I mean, I've made several mistakes. I was teaching a student once—I was soloing next to him—and I fell off. A guy about ten feet below me hit me on the back as I went by and shoved me into the wall on to a ledge. His action was nothing but a reflex; he wasn't trying to save my life or anything, but what can I say? I made a mistake. I was lucky. So was Rob, in a more extreme way because he had to work incredibly hard to maintain himself so as to make it down. I guess that I could have blamed that student for causing the accident. But it's only your own ego that pushes you. It's never anything else.

You wouldn't argue that competition pressures between partners, in a situation like the one in which Rob and yourself were in, don't exist?

No. You're right, the pressures do exist. But in this instance, I don't think so because Rob Taylor is one of the most uncompetitive climbers around. He's never made a point of trying to get his name around. He's very unselfish in his climbing.

Do you see parallels between this situation and that involving Reinhold Messner and his brother on Nanga Parbat?

Only in that there was some writing done in which Messner was, in a vague way, blamed for his brother's death. Decisions were made and carried out. It's a clear-cut thing. People have to live with their decisions, and that's what Rob and I are doing now.

from CLIMBING 55 *1979*

The End of a Chapter

SIR ARNOLD LUNN

On the following day Lindsay felt like a rest, so I set off alone and climbed the East Ridge of Cyfrwy, off which I fell two days later. It is an interesting climb, not very difficult judged by modern standards, but quite amusing. A steep face, shown in the illustration, looks sensational but is really quite easy. The best thing on the ridge is a miniature Mummery crack which calls for skill if one wishes to climb it without disproportionate effort.

On August 28 I started for my last climb. Lindsay was not feeling fit, and he left me near the top of Cader Idris. I decided to descend the East Ridge and climb the North Ridge of Cyfrwy. I was carrying a short rope which I had brought along on the chance that Lindsay might join me.

The day was perfect. The burnished silver of the sea melted into a golden haze. Light shadows cast by scudding clouds drifted across the blue and distant hills. The sun flooded down on the rocks. I slid down the crack and reached the top of the steep face of rock above 'The Table'. The usual route dodges the top 15ft. of this face, and by an easy traverse reaches a lower ledge. But on that glorious afternoon I longed to spin out the joys of Cyfrwy, and I found a direct route from the top to the bottom of this wall, a steep but not very severe variation.

It was one of those days when to be alive is very heaven. The feel of the warm, dry rocks and the easy rhythm of the descending motion gave me an almost sensuous pleasure. One toyed with the thought of danger, so complete was the confidence inspired by the firm touch of the wrinkled rocks.

I was glad to be alone. I revelled in the freedom from the restraints of the rope, and from the need to synchronise my movements with the movements of companions.

I have never enjoyed rock-climbing more. I have never enjoyed rock-climbing since. But, at least, the hills gave me of their best, full measure and overflowing, in those last few golden moments before I fell.

A few minutes later Lindsay, who was admiring the view from Cader, was startled by the thunder of a stone avalanche. He turned to a stray tourist, urging him to follow, and dashed off in the direction of Cyfrwy.

And this is what had happened. I had just lowered myself off the edge of 'The Table' — conspicuous in Mr. Abraham's excellent photograph. There was no suggestion of danger. Suddenly the mountain seemed to sway, and a quiver ran through the rocks. I clung for one brief moment of agony to the face of the cliff. And then suddenly a vast block, which must have been about ten feet high and several feet thick, separated itself from the face, heeled over on top of me and carried me with it into space. I turned a somersault, struck the cliff some distance below, bounded off once again and, after crashing against the ridge two or three times, landed on a sloping ledge about seven feet broad. The thunder of the rocks falling through the 150ft. below my resting-point showed how narrow had been my escape.

I had fallen a distance which Lindsay estimated at 100ft. It was not a sliding fall, for except when I struck and rebounded I was not in contact with the ridge. The fall was long enough for me to retain a very vivid memory of the thoughts which chased each other through my brain during those few crowded seconds. I can still feel the clammy horror of the moment when the solid mountain face trembled below me, but the fall, once I was fairly off, blunted the edge of fear. My emotions were subdued, as if I had been partially anaesthetised. I remember vividly seeing the mountains upside down after my first somersault. I remember the disappointment as I realised that I had not stopped and that I was still falling. I remember making despairing movements with my hands in a futile attempt to check my downward progress.

The chief impression was a queer feeling that the stable order of nature had been overturned. The tranquil and immobile hills had been startled into a mood of furious and malignant activity, like a dangerous dog roused from a peaceful nap by some inattentive passer-by who has trodden on him unawares. And every time I struck the cliff only to be hurled downwards once again, I felt like a small boy who is being knocked about by a persistent bully – "Will he never stop? . . . surely he can't hit me again . . . surely he's hurt me enough."

When at last I landed, I tried to sit up, but fell back hurriedly on seeing my leg. The lower part was bent almost at right angles. It was not merely broken, it was shattered and crushed.

I shouted and shouted and heard no reply. Had Lindsay returned home? Would I have to wait for hours before help came?

Solitude had lost its charm. I no longer rejoiced in my freedom and called upon society to come to my assistance. I set immense store on my membership of the Human Club, and very urgently did I summon my fellow-members to my assistance.

And then suddenly I heard an answering cry, and my shouts died away in a sob of heartfelt relief.

And while I waited for help, I looked up at the scar on the cliff where the crag had broken away, and I realised all that I was in danger of losing. Had I climbed my last mountain?

During the war the cheery dogmatism of some second lieutenant home from the front was extremely consoling, for the human mind is illogical and the will to believe very potent. And so when Lindsay arrived and replied with a hearty affirmative when I asked him whether I should ever climb again, I was greatly comforted, even though Lindsay knew less of broken legs than the average subaltern of the chances of peace.

Lindsay was preceded by an ancient man who keeps the hut on Cader. He examined my leg with a critical eye and informed me that it was broken. He then remarked that I had been very ill-advised to stray off the path on to 'rough places' where even the natives did not venture. He grasped my leg, and moved it a little higher on to the ledge. This hurt. He then uncoiled my rope and secured me to a buttress which overhung my narrow perch.

Then Lindsay stagged onto the ledge, gave one glance at my leg, turned a curious colour, and sat down hurriedly. He suggested breaking off a gate and carrying me down on it. The ancient man of Cader hazarded a tentative suggestion in favour of sacks. I demurred, for a sack may be appropriate to a corpse but is not conducive to the comfort of a wounded man.

Lindsay, by a lucky accident, remembered Warren's address, and so I sent him off to find him. He left me in charge of the tourist who had followed him, and departed with the man of Cader.

Lindsay's chance companion was useful while he stayed, for I was lying on a sloping ledge, and was glad of his shoulder as a pillow. Ten minutes passed, and my companion remarked that he thought he ought to be going. I protested, but could not move him. His wife, he said, would be getting anxious. I hinted that his wife's anxiety might be ignored. "Ah, but you don't know my wife," he replied, and, so saying, left me.

He consented to leave his cap behind as a pillow. A month later he wrote and asked me why I had not returned it. This struck me as unreasonable, but—as he justly observed—I did not know his wife.

I fell at 4 p.m. About 7.30 p.m. it became colder, and shivering made the pain worse. About 7.45 p.m. the old man of Cader returned with some warm tea which he had brewed for me, and for which I was more than grateful. Half-an-hour later the local policeman arrived with a search party and a stretcher.

Luckily the ledge ran across on to easy ground, but it was not until midnight—eight hours after my fall—that I reached the Angel Hotel.

My leg was broken, crushed and comminuted. Twice the preparations were made for amputation. Twice my temperature fell in the nick of time. At the end of a week I was taken home, and lay on my back for four months, much consoled by a Christian Scientist who assured me that my leg was intact. But it was not to Mrs. Eddy, but to the faint hope of the hills that I turned for comfort in the long nights when pain had banished sleep.

from THE MOUNTAINS OF YOUTH *1925*

The Green Lake

MICHAEL ROBERTS

Eloquent are the hills: their power speaks
In ice, rock and falling stone;
The voices of croziered fern, wood-sorrel, gentian, edelweiss
Lead upward to the summit or the high col.

The mountain lake mirrors the hills, and the white clouds
Move in a blue depth, the hut stands empty:
No one appears all day, nothing disturbs
The symphony of ice and yellow rock and the blue shadow.

And at dusk the familiar sequence: the light
Lingering on the peak; and near the horizon
Apricot-coloured skies, then purple; and the first stars;
An hour of bustle in the hut, and then silence.

Only at two in the morning men stir in the bunks,
Look out of the windows, put on their boots,
Exchange a word with the guardian, curse the cold,
And move with a force beyond their own to the high peaks.

Be still for once. Do not sing,
Let the blood beat its symphony unanswered;
Remain here by the lake for a whole day
With the sky clear and the rocks asking to be climbed.

There is music in movement, in the song, the dance,
The swing of the accordion in the crowded hut,
The swing of the axe in the icefall; but be still.
Listen. There is another voice that speaks.

from ORION MARCHES

PART 6

Controversies, Tactics, Histories, Distractions

This final section of the book in essence is a summary of all that has gone before. Here the climbers talk about the significance or validity of their sport, quarrel amongst themselves, mock each other's and their own foibles, inflate importance or discuss appetite. You will probably find—in articles such as Mike Thompson's *The Aesthetics of Risk* or Michael Roberts' *The Poetry and Humour of Mountaineering*—some of the most considered writing in the book. You should also seek out, in Robert Reid's *No Wonder Mallory Didn't Make It*, a joyful collection of what are undoubtedly the worst jokes ever foisted upon an unsuspecting public.

The Aesthetics of Risk

MIKE THOMPSON

The real physical risks in Himalayan mountaineering – the avalanches, the frostbite, the verticality, the cerebral and pulmonary oedema, even the leeches and the Nepalese food — would probably be all too apparent to non-mountaineers even in the absence of the books and slide lectures which, with their relentless and emphatic rehearsal of these horrors, are the favoured means by which those climbers who have survived recoup the financial losses incurred in their latest exploit and accumulate something towards the expenses of the next.

But sometimes an expedition will entail, as well as these physical risks, financial risks that in their own way are every bit as great. When Barclays Bank agreed to back the 1975 British Everest Expedition there had already been six attempts by powerful teams, including one led by Chris Bonington who was also to lead our 1975 attempt, all of which had failed by a considerable margin to climb the South-West Face: the formidable 'last great problem' on Everest. Obviously, Barclays were ill-equipped to assess our chances of success but there were plenty of experienced mountaineers, and many a self-appointed pundit, only too willing to bend their corporate ear. Most were strongly pessimistic but prudently elected not to pronounce too specifically on the likely outcome. But our journalist, Chris Brasher, actually went so far as to quote the odds as fifty to one against.

The full enormity of Barclays' financial risk beomes apparent when you see the same institution that is so reluctant to lend a customer just a few hundred pounds against the ample security of his freehold house, calmly handing out £150,000, completely unsecured, for a madcap scheme that they know has only a fifty to one chance of succeeding. Of course, Barclays will point out that this is not what they were doing and that the money, in fact, came entirely from that part of their budget allocated to advertising and public relations. But the fact that they were bombarded with letters from incensed customers suggests that the general public has difficulty in visualising the Big Five banks as benign grannies with the cash they have earmarked for various purposes distributed between different tins and vases on their mantelshelves. Rather, they employ a simple input-output model. They see their money going into the bank and they see that same money being dished out to Chris Bonington, his friends and a whole lot of opportunistic Sherpas on the other side of the world.

In the event the prophets were confounded, the South-West Face was climbed and Barclays' great gamble paid off in the sense that they have now got back much more than the £150,000 that they laid out. I hasten to add that these profits have not disappeared into their coffers but have all been carefully placed in a little tin on Grannie Barclay's mantelshelf and are to be devoted to the encouragement of youthful adventure.

There can be no doubt that Everest climbing involves massive physical and financial risks. The reason why Everest climbing, unlike say air travel, has not got safer with the passage of time is to be found in its uselessness. Once air travel became useful there were powerful economic incentives to increasing the likelihood of a passenger being delivered live to his destination. Technology, management, the selection and training of personnel, even international law, were all bent towards this paramount aim of increasing the probability of a passenger arriving safely and on time in the place where he wished to be. Mountaineering has been mercifully free of such utilitarian constraints . . . until recently.

The first ascent of Everest (twenty-three years before ours), coinciding as it did with Queen Elizabeth's coronation, was one of the great imagination-capturers of this century. Almost every child in Britain saw the film: *The Conquest of Everest* . . . the members of the expedition regrouped into lecture teams to visit every corner of the Kingdom. Plain men with simple tastes became Knights of This and Companions of That, and found themselves sustained on a diet of champagne and smoked salmon. "We knocked the bastard off" entered the Oxford Dictionary of Quotations.

Every man destroys the thing he loves: the leader, Brigadier John Hunt, left the army and, as Sir John (later, Lord) Hunt, headed the Duke of Edinburgh's Award Scheme designed to channel the pure spirit of the great achievement to every schoolboy and schoolgirl in the land. Outdoor Pursuits arrived in education and with it came a whole new profession: Outdoor Pursuits Instructors: hideous Frankensteins, half teacher half mountaineer.

One result of all this was that a small number of children, who left to themselves might never have gone near a mountain, died. Mountaineers are an irresponsible lot, teachers are responsible: the faces of the Frankensteins were contorted with anguish. In vain did they hold Official Inquiries, introduce Codes of Safety, initiate Mountain Leadership Certificates and weigh down their charges' rucksacks with devices that would enable them to extricate themselves from every conceivable eventuality. Some children still died.

In desperation they even asked the mountaineers why this should be so. They replied: "Some children die because mountaineering is dangerous." The message was clear: there is no place for mountaineering in education. It was also unacceptable. If mountaineering was removed from education Outdoor Pursuits Instructors would be left with no children to instruct and Mountain Leadership Certification Boards would have no candidates to certify. The solution was simple and obvious: *mountaineering must be made safe*.

In this way, a programme originally inspired by a great achievement is now poised to bring about a situation in which such an achievement will be impossible. Nearly all the Buddhists have been converted to Hinduism: there are very few of us left. Before we become extinct, and before achievements involving a high level of risk become impossible, let me enter a plea for our preservation. I do not ask that we be recognised as yet another oppressed minority and granted the security of a Buddhist sanctuary: to make such a request would be to capitulate and to join the Hindus in their prescription-ridden and risk-free world. Rather, I would urge that we understand the Hindu-Buddhist cycle, and its switching mechanisms before it finally breaks down. If we understand it we can rebuild it and so retain access to the full range of capabilities that it alone can generate.

The aesthetics of high-standard mountaineering are such that a proposed route is only felt to be worthwhile if there is considerable uncertainty as to its outcome. It is for this reason that we wished to climb the South-West Face. Advances in equipment and technique, and the familiarity resulting from its many ascents, have rendered the original route by the South Col of little interest to the leading climbers of today (unless it be an attempt with a very small party or without oxygen). To repeat the original route with a large party or with helicopters to ferry loads into the Western Cwm, as happened recently, is simply to do less with more and to render the outcome almost a foregone conclusion. The traditional mountaineering response to this aesthetically repugnant behaviour is ridicule, and I was interested to discover that the Sherpas who accompanied us on the South-West Face also entered into this aesthetic framework and disparagingly referred to the line by which Hillary and Tensing first reached the summit as 'The Yak Route'.

In sharing this little joke, European climbers and Nepalese Sherpas are both revealed as Buddhists poking a little malicious fun at some European Hindus. For a moment, as we chuckle, the mists of cultural difference clear and we see through to the universal mountain that usually they obscure. These mists are formed by our personal processes of risk management. Risks, it turns out, come in several different forms and the way in which we emphasise one and play down another often clouds our understanding of what is actually going on.

As well as physical risk and financial risk there is a third type, intellectual risk. A person takes an intellectual risk when he sets out to provide an adequate explanation for something where previous attempts have failed, and he takes an intellectual risk when he sets out to question the validity of some explanation which most people believe to be perfectly adequate. In taking an intellectual risk a person stands to lose neither his life, nor his fortune, but his credibility. Since knowledge, like air travel, is usually believed to be useful there are strong disincentives to intellectual risk-taking, and anyone who wishes to take such risks would be well-advised to immerse himself in some relatively useless area of knowledge, such as anthropology.

If Everest-climbing and anthropology are united to the extent that they are both pretty useless, they are set apart by the very different kinds of risk-taking that each encourages. The picture is further confused by the intrusion of financial considerations. Though neither the Everest-climber nor the anthropologist is particularly interested in financial risk both need money to indulge in the sorts of risk-taking that do interest them. When it is not forthcoming the problems they face and the risks they must run are compounded. For example, Don Whillans, in the first batch of mail to arrive at Base Camp after he and Dougal Haston had returned exhausted but triumphant from the summit of Annapurna, received just two letters. One, from the Lord Mayor of Rawtenstall, offered him the freedom of his native borough, the other, from a different room in the same Town Hall, informed him that if he did not pay his rent arrears he would be evicted from his council house.

An example of intellectual risk-taking in the face of financial difficulties every bit as severe as those besetting Whillans is provided by the application, by Professors Hoyle and Wickramasinghe, to the British Science Research Council for funds to investigate their hypothesis that life originated in outer space and arrived, and is still arriving, on earth by meteorite. Although the credentials of these two gentlemen are quite impressive, and although £8,000 is quite a small price to pay for evidence that might upset widely held beliefs about evolution, the application was rejected. By the simple expedient of saving itself £8,000 the Science Research Council stood a good chance of preventing the evidence being gathered, thereby avoiding the risk that the amount of certainty in a wide field of very useful knowledge might be suddenly and dramatically reduced. At the same time it could avoid the risk, inherent in approving the application, of itself losing credibility and becoming, in the eyes of its faithful, the Science Fiction Research Council.

Now intellectual risk-taking is not usually much in evidence on Himalayan expeditions. A climber *knows* he wants to climb Everest and his main concern is to try to do it in as aesthetically pleasing a way as possible. If he were all the time asking himself *why* he wanted to climb Everest he would probably not get far beyond Base Camp, and might well fall down a crevasse if he did. Mallory's famous reply: "Because it's there": was not an answer to the question: "Why climb Everest?": it was a way of stopping people asking it for long enough for him to have a stab at doing it. The charm of the Sherpas' little 'Yak Route' joke is that, by momentarily clearing those mists, it encourages me to take a large and exciting intellectual risk. In anthropological terms I want to try to formulate a general theory of risk. In everyday terms I would like to have a go at answering that perennial question: "Why climb Everest?"

It is perhaps only appropriate that that ugly pyramidical lump which happens to terminate in the highest point on earth should act as a focus not just for physical risk but for financial and intellectual risk as well.

Aesthetics, of course, have always been recognised as an important part of mountaineering. The aesthetic form may change, from the stiff upperlips of the pre-war Everest climbers, through Smythe's 'spirit of the hills',' Winthrop Young's 'craftsmanship' and Whillan's 'job-of-work-to-be-done', to Bonington's shameless exposure of his inner states, but, whether it be the aesthetic of reticence, nature mysticism, esoteric skill, hard graft, or of letting it all hang out, there can be no doubt that more than just economic considerations motivate the mountaineer.

Yet, curiously, such aesthetic niceties are not assumed to extend to the Sherpas who throughout the history of Himalayan mountaineering have carried the Sahibs' loads, and sometimes the Sahibs themselves, up their chosen peaks. True, virtually every expedition book is full of praise for the Sherpas' fortitude, courage, cheerfulness and dependability, but at the same time there is always something rather stereotyped about this handsome expression of credit and inevitably the reader finds the Mingmas, the Dorjes, the Pasangs and the Kanchas merging into a succession of indistinguishable brown, hairless, smiling faces. The same convenient anonymity permits their formidable achievements to be condensed into a statistical table of loads carried and altitudes reached somewhere among the appendices on food, health, logistics, communications and the like, towards the end of the book. Despite the numerous best-selling accounts of expeditions, and despite the real bonds of affection and admiration that link many a Western climber and his Nepalese counterpart, the Sherpa still remains the Cheshire cat of mountaineering literature: little more than a big smile at the opposite end of the arm to the Sahib's pre-dawn mug of tea. The basic assumption is that the Sahib climbs Everest because it is there whilst the Sherpa climbs it for the money.

It is a convenient assumption. If climbing is mostly about aesthetics and if the Sherpas are concerned only with economics, then their contribution to any mountaineering achievement can be equated with that of, say, Barclays Bank. You need money to climb Everest so the argument runs, and you need Sherpas to climb Everest, but both are simply the pre-conditions for Himalayan mountaineering: neither has anything to do with its essence, with what climbing is *really* about.

In other words, our personal risk management leads us to expand the aesthetic scope of our own actions and to contract that of the Sherpas: East is East, we say, and West is West and cultural difference explains all. But, of course, all that this appeal to cultural difference does is set a limit to what we are prepared to explain. Sharing a joke with Sherpas overrides these distortions produced by our risk management and reveals that the frames of our aesthetic scopes are identical. Suddenly, appeals to cultural difference are of no avail: we can no longer call upon Kipling to bail us out when the intellectual risks become too great.

Probably the greatest achievement of anthropology has been to shatter the convenient assumption that in the same sort of situation people will tend to do the same sort of thing, and no sooner does an economist, a psychologist, a sociologist or a political scientist produce some elegant universal model of some aspect of human behaviour than an anthropologist will jump up to spoil his fun by adding the carping codicil: "in our culture." Anthropologists have become so carried away by their spoilsport success that they have almost completely lost sight of the really interesting, and difficult, question which is: "Granted that different people in the same sort of situation may do different things, *why* do they do the different things that they do!" This is the question that a general theory of risk will have to answer. It will have to offer some satisfactory reason why Mallory wanted to climb Everest, and why Mingma wants to climb Everest, and it will have to give some satisfactory reason why all sorts of other people *don't* want to climb Everest.

Risk-taking and risk-avoiding

Since climbing Everest is both a voluntary and a risky business, an explanation of why some people accept risks and others avoid them will go a long way towards answering these questions. The answer to the secondary question, "Why climb (or avoid climbing) Everest, in particular?" is simply that Everest-climbing is very risky and very useless. The risk-taker, anxious to expand the pure aesthetic scope of his preferred style, could not ask for a more perfect objective. There is nothing peculiar, or hard to understand, in his choosing Everest. On the contrary, if Everest did not exist it would probably be necessary for him to invent it. The risk-avoider is positively repelled by these very same properties that the risk-taker finds so attractive. For him, risk of any kind is nasty and a useless *and* voluntary risk is just about the nastiest thing there could be. So the whole explanation hinges upon these two personal styles: risk-taking and risk-avoiding.

For every proverb and catch-phrase there is, it would seem, a contradictory counterpart: 'Look before you leap' versus 'He who hesitates is lost,' 'There's safety in numbers' versus 'Only a dead fish swims with the current.' If we were to collect these contradictory pairs and line them up with one another we could sketch out the world views: the sorts of predictive frameworks: that the risk-taker and the risk-avoider use in choosing, and justifying, the very different courses of action that each follows. The risk-taker's world view corresponds to that of the adventurous Himalayan trader: the Buddhist. The risk-avoider's world view corresponds to that of the cautious stay-at-home cultivator: the Hindu. One grants credibility to one set of proverbs, the other to the opposing set. Once equipped with these very different percep-tions of the world it is hardly surprising to find that, when confronted with uncertainty, they operate very different strategies.

The Buddhist is an optimist: his response to uncertainty is positive. He acts boldly, but not foolhardily, in the hope of reaping rich rewards. The Hindu is a pessimist: his response to uncertainty is negative. He prefers not to act for fear that one thing may lead to another. He subscribes to a 'domino theory' that insists on the connectedness of everything. The Buddhist operates on a 'one-off theory' that allows him to disregard those possible consequences that lie outside his immediate concern. He goes in for risk narrowing: 'Spot on he wins, way out he loses.' The Hindu goes in for risk spreading: 'A trouble shared is a trouble halved.' Why should one be led to adopt the risk narrowing-strategy, the other the risk-spreading strategy?

First of all, it is not because one is a Buddhist and the other is a Hindu. 'Buddhist' and 'Hindu' are simply convenient labels to identify a person's commitment to one or other set of proberbs.

No, the answer to why a person accords credibility to one set of proverbs rather than the other is quite ridiculously simple, and has nothing to do with cultural difference.

The Hindu adopts a risk-sharing strategy, and subscribes to the pessimistic all-embracing world view that justifies such a strategy, because he has someone to share with. The Buddhist adopts a risk-narrowing strategy, and subscribes to the optimistic piecemeal world view that justifies such a strategy, because he has no one to share with.

Social context is enormously persuasive. If there is no-one there to share your risks with you, you cannot go in for risk-sharing and, conversely, only a mug would take a huge personal risk knowing that, if he was successful, he would have to share the rewards among all his cautious risk-shunning fellows. Of course, a risk-avoider may, in certain circumstances, be prepared to take certain risks: those that are not for personal gain but for the survival, the glory or the honour of the group. These altruistic acts can sometimes be so risky as to be suicidal: the team spirit of Horatius and his comrades and the selfless heroism of the Kamikaze pilot typify the risks a risk-avoider may accept: 'Never volunteer for anything, except certain death.' Paradoxically, the risk-acceptor has a strong aversion to these sorts of risks. As a perceptive mountaineer, Tom Patey, once put it: "He should never underestimate the importance of staying alive."

I can foresee two possible objections to this devastatingly simply answer to the question, "Why climb Everest?" The first is that, if my theory states that individualism encourages risk-taking and collectivism encourages risk-avoidance, then, in equating Everest-climbing with individualism, I have got it all wrong because Everest-climbing is a collectivist activity wholly dependent for its success upon superlative team work and upon highly-motivated and skilled individuals selflessly surrendering their personal ambitions (to be *the* man on top of Everest) to the common cause (getting *a* man on the top of Everest). Now, though this heroic picture is often what those who do not go on Everest expeditions choose to see and, indeed, is often what those who do go on them are happy to paint for their armchair public, Everest expeditions are not like that at all.

High-standard mountaineers are extraordinarily individualistic and are only prepared to join together to form an expedition in the first place because they know that, regrettably, they can't got to the top of Everest unaided. The steady progress of an Everest assault can only be maintained by continually changing the lead climbers: those who have done their stint returning to Base Camp for a rest whilst others, still fresh, take their place. Going down to Base Camp takes one or two days, coming back to the sharp end is at the rate of one camp per day. It is most fortunate that the total amount of time it will take to climb the mountain is unknowable; if the members of an expedition knew just how many days lay between the first pair of climbers setting out from Base Camp and the placing of a man on the summit, they could quite easily work out which position in the sequence of lead climbers they should take up in order to end up on the summit. Having myself watched and been involved in these complex dynamics, I am quite certain that, if the optimum position happened to be that of the first pair to set out from Base Camp, all the members of the expedition would hurl themselves simultaneously at the mountain and that, if this was not the optimum position, not a soul would stir from his sleeping bag.

Of course, as the climb proceeds so this degree of uncertainty decreases and towards the end it becomes quite predictable, either that the summit will not be reached, or that it will be reached in a certain number of days. But, by this time, it is usually too late for the individualists to be able to do much about it. If they are resting at Base Camp they have had it: if they are moving up towards the top camp they are in luck. Of course, those in the top camp, sensing victory, could if they were selfish enough refuse to return to Base Camp and this, indeed, is often what happens. On one brilliantly successful expedition Base Camp contained only the Sherpa cook and a Yorkshireman with a wooden leg: all the other members were crammed into the top camp and the last one to drag himself up to this over-populated spot received for his pains, not a steaming mug of tea, but a punch on the nose.

But, usually, events move too quickly and many of the members are stranded without any real hope of getting to the top camp in time. It is at about this moment that they turn their hands to good works—selflessly ferrying essential supplies to the higher camps . . . manning the Base Camp radio (in their sleeping bags) in case the summit party should suddenly come on the air . . . getting a good sweet brew ready for the returning victors. The leader for his part plans increasingly unrealistic second, third, fourth and even fifth summit parties in a pretence of fair shares for all, and the Sherpas, sensing the end of the expedition, lose their upward momentum and divert their energies to the stripping of the camps and the accumulation of staggering loads of personal booty.

The second possible objection is that, if the answer to this perennial question really is so simple, how come somebody hasn't come up with it sooner? The reason is twofold. First, people are usually very strongly committed to their view of how the world is, and this commitment is partly maintained by denying the validity of other ways of seeing the world. Second, though the world view to which they are committed depends upon their social context, they're unaware of this dependence. As far as they are concerned, their world view is not some artificial construction, it is an accurate factual account of how the world is. One might say that the collectivised context is to the Hindu what the earth is to the worm and that the individualised context is to the Buddhist what the air is to the bird. Each is as firmly and unquestioningly committed to his world view as are the worm and the bird to their respective eye-views.

But there is a crucial difference. For worms and birds the environments are natural: for risk-avoiders and risk-takers the environments are social. No matter what actions worms and birds take they will never find themselves living in one another's media but, for the risk-avoider and the risk-taker, there exist the possibilities equivalent to the worm sprouting wings and the bird slithering into the soil. Social contexts can change, either as a result of the actions of the individuals who constitute the totality, or as a result of external natural or social pressures. This means that, whilst wormhood and birdhood are two clearly separate and unrelated states, risk-avoiders can be transformed into risk-takers and risk-takers into risk-avoiders. Yet the path to risk-acceptance is not the reverse of the path to risk avoidance: there is a cyclical relationship between the two states: a Hindu-Buddhist cycle.

Though people are convinced that the view they have of the world is something natural — something self-evident — they have in fact worked very hard to make it appear like that. The Hindu in his collectivised context *learns* to avoid risk-taking. Since he learns from his mistakes, as well as by getting it right, he will have built up a considerable profit-and-loss account by the time he is firmly locked onto the set of proverbs that makes sense of his world. In the same way, the Buddhist will build up his distinctive pattern of investments that commits him firmly to the other set of proverbs. The consequence of all this work – all this aesthetic investment – is that, in order to let go of the Hindu world view and acquire a firm grasp on the Buddhist world view, you have to dismantle one investment structure and build another. This means that, if you went right round the cycle from Hindu to Buddhist to Hindu again, you would, on the first leg, cling to your risk-avoiding strategy long after you had passed the mid-way point between collectivised and individualised contexts and, on the return leg, you would similarly over-persist with your risk-accepting strategy.

Taking someone from Hinduism to Buddhism and back again is rather like that school experiment in physics in which you start off with an iron bar magnetised north-south, demagnetise it, magnetise it south-north, demagnetise it and then magnetise it north-south again. Such cycles can be depicted by a graph called a 'hysteresis' in which the area enclosed by the paths between the two magnetised states provides a measure of the work done in going round the cycle.

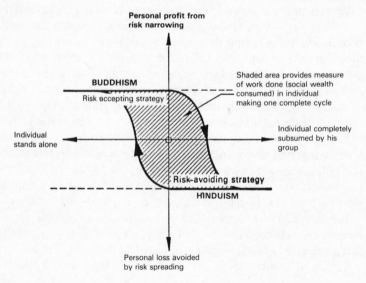

Apart from providing some sort of answer to the question: "Why climb Everest?" what does this little diagram tell us that we don't already know?

It tells us:

1. That changing people's social contexts is a costly business.

2. That, though risk-taking and risk-avoiding strategies are contradictory, little is to be gained and a great deal could well be lost by insisting that one is right and the other is wrong. Rather, each is appropriate in a particular kind of social context.

3. Though each is convinced that his view of the world is the right one, Buddhist and Hindu each stand to gain, as well as lose, from the activities of the other. This means that in all probability there will be, in the distribution of Hindu and Buddhist contexts, some optimum arrangement at which the gains minus the losses for the totality reaches a maximum.

4. Since a modern industrial society inevitably generates both sorts of social context, and since the social policies that such societies implement inevitably result in the transformation of some individuals' contexts, there exists the possibility of evaluating these policies according to whether they will bring us nearer to, or take us further from, this optimal.

Having put forward these few suggestions, I am assailed by awful premonitions. Could it be that I am about to destroy the thing I love: have I got something *useful* out of Everest climbing?

from SOCIETAL RISK ASSESSMENT *1980*

The Final Game

GLEN RANDALL

The Naked Edge dominates Colorado's Eldorado Canyon. Every pitch is in full view, from the 5.11 finger-crack at the base to the hand-crack splitting the final overhanging prow, 600ft. off the ground. Before 1978, everyone who attempted the Edge considered the challenge quite sufficient to warrant a rope. Then, early on a summer morning, Jim Collins decided to try it solo.

"You know, I never consciously planned to solo the Edge," he said. "I think if I had planned it I would either have backed off the the first pitch or got nervous somewhere and blown it. And all the way up I never really thought about finishing the route. I had planned to finish on Jules Verne. But I got up to the base of the fourth pitch and just started bouldering up it. I got that little finger-lock at the top of the dihedral and by then I was kind of committed. It was pretty scary, actually, but I knew I could do the chimney and stuff. I got to the little ledge at the base of the fifth pitch (the overhanging hand-crack) and that's where I started thinking.

"I'd done the climb five times before, but I'd only done the fifth pitch once before without falling. There were three thoughts in my head as I started the pitch. One was that I was scared and that I didn't really want to do it. Another was that I did want to do it. I was having one of the best days of climbing in my life and I just wanted to climb, to keep going and finish it. And another thought was that I just didn't care. I had had a fight with my ex-girl-friend in the early morning hours the night before. I was thinking that there wasn't much outside of climbing that I cared about then. It wasn't a suicidal thing. I was pretty bummed out, though.

"I started up the hand-crack thinking that I would just go to a really solid-looking fixed pin and clip in to it and wait for a rescue. But every time I got to a pin I always trusted my climbing ability more than just one fixed pin, and so I would keep going. I got to the rest, and then it's only 5.8 or so to the top, so I finished it. There wasn't even that much elation, really."

Collins' solo of the Edge was no isolated incident. A number of climbers have recently soloed routes once considered extreme for a roped party of two. I asked several of these climbers about their fascination with this potentially deadly game, and got some interesting and wide-ranging responses.

Some solo, at times, for the simple joy of moving unfettered. Boulder climber Charlie Fowler recalled the first time he did a lot of soloing.

"I went to Eldorado one day and did the Bulge, the Bastille Crack, Pseudo Sidetrack and T2, about twenty pitches, in about four hours. It just blew my mind. It seemed so easy, in a technical sense, not hassling with hardware."

Duncan Ferguson from Estes Park, said, "Soloing removes all the impedimenta of climbing. Some of my most enjoyable solos have been done with no shoes, even no clothes."

As the difficulty of the solo approaches a climber's sight-leading ability however, challenge increasingly becomes the motivation. Fowler said flatly of Perilous Journey, a totally unprotected face-climb near Boulder with a 40ft. 5.11 approach to a 5.11 + crux, "The risks are unjustifiable unless you approach it as a challenge." Fowler made the second ascent in 1977.

The challenge motivated many of Jim Erickson's solos as well. Like most soloists, he began with easy routes he'd done before.

"At first I wasn't achievement-oriented," he said. "After a while, of course, you become addicted."

After soloing Grond, a 5.10 hand-crack in Llanberis Pass where "if you fell and took one bounce, you'd go all the way down Cenotaph Corner," Erickson began thinking of soloing "something more serious" — something no one had done before.

"In terms of rock-climbing, soloing a new route was the ultimate commitment."

After soloing a few 5.9 new routes, Erickson soloed an "easy" 5.10, Sooperb. Two months later he spotted a hand-crack slicing a roof on a crag near Golden. He named it Cassandra.

"I thought it would be the next ultimate," he said. "It's solid 5.10 by today's standards. I would have gone 200ft. if I'd fallen. It was pretty freaky, but at that time I was convinced my hands would never slip out of a hand-crack.

"Spiritually, Cassandra was the high point of my climbing

career. I felt I didn't need to prove anything more to myself. I also realised that if I kept soloing I wasn't going to live much longer. I felt like that climb was as far as I wanted to go."

Some climbers have had strange experiences pushing close to that edge. Collins asked me once:

"Have you ever got the desire when you were in the middle of a climb, soloing, to just jump? I have. I got this incredible urge when I was in the middle of Hair City (a 5.9 in Eldorado) to just jump. I mean, you're up there defying death, and it's really neat, and I thought, wouldn't that be the ultimate test of what you could survive, to just jump off something? Obviously, the urge was quickly suppressed."

Ferguson related a similar experience during a summer when he was soloing harder and harder things in Eldorado.

"I had just done the West Face of the Bastille (a 5.9+), and I was sitting on the ledge at the top. I realised that, ultimately, the next step would be to fall off something. First I'd soloed routes I'd done, then routes I hadn't done, then new routes. If I could have hopped off without hurting myself, I would have. You're playing so close to the line, and the line is falling off. It's like a kid brother. It's always there. The feeling had nothing to do with wanting to hurt myself, because I've felt that way too. I sat up there and thought, "That's really weird," then I reversed the route and went home. I took a much lighter approach after that to soloing, though I've soloed much harder climbs since then."

Just how dangerous is soloing? Other than the risk of holds breaking, the danger comes from within: panic, misjudgment, lapses in concentration. Ferguson's comments are interesting in light of Erickson's thoughts just before he took a near-fatal fall in 1973 from a new route on the Boulder Flatirons.

"I stopped soloing for six months after I did Cassandra in 1973. This may sound silly, but I didn't want to kill myself before I tried Half Dome free again. After Art Higbee and I didn't get very far, I got depressed and started soloing again."

Later that summer, Erickson tried to solo a short new route on the Fourth Flatiron.

"There was a huge stick with a sharp end sticking up like a marlin spike right where you'd land if you fell. I went through these psychological conundrums with myself. I thought, if you fall, you're going to be impaled on that stick. Then I thought, maybe if you think you're going to fall, you shouldn't climb. Then I thought, well, I came here to climb, let's do it.''

Erickson started up the route—after moving the stick. Forty feet up, his hands slipped from the crack. He crashed on sloping talus and broke both ankles and his left wrist.

''I've always wondered if my subconscious took the opportunity to get me to slow down by making me fall in a place where it wouldn't be fatal. Maybe my psyche realised that I'd gone a little too far along the thin edge.''

Erickson did not give up soloing after his accident. In fact, he has soloed 10 or 15 new routes since then, most of them 5.9. But his attitude has changed. ''It's just a game of Russian Roulette,'' he says.

''It's a question of how many cartridges you want to put in the gun. You can get away with a few spectacular climbs, but if you go up and do ten or twenty of them, you're stacking the odds against yourself. Since I value my life more now, and have more responsibilities, I don't solo as much.''

Erickson is thirty-one now, with a wife and child.

Other soloists consider the game less risky than Erickson. Fowler said, ''I would give up soloing in a minute if I ever had a bad epic.'' And Dave Breashears said of his first ascent of Perilous Journey in 1975:

''There was no point in going up there if I even thought I could fall off. It wouldn't have been worth it if I scared myself. I would have considered it a failure.''

Ironically, Breashears says he learned his approach to soloing from Erickson. ''Erickson thought you should always be able to downclimb anything you soloed up.'' Though Erickson does say he has soloed climbs he couldn't reverse, his mastery of climbing down is well-known. He fell not through an inability to retreat, but through a completely unforeseen slip of his hands. Breashears and Fowler seem to discount that possibility, though Fowler admits, ''I've fallen off lots of climbs (with a rope) that were easier than climbs I've soloed.'' He also says, however, that he climbs best when he is soloing. Collins agrees.

''It was much more terrifying going back and leading the first pitch of the Edge with a rope than it was to solo it. I kept thinking.

'God, I can't believe I soloed this.' You know how when the second you get sloppy and fall off things you would never fall off leading? When you're leading you think a lot more and climb in better style. You concentrate more. I think you get a still higher level of concentration when you're soloing.''

For both Fowler and Collins part of that heightened concentration seems to be a conscious determination to erase all doubt before starting up a climb. Fowler says:

"I think it's foolhardy to solo when there's doubt in my mind. If I start up a route to solo it, it's perfectly clear in my mind that I can do it. I don't think about retreating. The reason people climb with a rope is because they have doubts they can do the climb. If you eliminate the rope you have to eliminate the doubt as well.''

For Collins, "The decision is, do I solo today or not? If I decide to solo I just do it. I don't think about reversing moves. I've always soloed on days when I felt really good and I knew I could do the climb. What I'm trying to develop and haven't done perfectly yet is to sense intuitively when I'm going to have that good day.''

Collins discovered how fallible intuition can be on the day he soloed the direct finish to the North-West Corner of the Bastille, a 5.10+ in Eldorado.

"I had done the route with a rope a few days before. I had heard that the direct finish was really hard, and so I was prepared, when I went up there with a rope, for something desperate. Then it turned out not to be so bad. But when I went up there without a rope, I did the mantel and grabbed this hold when I wasn't in balance. My hand just popped off the hold – my hands just flew off the rock and I basically fell over backwards. I had a split second to think about whether to jump and try to grab the ledge about 10 or 15ft. down. Then my toe levered into the horizontal crack and my other foot scraped down onto a hold and I caught myself. But I nearly fell off. I would have gone to the ground from the top of the Bastille.''

Like Collins, Fowler only solos at certain times:

"Both the DNB (Direct North Buttress of Yosemite's Middle Cathedral, a 1,600ft., 5.10) and the Diamond were real spur-of-the-moment things. Things were right at that moment.''

Fowler had originally planned to climb the Right Side of the Folly on the day he did the DNB.

"I got up at sunrise, and I thought, 'I don't really want to do the Folly. I want to do the DNB.' The idea of doing something like that had occurred to me before, but I hadn't specifically thought of the DNB.

"The hardest part, psychologically, was starting If you can overcome the fear it's much easier to climb without a rope. On the climb I just remember I was continuously climbing and how enjoyable that was. I'd focus just on the climbing. When I got to the top I was sort of spaced out, like I'd gotten away with something. I'd been concentrating so hard."

Fowler was at a party until midnight the night before he soloed the 'Casual Route' on the Diamond. He left the Long's Peak parking lot at 2 a.m. and made the six-mile approach by head-torch.

"When it was just light enough to see I started up the route. I climbed continuously up to the Yellow Wall bivy ledge and hung out there for a while, took some pictures. I had my cagoule tied around my waist and my camera around my neck. I felt like a tourist. "Oh, is this the cables route?"

Fowler describes his feelings at the top of a hard solo like the Diamond as "a mixture of elation, exhaustion and satisfaction."

"It's almost like I'm tripping. It's an altered state of consciousness. I'm not sure if it's good or bad. It's like you face reality again after being completely focused on the climbing. Or maybe the climbing is the reality. When I solo I'm so utterly focused that my mind is in a totally different place when I stop."

Are the rewards of soloing worth the risk? Breashears and Fowler, convinced they aren't actually laying as much on the line as their climbs make people think, say yes. Collins says no.

"I've really got a lot out of soloing. The rewards have been great. But when I think back on the risks I've taken on some of the climbs I've done, like the Edge and the North-West Corner, I think the rewards haven't been worth the risk."

Erickson agrees:

"You have to ask yourself, how will I feel about it in five years? How will my friends and family feel? I think five years after these people do their solos they'll think the same thing I do, 'God, it was really stupid of me to do these things.'"

Ferguson comes at the question from a different perspective:

"Like everything, the more you put into soloing, the more you get out, but difficulty doesn't have much to do with it. If I put my whole being into something, then I get the most out of it. I've done easy solos that were wonderful, and I've done desperate solos and got little out of them. Soloing acts so much like a mirror. It reflects my own attitudes and feelings."

Soloing is indeed a mirror, and Ferguson's final comment may explain much of the diversity in opinion. Even more than roped climbing, soloing reflects a climber's strengths and flaws with pitiless clarity. As Tom Patey once said of soloists:

"If they're not good, they're dead."

from MOUNTAIN 80 *1981*

Bouldering as Art

JOHN GILL*

We have commented that bouldering is an art, that it is born of discipline and feeling. How far can we go with the concept of bouldering as art?

I would not want to add too much of a sophisticated veneer to it. At one time, I quite seriously did consider it an art form similar to ballet or formal, competitive gymnastics. When one sees good bouldering, one sees a graceful display of athletic ability. There is the same sort of precision that is apparent in good dance, the same sort of balance, coordination, and strength. I've found bouldering to be therapeutic. It might be interpreted as a kinesthetic art form. An observer can, even with very little knowledge of climbing, appreciate the artistry in bouldering, just as a person unacquainted with gymnastics is able to appreciate artistic composition and grace in a good exhibition.

Is is possible to correspond B 2 with a 5th-class rating?

A B 1 might be 5.11, somewhere in there. B 2 is quite a bit harder. And B 3, my feeling is now, should be a completely objective climbing rating. B 3 is something that is done once, is tried

*Responding to questions from Pat Ament

frequently, but is not repeated. If it is repeated, then it drops automatically either to B 2 or even B 1. B 1 and B 2 are really the two more or less subjective standards for bouldering, as far as I'm concerned. B 1 is pretty damned hard, and B 2 is really damned hard! And B 3 is an objective standard. I don't think of B 3 as being the supreme technical limit. Once you reach these very esoteric bouldering levels, it becomes increasingly a matter of body-size and reach. It is a little absurd to try to keep breaking difficulty down into finer and finer subdivisions. I've had real difficulty with routes that other climbers have done without much effort. So I feel as though, once you get up to those high levels of difficulty, there should be perhaps two, at the most three, grades. Beyond that, there should be a very objective classification which puts climbs in a particular realm of their own without any sort of judgment being required on the part of the climber. You're quite familiar with gymnastics, you know, A-B-C difficulty levels. As far as I know, they haven't enlarged on that.

What advice would you give to climbers as to how to progress?

It depends upon basic bodily structure and physiology as to how one can progress. You have to keep in mind what your end goals are. With regard to bouldering, the person is going to have to develop strength. I firmly believe that most people who wish to pursue bouldering can really benefit from formal gymnastics: rope climbing, still rings, parallel bars, some high bar, free exercise . . . I think that these are excellent activities with regard to developing acrobatic dexterity, poise, gracefulness, and balance, various attributes which a good boulderer should possess. I personally have never used weights for training except to do a one-arm pull-up with 20 to 30 pounds of weight in the other hand. I've avoided doing well-regimented exercises, the classical curls and military presses. I'm not going to emphatically say that a person would not progress quite nicely using these means. But it depends upon the individual very much.

What's worked best for me has been a combination of actual bouldering and certain forms of gymnastics. The weakest link between the climber and the rock is the fingers. Most climbing does require finger strength. However, you know from your own experience that there are a lot of crack climbs that do not directly involve finger strength but rather certain cross-pressure strengths utilising various upper torso muscles. Unfortunately, finger strength is probably the most difficult to develop and keep. It is the first thing to go with increased age. I'm thirty-nine now, and my finger strength has not diminished severely over the last ten or fifteen years, but I can't be too optimistic about the future. There are exercises that I have used to develop my fingers—fingertip chins on doorjambs and, ultimately, one-arm chins on the first joint of the fingers. This, I want to point out, tends to develop power more than stamina. In most instances, a boulderer is concerned with a sudden burst of power, as opposed to long-term stamina, but not always. The sort of strength one develops when working on the still rings seems to carry over to climbing. It gives you a certain amount of poise when under stress, on overhangs for example. For a number of years, the sort of gymnastics that I did was geared to routines done in actual competition on the various pieces of apparatus. I was able to do butterfly mounts on the rings moderately easily and an iron cross. I did an inverted cross on occasion. Over the past few years, I've gotten away from gymnastics and at present don't do any. I haven't climbed the rope in about ten years. I do traverses across long doorjambs when they are available. I'm getting a little out of shape on front levers, haven't done one recently. I used to do quite a bit of handbalancing but don't do any now. I haven't done a hand stand in perhaps three years. Upon occasion I will do—or at least attempt to do—a one-arm mantelshelf on a low rock wall. Just one or two of these per session, I have found, keeps me in fairly good shape as far as that sort of pressing is concerned. I've never been terribly good at mantels, one of the reasons being that my legs are too long.

How did you learn the one-finger, one-arm pull-up?

I actually learned it as the result of hearing a rumour. I have no idea whether or not the rumour is true. But, during the year that I spent at the University of Chicago, I went climbing several times with a German mathematician, Helmut Rohrl, a very competent mathematician and quite a good climber. Those were the days, of course, when Hermann Buhl's reputation was so phenomenal. Helmut had known Buhl—at least in tangential manner—and told me in one of our conversations that Buhl was able to do a one-finger pull-up. That was the first time I had heard of a climber – or anybody else – doing it. I had been working on one-arm pull-ups. One does those occasionally when training for rope climbing competition. It is an attribute that you develop after awhile from climbing the rope. But, as for doing a one-finger, I hadn't really thought much about that. However I found it to be a very provocative idea. It wasn't that difficult to learn. I think once a person knows how to do a good solid one-arm pull-up, doing it on one finger (and, of course, I ordinarily use the middle finger of my right hand) is not all that hard. I don't do it on a ledge. People have told me that they understand I can do a one-finger pull-up on any finger just on a slim ledge. That is completely false. I was able to do it over a horizontal bar with the middle finger of my right hand, also with the index finger, and I've done it with the middle finger of my left hand. But I never tried pushing it beyond those limits. As to whether I could have gone farther and accomplished more, I don't know. It gets pretty silly after awhile, really. The carry-over to climbing is not that great. It's just a little circus gimmick, something to impress other climbers or gymnasts with.

from MASTER OF ROCK *1977*

Love in the Mountains

KARL LUKAN

"Then he knelt down in front of her and buried his face in her lap. He looked up at her angelic face, gazed deep into her glowing eyes and said:

'My poor little Magda, at last your torment is over; never again will you slip away from me, I want to hold on to you forever!''

Her silky soft hands brushed his skin, and she replied without fear, a heartfelt

'Yes.' . . . . ''

These are the final words of *Hochtor*, a climbing novel which appeared about four decades ago. Alone, the hero has climbed the North Face of the Hochtor and has won the hand of his loved one.

Love in the mountains?

Inscribed on an armchair in a small room in the Weichtalhaus at the foot of the Rax is the following message:

"Our guests are politely requested not to rent rooms by the hour." In the Hubertushaus on the Hohe Wand, visitors are reminded that an extra amount will be charged for any:

". . . immoral stains on the sheets."

Love in the mountains?

Once upon a time my friend Sepp wanted to climb an exceptionally difficult route on the Rax. However, his partner was too weak, and Sepp and his friend found themselves 'pinned' (in the most literal sense of the word) to the wall with night approaching. So we all climbed up to fetch Sepp, which involved a most exciting abseil manoeuvre. We hauled Sepp and his partner, dangling free, off the wall. In the middle of the dozen or so men who were pulling in the rope sat the young lady whom Sepp loved. It takes a long time for a group of rescuers to winch a climber up an overhanging wall with nothing but bare hands and elbow grease. The rope cut into his chest; that hurt, and meant that he could not breath. When we dragged him over the last overhang, Sepp was exhausted. We untied him from the rope and he staggered over to his girlfriend and:

". . . buried his face in her lap."

just like the hero in the novel, *Hochtor*. Sepp had never read this novel; all he wanted was his woman.

Love in the mountains. . . .

The summer of 1968 was not a good summer. Lots of rain, lots of fresh snow, little opportunity for big routes. A few months later there was an outbreak of marriage fever among the young Viennese climbers. The tough young lads who had always got along without female company congratulated the fathers-to-be, re-asserting once more that the summer of 1968 had not been a very good one for climbing.

Love in the mountains!

"We got to know each other in the mountains!" You often hear it from married couples. And every Sunday many of them are still to be seen, with or without offspring, out on the hills. . . . "My best climbing partner is my wife!". . . . "All my best climbing trips have been with my husband!"

Love in the mountains—a theme with many variations. Yet in climbing literature (in thousands of books and many thousands of articles) it hardly gets a mention.

In 1909, in the preface to his *A History of Morals*, Eduard Fuchs wrote:

> The present moral code and the present opinions and regulations concerning moral conduct which control or condone man's sexual behaviour within a certain period of time are the most significant and characteristic manifestations of this era of development. For man's sexual behaviour is indicative not only of certain important principles, but also of the law of life itself.

A young, active climber who is out every weekend and, in addition, for the whole of his holidays spends about one third of his life in the mountains. He loves the mountain.

But: does he love only the mountain?

In his youth Edward Whymper loved only mountains. Frank Smythe, in his biography of the Matterhorn conqueror, had this to say:

> Throughout his life, Whymper formed no deep and lasting relationships. Women did not speak to him and could exercise no influence over a man who dealt only in cool calculation and logical conclusions. He had no time for the weaknesses of the fairer sex.

At the age of sixty-five he did in fact marry a twenty-year-old girl and became the father of a baby girl, but the marriage broke up after only four years. Whymper's life showed that to love only the mountains does not make for a full and happy life. Another great mountaineer, Henry Hoek (1878-1951) confessed with some remorse at the end of his life:

"If only I had not wandered so much, I would have loved more!" Dr. Karl Prusik, however, in a climbing guidebook which appeared in 1929, voiced the opinion that an active climber should live a life of celibacy.

Now for the 'expert opinion' of two present-day doctors: Doctor Number One (a fine figure of a man!): "Sex weakens the constitution!" Doctor Number Two (who strangely enough wears horn-rimmed spectacles): "Sex stimulates one's constitution and leads to higher levels of performance!"

Who is correct?

The hut custodians probably know far more about it, but they merely smile and remain discreetly silent. Or else they say, almost apologetically: "Well, that's as much a part of climbing as anything else!" There are huts with separate rooms for male and female visitors but in the majority of huts one finds boys and girls sleeping together. Generally very close together. Furthermore, it is dark.

I was seventeen years old and was lying next to a girl. She belonged to the same climbing school as me. I was thinking about the routes I would do the next day, but it also crossed my mind that I ought not to lie like a block of wood next to a young lady. I was still very new to climbing but this much I had learned from the 'old men's' conversations: lager beds were made for kissing on. The girl next to me was also still awake. I kissed her on the cheek. "At last!" said the girl. And with that we drifted peacefully off to sleep.

But: it is not only cheeks that get kissed on lager beds! "All sorts of things were going on on our bed last night!" The neighbours complain bitterly in the morning. "Indelicate" is the word which many older people use to describe these love-scenes in a room full of twenty or thirty sleeping people. And indeed they are. But young people are an impulsive lot; the lad is lying there, the girl there—it is dark, everyone is asleep. At least they think that everyone is asleep. . . . The recently-deceased climber and raconteur, Kurt Maix, once recounted the following conversation which he overheard on a *Maträtzenlager* (lager-bed):

A whispered voice, male: "What's your name?"

A whispered voice, female: "Steffi!"

A whispered voice, male: "I'm Michl!"

There follows a brief, but restless, quiet.

A whispered voice, male: "Stefferl! How about it?" (translation into Queen's English: Would you care to. . . .)

A whispered voice, female: "Yes . . . Please!"

Lying close to each other, in the dark, far away from the worries of everyday life—these and many other things lead to 'Love on the Lager-bed.'

A few years ago we held a discussion on this subject in our climbing club.

One opinion: "The majority of people who conduct themselves thus in huts are quite simply barbarians. That is not intended to be an outright condemnation, but those who live in the country, the 'natural men', do have less moral scruples."

A contradictory opinion: "Young people living in towns behave like that as well. . . ."

Yet another opinion: "All youngsters today are the same—no moral scruples!"

An elderly man offers his view: "Rubbish! Exactly the same thing went on when I was young!"

Probably the hut custodians are right when they say: "Well, it's as much a part of climbing as anything else!"

In the last century, the white-coated doctor was the great 'ladies'-man', along with the army officer in his dress-uniform, and the twentieth century, too, has its 'lovers by profession'—the airline pilots, the racing drivers, the film star, the television personality, the ski instructor. . . .

The ski instructor: he is sunbronzed and immaculately dressed. He is a ski-god, revered and loved, living his life between piste and bed. . . .

"But we are not like that!" said Wendel, a friend of mine who is a ski instructor at an Austrian winter resort. "We are not like that—really."

During the skiing season the instructor wants to earn money. Therefore he has to teach people how to ski. His classes do not consist entirely of twenty-year-old girls with a lot of money or a roving eye; the fat garage owner from Düsseldorf also wants to learn how to ski. Thus the instructor has to see to him as well. Were he to spend all his time flirting with the twenty-year-old girls the gentleman from Düsseldorf would soon get disgruntled and this would lead to a massive complaint being lodged with the town's tourist authorities. Wendel: "Like any other teacher, the ski instructor has his timetable to stick to. Age and sex are of secondary importance; the main thing is that the pupils learn the ins and outs, of skiing, I mean. . . . What about après-ski?

Wendel again: "There are about fifty instructors here, of whom two or three younger ones frequent the bars. The rest go home to their wives in the evenings, for most of us are married. The pub prices here are so steep that if we were to hang around the bars and buy the girls' drinks every night we'd hardly have enough left to buy a new ski jumper!" The reason why ski-instructors get labelled as the 'Casanovas of the piste' has to do with our patter (part of the job!). The clients are on holiday, the sun is shining, the snow is gleaming white—all this makes them feel adventurous and the instructor obviously plays along with his: "Baby, you look good enough to eat today. . . .!" But that's just our patter. Understand me?

'Patter' or not, the modern ski instructor is still seen as a sex symbol, a ladies' man.

The climber; his rope slung loosely about him, has always enjoyed the reputation of being a rather rugged sort of chap and in the days when Luis Trenker was making his great climbing films the climber almost reached the status of 'ladies'-man'. Even women for whom climbing one flight of stairs involved a considerable effort fell madly in love with Trenker's sunburnt 'North Face face' and soon the Alps were full of aspirant Trenkers, each with a broad-brimmed hat and a pipe set between his teeth. No matter what great climbing feats they had performed, no other climber (no, not even Whymper, or Emilio Comici, or Anderl Heckmair, or Dietrich Hasse, or, or . . .) epitomised the image of the manly climber more than Luis Trenker. Perhaps in years to come when we speak of the cultural history of alpine climbing we will have to speak, too, of 'Trenkerism'.'

But the years went by, and Trenker stopped making his films. However, prodigious things continued to be done in the mountains . . . 1966 . . . a thirty-one days' struggle on the Eiger Direct in winter; by 1970 this had reached forty-two days. Press photographs of this expedition-scale venture generally showed the climbers in the company of beautiful women. Toni Hiebeler wrote this report:

> Parisienne, Madame F. R., twenty-five, staying in Room 98, chalk-white despite the previous days of sunny weather, has by all accounts a 'hard life' in Scheidegg: she has made it her business to see to the spiritual welfare of the climbers.

For the majority of climbers who read this piece, the phrase 'spiritual welfare' provoked only knowing smiles: "spiritual welfare' – I've never heard it called *that* before!" But it really was 'spiritual welfare' and whether or not the Parisienne Mme. F. R. went to bed with any of the Eiger-men is beside the point. During the climb one of the best alpinists of our time, the thirty-one-year-old American John Harlin, fell to his death. Any one of the thirteen climbers could have died on the Eigerwand — and each of them knew it. Men who live dangerously either need a woman passionately, or not at all. Either – or.

In the script of the erotic film *Roma Amor* the French archaeologist Jean Marcadi talks of: "the secret chemistry of human love," and in the more subtle literary works of the past one often comes across the phrase: "he knew her as a woman." And the woman referred to 'had' (in the real sense of the word) her child. Men who love adventure are children (or at least in their second childhood) too. According to Freud, what every man looks for in a woman is his mother. Goethe surely put it better—he called it "Eternal feminism." But a friend of mine, a top climber called L. was even more lucid: "When I'm on a hard route, I want a bird at the bottom!"

I once observed L. when he was with his 'bird'. He hardly looked at her. Occasionally, when he thought he wasn't being watched, he nodded to her. He talked about bolts and overhangs with the other experts. And was glad to have his woman sitting next to him. About four in the morning he crawled out of his sleeping bag and looked around for his boots, his rope and his gear. . . . "When will you be back?" asked his girlfriend. "Oh . . . about three o'clock. The route should be well pegged-up!" "I'll have a meal ready for you then!" "You don't have to do that. Just make sure you're there!" Then a kiss, just a brief little kiss. But L. knew that here was a girl he wanted to come back to.

Penelope waited years for Odysseus to return from his adventures. The wives of today's astronauts have to wait only six, seven, eight days for their high-flying husbands to get back. The climbing wife also has to wait. The modern wife, however, does not like waiting. She becomes liberated.

"Der Gipfel fiel im Sturm,
    Wir brauchen keine Buam!"*
wrote one all-women party in the summit book on the Hochschwab. Just how liberated women climbers can be is shown by Felicitas von Reznicek's book, *From Crinoline to the Six Grade*, published a few years ago. It talks about 100 women who are better climbers than 100,000 men, and also established that chivalry in the mountains is finally dead . . . or rather, not quite dead, for the book ends with this message to women: "Treat your man with coutesy!" In this book about women climbers there is, however, no mention of 'guiding fees'. To many climbers, doing a route with a girl was, and indeed still is, just a diversionary tactic to lure her into bed. Once upon a time climbers used to complain—man to man—that only ugly women went climbing. One hears the same complaint these days, but amongst the top 'climberesses' there are some really lovely girls, sex symbols in patched climbing trousers with a helmet sitting on top of their long hair.

*Roughly translated: "The summit fell in the wind and rain, what need have we for silly men?"

Above all, the general 'sex boom' has hit climbing . . . girls in tight jeans which accentuate every curve of thigh and bottom and pullovers designed with frontal elevation in mind. This emphasis on a woman's exterior shape has also changed her 'inner shape'. The 'climbing-wife' who wants only to 'serve her husband' is no more. Even in the mountains, the woman wants to remain a woman.
   "Der Gipfel fiel im Sturm,
      Wir brauchen keine Buam!''
Beneath this entry is another, written in a strong male hand:
   "Ihr lieben Frauenzimmer.
      An Buam, den brauchts ihr immer!''*

The 'grope rope' (every stance an arbour of love) has been around for years. Generally, however, one only came across them on the easier routes. A relatively modern thing is that one now comes across the 'mixed rope' of bloke and bird, man and wife, far more often than before on the harder routes. The woman has become so liberated that she no longer has to point this out. She is no longer "tied on by her boyfriend and dragged up the route" as one old climbing song put it. She ties herself on and accompanies her fella through thick and thin.

If two men climb together they are called partners, comrades, friends. Not so a man and a woman (even if they are not lovers)—then there is always more to it. Each of them is attracted to the other: Adam and Eve on high hills. This increases the possibility of romantic involvement, for Adam and Eve's heartbeats are most definitely quickened when there is a nice view, and difficulty and danger awake in them the desire to be nice to each other. . . .
   I was once doing an easy route with a lady (the mother of two children) when the party ahead started a veritable avalanche of rocks. We had no protection from them. Fist-sized rocks rained down to left and right as the pair of us snuggled up to each other and . . . kissed each other! I don't know why, but we kissed each other! I usually meet this lady about once a year, and we always talk about that "first and only kiss." I know it sounds like a load of rubbish – but it's true. As is the following story:
   We were out climbing one Sunday with a young married couple.

*Translate this for yourselves. It's quite rude.

Afterwards we wanted to invite them both for a cup of coffee. They declined: "It was such a good route today that we just want to get straight off home. . . ." said the young girl. "You know what it's like after a good route!" We knew. . . .

from ALPINISMUS *1970*

FRCCJ 1944

The Blue Crampon Brigade

ANNE SAUVY-WILKINSON

Once, at the age of about twenty, I found myself one day in a cable car with a young man of imposing mien. Waving a lordly arm dismissively over the surrounding countryside, he gave me to understand that of course it was lovely, but not a patch on the mountains in summer. I agreed wholeheartedly, delighted to find a kindred spirit. At that time I already had four Alpine seasons to my credit (although only a very limited number of north faces); but even though most of my friends were excellent climbers, I was conscious of my own limitations and quite ready to find virtue in a new acquaintance.

And this new acquaintance seemed an epitome of all the virtues. His words were simple but sincere, his tone warm, and his account of the passions inspired in him in his Alpine career touched a chord in me. I was of course perfectly aware that he was setting his experience as a snare to catch a young woman hanging on his every word. He was in fact shooting a line; I was not to know how very fragile the line was. . . .

On the surface he was splendid. He spoke fluently, eloquently: the warmth and companionship of the climbing team, the slender ridges, the delicate flowers of the rhododendrons greeting the climbers as they paced back to the valley, at peace after their struggles against the storm. . . . But still at the back of my mind was a niggle: nothing he had said enabled me to place him accurately or in any precise context. It was ignoble, of course: here was a poet of the Alps, and yet my prosaic mind was insisting on asking questions; it wanted some geography, even a statistic or two. I could not resist a few unkindly queries. Where had he done his climbing? In the Mont Blanc massif! Now, I'd spent some time there myself, and I'd be able to recognise his routes. What exactly *had* he done?

The young man fell headlong into his own trap, lured to his doom by my breathless interest in his exploits. Descending from the realms of poetry to those of fact, he confided that he'd done a lot of climbing on the Rocher des Gaillands, and that he'd done a particularly fine route—I wouldn't have heard of it, it was the sort of thing only a specialist would venture upon—the main summit of the Dômes de Miage.

I fear that I failed that day in the virtue of charity, but it was irresistible.

"Yes, of course I knew the Miages, in fact I'd had an excellent view of them (a couple of years back) from the top of the North Face of the Bionnassay. Well, they did look a little flattened from up there, but of course you could see that they were a mountain of sorts. A good climb, incidentally, the North Face of the Bionnassay—a shame it wasn't a bit longer. Even if you went on up the ridge to the Dôme, you could still be back in Chamonix for lunch. We hadn't gone on as far as Mont Blanc that day—primarily because I'd already done it, but also because we were intending to come back the next day to do the traverse. Quite a good traverse, too—the Aiguille du Gouter to the Montenvers, with a side-step to take in the top of the Tacul. Not bad at all—he would enjoy it one day, being such an expert. Not a really great route of course—but how were you to define a really great route? Now when I'd done the Aiguille Verte by the Couturier Couloir (nothing much really, just the third female ascent) well . . .

Seldom have I seen a young man so discomfited: just one of the perks that fall to the woman climber.

My intention here, however, is to speak not of the perks of female climbing but of its essence.

The title at the head of this article seemed particularly opposite. If a female cook can be described as a *cordon bleu* and if an intellectual female can be termed a *blue stocking*, why not *blue crampon* for a female climber? More particularly for a somewhat militant female climber. And in the context, the phrase has the virtue of tempering by a touch of fancy the brutally prosaic *Front for the Liberation of the Female Climber*. FLFC itself is a dual-purpose title, being simultaneously neat, mysterious and efficacious. Efficacious particularly in that a few discreet soundings among my friends and relatives have shown that I shall lose the sympathy of all male readers because of the militancy of my title, and of all my female readers because the content of the article will turn out to be so mildly un-militant. Secure therefore in the knowledge that I have alienated virtually all my readership, I can allow myself to be rude both to men and to women. My only dilemma is with which to start — a modern dilemma, this, since once upon a time, when men were universally recognised as the stronger sex and women in their weakness were given certain advantages, the latter could have expected to be put first. But now that fashion seemingly dictates that this order be reversed, I shall round first of all on the men; on two of them in particular, who have apparently failed to grasp the subtleties of the problem of female climbing.

The first of them is a certain Samivel, who describes the woman climber in his *L'Amateur d'Abîmes*: "Oh yes, we have all come across them, unhappy ladies of the heights, like crows haunting huts and rock faces, their faces ecstatic in the wind, their arms hugging the rock like a lover." This one I have no compunction in leaving to the tender mercies of my sisters-in-arms.

The second is Alain de Chatellus, in those published work we find a number of interesting remarks:

> In that strange world of stern pleasures, of shadows, of passing gleams of light, are a few women. How did they stray so far out of their true and predestined path? Nothing in the feminine psyche seems to predispose a woman for the great routes. A man whose face is beaten and weathered by fatigue retains a masculine beauty, compounded of strength and virility. Not so a woman, her face drawn and prematurely aged by the struggle . . .

I must admit that with a healthy disregard for my own womanly beauty, I grind my teeth at statements such as these. I wonder if he had ever really studied those "faces beaten and weathered by fatigue?" Do you know that famous photo of Gaston Rebuffat in *Starlight and Storm*: "After the second bivouac?" Not, as far as one can discern, the portrait of a young lady . . .

For my part, I did a lot of climbing at one time with a friend who was a guide and who was once described by a sensation-seeking journalist short of copy as being "remarkably handsome." Now, if we were ever in danger or difficulty, I had no need to consult the weather conditions — I had only to look at Claude, and when he started looking like my Uncle Edouard, I knew that things were going badly. Actually I was very fond of my Uncle Edouard, and had the circumstances been different, would have been delighted to note so pleasing a family resemblance. But Uncle Edouard was forty years older than Claude and looked it . . .

I should welcome the opportunity of examining photos of M. de Chatellus at moments of struggle—but recognise that photos are rarely taken at such moments, however virile and strong the climber. . . .

But these are incidentals. What is more interesting is the question that M. de Chatellus poses in my first citation, and the challenge that he subsequently issues: "This is an enigma we cannot resolve; let us hope that one of the women climbers will have sufficient immodesty to offer an explanation." I pass over the point that it ill becomes someone who has spent some 200 pages searching for the well-springs of masculine climbing to accuse others of immodesty; I will simply try, immodestly, to give some answers:

The motives which inspire a girl to climb are of course as various as those which inspire a boy: friends, books, skiing, climbing courses etc. In my case it was the dazzling sight, at Christmas in my thirteenth year, of the Matterhorn. For me that was enough, and from then on the mountains were to be irrevocably and in some form or another an integral part of my existence. Even as early as that, I realised that I would one day be a climber, though the prospect then seemed as remote as that of being an astronaut. But as far as my sex goes, I was offered no choice, and however preferable it would have been (in this domain at least) to be a large and hairy muscle-man, I had to make do with what I had.

There is no point in looking for some other, more esoteric motive. Mallory said that mountains were to be climbed, "because they are there"; a woman who wishes to climb automatically becomes a woman climber. There is no need to find this surprising, or to go in for Freudian explanations, or to make the matter an excuse for dubious humour. Samivel and Alain de Chatellus might have remembered that had the fates so decided, they too would have been born women and would then have become women climbers . . .

The whole problem therefore seems to me badly formulated. Quite simply, climbing is something done by climbers of different sorts. It makes just as much, or as little, sense to talk of young as opposed to old climbing, capitalist as against communist climbing, and so on. I suggest that it is up to the woman climber to proceed in such a way that it will no longer seem necessary to apply to her any distinction other than the natural ones of strength of arm and of character (remembering that these can differ from causes other than sex, such as age) — rather than brandishing the fact that they are women as some sort of battle slogan.

I would rather turn to something else, something between masculine and feminine excesses, namely something I would call marital climbing. This is a melting-pot for all sorts of experience, strange, remarkable, picturesque — and frankly I have always felt that the cleric who devised the formula 'for better, for worse' must have had some Alpine experience behind him.

The worse is the epitome of all those masculine tendencies I described above, exacerbated by that extra irritability typical of high altitudes. As dawn in russet mantle clad creeps over the Alps, only too clearly there come floating up, sharp and distinct, the words of husband to wife toiling in his wake:

> Get a move on, for God's sake! Surely you could make a bit of an effort. . . . If you can't keep up you shouldn't have come. . . . No, I can't slow down. I get tired if I slow down. . . . No, we can't rest before the top, at the speed we're going we'll be bloody lucky to make the summit at all. . . . Your crampon strap's loose? God, I'd have thought you'd have learnt how to put your crampons on by now! What do you mean, I didn't leave you enough time to do it properly? *I* had enough time, didn't I? And now I suppose you'd like me to put it on for you? Wouldn't like a butler too, I suppose? All right, so it's come off, so you can carry the bloody thing, can't you? Next time perhaps you'll remember to put it on properly in the first place! What do you mean, you keep on slipping? Watch what you're doing then, otherwise I'll unrope and leave you to get on with it! Oh well, that's it then, isn't it? You don't like climbing with me? That's the bloody limit, that is. . . !

Any wife who recognises her husband in this monologue is at liberty to join the Women's Movement, or the FLFC, with my most heart-felt good wishes.

But let us be clear that the better, too, thankfully, exists. The husband who realises his wife's capabilities, who, if necessary, weighs up her sack at a halt and says: "This probably *is* a bit heavy for you" and takes over her water-bottle and crampons. The sort of gratitude felt in such circumstances has repercussions far beyond the route itself. A smile. "OK?" "Yes, OK." "Shall we go, then?" "Yes, let's go!" The sort of harmony created by meeting difficulties together, by making sacrifices one for the other, by achieving success on a route, can make an unequalled bond for any couple.

This was something I thought about a lot one day, or more precisely one night, when John and I were walking at about 2 a.m. over the Oberaletsch Glacier. The night was velvet dark, we were walking unroped, and in the gleam of our head-torches ice-crystals glittered and glimmered like stars.

John had thought up a little game to pass the time. It consisted in standing every so often in a hole full of melt-water in order to have a pretext for a string of exclamations in his native tongue. He was displaying an admirable virtuosity, creating striking conjunctions between glaciology, the Anglican liturgy and human reproductory systems, with occasional reference to unnatural vice. I was amused, but not emulating, since the required pretext seemed to me detrimental to comfort, and that is something I consider important.

I was walking along sedately, therefore, placing my own feet with some care and thinking about marital climbing. I told myself that for a couple it is a most extraordinary experience. Each of us had made the same series of moves dozens of times, each of us had done the same sort of glacier walk, and yet even so we still felt, both of us, that sense of delightful adventure. Can there be many couples to whose lot it falls to walk before dawn over the ice, with a glittering sky and an occasional shooting star overhead? To walk absolutely alone, through a silent, steel-cold night? To watch together the birth of a new and perfect day, and together, to smile as by unspoken agreement they turn off their head-torches?

That day turned out to be too late in the season for our intended route; the way was barred by a maze of crevasses and seracs. But our failure was irrelevant. We crossed a col and came down into a valley we did not know. All day we walked in perfect peace and harmony, alone in the mountains, and met nothing more obtrusive than a butterfly. That day forms one of my most cherished memories.

The reason why I have chosen to speak of marital climbing is because it seems to me to reconcile what so many insist on calling masculine climbing and feminine climbing. True the first of these phrases seems unfamiliar; the second is the one we hear so much of, and that seems to me the responsibility primarily of the women themselves. Let me say outright that I find the militant feminists profoundly exasperating. They seem to me shrill rather than enthusiastic, vehement rather than fulfilled, demanding rather than generous, and overall entirely boring. Was it too much to hope that women climbers would avoid being contaminated by this particular infection? I fear it was. Time and again I have heard some young woman claiming that physically women are capable of every exploit open to men, and putting herself forward as evidence. Time and again I have heard her husband or fiancé or brother point out with great good humour and total lack of tact that on such-and-such a route or such-and-such an extreme pitch, the air had resounded with feminine squeaks for help.

Surely we should try and be rational about the matter. there is no point in denying nature, and nature has so willed it that the female body (with a few exceptions which merely serve to prove the rule) is not built to the same pattern as the male, and does not have the same musculature. To try and claim the opposite is simply absurd. Moreover it seems probable that there are certain psychological traits which women possess less than men and which are fundamental for extreme climbing, such as aggressivity and competitiveness. I shall, of course, be told that this is simply social conditioning, but this is surely not valid today when education has narrowed the gap between the sexes. And this argument, in any case, I have only ever heard put forward by women – young or old, single or married – who have had no close contact with children. Anyone else is perfectly well aware that the masculinity or femininity of a small baby is established long before any social conditioning or educational process can be brought to bear.

We are often told that one of the greatest advances made by women since the last war is the fact that in certain countries they can now do all the jobs open to men – work as labourers, empty rubbish bins, go cod fishing in the North Atlantic. I feel that all-female expeditions to the Himalayas are in something of this league. I find it difficult to see in what sense this constitutes an advance. On the contrary, it seems to me a quite senseless triumph, and I would be more impressed by a militant feminism which did its best to see that women were protected from the more arduous and painful professions. I should add that when Lucien Berardini dismissed the first French women's Himalayan expedition as "Operation Tampax", I was inclined to be amused rather than indignant. . . .

It seems to me vital too that one should not judge the success of a climb simply by the degree of difficulty of the route involved. Climbing is after all only a game, not a scale of values, and consists prosaically in climbing up one side of an acclivity and down the other. Certainly, as I have already said, climbing has been of paramount importance in my life, but it has never been a religion. Climbing must be placed in some perspective, and that any woman should refuse the amazing adventure of motherhood in favour of an ephemeral experience like an Alpine season passes my comprehension. One of the most admirable people I have ever known was an excellent climber, certainly, but also a charming woman, a mother of four, and a most witty and welcoming hostess. If a prize were to be awarded to a female climber, I would quite unhesitatingly award it to her.

It it therefore absurd to assess a climber merely according to how nearly she climbs at Grade 7. I do not begrudge their success to those who reach it, or who make it their life's work to reach it, but they remain the exception. I have often noticed, myself, that my enjoyment of a climb is in no way directly proportional to its degree of difficulty. Sometimes of course a relatively easy route can be boring, and I admit that this is never the case when the climb is something of a struggle. But struggle is not equivalent to enjoyment. There are high-standard routes you enjoy only in retrospect, and then only in the sure knowledge that you will never have to repeat them. The climbing persona is only partly a matter of strength and technique; we have all known climbers of the utmost competence whose bad temper and repulsive personality make a mockery of their physique. And this part of the equation should never be neglected by the female climber. Another of my friends, Denise Esconde, typifies this: she is certainly an excellent climber, but at sixty-two notable primarily for her charm and her enthusiasm: an admirable specimen of the female climber.

Another thing that annoys me: the present-day lack of historical perspective, so that it is felt that the late twentieth century has invented everything from communism to the paperback. Feminism is as old as time, yet one would imagine that women had only just screwed up their courage to venture into the mountains. I quote: "We can no longer ignore the woman climber, since she is now proliferating in all areas of climbing" — and this from a climbing manual published in 1904. And let me point out too, that the first article in the first number of *La Montagne* was the work of a woman founder-member. She was called Aurore—though admittedly she signed herself George Sand.

We have always been as free to climb as we have been to write. Simply, we must make the effort to do so, and not impute to others the blame if we fail (something else which has recently become all too fashionable). Nothing prevents women from proving themselves, climbing intensively, taking up weight and circuit training if they so wish, even taking hormones, if they like, to develop muscular, hairy arms like those of their rivals. There is no reason why they should not lead, solo, climb as *cordées féminines*. None of these particularly appeals to me—I have for instance soloed nothing more daunting than the North Face of the Tête Blanche—but that does not prevent others from making their own decisions. And it is then and only then that the most recalcitrant males will be convinced—by practice, and not by theory, however vociferous.

Let me end with a little anecdote designed to appeal to the Blue Crampon Brigade. I am very fond of Simone Badier – and her fame in climbing circles, incidentally, does not preclude her possessing all sorts of other qualities. I particularly admired her, for instance, once when I met her in Chamonix in an elegant cornflower-blue dress and perfectly groomed hair, asked her how her season was going and was told that she had done the North Face of the Matterhorn the day before. What is less well-known is that she has a charming husband called Jean. Not so long ago, I married a charming husband of my own, John Wilkinson. I had introduced him to Simone, and a few days later the two of them were in the same cable car in Lognan. John went over to say hello to Simone, who stared at him with that friendly but slightly glassy look we reserve for people we cannot remember ever having met before.

"I'm John Wilkinson," offered John.

The look stayed just as friendly, but just as perplexed.

"Anne Wilkinson's husband," John persisted.

Still no reaction.

"Anne Sauvy's husband," John tried as a last resort.

"Of course!" said Simone.

They started talking. John luckily has an excellent sense of humour, and he launched into a brilliant tirade on female empire-building, and on the fact that any man wishing to make himself known these days has no longer any recourse other than naming his wife. It was at that point that a gentleman who had been standing behind Simone came forward smiling and introduced himself:

"Jean Badier!"

from LA MONTAGNE *1976*

"Guess what we girls did today?"

No Wonder Mallory Didn't Make It

ROBERT REID

Beginnings: Genesis, Exodus, Leviticus, Et Al.
In the beginning there was nothing. Then on the third day God created the mountains. This was good. God formed the ridges and the couloirs, the chimneys, the dihedrals and the overhangs. Then on the sixth day God created the climbers.

The first man was named Adam. His wife was Eve. Adam had no time to climb mountains. He spent his days resisting temptation. But Eve was different. She wandered hither and yon searching for hills to ascend. When there were not hills to be found she settled for dales. Although not greatly renowned as a technical climber, Eve is remembered for making history's first aid descent. She bolted down an apple.

In the climbing world today, this is generally regarded as Original Sin.

Nothing much happened during the next 4,000 years. With the exception of Moses, who ascended Mt. Sinai and received ten commandments, none of which he was anxious to keep, mountaineers stayed in the lowlands and practised their moves in secret. Climbers came to be viewed with suspicion and the mountains themselves began to be regarded as unhealthy places, full of ice, snow and commandments.

The Dark Ages: A Slow Period
Many ages passed. Finally the Dark and Middle Ages arrived, at nearly the same time. Knowledgeable people claimed that these were the same, thus inspiring lively conversation but ultimately great confusion. Of the two ages, mountaineers preferred the Middle as it is nearly impossible to climb in the Dark.

Objective hazards for climbers during this era were numerous. Dragons inhabited the high country. Ghosts flew about in a terrible rage and frightened innocent mountain travellers. Crazed scientists studying barometers lurked near every pass. As a result of these dangers first ascents were almost unknown, the cautious mountaineers of the day preferring second and third ascents.

Everyone agreed that the sport of mountaineering was mouldering in the doldrums. It was morbose and peccant. What was needed was a colourful figure who could generate some excitement. Fortunately, at just this moment, Leonardo da Vinci arrived on the scene. Not only was Leonardo colourful—mostly pink, with blue eyes and touches of grey around the temples—he also possessed a large set of lungs and with these he breathed life into the sport. Leonardo took time off from a busy schedule to explore the high peaks and glaciers. One day he found himself in great difficulty near the Col d'Olen. Unable to save himself but luckily spying a British scientist in the pasture below, Leonardo screamed in his best English, "Elp! Elp!" In a short time he was rescued and the mountains henceforth came to be known as the Elps.

(Well . . .)

Maps: Hard to Read

At about this time, maps were invented. The first of these were primitive affairs which consisted of blank sheets of paper. To distinguish one from another, each map was labelled with the name of the area is purported to cover. 'Himalayas', for example, was popular, as were 'Appalachians' and 'South Chicago.' Unfortunately these maps were impossible to interpret and mountaineers became despondent. After all, without squiggly lines to follow, where could they go?

Soon there were answers to this haunting question. Intrepid explorers moved into the interior. The country came to be better understood. Where formerly there had existed only blank spots on the maps, mountains suddenly sprang up. This amused the natives but ruined the crops. One such mountain rose near a blank spot on the French-Swiss border. To commemorate the event, local peasants named it Mt. Blank.

Mt. Blank was the first great problem. Ironically, the simple-minded mountaineers in the neighbourhood referred to it as the Last Great Problem. It is well to note that there have been many Last Great Problems throughout the history of mountaineering. This was the first of them.

The problem with Mt. Blank was that it was forbidding. Children were forbidden from touching it. Husbands were forbidden from climbing it. So much was forbidding about the mountain that the people decided it should be put up for bids. The highest bid was entered by a kind gentleman named Horace Benedict de Sausseur. He offered a huge reward to the first person to climb Mt. Blank. Because the mountain was no longer forbidding, many climbers attempted to reach the summit. The first to succeed were Doctor Michel Paccard and Jacques Balmat. While on the mountain these two climbers discovered a Grand Plateau and some Grands Mulets. And when they returned to the valley their received five grand from de Sausseur. Both of them agreed that they had had a grand time.

The Golden Age: Old Timers

Ages continued to come and go. At last the Golden Age arrived. This colourful era derived its name from the strange fact that the only mountaineers then active were all at least eighty years old. Most of them are now even older.

Some of the mountains first ascended during this period included the Wetterhorn, the Weisshorn and the Finsteraarhorn. When all of these horns resounded simultaneously people said that the hills were alive with the sound of music.

One golden-ager was Edward Whymper. Whymper heard the call of the wild. After recovering from the shock, he set off to climb the Matterhorn. This mountain was considered by the golden-agers to be the Last Great Problem. The story of its first ascent is an exciting chapter in our story, filled with periods, commas and vowels. Whymper had been eyeing the Matterhorn for some time. So far he had received no response but Whymper was not one to give up easily. By chance one afternoon he happened to meet two guides, Old Peter Taugwalder and Young Peter Taugwalder. Whymper inquired as to which of the two was older and was told that in fact it was Old Peter who was older. At this, Whymper, an immensely logical man, became very excited and pursued the same line of questioning. Which of the two, then, was younger, he asked. Young Peter smiled. "I am," he responded. Whymper leapt into the air gleefully. "At last!" he shouted, "At last I shall climb the Matterhorn!"

Fortunately for Whymper, the Taugwalders were crazy, too. Immediately they realised that they had found the man who would conquer the Matterhorn. The Last Great Problem would be solved.

Eagerly, they joined Whymper's expedition.

The following day the trio set off for the summit, accompanied by four other men, Hadow, Croz, Hudson and Douglas. The route was fraught with peril. Couloirs and arêtes threatened the party each step of the way. But they were brave men, dauntless and fervent. They refused to be discouraged. The following afternoon their persistence paid off. Whymper and his party reached the summit of the Matterhorn. Victory was theirs!

The descent was uneventful, except for one small slip by Hadow. Whymper returned to the valley a hero. The Matterhorn was conquered.

The Alpine Club: Stuffy

At about this time the Alpine Club was formed. This was a group of elderly and pretentious climbers who sat around all day in large overstuffed chairs exclaiming, "Icy, old chap!" Alpine Club members were required to smoke pipes, glare contemptuously and engage in light-hearted banter. Unruliness was ruled out.

The Alpies spent their holidays in the Elps where they tested new and highly specialised pieces of equipment. Although their inventions were simple and crudely designed, they were the forebears of today's complex technical mountaineering gear. For example, the Alpies developed the forerunner of the ice axe, which they called the alpenstock; the forerunner of the Vibram sole, which they called hobnails; and the forerunner of the hauling bag, which they called the porter. This latter invention recently has seen considerable service in the Himalayas, where the hauling bag is known as a Sherpa.

Women: Skirts come to the Hills

Although they began slowly, women climbers soon became an important part of the mountaineering scene. In the Elps, brave women such as Lucy Walker, Henriette d'Angeville and the Pigeon sisters made important ascents. The fine achievements of women have continued to the present day with Dolly Giri, Chrome Molly, Fifi Hook and Patty Gonia all making important recent contributions. Among these contributions have been the development of many interesting pieces of equipment, the most important of which is the double sleeping bag.

While in the mountains women took part in numerous exciting and harrowing adventures, many of them in small tents after returning from a climb. Often a number of these tents were pitched together at the foot of a mountain. Because of the activities which took place there, these sites became known as 'base camps'. A climber spending a night there was said to have 'belayed'.

Gripons and Eggies: Cracked

Surrounding Mt. Blank were numerous ovoid-like pinnacles. These pinnacles so much resembled eggs that they came to be known as 'eggies'. There was the Eggie du Midi, the Eggie du Plan and the Eggie Verte. When a climber managed to scramble to the top of one of these . . . well, you can guess that one.

Not all the eggies were scrambled, however. The Gripon, for example, had rappelled the greatest climbers of the day. At last fate intervened. Alfred Mummery, an ambitious but nervous Victorian mountaineer, arrived on the scene resolved to get a Gripon himself. When he reached the crux of the climb, Mummery was vastly relieved to find that the eggie was cracked. His greatest surprise, however, was still to come. Mummery, an unusually superstitious man, was stunned to speechlessness when informed by his guide that the flaw in the eggie had a name—the Mummery Crack! What a coincidence! Recognising the significance of the freakish set of events, Mummery, a man of action, acted. Placing himself in the crack, he surmounted its difficulties with ease and moved upward rapidly. In a moment he stood at the summit of the eggie. Triumph was his!

Mummery made other first ascents, including an unbelievably dirty climb of the Matterhorn's 'Smut' Ridge. Feculance, swill and quagmire pester the mountaineer who attempts this drecky route. Smudge is so rampant that discouraged seconds often report an almost complete inability to clean the pitches.

Chomolungma: Growing Pains

Located far away in a corner of the strange country of Tibet was an insignificant peak named Chomolungma. No one noticed Chomolungma and it lay in obscurity for years. Then the surveyor-general began to measure the heights of all the mountains in the neighbourhood. Each time Chomolungma's height was measured the results were more and more impressive. The surveyor-general could not believe his eyes. Something weird was happening! Chomolungma was growing! Before long it was found to be the highest mountain in the world. That's the mysterious East for you!

Because they thought that Chomulungma was still growing, the British, whose empire was shrinking, wanted it for themselves. Privately most of them admitted that until the mountain belonged to them they didn't think they could ever rest. Soon after this the mountain came to be known affectionately as Mt. Ever-Rest.

As occasionally happens, however, men of principle intervened. They pointed out that the mountain belonged to the Tibetan people and should be left to them. George Leigh-Mallory, who was used to standing on tall mountains and was therefore a man of high standards, stated the case most succinctly. Ever-Rest should remain with the Tibetans, he said, "because it is theirs."

Everyone agreed that Ever-Rest was the Last Great Problem. The story of the heroic attempts to reach its summit is one fraught with adventure, heartbreak and leeches. Monsoons abounded. Brave men like Epic Shipton and Namche Bazar struggled with the elements and lost. Expedition after expedition fell victim to the intense cold, oxygen deficiency and especially to the sherbits, a cold people who resided nearby. Many of these sherbits were tigers, whose ferocious presence made the climb doubly difficult.

George Leigh-Mallory was the most famous mountaineer to attempt Ever-Rest. He discovered the Yellow Band, a Chinese orchestra that had perished high on the North Face. He also discovered the First and Second Steps leading toward the summit. Unfortunately he failed to find the Third and Fourth Steps.

Other climbers searched for these steps. Men like Frank Smythe and Wind Harris took decisive steps but these were not enough. Finally Epic Shipton decided to look on the other side of the mountain. This was a step in the right direction. Shipton discovered that the route to the summit lay through the Western Cwm. Now only one problem remained: Find someone who could pronounce the word Cwm!

A search was begun. At last Edmund Hillary was suggested for the task. Since Hillary was a B-keeper by profession, it was felt that he might have a chance with C's, W's and M's. As it turned out, those who believed in Hillary were correct. He negotiated the Cwm flawlessly and together with the Scandinavian climber, Tenzing Norway, fought his way toward the summit of Ever-Rest. The two men complemented each other perfectly. Despite the incredible difficulties, they never argued. Neither man believed in friction climbing. On they trod. And then . . . they were there. Hillary and Norway had knocked the bastard off! The prize had been won. Ever-Rest was in the bag at last!

Why and Wherefores: An Analysis

Ever-Rest is now behind us. Historians are looking back to reflect on the success of Hillary and Norway, to enumerate the errors of previous expeditions and to place the final victory over the mountain in its proper perspective. It is now apparent that each of the unsuccessful attempts on Ever-Rest, having placed as many as nine camps on the mountain, was ultimately defeated by the debilitating effects of the oxygen-thin air. At the climactic moment in each of these expeditions the confused leader would inevitably be seized by an attack of convoluted logic and would order the best climbers to descend from Camp 9 to Camp 8 and so on all the way down to Camp 1. There it was quickly apparent to all that the bottom of the mountain had been reached rather than the top, thus effectively ending the expedition. To understand the strength of this argument consider now the case of Hillary and Norway. They chose to climb from Camp 1 to Camp 9 in more or less consecutive ascending order. This was logical. This was reasonable. It left them a chance. It left them a loophole. Most importantly, it left them pointed in the right direction.

After Ever-Rest: Let's Give Credit

When Ever-Rest had been conquered, it became customary for members of the successful expedition to point out to admirers that their success was due chiefly to the groundwork that had been laid by earlier expeditions. In a sense, they said, Hillary and Norway climbed on the shoulders of Epic Shipton and Shipton climbed on the shoulders of Frank Smythe and Smythe climbed on the shoulders of Wind Harris and Harris climbed on the shoulders of George Leigh-Mallory.

With so many people climbing on his shoulders, it is no wonder that Mallory didn't make it.

North Faces: Which Way Do They Face?

One of the strangest periods in mountaineering history was the era of north faces. During this period all climbers, for reasons that have never been fully explained, exhibited fanatic enthusiasm for north faces. Under close examination nearly all of these were revealed to be facing north. What's so exciting about that? Why didn't they discuss south faces anyway? The mountaineers of the day refused to answer such questions. These men were deceptive, mealy-mouthed and venal.

All of the north faces were called "wands." The most famous were the Eigerwand, the Matterhornwand and the Grand Jorassewand. Men who attempted to climb them were called wanderers. Wanderers faced great hazards — storms, rockfall and publicity.

The Matterhornwand and the Grand Jorassewand were the first wands to be polished off. This left them with a high sheen and an attractive finish. Now only the Eigerwand remained. With little doubt, it was the Last Great Problem. Mountaineers stormed its ramparts and pummelled its bulwarks. Those who could find them ran full tilt against its parapets. Finally someone tried to climb it. This was the key that had been overlooked! In short order the Eigerwand fell, narrowly missing the Austrian climbers Heckmarr, Kasparek, Vorg and Harrer, who were on it at the time. Their success was due principally to the fact that Harrer had studied entomology at the University and was thus able to tame the large white spider which lurks near the top of the face. The Austrians were so happy to avoid the spider's tentacles that they joked and bantered the remaining way to the summit. Their light-hearted jests, now traditional among successful climbers of the Eigerwand, came to be known as 'exit cracks'.

England: Gritstone and Scholarships

Although Britain possessed no large mountains she was blessed with numerous outcroppings and pubs. Most climbers started off on the former and ended up in the latter. A few, however, started off on the former and ended up in the latter. It is well to note that no one started off on the former and ended up on the former.

The gritstone cliffs that abounded in the pleasant English countryside were perfect for the kind of equipment which the typical British climber brought to the sport, namely, PAs, chockstones and recklessness. Because some mountaineers regarded these crags as mere training grounds for more complex climbs elsewhere, they were called 'nurseries'. Climbers who graduated from the nurseries moved on to the Elps where they attempted Grade I through Grade VI. This kind of schooling required money so that funds were set up to support the studies of some of the better climbers. These men were said to be climbing 'with aid'. The less fortunate had to search out the cheaper outcroppings, where there was abundant free climbing.

The Hard Men: Tenacious
Some of the British climbers developed huge bulging muscles. These men were tough as nails. The bigger they were, the harder they fell. Because of this they were called the hard men.

Everything these men did was hard. They liked their eggs hardboiled and their women hardhearted. Instead of underwear they wore hardware. These men were hard to believe.

One of the hardest of these climbers was Joe Brown. He had great courage and long arms. Brown invented the justly famous 'fist jam,' a sticky substance similar to strawberry jam which when applied to the fist caused a climber to adhere to the rock. Many British cracks became clogged with this substance, including the most famous, now known affectionately as 'Cloggy'. A few climbers, horrified at the thought of all those gooey cracks, refused to carry hand jam. These men were called clean climbers.

For some reason the typical hard man never ventured far from home. He was shortsighted, unable to see beyond his local crag. He had no vision. Some critics said he lacked idealism, others said he lacked purpose. All agreed that he could use a good pair of glasses.

But Joe Brown was different. His long arms enabled him to branch out. He was a cut above the other hard men. From that altitude he was able to see considerably farther than they could. Brown decided to venture abroad. He needed a climbing partner and luckily discovered Don Willing, who was willing to try anything. The two ranged far and wide. They climbed here, there and everywhere. After a time, however, they grew weary of all this activity and only climbed here and there. Willing settled down and invented a Willing Harness which his friend Brown used to capture a huge horse named Mustang Tower.

The Eight-Thousanders: Expensive

Throughout the Himalayas were scattered the legendary 'Eight-Thousanders', those mountains which had never been ascended for an outlay smaller than $8,000. These were the mountains of the wealthy. A group of poor Frenchmen led by Maurice Herzog developed a plan to raise the funds necessary to climb one of these expensive peaks. For months these dedicated men hiked in the French Elps building up calluses on their feet. Finally they were well-heeled. They decided to attempt Dhaulagiri, $8,167, an elusive mountain which regrettably they were unable to find. As this turn of events made climbing it impractical they turned their attention to Annapurna, $8,091, a mountain that nearly all of them could find since their base camp lay at its foot. Annapurna was an appealing mountain as it was cheaper than Dhaulagiri by $76. After pooling their remaining resources the lucky Frenchmen found to their delight that they had just enough left to make a bid for the summit. After great hardship and harrowing adventure, Herzog and Louis Lachenal succeeded in humbling the mountain, a favour that the mountain returned during their descent.

Another Eight-Thousander was Kangchenjunga, $8,598. This mountain was situated in a region of confused topography. Climbers wandered around in circles and became lost. Many of them didn't know what was up. A British expedition moved to and fro in fits and starts. The issue remained in doubt. Fortunately Joe Brown had decided to come along. Of course, he reached the summit of Kangchenjunga. When he arrived the level-headed Brown knew exactly where he was. He peered over the edge and shouted down to his climbing partner George Band, "George, we're there!" Band, however, was still sceptical. He regarded Brown quizzically. An impasse ensued. Finally Band was persuaded to climb on. At last he too reached the summit. Only when he looked around at the view which unfolded before his eyes was Band willing to admit that Brown had been correct. They were there.

Other expensive mountains stretched to the west. Chief among them was K2, a peak owned by the Americans. K2 was a very cold mountain. Americans on K2 stayed warm by hovering around House's Chimney. When it was time to become cold again the Americans would attempt to climb K2. Each attempt turned into an epic battle for survival, full of storms, freezing temperatures and smoke from House's Chimney. Finally the smoke cleared. The Americans were surprised at what they saw. They saw the Italians. The Italians were standing on top of K2. These men had not needed House's Chimney as they were hot-blooded and possessed fiery temperaments.

The last Eight-Thousander worthy of consideration is Nanga Parbat, $8,125. This mountain gained its greatest fame when Hermann Buhl made a solo climb to its virgin summit. Although the leader of Buhl's expedition, Dr. Herrligkoffer, claimed that Buhl was driven to his remarkable achievement solely because of an obsession to reach the top, Buhl later admitted in private that he was only trying to get as far away as possible from Dr. Herrligkoffer.

Other climbers have been emulating Buhl ever since.

America: Rags to Riches

In America at first there were no mountains. Frustrated alpinists began climbing the walls. No one was happy with the situation. It was a dreary era, characterised by boredom, surliness and loathing.

Then word arrived that explorers in the Hinterlands had discovered the Rocky Mountains. Other ranges were quickly uncovered—the Sierra, the Cascades and the Olympics. Mountaineers rejoiced. There were mountains in abundance. There were even a few in Texas.

It was soon apparent that the Rockies were best for mixed climbing. Sometimes this meant climbing on mixed rock and ice. At other times it meant climbing on mixed free and artificial terrain. Climbers who weren't sure which was which were said to be mixed up. Some of them didn't know their head from their adze.

The best rock climbing was in Yosemite. This area was named for the great shaggy grizzly bears, the uzumatis, that once lived there. In memory of these animals climbers in Yosemite spent their time doing bear climbs.

Yosemite's top climbers could literally fly up the walls. This was not as difficult as it sounds since most of them wore Robins on their feet. These climbers spent so little time walking horizontally that they developed a painful foot affliction called Royal's Arches.

Some of Yosemite's best climbs were on domes. There were half domes, quarter domes, eighth domes and sixteenth domes. In order to ascend one of these a climber needed to purchase a large quantity of expensive equipment from two men named Yvon Chouinard and Tom Frost. Many climbers completely exhausted their resources in making such purchases and were said to be Frost-bitten.

To the north of Yosemite loomed Alaska, a land of terrifying glacier-covered peaks. The first mountaineers to visit the area were surprised at the lack of vegetation they found and vowed to do something about it. They chartered airplanes to fly in bushes to be planted on the mountainsides so that climbers would have something to hold on to besides glaciers. The pilots who brought in these plants were called bush pilots.

The mountaineers of the north were tough buzzards who lived for months at a time on sourdough, pemmican and icicles. The toughest of these men was Duke Abruzzi. Duke made the first ascent of a difficult peak named Mt. St. Elias. At one point during the climb he had to traverse beneath an arête in order to avoid some rock pinnacles. Duke is remembered as the mountaineer who was placed under arête by the gendarmes.

South America: Devout

South America was inhabited by a religious people known as the Catholics. They named their villages for saints, such as Santa Maria and Santa Lucia. Their mountains were named for St. Andrew and were referred to affectionately as Andy's. Andy's mountains stretched from Colombia to Argentina, quite a stretch by any stretch of the imagination.

The biggest of Andy's mountains was Aconcagua. Mattias Zurbriggen, who made the first ascent, thought that the mountain would contain solid rock suitable for high-angle climbing. Zurbriggen was wrong. He was guilty of taking the mountain for granite. In fact he discovered that there was nothing gneiss about the climb at all. Aconcagua was full of schist.

At the southern end of Andy's mountains in the country of Chilly lay a fearful peak named Cerro Torre. Cerro Torre's precipitous overhangs gave many climbers hangovers. Her terrifying ice flutings could be heard for miles. Mountaineers gazing up at the Torre from the depths of a Patagonian ice storm winced and faltered. Such erratic behaviour was considered bad form and made Vibram soles useless. The proud Torre remained inviolate.

Finally, along came Toni Egger and his companion Cesare Maestri. These ferocious Italians, applying courage, audacity and derring-do, managed to climb the Torre—but in so doing unwittingly unleashed one of the greatest scandals in the history of mountaineering. For on the descent the two brave climbers dropped their camera! From all corners of the world rose a hue and cry. Children wept. Publishers gnashed their teeth. And why not? After all, now there could be no book about the climb! Who ever heard of a book without pictures anyway?

Maestri, humiliated and exasperated, languished and festered at his home in Italy and acquired a snarling demeanour. He also acquired a pneumatic drill from a dentist in Milan. This kindly gentleman had spent months attempting to repair the gnashed teeth of the world's publishers. Now he convinced Maestri to return to Patagonia with the dental drill and use it to fight tooth and nail against Cerro Torre. Maestri saw the logic of the dentist's argument. He returned to the Torre. As expected, the drill proved useful during the epic battle which ensued. It augured well. Maestri again was up to the challenge. A few minutes later he was up to the summit. But his remarkable success quickly turned to failure again. The unfortunate Maestri was unable to find the camera that had been dropped!

The incident left Maestri with a bad taste in his mouth. The incident left everyone with a bad taste in his mouth. Even Maestri's friend the dentist was unable to do anything about all of this bad taste. Most people agreed that with everything tasting as it did, the only thing that was tasteless was Cesare Maestri.

Ethics: Endings

Inevitably the question of ethics arose. Ethics were rules which governed how one should act. In the past mountaineers had lived by a number of rules. There were the Golden Rule, the General Rule and the Rule of Law. For the fist jammers there was even the Rule of Thumb.

Now it was hoped to find a set of rules that would assist climbers in making their decisions. Everyone offered suggestions. Some said that all pitons should be banned. Others disagreed. Some said that the climbing community should be a closed society. Others disagreed. Some said that large expeditions should be discouraged. Others disagreed. Exasperated at all of this disagreement, a few climbers threw up their hands and asked the single question which summed up all of their frustration: Where do we go from here?

This was known as the Last Great Problem.

from MOUNTAIN GAZETTE 37 *1976*

Large or Small?

ERIC SHIPTON

In 1933 I formed a deep conviction of the fallacy of tackling Mt. Everest with such a huge organisation. In the first place no expedition had in practice launched more than two attempts on the summit; it was agreed that the best number for an attempt was two, therefore it seemed improbable that in any expedition more than four men would be required to make the actual attempts. Why then should a party consist of fourteen climbers? It was argued that there must be reserves in case some of the climbers went sick. But in no case had a man, who was known to be capable of climbing to great altitudes and who had been relied upon to take part in the final climb, actually succumbed to sickness before the attempt. It seemed clear, then, that this risk was insignificant compared with the enormous chances against any one expedition finding the mountain in a climbable condition. Reserves yes, but not three reserves to every one man who was expected to go high. Again, this question of sickness should surely be regarded against a background of individual experience. In all the dozens of expeditions and climbing holidays that I have done I do not recall a single occasion on which sickness of any member of the party has prevented us from reaching our objective. I believe that most climbers can say the same, or at any rate will agree that such a misfortune is a rare occurrence. Further, when a man is sent on an important job during which he has to live, perhaps for years, in a bad climate the appointment is not duplicated in case he goes sick. Why, then, this extraordinary expectation of disease and accident on an Everest expedition? I refer of course to the approach and not to the final attempt on the summit.

But it was mainly on psychological grounds that I was opposed to large expeditions. It is vitally important that no member of a party should at any time feel that he is superfluous, or that he is simply there in case someone else breaks down. Such a state of affairs imposes an intolerable strain on everyone, and is bound to lead to friction and a consequent loss of efficiency. This matter is easily overlooked by a leader who has all the interest of the organisation and is constantly busy with his plans. On a scientific expedition each man is, or should be, absorbed in his particular line of research; the party can easily be split up into self-contained units each with its special task and responsibility. But when the sole object of a venture is to reach the top of a particular mountain, the problem is entirely different. It is merely tactless to remind a man that he is lucky to be there at all, and that there are hundreds of equally good climbers at home who would be only too glad to take his place. You cannot argue an expedition into running smoothly, nor avoid a competitive feeling by appealing for the 'team spirit'. The strongest mountaineering party is one in which each member has implicit confidence in all his companions, recognises their vital importance in the common effort and feels himself to have an equally indispensable part to play. This ideal is no less important on a Himalayan expedition than on an Alpine peak. To my mind it can only be achieved with a relatively small, closely-knit party. Only then can you talk (if you must) about 'team spirit'. How is it possible, when at least fifty per cent of the members are destined to remain in reserve, to avoid a feeling of competition? Only a saint could expunge from deep down in his soul all hope of another man falling sick, that he might take his place. How different from the joyous partnership we have known on other climbs!

For my part I loathed the crowds and the fuss that were inseparable from a large expedition. I always had the ridiculous feeling that I was taking part in a Cook's tour or a school treat, and I wanted to go away and hide myself. Of course this did not apply to the few days or weeks when one was actually doing a hard job of work, but unfortunately such spells occupied a very small proportion of the whole time. The small town of tents that sprang up each evening, the noise and racket of each fresh start, the sight of a huge army invading the peaceful valleys, it was all so far removed from the light, free spirit with which we were wont to approach our peaks. And I believe that spirit plays an important part in the success of any mountaineering venture. Remove, then, the impression that one is engaged in a vast enterprise upon which the eyes of the world are focused, realise that one is setting out to climb a mountain, higher perhaps, but fundamentally no different from other mountains, and one will add greatly to one's chances of success, and, more important still, enjoyment.

Finally, the disadvantage of large expeditions lay in the fact that the necessity of raising big funds made it difficult to control publicity. The expeditions became invested with a glamour foreign to the fundamental simplicity of the game. It was quite natural that mountaineers should wish to climb the highest peak in the world, or at least be interested in the project. But unfortunately Everest's supremacy among mountains appealed to the popular imagination of a record-breaking age, and gradually the expeditions began to receive a press publicity out of all proportion to the value of the undertaking, and certainly out of keeping with what used to be regarded as 'the best traditions of mountaineering'. It was claimed that the enterprise symbolised the spirit of modern youth, and that its success would represent a triumph of humanity over nature. In fact, of course, the first part of the venture was an intensely interesting piece of geographical exploration, and the second an absorbing mountaineering problem – no more, no less; both were on the same plane as any similar project.

Mountain climbing has its roots in mountain exploration, and it is not unnatural that in little-known ranges the mountaineer should tend to revert to the basis of his pursuit. It would be difficult for anyone with an interest in a strange country to go all the way to Mt. Everest without feeling some desire to leave the route and wander off into the labyrinth of unmapped ranges that stretch away on every side. On the way back to India in 1933, Wager and I left the main party and made our way across a small strip of unexplored country to the south, and crossed into Sikkim by a new pass. My chief interest was in climbing peaks. Wager, on the other hand, as a geologist, had a wider view. He had already tasted the joys of serious exploration in Greenland, and his main enthusiasm was for the country itself. Though I disputed the matter hotly at the time, I gradually became converted to his way of thinking. Something of my early feeling for mountains began to revive.

Then the thought occurred to me, "Why not spend the rest of my life doing this sort of thing?" There was no way of life that I liked more, the scope appeared to be unlimited, others had done it, vague plans had already begun to take shape, why not put some of them into practice? It was a disturbing idea, one which caused me much heart-searching and many sleepless nights. The most obvious snag, of course, was lack of private means; but surely such a mundane consideration could not be decisive. In the first place I was convinced that expeditions could be run for a tithe of the cost generally considered necessary. Secondly if one could produce useful or interesting results one would surely find support; and as experience grew, so too would the quality of the results. No, lack of money must not be allowed to interfere. The fact that I had no training in any particular branch of science was a more serious obstacle. But might not this defect be remedied as one went along, or in spare time between expeditions? Also there is much to be said against the organiser of a scientific expedition being himself a specialist; firstly because he would tend to take a narrow view of the work of the expedition, and secondly because the running of an expedition is in itself nearly a whole-time job. For I did not expect to have to hunt alone – I anticipated no difficulty in finding men willing to join me on an attractive project.

I do not know how much I fought the temptation. I certainly suffered qualms of conscience, but they were due more to the mere prospect of such exquisite self-indulgence than to fear of the consequences of abandoning the search for an assured future, provision for old age and other worthy ambitions. I had always rather deplored the notion that one must sacrifice the active years of one's life to the dignity and comfort of old age. Also the less conservative of my monitors assured me that things had a way of panning out so long as one knew what one wanted. So the decision was taken, albeit with a faint heart.

from UPON THAT MOUNTAIN *1943*

T. Graham Brown and the
Brenva Face

LORD TANGLEY

There can be no doubt that both in achievement and character Graham Brown was one of the most outstanding (perhaps the most outstanding) amongst British climbers in the Alps during the inter-war period. Indeed, in my humble opinion his imagination and determination concerning, and his concentration on, the Brenva face of Mont Blanc has been equalled only by Whymper's similar concentration on the Matterhorn. The result was that this glorious face became an arena in which the Alpine Club's approach to mountaineering was displayed in all its purity and without inter-national competition, although, with the last and greatest ascent, the Pear Buttress, this unhappy element was only narrowly and most fortuitously avoided. The Brenva face became Graham Brown's own, and the history of its exploration flows directly from G.B.'s own personality. His was one of the most complex person-alities I have even known. There was the rigorous scientist whose work in physiology earned him a Fellowship of the Royal Society. There was a deep humility in the presence of the great mountains, amounting to awe. There was a deep capacity for friendship. There was a soaring ambition which quite naturally made him wish that the world should know that the great Brenva climbs were his. There was also a touchiness which made him at times a difficult companion and resulted in interruptions of friendship. I remember one fine morning, high up on Mont Blanc, I ventured to comment on the beauty of the sunrise. Receiving no answer and seeing G.B. with head bent over his ice-axe, I asked him if he was all right. The reply (without looking up) was, "Yes, perfectly, except that I object to your conversation." Fortunately, I then know him well enough to realise that I had interrupted one of his deep meditations which were the mainspring of his actions.

His physical characteristics were no less remarkable. He was very short in stature and had particularly short legs. In 1926 he was already in early middle-age, but weighed little over nine stone. He

621

had had some experience of rock-climbing but little of snow or ice work. In 1926, helped by his minute weight, he was able to scramble up rocks quite well. On snow and ice he was really quite poor, and in addition was handicapped by his very short legs. His great strength was his ability to go on indefinitely without any apparent fatigue. I recall two descents of the Nantillons Glacier in one week in 1927 and the painful slowness of his descent of the dangerous passage. Neither in 1926 nor in 1927 was Graham Brown in my opinion fitted to lead a serious expedition. I mention these limitations, not for the purpose of detracting from Graham Brown's achievements, but on the contrary to emphasise the fact that his will and imagination were capable of transcending his own limitations and those of others.

I never met or heard of Graham Brown before 1926. In that year I met R. J. Brocklehurst and Graham Brown in Grindelwald, and we did the Wetterhorn together. They did the Jungfrau while I had a couple of days flesh-potting on the Lake of Thun. We then did the Schreckhorn, passed over to Fionnay, traversed the Grand Combin and Mont Velan and descended to the Great St. Bernard where we passed the night. It is at this point that Graham Brown's account of Brenva in his book begins. We were delayed in our descent to Aosta by the breakdown of the post wagon and started up for Courmayeur by the post wagon late in the evening. It is a night none of us will ever forget and is well described by Graham Brown in *Brenva*. This was the first moment that any of us had seen the south side of Mont Blanc except from distant mountains. I did not then know that, on the basis of *Running Water* and the map in Baedecker, Graham Brown had already been captivated in imagination by the Brenva Face. But his excitement was more than could be accounted for, even by the magnificence of what we saw before us. At Courmayeur we duly met Baker and proceeded to the Dôme Hut. On the way we passed Purtud. The halt at Plan Ponquet is well described in the first chapter of *Brenva*. Many times have we talked about this moment and many times have we examined the photographs taken from that point on that day. I have no doubt that what Graham Brown writes there is absolutely accurate, that the picture in Graham Brown's mind built up from the Baedeker map was destroyed and at the same moment the conception of Route Major was born. I am equally certain that it was an absolutely original conception on the part of Graham Brown and this I believe is an excellent illustration of the combination of his vivid imagination and his scientific mind. To abandon an imagined topography and instantly to substitute a new and, as it turned out, true one was a remarkable feat.

We went on to the Dôme Hut on a superb, cloudless day. Going on by full moonlight, we completed the traverse to the Grands Mulets without ever lighting a lantern or cutting a step. I had to depart for London the same evening, but Brocklehurst and G.B. went on over the passes and ascended the Tour Noir. Before we parted, both Graham Brown and I had decided that we would like to climb together again next year. We also knew that we would like to have Bernet and his uncle Jossi as guides. After we left Purtud on the way up to the Dôme Hut, there was little time left for discussion, though there was no doubt that we had seen the Route Major.

During the winter, Graham Brown read all the alpine literature there was on the subject and in particular was struck by the photograph of the Brenva Face from the Col due Géant taken by Finch. This crystallised the route in his mind and when we met at Simpson's in the Strand to make plans, as he records in his book, he was anxious that we should attempt this route. I had a vague idea that the entire Brenva Face was extremely dangerous from stone-fall and falls of ice from the upper séracs. From a study of what photographs existed, Graham Brown was quite sure that under the right conditions there could be no stone-fall, and that Route Major would be entirely safe from falling ice provided the foot could be reached early enough in the morning. In retrospect, this seems to me to be quite a remarkable exercise of what I might call the scientific imagination. All subsequent experience has confirmed what Graham Brown that night said would be the fundamental physical conditions of the Brenva Face. His practical proposition was that we should do what he called the "southern zig-zag" of Mont Blanc. This was to ascend by the Brouillard Arête, do a descent of the Peuterey and an ascent of his proposed new Brenva climb. All this was to be undertaken after a suitable training course.

I was to engage Jossi and Bernet, which I duly did, and the party foregathered at Lac de Champex. We were dogged by deplorable weather. We first made the traverse of the Grand and Petit Darrei and hoped to traverse the Aiguille d'Argentière, but a deterioration in the weather made us choose the Col du Chardonnet instead. We then went up to the Montenvers which we made our base. We first did the l'M and the Petits Charmoz. Next we did the Requin, in the course of which we suffered from the accident to another party described by Graham Brown in *Brenva*. What he did not mention was the splendid skill, courage and determination he displayed during the recovery of the body and the rescue of the survivor, who, though uninjured, was in a state of serious shock and hysteria. The news of the death of friends in the Lake District and the Dauphinè coming on top of this experience on our arrival back at Montenvers certainly had the unnerving effect which G.B. describes. The alternative was either to abandon the mountains or to regain our nerve. We chose the latter course, and during the next few days made ascents of the Grands Charmoz and the Aiguille de Blaitière. It is the descents from these two peaks over the Nantillons glacier to which I have referred above.

The weather had broken and now got worse. We had to turn back from the Moine ridge of the Verte and to abandon any idea of the Grandes Jorasses. Instead, we went up to the Torino hut and down to Mont Fréty, having, from the Torino hut, for the first time for either of us, seen something of the Brenva Face.

In view of the bad weather, it was obvious that the South Face of Mont Blanc was impossible, so we decided to make a circuit of Mont Blanc and to see it from as many angles as possible. With this object in view, we walked up to the Cantine de la Visaille in order to ascend the Aiguille de Trélatête. Graham Brown mentions this expedition but omits to explain why, in the late afternoon and early evening, we descended the Col de Trélatête at all. This was a pure error. We intended to go down the easy Col des Glaciers, and indeed thought that that was what we were doing! But we found that we were inextricably involved in the difficulties of the famous col. In the result, we were not down on to the glacier until well after dark, and did not reach the Pavillon de Trélatête until about ten o'clock that night, having been out for twenty-four hours. Jossi's route-finding through the séracs in the dark was remarkable. This brings out (and I think it must be mentioned) Graham Brown's touchiness. He could not bear to admit an inadequacy or an error and suggests in his book that we set out to cross the Col de Trélatête.

Having now seen this end of Mont Blanc, our intent was to get back to the Torino Hut as fast as possible. For this purpose we went down to St. Gervais in sunshine – with swallow-tailed butterflies sunning themselves on the stones – and from there ascended the Tête Rousse, intending to cross Mont Blanc and descend via Mont Maudit to the Torino. All being well, we would then attempt the 'new Brenva Route'. Unfortunately the weather broke again and we went round by train to the Montenvers, where the weather continued bad and my own time and that of the guides was up. I felt extremely sorry for Graham Brown that his dream should not have come true, and when Smythe came back to the Montenvers with Ogier Ward off the Old Brenva Route, it was with a good deal of pleasure that I introduced him to Graham Brown. I had known Smythe well for some years although I never climbed with him, believing (quite rightly) that I was nowhere near his class. Seeing him and Graham Brown left at the Montenvers, each at a loose end, I believed that Smythe was competent to lead the new climb and Graham Brown to follow him. Graham Brown's heart was set on Route Major but he knew nothing, any more than I did, about the state of the ground between the Torino and the foot of the climb. Smythe had recent knowledge of the section between the Torino and the start of the Old Brenva, but so far as I could judge, had never looked at or interested himself in anything beyond. In the end, as we all know, they did neither Route Major nor the variation of the Brenva route which Smythe had in mind, but an intervening climb, which they called the Sentinelle Rouge. This was a fine climb in itself. In the book it is suggested that they saw this route from the Torino Hut and settled there to attempt it.

Although Smythe and Graham Brown fell out and indeed quarrelled violently, I was fortunate to be able to remain on terms of close friendship with both. Each of them published separate accounts of the Sentinelle climb, but each talked with me intimately about it, as happened in the subsequent year with regard to the Route Major. I am forced to the conclusion that the decision to attempt the Sentinelle route was not nearly as clear-cut as *Brenva* suggests. Graham Brown in his heart of hearts wanted to go for Route Major. Smythe was really after a variation of the Old Brenva. The Sentinelle was somewhat of a compromise between the two and neither had done what he set out to do. Of these two disappointments, G.B.'s was by far the greater. He and Smythe turned upward prematurely before even trying to get to the base of the Route Major. Nevertheless, the Sentinelle is a fine route and Smythe undoubtedly regarded it as his. He also believed that it was only owing to his superior skill as a leader that Graham Brown was got up the climb! Here were evident seeds of a dispute between two highly strung men, and Graham Brown raised strong objection to some of Smythe's published accounts of the climb. Certainly by the time the climb was over Smythe had made up his mind not to climb alone with Graham Brown again.

In 1926 and 1927 I had already entered on a period of severe personal and business strain accompanied by gross overwork and in consequence, holidays for three or four years had to be treated as recuperative. During those years I had some excellent ordinary seasons in the Alps, but it was obviously impracticable that I should seek to rejoin any Brenva efforts. Nevertheless, I think that both G.B. and Smythe felt that I was one of the few who had been in on the original conception, and both used to come to me with their plans beforehand and their accounts afterwards.

I must confess that, looking back at that time, now so long ago, I still feel a pang of disappointment that I should have so narrowly missed what I am sure would have been the first ascent of Route Major by our 1927 party.

It is to be noticed that, for the attack on Route Major in 1928, Smythe proposed a party of four. This was in fact reduced to the original pair owing to the inability of Ogier Ward to come out, and the sickness of Blakeney. I know that Smythe was very unwilling to attempt Route Major with Graham Brown alone, but partly he felt that he was committed and partly I think the appeal of the Buttress had laid its hand upon him. Probably also, Graham Brown's indomitable will-power had imposed itself upon his partner, who was the stronger climber but the weaker character. Certainly, after Route Major, the two men never climbed together again, and were scarcely on speaking terms. The crux of the climb was the cutting down into the couloir round the tongue. Either this was nothing like as difficult as Graham Brown thought it to be or Graham Brown's cutting was much slower than Smythe could easily tolerate. Knowing G.B.'s 1926 form and the highly strung dispositions of both men, the opinion I formed at the time was that both these views were correct. Again, each man published accounts at the time which diverged in some respects. The mutual disappointment between them was no doubt subconsciously aggravated by the fact that Smythe felt that the climb was virtually his by reason of his greater contribution to the climbing, whereas Graham Brown regarded the climb as his, as the materialisation of his long dream. Thereafter, each man went his own fruitful way, and the history of each is well-known. I was particularly glad that Graham Brown's wise decision to climb with guides led to such splendid results. It was also a source of gratification that my two friends, whom I introduced at the Montenvers, should have had these two great climbs together. Unfortunately, as the years went by their attitudes hardened and their mutual feelings grew no softer. When Graham Brown was writing *Brenva*, he consulted me on innumerable points concerning 1926, 1927 and 1928, and I hoped that all would be well. However, the proofs were shown to Smythe, who reacted violently, even to the point of talking about legal proceedings. Eventually they both agreed that they would accept publication in any form I approved. This involved quite substantial revision, with the result that parts of the early chapters of *Brenva* contain considerable elements of my writing.

Now that both men are dead, it seemed to me worth while to record the foregoing as a footnote to Alpine history.

I am pleased to say that my friendship with Smythe and his family remained unbroken. That with Graham Brown suffered a sad interruption.

It was one of my duties on becoming President of the Club to communicate to G.B. the decision of the Committee that the time had come for a change in the editorship of *The Alpine Journal*. At the time, unbeknownst to me he was in hospital, recovering from the effects of an accident on Ben Nevis. This is another example of his extraordinary touchiness. He could not bear to have it known that he had been involved in an accident. He took my communication, when he ultimately received it, very badly and for some years refused to speak to me or even to acknowledge my presence. This was sad, but there was nothing I could do about it. Suddenly one day out of the blue I had a little note from him saying that we were far too old friends to quarrel, and what about having lunch together? We lunched at the Athenaeum as though nothing had happened and our friendship was thus resumed.

And so I now look back over a period of forty years to two men, both friends, who in their various ways and according to their diverse abilities and personal characteristics added lustre to British mountaineering.

from THE ALPINE JOURNAL *1966*

Backdoor Diplomacy

ERIC SHIPTON

On July 28, a week after I had returned to England, the Himalayan Committee met to hear my report on the training expedition and to consider plans for the organisation of the attempt on Everest the following spring. It was clear that the Committee assumed that I would lead the expedition. I had, however, given a good deal of thought to the matter, and felt it right to voice certain possible objections. Having been to Everest five times, I undoubtedly had a great deal more experience of the mountain and of climbing at extreme altitudes than anyone else; also, in the past year I had been closely connected, practically and emotionally, with the new aspect of the venture. On the other hand, long involvement with an unsolved problem can easily produce rigidity of outlook, a slow response to new ideas, and it is often the case that a man with fewer inhibitions is better equipped to tackle it than one with greater experience. I had more reason than most to take a realistic view of the big element of luck involved, and this was not conducive to bounding optimism. Was it not time, perhaps, to hand over to a younger man with a fresh outlook? Moreover, Everest had become the focus of greatly inflated publicity and of keen international competition, and there were many who regarded success in the coming attempt to be of high national importance. My well-known dislike of large expeditions and my abhorrence of a competitive element in mountaineering might well seem out of place in the present situation.

I asked the Committee to consider these points very carefully before deciding the question of leadership, and then left them while they did so. When I was recalled the Chairman informed me that they had reached the unanimous decision that I should be asked to lead. He was kind enough to add that I had the full confidence and backing of the Committee, who considered that my prestige alone, particularly among the Sherpas, made it most desirable that I should accept. I did so, and at the same time asked that Charles Evans should be appointed deputy leader. Incidentally, if the Committee had asked me to withdraw I would have recommended most strongly that Charles should be invited to take my place, for I had formed the highest opinion of his ability and temperament.

To take full advantage of the many technical advances made during the war in such things as cold-weather clothing, diet and oxygen, a great deal of research and experiment would be needed in addition to the normal work of preparation. For this reason, it was decided to appoint an organising secretary, preferably a mountaineer qualified to take part in the expedition itself. The first choice was John Hunt, whom I interviewed a few weeks later. We had a frank discussion, and John told me that he did not feel able to accept the position unless he were made deputy-leader. While I understood his point of view as a high-ranking Army officer, I could not, of course, agree to his terms, since I had already nominated Charles Evans as my deputy. Also, it was clear to both of us, and admitted, that our approach to the enterprise, both practical and temperamental, was so fundamentally different that we would not easily work together. We parted, however, on friendly terms. The post of organising secretary was filled by Charles Wylie, and we started work at the Royal Geographical Society.

The next meeting of the Himalayan Committee was on September 11. I was surprised to find that the first item on the agenda was the 'Deputy Leadership', and still more so when I was asked to go out of the room while this was discussed. An hour later I was recalled and told that John had been appointed 'Co-leader' with me. Then, for the first time, it dawned on me that there must have been a great deal of backdoor diplomacy since the last meeting, of which I had been totally unaware. It seemed particularly strange to me that I should have been expected to accept the proposal, especially remembering the views expressed the previous winter on the subject of joint leadership by most of the Committee and by myself. In declining, I told the Committee that if they wished to reconsider their former decision regarding the leadership, they were, of course, free to do so. I then withdrew for a still longer period. I returned to be told that it had been decided to appoint John Hunt in my place.

The influences which caused the Committee's *volte face* are still obscure. Assuming both the need and the desirability for a large heavily organised expedition, their ultimate decision was right. My taste for simplicity would certainly have influenced my conduct of the enterprise. Moreover, partly because of this disposition, I am neither an efficient organiser of complicated projects nor a good leader of cohorts. Even so, the chagrin I felt at my sudden dismissal was a cathartic experience which did nothing to increase my self-esteem. I had often deplored the exaggerated publicity accorded to Everest expeditions and the consequent distortion of values. Yet, when it came to the point, I was far from pleased to withdraw from this despised limelight; nor could I fool myself that it was only the manner of my rejection that I minded. I was further humbled by the loyalty of Tom Bourdillon, who was so incensed that, without telling me, he wrote to the Committee resigning from the expedition. Knowing how desperately keen he was to take part in the attempt on Everest, I was fully aware of the extent of his sacrifice. It took me a long time to persuade him to retract.

from THAT UNTRAVELLED WORLD *1969*

Two Everest Reviews

H. W. TILMAN AND ROBIN CAMPBELL

Mr. Ullman has written several mountaineering books, of which *The White Tower* is the best known. His book, *Americans on Everest*, is therefore a professional job. Although he did not accompany the expedition beyond Katmandu, he had been associated with it from the beginning, knew all the members, and from their first-hand experiences has put together a full, fair, intimate account. It is pleasant to record that he pays due tribute to earlier expeditions. The book is meant to have a popular appeal — and one can't quarrel with that — so that those with sober tastes may find the writing florid, over-dramatic, lapsing frequently into National Geographic Magazine style. A style, no more than a man, that is popular, cannot be excellent, cannot have distinction, and therefore the publisher's claim that this is one of the classic mountaineering books is as wide of the mark as are most such claims. For the price of 50 shillings the illustrations are disappointing. There are six untrue colour plates while the black-and-white are not well reproduced and have been crammed together three or four to the page. Two minor points — will any British reader know of "the late C. B. de Mille" who on p.55 starts turning in his grave?* And is "by happenstance" the American for "by chance?"

The fortunes of the various parties at work on the mountain are easy to follow. One of the main difficulties in describing a large expedition, that of showing where everyone is at a particular time, has been well overcome. The author appreciates the contradictions inherent in an Everest expedition — small parties or large, the mingling of mountaineering with science, flag-waving; and having discussed them he inevitably justifies the means. "No climber worth his salt," we are told, "wants to climb in a crowd," but the party numbers twenty. "Norman (the leader) preferred his mountainering 'straight'," but nevertheless takes with him four scientists. "Mountaineers are not jingoistic flag-wavers," but Old Glory and the flag of the National Geographic are duly waved.

So much for the book. The expedition itself, like many others, met with mixed fortunes. The fatal accident in the first few days on the icefall might well have taken the steam out of a less resolute party. To have to pass repeatedly over the spot where Breitenbach lay buried under the ice cannot have been encouraging. The changing of the original ambitious plan of mounting simultaneous assaults by the West Ridge and the South Col led to trouble, setting up stresses and strains that, but for the good sense and goodwill of all concerned, might have ended in disintegration. After the establishment of Advanced Base at 21,350ft. Dyhrenfurth seems to have feared that to allot equal resources to both the West Ridge and

*Tilman is reputed never to have set foot in a cinema.

the South Col parties might jeopardise success. He decided to give the latter priority and in spite of the protests of the West Ridge adherents and the bitter arguments that ensued he stuck to his decision, a decision that was probably right and in the circumstances almost inevitable. Had it been a private expedition, answerable to no one, success would have been of less moment and both assaults might have been given equal chances. In which case it is conceivable that the West Ridge party might not only have succeeded, as they did, but by having enough Sherpas to establish a camp higher than 27,250ft. from which to start, might have been spared the night out at 28,000ft. on the South Ridge with its unhappy consequences of frostbite.

The reasons for the ten days of inaction at Advanced Base (21,350ft.), while the unescorted Sherpas carried to the South Col, are not made clear. This seems to be carrying to an extreme the principle of the conservation of energy and cannot have been good for the morale. Judging by the account, long before the ten days were up, 'cafard' was oozing out of the tents. Our member J. O. M. Roberts, in an entertaining note about the transport problems, also remarks on this long pause.

The author rightly and repeatedly stresses the work of the whole team in getting men to the top. Nevertheless it is hardly possible not to single out Unsoeld and Hornbein, obviously the fittest members of the party, the moving spirits on the West Ridge, who from the start chose to be beaten if necessary by that, rather than succeed by the South Col route. In spite of having to make do with the scrapings of the barrel in the way of Sherpas and support parties, they stuck to their resolution through thick and thin and brought it to a triumphant conclusion. It needed audacity to persevere by their route and even more audacity when at a point 800ft. below the summit at three in the afternoon, with no sure retreat by the way they had come, they decided to push on and descend by what was to them the unknown South Ridge. This West Ridge climb lifts the expedition to a high plane, a plane level with that of the first ascent of the mountain in 1953.

No Everest book is complete without appendices. Here we have the lot — finance, food, equipment, transport, health, oxygen, photography, communications, geology, glaciology, physiology, psychology, and (God save us) sociology. The tents are highly praised, yet at Camp 4W, "a broad level platform of snow, and idyllic camp site," three tents, one with four men inside, were blown 50 yards down the mountain. The butane stoves, too, are given full marks in spite of an explosion at Camp 6 which nearly put paid to the second summit party's effort.

That science is madness, if good sense does not cure it, is surely plain when psychologists and sociologists are found accompanying a mountaineering party. Physiologists have been there before. In this case Doctor Siri, after several pages of mumbo-jumbo, arrives at two conclusions neither of them new — that high on Everest a man has no appetite and consequently is half-starved, and that fresh food is more palatable than processed food. In America, where they invented processed food, the latter may well be news. Doctor Siri remarks that, "No one would argue that without oxygen life at 29,000ft. could be anything but short." How short is short? Ten days, a week, a day, or a couple of hours? This reviewer likes to think that one day Everest will be climbed by a small party of really tough men without oxygen. Were it not that for centuries past they have been addicted to going about in hordes, and still do, the Russians or the Chinese would be the best bet. Perhaps a party of Sherpas would succeed. Before they caught the oxygen habit from their employers these men could carry 30lb loads to over 27,000ft. Carrying nothing they might well get unaided to the summit.

On the whole this expedition is better to read about than to have taken part in. How many members of the Alpine Club would consent — as these Americans did — to a session at the Institute of Personality Research (IPAR), and how many would emerge from it unbroken in mind or body? A party of 20 climbers, 900 porters, costing 40,000 odd quid! Having faithfully perused the book to the last appendix your reviewer's thoughts turned reluctantly but sympathetically towards Maurice Wilson. He may have been mad, or as our sociologists put it, "not fully in touch with reality," but at any rate he had in him the root of the matter. And if he was mad he had probably been reading too many Everest books.

from THE ALPINE JOURNAL *1966*

Everest South-West Face, Chris Bonington (Hodder and Stoughton, £3.95)

> *Interviewer*: Why are you going to climb the South West Face of Everest?
> *Bonington*: Because it offers an interesting mountaineering challenge: to do it will involve technically difficult climbing at an altitude requiring constant use of oxygen, thus posing extraordinary logistic problems of supply and support.

Most of us will prefer Mallory's answer, but the occasion for it has passed. Poor Bonington had to choose between the one given in the book (and paraphrased above) or the blunt honesty of "Because it's all that's left there," or the subtler, less palatable truth of, "Because I've sold a book about it."

This last reason illustrates the paradoxical nature of the *South-West Face*. In fact, it is a new art form—a work of imagination upon which facts are based! Unlike other novels of fact such as Norman Mailer's this one was conceived, planned and sold *before* the 'events' described occurred. Bonington and his men then went to Everest to follow the plot as best they could, eventually returning to complete the book in accordance with what actually happened. The climbers may not see it in this way, but given their financial circumstances, the eventual existence of the book was a necessary condition for a successful expedition, and not conversely, so the issue of logical priority is clear. Thus, the events on the mountain should be seen as an outgrowth of the book (and other media objects). Of course, this topsy-turvy 'pseudonews' is not a new phenomenon, nor confined to mountaineering: one suspects, for instance, that many recent sailing ventures have a similarly dubious motivation.

To be fair to Bonington, he does not completely gloss over the Janus-faced nature of modern Greater Mountaineering. It is made clear to the reader by reference to his 'agent', to the prior selling of book, film, television rights, etc., to the complex arrangements for getting the 'news' out fast that not only mountaineering values are involved. However, much is still left unsaid. For example, nowhere is the *quality* of the route discussed—a factor considered important in mountaineering circles—and the quality of the South-West Face is exceedingly low.

Most of it is straightforward snow slopes and gullies. The

technical difficulties (not yet really tackled, despite four major expeditions) are likely to be extreme but are confined to a short section which, apparently, may be by-passed by traversing off the face. Moreover, in appearance the face resembles nothing so much as a huge coal bin under snow! Small wonder that the specialist mountaineering journals have shown little interest in the route, since many finer routes are made in the Himalayas each year. Why then was it chosen? I imagine because it is well-known to the public, because Germans and the like had failed on it, affronting good selfless British chaps like Whillans in the process with offensive nationalistic displays, because it is the only new route left to Everest from the Khumbu glacier (the only presently-available approach): in short, because of its news value.

The standards which must be applied to *South-West Face* are therefore those which apply to any contemporary adventure thriller. How has Bonington coped with plot, characterisation, tempo etc., bearing in mind that the expedition was a total failure due to impossible weather conditions? Pretty well, under the circumstances. The story has a good deal of human interest: blazing rows flare up periodically between Bonington and the other English members Burke, Estcourt and Scott and these inject some tension into what would otherwise have been a fairly dull tale (it is inconceivable that these could have been 'staged', I suppose). Narrative responsibility shifts occasionally to other members, all of whom keep diaries (they couldn't have been asked to keep them, could they?) and this also helps the story along. The Sherpas provide useful light relief: much is made of the similarity between them and the modern Western worker since they seem thoroughly familiar with strikes, demarcation disputes, bonus schemes, etc.; at the same time not enough (except in the excellent appendix by Roberts — the only really objective comment on climbing Everest in the book) is made of their evident ability to climb the mountain several times over were it not for the fact that they have to hump these great loads of rich food and oxygen around for the Europeans! Those essential ingredients of the modern thriller, sex and violence, are more difficult. However, Bonington does his best by substituting several anal adventures (in which he stars) for the first. As for violence, there are the various accidents — Scott's lucky escape at Camp 5 when he walks backwards off the mountain taking photographs (for the book, of course).

One might fault some of the characterisation. The hero himself is not terribly likeable – for example he gratuitously and brutally insults Tiso and Kent, both of whom served him well. Of the other characters, Burke, Bathgate, Estcourt and Scott are well drawn but Haston, MacInnes and Tiso remain shadowy figures. One wonders what Tiso thought about during his long solitary vigil at Camps 3 and 4 (surely he didn't neglect his diary?) But, all in all, it is not unworthy of, say Alastair MacLean.

from THE SPECTATOR *1973*

Hanging Around

DAVE ROBERTS

One cringes at belabouring the obvious. But every once in a while the need for such an article as this arises. Traditions grow fuzzy, and the legends of one generation need footnoting in the next. In my recent rambles around the climbing world, a melancholy fact has gradually nagged its way into my consciousness.

The fact is this: there is emerging upon us right now a whole new crop—one would be tempted to call them a 'school', but for their woeful ignorance—of young, dedicated climbers who have got the most central tenet of mountaineering ass-backwards. For their benefit, and at the risk of sounding pontifical, I here reaffirm that tenet. Namely, that the very object and essence of mountaineering, its be-all and end-all, is Hanging Around. All else is peripheral, a distraction.

The youngsters, it grieves me to report, can be seen everywhere these days obtusely infringing upon the long-established conventions of Hanging Around. Some of them, for instance, behave in a climbing store as if it existed in order to sell them equipment to go out and abuse the cliffs with—not as a hanging-around scene for its own sake, sufficient unto itself. Others can be observed leaving a bar at 10 p.m. in order to get "an early start" in the morning. Some actually come to slide shows to get ideas for expeditions. I do not exaggerate. In general, there is a disturbing tendency among the younger generation to take climbing itself altogether too seriously—which cannot but lead to a deplorable loss of finesse and subtlety when it comes to hanging around.

For their sake, then, and for the sake of posterity, which seems to have a knack for losing track of the most obvious facts of the past—it takes *My Secret Life*, for example, to remind us that English women wore no underpants before the eighteen-seventies—I shall set down here in cold print the hows and whys of Hanging Around, as it was practiced in the golden heyday of mountaineering, by the best climbers in every civilised nation, some few of whom I was privileged to loiter and vegetate with in their best days.

The Climbing Store

It is important to realise that the climbing store exists not to sell equipment, but as a mutual sniffing ground in which mountaineers establish their credentials. The essence of proper behaviour, as in so many climbing scenes, is not to try too hard. The climbing store is articularly effective in allowing the local talent to size up the visiting outsider, and vice versa. The game is harder to play for the outsider, since indifference and disdain come automatically to the proprietors, who are sick to death of selling Gerry Kiddie-Packs and Richmoor beef stew. There are a few tricks, however.

For instance, in Southern California you can usually get away with talking tents. A successful dialogue might proceed as follows:

Customer (musing over the store's own design, prominently pitched in the front foyer): Very pretty. Nice colours.

Owner: Notice the extra-long sleeve door. And optional mosquito netting.

Customer (with a chuckle): Ah, yes, mosquito netting. What won't they think of? I was wondering if you have something with a ridge pole, you know, a little sturdier? (At this point it doesn't hurt to push sceptically against the tent wall.)

Owner: We do sell the Glacier Designs four-man. It's very popular with Sierra Club outings.

Customer: I was thinking of a two-man. With snow flaps.

Owner: I see. For winter use—

Customer: Well, yes, of course, but really for next summer. Up North. I hate to spend so much money, but my old Alp Sport's in tatters.

And so on. In the East, talk Jumars vs. Gibbs ascenders. In Boulder, cagoules. In Jasper, bivouac hammocks.

In the climbing store, of course, it is essential not to hang around too long. Twelve to eighteen minutes is about right. Longer brands you an equipment freak. And, of course, one does not browse among the books (implying unfamiliarity with the few good ones), but only among the magazines (implying that you would never subscribe to one).

Another gambit is to dash in and ask abruptly for a very specific item. Half a dozen nuts of the same size, say. If questioned, it is legitimate to mumble something about "taking the aid out of Steppenwolf" — but never volunteer this information.

It goes without saying that proper attire is vital. The sort of fellow who shows up in a climbing store with a nylon runner for a belt has blown it irrevocably. Likewise with worn klettershoes, frayed knickers, or too conspicuous cuts and scratches on the backs of the hands. Greasy down jackets, however, are OK.

The Local Climbing Area

Here, the important thing is not to get conned into climbing anything hard. A once-clever gimmick, now ruined by over-use, is to show up in sandals. (Future guide books will list first sandalled ascents; the standards are already tough.) However, fresh variations on the nonchalant just-happened-to-drop-by approach still work. A friend of mine recently scored valuable points at Carderock (near Washington DC) by becoming the object of awe-struck whisperings: "You know ———? He doesn't even use chalk."

In the old days, a favourite way of beefing up local prestige was to take the visiting celebrity out to the local area, ostensibly "just for a little climbing," but really to see what the hot-shot could handle. It's sad to reflect that even champions like Terray and Robbins fell for this trick, and struggled valiantly on 5.10's some local wizard had spent the last half-year perfecting. By now, of course, the visitor knows that all the hardest local climbs are hopelessly beyond him, and that the way to play the game is with studied magnanimity. Thus, the locals are in danger of blowing it themselves — as happened here a year or two ago, when, following a visit by Chouinard and Frost to the nearby climbing area, the local store wore its hero-worship on its sleeve, immortalising the visit in a poster-board display (photos of Chouinard's shoe poised exquisitely on a foothold) and repeating fervently to all who would listen to Frost's assessment of a 15ft. aid climb, "Yessiree, we don't do much in the Valley that's that hard."

The local climbing area is an ideal place to show up with an ulterior motive: say, hustling a touch football game, or (although this is a trickier tack to take) soliciting information about the big climb planned for the next weekend at the Gunks. "Anybody know about the top pitch of Carcinoma? How's the protection?" The danger, of course, is that someone there will have done Carcinoma, or that someone else will remember two weeks later that you were going to do it last weekend.

If forced to climb, it is best to wander absent-mindedly along traverses five feet off the ground. If you fall off, you can usually imply that you were trying it one-handed. Never bring a rope. The reason for not soloing climbs, naturally, is for fear of encouraging beginners who may not know any better. Groups of beginners have other uses, too: you can often claim that you showed up (and can persuade others to join you) just to watch the University Outing Club practicing prusiking.

The AAC Board of Directors' Meeting

A very strange scene, one which, for better or worse, most mountaineers will never be privy to. The weekend of a Directors' Meeting begins with a Friday evening cocktail party. The principle of the disguise, developed originally for use in climbing stores, seems to have reached macabre perfection here. Most of the Directors show up in business suits, wearing shiny black shoes, carrying attache cases, talking committee reports. At the party, after hearty back-slapping, they drink—not beer or cheap wine, as in campgrounds the world over—but real cocktails, scotch-on-the-rocks in hefty belts.

The next day, during the business meeting, the Directors continue the masterly charade. All of them display an astonishing familiarity with parliamentary procedure, and they sling around with Congressional pomp phrases like, "If the chair can prevail upon the head of the Rocky Mountain Section to instruct his membership that. . . ." They seem to know about budgets.

There used to be a dangerous pressure at Directors' Meetings to knock off Sunday and go climbing together. Fortunately, the business of the Club has grown to such proportions that it can be counted on to spill generously over into Sunday afternoon. Thus the Board need not be haunted by the spectre of an aging Director securing the token Yosemite youngster with a classic European over-the-shoulder standing belay, or of a boozy ex-hard-man developing sewing machine leg on a 5.4 move the day after a hard night arguing membership qualification standards for the AAC.

The Slide Show

Slide shows used to be fun, easy-going. No longer. There was a

time when you could get away with sunsets. Tilted climbing shots.
Under-exposed bad-weather shots. There used to be a gentle give-
and-take; the audience was on your side. In fact, I can remember
the hoary days when you could get a chuckle out of old chestnuts
like, "The belay I gave Joe was a strictly psychological one," or,
"Ten minutes after we climbed this slope it was swept away by an
avalanche."

Nowadays a slide show audience is hostile in proportion to its
sophistication. This makes it very hard to give slide shows. Good
photos are suspect; if you have time and the weather to take a
beautiful picture, obviously it was posed, or at least you weren't
spending all the effort you should have getting on with the
desperate business at hand. Bad photos (poorly-centred, out of
focus, dusty, over-exposed) have their integrity. In fact, the perfect
slide show, like Apollinaire's perfect poem, would have no pictures
in it.

The right tone is extremely difficult to strike. One must imply
that he is somewhat bewildered by all the fuss being made about
some climb he and his buddies happened to blunder up last
summer, that he is quite astounded to find anyone interested in the
fact that he woke up one morning last January to discover himself
in Patagonia at the base of Cerro Torre. The "what am I doing
here?" tone is best, which modulates easily into, "Wouldn't it be
more fun if we all went out to the local bar?" tone, which lends
itself admirably to a transition to:

The Climbers' Bar

The bar, it is understood, is the place one goes to commiserate with
other climbers when, darn it all, the awful weather has spoiled the
climbing. Like the climbing store, it also serves as a mutual sniffing
ground. Here the game is to figure out what route the other guys
have up their sleeves, or, failing that, to imply that you have their
much-coveted route up your own sleeve. I recall a conversation in a
brightly-lit bar in Banff (all Canadian bars are brightly-lit) a few
years ago with the resident master, who was quite suspicious of our
plans. After the ritual pleasantries, he said:

"Well, what brings you chaps up here?"

"Oh, nothing much," we answered cheerfully. "Some of the
classic routes. Robson, maybe."

"Lovely mountain. We had a great weekend there in May."

Thus we had established that we were both after the same new route. Now the sniffing got sharp. After half an hour's banter, we managed to compliment the old hand's route of a few years before on our intended mountain's north face. "Must have been a fine climb," we said.

"Nothing special."

"That route up the middle of the face would be something else. Scary, I'll bet."

His eyes glinted. "Suicide, I suspect. When we were on our route, we saw this huge bloody rockfall sweep the whole thing."

He had scored there. We must have betrayed a little panic. "That's what I figured," one of our group managed lamely. "Anyway, after all this weather, a thing like that wouldn't be in shape till August. If then."

"Maybe not too hard a climb," the master said as he got up to play shuffleboard. "Just suicidal."

That we were out the next day, nursing our hangovers on the hike in, was irrelevant. The essential battle had been fought the night before. The master had won, by insinuating that we were crazy if we tried the route and chicken if we didn't.

Bars, too, serve as scenes for epic gross-outs and obscene displays. These are a speciality of the British. A rule of thumb to follow is, if you can't be spectacularly offensive, then get quietly drunk in your corner. Anything in between is bad form, and smacks of seeking attention.

Corollaries: make sure you show up in the bar on marginal days—defined as days with any clouds in the sky. Only perfect weather, you want to imply, will lure you into attempting a scheme of the boldness, of the one you and your cronies have been hatching. And you need a few days of sun to get 'the summit snowfields' in shape. There is a whole style of slouching, of brooding pensively, that reeks of hoarding-strength and of building-up-psychologically. Cultivate it.

Bush-pilot Hangars

A scene requiring very adroit one-upsmanship. The politics of hangar-waiting in Alaska, for example, during the mandatory three-day storm after arrival, leading to the automatic assumption that he will take your party in first as soon as the weather clears, no matter when you showed up. Meanwhile, an air of calm confidence attends your perusal of the other groups' gear. The Japanese in Alaska always used to provide a few laughs. "Very interesting pickets," you would say, grinning, as you dubiously flex their hopelessly flimsy stakes. "Pickets, yes," the Japanese would grin back. "Much snow McKinley."

In Don Sheldon's hangar there were archaelogical layers of leftover rations from past expeditions. There, behind the cartons of Pepsi, were Terray's lemon drops; and, yes, under them, could those be some of Cassin's meat bars? One liked to strike a pose of being willing to donate, say, an extra loaf of logan bread to that food museum.

Relations with the pilot himself are carefully ritualised. Self-evidently gauche is any palaver about how-soon-do-you-think-you-can-take-us-in — in a category of crudeness, really, only with haggling over rates. On those rare occasions when the man himself comes in view, one hallos out a hearty greeting, as if you are quite surprised to find him there, in the middle of your summer's food-boxing and equipment-puttering. Most coveted of all: the special invitation to have dinner in the pilot's own house, there beside the air strip. The green looks of envy on the others' faces, as they labour over their Sveas, are worth a whole expedition.

Finally:

The International Scene

Having never climbed in the Alps, I consulted a friend just back from three years in Europe about the international scene. He had done some of his best hanging around in Chamonix. I was curious to know whether European climbers understood the traditions of the activity as well as Americans do. He was reassuring.

"Basically, in Chamonix," he told me, "the scene centres around two bars: the 'Nash,' or Bar National, and Le Drug Store. Only the English hang out at the Nash, which is a pretty raunchy place, small and seedy, with a fussball game and a one-eyed waiter named Maurice. At Le Drug Store you find all nationalities. That's where the English go when they're looking for a fight."

"A fight?" Never in my climbing days had I seen a fight. American climbers are pacifists.

"Yeah. They hate the French. They get drunk and stand up on the tables and sing foul songs. One day I was walking to this climb with some English guys, and they saw two other climbers in the distance. Naturally, they assume they're French. So they shout out, in inimitable Cockney, 'S'enculer!'"

."Which means?"

"Roughly translated, 'Up yours!' There's a pause. Back comes a voice, in inimitable French, 'Sheeet!'"

"Why do they hate each other?"

"God knows. They're English. It's English to hate the French. When I was there, I helped them heist a table from the Drug Store to take out to their campground."

"A whole table?"

"Yeah. They camp on this private land owned by Snell's, the local climbing store. Snell's has a tacit agreement with the English: they can camp on the company's land, and in return they won't shoplift from the store."

"Weird. What about the others? Say, the Germans?"

"Oh, the Germans. They all camp in another campground, tents in perfect rows, neat and tidy. And the climbers are all very hardy-looking, neatly-dressed."

"But they hang out at Le Drug Store."

"Yeah. All except the Japanese, who are far too serious for the bars. The Japanese only know two words in English: 'North Wall'."

"Not like the old Japanese in Alaska."

"Nope. A different generation."

"How about Americans? Besides yourself."

"Oh, there's a typical kid from Washington who's done all the 5.9's in the Seattle area. He's come over to do the Bonatti Pillar. The day after he gets there he hears two people are killed in the approach couloir. He manages to sprain his ankle falling off the boulder in the campground parking lot."

"I see why you associated with the English."

"Yeah. Hey, did I ever tell you the story of how MacInnes inherited Terray's down jacket after he fell off the statue and broke his leg?"

At least the English, I concluded, have the proper respect for the grand traditions of Hanging Around. While we were talking, a fifteen-year-old kid had just made the crux move on Amanita. Two seventeen-year-olds beside us were planning their expedition to Nuptse. An eight-year-old girl in tennis shoes were perusing a well-thumbed guide book. We shook our heads, finished our peanut-butter sandwiches, and headed down to Ramon's for a morning beer.

from MOUNTAIN GAZETTE 19 *1974*

A Clandestine Plea

RICK SYLVESTER

I have another more specific reason for desiring this communication, this accurate conveying of the pursuit of mountaineering to the outside world. And this is where I find myself in perhaps irreconcilable disagreement with viewpoints which profess concern about "unduly [opening] a special lifestyle to the rapacious general public," with the sneer of those who write against offering "a necessary explanation of the Yosemite scene to the misinformed public (the benevolent educationalist school)." This is where I might be accused of being a dyed-in-the-wool wide-eyed idealist, or worse, the ultimate insult, a card-carrying true believer (see Eric Hoffer; also Pär Lagerkvist's *Barabbas*). Nevertheless, here goes. I have strongly felt, from almost the very inception of my involvement with climbing, that it serves not only as an end in itself, a source of limitless joy and satisfaction, but as a means as well, a vehicle powerful in leading individuals to self-control, discipline, self-knowledge, in short, quite a few of the goodies. Climbing can help form many of the personal attributes which make for strong healthy self-sufficient individuals, knowledgeable of themselves and thus insightful into the world and society, if not necessarily well-adjusted to that society (see R. D. Laing's *The Politics of Experience*). What climbing can do to the mind as well as the body might be likened to the combined effects of much of zen and yoga. Many of the postures in climbing approach yoga, such as the concentration and quiet needed to stay on small holds. But different from the practice of these traditional disciplines the transformation arises spontaneously and unsought, more as by-product. Thus the often self-defeating problems associated with conscious striving are avoided. I would never claim climbing to be the one exclusive path to certain insights, truths, and personal transformations; yet from what it requires of the climber it certainly accomplishes much that the traditional and more rigidly structured disciplines assert to yield. Also, this is not to state or claim that one should climb primarily to gain these attributes, essentially by-producuts however valued, of the experience. Ultimately one would be foolish to climb for anything but the climbing.

Some may argue with merit that it is not the thing itself but rather what one puts into it. They may cite breathing, fasting, chanting, yoga, meditation, zen archery, zen snow-shovelling or climbing if I insist as all potentially equal in effect, all possible means to reach Tao, Buddhahood, enlightenment, union, It, whatever. Nevertheless I would place climbing high among these. "Truth can be defined in many ways. But if you define it as understanding (and this is how all the masters of the spiritual life have defined it), then it is clear that 'truth must be lived'." Or as Shaw put it, "Activity is the only road to knowledge." Of course activity interpreted in its broadest sense can include even such as meditation. But in such pursuits there exists a strong potential for self-delusion. The measuring rods are less exact, more nebulous than in climbing where feedback is quite definite. You get up or you don't. And even if you got up you are quite aware of how you got up. There is no fooling yourself, no matter how it looked from the ground. You know if you had insufficient control of your mind, if you panicked or were on the edge of panic, if you clambered up, emotions in turmoil, gripped, despite outward appearances of calm and cool. You cannot hide from yourself a thrutch effort, strength used incorrectly or excessively, unable to keep on that that thin edge (figuratively more than literally). Even the minimum climb often requires so much of a person. Even a slight exposure to climbing seems to cause beneficial changes which from other disciplines might result only after years of concentrated effort. To be frank I must admit that my thinking on this is not finished or complete. It may be the cheapest crassest bullshit; it certainly has that appearance. Yet, so many times I have strongly felt the truth of these matters while engaged in the act (climbing, that is). Again, this is not the proper context to more than introduce this subject. I recommended Aldous Huxley's *Island*. In his plan for a utopian society Huxley, who has perhaps pondered such matters at greater length than you and I, interjected climbing as an essential facet of the whole scheme. Climbing is presented as the physical discipline, the *sport* if you will, indispensable for the attitudes it helps inculcate. Without the shaping of men and women that climbing leads to, the utopian society Huxley envisioned and carefully planned (with far more depth and insight than Skinner in *Walden Two* I might add) has no chance of flourishing. After studying *Island* you may fault Aldous, and me, possibly for being idealistic or naïve enough to think along lines of saving, i.e. changing, the world. Further fault might be found in that the cost could well be climbing as we know it today, where solitude is still the rule and not the exception, *all* climbing settings considered (e.g. the Himalayas, Alaska, Turkey, Patagonia, the Southwest desert, much of the Canadian Rockies, not just Yosemite, Llanberis Pass, Chamonix, the Gunks, the En Vau Calanque, the Banff area). It is quite possible the opinion I hold of climbing and its potential to transform men and women is unrealistically exalted. But it is a view that can, and should, be debated. And as long as I continue holding this view I will always look with at least mixed emotions on attempts to keep mountaineering clandestine, to stifle exposure and, of relevance here, to disseminate anything but a wholly accurate picture.

from THE CANADIAN ALPINE CLUB JOURNAL *1976*

The Climber as Visionary

DOUG ROBINSON

In 1914 George Mallory, later to become famous for an off-hand definition of why people climb, wrote an article entitled 'The Mountaineer as Artist', which appeared in the *Climbers' Club Journal*. In an attempt to justify his climber's feeling of superiority over other sportsmen, he asserts that the climber is an artist. He says that "a day well spent in the Alps is like some great symphony," and justifies the lack of any tangible production—for artists are generally expected to produce works of art which others may see—by saying that "artists, in this sense, are not distinguished by the power of expressing emotion, but the power of feeling that emotional experience out of which Art is made . . . mountaineers are all artistic . . . because they cultivate emotional experience for its own sake." While fully justifying the elevated regard we have for climbing as an activity, Mallory's assertion leaves no room for distinguishing the creator of a route from an admirer of it. Mountaineering can produce tangible artistic results which are then on public view. A route is an artistic statement on the side of a mountain, accessible to the view and thus the admiration or criticism of other climbers. Just as the line of a route determines its aesthetics, the manner in which it was climbed constitutes its style. A climb has the qualities of a work of art and its creator is responsible for its direction and style just as an artist is. We recognise those climbers who are especially gifted at creating forceful and aesthetic lines, and respect them for their gift.

But just as Mallory did not go far enough in ascribing artistic functions to the act of creating outstanding new climbs, so I think he uses the word 'artist' too broadly when he means it to include an aesthetic response as well as an aesthetic creation. For this response, which is essentially passive and receptive rather than aggressive and creative, I would use the word visionary. Not visionary in the usual sense of idle and unrealisable dreaming, of building castles in the air, but rather in seeing the objects and actions of ordinary experience with greater intensity, penetrating them further, seeing their marvels and mysteries, their forms, moods, and motions. Being a visionary in this sense involves nothing supernatural or otherworldly; it amounts to bringing fresh vision to the familiar things of the world. I use the word visionary very simply, taking its origins from 'vision', to mean seeing, always to great degrees of intensity, but never beyond the boundaries of the real and physically present. To take a familiar example, it would be hard to look at Van Gogh's *The Starry Night* without seeing the visionary quality in the way the artist sees the world. He has not painted anything that is not in the original scene, yet others would have trouble recognising what he has depicted, and the difference lies in the intensity of his perception, heart of the visionary experience. He is painting from a higher state of consciousness. Climbers too have their 'Starry Nights'. Consider the following, from an account by Allen Steck, of the Humming-bird Ridge climb on Mt. Logan: "I turned for a moment and was completely lost in silent appraisal of the beautifully sensuous simplicity of windblown snow." The beauty of that moment, the form and motion of the blowing snow was such a powerful impression, was so wonderfully sufficient, that the climber was lost in it. It is said to be only a moment, yet by virtue of total absorption he is lost in it and the winds of eternity blow through it. A second example comes from the account of the seventh day's climbing on the eight-day first ascent, under trying conditions, of El Capitan's Muir Wall. Yvon Chouinard relates in the 1966 *American Alpine Journal*:

> With the more receptive senses we now appreciated everything around us. Each individual crystal in the granite stood out in bold relief. The varied shapes of the clouds never ceased to attract our attention. For the first time we noticed tiny bugs that were all over the walls, so tiny they were barely noticeable. While belaying, I stared at one for fifteen minutes, watching him move and admiring his brilliant red colour.
>
> How could one ever be bored with so many good things to see and feel? This unity with our joyous surroundings, this ultra-penetrating perception gave us a feeling of contentment that we had not had for years.

In these passages the qualities that make up the climber's visionary experience are apparent: the overwhelming beauty of the most ordinary objects—clouds, granite, snow—of the climber's experience, a sense of the slowing down of time even to the point of disappearing, and a "feeling of contentment," an oceanic feeling of the supreme sufficiency of the present. And while delicate in substance, these feelings are strong enough to intrude forcefully into the middle of dangerous circumstances and remain there, temporarily superseding even apprehension and the drive for achievement.

Chouinard's words begin to give us an idea of the origin of these experiences as well as their character. He begins by referring to "the more receptive senses." What made their senses more receptive? It seems integrally connected with what they were doing, and that it was their seventh day of uninterrupted concentration. Climbing tends to induce visionary experiences. We should explore which characteristics of the climbing process prepare its practitioners for these experiences.

Climbing requires intense concentration. I know of no other activity in which I can so easily lose all the hours of an afternoon without a trace. Or a regret. I have had storms creep up on me as if I had been asleep, yet I knew the whole time I was in the grip of an intense concentration, focused first on a few square feet of rock, and then on a few feet more. I have gone off across camp to boulder and returned to find the stew burned. Sometimes in the lowlands when it is hard to work I am jealous of how easily concentration comes in climbing. This concentration may be intense, but it is not the same as the intensity of the visionary periods; it is a prerequisite intensity.

But the concentration is not continuous. It is often intermittent and sporadic, sometimes cyclic and rhythmic. After facing the successive few square feet of rock for a while, the end of the rope is reached and it is time to belay. The belay time is a break in the concentration, a gap, a small chance to relax. The climber changes from an aggressive and productive stance to a passive and receptive one, from doer to observer, and in fact from artist to visionary. The climbing day goes on through the climb-belay-climb-belay cycle by a regular series of concentrations and relaxations. It is of one of these relaxations that Chouinard speaks. When limbs go to the rock and muscles contract, then the will contracts also. And at the belay stance, tied in to a scrub oak, the muscles relax and the will also, which has been concentrating on moves, expands and takes in the world again, and the world is new and bright. It is freshly created, for it really had ceased to exist. By contrast, the disadvantage of the usual low-level activity is that it cannot shut out the world, which then never ceases being familiar and is thus ignored. To climb with intense concentration is to shut out the world, which, when it reappears, will be as a fresh experience, strange and wonderful in its newness.

These belay relaxations are not total; the climb is not over, pitches lie ahead, even the crux; days more may be needed to be through. We notice that as the cycle of intense contractions takes over, and as this cycle becomes the daily routine, even consumes the daily routine, the relaxations on belay yield more frequent or intense visionary experiences. It is no accident that Chouinard's experiences occur near the end of the climb; he had been building up to them for six days. The summit, capping off the cycling and giving a final release from the tension of contractions, should offer the climber some of his most intense moments, and a look into the literature reveals this to be so. The summit is also a release from the sensory desert of the climb; from the starkness of concentrating on configurations of rock we go to the visual richness of the summit. But there is still the descent to worry about, another contraction of will to be followed by relaxation at the climb's foot. Sitting on a log changing from klettershoes into boots, and looking over the Valley, we are suffused with oceanic feelings of clarity, distance, union, oneness. There is carryover from one climb to the next, from one day on the hot white walls to the next, however punctuated by wine dark evenings in Camp 4. Once a pathway has been tried it becomes more familiar and is easier to follow the second time, more so on subsequent trips. The threshold has been lowered. Practice is as useful to the climber's visionary faculty as to his crack technique. It also applies outside of climbing. In John Harlin's words, although he was speaking about will and not vision, the experience can be "borrowed and projected." It will apply in the climber's life in general, in his flat, ground, and lowland hours. But it is the climbing that has taught him to be a visionary. Lest we get too self-important about consciously preparing ourselves for visionary activity, however, we remember that the incredible beauty of the mountains is always at hand, always ready to nudge us into awareness.

The period of these cycles varies widely. If you sometimes cycle through lucid periods from pitch to pitch or even take days to run a complete course, it may also be virtually instantaneous, as, pulling up on a hold after a moment's hesitation and doubt, you feel at once the warmth of sun through your shirt and without pausing reach on.

Nor does the alteration of consciousness have to be large. A small change can be profound. The gulf between looking without seeing and looking with real vision is at times of such a low order that we may be continually shifting back and forth in daily life. Further heightening of the visionary faculty consists of more deeply perceiving what is already there. Vision is intense seeing. Vision is seeing what is more deeply interfused, and following this process leads to a sense of ecology. It is an intuitive rather than a scientific ecology; it is John Muir's kind, starting not from generalisations for trees, rocks, air, but rather from *that* tree with the goitre part way up the trunk, from the rocks as Chouinard saw them, supremely sufficient and aloof, blazing away their perfect light, and from that air which blew clean and hot up off the eastern desert and carries lingering memories of snowfields on the Dana Plateau and miles of Tuolumne treetops as it pours over the rim of the Valley on its way to the Pacific.

These visionary changes in the climber's mind have a physiological basis. The alternation of hope and fear spoken of in climbing describes an emotional state with a biochemical basis. These physiological mechanisms have been used for thousands of years by prophets and mystics, and for a few centuries by climbers. There are two complementary mechanisms operating independently: carbon dioxide level and adrenalin breakdown products, the first keyed by exertion, the second by apprehension. During the active part of the climb the body is working hard, building up its CO_2 level (oxygen debt) and releasing adrenalin in anticipation of difficult or dangerous moves, so that by the time the climber moves into belay at the end of the pitch he has established an oxygen debt and a supply of now unneeded adrenalin. Oxygen debt manifests itself on the cellular level as lactic acid, a cellular poison, which may possibly be the agent that has a visionary effect on the mind. Visionary activity can be induced experimentally by administering CO_2, and this phenomenon begins to explain the place of singing and long-winded chanting in the medieval Church as well as the breath-control exercises of Eastern religions. Adrenalin, carried to all parts of the body through the blood stream, is an unstable compound and if unused, soon begins to break down. Some of the breakdown products of adrenalin are capable of inducing the visionary experience; in fact, they are naturally occurring body chemicals which closely resemble the psychedelic drugs, and may help someday to shed light on the action of these mind-expanding agents. So we see that the activity of the climbing, coupled with its anxiety, produces a chemical climate in the body that is conducive to visionary experience. There is one other long-range factor that may begin to figure in Chouinard's example: diet. Either simple starvation or vitamin deficiency tends to prepare the body, apparently by weakening it, for visionary experiences. Such a vitamin deficiency will result in a decreased level of nicotinic acid, a member of the B-vitamin complex and a known anti-psychedelic agent, thus nourishing the visionary experience. Chouinard comments on the low rations at several points in his account. For a further discussion of physical pathways to the visionary state, see Aldous Huxley's two essays, 'The Doors of Perception' and 'Heaven and Hell'.

There is an interesting relationship between the climber-visionary and his counterpart in the neighbouring subculture of psychedelic drug users. These drugs are becoming increasingly common and many young people will come to climbing from a visionary vantage point unique in its history. These drugs have been through a series of erroneous names, based on false models of their action: *psycho-tomimetic* for a supposed ability to produce a model psychosis, and *hallucinogen*, when the hallucination was thought to be the central reality of the experience. Their present names means simply 'mind manifesting,' which is at least neutral. These drugs are providing people with a window into the visionary experience. They come away knowing that there is a place where the objects of ordinary experience are wonderfully clear and alive. It may also be that these sensations remind them of many spontaneous or 'peak' experiences and thus confirm or place a previous set of observations. But this is the end. There is no going back to the heightened reality, to the supreme sufficiency of the present moment. The window has been shut and cannot even be found without recourse to the drug.

I am not in the least prepared to say that drug users take up climbing in order to search for the window. It couldn't occur to them. Anyone unused to disciplined physical activity would have trouble imagining that it produced anything but sweat. But when the two cultures overlap, and a young climber begins to find parallels between the visionary result of his climbing discipline and his formerly drug-induced visionary life, he is on the threshold of control. There is now a clear path of discipline leading to the window. It consists of the sensory desert, intensity of concentrated effort, and rhythmical cycling of contraction and relaxation. This path is not unique to climbing, of course, but here we are thinking of the peculiar form that the elements of the path assume in climbing. I call it the Holy Slow Road because, although time-consuming and painful, it is an unaided way to the visionary state; by following it the climber will find himself better prepared to appreciate the visionary in himself, and by returning gradually and with eyes open to ordinary waking consciousness he now knows where the window lies, how it is unlocked, and he carries some of the experience back with him. The Holy Slow Road assures that the climber's soul, tempered by the very experiences that have made him a visionary, has been refined so that he can handle his visionary activity while still remaining balanced and active (the result of too much visionary activity without accompanying personality growth being the dropout, an essentially unproductive stance). The climbing which has prepared him to be a visionary has also prepared the climber to handle his visions. This is not, however, a momentous change. It is still as close as seeing instead of mere looking. Experiencing a permanent change in perception may take years of discipline.

A potential pitfall is seeing the 'discipline' of the Holy Slow Road in the iron-willed tradition of the Protestant ethic, and that will not work. The climbs will provide all the necessary rigour of discipline without having to add to it. And as the visionary faculty comes closer to the surface, what is needed is not an effort of discipline but an effort of relaxation, a submission of self to the wonderful, supportive, and sufficient world.

I first began to consider these ideas in the summer of 1965 in Yosemite with Chris Fredericks. Sensing a similarity of experience, or else a similar approach to experience, we sat many nights talking together at the edge of the climbers' camp and spent some of our days testing our words in kinesthetic sunshine. Chris had become interested in Zen Buddhism, and as he told me of this Oriental religion I was amazed that I had never before heard of such a system that fit the facts of outward reality as I saw them without any pushing or straining. We never, that I remember, mentioned the visionary experience as such, yet its substance was rarely far from our reflections. We entered into one of those fine parallel states of mind such that it is impossible now for me to say what thoughts came from which of us. We began to consider some aspects of climbing as Western equivalents of Eastern practices: the even movements of the belayer taking in slack, the regular footfall of walking through the woods, even the rhythmic movements of climbing on easy or familiar ground; all approach the function of meditation and breath-control. Both the laborious and visionary parts of climbing seemed well suited to liberating the individual from his concept of self, the one by intimidating his aspirations, the other by showing the self to be only a small part of a subtly integrated universe. We watched the visionary surface in each other with its mixture of joy and serenity, and walking down from climbs we often felt like little children in the Garden of Eden, pointing, nodding, and laughing. We explored timeless moments and wondered at the suspension of ordinary consciousness while the visionary faculty was operating. It occurred to us that there was no remembering such times of being truly happy and at peace; all that could be said of them later was that they had been and that they had been truly fine; the usual details of memory were gone. This applies also to most of our conversations. I remember only that we talked and that we came to understand things. I believe it was in these conversations that the first seeds of the climber as visionary were planted.

William Blake has spoken of the visionary experience by saying, "If the doors of perception were cleansed everything would appear to man as it is, infinite." Stumbling upon the cleansed doors, the climber wonders how he came into that privileged visionary position vis-à-vis the universe. He finds the answer in the activity of his climbing and the chemistry of his mind, and he begins to see that he is practising a special application of some very ancient mind-opening techniques. Chouinard's vision was no accident. It was the result of days of climbing. He was tempered by technical difficulties, pain, apprehension, dehydration, striving, the sensory desert, weariness, the gradual loss of self. It is a system. You need only copy the ingredients and commit yourself to them. They lead to the door. It is not necessary to attain to Chouinard's technical level—few can or do—only to his degree of commitment. It is not essential that one climb El Capitan to be a visionary; I never have, yet I try in my climbing to push my personal limit, to do climbs that are questionable for me. Thus we all walk the feather edge—each man his own unique edge—and go on to the visionary. For all the precision with which the visionary state can be placed and described, it is still elusive. You do not one day become a visionary and ever after remain one. It is a state that one flows in and out of, gaining it through directed effort or spontaneously in a gratuitous moment. Oddly, it is not consciously worked for, but comes as the almost accidental product of effort in another direction and on a different plane. It is at its own whim momentary or lingering suspended in the air, suspending time in its turn, forever momentarily eternal, as, stepping out of the last rappel you turn and behold the rich green wonder of the forest.

from ASCENT *1969*

The Poetry and Humour of Mountaineering

MICHAEL ROBERTS

On a foggy August morning some years ago, three of us set out from the Vittorio Sella hut intending to do the Grivola by the ordinary route. For guidance we were relying mainly on an Italian 1:100,000 map, a picture-postcard view of the South Face, and our own determination to avoid the 'deceptively easy-looking' North-East Ridge. As we came up to a plateau at the foot of the mountain, the mist lifted for a moment: "That peak's as good as ours," said No. 3, with unusual rashness; but all went well till we got to the foot of the rocks. True, we crossed the glacier in five minutes instead of the twenty we had expected, and the ribs of the mountain seemed to be running up the wrong way; but the map made it clear that this *must* be our mountain, and after some glib talk about retreating glaciers and the curious effects of perspective, up we went. I knew there were falling stones on the South Face of the Grivola, and when I found myself with one finger and the toe of one boot in a small crack with crumbling edges, I had leisure to listen to their vicious 'whing' as they invisibly whistled by at the rate of fifteen a minute. I did not like them. No. 2 announced that I could not be held: No. 3 pointed out that some of the stones were hitting the next ledge, 50ft. up. The mist lifted again; anybody would have sworn that one could walk up the North-East Ridge in half an hour. But we remembered the words of Coolidge, and, very much ashamed of ourselves, wriggled down and went over to the South Ridge. That was grand: towers, spurs, caves, all littered with letter-box and jug-handle holds; there seemed to be stirrups, ears and noses everywhere; sometimes, when the mist thickened for a moment, we climbed a gendarme by mistake; then the caravan would reverse and No. 3 would lead us into a pulpit or up a flying buttress. The sun burned its way through a few remaining wisps of vapour; rock towers and gargoyles stood out bright red against the deep blue of a clear sky; and suddenly No. 3 climbed up into a cave and emerged through a trap-door on to the summit. "We are deceived in our peak," he said; and sure enough, a mile away and 1,000ft. above us, we saw the Grivola, and at our feet there was the Trajo Glacier, the best part of a kilometre wide. We were on a peak not marked on the Italian map. We ran down our 'deceptively easy-looking' North-East Ridge in 10 minutes and did the Grivola next day.

Better men than myself have done that sort of thing: it is annoying and humiliating (it happens even to airmen flying round Everest), but these exhibitions of our own foolishness are an intrinsic part of climbing, and some malicious humorist might well take a number of narratives, like my story of the accidental ascent of Punta Rossa, and work them up into a useful and chastening book, 'The Climber's Guide to the Wrong Mountains'.

Whilst we are thinking of that great unwritten work we might turn aside for a moment to consider its companion volume: 'The Climber's Guide to Imaginary Mountains'. It would deal not with mountains like the 13,000ft. Mont Iseran, whose existence (like that of some Alpine huts) is purely cartographical, but with those nameless symbolic mountains that haunt our imagination. As the Wrong Mountains belong to the domain of humour, so the Mountains of Imagination (if we are cautious enough about the word 'imagination') belong to poetry. One can go astray among these mountains as easily as one can among the more material Alps, and our sense of humour, which often helps us to deal with hardships and humiliations, can also serve to check our wilder expeditions into the Mountains of Imagination, and to give us warning when we approach too near the point at which the sublime turns into something else.

I am not altogether a disciple of Hobbes: I do not share his distrust of poetry, his grimly practical view of religion, and his gloomy view of human nature; and though I agree, as any climber must, when he says that "men are wont to laugh at mischances and indecencies wherein lieth no humour at all," I wonder what he means by humour, and whether he would prefer us to weep and curse at all misfortune. For it is plain enough that most jokes *are* concerned with difficulties and mishaps: they remind us brutally of human limitations, they preserve our sense of proportion, or give it expression, and they restore us to reason when we are thinking of suicide or murder because we have stubbed our toe. Humour is often the seamy side of poetry, and a poem that cannot stand up to a joke or a parody with its brutal recollection of 'mischances and indecencies' is a bad poem.

Hobbes would have been a bad companion on a rope: there is a wildly non-utilitarian element in mountaineering which finds no place in his philosophy; there is a good deal of scope for poetry; and there is also something inherently funny in a sport in which you get up at 2 a.m., bruise your shins, blister your face, get one ear nicked by a falling stone and, after getting soaked in a rainstorm on a three-mile-long moraine, blunder into a hut after dark, only to find the Chasseurs Alpins sleeping on every inch of floor and table. When we explain that we do all this for pleasure, the psychoanalyst will always give us a special kind of look, and the ordinary citizen will feel that there is a joke lurking about somewhere, and that if there isn't, there ought to be. But this joke is the one joke that is missing: each of the separate pains and penalties of climbing has its classic joke, but the transcendental joke, the joke of transfinite order that would reconcile outsiders to our incomprehensible passion, does not exist. Our justification, if it is to be found at all, must be found in poetry; but the English as a race prefer humour to poetry, and we might find that if we billed ourselves as the world's ultimate practical jokers we would more often escape the awkward, "But *why* do you do it?"

Meanwhile we have all the separate constituent jokes of mountaineering: the Alpine flea, now less virulent than in the sixties (or are we a more hardy generation?), the sardine-tin on the virgin summit, the glacier that goes down faster than the climbers go up, the mountaineer who doesn't feel very well at the foot of the big crack. There is even the search-party joke — and anybody who has ever taken part in an unnecessary search party knows how necessary that joke is. It takes its best form, I think, in Dorothy Pilley's *Climbing Days*:

> The ground above the Cascade des Ignes is famous as a place for benighted parties. There is the remarkable story of the man the search party could not find. When in despair they went back to Arolla, there he was sitting in the hotel garden. "Wherever have you been? How did we miss you? Didn't your hear our shouts?" they asked. "Yes," replied the benighted one, "but they sounded so terrible and angry that I hid under a rock till you had gone by."

All these are what I would call functional jokes; I do not know whether to include in this category the story of Mrs. Aubrey Le Blond's traverse of the Zinal Rothorn, in which she got nearly down to Zinal, and then had to go back over the mountain to Zermatt because her skirt had been left under a rock on the Trift Glacier. It can hardly have been a joke at the time; in the middle distance it may have seemed excruciatingly funny; and now, when ladies are allowed to enter hotels in trousers, it seems quaint rather than funny, and creeps into the class of historical anecdote concerned with personal peculiarities rather than with climbing itself. The same may be said of the description of Coolidge as "the American who climbs with his aunt and his dog," or of that former President of the Club, to whom the innkeeper ascribed immense political powers as "il presidente di Londra." Conway's guide, too, will be remembered as the man who said, "It is the natural instinct of man to run from gendarmes"; and Hope and Kirkpatrick will always survive in Alpine legend as the inventors of the aluminium collar-stud. But a whimsical, nostalgic flavour finds its way into these anecdotes and appellations: they become tinged with regret for an age in which men could roam over the Alps making new ascents every other day, when frontier guards were a nuisance, but not a danger, and when male climbers would no more think of entering a hotel without a collar-stud than Mrs. Le Blond would go down to Zinal without a skirt.

The personal anecdote, the incident or phrase that reveal a character and at the same time helps us to make light of our own troubles and difficulties, finds a natural home in narratives of climbing. Tilman, in *Nanda Devi*, after weeks of difficult climbing and still more troublesome descents through bamboo jungle, exclaims characteristically at the sight of the first mud village, "We shall be down in time for tea." A more scholarly and no less effective manner was that of Buxton on the first ascent of the Aiguille de Bionnassay. He spent the day arguing about Greek and Sanskrit roots, and halfway through a cold, uncomfortable bivouac he first agreed with Craufurd Grove that inasmuch as all things have an end, even a night on the Bionnassay must finish some time, then added thoughtfully, "that in the present case the question was, which would finish first, the night or ourselves."

The deep satisfaction that we get from climbing is something that many of us would like to express in poetry rather than in prose, partly because the rhythm of poetry is the more memorable, and partly because poetic rhythms encourage us to pitch our sentiments a little higher than we can do in prose without falling into the lush verbiage of that familiar purple bog. Those who have tried know it is very hard to write that kind of poetry. There is a poem by James Reeves, called *Climbing a Mountain*, but that scarcely meets our need, for it describes the feelings of an inexperienced amateur. In the more traditional measures appropriate to unqualified enthusiasm there are the poems of Douglas Freshfield and Geoffrey Winthrop Young. Even the most modest descriptive poetry has its dangers: the rhythms run away with us, the mood sweeps up into the false heroic, familiar epithets come away in our hand, and before we know where we are we have stepped off into the empty air.

Most of us would be content to avoid the problem if we could escape as elegantly as Godley, who uses the familiar, high-sounding epithets half-comically, half in earnest. He pokes fun at himself and his friends for feeling so strongly about it all, and he reminds them that, "They will dine on mule and marmot and on mutton made of goat." It is a mood familiar in the light verse of English academic writers – among others, Calverley and J. K. Stephen. It is not the mood of enthusiasm, but the mood in which one smilingly deprecates one's own enthusiasm, without being ashamed of it.

The central problem, of plain unwhimsical description, remains; and beyond that there is the problem of imaginative writing. Wordsworth's lines on the Simplon, Shelley's *Mont Blanc*, and Coleridge's *Hymn before Sunrise* all contrive to express imaginative insight without falsifying or distorting the material vision; but all these belong to the poetry of mountains rather than the poetry of mountaineering. Perhaps, in the end, pure descriptive poetry, whether of mountains or of mountaineering, is not possible: the underlying significance that we read into our experience is inseparable from the experience itself. Certainly Freshfield and Geoffrey Young are seldom content with simple physical description. But it is just here that the dangers of falling into empty air are most acute: the precision and brevity of prose are lost; writers who would never venture to exaggerate or over-emphasise in a 'paper communicated', are tempted to throw off the rope and abandon honest climbing for a titanic struggle with the infinite cliffs of the wildly impossible. Poetry, when it rises above the level of accurate reporting, differs from common speech in something more than the use of metaphor and rhythm, for the poet writes under a sense of compulsion, and sometimes disregards the claims of reason and material fact; but the poet who will not take the trouble to make accurate concrete observations is not likely to get any depth of meaning into his allegories and metaphors. 'Aesthetic distance' is not the same thing as a colourless abstraction; and a strong and precise emotion is not communicated by a hackneyed style eked out by wild exaggeration. Like the prophet and the dreamer, the poet is all the better for keeping his eyes wide open in his ordinary waking moments.

In this matter the prose writers of mountaineering have something to teach the poets: consider the accuracy of Tyndall's observations, and the vigour of his images: "Veils of the silkiest cloud began to draw themselves round the mountain, and stretch in long gauzy filaments through the air, where they finally curdled to common cloud, and lost the grace and beauty of their infancy." Or turn to Craufurd Grove, when he speaks of "the gradual extinction of sound all over the glacier as the cold became more intense." The word 'extinction' is right not only scientifically but also sensuously: the middle syllable suggests both the cold and the last sharp cracks as the glacier freezes; and imaginatively also, for the sound does not merely *stop*: it is extinguished in another element, the encroaching silence.

In modern writers we find the same capacity to choose the illuminating word or phrase: Dorothy Pilley tells us that the rocks of the Devil's Kitchen are "rather like slippery and brittle toffee," or that she herself, after being pulled out of a crevasse, walked, "for the rest of a day as though on a soap-film." If we try to give the impression of extreme delicacy by direct description — "I walked more carefully than I have ever done before or since" — we are left with the same information, but we no longer have the *feeling* of the experience. A good metaphor or simile plays upon our senses, and no amount of exaggeration, no deliberate working up of the tawdry vocabulary of purple patches, will do the work of one apt phrase.

Wordsworth, Coleridge, Tennyson find such phrases when they write of mountains, and so at times does F. W. H. Myers, but on the whole the poetry of mountains shows all the vices of bad description. It is bloated, pompous and sugary, and the explanation seems to be that it deals with the Wrong Mountains — not the Wrong Mountains of material reality, but the Wrong Mountains of imagination. It expresses a kind of sham religion, a sentimental daydream in which brutal realities are not transcended but conveniently ignored; and as one kind of blindness or evasion leads to another, this easy-going religiosity finds expression in images and rhythms that are as crude and limited as its theology.

The phrase, "the religiosity of mountains," is Mr. Arnold Lunn's, not mine, but I would like to explain more fully what I understand it to mean. From the earliest times the loneliness, immensity and permanence of mountains have made men think of a power beyond themselves. The superhuman force of cataract and glacier, the gloom of mountain forest, the sudden contrast of the minute mountain flower, and the pure contradiction of snow and sunlight, have all helped to fascinate and terrify; and the difficulty of reaching the heights, with their wide vision over a landscape of towns, fields, rivers and all the world of ordinary life, has made the climbing of mountains an image of life itself, with its difficulties, dangers, and moments of unexpected insight.

Material imagery is always necessary to the writer who is concerned with spiritual reality; and it is natural that the religious writer should turn to mountains for his imagery — the gods dwelt on Olympus, and Dante's Earthly Paradise was set on a mountain. The Austrian poet Rilke, in one of his poems,* uses mountains explicitly as symbols of human existence and the struggles of the human spirit:

> Exposed on the mountains of the heart. Look, how small there,
> Look: the last village of words, and higher,
> But still how small, yet one remaining
> Farmstead of feeling. Can you not see it?
> Exposed on the mountains of the heart. Bare rock
> Under our hands. Yet here too
> Something blooms: from the dumb precipice
> A plant unknowing blooms singing into the air.
> And the knower himself? Ah, he began by knowing,
> Now silent, exposed on the high hills of the heart.
>
> And here, with undistracted mind,
> Roam many creatures, sure-footed mountain beasts,
> Pausing and passing. And the great bird dwelling in secret
> Soars round the pure, forbidding summits—beyond all shelter,
> Here, on the high hills of the heart.

More often, as in Wordsworth, the symbolism is implicit, but whether the symbolism is explicit or implicit, people are apt to take the imagery for the reality, and the great nineteenth-century movement against the Christian religion, influenced perhaps by the kind of pantheism that we find in Wordsworth, served to encourage the error. The symbol was taken for the reality, and while ordinary people talked of listening to the sermons of Doctor Greenfields, the climber talked about mountaineering as a religion.

*The translation given here is adapted from Mr. J. B. Leishman's version.

Mountaineering is a game, a sport, a recreation, the best of recreations. It takes all our energy and attention, it sets us a job that we can do, but only just do; for the time being it reduces the complexities of life to neat simplicity; it calls for qualities that are valuable in civil life; it gives a harmless outlet to instincts and desires that might otherwise turn to evil; and it offers an experience rich in symbolic significance. But it is not real life and it is not religion. There is no virtue in the exercise that it gives to valuable qualities unless we turn those qualities to good account when we are no longer playing; and there is a real danger in the experience if we confuse the act of submitting ourselves to the conditions and difficulties of mountaineering with the act of submitting our will to a spiritual power beyond ourselves. Mountains may be symbols or images of some other reality, but the worship of images as if they were something more than images is a form of superstition.

Often, in mountaineering poetry (and sometimes in prose), this pantheistic heresy is combined with another. I mean, the doctrine of the unreality of evil. There is a sense in which the religious poet is concerned to show the transcendental good arising from the struggle of good and evil; but to say this is not to deny the reality of evil. The existence of evil, in the world and in ourselves, is as real and demonstrable as the existence of crevasses in the Mer de Glace and bad rock on the Matterhorn; and to ignore it is to live in a fool's paradise. It is natural that the kind of poetry which expresses what is sometimes called an optimistic view should ignore the real humiliations of climbing—the blisters, the occasional belly-ache, the foul air in the huts. A make-believe religion is imaged by a world of make-believe—a world in which all Hobbes's "mis-chances and indecencies" are not transcended, not treated as part of the material out of which transcendent good arises, but merely ignored. To select pretty details, as Tennyson does in his lines on Monte Rosa, is harmless: a selecton of that kind is still funda-mentally true, and it would not be wholly upset by the intrusion of some realistic detail taken from the seamy side. Poetry can be honest without treating the intrinsically ugly equally with the beautiful. The danger begins when selection becomes distortion of fact, so that the poem falsifies both the sentiment and the world described, and rests on a religion that is bad because it cannot be applied to the real world.

Judging from internal evidence, the writers of this sentimental poetry are seldom climbers. It would be unkind to take an example from the minor offenders of our day, and for me it would be unfair, for I have served my time as a reviewer and my feelings about bad poetry are exceptionally strong. Let us turn to Matthew Arnold, who would certainly agree with most of our contentions, but sets us a bad example in *Rugby Chapel*. In that poem he has a long descriptive passage:

> Cheerful with friends we set forth:
> Then, on the height, comes the storm —

Bad judges of the weather, evidently, Arnold and his friends; and they pay for their imprudence:

> Friends who set forth at our side
> Falter, are lost in the storm.

But there is no practical nonsense about trying to rescue them: the note is too romantically heroic to admit common sense:

> With frowning foreheads, with lips
> Sternly compressed, we strain on,
> On, and at nightfall at last
> Come to the end of our way —

Happily, they arrive at an inn, and the innkeeper, who knows this kind of traveller, asks whom they have left in the snow:

> Sadly we answer: We bring
> Only ourselves! we lost
> Sight of the rest in the storm.
> Hardly ourselves we fought through,
> Stripp'd, without friends, as we are;
> Friends, companions, and train,
> The avalanche swept from our side.

We don't really talk of disasters in that tone of voice, and, to put it mildly, disasters don't happen like that in a well-organised party. Arnold knew quite well that the whole passage was only a metaphor for his real meaning: he was trying, as he always did try, to say that life was a struggle, and that difficulty and danger were inseparable from life, or at all events from any life of value; but it would have been far more convincing if it had been more practical, and if it had contained less of the Excelsior spirit and more of the cheerful acceptance of real indignities and sufferings.

There is another interesting point in *Rugby Chapel*. Here, as in many passages of this kind, the heroes are travellers, presumably with some good reason for making the journey. The mountaineer seldom has any such reason: his climb has to be its own justification, and in this it symbolishes life even better than a journey does. Climbing derives its most profound symbolic meaning from its gratuitousness, its apparent pointlessness. The climber, however tentatively and reluctantly, accepts risks as well as discomforts and indignities, and unless he is a professional he cannot say that he is compelled to do so. He makes a free choice, and deliberately rejects greater safety for less. The final entry in Hartmanns Nanga Parbat diary is one that inevitably turns our attention to this aspect of climbing. Hartmann had spent the day making a track up to Camp 5, and in his diary he writes:

> June 14. It was wonderfully fine and I was making height so easily without breathing spaces, and that moreover in snow where usually I broke in more deeply than the others and had consequently to undergo greater fatigue. I wondered at all this and was confident and grateful. I think moreover that I smiled all day to myself—well, it was because of my son's birthday! Slowly, one after the other, came the Sherpas, each throwing his load down on the ice nose.

Hartmann had no designs on the reader, and it is only our knowledge that those were his last words, and most likely his last thought, that gives them their special poignancy. "I think moreover that I smiled all day to myself." The words are not poetry, yet they make a great deal of mountain poetry look silly. They are not sentimental, for the sentiment is neither exaggerated nor misplaced, and yet it would be almost impossible for them to occur in poetry without being grossly sentimental. No one could use such an incident in poetry without first answering the question the whole disaster makes us ask: What right has anyone to throw away his life like that? Granted that a good climber, once he decides upon his mountain and his route, uses all his skill and knowledge to minimise every kind of risk, what right had he to take the risk at all?

I think there is an answer: but all the subsidiary reasons we give, all the adequate reasons that justify our scampering up and down familiar Alpine peaks, are ruled out. It is plainly inadequate to talk of the view, the exhilaration of physical effort, the satisfaction of escaping for a time from all the problems and annoyances of daily life and losing oneself in a job that takes all one's thought and skill. If climbing were nothing more than a brief escape from worry and responsibility it would be the same as any other sport, but the fact that we can talk of the poetry of mountaineering and keep near to the subject of great poetry shows that there is an element in climbing that is lacking in golf or motor-racing. If climbing were valuable merely for its contributions to scientific knowledge, there would be no excuse for our prejudice against dynamite and iron ladders. If it were merely a healthy exercise, there would be no excuse for occasionally risking our necks. To justify mountaineering in the fullest sense, we must justify the loss of life, the deliberate taking of risks. And I think the only answer is in the sheer uselessness of the loss: man can preserve his dignity only by showing that he is not afraid of anything, not even death.

To take a stupid risk in crossing the road or to amuse ourselves by drawing lots for suicide would not satisfy the condition, for it would show merely that we did not value life at all. There must be something to set against the risk, and something adequate; and there, I think, all the other reasons for climbing are thrown into the scale. The sacrifice is not necessary: the risk brings no material gain, but it offers something—the exhilaration, the sense of clear vision—which partly excuses the risk. And then, for the rest, the risk excuses itself. It is a demonstration that man is not wholly tied to grubbing for his food, not wholly tied by family and social loyalties; that there are states of mind and spirit that he values more highly than life itself on any lower level.

A simpler explanation might be offered: it may be said that our appreciation of life is keenest when our hold on it is most precarious; and certainly a psychopathic passion for living in a state of artificial intensity may account for the conduct of some climbers. But for most people it is only a small part of the explanation: the whole explanation cannot be grasped unless we have a sense of intrinsic value such as we find in religion. A thing is not good for any purpose or end, but just because; and sacrifices are good because they show superiority to all mere utilitarian values: they show an excess and overflow which is really a gesture of confidence and vitality. The primitive man who sacrifices his last loaf to the gods is not necessarily a fool: he may die of starvation, but he shows the spirit of a race that will not die.

This relation between mountaineering and religion is one that almost everyone has felt, but it need not be mistaken for identity. If we are to use mountaineering as a symbol, let us keep clear the distinction between symbol and reality, and let us at the same time preserve the vitality and scope of the symbol by frankly admitting both the mischances and indecencies of climbing. In this way we can do something to ensure that our interpretation of life is not a sentimental daydream but a comprehensive and adaptable philosophy: if we use our sense of humour wisely, we can use it not merely to save us, as it saved Godley, from an embarrassing public exhibition of private sentiment, but also to remind us that mountaineering, even when it supplies the symbols of our religious thought, is still distinct from religion. The Guide to the Mountains of Imagination is distinct from the works of Ball and Coolidge, but it should be not less practical, and to guard against our own vanity and exaggeration this Guide to the Sublime should be read in conjunction with the Guide to the Ridiculous.

from THE ALPINE JOURNAL *1941*

Scafell Pike

NORMAN NICHOLSON

Look
Along the well
Of the street,
Between the gasworks and the neat
Sparrow-stepped gable
Of the Catholic chapel,
High
Above tilt and crook

Of the tumbledown
Roofs of the town—
Scafell Pike,
The tallest hill in England.

How small it seems,
So far away,
No more than a notch
On the plate-glass window of the sky!
Watch
A puff of kitchen smoke
Block out peak and pinnacle—
Rock-pile of volcanic lava
Half a mile thick
Scotched out
At the click of an eye.

Look again
In five hundred, a thousand or ten
Thousand years:
A ruin where
The chapel was; brown
Rubble and scrub and cinders where
The gasworks used to be;
No roofs, no town,
Maybe no men;
But yonder where a lather-rinse of cloud pours down
The spiked wall of the sky-line, see,
Scafell Pike
Still there.

                        from SEA TO THE WEST

Postscript

CLAUD SCHUSTER

The great heat on the walk up to the hut was a warning of what was to come. The hut itself was even hotter and stuffier than huts usually are. There was a lifelessness in the air outside and the stars seemed dim. A lassitude verging on peevishness, hung on the party. The hay seemed lumpier, the boards harder, and the snores of others less tolerable. Thus, as might have been expected, the early morning was very dark and uninspiring. The snow in the great couloir was hardly frozen; about it, on the face which leads to the ridge, the going was worse. The snow patches were unstable; little stones slipped, and feet stumbled; the other fellows seemed to let the rope catch and drag; the pace was always too fast or too slow. It was difficult to refrain from hard words. But the moment's pause at the bergschrund, as the first man cut a step or two and cleared it, and each man had to reach well out to follow, pulled the party together, and, once on the ridge itself, they began to move like a team. The rocks were dry and firm and good. The holds were small and far apart, far enough to stretch the muscles and every now and then to call for that little extra exertion which gives the delightful sense of accomplishment as each obstacle is surmounted. Every now and then the ridge suddenly steepened and presented itself as a sheer face, and, when this happened, sometimes the leader attacked it frontally, taking perhaps a shoulder or a knee from his immediate follower; or sometimes, with a long reach into apparent vacancy, he disappeared round the corner and his rope was seen wriggling away out of sight to the sound of grunts and scratches until, freed from the belay, it pointed upwards, and his brown beard and his merry eyes looked over the wall at his companions. Whichever course was taken the rest of the party was glad of the respite, for the pace was too hot to last for ever.

Halfway up the ridge there was a halt for food, and someone said something about the weather, but none paid much attention. Then the march was resumed. It was one of those climbs which are said to present no technical difficulty. Everyone felt he was climbing as he had never climbed before in his life, and that everyone else was doing the same. One rhythmic soul animated the party. They climbed as one man, perfectly confident, perfectly fit, thrilled with physical delight and expectation. As they neared the summit there was a pause. The leader pulled from his pocket a handkerchief which had once been white, and bound it over his hat and under his chin. The followers took each his own precaution. The leader grasped the great rock which barred their progress and with a heave, his legs dangling behind him, flung himself upwards. Each followed, grasped from above and pulled onwards, and met the gale and rolled over to what shelter could be gained from the summit cairn, and lay there panting. The wineskin passed round without a word; indeed the roaring of the wind forbade intelligible speech. The great ritualists of the party filled and sucked vainly at their pipes to give the mountain the due incense of tobacco. The leader yelled unintelligibly at his companions what were probably meant to be words of caution, and the descent began.

This was a very different affair from the ascent. The tilt of the strata running through the mountains set every hold the wrong way. The little stones, loosely balanced on the sloping surfaces, slipped under the feet, or of their own volition. Everything was rotten, and the towers which crowned the ridge were undercut and trembled at a touch. The passage, which would have been merely unpleasant in calm weather, was horrible in the storm. Underfoot the stones were coated with a light film of frozen damp. Below the wind came howling upwards, dislodging pebbles and snow, throwing them upwards and curling back from the ridge like a retreating wave. The rope, soon frozen stiff, swung out before the tempest, catching on every projection, trammelling, dragging. Very little snow was falling; but what there was lashed the face, clogged the glasses and filled what holds there were. The cold was bitter. Yet speed was impossible. Every step must be made good. Every man must secure himself at every instant, and be ready to secure his friends. The sun was blotted out. Every familiar landmark had disappeared. Only now and then the gale tore the mist asunder and showed some fantastic form upon the ridge, or disclosed some apparently bottomless precipice below. All sense of time was lost. It seemed as though the party had already entered into hell and must toil for ever downwards in an eternity of peril and of fear.

Suddenly the leader stopped. He seemed to yell something. His followers joined him and he pointed his finger below. By his gestures it was possible to discern with aching eyes that here the ridge stopped sharp, as if cut off with a knife, and descended in an unbroken and impassable face whose base was shrouded in the fog. Intelligible speech was inaudible, but the course to be followed was clear. The side of the face must be descended into the funnel between the converging ridges, and the glacier gained. It seemed pleasant to feel that so much had been accomplished, and any change from the ridge was a welcome as a relief. But those who harboured such thoughts soon had occasion for repentance. The slope was extremely steep, devoid of handholds, and garnished with stones, stuck loosely in thin ice or unstable snow. Furthermore, though on the ridge nothing could hit you except what the wind slung through the air or your companions or you yourself dislodged from the towers, here everything at once seemed to fall; the mountain seemed in dissolution; your feet slipped and sent down pebbles on those below, and, the further you descended, by so much more terrible was the rattle of the stones projected by those above, and the scream of the heavier, invisible missiles whizzing through the air from the rampart of the mountain. In this infernal cannonade some degree of speed was essential. Everyone, as soon as he had attained some precarious security, must wave his companion on, and, as he best might without belay, play out the rope to him inch by inch, taking his weight and trusting vaguely that, if the strain suddenly became a jerk, he could avert catastrophe. Then, casting off false pride, he must himself bear on the rope and yet keep his body erect and his feet firm on the treacherous surface. With a frozen rope, kinking and intractable, these manoeuvres were peculiarly difficult to perform.

The distance to the glacier was not great and the time occupied not so long as it appeared to all. The moment came when the second man found the leader standing motionless. He came close up to him. The leader jumped apparently into space. The third man came close to the second. The second, as an act of faith, imitated his leader and instantly found himself on his face in deep snow, with his feet sliding away into nothing. Number three and number four followed, and wasting no time in the recovery of breath or in shovelling snow out of neck or pockets, for stones of every size, some embedded in the soft snow, some lying on the surface, proclaimed what kind of place this was, all rushed down. Again, however the slope broke off abruptly. They were come to the overhanging lip of the bergschrund. Anchored as best he could and leaning on the rope, the leader extended his rigid body and peered over. The prospect was not alluring. Turning to one side he cut steps on a level along the upper edge—such steps as no one would have dared to use save in extremity. Then suddenly he turned downwards again. Balanced on nothing he struck with his whole force on the rotten ice. Once he struck, and twice, and thrice, and then sprang back as a huge piece, compacted of ice and snow and little stones, broke off with a crack. Down it went with a boom and dissolving into fragments, tinkled into the gulf. "Come, quick, quick," he cried and jumped again, this time a little outwards as well as downwards, pulling the next man out of his steps, so that his jump was more than half a tumble, and he would have rolled down on to the flat glacier but for the arms that received and held him fast. Then breathless, he could at least look round and observe the lack of elegance of those who came after.

Now for the first time all could realise that the snow, which had seemed to fall but thinly on the ridge was coming down in thick heavy flakes. The wind, though it could be heard roaring beyond and over the great wall from which they had descended, could not reach them. Whatever might yet lie before the party, some rest and some restoration of their strained energies seemed imperative. Walking along the lower lip of the great crevasse until they reached a place which afforded some refuge from the mountain's artillery, they halted and took shelter in the rift itself. They scraped off the snow, rubbed, banged and kicked half-frozen noses and fingers and toes, contemplated cuts and bruises and inspected the damage. One stone had cut through a knapsack and penetrated a wine-skin from which the precious fluid was slowly oozing. The rope was all but severed in two places. The bread was frozen and the butter stiff. Everyone was strained and tired, but all were happy. They ate sardines whole with their fingers and didn't care that the oil ran down their chins. They congratulated one another exuberantly and extravagantly, and made feeble jokes, which seemed to them the height of wit, and laughed excessively. There was toil before them, but the danger was over. Perhaps it had never been so great as it had seemed, but it had hung round them and penetrated their sub-conscious minds, each perilous step the prelude to destruction. Now it was gone and forever. Its departure released the thousand trivialities which make up the life of man. It was not a moment for solemn thoughts. They had come to safety out of death, and life, rough jokes, rough wine, coarse food made up their being.

The march over the glacier must be begun. It was interminable. Excitement and fear were past. Nothing remained but labour and discomfort, snow sometimes to the knees, the shinbone striking against the edge of the small concealed crevasse, the sudden deviation from the direct line as the axe of the leader revealed a crevasse too wide to pass; the eyes aching from the effort; the muscles released from the exertion of the ridge; the clinging damp of the snow as it melted through their coverings, the lurking fear that in the fog they might not have hit the right direction, and the effort not to say so lest the leader should be disheartened and the party discouraged; the general feeling of anti-climax; all these made it difficult to keep going, vexed, depressed. To these succeeded a period of sheer boredom. Nothing seemed worth while except to stop, to have done with all this nonsense, to do something violent so as to break the monotony of ceaselessly dragging one foot after another, of bending under the weight of the sack, of treading an eternal path which led nowhere. Again suddenly it had led some-where. They were at the foot of a rock. The wind had dropped enough to allow one to hear oneself speak. Someone said that the hut was up there. Then why the devil didn't one climb up? No!— the leader must needs circle round. He came to a cleft running transversely upwards. Had one to begin climbing again!! The rocks were all icy, but he began quickly and lightly. Why the devil did he want to go so fast? It wasn't fair. There's lots of time. There's a knee banged against the side of the cleft. They are up. Where's the beastly hut? We've come wrong after all. No! there it looms. This path is very rough. Why couldn't we stick to the snow? Heavens! is the hut locked? No! He's pushed the door open. We have had a day.

To dwell on what one eats and drinks, though often pleasant to oneself, is always tedious, and may be nauseating to others. So the details of the next period can be passed over. But its emotions remain in the memory, perhaps for that short span of human life which we call 'forever'. Night has come; and, according to all the canons, the climbers should have been addressing it in apostrophe:

> Oh Night
> And storm and darkness, ye are wondrous strong,
> Yet lovely in your strength, as is the light of a dark
> eye in woman.

But to the mountaineer, unless he has been extraordinarily fortunate at cards, nothing could possibly be less like an eye of any kind in woman than a storm among the hills. To our party it had meant not only an emotional disturbance, but a practical fear. To them admiration of the power of nature had been subdued by a lively anticipation of rheumatism. Their wet knickerbockers, clinging round their legs, their boots, squelching with water, forbade them to ask the night to be to any of them

> A sharer in the fierce and far delight
> A portion of the tempest and of thee.

Sensible men, in these circumstances, however fully charged with sensibility, ask to share nothing with anyone but a roof, a wisp of hay, some hot soup, and, if no beer is available, the last dregs of wine, still redolent of the goatskin from which they came. The party, having tasted these delights, delivered from the instant peril and the chilling fatigue, can open the hut door and contemplate the night. The storm has died, though the winds are still fierce round the ridges on which the climbers lately gasped and clung. They still drive small white clouds across the summit, and, from time to time, obscure a moon that looks on Italy. From afar below comes the roar of the cataract, swollen by the rains of the afternoon. Nearer, but still in the deep shadow of the peak, and the more deeply hid because of the sharp brilliance of the foreground, lie the highest pastures; and you can guess that the cows are mooing uneasily and can catch at intervals a round note from a bell. Otherwise it is very still and very cold. The mystery of the struggle through which they had passed, and of the ease and peace now so hardly gained, were upon them. They crept back into the hay and fell asleep in the full companionship of the hills.

Or shall we tell the story like this?

4 August 1890. *Verfluchtighorn* (4,159m., 13,626ft.). *First ascent of the North-East Ridge, descent by the South-West Ridge.* Same party, with Abraham Beidenblatten and Jakob Schnorr as porter. Left Amicitia hut at 1.30 a.m. and immediately took to the great couloir which gives access to the upper Wasserlein glacier (3 a.m.), crossed the glacier and ascended the rocky face above it to the foot of the great North-East Ridge (reached at 7 a.m.). After half-an-hour's halt for the breakfast, began to climb the ridge. Though steep it presents no technical difficulties and can be followed, almost in its entirety, to the summit. The most interesting portions of the ascent consist in the passage of the three great gendarmes which are conspicuous from the valley or in the panorama from the Aussichtshorn. These occasioned some loss of time and were, in each case circumvented by traverses on one side of the ridge or another. The summit was reached at 11 a.m., and the well-known South-West Ridge was then followed until it breaks off. A traverse was then made on to the Upper Zwischengrat glacier (reached at 2 p.m.), and that glacier was descended to the bergschrund. Some difficulty was experienced in hitting off the best place to cross the 'schrund, but the lower glacier was reached at three, and, after a short halt, was crossed in deep snow and the Friedenshütte attained at 5.30 p.m. Throughout the descent the party were greatly hampered and delayed by storm and fog.

You will have perceived that, whichever method of description be preferred, the whole of this story is ficticious, a kind of pot-pourri of many Alpine memories, drawn some from the experience of the writer, and some from those of others. Perhaps even it might be taken to be in some sense an allegory, illustrating human life, and, in particular, the Alpine career—the high hopes, a little dashed with apprehension, of the early morning, the glorious achievement of full day, the fierce struggle of the early afternoon, the dull relentless endeavour as the day wears to evening, the calm acceptance of the night in peace and hope. Only, unhappily neither life nor mountains are in the least like that. We are not, nor ought we to be, satisfied. "I've had my day, I've had my day; and nothing on earth can take away the taste of that," said Learoyd (or was it Ortheris?). But, in uttering the sentiment (recorded by one who was then a very young man), he, like Oliver Twist, betrayed his appetite for more. It is a mistake to suppose that old age brings its consolations, or that passage of years brings peace. There comes a partial and resentful resignation. Hear also what Voltaire says:

> L'amitié vint à mon secours
> Elle n'était peut-être aussi tendre
> Mais moins vive que les amours.
> Touché de sa beauté nouvelle,
> Et de sa lumière éclairé,
> Je la suivis; mais je pleurai,
> De ne pouvoir plus suivre qu'elle.

There is a further matter to be borne in mind when planning for senectitude and listening to those who recommend water-gruel and a crutch. A friend writes to me, commenting on the fact that, my legs failing, I have taken to a horse, "as to this Jorrocks business, I get your point, and there is a good deal in it. If you persistently fall down, into, over, or under everything that appears in your path, it is at any rate probable that you will avoid a painful and peevish old age; which is probably the most unpleasant thing in nature. My only resource will be to get under a No. 11 bus."

Everything however, comes to an end, and the time arrives when

> You grow so very fat
> That you climb the Gorner Grat
> Or perhaps the Little Scheideck
> And are rather proud of that.

when you take more pleasure in other people's prowess than your own, and nestle more comfortably as you turn in bed before you put out the light, at the thought that someone else is sleeping in a stuffy hut, and will, before you wake next morning, have already endured unspeakable discomforts and unnecessary privations. There are few more delightful exercises than to sit below the top of the Riffelhorn on warm rocks and to lower your grand-daughter down the first hundred feet of the glacier couloir, and then hold the rope for her to ascend, pointing out her faults in style and remembering how rigorous teachers seized 'your' youth,

*Editor's Note: Compare this with Sophocles' Great Synthesis of the same poetic commonplace — "Desire is an insane and cruel master."

And purged its faith, and trimmed its fire
Showed you the high, white star of truth,
There bade 'you' gaze and there aspire,
Even now their whispers pierce the gloom.

And you can hear their adjurations to stand up and lean out from the rock across some fifty years. When all this comes upon you, and you feel a fatal tendency to reminiscence and anecdotage, and you are commanded to sing, or at least to read, for your supper, what is left to you? Long ago you have written all that was in you and spilt your experience in a hotch-potch of adventure and emotion. The letter to a friend is finished. It has set out fully all that was done and thought and felt. You read it through again and find something missing, something which you have tried to say over and over again, now in simple words, now in elaborate phrases. It is not likely that you will succeed where you have failed so often. But you must make the attempt and say, once more, how well worthwhile it was. Much of your time was wasted through sloth, or failing courage, or lack of imagination. But, where you seized on life with both hands, whether you succeeded or failed, there you triumphed.

I do not mean by this that it is a rational pastime, or even good mountaineering, to come down the Couloir du Lion in the middle of a hot August afternoon. I have myself chosen a night in the Bergli Hut in preference to the great wall below it when the avalanches were thundering down to the Lower Grindelwald Glacier. The dangers in these two places can neither be averted nor subdued and I cannot see that any advantage is gained by incurring them. "Who," says the wise man, "will pity a charmer that is bitten by the serpent, or any such as come nigh wild beasts?" The last thing to be inculcated is a challenge to danger for its own sake or for the sensation to be plucked from it. There must be dangers in this as in all forms of bodily activity. It is good mountaineering to acquire the knowledge to recognise, and the skill and endurance to overcome them. And the infinite delight of the pursuit is not lessened but enhanced because forethought and care are necessary elements in an alpine equipment.

I have wandered from my text and from the material of my post-script. Let me repeat it. All was very good. All the labour as well as the joy, knit into the very frame of the mountaineer, gives him not only a more vigorous body, but a richer mind, a fuller life; and however feeble his limbs may grow, however faint his courage, still, as he looks backwards and forwards, he would ask nothing more for those whom he wishes well than that they, like he, should be carried away in the spirit to a great and high mountain, and should find the things which were revealed to him.

from THE FELL AND ROCK JOURNAL *1940*

Notes on the Articles

Coast to Coast on the Granite Slasher
An impressionistic account of some of the harder big-wall aid-climbs in California's Yosemite Valley, by a young Australian climber now resident in the USA.

End of a Climb
John Menlove Edwards was a profoundly innovative explorer of the rock faces of North Wales in the 1930's and 1940's, who brought about a major re-assessment of what could be considered climbable. A practising psychiatrist, he was a conscientious objector in the Second World War. The break-up of a love affair with Wilfrid Noyce precipitated a mental collapse from which he never really recovered. He died by his own hand in 1958.

On the Profundity Trail
Doug Scott wishes to acknowledge his debt, in this account of an ascent of Salathé Wall, to Doug Robinson's seminal article *The Climber as Visionary* (q.v.).

Nightshift in Zero
The second ascent of Zero Gully on Ben Nevis, by the formidable team of Haston and Smith, with the novice Wightman. Highly evocative of the atmosphere of Scottish ice-climbing in the early sixties.

Speeding Down South
Jim Bridwell is acknowledged as a leading Yosemite climber. Latterly his career has taken off into the realms of super-alpinism, the account here of his extremely fast ascent of Cerro Torre being one of his most impressive achievements.

No Big Cigar
The Peak District of Derbyshire has always been a forcing-ground for British rock-climbing. This article charts the competition for first free ascents of some of the old aid routes, and describes the second ascent of one of the most important of them.

Snakes and Ladders
The first British ascent of the Swiss-Italian Route on Cima Ovest, by Robin Smith and Dougal Haston.

The Only Blasphemy
Solo climbing on the hard test pieces of Joshua Tree – a granite climbing area in Southern California. The title of the article obviates the need for comment.

On Tree Climbing
In company with George Mallory, often as leader, Harold Porter made many of the hardest pre-First World War ascents in Snowdonia and was a champion of guideless alpinism. But this piece is in more playful vein.

Trapdoor Fandango
Although this is well-back-from-the-edge compared to *The Only Blasphemy*, it is interesting to speculate on whether putting these thoughts down on paper is yet another aspect of the doom-testing, the dance on the trapdoor?

Fortunatus
Dorothy Pilley, wife of the literary critic I. A. Richards, here describes an incident on the Direct Route of Glyder Fach. When pressed for the identity of 'Fortunatus' she replied that "I had better not divulge this as he was a member of the Alpine Club and his daughter has been a friend of mine for fifty years and could easily be upset."

All That Glory
Bettembourg's book, *The White Death* from which this passage is taken, is one of the more honest accounts of Himalayan climbing to have appeared in recent years.

Pass the Mirror
For all that this expedition opted for a pretty tedious route up the mountain, the book contains some delightful vignettes, the one printed here being my favourite.

Welsh Interlude
Jean Morin, Nea's husband and a well-known alpinist and GHM member in the inter-war period, was shot down in 1943, whilst on a secret mission with Free French forces.

Beltane Fire
An account of some early ascents of the hard Lakeland routes of the late seventies and an interesting commentary on the peculiar problems of seconding difficult rock-climbs.

States of the Art
The title says it all – this is the super-athletic style which transformed rock-climbing from the mid-seventies onwards. Compare it to the traditionalism of the next piece.

Solo on Cloggy
Wilf Noyce, killed in the Pamirs with Robin Smith in 1962, was a gifted mountaineer and respected climbing writer. Curving Crack, first climbed by Colin Kirkus ten years before Noyce's solo ascent, is graded Very Severe.

Kamet Seen and Conquered
The 1931 expedition to Kamet (25,447ft.) put seven members on the highest summit then reached by man.

Robbins – On the Plank
Pat Ament, multi-faceted Colorado rock-star, is at his best in capturing the character and mannerisms of his fellow American climbers.

Asgard Outing
As a clear, succinct, and strong-mindedly reasonable account of a small expedition to a relatively unknown area, this could hardly be bettered. Nunn has been a potent and enthusiastic force in British mountaineering for several decades.

Hetch Hetchy: First Impressions
It is very refreshing, amongst the aridity of much mountain writing, to encounter an author as stimulating in his approach to the mountain environment as Rowell. .

African Escapade
When the remote situation, length of rock, height of the mountain, and relative inexperience of the two climbers are taken into account, this first ascent of the West Ridge of Mount Kenya must rank with the major alpine achievements of the time.

Potato Medallist
Kirkus's delightful little instructional book, *Let's Go Climbing*, from which this account is taken, has probably lured more people into the sport than any other volume. Modern ascensionists of Clogwyn du'r Arddu's Great Slab will scarcely recognise the bare and polished present-day climb from Kirkus's description.

Jack of Diamonds
An interesting counterpoint to Robbins' celebrated *Tis-sa-ack* – this time the record of an ascent undertaken in sympathetic company, with one of the legendary figures of American climbing.

Wintering Out
Alan Rouse, golden boy of British rock-climbing in the late sixties and early seventies, successfully made the transition to alpine and greater ranges mountaineering. Here he describes an ascent with Rab Carrington of the North Face of the Pelerins.

The Mask of Death
Originally published under the title *Miracle on the Civetta*. Mazeaud here chronicles a first ascent on the Quota IGM (North Face of the Civetta) which all but ended in disaster. Mazeaud was later to achieve celebrity as a French government minister.

Gentlemen's Relish
Tilman's *The Ascent of Nanda Devi* is probably the finest of all expedition books, the quality deriving as much from the idiosyncratic and humorous nature of the author as from the events described. At times a plangency creeps in behind the characteristic irony, as in this summary of his feelings on reaching the highest summit of the day.

Dangerous Dancing
Alex MacIntyre, unhappily, lost his life on the South Face of Annapurna in 1982. He had been in the *avant-garde* of Himalayan mountaineering for several years before his death.

Henna Horror
Fowler's Cornish depravities have received acclaim rather than established popularity amongst the sea-cliff *aficionados*. More recently he and his friends have been tackling the huge chalk cliffs of Southern England using full ice-climbing equipment.

Boredom and the Big Numbers
Reinhard Karl, one of Germany's leading climbers, was killed in 1982 when his tent was overwhelmed by an ice-avalanche on Cho Oyu. The tedium and curiously masochistic appeal of Himalayan mountaineering come strongly across in this extract from his book. Karl promised to develop into one of climbing's leading writers and photographers.

Imagined Heights
Probably not the first, and certainly not the last, of the periodic hoaxes with which climbing has been bedevilled throughout its history.

Once in a While
Reasons of space prevent me from including more by Dutton. Suffice it to say that his Doctor seems to me one of the most amusing characters of climbing fiction, and that there is a Dickensian gusto about the writing which never fails to leave me entranced. Dutton is a Professor of Biochemistry at Dundee University and a stalwart of the SMC.

Uninvited Guests
For all that Tilman is one of the very best mountaineering authors – *Nanda Devi* being the best expedition book ever written and *Everest 1938*, according to Jan Morris, "manifestly the best of all books on Everest", he seems to me to belong more fittingly in the genre of travel-writing. The succinct presentation of scene, urbane wit, and appreciation of all points of view, is entirely typical of the man.

Hitler and Leni
Most readers to whom this extract has been shown voice envy when they come to the point where Heckmair describes how "Xaver had to spend the rest of the night comforting and rubbing Leni to keep her warm." It is interesting to consider that in recent years the subject of Ms Riefenstahl's political commitment has been frequently aired, and the conclusion drawn that she was independent of all links with the Nazi party. This would seem to be borne out neither by her films nor by Heckmair's account. It is also interesting to ponder on the political momentum generated prior to the Eigerwand ascent in 1938.

An Excursion in Scotland
Robbins is a wonderfully fresh-eyed observer of scenes, with a gift for the perfectly-turned phrase – a welcome change from the in-jokery of much mountain writing.

The Mountain Tourists
Putting aside the matter of *The Playground of Europe* being an established classic, Leslie Stephen is an interesting case to contemplate along the lines of whence does a man's fame derive. Author of a mountaineering classic; object of a Thomas Hardy poem; editor of The Dictionary of National Biography; or father of Virginia Woolf? I doubt if the question would have exercised him very much, and this outburst of spleen is still relevant and vastly entertaining.

Alaska: Journey by Land
If writing of this quality were produced with more frequency about the actual climbing of routes, no mountaineer would ever need to feel in the slightest degree apologetic about the literature of his sport.

Travels With a Donkey
Livesey revolutionised British rock-climbing almost single-handedly in the mid-seventies through his unashamedly professional approach. This totally scurrilous piece of writing shows him in lighter mood. I doubt if Robert Louis Stevenson, from whom he thieved the title, would have approved. Parts of this team's itinerary might be plagued with more difficulties these days.

The Soloist's Diary
This elliptical masterpiece is one of Jeff Long's earlier works, and is widely acclaimed.

Confusions of an Odium Meeter
Unpublished Smith, included to complete the canon.

Crooked Road to the Far North
This is a shortened version of the original article, large sections of free verse having been left out for reasons of space. It remains a most touching story of unrequited love. Proust would surely have approved.

Your Lovely Hills Are Very Dangerous
I doubt if anybody but Kevin Fitzgerald could have constructed such a delightful entertainment out of what is essentially an eight-mile walk along a main road.

But I Never Returned . . . (A Thirties Idyll)
Raymond Greene, who died early in 1983, was an eminent Harley Street endocrinologist whose important work on pre-menstrual tension re-emphasized a lifelong interest in the opposite sex. He was the brother of Graham Greene, and shares something of his lyrical wryness.

Climbers
James Morris I think first encountered mountaineering as the Times correspondent to the 1953 British Everest Expedition. A very accomplished and cultured travel writer, he underwent a sex-change operation in the seventies and came into the public view with a frank and sensitive account of this entitled *Conundrum*. Jan Morris, as she now is, lives in Gwynedd and writes chiefly nowadays about Welsh affairs.

Letters from Herbert
At this point the anthology editor must perforce reveal a rift with his publishers. Lauria says "I will not apologise for TM's choice of words, because those who know him realise that to edit Herbert is to mute Beethoven." – With which sentiment, and having no personal reputation for purity of vocabulary, I thoroughly agree. However, the publisher seems to think that Mary Whitehouse, the Daughters of the Revolution, the John Birch society or whoever might think such red-blooded expression an affront or political plot. So the article therefore submits itself to the indignity of the dash.

Who Was Oscar Eckenstein?
David Dean's account of Eckenstein is included not only for the fascinating and exemplary manner in which he goes about his research into this shadowy figure, but also for the light which it throws on the personality of Aleister Crowley, the mountaineer and black magician.

A Short Walk with Whillans
In the early decades of this century, when American scholarship on *Boswell's Life of Johnson* was at its peak, one of the much-discussed questions was that of *ipsissima verba* – were the words which Boswell recorded those which Johnson actually spoke? You can raise the same question with regards to Patey on Whillans, and the best response is equally applicable. If they sound right and take on the personality of the subject, they're as true as any tape-recording. Selectivity and imaginative re-creation are the province of art, as Patey amply proves in this, his best essay.

Tenzing Norgay and *Sahibs and Sherpas*
When the arcane mists clear, Tobias is a fine mountain writer, with a groping energy so typical of the best American writing. Compare this account of Tenzing with the Tilman extract, *Uninvited Guests*.

When we come to Mike Thompson's essay the accent changes and the fundamental concerns are perhaps more clearly delineated. One wishes that Thompson wrote more on mountain subjects (his major area of interest is anthropology). Thompson gives a fuller exposition of his preoccupation in *The Aesthetics of Risk*.

The Llanberis Movement
Factionalism has always existed in climbing, though this is a quite surprisingly vehement expression of it.

Brick-Edge Cruiser
MacIntyre's sharply sardonic and humorous observations on the climbing scene, whether rock-gymnastics or the International high-finance expedition league, will be sorely missed by all who knew him.

True-Born Englishmen and *A Superiority Complex*
Let the second's title do battle with the first's content. Strutt's great contribution was as, perhaps, the best ever Alpine Journal editor. Schuster's mountaineer-writing (see also *Postscript*) is surely due for re-appraisal.

Ross Talks . . . and *New Breed*
Paul Ross was the leading Lake District climber at the end of the fifties; Kim Carrigan is the top Australian climber in the early eighties. *Plus ca change, plus c'est la même chose?*

A Word For Whymper and *Whymper Again*
The exhaustive detail laced with feline spite that is focussed on arguments and incidents nearly a hundred years old is breathtaking—proving yet again that the Alpine Club daggers are the sharpest and most carefully aimed of all.

On the Edge
Sue Geller's frightening experience took place on the Naked Edge, Boulder, Colorado. (see also *The Final Game*, p. 574.)

The Beginning of a New Life
Fred Rölli's strong and moving account of his accident and its aftermath.

Salt-Water Cure
I bullied Pat Littlejohn into writing for the anthology this account of one of his adventures on Carn Gowla in Cornwall. The most prolific explorer of new rock in the history of British climbing, with a tally of over 800 routes to his credit, his most fruitful partnership was with the madcap Westcountryman, Keith Darbyshire. Darbyshire died shortly after the experience described here – drowned in a rough sea having fallen whilst soloing on Dodman Point in South Devon.

Shuffling Off This Mortal Coil
The subject of this extract is William Paton Ker (1855-1925), Quain Professor of English Language and Literature in the University of London and author of the seminal work of literary scholarship and criticism, *Epic and Romance* (1897). He was an important influence on the pre-First World War côterie-culture of mountaineering.

Prisoner of War
A fascinating account of the genesis of a mountaineering classic.

A Breach of Faith and *Henry Barber Replies*
Whatever the pundits care to say on this one, both men seem to me to come out of it with unblemished reputations, the magnanimity of Henry Barber in response to Rob Taylor's impassioned complaint being especially noteworthy. All that can really be said is that these situations will inevitably arise where differently powerful personalities are placed together in perilous situations.

The Final Game
Soloing has always been around, and had underlying recognition as the sport in its
uncluttered perfection. Its growing popularity is probably best explained as a
compensation-factor generated against the increasing sophistication of rock-
climbing protection.

Bouldering as Art
John Gill, an American academic mathematician, was a climbing phenomenon
whose hardest problems went far beyond the established abilities of his generation.

Love in the Mountains
Karl Lukan is a German alpinist well-known for his humorous articles on
mountaineering. The title is a misnomer – it's really all about sex.

The Blue Crampon Brigade
A very suave and urbane account of climbing from a traditionally feminine
viewpoint.

No Wonder Mallory Didn't Make It
Robert Reid works on the principle that if you say it with a smile, you can get away
with almost anything. Long live this style of anarchy – I groaned so much it hurt.

Large or Small?
The definitive statements on this continuing debate are probably those made by
H. W. Tilman, who thought that the ideal expedition consisted of one member, and
could be planned on the end of a matchstick.

Backdoor Diplomacy
A dignified insight into the skulduggery often attendant upon the planning of major
expeditions.

The Climber as Visionary
This very important article gave rise to a host of lesser imitations. Doug Robinson
asked that the following note be included as a retrospective comment on the piece:
"The years since writing this have only strengthened my conviction that climbing is
among the best of all activities at evoking the visionary within each of us. Excursions
into biochemistry are buttressing my contention that adrenaline transforming into
mescaline is at least part of the cause. I now think that increased oxygen, not carbon
dioxide, in the brain encourages the process, but the detailed reasoning is too
involved to insert here. Anyone interested in the mechanics should look out for my
book, *Adrenaline*, which I am currently knitting together from rucksack notebooks
and scientific journals."

The Poetry and Humour of Mountaineering
William Edward ("Michael") Roberts, Socialist, poet, teacher, polemicist and
mountaineer is certainly the finest poet climbing has yet produced. He is an
interesting and important figure in twentieth century letters, and a man whose every
literary expression is imbued with lucid intelligence and concern. He was what
nowadays would be called an ecologist long before it was fashionable to be so, an
influential anthologist, and a sensitive and informed critic of modern poetry. He
was married to the writer Janet Adam Smith (v. *Othon Bron*) and died of leukaemia
at the age of 46 in 1948. The essay included here is one of his most finished works.

Subject Index

Listed in page order

ROCK-CLIMBING

Coast To Coast on the Granite Slasher
  Greg Child 19
On the Profundity Trail *Doug Scott* 41
No Big Cigar *Geoff Birtles* 66
Bernat's Horse *Harold Drasdo* 95
Cengalo, Cengalo *Emil Zopfi* 101
Trapdoor Fandango *Ron Fawcett* 115
Fortunatus *Dorothy Pilley* 133
Glasgow *John MacKenzie* 136
Ball's Pyramid *Keith Bell* 141
Welsh Interlude *Nea Morin* 145
Moses *Fred Beckey* 148
Beltane Fire *Geoff Milburn* 152
States of the Art *Max Jones* 155
Solo on Cloggy *Wilfrid Noyce* 159
Day of the Fox *Chris Baxter* 171
Botterill's Slab *Fred Botterill* 175
Robbins — On the Plank *Pat Ament* 178
Asgard Outing *Paul Nunn* 181
Hetch Hetchy — First Impressions
  Galen Rowell 185
Potato Medallist *Colin Kirkus* 197
Patagonian Virgin *Chris Bonington* 200
Jack of Diamonds *Royal Robbins* 204
The Mask of Death *Pierre Mazeaud* 213
Taxation no Tyranny *Jim Perrin* 229
Henna Horror *Mick Fowler* 234
Reflections of a Broken-Down Climber
  Warren Harding 421
Brick-Edge Cruiser *Alex MacIntyre* 429
Ross Talks . . . *Paul Ross* 440
New Breed *Kim Carrigan* 453
Salt-Water Cure *Pat Littlejohn* 524
The End of a Chapter *Sir Arnold Lunn* 554
The Final Game *Glenn Randall* 574
Bouldering as Art *John Gill* 580

ICE-CLIMBING AND ALPINISM

Nightshift in Zero *Dougal Haston* 51
Speeding Down South *Jim Bridwell* 60
The Inscrutable Bregaglia East
  Robin Campbell 71
With God On Our Side *Terry King* 75
With Two Men on the Matterhorn
  Yvette Vaucher 91
The Shroud Solo *Ivan Ghirardini* 121
African Escapade *Eric Shipton* 190
Wintering Out *Alan Rouse* 209

Dangerous Dancing *Alex MacIntyre* 226
A Short Walk With Whillans *Tom Patey* 371
Under Starter's Orders *John Barry* 381
A Crevasse on the Ecrins
  Geoffrey Winthrop Young 487
The Beginning of a New Life *Fredi Rölli* 496
A Breach of Faith *Rob Taylor* 540
T. Graham Brown and the Brenva Face
  Lord Tangley 621

EXPEDITION CLIMBING

The Last Step *Rick Ridgeway* 54
Momentum on Makalu *John Roskelley* 117
Above and Beyond *Reinhold Messner* 126
All That Glory *Georges Bettembourg* 135
Pass the Mirror *Arlene Blum* 139
Kamet Seen and Conquered *Raymond Greene* 169
Patagonian Virgin *Chris Bonington* 200
Gentlemen's Relish *H. W. Tilman* 217
Consolation for a Tragedy? *Dave Roberts* 221
Boredom and the Big Numbers *Reinhard Karl* 238
Himalayan Hopefuls *Greg Child* 331
The Death of Gary Ullin *Robert W. Craig* 503
A Few Moments *Merv English* 515
Nanda Devi Unsoeld *Willi Unsoeld* 518
Five Into Eight Won't Go
  Georges Bettembourg 528

IMAGINATIVE ARTICLES

End of a Climb *John Menlove Edwards* 28
The Soloist's Diary *Jeff Long* 288

HUMOROUS AND SATIRICAL ITEMS

The Inscrutable Bregaglia East
  Robin Campbell 71
On Tree Climbing *H. E. L. Porter* 110
Once in a While *G. F. Dutton* 251
Notes From a Fund-Raising Brochure *Anon.* 272
A Short Walk With Whillans *Tom Patey* 371
The Eyeglass *Tom Longstaff* 385
Your Lovely Hills Are Very Dangerous
  Kevin Fitzgerald 326
Arnold Küpfer *Claude Benson* 400
Sahibs and Sherpas *Mike Thompson* 405
"Sir, I Refute It Thus" *Sir Douglas Busk* 490
No Wonder Mallory Didn't Make It
  Robert Reid 603
Hanging Around *Dave Roberts* 636

ROMANCE, EROTICISM, BACCHANALIA

Cengalo, Cengalo *Emil Zopfi* 101
Hitler and Leni *Anderl Heckmair* 259
Travels With a Donkey *Pete Livesey* 281
Crooked Road to the Far North
  Lito Tejada-Flores 319
But I Never Returned . . . (A Thirties Idyll)
  Raymond Greene 338
Letters From Herbert *Don Lauria* 348
The Llanberis Movement *John Cleare and
  Robin Collomb* 418
Love In The Mountains *Karl Lukan* 584

PERSONALITIES

Three Beginnings *Jeff Schwenn, Gwen Moffat
  and Dennis Gray* 161
A Short Walk With Whillans *Tom Patey* 371
Le Grand Melchoir *Ronald Clark* 385
Tenzing Norgay *Michael Tobias* 401
Reflections of a Broken-Down Climber
  Warren Harding 421
True Born Englishmen *Claud Schuster* 430
Pratt *Pat Ament* 435
Ross Talks . . . *Paul Ross* 440
New Breed *Kim Carrigan* 453
T. Graham Brown and the Brenva Face
  Lord Tangley 621

TRAVEL TO AND FROM THE MOUNTAINS

Uninvited Guests *H. W. Tilman* 257
An Excursion in Scotland *Royal Robbins* 265
The Mountain Tourists *Sir Leslie Stephen* 271
Alaska: Journey by Land *Galen Rowell* 274
Travels With a Donkey *Pete Livesey* 281
Rawalpindi to Rawtenstall *Don Whillans* 308
Crooked Road to the Far North
  Lito Tejada-Flores 319
But I Never Returned . . . (A Thirties Idyll)
  Raymond Greene 338

CONTROVERSY

Imagined Heights *Hudson Stuck* 247
A Superiority Complex *E. L. Strutt* 437
A Word For Whymper: A Reply to Sir Arnold
  Lunn *T. S. Blakeney and D. F. O. Dangar* 456
Whymper Again *Sir Arnold Lunn* 478
A Breach of Faith *Rob Taylor* 540
Henry Barber Replies *Henry Barber* 550
Backdoor Diplomacy *Eric Shipton* 628

DISCURSIVE ARTICLES

Boredom and the Big Numbers *Reinhard Karl* 238
Who Was Oscar Eckenstein *David Dean* 361
Sahibs and Sherpas *Mike Thompson* 405
The Aesthetics of Risk *Mike Thompson* 561
The Blue Crampon Brigade
  Anne Sauvy-Wilkinson 593
Large or Small *Eric Shipton* 617
A Clandestine Plea *Rick Sylvester* 645
The Climber as Visionary *Doug Robinson* 648
The Poetry and Humour of Mountaineering
  Michael Roberts 656
Postscript *Claud Schuster* 670

GRAVITAS

The Only Blasphemy *John Long* 107
The Shroud Solo *Ivan Ghirardini* 121
The Mask of Death *Pierre Mazeaud* 213
Consolation for a Tragedy? *Dave Roberts* 221
Glacier Pilot *Jim Sharp* 353
I'm Alive — How Can He Be Dead
  Dietrich Hasse 356
On the Edge *Sue Geller* 491
Othon Bron *Janet Adam Smith* 495
The Beginning of a New Life *Fredi Rölli* 496
The Death of Gary Ullin *Robert W. Craig* 503
A Few Moments *Merv English* 515
Prisoner of War *W. H. Murray* 530
The Pity of War *Lionel Terray* 536
War Ironies *Armand Charlet* 539
A Breach Of Faith *Rob Taylor* 540
The Final Game *Glenn Randall* 574

Index of Authors

Adams Carter, H., 521
Ament, Pat, 178, 435
Anon, 273

Barber, Henry, 550
Barry, John, 381
Baxter, Chris, 171
Beckey, Fred, 148
Bell, Keith, 141
Benson, Claude, 400
Bettembourg, Georges, 134, 528
Birtles, Geoff, 66
Blakeney, T. S., 456
Blum, Arlene, 139
Bonington, Chris, 200
Bonney, T. G., 417
Botterill, Fred, 175
Bridwell, Jim, 60
Busk, Sir Douglas, 89, 490

Campbell, Robin, 71, 630
Carrigan, Kim, 453
Charlet, Armand, 539
Child, Greg, 19, 331
Clark, Ronald, 385
Cleare, John, 418
Collomb, Robin, 418
Craig, Robert, W., 503

Dangar, D. F. O., 456
Dean, David, 361
Drasdo, Harold, 95
Drummond, Ed, 82
Dutton, G. F., 251

Edwards, John Menlove, 28
English, Merv, 515

Fawcett, Ron, 115
Fitzgerald, Kevin, 326
Fowler, Mick, 234

Geller, Sue, 491
Ghirardini, Ivan, 121
Gill, John, 580

Gray, Dennis, 161
Greene, Raymond, 169, 338

Harding, Warren, 421
Hasse, Dietrich, 356
Haston, Dougal, 51
Heckmair, Anderl, 259

Jones, Max, 155

Karl, Reinhard, 238
King, Terry, 75
Kirkus, Colin, 197

Lauria, Don, 348
Littlejohn, Pat, 524
Livesey, Pete, 281
Long, Jeff, 288
Long, John, 107
Longstaff, Tom, 385
Lukan, Karl, 584
Lunn, Sir Arnold, 478, 554

MacIntyre, Alex, 226, 429
MacKenzie, John, 136
Mazeaud, Pierre, 213
Messner, Reinhold, 126
Milburn, Geoff, 152
Moffat, Gwen, 161
Morin, Nea, 145
Morris, James, 347
Murray, W. H., 530

Nicholson, Norman, 669
Noyce, Wilfrid, 159
Nunn, Paul, 181

Patey, Tom, 371
Perrin, Jim, 16, 229
Pilley, Dorothy, 133
Porter, H. E. L., 110

Randall, Glenn, 574
Reid, Robert, 603
Ridgeway, Rick, 54
Robbins, Royal, 13, 204, 265

Roberts, Dave, 221, 636
Roberts, Michael, 558, 656
Robinson, Doug, 648
Rölli, Fredi, 496
Roskelley, John, 117
Ross, Paul, 440
Rouse, Al, 209
Rowell, Galen, 185, 274

Sauvy-Wilkinson, Anne, 593
Schuster, Claud (Sir, later Lord) 430, 670
Schwenn, Jeff, 161
Scott, Doug, 41
Sharp, Jim, 353
Shipton, Eric, 190, 617, 628
Smith, Janet Adam, 495
Smith, Robin, 85, 306
Smythe, Frank, 522
Stephen, Sir Leslie, 271
Strutt, E. L., 437
Stuck, Hudson, 247
Sylvester, Rick, 645

Tangley, Lord, 621
Taylor, Rob, 540
Terray, Lionel, 536
Tejada Flores, Lito, 319
Thompson, Mike, 405, 561
Tilman, H. W., 217, 257, 630
Tobias, Michael, 401

Unsoeld, Willi, 518

Waterman, Laura and Guy, 351
Whillans, Don, 308

Young, Geoffrey Winthrop, 487, 529

Vaucher, Yvette, 91

Zopfi, Emil, 101